SELF-DEFENSE LAWS OF ALL 50 STATES

With Plain-Talk Summaries
by
Attorney James D. "Mitch" Vilos
and Evan John Vilos

Compiled, written and published in the United States of America
by Attorney James D. Vilos and Evan John Vilos for Guns West Publishing, Inc.

2nd Printing, December 2010

ISBN 978-0-9845058-0-7

James D. "Mitch" Vilos, P.C.
Evan John Vilos
PO Box 1148
Centerville, UT 84014
E-Mail: mitchvilos@gmail.com
1(800) 530-0222
www.utah-injurylaw.com
www.firearmslaw.com

TABLE OF CONTENTS

DEDICATION AND ACKNOWLEDGMENTS

To my lovely wife Bonnie who has tolerated with good humor my consuming fascination with firearms law ever since I turned forty, chalking it up, I'm sure, to mid-life crisis. She astutely recognizes shooting as a relaxing diversion for a trial lawyer who stresses over the rights of the "little guys." Thankfully, she has bought into my excuse of playing cowboy and hunting varmints for medicinal purposes. She even refrains from initiating commitment proceedings when I don the sombrero, leather bandoliers, holsters, guns and bullets ("booolets") of the notorious pistolero "Pancho Vilos" and shoot it out with the members of the infamous Cold Water Gang. What a woman, every gunslinger's dream girl!

To my sons Evan and Jason. Without Evan's research, writing, editing and help hiring talented and able legal researchers, this work could have NEVER been completed. He has not only been a calming and stabilizing force in the office, but at home as well. His political science degree at BYU Hawaii prepared him for the rigorous research schedule we've had to endure to make the deadlines we set for ourselves. Not bad for a college kid who minored in head-banger guitar and surfer dude! He's an all around nice person who has been a joy to work with.

Jason helped write the entertainment package to keep readers' brain cells sufficiently oxygenated in their quest for self-defense-law nirvana. He recently livened up our West-Desert rabbit hunt by sparking his flintlock after forgetting to cap his authentic-hand-carved-mountain-man powder horn containing a pound of black powder. Miraculously he sustained only minor injuries while emphasizing the instability of pre-1900 propellants. My sons' pursuit of their passions, almost at the exclusion of everything else, has given me the assurance that it is okay to divert occasionally from the pursuit of earning a living, to "roll with it," and play with big-boy toys. Both of my sons completed two-year missions for the Church of Jesus Christ of Latter-day Saints, a fact of which I am very proud.

To my three exquisitely beautiful daughters, all accomplished dancers, who have leavened my life with music and culture. But back off boys, they know how to shoot! That's why they're known as Pancho's Angels.

To my cousins Mike and Randy who have a tendency to say what they mean even though it takes days or weeks for the shock to wear off. To all of Mike's Idaho and Utah friends at "Psychos-R-Us" who encourage my politically incorrect bad behavior.

A special thanks to J. Ruben Clark Law School legal researchers Chris Whittaker, Wiley Barker, Pierce Andrews and Matt Newbold whose help is much appreciated; my cover and website design artist Clarence Bowman of Bowman Design (www.ClarenceBowman.com); my print formatters at DTS; my grammar editor, Jake Wilcox, and the superb and hardworking printers at Artistic Print in Salt Lake City.

We give thanks to and acknowledge our excellent legal research services, Loislaw and Westlaw (Thomson Reuters), which made it possible for us to find and cite the large number of statutes and cases comprising the law of self-defense. Furthermore, without the jury-instruction search data base of Westlaw, obtaining many of the jury instructions we used to confirm and explain the rules of self-dense would have been extremely difficult.

Finally, this book is dedicated to the Right to Defend Ourselves and Our Loved Ones. Without It, What Else Matters?

PREFACE

WHY WE WROTE THIS BOOK – One of the most common reasons we are hired to defend people involved in defensive incidents is because they did not fully understand the limitations of the law of self-defense. The requirements of legal self-defense are often vague and difficult to understand. There are countless hidden legal traps causing a multitude of misconceptions. The consequences of such ignorance of the law can be disastrous. If you get convicted like the hapless fellow whose tale is told in Chapter 2, your life as you now know it will be OVER (life in prison with no possibility of parole)! The cost of paying a competent attorney to go "all out" to defend against allegations of murder or attempted murder can be an excursion into the world of bankruptcy.

Rather than meeting a client after he has made a serious legal mistake, our goal is to educate him before he tears his Taurus out of his Thunderwear! We want to be like the fence at the edge of a sea cliff that prevents people from falling into the ocean, rather than coast guardsmen at the bottom of the cliff who dredge up torn and dismembered corpses ripped apart by feeding frenzies of sharks and barracudas (figurative for homicide detectives, prosecutors and personal injury lawyers).

Our Unusual Writing Style – We're not writing this book to impress our colleagues, lawyers and judges. We hope its plain enough so that every person who keeps any weapon for self-defense will understand. This book is a private conversation between you and us. We don't want an impersonal, complicated writing style to get in the way of helping you avoid the indescribable horror of being arrested, prosecuted or convicted. So we use the personal manner of addressing you as "you" (think of it as ya'll, if you're from Dixie) and us as "we" and "us." After all it's **YOUR BRASS** THAT'S ON THE LINE! You must understand the rules of law so well that you can apply them in the one and one-half seconds we refer to as perception and reaction time before some thug whacks you or a loved one. Some may consider our writing style tacky for highlighting **ABSOLUTELY CRUCIAL CONCEPTS** using ALL CAPS, **bold**, *italics*, underlining; **different fonts,** [colors and brackets]. Hopefully you'll appreciate the over emphasis as long as it keeps your posterior out of the hoosegow and ambulance chasers out of your wallet.

Why We Cited Statutes, Jury Instructions and Excerpts From Cases Rather Than Simply Summarizing – The ultimate responsibility of knowing what the law says rests upon you, not us. We could have reduced the size of the book considerably by generalizing or simply providing you with our "plain-talk" explanations, but we wanted you to have access to the actual words by which your acts of self-defense will be judged. We have given you references to the laws we have cited, hoping you will check for changes that might occur between now and the next edition of this book. Any crucial information that becomes available to us, will be posted on the internet as we have described in Chapter 19.

ME vs. We – When referring to my experience and insights as a trial lawyer, I speak in terms of "I and me." When describing research findings, the term "we" is used to acknowledge the exhaustive research of my son, Evan, and the impressive team of law clerks he helped to assemble. He is not yet a lawyer, but this book would have never been completed without his focus and tenacity.

HUMOR (Entertainment) – Finally, you'll notice a little levity interspersed throughout the book (OK, some of it's really corny). Bluntly put, this law stuff can be VERY DRY. We thought a little light humor might "help the medicine go down" as Mary Pop 'Em (ugh!) used to say. Hopefully, it will help you remember the material better because you didn't nod off while soaking it in. At the same time, we pray the funny stuff doesn't cause you to misjudge the seriousness of the topic or fail to tremble at the dire consequences if you do.

Who the heck is Pancho Vilos and what in the world is "Pancho's Wisdom?" The character Pancho Vilos started as a Single Action (Cowboy Action) Shooting Society membership persona. However, in the process of writing previous books on Utah's Gun laws, Pancho became the leavening agent in the bread, the comic relief that made reading law bearable. He also became a symbol for the frustration and anger that many gun owners feel when they are confronted with naysayers and anti-self-defense politicians who have no common sense when it comes to the Second Amendment. Pancho sports a sombrero and a poncho, which he defines as a "South of the border concealed arsenal permit!" Tourists happening on wanted posters tacked to fence posts, trees and cactus swear that Pancho bears a striking similarity to the attorney-author of this book. He is often filmed riding with the infamous Cold Water Gang that terrorizes civilized folk along parade routes, historical sites, pioneer celebrations and commercial grand openings. He is an enigma whose wisdom and photos grace what would otherwise be the blank spots in the text of this literary work. Pancho is most certainly on Secretary Napolitano's Right-Wing Extremist Watch List (and Proud of It!), having had written communications to his compatriots like the following seized by Federales patrolling the historical Pony Express Trail:

Pancho's Wisdom

I love God, my family, my country, my guns, my dogs and my truck; oh, and my fellow man, as long as he KEEPS HIS MITTS OFF all of the above!

Pancho's "Gunnut" Quips are comedy relief to keep your spirits lifted as you tackle a serious subject carrying a heavy responsibility. If you truly are a gunnut, you will understand all the hidden meanings (e.g., only a gunnut would know what Hoppes No. 9 is) and maybe crack a smile. (You just might be a gunnut if your girlfriend thinks the smell of Hoppes No. 9 is your aftershave!) But there is a serious purpose to these as well. **Typical judges, jurors and prosecutors do not view life through the same optics we do!** They don't see the need to remain vigilant to vanquish villains with a Vaquero. This could, in turn, affect the way they perceive whether it was reasonable or necessary (see critical discussion about these terms in Chapter 3) to use deadly force during a defensive incident. Please remember this as you face up to the fact that you just might be a gunnut if you don't give a hoot what Brangelina or Lady Gaga did last weekend!

Our goal is to make this book and our website the most accurate, helpful, insightful, entertaining and valuable information EVER assembled concerning the right of self-defense. With your assistance and feedback (see Chapter 19, About Future Additions), we believe this is not an impossible dream.

Grammar? We don't need no Stinkin' Grammar!

A WORD OF CAUTION AND DISCLAIMER

Every attempt has been made to ensure the accuracy of this book, but state statutes, cases and jury instructions can be vague and subject to different interpretations. Statutes are often amended, changed by judicial interpretation, replaced and repealed with little notice to the public. Cases are often overturned. Committees rewrite jury instructions.

Disclaimer: Therefore, the authors, their agents, publishers, contractors, employees, heirs, assigns, distributors, wholesalers and retailers of this book accept no liability, express or implied, for damages of any kind resulting from reliance on any aspect of this book, including but not limited to, consequential damages. This book should be used as a guide only and not considered as legal advice. Attorney Vilos is currently licensed to practice law in Utah only. You should seek legal advice from competent, experienced attorneys practicing criminal law IN YOUR OWN STATE. There is no guarantee that police, prosecuting attorneys, wildlife officers, courts or juries will agree with the authors' interpretations. Even if our interpretation is right, you may still have to pay attorneys to defend you. We encourage the reader to use the citations given in this book to check for changes in the law. Nothing in this book is intended to suggest that you may violate any state or federal law governing the possession of firearms or other weapons. Because you may have the right to use deadly force does not imply you may lawfully possess a firearm or other weapon in any given jurisdiction. Weapons possession issues are beyond the scope of this book.

Corrections: We have created a page on our website at www.firearmslaw.com so we can post critical corrections or updates as soon as we become aware of them. We will list any corrections by chapter and by state alphabetically. Of course, we will incorporate all corrections into the very next edition of the book. **If you become aware of anything you believe to be in error, please do not hesitate to contact us immediately at mitchvilos@gmail.com.** Of course, we reserve the right to control the actual content of our book. We are anxious to combine efforts with our readers to make this the most accurate and complete compilation of self-defense laws for non-lawyers ever written.

Pancho and Tom standing guard over the Right of Self-Defense.

1

INTRODUCTION

We published our first "gun-law" book in 1998 to help non-lawyers have quick access to Utah's weapon laws. To aid in understanding, we summarized each law in simple terms referred to as "plain-talk." Not long after our first book was published, clients from the high desert charged with weapon offenses began drifting into our office. Their statements to investigators, from time to time, reminded us of something that might have been recorded in the Tombstone Epitaph, "He crawfished a bet and called me a liar, Sheriff!" Not always picture perfect, we see the claim of self defense quite often in our office.

While researching the law of self-defense in preparation for trial, we shudder at all of the potential hidden legal traps. We have begun teaching legal seminars and certifying students for concealed firearm permits to illuminate the uninformed. Our objective is to help avoid the legal nightmare.

A. Avoiding the Legal Nightmare

During our interaction with clients and students, we became aware of a shocking number of misconceptions about the law of self-defense. Perhaps you have heard or read "legal conclusions" uttered by *Law and Order* wannabees that sound something like this:

- "If you shoot someone breaking into your home and they fall outside, drag them back into the house."
- "If you shoot someone in self-defense, make sure you kill them. Otherwise, they'll sue you for all you are worth."
- "Don't draw your gun unless you intend to shoot to kill."
- "I have a concealed weapon permit; I don't understand why they arrested me for brandishing."
- "He was twice my size; I felt threatened, so I shot him." (Explanation why the defendant charged with attempted murder shot an unarmed assailant.)
- "Trespassers will be shot; survivors will be prosecuted."

These myths, half-truths and misapplications of the law of self-defense stem from incomplete knowledge and training. Some of the reasons citizens have a hard time finding and understanding self-defense law include:

- Self-defense statutes can be very difficult for non-lawyers to find. It's easier to rely on what others claim the law says than to look it up and study it for one's self.
- Not all states have self-defense statutes and the statutes of those that do can be quite incomplete.
- Some statutes are so old and broadly worded that courts have changed their meanings.
- Self-defense law can be buried in pattern jury instructions which are not readily available to the public.
- No state's self-defense laws are exactly like those of any other state.
- Cases changing the meaning of state self-defense statutes are not easy to locate or understand.

We wrote his book to help non-lawyers quickly find and thoroughly understand the laws of self-defense in their home states and in states where they will eventually travel. There is no longer any reason for you to speculate or rely on rumors. You can read the law for yourself straight from the mouths of legislators and judges. And we use "plain-talk" summaries to help you cut through the thicket of legal mumbo jumbo. This is the most comprehensive compilation of self-defense laws ever assembled for non-lawyers under one book cover. The stories behind the cases we summarize illustrate legal principles that would otherwise be difficult to understand or remember. Our ultimate goal is to reduce the number of tragedies like the one described in Chapter 2.

B. Staying Alive

Staying out of trouble is important, but staying alive is paramount. Police academies are now revealing the brutal truth to their cadets that "action always beats reaction." Officers who don't understand the realities of perception and reaction time are at the complete mercy of suspects who know no mercy. It's the exact opposite of Hollywood westerns where the good guys always outdraw the bad guys even though the bad guys go for their guns first. For a detailed description of the training exercise often used to convince police trainees of this reality, see Chapter 11, Perception and Reaction Time. The point is that fractions of a second could make the difference between life and death. If trained officers are dying because of failure to account for perception and reaction time, imagine the challenge facing ordinary citizens who have not been through a police academy. Citizens should know the law of self-defense well enough to apply it without unnecessary delay. What good is it to be armed, if you are killed during the legal analysis?

To combat this problem, state legislatures in many states have passed laws giving innocent citizens an advantage during a criminal attack. These laws come in the form of presumptions and reduced thresholds triggering the right to use deadly force sooner under certain conditions. These laws could give citizens and their loved ones the split second advantage needed to survive. They are worth knowing. If your state has not adopted such laws, we encourage you to use the knowledge gained by studying this book to educate your state's lawmakers. Working together, we can make our communities safer. See Chapter 20, The Mother of All Self-Defense Laws.

C. Quick-Draw Self-Defense Law

We wanted to make access to the self-defense laws of any state quick and easy. To do this we organized the book like a reference manual. The heart of this book, if you will, is Chapter 5. Chapter 5 contains the complete text of every state's self-defense laws, with "plain-talk" summaries. The states are listed alphabetically from Alabama to Wyoming. All the information you will need to fully understand the material in Chapter 5 is explained in Chapters 3 and 4.

- Chapter 3 contains an explanation of the terms and concepts most commonly found in the law of self-defense.
- Chapter 4, to create some degree of uniformity and logic, we created a simple outline containing the main topics, such as the elements of and exceptions to the law of self-defense. We refer to this outline as our TEMPLATE.
- Chapter 6, the State Deadly Force Comparison Chart, succinctly summarizes, in table format, the issues thoroughly explained in Chapter 5. This chart and the accompanying map make it easy to see which states require retreat before using deadly force.

The remaining chapters will assist you in the application of principles contained in Chapters 3 through 6. These include topics such as: factors that most often lead to arrest and prosecution, conflict avoidance, perception and reaction time, an analysis of different levels threat and the potential legal ramifications of such reactions, use of Tasers, self-defense from animals particularly those listed as endangered, domestic violence, civil liability, and dealing with the aftermath of a shooting. We also point you to a wealth of additional resources related to self and home defense. For those who wish to participate in the political process, we provide an all-star list of favorable self-defense provisions that your state legislature could choose from.

D. Shock and Awe

Larry Harmon thought he knew what the laws of self-defense were in his state. After all, he lived in Fillmore, Utah, about as close to the Old Wild West as any man can be in this day and age (OK, and then there is Texas!). His objective that fateful day was simply to watch his neighbors' cabins and keep two ruthless-looking young toughs from beating him up and taking his gun away. Why is he sitting in the Utah State Penitentiary doing life without parole? His shocking story is in Chapter 2. Could the next sad story involving a defensive incident be yours?

Join Pancho's revolution to make our nation's self-defense laws MORE protective of the INNOCENT, and LESS protective of CRIMINALS. See Mother of All Self-Defense Laws, Chapter 20.

2

FROM NEIGHBOORHOOD WATCH TO LIFE IN PRISON

(The *"HARMON"* Case)

(Dramatization) Larry Harmon knew they were up to no good. They tried to break into his place and then went through the neighborhood of cabins peeking into windows and rattling doors. The tall thin one had on a black motorcycle jacket with chains hanging off of it. The muscular one with long hair looked like he was high on something. They kept coming straight at Larry even though his pistol was clearly visible. He had no doubt they were capable of overpowering his aging, 57-year-old frame and pistol whipping him, or worse, with his own gun. He yelled, "Stop! Don't come any closer; what's your business?" But it didn't phase them; they kept coming. The one on Larry's right started to circle. Larry's truck with an open door was behind him and to the left; he had nowhere to run. Larry gripped his old 1911 tighter just in case they lunged for it. When the longhaired one was within 3 feet of him he raised his .45 pulling the hammer back, praying they'd turn and run. Nothing. With the attacker on the left literally an arm's-length away, there was no more time for waiting. Larry pulled the trigger. He swung right to stop the attack from that side. He spotted a blur of black leather filling his peripheral right. Too close for aiming, he spun and jerked the trigger, firing several more shots as the dark form disappeared into the trees. That's how Larry remembers it as he sits out his sentence of life without parole at the Utah State Prison near Salt Lake City.

Twenty-seven-year-old Douglas Greer, a felon convicted of methamphetamine possession, lay dead in the road, shot through the face. His companion, Ray Thomas, whose past included allegations of domestic assault, escaped with a bullet hole through the back of his arm. Larry called 911 to report the shooting. The Utah Supreme court summarized the official but conflicting versions of what happened as follows:

> The homeowners in the rural Frampton Heights area had an informal "neighborhood watch" system of keeping an eye on one another's properties and investigating the names, license plate numbers, and

activities of strangers seen in the area. Harmon, the only year-round resident, participated in the watch and reported suspicious tracks or people to the owners of the five other cabins in Frampton Heights.

At trial, Harmon and Thomas gave conflicting testimony regarding the events leading up to and following the shooting.

Harmon testified as follows: He was awakened from a nap by knocking on the front and side doors of his cabin. When he looked outside, he saw two young men, Greer and Thomas, whom he did not know. Thomas was jerking on the side screen door, which was locked from the inside, apparently trying to open it. Harmon watched the two men walk away from the cabin toward a gate exiting his property. The two men then walked back toward his cabin and began looking at one of his automobiles. Harmon called out to them to state their purpose and told them to leave. Without verbally responding, they walked back toward the gate and exited his property. Harmon set out in his truck to check his neighbors' homes and to get more information about the two men and what they were doing in Frampton Heights. After checking the homes and finding nothing amiss, he spotted Greer and Thomas walking along the road leading to Fillmore. He drove past them, parked his truck on the side of the road, got out, and asked them their names and what they wanted. Greer and Thomas did not respond to his questions but continued to approach him with "unfriendly expressions," without heeding his requests that they stop. Greer approached straight on while Thomas circled around to Harmon's side. They continued to approach, even though Harmon was displaying a .45 caliber handgun he had retrieved from his truck. Backed against the door of his truck, Harmon feared for his life inasmuch as the two men were not responding to his requests to stop advancing, and it appeared that they could disarm him. Thus, in self-defense, he shot Greer once in the face and then turned and rapidly fired at Thomas. After the shooting, Harmon returned to his cabin, called 911 on his cellular phone, and reported that he had shot someone who had been trying to break into his property. [After a defensive incident, do you think your version is the only story law enforcement officials will hear? Think again.]

In contrast, Thomas testified as follows: He and Greer were on their way up to Twin Lakes, above Fillmore, when their vehicle became stuck in the mud. After unsuccessfully attempting to free it, they decided to walk back to town. To save time, they took a shortcut down a mountain and found themselves in Frampton Heights. They followed a fence line until they came to Harmon's property, and though neither Greer nor Thomas knew Harmon, they jumped over the fence and entered his property, hoping that the property owner might be able to help them pull their vehicle from the mud. Thomas walked up to the porch of the

> cabin and knocked on the door. Receiving no answer, he went around to the side door of the cabin and again knocked. When no one responded, he and Greer began walking down the road, away from the cabin. However, Harmon called out to them, and they walked back toward the cabin, believing they could still solicit help. When they were twenty to thirty feet away, Harmon began yelling at them from behind the screen door. Harmon asked them if they were ignorant and couldn't read, ...and he told them that they were on his property and ordered them to leave. They then left Harmon's property and began walking on the road toward Fillmore. As they were walking, Harmon's truck approached from behind, passed them, and stopped about six or seven feet in front of them. Harmon got out of the truck wielding a .45 caliber handgun. Thomas and Greer stood still.
>
> Harmon held out the gun and asked Thomas if he knew what it was. Thomas replied that he did. Harmon then told him that the gun was a .45 and asked Thomas his name. After Thomas responded, Harmon turned and said something to Greer. Thomas heard the hammer go back on the gun and saw Harmon raise it and shoot Greer in the face from a distance of six to twelve inches. Harmon then pointed the gun at Thomas, asked him if he wanted to get shot, and told him to "take off running." As Thomas was running away, he heard the gun fire and felt a bullet strike his arm. He also heard several more shots and saw dirt flying in front of him.
>
> During the trial, the medical examiner testified that Greer had been shot once in the face at a distance of six to twelve inches from the end of the gun. Thomas's physician indicated that the bullet which struck Thomas entered from the back of his arm and exited out the front. The evidence introduced at trial further indicated that Harmon fired a total of five shots from his gun, which held a maximum of eight rounds.

State v. Harmon, 956 P.2d at 264, 265. A rural jury in Fillmore, Millard County, Utah convicted Larry Harmon of First Degree Felony Murder for killing Greer and First Degree Felony Attempted Murder for shooting at and wounding Thomas. Greer's mother and Thomas obtained a combined civil judgment against Harmon for $1.5 million dollars and executed on everything he had saved or owned. In October of 2008, the Utah Parole Board decided that Harmon would spend the rest of his life in the Utah State Prison without the possibility of parole. An October 2008 article entitled *Convicted Killer to Spend Natural Life in Prison*, by Ben Winslow of the *Deseret News* in Salt Lake City reported:

> "He had a truck, a gun and a cell phone. He chose to use the gun instead of call for help," Greer's mother, Juanita McCall, said at his parole hearing on Sept. 2.
>
> Harmon, who is now 70, apologized and said it was a "tragic

> error in judgment." ...the five-member [parole] board ruled against [ever] releasing him [from prison] because of the number of victims, the aggressive act itself and that Harmon minimized it, instead of accepting responsibility.

Did the jury completely discount a legitimate concern I hear from gun owners all the time—being rushed and overpowered by multiple unarmed assailants? Harmon claimed he only fired his gun because Greer and Thomas wouldn't stop at his commands. Assuming it happened the way he described, what was he supposed to do at that point? Had they disarmed him, they could have killed him with his own gun. He had a right to confront them and find out why they were going around trying to get into houses. He had a right to arm himself before approaching them. If they rushed him, he had a right to use reasonable force to defend himself. It wasn't clear from the record of the court how large Greer and Thomas were. Nevertheless, there were two of them and only one of him, sometimes referred to by concealed weapon instructors as "disparity of numbers." They were obviously much younger, stronger, and more agile. It seems likely that they could have easily overpowered Harmon and taken his gun. Why was Greer so close to Harmon unless he refused to stop or back off? I do not recall reading any evidence in the 1500 page trial transcript that Harmon, after he stopped his truck, approached the boys. The evidence was that the .45 casings fell fairly close to the truck. These are very troubling issues for those who carry a weapon for self-defense.

How do you legally deal with multiple assailants who are not exhibiting weapons but are refusing to obey your command to stop? Several plausible acceptable legal solutions to this problem are discussed more fully in Chapters 9 through 11. There were several Thumbs-Down factors in this case that we would not have known about had I not spent a day and a half reading the transcript at the Millard County Courthouse. See Thumbs-Down Factors, Chapter 7.

This case is a dramatic and solemn reminder to gun owners of the legal, moral and psychological risks of using deadly force. It is one of many cases reported in this book in which gun owners were found to have acted with excessive force resulting in the conviction of a crime and making them liable in damages. A careful study of these cases, compared to incidents in which there was no arrest, will help the reader see how police, prosecutors, judges and juries thread the needle through the intricate wording of each of the states' self-defense laws. The stories of how the law was applied to the defensive incidents described in this book will add "flesh" to the bare-bone self-defense statutes and aide in understanding. Additionally, staying with our cliff analogy in the preface, we hope to show you right where the edge is so you don't step over it. The problem is, sometimes the edge is not very well defined; you get too close —GOTCHA!

3

UNDERSTANDING THE CRUCIAL TERMS AND CONCEPTS OF SELF-DEFENSE LAW

(CAUTION! Read this Chapter and the Next Before Reading Any of the States' Subchapters!)

Introduction

Although we could not find two states with exactly the same self-defense laws, we found that all of them contain a few common, vital, core concepts as well as many similar terms. To understand the self-defense laws of any of the states, it is absolutely critical for you to understand these concepts. That is why we have asked you to read, comprehend and remember the content of this chapter and the next before proceeding.

WARNING: It would be impossible for any author to anticipate ALL the variables in any given case that could result in a criminal prosecution, conviction or civil damage award. A slight change in the facts could effect whether police arrest, prosecutors prosecute or whether jurors and/or judges convict. Unpredictable variables that could affect whether you are arrested, prosecuted or convicted could include the personalities of the persons making decisions about what you did, the emotions of such persons at the moment these decisions are made, and even societal factors, such as recent heinous crimes shocking the community or hateful attitudes about guns and gun owners. Race, religion, national origin and sexual preference of the defender or victim can affect the outcome of a case despite the best attempts by lawyers or judges to keep it from happening. Police, prosecutors, judges and jurors are only human and make mistakes. There is no such thing as ABSOLUTELY PREDICTABLE justice. Therefore, the examples we use in this book illustrating situations where a person might be justified in using deadly force should not be taken literally. They are simply to illustrate the legal principle being discussed. They are NOT to make you believe you have a license to use force when dozens of other variables not mentioned in the example could affect

whether there is an arrest, prosecution or conviction. Even though your actions fall within THE-PERFECT-TEXT-BOOK-DEFINITION OF SELF-DEFENSE (if there is such a thing) if you get the wrong arresting officer, prosecutor or jury, you could be arrested, prosecuted or convicted.

> ***Example:*** **Texas has one of the most protective home defense statutes in the country. Most folks have been led to believe that homeowners may always legally shoot intruders who break into their homes at night. At least one would think it's true in a place like Texas, where, according to *Miss Congeniality,* "everyone has guns." One night several teens broke into the trailer of an elderly man, Jose Gonzalez, age 63. Fearing for his life, the homeowner shot and killed one of them. It turned out the deceased boy was only 13 and his friends told the police they only broke in to steal candy and a soda. Despite an uproar from the community that this man was even charged, he was tried for murder.** *Deseret News, Sept. 28, 2008.* **Why was he prosecuted? Was it the age of the boy, an anti-gun prosecutor, or racial undertones at work? Who knows? Unless he qualified for a public defender, the trial cost him a fortune. The outcome of the case is reported in Chapter 7, Thumbs-Down Factors.**

History and Background

The philosophy behind most of the states' self-defense laws comes from English common law. When British settlers immigrated to the original Thirteen Colonies, they brought their knowledge of the law of England with them. These rules of common law began to take shape in both the statutes and cases of the American states. Although some states like Virginia and Washington D.C. never did enact self-defense statutes, cases from those two jurisdictions have passed on common law rules from case to case until the present. In the law, we refer to these cases as "legal precedents." The law used in a previous case is generally applied in later cases unless there is a good reason to change it.

The differences we see in states' self-defense laws are because courts and legislatures of each state have adjusted common law according to their values and beliefs. In many Western and Southern states, citizens are allowed to use deadly force more readily than in other parts of the country. Laws that justify the use of deadly force to prevent the commission of violent felonies or that lower the threshold for the use of deadly force in special places, such as homes or occupied vehicles, may allow defenders to react more quickly and thus increase their chance of survival. From a tactical standpoint, they are worth knowing. Such laws not only protect the innocent, they serve as a warning of potential injury or death to criminals.

Purpose

The next two chapters are to help you understand basic self-defense principles common to all states. This prevents us from having to repeat them for each of the fifty states.

Approach

Chapter 5 contains a subchapter for every state, starting with Alabama and ending with Wyoming. In each state we divide the discussion of self-defense into several topics. These topics include the use of non-deadly force, deadly force, the duty to retreat before using defensive force, limitations on the use of force, the right to use deadly force to prevent serious felonies and to defend persons in your home and other special places. Defense of property is also addressed. For each state we created an outline of sub-headings that we refer to as our "TEMPLATE." These topic sub-headings alert you to the subject being addressed and are flagged by **[brackets, red ink and bold print]**. The TEMPLATE makes it easier for the reader to understand how the law differs in each state in relation to each of these vital topical areas.

Statutes – Most states have self-defense statutes, or laws that were written by their respective state legislatures. All state statutes are preceded by this symbol – **§**. For example, Alabama's general law of self-defense is cited as **Alabama Code § 13A-3-23. Use of force in defense of a person.** Of those states that have statutes, some states statutes are quite complete and address most or all of the topics listed in the TEMPLATE below (e.g., Texas, Utah). Others have statutes that are short and relatively incomplete (e.g., Vermont, Wyoming). A few have no statutes at all (e.g., Virgina and Washington, D.C.). Unfortunately, some states' self-defense statutes have been interpreted by courts to mean something different than the plain language of the statute. For example, one of California's statutes says you can use deadly force "to apprehend any person for any felony committed, or in lawfully suppressing any riot, or in lawfully keeping and preserving the peace." On its face, the statute gives the impression you would be totally justified as a vigilante sniper who picks off rioters and felons all day long from the top corner of a skyscraper. This statute has been dramatically limited by case law. We alert you what effect case law has had upon such statutes. **This is vital information that you could not find on your own without an enormous investment of time and money.**

Case Law – For those states that do not have self-defense statutes, or whose self-defense statutes are short and comparatively incomplete, we have conducted exhaustive research to find whether each state's court cases address the topics outlined in our TEMPLATE. If a rule of self-defense is contained in a case, the name of the case is cited in *italics* as in the following Vermont case, *State v. Wheelock*, 609 A.2d 972 (Vt. 1992). These rules are created by appellate court interpretations of statutes or previous cases.

Jury Instructions – If a rule is contained in a jury instruction, we will tell you it is a jury instruction, where the instruction can be found and whether it is generally accessible to the public. **What are jury instructions?** When a case goes to trial, it is the job of jurors to listen to the witnesses and decide what really happened. After they decide what the facts are, the trial judge tells them what the law is. They apply the law to the facts and arrive at a verdict. The judge either reads the law to the jury or gives it to them in writing. These oral or written restatements of the law are referred to as "jury instructions" or "charges to the jury." In states that have statutes defining the laws of self-defense, the jury instructions will generally be worded using the language of the statutes. Where there is no statute covering a particular issue of self-defense (e.g., duty to retreat before using deadly force), the courts and lawyers look at previous cases that have decided that particular issue. The court then takes the rule of law found in the case or cases and drafts jury instructions informing the jurors what the law is regarding that particular self-defense issue.

Jury instructions are not law. They are simply attempts by lawyers and judges to define the law for the jury in any given case. In each case, the lawyers argue to the judge what the instructions should say and the judge makes a final decision based upon his reading of the self-defense statutes and/or cases in his particular state (or neighboring states, if no cases in his state can be found speaking to that particular self-defense issue).

Although jury instructions are not considered laws like state statutes are, some states like California rely heavily upon them. In such states, they are updated frequently to reflect appeals court cases that either approve the instructions or change them. When a particular jury instruction or part of an instruction best states the rule we are informing you of, we will cite the instruction rather than a statute or case. In other words, we use the most correct statement of a state's law of self-defense, whether it be a state statute, a law case, or jury instruction.

The TEMPLATE – The Order of Presentation of Each State's Self-Defense Law

We have attempted to present each state's self-defense law using the following outline or TEMPLATE. We say "attempt" because not every state addresses all of the topics nor do the topics appear in the same order in every state. Rather than force a state's self-defense law into the outline where it would make no sense, we often just insert the concepts in brackets (for example, **[Duty to Retreat]**) into the statute to alert you to what concept is being addressed. Notice we highlight these TEMPLATE topics in red. In the TEMPLATE section of each state's subchapter black print indicates the actual statute, case or jury instruction which describes that state's self-defense law. The use of the color red alerts you to TEMPLATE topics and our commentary. TEMPLATE topic headings appear **[In Red, Bold, Initial Caps, and In Brackets]**. We list the topics for which we could find neither statutes nor case law at the bottom of that state's subchapter under the heading **[TEMPLATE Topics We Could Not Find Explained in Statutes or Cases]**. For such states, we suggest you look to neighboring states to see how their courts have decided the issue. Courts often rely on case decisions in bordering states if their own state law doesn't say anything about the issue. For example, it's not uncommon for lawyers and judges in many of the less populated Western states to cite California cases or jury instructions when a statute or case precedent can't be found in their own state. The following TEMPLATE shows the topics and order of presentation we attempt to use for each state, where possible. We purposely did not assign consecutive numbers or letters to the TEMPLATE topics because the laws of every state may be arranged in quite different order.

TEMPLATE

NAME OF STATE

[Defense of Self and Others]

  [Non-Deadly Force]

  [Deadly Force]

[Use of Deadly Force to Prevent Serious Felonies]

[Defense of Third Persons]

[Exceptions to Justifiable Self-Defense]

    [Initial Aggressor]

    [Provocation]

    [Committing Felony or Unlawful Act]

    [Mutual Combat]

    [Exceptions to the Exceptions]

      [Withdraw and Communicate]

[Duty (or No Duty) to Retreat – Generally]

[Defense of Person(s)s in Special Places – (e.g., Home, Business, Occupied Vehicle)]

  [Duty (or No Duty) to Retreat From Special Places]

    [Co-Habitants; Co-Employees – Duty to Retreat]

  [Presumption of Reasonableness in Special Places]

[Responsibility to Innocent Third Parties]

[Civil Liability]

[Defense of Property]

[Helpful Definitions Relating to Self-Defense Statutes]

[TEMPLATE Topics We Could Not Find Explained in Statutes or Cases]

(For a detailed explanation of each topic mentioned in this TEMPLATE, please refer to the following chapter.)

Core Concepts Explained

Before we give you a detailed explanation of each topic contained in the TEMPLATE, we need to make sure you understand the "Core Concepts" of the law of self-defense. The terms *Justification, Reasonable, Necessary, Imminent, Serious Bodily Injury, and Deadly Force* are critical to the understanding of self-defense law.

JUSTIFICATION

Justification in simple terms means not guilty or not liable. Killing another person without justification is murder or manslaughter. Killing without justification will also subject the killer to liability for wrongful death. Killing another person in lawful self-defense is justifiable and is not a crime. Justification can be a defense to a civil lawsuit as well. *Only judges and juries have the authority after a defensive incident to decide if a person's actions were justifiable.* No attorney or firearms instructor, no matter how smart or talented, can predict with certainty whether a person's reaction to any particular threat will be judged as justifiable. No two defensive incidents will ever be exactly alike. There are simply too many variables.

REASONABLE

Every self-defense law requires a defender to act reasonably. **Example:** The law is not going to allow a person who is unreasonably afraid of germs to wander through public areas shooting people who come too close. The fear has to be a reasonable fear. Someone with a broken bottle standing within arms length threatening to "cut your face off" would invoke a reasonable fear of death or serious injury in most people. A person may honestly believe his life is in danger, but if his belief is unreasonable and he responds with deadly force, he will be convicted of a crime. Just in case you're into dictionary definitions:

> **Reasonable person.** 1. A hypothetical person used as a legal standard, esp. to determine whether someone acted with negligence; specif., a person who exercises the degree of attention, knowledge, intelligence, and judgment that society requires of its members for the protection of their own and of others' interests. The reasonable person acts sensibly, does things without serious delay, and takes proper but not excessive precautions. Also termed reasonable man; prudent person; ordinarily prudent person; reasonably prudent person; highly prudent person.

See reasonable care under CARE. *Black's Law Dictionary* (8th ed. 2004), reasonable person. A reasonable fear of serious injury or death alone is not enough to justify the use of deadly force. The threat must be imminent and the defender must be without fault in causing the conflict.

Reasonable belief and actual belief – You'll notice in Chapter 5 that some state's self-defense statutes say you have to have both a reasonable belief as well as an actual belief. Whether the state statute requires it or not, you should never use defensive force unless you actually believe it is necessary. Because this is our advice, we don't believe it's important for us to include a scholarly dissertation about the subtle differences between state statutes that require only a reasonable belief and those that require both a reasonable and actual belief.

Keep in mind that the reasonableness of your actions will ultimately be decided by a jury of your peers. Your peers, in this context, are not your fellow students at the superb shooting school you attended. Depending upon where in the country your trial is held, many prospective jurors may have the mindset that they would rather die than take another person's life. What's reasonable to you will not appear reasonable to them. This underscores how important it is for your attorney to have a strategy to keep such people off your jury. See the strategies we used in the high-profile case transcribed in Chapter 12.

NECESSARY

When you were a kid and hurt a sibling or classmate unnecessarily, do you remember your mother or your school teacher asking you in a sharp, scolding tone, "Was that necessary?" If you learned your lesson, it may have been one of the best lessons you ever learned.

Police, prosecutors and jurors will be asking themselves the same question if you make Swiss cheese out of someone with your Sturmgewehr 90. Most self-defense statutes include the word necessary somewhere in the code section. If you are lucky enough to live or be traveling in the states that allow deadly force against serious felonies, the question will be "was it necessary to use deadly force to stop the progression of the forcible felony?" Any force beyond what is necessary to stop the unlawful force being used against you is considered excessive force. The following case quote is perhaps one of the best explanations we've seen concerning what qualifies as necessary action.

> "It is well established that the privilege to use deadly force is not unrestrained, but rather subject to limitations of scope and manner exercised, and when self-defense is claimed, the actor is not privileged to use any means which is intended or likely to cause bodily harm in excess of that *which he correctly or reasonably believes to be necessary for his protection." Coghlan v. Phillips,* 447 F.Supp. 21, 28 (D.C. Miss. 1977). (Emphasis added.)

Example: Suppose you have justification to use deadly force against an assailant attacking you with a deadly weapon. Further assume your first shot wounds your attacker and he falls to the ground writhing in pain. Because of the tremendous impact of the hunka-hunka burning lead you fired (.500 S&W!), the weapon he had been wielding flies from his grasp and out of reach. You are absolutely certain he no longer imposes a threat. Can you shoot him again just because your self-defense instructor has told you that the standard drill when faced with an imminent threat of deadly force is to "shoot a controlled pair at center mass?" NO! You may not cause additional bodily harm in excess of what you reasonably and actually believe to be necessary to protect yourself. Remember, your intent is not to kill even though it may be the natural result of your deadly force. Your intent should only be to stop the progression of deadly force to prevent seriously injury or death.

What if he threatens to sue your @#$@T% @$#@ but is totally physically unable to hurt you or anyone else? Can you "finish the job?" After all, dead men tell no tales. Absolutely not! Anything you do to prevent testimony or to tamper with the evidence is generally by itself a serious crime and strongly suggests a guilty conscience. It is never necessary to execute someone you have rendered helpless by your use of defensive force. If you do and crime scene investigators (CSI) figure it out, you'll fry like a chicken gizzard on a hot Sunday afternoon in the Deep South!

Never say "kill" – How does a jury determine intent? Certainly by what you do. But they also surmise your intent by what you say. In the instant before your use of force to stop an attack, we hope you are saying things like, "Stop! Or I'll Shoot!!!!" not, "You dirty @#%$&, freeze or I'll kill your #$@^%& !!!

Revenge – You must never act out of revenge for someone having committed an act of aggression against you or someone you love. **Example:** Heaven forbid you walk in on an intruder that has just finished molesting your 4-year-old granddaughter. You are not justified in sending him to Hades on the Winchester Express. Your act would be one of revenge, not an act of prevention. **Another Example:** The footnotes to the Connecticut Jury Instructions say if a person commits arson by setting fire to your home, you may not use deadly force against him "one second after the blaze has begun." *Connecticut Jury Instructions*, Paragraph 2.8-4 Defense of Premises — § 53a-20, note 4. (Used with permission of the State of Connecticut Judicial Branch, Copyright ©2010, State of Connecticut Judicial Branch.) An act of revenge is never justifiable. See our advice in Chapter 4 advising not to chase after fleeing felons.

IMMINENT

For a term that is so critical to understanding the law of self-defense, it's frightening how its definition varies.

Here's Utah's definition:

(5) In determining imminence or reasonableness under Subsection (1), the trier of fact [jury] may consider, *but is not limited to*, any of the following factors:

(a) the nature of the danger;

(b) the immediacy of the danger;

(c) the probability that the unlawful force would result in death or serious bodily injury;

(d) the other's prior violent acts or violent propensities; and

(e) any patterns of abuse or violence in the parties' relationship.

Here's Oklahoma's:

Imminent Danger – Danger that is pressing, urgent, or immediate. OUJI-CR [Oklahoma Uniform Jury Instructions – Criminal] 8-56 Defense of Self-Defense – Definitions.

Virginia and Massachusetts cases tell us imminence requires an *overt act.* In, *Commonwealth v. Sands,* 553 S.E.2d 733 (Va. 2001), a husband abused his wife for hours, shot a gun next to her head twice, stuck the barrel of the gun up her nose and told her "I promise you, you will die." He then put the gun in a kitchen cabinet and plopped his machoness in front of the TV. Less than an hour later, the wife opted for a "pre-emptive strike" and unloaded five caps into his cocaine-induced catnap with his own pistol. She was convicted of murder and appealed. The Virginia Supreme Court said there was no way she acted in self-defense because the threat on her life was not imminent. It said imminence required an overt act from the husband besides just laying horizontal, grunting and snoring.

Whatever imminent means, it seems to us the definition sits somewhere between immediate and damn near immediate. A Kansas case defines imminent as being a little bit longer than immediate, but no longer than "near at hand."

> "Although the term "imminent" describes a broader time frame than immediate, the term "imminent" is not without limit. The danger must be near at hand." *State v. White,* 161 P.3d 208, 210 (Kan., 2007).

A few of the western and southern states may have adopted the simplest solution. They substitute the words *about to* instead of *imminent*. For example, Alabama allows the use of deadly force against a person "using or about to use unlawful deadly physical force."

Example 1: Angry Deano the Drunk threatens with a broken, jagged Jack Daniels bottle from a block away. You are sitting in the driver's seat of Richard Petty's Ol'43 fully gassed and screaming, "Dixie!" If you put the cross hairs on Deno with your new .204 Ruger, we suspect police and prosecutors would seriously question whether the threat to you was imminent.

Example 2: Let's change the facts somewhat. Deano's a world class runner, drunk or sober, and he's closing on you fast with a machete in his hand at 25 yards. You're confined to a manually operated wheelchair with your left arm in a sling. Most would agree that the threat is imminent. Imminence does not mean you have to let your attacker clobber you before you use defensive force.

> "Under the law relating to self-defense, one may defend oneself whenever one reasonably believes that he or she is in imminent danger of bodily harm at the hands of another. Such a person, having the fear, *need not wait for the other to strike the first blow." State v. Hallenbeck*, 878 A.2d 992 (R.I., 2005) (citations omitted, emphasis added).

Example 3: Victor whips out an UZI and tells Richard (in the presence of several credible witnesses, hopefully) the next time he sees him, he'll shoot him. Days later Victor approaches Richard while reaching under his coat growling, "I told you the next time I saw you, I was going to kill you!" Richard, honestly believing Victor is reaching for a machine-gun, draws and fires. Under these circumstances, Richard has an argument that he had a reasonable belief that death was imminent because of Victor's past threats. Reaching under his coat is an overt act. (Unfortunately, if there turns out to be no weapon, he'll probably be arrested. It seems like half of the cases we have read involving murder convictions involve defendants who claimed, "I thought he was reaching for a weapon!")

SERIOUS BODILY INJURY

Serious bodily injury – injury that is life threatening, causes permanent disfigurement, or results in permanent disability. **Examples:** Being stabbed with a knife, shot with a firearm, beaten with a tire iron or baseball bat or filleted by a samurai sword. Many states use variations of this term such as "great bodily harm," but the concept is the same. This is phrase is defined by several of the states in Chapter 5.

DEADLY FORCE

Force that could cause *serious bodily injury or death.* Shooting a firearm at someone is considered the use of deadly force in every state. Also, see the definitions included in the codes of several of the states in Chapter 5.

BURDEN OF PROOF

This is of more concern to your lawyer than it is to you, so you won't see it discussed extensively in this book. But we mention it because it's something that you will eventually wonder about while studying the subject of self-defense. In all states except Ohio, the state has the burden of proving beyond a reasonable doubt that the defendant did not act in self-defense. If the state proves beyond a reasonable doubt that you failed to meet just one of the requirements of self-defense (e.g., you failed to act reasonably, the threat was not imminent, you used more force than was necessary), then you will not win on the theory of self-defense. In Ohio, the defendant must first prove the elements of self-defense by a preponderance of the evidence (more likely than not). If he does so, then the state has the burden of disproving self-defense beyond a reasonable doubt.

4

TEMPLATE *[Subheadings]* DESCRIBED IN DETAIL

This chapter *explains* the *legal issues* that we discuss under each of the TEMPLATE topics for each state. It does *not* tell you how to conduct yourself during a defensive incident in any *particular* state. After you understand the issues, you'll need to turn to each state's subchapter to find out what that state's specific rules are for each TEMPLATE topic.

NAME OF STATE

The state self-defense laws appear alphabetically from Alabama through Wyoming in Chapter 5, each state having its own subchapter. As the key in each subchapter indicates, except for a short introduction, state statutes, cases and jury instructions appear in black ink. The TEMPLATE subheadings are in red, **bold**, in Title Case and in [brackets] e.g., **[Deadly Force]**. Our commentary appears in red and [in brackets].

[Defense of Self and Others]

This TEMPLATE heading indicates the beginning of the discussion of defense of persons as opposed to defense of property.

[Non-Deadly Force]

You can generally threaten or use as much force as reasonably necessary to stop unlawful, non-deadly force against you or someone else, but you cannot use deadly force. **Example:** On Black Friday, just after Thanksgiving, you get to the toy store before anyone else and snag the last, newest, and hottest "Drag Queen Bobbie" doll off the store shelf. Another woman is angry and starts slapping at you and your 8 year-old daughter. You can use whatever force is *reasonably necessary* to keep her from striking you or your daughter. This might include pushing her away or slapping her to make her stop her attack. But you cannot use force *likely to cause death or serious bodily injury* (meaning leave your new, pink .38SPL Lady Smith holstered in your purse). If your assailant falls down as you push her away and it's clear you have knocked the fight out of her, you cannot kick her in the face with your high heel while she's down "to teach the crazy b@&^h a lesson!" You certainly also cannot fire a warning shot from your Lady Smith. In virtually every state, shooting a gun is considered the use of deadly force and is almost never justifiable when used against a non-deadly threat.

Hidden Trap Regarding Brandishing and Assault with Deadly Weapon – Caution – Especially in Kansas. Just before this book went to print, we discovered a Kansas case that held that self-defense does not apply to crimes that involve the threat of force rather than the use of force. Such crimes include brandishing and aggravated assault. The term "threaten" is not found in the Kansas self-defense statute. Therefore, the Kansas Supreme Court held that a person who threatens deadly force cannot claim self-defense. *State v. Hendrix*, 289 Kan. 859, 218 P.3d 40, (Kan.,2009), followed by *State v. Flint*, 2010 WL 445934 (Kan. App. Jan 29, 2010). Fortunately, we have not found any cases in other states that have followed this reasoning even though several states' self-defense statutes do not expressly address the act of threatening. *Pancho's Wisdom* – This is a hair-brained decision. It suggests you are better off shooting someone than threatening him. If you have access to legal cases, see Justice Davis' dissent in *Hendrix*. Read UCLA law professor Eugene Volokh's stinging criticism of the *Hendrix* and *Flint* decisions at http://volokh.com/2010/02/12/if-you-brandish-a-gun-in-self-defense-in-kansas-youd-best-shoot-it/.

[Deadly Force]

The typical self-defense statute says you cannot use force *likely to cause serious bodily injury or death* unless you *reasonably believe* there is an *imminent threat* that someone is "about to" cause you or another person *death or serious bodily injury*. **Example:** You're in the mall with your daughter and a fellow clad in a black trench coat begins to pull a semi-automatic Bullpup out of his U.S. Postal Service cloth bag as he shouts he is going to "make Hamburger Helper out of the both of you!" Such a threat, accompanied by the showing of a scary-looking firearm, would normally be considered an *imminent threat of death or serious bodily injury*. Assuming all elements for self-defense are legally satisfied, you would be justified in quickly (hopefully) responding with enough shots out of your Smith &Wesson to neutralize the attacker.

[Use of Deadly Force to Prevent Serious Felonies]

Many states recognize that certain felonies are so serious and harmful that they give their citizens the right to use deadly force to prevent or interrupt them. Some states list these serious crimes in the self-defense section of their codes and others mention them in the section relating to defense of special places such as homes, occupied vehicles, and places of employment. These statutes give the defender the right to use deadly force if he *reasonably believes* it is *necessary* to prevent the commission of *imminent violent felonies*. Other states use the term *"forcible felony."* There are states that actually name the felonies that apply. See the Utah and Florida subchapters. Common felonies include murder, manslaughter, rape, forcible sodomy, sexual abuse of a child, kidnapping, assault with a deadly weapon, arson and burglary. At common law, these types of felonies were punishable by death. Hence, the rationale at common law for allowing the defender to use deadly force was that he was simply speeding up the inevitable death of the perpetrator of the crime. The definitions of the felonies authorizing the use of deadly force, if any, are found at the end of the state's subchapter under the heading **[Helpful Definitions Relating to Self-Defense Statutes]**. For these felonies, we give the gist of the definition and then cite the statute where these crimes can be found in your state code books or on the internet. Our commentary [in red and in brackets] is to give you a general idea in plain English what these code sections say. You would do well to read each actual forcible felony statute at some point so you know specifically what every element of each crime is.

Special Concern – Sexual Crimes: A potential hidden trap exists in those states that do not specifically authorize the use of deadly force against sex crimes such as rape or forcible sodomy, but only authorize the use of deadly force to prevent "death or serious bodily injury." The trap is that it is not always clear that a sexual assault will be considered by the courts to constitute a threat of serious bodily injury. *Pancho's Wisdom*: Fix it! If your state does not specifically authorize the use of deadly force against forcible sexual assaults, perhaps it's time to pressure your legislature to make the change. In this day and age it is unacceptable for a woman to have to wonder whether or not the law might punish her for using deadly force to keep from being sexually assaulted.

Fleeing-Felon and Any-FelonyTraps – The wording of some states' self-defense statutes seem to give a defender the right to use deadly force to prevent the commission of *any felony*, or to pursue *a fleeing felon*. If you rely on the wording of these statutes, you might be lulled into believing you can shoot an unarmed, non-dangerous person committing a non-violent felony or one running away after the commission of such a felony. This could have disastrous legal and economic consequences for you. The U.S. Supreme Court in a civil rights case held that "statutes allowing use of deadly force against apparently unarmed, non-dangerous suspects is *constitutionally unreasonable* and a violation of the Fourth Amendment of the United States Constitution." *Tennessee v. Garner,* 471 U.S. 1, 11 (1985). In 1993, the Nevada Legislature, based partly upon the holding in *Garner,* repealed Nevada's fleeing-felon statute and enacted a statute limiting a police officer's use of deadly force. The defendant, a private citizen, in the case of *State v. Weddell,* 118 Nev. 206, 43 P.3d 987 (2002), unaware of the changes occurring in the law, attempted to stop a fleeing felon by shooting at him. He was arrested and charged with felony assault with a deadly weapon. Although the trial court dismissed the charges, the Nevada Supreme Court reinstated them holding that the law of Nevada no longer allowed private citizens to use deadly force to stop fleeing-felons. The research conducted by the attorneys in the case and the discussion of that research by the Nevada Supreme Court leads us to believe that there is a trend nationally to repeal (get rid of) fleeing-felon statutes for private citizens. In the *Weddell* case, the Nevada Supreme Court explained how the nature of felonies has changed since the enactment of Nevada's original fleeing-felon statute in 1931 (footnotes omitted):

> At common law, the fleeing-felon rule permitted a private person to use deadly force to apprehend a felon. The use of deadly force was permitted to prevent the commission of a felony or to arrest someone who had committed one. The rule was developed at a time when felonies were only the very serious, violent or dangerous crimes and "virtually all felonies were punishable by death." As the United States Supreme Court noted, "Though effected without the protections and formalities of an orderly trial and conviction, the killing of a resisting or fleeing felon resulted in no greater consequences than those authorized for punishment of the felony of which the individual was charged or suspected." Today, however, many crimes which are punished as felonies do not involve dangerous conduct or violence and are not punishable by death. As the United States Supreme Court observed in *Tennessee v. Garner*, the modern distinction between felonies and misdemeanors is "minor and often arbitrary." For example, a person who works at a voter registration agency and who wears a "Vote for Jane Johnson" button at work is guilty of a felony. A person who steals $255 worth of bedding from a hotel is guilty of a felony. A person who buys $250 worth of food stamps from someone when not authorized to do so is guilty of a felony. These felons, like many others, will not receive the death penalty. Society would not tolerate the use of deadly force to prevent the commission of any of these crimes or to apprehend someone suspected of any of these crimes. The modern arbitrary and expanded classification of crimes as felonies has undermined the rationale for the old common law fleeing-felon rule, which, as mentioned, was to prevent the escape of a felon by inflicting the punishment that was inevitably to come.

State v. Weddell, 118 Nev. at 211,212 (2002). If you threaten with a weapon, shoot at, injure or kill an unarmed, non-dangerous felon who has not committed a serious felony while relying on the any-felon language of your state's self-defense or fleeing-felon laws, you could be prosecuted and convicted. **Our advice that could save your freedom and your fortune:** Don't shoot obviously unarmed, non-threatening, non-violent felons you have accosted, even if they bolt and try to get away.

[Defense of Third Persons]

Most states permit you to protect another person, whether they are related to you or not, just like you would defend yourself. However, California, Idaho, Nevada, Oklahoma, South Dakota, and Vermont limit the right to protect third persons to a select group, including some but not all relatives and one's master and mistress. We believe the terms "master" and "mistress"to be the titles of male and female employers. A mistress under these statutes does NOT refer to your adulterous lover(s) (Tiger, listen up here). "Under the provisions of Title 21, § 733, O.S. (Oklahoma Statutes)1951, the term 'mistress' defines a lawful relationship as between mistress as the female head of a household, or lawful institution, having power or command over another as the servant, which relationship may constitute the legal basis for justifiable homicide by the mistress in defense of the servant or vice versa." *Haines v. State,* 275 P.2d 347, 349 Okl.Cr.App. 1954. In those states, a person would be taking a legal risk to defend a third person not defined in the particular group referenced in the statute.

Some states only allow you to defend a third person if the third person could have defended himself under the same circumstances. The following section lists several examples of how a person can lose the right to defend him or herself. One way is by starting a fight (initial aggressor). In some states, because an initial aggressor has no right to defend himself, you also have no right to defend such person, even though you didn't know he started the fight. Unfortunately, this rule of law adds substantial legal risk to being a Good Samaritan. Carefully read your state's statute relating to defense of third persons so that you will be aware of such issues.

[Exceptions to Justifiable Self-Defense]

If you are at fault in starting or escalating a fight, you risk losing the legal right to defend yourself. Most of the self-defense laws deprive or diminish one's right to claim self-defense if he starts a fight, shares guilt in escalating it, agrees to a duel or commits an unlawful act which, in turn, culminates in an act of self-defense. The combinations of these limitations vary from state to state. Our experience has been that if your opponent or any witness claims you started or escalated the conflict, you will generally be arrested and prosecuted. The word to the wise is don't start fights and control your temper. If anyone claims (truthfully or not) you are at fault in starting, provoking or escalating an event that ends with deadly or potentially deadly consequences, you WILL be arrested and you WON'T be able to talk your way out of it. Telling the police anything other than you want to talk to your lawyer will only hurt your case. SHUT UP!!!!!

[Initial Aggressor] – The *initial aggressor* is the guy who started the fight. He's not allowed to claim self-defense. New York's Justification jury instructions contain one of the most complete and just definitions of the term:

"Initial aggressor" means the person who first attacks or threatens to attack; that is, the first person who uses or threatens the imminent use of offensive physical force. *The actual striking of the first blow or inflicting of the first wound, however, does not necessarily determine who was the initial aggressor.*

A person who reasonably believes that another is about to use physical force upon him need not wait until he is struck or wounded. He may, in such circumstances, be the first to use physical force, so long as he reasonably believed it was about to be used against him. He is then not considered to be the "initial aggressor," even though he strikes the first blow or inflicts the first wound. *Arguing, using abusive language, calling a person names, or the like, unaccompanied by physical threats or acts, does not make a person an initial aggressor and does not justify physical force.* (Emphasis added; alternate personal pronouns omitted.) New York Justification Jury Instructions, JUSTIFICATION: USE OF PHYSICAL FORCE IN DEFENSE OF A PERSON, PENAL LAW 35.15 [This jury instruction clarifies two excellent points. First, you don't have to let someone clobber you first just to prove that you are not the initial aggressor. Second, your swearing or name calling doesn't necessarily make you the initial aggressor. But using obscenities or fighting words is certainly a "Thumbs-Down Factor" that could escalate a fight and cause you tremendous legal grief. See Thumbs-Down Chapter 7. Finally, don't forget, not every state has adopted this excellent definition.]

[Provocation] – Some states use the term *"provocation"* interchangeably with the term *"initial aggressor."* But it is most often used in the sense of starting a fight AS AN EXCUSE to hurt the other person after he reacts to the provocation. Obviously, under those circumstances the provoker is not justified to use force in self-defense.

[Committing Felony or Unlawful Act] – If you rob a convenience store and the clerk defends his cash register with a shotgun, you can't claim you shot him because he was threatening deadly force.

[Mutual Combat or Combat by Agreement] – Agreeing to meet another behind the gym to duke it out or in front of the saloon at high noon to slap leather is no excuse for smacking or shooting another, even if he threw the first punch or he drew his Peacemaker first. You kill someone under those circumstances and it is considered murder or at least manslaughter in virtually every state. In modern times, prosecutors sometimes claim road rage is combat by agreement. It usually begins with vulgar language and obscene gestures and then escalates to more dangerous conduct like swerving cars and brandishing weapons. Acting or reacting like this will almost always get you arrested and prosecuted. We estimate that over 50% of our brandishing cases come from some sort of road rage incident.

[Other Exceptions – Resisting Arrest – Claim of Right to Property] – You are not justified in using force in self-defense to resist arrest by a peace officer, even if you believe the arrest is unlawful. Resisting arrest can result in a felony conviction and wipe out your right to possess a firearm.

Another exception that restricts the use of defensive force is when your opponent claims a right to real estate or personal property. For example, your landlord serves you with an eviction notice and claims he has a right to inspect your apartment. You could both be in trouble if the pushing and shoving turns into a WWF SmackDown! That's because you are both claiming a right to the property and the law expects disagreements like that to be worked out in the civil courts, not in the ring or with dueling pistols. And, no, you can't kill the repo man knowing you are three payments behind on your Harley.

[Exceptions to the Exceptions] – Although one who starts or voluntarily participates in a fight is not normally entitled to claim self-defense, there are a couple of possible exceptions. **[Withdraw and Communicate]** He must completely stop his aggression and clearly communicate his intent to stop fighting to his opponent. Then, if his opponent continues to use force, most states allow him to repel the attack, some even with deadly force. **[Escalation]** In some states, even though a person is the initial aggressor, if he does so with non-deadly force, but his opponent responds with deadly force, the initial aggressor can respond with deadly force. Whenever there is a possible exception to an exception, there are so many facts to sort out that police and prosecutors will almost always arrest and prosecute. It's all so complicated that they simply let the jury sort out who's telling the truth and who's to blame. From a legal standpoint, it's best to be completely without fault before taking defensive action.

Perception of Fault, Words and Witnesses – What you say can influence how witnesses perceive whether you were somehow at fault in causing or escalating an incident. As you step up force to meet the threat (Chapter 10), make sure what you say doesn't lead eye witnesses to believe you are the one who started or escalated the conflict. **Wrong things to say:** "Come on B^**^, I'm gonna kick your @#$." Avoid "macho" language if at all possible. **Right:** "Stop right there! Don't come any closer! *I'm leaving and don't want trouble!*" And finally, "Don't come any closer or I'll shoot!"

[Duty (or No Duty) to Retreat – Generally]

At common law, a citizen attacked while outside of his own home had a duty to retreat from his attacker before he could use deadly force. He was required to "retreat to the wall," meaning until he could no longer retreat safely, and only then could he resort to the use of deadly force. A citizen was not required to retreat from his home or "castle," hence the term "castle doctrine." The states have changed these rules in a whole host of ways since the days of common law in Jolly ol' England.

Make-My-Day Laws – Many states have done away with the duty to retreat as long as the defender is acting lawfully. Elimination of the duty to retreat is sometimes referred to as an extension of the castle doctrine. In remembrance of the great line in the Clint Eastwood movie, *Dirty Harry,* a law eliminating the duty to retreat when attacked outside of one's home is also referred to as a "Make-My-Day law." Under this doctrine, instead of retreating, a person can stand his ground as long as he has a legal right to be in the place he is located when he is attacked. He can then meet force with force, deadly force with deadly force. Picture ol' Clint being robbed at gunpoint on the streets of Tallahassee, drawing his .44 from his shoulder holster, cocking it with that famous grimace on his face while rasping the immortal warning, "Make My Day . . . . Punk!"

There are exceptions to this rule. For example, trespassers must retreat. Also, if you are committing a crime, you start the fight, agree to a duel or provoke the conflict as an excuse to kill your opponent, not only must you retreat but you may lose the right of self-defense altogether. Whenever it gets that complicated and your opponent dies, you can count on being arrested, prosecuted and probably convicted of something ugly, if not murder, then manslaughter. See "Thumbs-Down" Factors, Chapter 7. The states that still require a person to retreat before using deadly force, only require retreat if it can done in complete safety.

Although there may be no duty to retreat, retreating may be the right thing to do if it can be done in complete safety. Tactically, retreating puts more distance between you and your attacker. This reduces the chances of getting shot or stabbed. It also gives your attorney something sympathetic to say about you. "Our client didn't have to retreat, but he did. He ran through the briars and he ran through the br... hum... huh? ...and he ran through the bushes where a rabbit wouldn't go; he ran so fast that the homees couldn't catch him; down the Chattahoochee to the Gulf of Mexico. And when he ran out of sand, then and only then did he draw his gun." You get our drift, even if we can't sing and don't remember the real words to the song!

[Defense of Persons in Special Places e.g., Home, Workplace, Occupied Vehicle]

Special Places – This is a phrase *we made up* to describe places in which states have given their self-defense laws a little more muscle. The most common *special place* is in the home. Under common law, landowners had the right to use deadly weapons, like swords and spears, to keep intruders out of their castles. A person was not required to retreat from his own castle before impaling a murderous invader. When outside of one's castle, a person was required to retreat before using deadly force. He was *not* required to retreat, however, unless retreat could be accomplished in complete safety.

Expansion of the Castle Doctrine and Curtilage – When modern states add places from which citizens do not have to retreat before using deadly force, this process is often referred to as an "expansion of the castle doctrine." For example, some states have extended the no-retreat rule slightly beyond the walls of one's own home to the area immediately surrounding the home, often called *the curtilage*. There is no way to know exactly what these special places are without reading each state's subchapter carefully in Chapter 5.

About one third of the states have expanded the castle doctrine or no-retreat rule beyond the home. Modern day castles may include one's *business, occupied vehicles, and buildings*. Temporary residences like hotels and campers can be considered castles as well, depending on the language of the state statute. Many state statutes say the occupants of such places are *presumed* to have a reasonable fear of death or great bodily harm if someone unlawfully breaks or sneaks into any of these special places.

A few states, like Utah, Florida and Texas extend the castle doctrine to *every place where a person has a right to be*. The flip side of that doctrine is that *trespassers* must retreat before using defensive force because they don't have the legal right to be on the property they are trespassing on. It's not their castle.

Lower Threshold for the Use of Deadly Force – Finally, in some of the more protective states like Utah, Florida and Texas, the threshold that triggers the right to use deadly force can be lower inside special places than outside. Under some conditions, a defender may use reasonable and necessary deadly force against an imminent threat of "personal violence" rather "an imminent threat of serious injury or death." For example, in Colorado, if certain strict conditions are satisfied, an occupant may use deadly force against an intruder when "the occupant reasonably believes that [the intruder] *might use any physical force, no matter how slight*, against any occupant." If Colorado residents learn the specific rules, this lower threshold could prove to be a lifesaver when split seconds count. For example, if all other conditions of Colorado's home and self-defense statutes are met (there are hidden legal traps, read the law carefully), a homeowner could arguably use deadly force against an armed home invader who is threatening harm but hasn't shown his weapon and hasn't yet threatened deadly force. According to Colorado and Illinois case law, before the lower threshold applies, there is a strict requirement of an "unlawful entry."

Unlawful Entry – Colorado and Illinois cases have interpreted the "unlawful entry" requirement in their defense-of-special-places statutes to require an actual unlawful entry by an intruder. A reasonable belief by the home owner, for example, that the entry was unlawful is not enough. This is a concern because the defense-of-special-places statutes of many states have similar language. **Example:** You live in a state that presumes you have a reasonable belief of imminent death or serious injury if someone unlawfully and forcibly enters your home. Your boyfriend, who does not live with you, has had permission in the past to enter your home without knocking if the door is unlocked. He enters and you perceive he intends to strike you with his fists. There is nothing to indicate he possesses a dangerous weapon or intends to sexually assault you. Because his entry was not unlawful, the lower threshold would not apply. Before you could use deadly force you would have to have a reasonable belief that his attack presented an imminent threat of serious bodily injury or death. If you used a deadly weapon to injure or kill him, an unarmed man, you would probably be prosecuted and convicted. See Chapter 7, Thumbs-Down Factors and Chapter 13 regarding domestic violence. **Example:** Assume the same facts as above except that your screen door is locked and a stranger bursts through the latched door. He appears as if he intends to assault you with his bare hands. This would be an unlawful entry and forcible entry. In those states that presume an imminent threat of deadly force, you would probably be justified in defending yourself with deadly force. Of course, states have different requirements, so be sure to identify the specific factors that trigger the presumption. The unlawful-entry requirement provides a good reason to keep your doors locked. And yes, we anticipated the next question many of you will have after reading this. If an uninvited person enters through an open window it's probably an unlawful entry. Whether it's a forcible entry would depend upon additional facts. In Utah, a secret or stealthy entry can satisfy the requirement as well as a forcible entry. Again, if your state has a lower threshold for the use of deadly force in special places, make sure you understand all of the prerequisites that trigger the presumption of an imminent threat of deadly force.

[Retreating from the Home or Other Special Places] – As mentioned above, most states do not require you to retreat from your own home. Check your state and those states in which you intend to travel carefully. Know what your legal and tactical options are.

Exceptions – Even in states where you don't have to retreat from your home or other special place, you will almost always have a duty to retreat if your actions place you within the following exceptions to the don't-have-to-retreat rule:

Initial Aggressor – If you start a fight in your home, you will be under a duty to retreat from your home if you ultimately expect to have any hope of reclaiming your right to defend yourself.

[Co-Habitant; Co-Employees]

People with a right to be in the home, workplace or on the property – You may be required to retreat from your home or other special place if the person who is attacking you has a right to be in the home. Such persons could include your spouse, a roommate, a live-in relative or someone who has custody or guardianship of a relative. This rule often applies to co-workers as well.

Exception to the Exception – If there is a restraining order or protective order against someone who has a right to be in the home, such as an abusive spouse, then there is usually no duty to retreat unless there is a general duty to retreat from your home or you started the fight. Please keep in mind that seriously injuring or killing a spouse or significant other who has a legal right to be in your home almost always results in arrest and prosecution regardless of the excuse for doing so. There is only one possible exception to this that we know of. See Chapter XIII.

No Weapons-in-the-Workplace Policies – Unfortunately, many employers prohibit their employees from bringing defensive weapons into the workplace or even into parking lots. If you value your job, you should research your company's weapon policies thoroughly before taking a weapon into a company building or company vehicle. Many employers even prohibit taking a weapon into company parking lot in the employee's own vehicle. Rather than ask specifically about your company's weapon policies, you might just ask to review the workplace policies. Some personnel managers are so freaked out by guns that they might consider you a safety risk for even asking. *Pancho's Wisdom* – After Utah's Supreme Court rejected our lawsuit challenging employer policies prohibiting employees from keeping firearms in their own vehicles, we went to work and passed a law in Utah reversing the Supreme Court. We encourage you to do the same in your home state. See Mother of All Self-Defense Laws, Chapter 20, under [**Protection of Persons in Special Places**].

[Presumption of Reasonableness in Special Places]

There are states that presume you acted reasonably if a person breaks or sneaks into your home and you fill him full of lead. This presumption can be rebutted, however. If you shoot someone in your home to whom you owe a gambling debt, your case will be investigated thoroughly. Most states do not apply the presumption if the person killed or injured is a member of the household. If you shoot your wife "by accident" just after you bought that huge life insurance policy for her—well, you get the point. In those states that have extended the castle doctrine to the workplace, there is usually no presumption of reasonableness if force is used against a currently employed co-worker who goes postal. However, if he's been fired and is trespassing when you light him up, there is a presumption you acted reasonably in those states that recognize the place of employment as a *special place.*

[Reckless Injury to Innocent Third Parties]

While murder, attempted murder or assault with a deadly weapon generally require proof of intent, criminal responsibility can also arise from reckless or negligent conduct. **Example:** You may be justified in using deadly force to prevent a bank robbery. However, praying and spraying with your MAC-10 in a crowded bank, thinking your bullets will be able to distinguish the guilty from the innocent, is reckless. Recklessness is generally sufficient to sustain a manslaughter conviction and a nasty civil suit.

[Civil Liability]

Civil liability refers to getting sued by persons you injure or the heirs of those you kill. Not being arrested, prosecuted or convicted doesn't mean you won't be sued. Ask Bernhard Goetz, the infamous "Subway Vigilante," who was found not guilty for the attempted murder of four toughs whom he claimed tried to rob him with a screw driver on New York's subway system. One of the thugs later recovered a 43 million dollar judgment claiming Goetz wounded him and then shot him in the head as he lay helpless.

How could Goetz have won the criminal case but lost the civil case? The burden of proof is lower in a civil case. Criminal prosecutors have the burden of proving their cases beyond a reasonable doubt. Injured people win lawsuits by a preponderance of evidence (more likely than not). Therefore, it's possible to win a not-guilty verdict in a criminal case and lose your shirt (and everything else you own) in the civil case that follows. See Chapter XV which delves deeper into the law of Civil Liability.

People in conservative states think it is outrageous for a violent felon to be able to sue his innocent victim for seasoning the felon's reprobate rump with 00 buck. These states have passed laws that protect those acting in lawful self-defense from lawsuits. An example of such a statute is included in Chapter XX. That's the good news. The bad news is that such protection against lawsuits doesn't apply if the felon has clearly retreated. This means that the seven exit wounds ripping through the delicate artwork of the battleship tattooed on a dead felon's shaven chest could spell L-A-W-S-U-I-T.

[Defense of Property]

Most state defense-of-property statutes limit the defense of cars, guns or electronic equipment (personal property) to the use of non-deadly force. But if the thief ups the ante with an imminent deadly threat, the state self-defense statutes kick in and may allow the property owner to respond with deadly force. *We strongly recommend against using force or threats to defend personal property.* If the attempted defense of property escalates, *very unpleasant* things could happen to you. You may have to shoot or kill the thief. Afterwards, the District Attorney may claim you used excessive force, indeed deadly force, to defend property. You could be prosecuted *and* sued. Even worse, you could be killed. If only personal property is involved, our advice is to get a good description of the thief and call 911. Keep photos and serial numbers of your property or mark it in hidden places so you can identify it later. If the theft happens on a Friday night, cozy up to a good novel, quick response time for a property crime could be four hours!

Consider the *Schanze* case chronicled in Chapter XII. Briefly, an assailant threatened to break out the tail lights of the defendant's black Jaguar. When the threatening man picked up a rock, the defendant drew his pistol out of concealment as a precaution. The man with the rock dropped it, but his friends called the police to report "a man with a gun." We beat the resulting brandishing charge, but instead of paying legal fees the defendant could have replaced the whole Jaguar let alone the tail lights. The financial, safety and legal risks of using a deadly weapon to defend personal property are almost never worth it.

[Helpful Definitions Relating to Self-Defense Statutes]

Most, but not all states, define the critical terms used in their self-defense statutes. Those definitions are included near the end of each state's section.

[TEMPLATE Topics We Could Not Find Explained in Statutes or Cases]

We list the TEMPLATE subheadings that we could not find explained in that state's statutes, cases or jury instructions at the end of each state's subchapter under this heading. When there is a defensive event that contains issues not addressed in a state's self-defense laws, judges and attorneys often look to neighboring states' cases to find what the law should be. This is how you could be held accountable for a rule of law used by another state that you had never known or anticipated. For this reason we recommend you not only read your state's self-defense laws in Chapter 5, but the laws of your neighboring states as well. If you plan to take a defensive weapon in your travels through neighboring states, you should know their self-defense laws anyway.

THE BOTTOM LINE

By now you may be asking yourself, "Is there a rule that would allow me to defend myself with deadly force no matter where in the country I am traveling?" Yes. Even in the states with the least protective self-defense laws, *if a jury* finds that *all* of the following conditions are met, you will be found *not guilty* on the theory of self-defense: (1) You are completely without fault in either starting, continuing or escalating the conflict; (2) You have a reasonable and actual belief that the force being threatened against you could cause serious bodily injury or death; (3) The threat is imminent; (4) You use only necessary force, not excessive force, and (5) Before using any force, you retreat until it is no longer safe for you to do so. This is the common law rule that applied when a person was *outside of his castle*. Whether any state's law of self-defense will give you any greater tactical advantage than this bottom-line, common-law rule, will depend upon which jurisdiction you are in when you are attacked. So study each state's laws carefully. If a state proves beyond a reasonable doubt that *any one* of its conditions for self-defense was not met, you lose.

Pancho's Wisdom

You just might be a Gunnut if . . .

. . . you have black rifles hermetically sealed and buried under your back lawn or secluded behind the sheet rock of an inner wall.

. . . yer neighbors refer to your vehicle as a carsenal.

. . . the first item on your "trip list" is your concealed weapon.

. . . you stole your first kiss while changing targets behind the 100 yard berm as bullets whizzed over your heads at a military-style shooting range.

5

SELF-DEFENSE LAWS OF ALL 50 STATES

Pancho Meditating and Levitating for Wisdom.

Pancho's Wisdom: Breaking into the home of a good ol' boy from Bama would subject you to more violence than playing dominoes on the line of scrimmage during an Alabama (Roll Tide!)/Auburn (War Eagle!) game!

Key: ■ commentary ■ original statutes, cases or jury instructions

---

[Defense of Self and Others] [Non-Deadly Force]

§ ALABAMA (ALA.) CODE § 13A-3-23 (a) (1) – (3).
Use of force in defense of a person.

(a) A person is justified in using physical force upon another person in order to defend himself or herself or a third person from what he or she reasonably believes to be the use or imminent use of unlawful physical force by that other person, and he or she may use a degree of force which he or she reasonably believes to be necessary for the purpose. . . [**Example:** You can push someone away who is trying to hit you in the face with his fist. You would NOT be legally justified in shooting a gun or thrusting a knife at that person, unless he was using his fist to commit one of the serious crimes specifically mentioned in the **[Deadly Force]** section below.]

[Deadly Force] [Defense of a Third Person]
[Use of Deadly Force to Prevent Serious Felonies]

[(a) continued. . .] A person may use deadly physical force, and is legally presumed to be justified in using deadly physical force in self-defense or the defense of another person pursuant to subdivision (4), if the person reasonably believes that another person is:

(1) Using or about to use unlawful deadly physical force. [In other words, like in most states, you can resist deadly force with deadly force.]

(2) Using or about to use physical force against an occupant of a dwelling while committing or attempting to commit a burglary of such dwelling. [You can use deadly force to defend someone in a dwelling who is being physically assaulted during a burglary, i.e. knowingly and unlawfully entering or remaining in a dwelling or building with intent to commit a crime therein. Notice the threshold for using deadly force is lowered when you are defending someone in your home. Outside your home you must be facing a threat of deadly physical force (such as an assault with a deadly weapon) before you can respond with deadly force. Even if an unlawful intruder has no weapon, if he threatens you or anyone else while committing or attempting to com-

mit a home burglary, you should be able to make him a painful participant in a shotgun-induced crimson tide!]

(3) Committing or about to commit a kidnapping in any degree, assault in the first or second degree, burglary in any degree, robbery in any degree, forcible rape, or forcible sodomy. [In most states, these are referred to as "forcible felonies" that trigger the justification to use deadly force. Assaults in the first and second degree are felonies including assault with a deadly weapon or with intent to cause serious bodily injury, assault on police officers, teachers, etc., Alabama Code – 13-6-20 & 21.]

. . .

[Exceptions to Justifiable Self-Defense]

§ ALA. CODE § 13A-3-23 (c).

. . .

(c) Notwithstanding the provisions of subsection (a), a person is not justified in using physical force if: [You can't claim self-defense if you . . .]

[Provocation]

(1) With intent to cause physical injury or death to another person, he or she provoked the use of unlawful physical force by such other person. [. . . provoke a fight as an excuse to injure or kill.]

[Initial Aggressor]

(2) He or she was the initial aggressor . . . [. . . start a fight. See Exceptions to Exceptions below]

[Exceptions to the Exceptions] [Withdraw and Communicate]

[You can't claim self-defense as an initial aggressor unless...]

[(2) continued . . .] he or she withdraws from the encounter and effectively communicates to the other person his or her intent to do so, but the latter person nevertheless continues or threatens the use of unlawful physical force. [. . . . . . you totally withdraw from the fight and make it clear to everyone around that you no longer want to fight. Then, if the bozo keeps coming, you can use reasonable force to stop him or her. You're still going to get arrested and probably prosecuted. The best advice is simply to NOT go around starting fights!]

[Mutual Combat]

(3) The physical force involved was the product of a combat by agreement not specifically authorized by law. [Dueling and face-to-face gunfights are not tolerated in modern law. If you are a willing participant in a gunfight ("meet me outside the saloon at high noon"), you can't claim self -defense even if you wear a white hat and let the bad guy "slap leather" first!]

[No Duty to Retreat – Generally]

§ ALA. CODE § 13A-3-23 (b).

. . .

(b) A person who is justified under subsection (a) in using physical force, including deadly physical force, and who is not engaged in an unlawful activity and is in any place where he or she has the right to be has no duty to retreat and has the right to stand his or her ground. [This no-retreat provision was added in 2006. Before that, in any place besides your home, you had to retreat (if it could be done safely) before you could use a deadly weapon to defend yourself. Because it's so new, we haven't found any case law that interprets it. Under the new law, you have no duty to retreat if you are in a place you have a legal right to be and are otherwise acting lawfully. Florida passed a similar law a few years ago and it received national media attention as the "Make-My-Day" law, named after a great line in the Clint Eastwood movie *Sudden Impact.* States like Utah and Texas have had such a law for years without blood running in the streets. Such laws act as a deterrent to hoodlums and muggers to leave law-abiding citizens alone.]

[Defense of Person(s) in Special Places – "Premises"]

§ ALA.CODE § 13A-3-25.

Use of force in defense of premises.

[Non-Deadly Force]

(a) A person in lawful possession or control of premises, as defined in Section **13A-3-20,** [see definitions below] or a person who is licensed or privileged to be thereon, may use physical force upon another person when and to the extent that he reasonably believes it necessary to prevent or terminate what he reasonably believes to be the commission or attempted commission of a criminal trespass by the other person in or upon such premises. [You can use reasonable force to keep trespassers off of your property, but not deadly force. *Pancho's Wisdom* – If someone trespasses into your garden to steal your turnip greens, don't run out and confront them with your squirrel gun. Why not just call the police? Does it make sense to risk a lawsuit or a serious criminal charge for a mess of turnip greens or polk salad?]

[Deadly Force]

(b) A person may use deadly physical force under the circumstances set forth in subsection (a) of this section only:

(1) In defense of a person, as provided in Section **13A-3-23** [see use of force in defense of persons above]; or

(2) When he reasonably believes it necessary to prevent the commission of arson in the first or second degree by the trespasser. [If someone is attempting to unlawfully burn a building down, you are justified in responding with deadly force. Arson in the first degree is starting a fire in a building knowing or having reason to believe someone is in the building; second degree arson is without knowledge or reason to believe someone is in the building.]

[No Duty to Retreat From Special Places]

[A person who owns or is in control of buildings or real estate obviously has a right to be there. Therefore, he has no duty to retreat from the premises. See **[No Duty to Retreat – Generally]** above.]

[Presumption of Reasonableness in Special Places – Home, Business or an Occupied Vehicle, or Federally Licensed Nuclear Power Facility.]

§ **ALA.CODE 1975 § 13A-3-23 (a) (4).**
Use of force in defense of a person.

(a) . . . A person may use deadly physical force, and is legally presumed to be justified in using deadly physical force in self-defense or the defense of another person pursuant to subdivision (4), if the person reasonably believes that another person is:

. . .

(4) In the process of unlawfully and forcefully entering, or has unlawfully and forcefully entered, a dwelling, residence, or occupied vehicle, or federally licensed nuclear power facility, or is in the process of sabotaging or attempting to sabotage a federally licensed nuclear power facility, or is attempting to remove, or has forcefully removed, a person against his or her will from any dwelling, residence, or occupied vehicle when the person has a legal right to be there, and provided that the person using the deadly physical force knows or has reason to believe that an unlawful and forcible entry or unlawful and forcible act is occurring. The legal presumption that a person using deadly physical force is justified to do so pursuant to this subdivision does not apply if: [This statute is patterned after Florida's very protective presumption statute. It's presumed you were justified if you use deadly force to keep yourself or others from being kidnapped from your home, a hotel room, RV or occupied vehicle and also to prevent sabotage of a nuclear power plant. But this presumption doesn't apply if . . . .]

a. The person against whom the defensive force is used has the right to be in or is a lawful resident of the dwelling, residence, or vehicle, such as an owner or lessee, and there is not an injunction for protection from domestic violence or a written pretrial supervision order of no contact against that person [Abusive husbands who have been court-ordered to stay away from their wives are not entitled to the legal protection of this exception].

b. The person sought to be removed is a child or grandchild, or is otherwise in the lawful custody or under the lawful guardianship of, the person against whom the defensive force is used; [This is to keep parents and grandparents who are fighting over custody of children from whacking each other.]

c. The person who uses defensive force is engaged in an unlawful activity or is using the dwelling, residence, or occupied vehicle to further an unlawful activity; or

d. The person against whom the defensive force is used is a law enforcement officer acting in the performance of his or her official duties. [Example for paragraphs c. and d.: Gangsters using their homes to deal drugs and their vehicles as getaway cars would not be "presumed to have acted reasonably" defending themselves from police attempting arrests in their homes or cars.]

[Reckless Injury to Innocent Third Parties]

§ ALA.CODE 1975 § 13A-3-21.

Basis for defense generally; injury to innocent person through negligence; civil remedies.

(a) *Defense.* – Except as otherwise expressly provided, justification or excuse under this article is a defense.

(b) *Danger to innocent persons.* – If a person is justified or excused in using force against a person, but he recklessly or negligently injures or creates a substantial injury to another person, the justifications afforded by this article are unavailable in a prosecution for such recklessness or negligence.

(c) *Civil remedy unimpaired.* – Any justification or excuse within the meaning of this article does not abolish or impair any civil remedy or right of action which is otherwise available.

[You own any bullet that leaves your barrel. If it happens to strike an innocent person, you can count on a lawsuit—period. If you negligently start a gunfight and innocents are struck by someone else's bullet, you will end up the defendant in a civil suit, even if you are not prosecuted.]

[Civil Liability]

(d) A person who uses force, including deadly physical force, as justified and permitted in this section is immune from criminal prosecution and civil action for the use of such force, unless the force was determined to be unlawful. [If you are justified in using force under Alabama's primary self-defense statute, you cannot be prosecuted for a crime or sued for civil damages. We are not sure how to reconcile the language of paragraph (c) above with this paragraph, nor could we find any cases to explain it. Nevertheless, if you injure an innocent person or use excessive force in self-defense, you will be sued.]

(e) A law enforcement agency may use standard procedures for investigating the use of force described in subsection (a), but the agency may not arrest the person for using force unless it determines that there is probable cause that the force used was unlawful. [Johnny Law doesn't usually arrest and prosecutors don't prosecute unless they believe they have probable cause. Certainly, if their investigation detects one of the thumbs-down factors identified in Chapter 7, you are probably going to be arrested.]

[Defense of Property]

§ ALA.CODE 1975 § 13A-3-26.
Use of force in defense of property other than premises.

A person is justified in using physical force, other than deadly physical force, upon another person when and to the extent that he reasonably believes it to be necessary to prevent or terminate the commission or attempted commission by the other person of theft or criminal mischief with respect to property other than premises as defined in section **13A-3-20.** [Like every other state, in Alabama you are not justified in using deadly force to defend personal property like a stereo, big screen TV or unoccupied vehicle. If you kill or seriously injure someone to defend something like that, attorney fees may cost you a hundred times more than what you could have bought the stolen item for brand-new.]

[HELPFUL DEFINITIONS RELATING TO THIS STATE'S SELF-DEFENSE STATUTES]

- **Building** – Any structure which may be entered and utilized by persons for business, public use, lodging, or the storage of goods, and includes any vehicle, aircraft, or watercraft used for the lodging of persons or carrying on business therein [Like an RV, motor home or trailer]. Each unit of a building consisting of two or more units separately occupied or secured is a separate building. **Ala.Code 1975 § 13A-3-20 (1).**

- **Deadly Physical Force** – Force which, under the circumstances in which it is used, is readily capable of causing death or serious physical injury. **Ala.Code 1975 § 13A-3-20 (2).**

- **Dwelling** – A building which is usually occupied by a person lodging therein at night, or a building of any kind, including any attached balcony, whether the building is temporary or permanent, mobile or immobile, which has a roof over it, and is designed to be occupied by people lodging therein at night. [More like a motel or hotel room; whereas your residence is your home.] **Ala.Code 1975 § 13A-3-20 (3).**

- **Felonies Mentioned Above** –
  - **Burglary** – [Unlawfully entering a dwelling or building with the intent to commit a crime.] **Ala.Code 1975 § 13A-7-5, 6 & 7.**

  - **Kidnapping** – [Abduction of another person with the intent to commit a crime against that person. Careful, this does not include lawful control over a relative, such as in a guardianship.] **Ala.Code 1975 § 13A-6-43 & 44.**

  - **Assault in the first or second degree** – [Felony assault with a deadly weapon or with intent to cause serious bodily injury, assault on police officers, teachers, etc.] **Ala.Code 1975 § 13A-6-21 & 22.**

  - **Robbery in any degree** – [Force or threatened use of force to commit theft.] **Ala.Code 1975 § 13A-8-41 - 43.**

- **Forcible rape** – [Intercourse with someone against his or her will.] **Ala.Code 1975 Code § 13A-6-61 Rape in the first degree.**
- **Forcible sodomy** – [Sodomizing someone against his or her will.] **Ala.Code 1975 § 13A-6-63. Sodomy in the first degree.**

- **Force** – Physical action or threat against another, including confinement. **Ala.Code 1975 § 13A-3-20 (4).**
- **Premises** – The term includes any building, as defined in this section, and any real property. [Notice this is even more broad than residence or dwelling and includes real estate. This could be your or your boss' business premises.] **Ala.Code 1975 § 13A-3-20 (5).**
- **Residence** – A dwelling in which a person resides either temporarily or permanently or is visiting as an invited guest. [Sweet Home Alabama, whether owned or rented.] **Ala.Code 1975 § 13A-3-20 (6).**
- **Vehicle** – A motorized conveyance which is designed to transport people or property **Ala.Code 1975 § 13A-3-20 (7).**

[TEMPLATE Topics We Could Not Find Explained in Statutes or Cases]

(For each of these topics that we could not find addressed in your state's statutes or cases, we suggest you review the same topics in the subchapters of surrounding states. Your state's courts may look to the law of neighboring states to see how their courts and legislatures have treated that particular self-defense issue.)

[Committing Felony or Unlawful Act]

[Co-Habitants; Co-Employees – Duty to Retreat]

Pancho's Wisdom

You just might be a Gunnut if . . . you had been born in Talladega and given the name of Ricky Bobby, your first words would've been "I wanna shoot fast!"

Key: ■ commentary ■ original statutes, cases or jury instructions

[Defense of Self and Others] [Non-Deadly Force]

§ ALASKA STATUTES (AS) § 11.81.330.
Justification: Use of nondeadly force in defense of self.

(a) A person is justified in using nondeadly force upon another when and to the extent the person reasonably believes it is necessary for self-defense against what the person reasonably believes to be the use of unlawful force by the other person, unless [If you grab someone by the arm hard without her permission, it is an assault. But if you do it to keep her from slapping you in the face, you would not be guilty of an assault unless . . . (see Exceptions below.)]

[Exceptions to Justifiable Self-Defense] [Mutual Combat]

(1) the person used the force in mutual combat not authorized by law; [. . .you both agree to fight . . .]

[Provocation]

(2) the person claiming self-defense provoked the other's conduct with intent to cause physical injury to the other; [. . . you shove her first, knowing she'll slap you, so you can punch her lights out . . .]

[Initial Aggressor]

(3) the person claiming self-defense was the initial aggressor; or [. . . you simply start the fight.]

[Committing Felony or Unlawful Act]

(4) the force used was the result of using a deadly weapon or dangerous instrument the person claiming self-defense possessed while

(A) acting alone or with others to further a felony criminal objective of the person or one or more other persons;

(B) a participant in a felony transaction or purported transaction or in immediate flight from a felony transaction or purported transaction in violation of AS **11.71;** or [Under (A) and (B), you can't claim self-defense if you possessed a deadly weapon (gun, knife, harpoon) while in the process of committing or seeking to commit a felony, no matter what happens afterward. The Exceptions to the Exceptions below only apply to paragraphs (1)-(3) above, not to this paragraph (4).

(C) acting alone or with others in revenge for, retaliation for, or response to actual or perceived conduct by a rival or perceived rival, or a member or perceived member of a rival group, if the person using deadly force, or the group on whose behalf the person is acting, has a history or reputation for violence among civilians. [This provision is obviously anti-gang, the Walruses v. the Polar Bears. It means if you go out with a deadly weapon looking for revenge on a rival gang, you can't claim self-defense.]

[Exceptions to the Exceptions] [Withdraw and Communicate]

(b) A person who is not justified in using force in self-defense in the circumstances listed in (a)(1)—(3) of this section is justified in using force in self-defense if that person has withdrawn from the encounter and effectively communicated the withdrawal to the other person, but the other person persists in continuing the incident by the use of unlawful force. [If you've agreed to or started a fight, you have to stop fighting and make it clear to your adversary that you quit. It would be nice if witnesses saw you put your hands up, retreat and yell, "I quit! I'm not fighting any more!" Then, if your opponent continues, it's his fault. Our experience and research shows that if you start a fight, no matter what you do afterward, you probably will be arrested and prosecuted.]

"[W]here an aggressor using non-deadly force (i. e., one who begins an encounter, using only his fists or some non-deadly weapon) is met with deadly force, the initial aggressor may justifiably defend himself against the deadly attack." *Castillo v. State,* 614 P.2d 756, 766 (Alaska 1980). [**Example:** You start a fist fight on the dock and begin to knock the sea salt out of your opponent. Humiliated, he picks up a large boning knife and charges you like a bull moose in a barroom. In desperation, you skewer him with a rusty harpoon just before he unzips your chest cavity. You might be found not guilty if the court applies the rule of law cited above, but you will certainly be arrested and tried for murder because you started the brawl. Knocking heads on a boring Friday night may escalate in ways you don't expect. Instead, vent your pent-up aggression on a caribou hunt.]

[Deadly Force] [Use of Deadly Force to Prevent Serious Felonies]

§ (AS) § 11.81.335.
Justification: Use of deadly force in defense of self.

(a) Except as provided in (b) of this section, a person who is justified in using nondeadly force in self-defense under AS **11.81.330** may use deadly force in self-defense upon another person when and to the extent the person reasonably believes the use of deadly force is necessary for self-defense against [As long as you comply with the requirements for non-deadly force (i.e. you are not the initial aggressor, provoker etc.), then you can use deadly force if you reasonably think it's necessary to defend against any of the following...]

(1) death;

(2) serious physical injury;

[The definitions of all of the following serious felonies are listed below.]

(3) kidnapping, except for what is described as custodial interference in the first degree in AS 11.41.320; [Custodial interference example – Mom can't hire a whaling crew to ice dad because dad violated the custody order by dragging little Johnny, kicking and screaming, into Canada.]

(4) sexual assault in the first degree;

(5) sexual assault in the second degree;

(6) sexual abuse of a minor in the first degree; or

(7) robbery in any degree.

[Duty to Retreat – Generally – Yes]

(b) A person may not use deadly force under this section if the person knows that, with complete personal safety and with complete safety as to others being defended, the person can avoid the necessity of using deadly force by leaving [retreating from] the area of the encounter except there is no duty to leave the area if the person is [You must retreat if you can do so in complete safety. You don't have to retreat if you are:]

(1) on premises

(A) that the person owns or leases;

(B) where the person resides, temporarily or permanently; or

(C) as a guest or express or implied agent of the owner, lessor, or resident; [This is sort of a repeat of the section above except it doesn't mention vehicles—you don't have to retreat before using deadly force if you're on your premises. "Premises" is defined as "real property and any building." (See Definitions section). Again, as long as you're on your land or in a building you own, you don't have to retreat.]

(3) in a building where the person works in the ordinary course of the person's employment; or [You also don't have to retreat from your workplace.]

(4) protecting a child or a member of the person's household. [No matter where you are, if you're defending a child or a member of your household, you have no duty to retreat first.]

"Alaska's self-defense statute, AS 11.81.330(a), does not specifically mention the requirement of imminency... *LaFave & Scott* cites this statute as one of the few 'self-defense provisions in the modern codes [that] fail to address [the requirement that the threat be imminent] explicitly.' However, as Judge Souter correctly perceived, AS 11.81.330 can be silent on this point because the legislature placed the requirement of imminency in the statutory definition of "force" contained in AS 11.81.900(b)(23) [actually (27)]. *Ha v. State*, 892 P.2d 184, 191 (Alaska App. 1995). [The definition of "force" is "any bodily impact, restraint, or confinement or the threat of imminent bodily impact, restraint, or confinement. 'Force' includes deadly and nondeadly force."

AS 11.81.900(b)(27). Thus, although Alaska's self-defense statute doesn't actually mention imminence, it's still required.]

[Defense of a Third Person]

§ (AS) § 11.81.340.
Justification: Use of force in defense of a third person.

A person is justified in using force upon another when and to the extent the person reasonably believes it is necessary to defend a third person when, under the circumstances as the person claiming defense of another reasonably believes them to be, the third person would be justified under AS **11.81.330** or **11.81.335** in using that degree of force for self-defense. [You can only defend another person if you (1) reasonably believe it's necessary and (2) that he legally could have lawfully defended himself (i.e. didn't start the fight, was facing a threat of unlawful force etc.)]

[Defense of Person(s) in Special Places – Home, Business, Occupied Vehicle]

§ (AS) §11.81.350 (c), (e) and (f).
Justification: Use of force in defense of property and premises.

(c) A person in possession or control of any premises, or a guest or an express or implied agent of that person, may use

. . .

(2) deadly force upon another when and to the extent the person reasonably believes it is necessary to terminate what the person reasonably believes to be a burglary in any degree occurring in an occupied dwelling or building. [Warning: Burglars in Alaska could end up in Cold Storage! You can use deadly force to prevent burglary in any occupied house or building on premises you control. Because Alaska defines "premises" as any building, this section can be interpreted to mean that you can use deadly force in your home or business. Guests and employees can defend a building with deadly force as well.]

. . .

(e) and (f) A person

(1) in a vehicle, or forcibly removed from a vehicle, may use deadly force upon another when and to the extent the person reasonably believes it is necessary to terminate what the person reasonably believes to be a carjacking of that vehicle at or about the time the vehicle is carjacked; [More states are adding carjacking to the list of serious felonies justifying the use of deadly force.]

(2) outside of a vehicle may use deadly force upon another when and to the extent the person reasonably believes it is necessary to terminate what the person reasonably believes to be the theft of that vehicle when another person, other than the perceived offender, is inside of the vehicle; this paragraph does not apply to a person outside of a vehicle who is involved in a dispute with a person inside of the vehicle who is a household member of that person; in this paragraph,

"household member" has the meaning given in AS **18.66.990.** [If you see someone trying to steal a car with a person in the car, you can use deadly force to prevent the carjacking. However, you can't do this if you are having an argument with a household member, which is broadly defined by the statute cited to the extent that it includes people who are dating or have dated. This statute is to prevent a jealous boyfriend or husband from claiming justifiable prevention of a car jacking after killing his girlfriend's or wife's new Prince Charming while whisking her away in his luxurious and amorous Pumpkin Carriage (orange Volkswagen bus – damned hippy anyway.)]

[No Duty to Retreat from Home, Vehicle, or Business]

(f) A person justified in using force under this section does not have a duty to leave or attempt to leave the area of the encounter before using force. [There is no duty to retreat before defending yourself or others while in the special places listed in this section.]

. . .

[Reckless Injury to Innocent Third Parties]

[Even if you're acting in justifiable self-defense, if you recklessly injure someone else, you can be prosecuted for that recklessness in Alaska. The state has to prove that you were aware of and consciously disregarded a "substantial and unjustifiable risk" of injury. *Ward v. State*, 997 P.2d 528, 532 (Alaska App. 2000).]

[Civil Liability]

§ AS § 09.65.330.
Immunity: Use of defensive force

(a) A person who uses force in defense of self, other persons, or property as permitted in AS 11.81 is not liable for the death of or injury to the person against whom the force was intended to be used, unless the person against whom force was used was

(1) a peace officer, whether on or off duty, who was engaged in the performance of official duties;

(2) a fire fighter, emergency medical technician, or paramedic engaged in the performance of official duties; or

(3) medical personnel, a health care provider, or a first responder in an emergency situation.

(b) The court shall award reasonable attorney fees, court costs, compensation for loss of income, and all expenses incurred by the defendant in defense of a civil action brought by a plaintiff if the court finds that the defendant is not liable under (a) of this section. [If you acted in justifiable self-defense, then you can't be civilly liable. As a deterrent to those who would sue you for justifiably defending yourself, Alaska law says the court must award you the attorneys' fees, court costs and lost income for having to defend the lawsuit.]

[Defense of Property]

§ (AS) § 11.81.350.
Justification: Use of force in defense of property and premises.

(a) A person may use nondeadly force upon another when and to the extent the person reasonably believes it is necessary to terminate what the person reasonably believes to be the commission or attempted commission by the other of an unlawful taking or damaging of property or services. [You can use non-deadly force to prevent a theft of property or vandalism. The property doesn't have to be yours. We don't recommend you do this because these situations may sometimes escalate to the point where deadly force is necessary. If that happens, you will usually pay more for attorney fees than the property you were trying to defend was worth.]

(b) A person may use deadly force upon another when and to the extent the person reasonably believes it necessary to terminate what the person reasonably believes to be the commission or attempted commission of arson upon a dwelling or occupied building. [Arson of someone's home or an occupied building involves an enormous risk that someone will die or be horribly disfigured for life. Therefore, the law justifies the use of deadly force to prevent such a vicious act.]

(c) A person in possession or control of any premises, or a guest or an express or implied agent of that person, may use

(1) nondeadly force upon another when and to the extent the person reasonably believes it is necessary to terminate what the person reasonably believes to be the commission or attempted commission by the other of criminal trespass in any degree upon the premises; [You can use reasonable force, but not deadly force to prevent criminal trespass.]

[HELPFUL DEFINITIONS RELATING TO THIS STATE'S SELF-DEFENSE STATUTES]

- **Building** – in addition to its usual meaning, includes any propelled vehicle or structure adapted for overnight accommodation of persons or for carrying on business; when a building consists of separate units, including apartment units, offices, or rented rooms, each unit is considered a separate building; **(AS) § 11.81.900 (b) (5).**

- **Deadly force** – means force that the person uses with the intent of causing, or uses under circumstances that the person knows create a substantial risk of causing, death or serious physical injury; "deadly force" includes intentionally discharging or pointing a firearm in the direction of another person or in the direction in which another person is believed to be and intentionally placing another person in fear of imminent serious physical injury by means of a dangerous instrument; **(AS) § 11.81.900 (b) (16).**

- **Deadly weapon** – means any firearm, or anything designed for and capable of causing death or serious physical injury, including a knife, an axe, a club, metal knuckles, or an explosive; **(AS) § 11.81.900 (b) (17).**

- **Defensive weapon** – means an electric stun gun, or a device to dispense mace or a similar chemical agent, that is not designed to cause death or serious physical injury; **(AS) §11.81.900 (b) (20).**

- **Dwelling** – means a building that is designed for use or is used as a person's permanent or temporary home or place of lodging; **(AS) § 11.81.900 (b) (22).**

- **Explosive** – means a chemical compound, mixture, or device that is commonly used or intended for the purpose of producing a chemical reaction resulting in a substantially instantaneous release of gas and heat, including dynamite, blasting powder, nitroglycerin, blasting caps, and nitrojelly, but excluding salable fireworks as defined in AS 18.72.050, black powder, smokeless powder, small arms ammunition, and small arms ammunition primers; **(AS) § 11.81.900 (b) (23).**

- **Felonies Mentioned Above**

    - **Kidnapping** – [The restraining of another person with the intent to commit a crime against him. Careful, this does not include lawful control over a relative or someone with legal custody/responsibility of a person, such as in a guardianship or caretaker.] **(AS) § 11.41.300.**

    - **Sexual assault in the first or second degree** – [Sexual contact with another person without consent or who is mentally incapable of consent.] **(AS) § 11.41.410 & 420.**

    - **Sexual abuse of a minor in the first degree** – [When someone 16 yrs or older engages in sexual intercourse with some one under the age of 13 OR sexual intercourse with someone younger than 18 by a parent or guardian OR sexual intercourse with someone under 16 by someone over 18 who has authority over the victim, like a teacher.] **(AS) § 11.41.434.**

    - **Robbery in any Degree** – [Threatening or using force to take or attempt to take the property of another against his or her will.] **(AS) § 11.41.500 & 510.**

    - **Arson** – [Intentionally damaging property by fire or explosion which recklessly puts another person at risk of serious injury.] **(AS) § 11.46.400.**

    - **Burglary in any degree** – [Entering or remaining unlawfully in a building with the intent to commit a crime.] **(AS) § 11.46.300 & 310.**

    - **Carjacking** – [A robbery involving the taking or attempted taking of a vehicle from a person.] **(AS) § 11.81.350 (g) (1).**

- **Force** – means any bodily impact, restraint, or confinement or the threat of imminent bodily impact, restraint, or confinement, "force" includes deadly and nondeadly force; **(AS) § 11.81.900 (b) (27).**

- **Household member includes –**
  (A) adults or minors who are current or former spouses;

(B) adults or minors who live together or who have lived together;

(C) adults or minors who are dating or who have dated;

(D) adults or minors who are engaged in or who have engaged in a sexual relationship;

(E) adults or minors who are related to each other up to the fourth degree of consanguinity, whether of the whole or half blood or by adoption, computed under the rules of civil law;

(F) adults or minors who are related or formerly related by marriage;

(G) persons who have a child of the relationship; and children of a person in a relationship that is described in (A)-(G) of this paragraph; **(AS) § 18.66.990 (5).**

- **Nondeadly force** – means force other than deadly force; **(AS) § 11.81.900 (b) (38).**

- **Premises** – means real property and any building; **(AS) § 11.81.900 (b) (49).**

- **Property** – means an article, substance, or thing of value, including money, tangible and intangible personal property including data or information stored in a computer program, system, or network, real property, an access device, a domestic pet or livestock regardless of value, choses in action, and evidence of debt or of contract; a commodity of a public utility such as gas, electricity, steam, or water constitutes property, but the supplying of such a commodity to premises from an outside source by means of wires, pipes, conduits, or other equipment is considered a rendition of a service rather than a sale or delivery of property; **(AS) § 11.81.900 (b) (51).**

- **Serious physical injury** – means:

  (A) physical injury caused by an act performed under circumstances that create a substantial risk of death; or

  (B) physical injury that causes serious and protracted disfigurement, protracted impairment of health, protracted loss or impairment of the function of a body member or organ, or that unlawfully terminates a pregnancy; **(AS) § 11.81.900 (b) (56).**

[TEMPLATE Topics We Could Not Find Explained in Statutes or Cases]

(For each of these topics that we could not find addressed in your state's statutes or cases, we suggest you review the same topics in the subchapters of surrounding states. Your state's courts may look to the law of neighboring states to see how their courts and legislatures have treated that particular self-defense issue.)

[Co-Habitants; Co-Employees – Duty to Retreat]

[Presumption of Reasonableness in Special Places]

ARIZONA

You're standing on a corner in Winslow, Arizona with seven women on your mind, when all of a sudden . . . !

Key: ■ commentary ■ original statutes, cases or jury instructions

[Defense of Self and Others] [Non-Deadly Force]

§ ARIZONA REVISED STATUTES (A.R.S) §13-404.
Justification; self-defense

A. Except as provided in subsection B of this section, a person is justified in threatening or using physical force against another when and to the extent a reasonable person would believe that physical force is immediately necessary to protect himself against the other's use or attempted use of unlawful physical force. [You may use reasonable force to defend yourself from a person using unlawful, non-deadly force against you. But you may not use deadly force except as explained in the **[Deadly Force]** section below.]

. . .

[Exceptions to Justifiable Self-Defense]
[Committing Felony or Unlawful Act]

[These exceptions to self-defense and exceptions to the exception are standard in most states. See discussion in Chapter 4.]

"In a felony-murder prosecution, a person who is found by the jury to be engaged in an attempted robbery must be considered the initial aggressor; it is immaterial whether the victim of the robbery or the defendant fired first." *State v. Celaya*, 660 P. 2d 849, 855 (Ariz. 1983). [If you rob a convenience store and the clerk pulls out a pistol, you can't claim self-defense if you blow him away before he shoots you. Duh!]

[Initial Aggressor]

"Also, as noted by A.R.S. § 13-404(B), an aggressor may not claim self-defense unless he withdraws from the combat in such a manner as will indicate his intention in good faith to refrain from further aggressive conduct." *State v. Lujan*, 664 P. 2d 646, 648-649 (Ariz. 1983). [This case clarifies that 13-404(B) bars the person who started the fight from claiming self-defense.]

§ A.R.S. §13-404 (continued).
Justification; self-defense

B. The threat or use of physical force against another is not justified:

[Provocation]

1. In response to verbal provocation alone; or

2. To resist an arrest that the person knows or should know is being made by a peace officer or by a person acting in a peace officer's presence and at his direction, whether the arrest is lawful or unlawful, unless the physical force used by the peace officer exceeds that allowed by law; or

3. If the person provoked the other's use or attempted use of unlawful physical force, unless:

[Exceptions to the Exceptions] [Withdraw and Communicate]

(a) The person withdraws from the encounter or clearly communicates to the other his intent to do so reasonably believing he cannot safely withdraw from the encounter; and

(b) The other nevertheless continues or attempts to use unlawful physical force against the person.

[Deadly Force]

§ A.R.S. §13-405.
Justification; use of deadly physical force

A person is justified in threatening or using deadly physical force against another:

1. If such person would be justified in threatening or using physical force against the other under section 13-404, and

2. When and to the degree a reasonable person would believe that deadly physical force is immediately necessary to protect himself against the other's use or attempted use of unlawful deadly physical force. [Same rules apply to use of deadly force as non-deadly force above, except that the following paragraph adds the requirement of a reasonable belief that deadly force is immediately necessary to repel a deadly attack.]

[Use of Force to Prevent Serious Felonies]
[No Duty to Retreat – Generally]

§ A.R.S. §13-411.
Justification; use of force in crime prevention; applicability

A. A person is justified in threatening or using both physical force and deadly physical force against another if and to the extent the person reasonably believes that physical force or deadly physical force is immediately necessary to prevent the other's commission of arson of an occupied structure under section 13-1704, burglary in the second or first degree under section 13-1507 or 13-1508, kidnapping under section 13-1304, manslaughter under section 13-1103, second or first degree murder under section 13-1104 or 13-1105, sexual conduct with a minor under section 13-1405, sexual assault under section 13-1406, child molestation under section 13-1410, armed robbery under section 13-1904 or aggravated assault under section 13-1204, subsection A, paragraphs 1 and 2. [In addition to being able to use deadly force to stop an imminent threat of death or serious bodily injury, the Arizona Legislature has added these serious felonies. This could give a law-abiding citizen the advantage if he is not quite sure the person has a deadly weapon, but is sure that one of these felonies is being committed. That way he doesn't have to wait around to be shot or clobbered before using deadly force. See Chapter relating to perception and reaction time, Chapter 11. We suggest you study and memorize these felonies. A summary of what they generally mean is provided in the definitions section below. We encourage you to look them up in the Arizona code. The citation is given right after the short summary.

Please do not disregard the language above which limits your use of force to that which is reasonably necessary. See our discussion of necessity in Chapter 3. Finally, with respect to a sexual crime against a loved one, don't miss our warning in the same chapter to NEVER act out of REVENGE. If the sexual assault is over, you are not justified in executing the pervert just because he deserves it! You may only use deadly force if it's reasonably necessary to stop the crime while it's in progress.]

B. There is no duty to retreat before threatening or using physical force or deadly physical force justified by subsection A of this section. [There is no duty to retreat before using deadly force to prevent the serious felonies listed above.]

C. A person is presumed to be acting reasonably for the purposes of this section if the person is acting to prevent the commission of any of the offenses listed in subsection A of this section. [Here is a presumption of reasonableness that is not limited to special places, but special circumstances, stopping the commission of serious crimes.]

D. This section is not limited to the use or threatened use of physical or deadly physical force in a person's home, residence, place of business, land the person owns or leases, conveyance of any kind, or any other place in this state where a person has a right to be. [This paragraph makes it clear that you can use deadly force to prevent such felonies and enjoy the presumption mentioned in paragraph C. This applies anywhere you have a legal right to be. It is a rather dramatic expansion of the "Castle Doctrine" explained in Chapters 3 and 4. It could also be referred to as Arizona's make-my-day law, named after the famous line in the Clint Eastwood movie.]

[Because police, judges and prosecutors tend to frown on what they perceive to be vigilantism, we don't recommend you go around looking for opportunities to use deadly force if the intended victim is not you or a loved one. But it's nice to have a statute this strong on the books. Violent predators BEWARE! Our congratulations to the Arizona Legislature for this strong statute protecting the lives of law-abiding citizens.]

[Defense of a Third Person(s)]

§ A.R.S. §13-406.
Justification; defense of a third person

A person is justified in threatening or using physical force or deadly physical force against another to protect a third person if:

1. Under the circumstances as a reasonable person would believe them to be, such person would be justified under section 13-404 or 13-405 in threatening or using physical force or deadly physical force to protect himself against the unlawful physical force or deadly physical force a reasonable person would believe is threatening the third person he seeks to protect; and

2. A reasonable person would believe that such person's intervention is immediately necessary to protect the third person. [This third-person provision is standard, see detailed discussion in Chapter 4, and applies to the use of both deadly and non-deadly force.]

[Defense of Person(s) in Special Places – Home, Occupied Vehicle]

§ A.R.S. §13-407.
Justification; use of physical force in defense of premises

A. A person or his agent in lawful possession or control of premises is justified in threatening to use deadly physical force or in threatening or using physical force against another when and to the extent that a reasonable person would believe it immediately necessary to prevent or terminate the commission or attempted commission of a criminal trespass by the other person in or upon the premises. [Wow! This paragraph recognizes that the THREAT of deadly force is not the same as the USE of deadly force (this comes from paragraph 3.11(2) of the Model Penal Code, "A threat to cause death or serious bodily injury, by the production of a weapon or otherwise, so long as the actor's purpose is limited to creating an apprehension that he will use deadly force if necessary, does not constitute deadly force.") Most states don't make this distinction. It is an important distinction because you should be able to threaten deadly force if someone unlawfully refuses to leave your property, and you don't know what mischief they are planning and don't want to find out. You can go out on your porch and rack one into the chamber of your 12 gauge. It is the universal language that almost always convinces the bad guys that they had better skedaddle off of your property!

You may NOT however USE deadly force, (see paragraph B. immediately below) unless the trespassers pose an immediate threat of deadly force as described above under the deadly-force statutes, A.R.S. §13-405 (self-defense), 406 (defense of others) and A.R.S. §13-411 (prevention of serious felonies).

What happens if they don't go away, they're not exhibiting weapons and there are not enough of them to be considered a deadly threat? Buddy, you're between a rock and a hard place. You don't have the justification to use deadly force. Hopefully, they'll be intimidated by your scattergun going "cha-chunk" as you chamber a shell. If they continue to come onto your property, our advice would be to run inside, bolt the door and call 911. If they use an instrument to break the door down, an instrument you hadn't seen before but could cause serious injury or death, then you may defend yourself in your home with your shotgun or other means of deadly force. See A.R.S. §13-418 below.

It's impossible to predict every scenario, but notice Arizona's home-defense statute does not reduce the threshold for a homeowner to use deadly force like some states. In some states like Utah, for example, in your home you only have to have a reasonable fear of an "assault or personal violence" before you use deadly force (see Utah Statutes 76-2-405. Force in defense of habitation). Arizona still requires a fear of death or serious bodily injury. Arizona should adopt Utah's Home Defense Statute and Utah should adopt Arizona's Threatening Statute.]

B. A person may use deadly physical force under subsection A only in the defense of himself or third persons as described in sections 13-405 and 13-406.

C. In this section, "premises" means any real property and any structure, movable or immovable, permanent or temporary, adapted for both human residence and lodging whether occupied or not. [As Yosemite Sam would say, "Git off my property, Varmint!" This applies even if you are in a temporary residence such as a motor home, rented or owned, or a pull trailer.]

[Defense of Person(s) in Special Places (cont.) – Home, Occupied Vehicle]

§ A.R.S. §13-418.
Justification; use of force in defense of residential structure or occupied vehicles; definitions

A. Notwithstanding any other provision of this chapter, a person is justified in threatening to use or using physical force or deadly physical force against another person if the person reasonably believes himself or another person to be in imminent peril of death or serious physical injury and the person against whom the physical force or deadly physical force is threatened or used was in the process of unlawfully or forcefully entering, or had unlawfully or forcefully entered, a residential structure or occupied vehicle, or had removed or was attempting to remove another person against the other person's will from the residential structure or occupied vehicle. [You cannot use deadly force to defend yourself or others in your home unless you reasonably believe the intruder poses an imminent threat of death or serious bodily injury AND (not OR) the entry is illegal (without your permission) or forceful (he breaks in) or tries to drag you out of the home. This applies as well to occupied vehicles (not a car burglary with no one in it).

Pancho's Wisdom – For a state that has such a fine use-of-deadly-force-to-prevent-serious-felonies statute, AZ sure has a WIMPY home-defense law! If someone is entering your home illegally, you should be able to use deadly force even if you are not sure if he has a deadly weapon. (For example, see Utah or Georgia's home-defense statutes. By the time you know for sure, he may have already killed you. Fortunately burglary is one of the forcible felonies you may use deadly force to prevent under the forcible felony statute (see A.R.S. §13-411 above).]

[No Duty to Retreat From Special Places]

B. A person has no duty to retreat before threatening or using physical force or deadly physical force pursuant to this section. [Obviously, you don't have to make like the Road Runner and retreat from your own home or occupied vehicle in the Grand Canyon State.]

C. For the purposes of this section:

1. "Residential structure" has the same meaning prescribed in section 13-1501. [13-1501 (11) "Residential structure" means any structure, movable or immovable, permanent or temporary, that is adapted for both human residence and lodging whether occupied or not.]

2. "Vehicle" means a conveyance of any kind, whether or not motorized, that is designed to transport persons or property.

[This statute permits someone to use deadly force to defend a person in a residential structure or an occupied vehicle if the assailant unlawfully enters or remains in the structure or vehicle and either threatens deadly force or tries to remove someone from the residence or vehicle against their will.]

[Presumption of Reasonableness in Special Places – Residential Structure or Occupied Vehicle]

§ **A.R.S. §13-419.**
Presumption; exceptions; definitions

A. A person is presumed to be acting reasonably for the purposes of sections 13-404 through 13-408 and section 13-418 if the person is acting against another person who unlawfully or forcefully enters or entered the person's residential structure or occupied vehicle, except that the presumption does not apply if:

[Exceptions to Presumption]

1. The person against whom physical force or deadly physical force was used has the right to be in or is a lawful resident of the residential structure or occupied vehicle, including an owner, lessee, invitee or titleholder, and an order of protection or injunction against harassment has not been filed against that person.

2. The person against whom the physical force or deadly physical force was used is the parent or grandparent, or has legal custody or guardianship, of a child or grandchild sought to be removed from the residential structure or occupied vehicle.

3. The person who uses physical force or deadly physical force is engaged in an unlawful activity or is using the residential structure or occupied vehicle to further an unlawful activity.

4. The person against whom the physical force or deadly physical force was used is a law enforcement officer who enters or attempts to enter a residential structure or occupied vehicle in the performance of official duties.

B. For the purposes of this section:

1. "Residential structure" has the same meaning prescribed in section 13-1501.

2. "Vehicle" means a conveyance of any kind, whether or not motorized, that is designed to transport persons or property.

[One has to wonder how much help such a presumption is because a person is already presumed innocent unless proven guilty beyond a reasonable doubt. But it's always nice, as a criminal defense attorney, to have more to discuss than less. If you shoot someone who has a right to be on the premises, like a family member in a domestic dispute or a police officer making an arrest, the title holder of the car repossessing it, the presumption does not apply. Furthermore, if you are committing an unlawful act, it does not apply. An estranged spouse who is the subject of a protective order telling him to stay away from his estranged-wife's home is treated just like a trespasser. She is presumed to be acting reasonably if he tries to break in.]

[Reckless Injury to Innocent Third Parties]

§ A.R.S. § 13-401.
Unavailability of justification defense; justification as defense

A. Even though a person is justified under this chapter in threatening or using physical force or deadly physical force against another, if in doing so such person recklessly injures or kills an innocent third person, the justification afforded by this chapter is unavailable in a prosecution for the reckless injury or killing of the innocent third person. [Although you can use deadly force to prevent the commission of a robbery, you can't just close your eyes, spray & pray with a Mac 10 in a crowded bank, and hope to get off scot-free if you injure or kill an innocent bystander. Any time you hit the wrong person you can expect bad things to happen in both the criminal and civil courts. It's another good reason to get additional training from one of the excellent firearm training facilities that exist throughout the country. See Chapter 18, Additional Resources.]

B. Except as provided in subsection A, justification, as defined in this chapter, is a defense in any prosecution for an offense pursuant to this title.

[Civil Liability]

§ A.R.S. §13-413.
No civil liability for justified conduct

No person in this state shall be subject to civil liability for engaging in conduct otherwise justified pursuant to the provisions of this chapter. [If your actions were justified under the criminal law, you're supposedly protected from a lawsuit by the person you shot or injured in self-defense. However, don't forget that the burden of proof is not as great in a civil lawsuit as it is in a criminal case. Just ask O.J. Simpson! He was found "not guilty," of murder, but was held to be liable for millions in the civil lawsuit. The same thing happened to the so called "Subway Vigilante" Bernard Goetz (see Chapter 15, for a discussion of civil liability).]

[Defense of Property]

§ **A.R.S. § 13-408.**
Justification; use of physical force in defense of property

A person is justified in using physical force against another when and to the extent that a reasonable person would believe it necessary to prevent what a reasonable person would believe is an attempt or commission by the other person of theft or criminal damage involving tangible movable property under his possession or control, but such person may use deadly physical force under these circumstances as provided in sections 13-405, 13-406 and 13-411. [This statute refers to defending your personal property, like your car, your table saw, your chest freezer, etc., as opposed to your real estate. You cannot use deadly force to defend such items of personal property.]

[HELPFUL DEFINITIONS RELATING TO THIS STATE'S SELF-DEFENSE STATUTES]

- **Damage** – means any physical or visual impairment of any surface. **A.R.S. § 13-1701(1).**

- **Deadly physical force** – means force which is used with the purpose of causing death or serious physical injury or in the manner of its use or intended use is capable of creating a substantial risk of causing death or serious physical injury. **A.R.S. § 13-105(14). Definitions.**

- **Felonies Mentioned Above –**
  - **Aggravated assault 1204 subsection A, paragraphs 1 and 2** – [Assault with a deadly weapon or causing serious physical injury to another.] **A.R.S. § 13-1204(A)(1)(2).**

  - **Armed Robbery** – [Taking someone's property by threat or force with a deadly weapon or a simulated deadly weapon.] **A.R.S. § 13-1904.**

  - **Arson of an occupied structure** – [Knowingly damaging an occupied structure by fire or explosion.] **A.R.S. § 13-1704.**

  - **Burglary in the first or second degree** – [Entering or remaining unlawfully in a residential structure with intent to commit a crime.] **A.R.S. § 13-1507 and 1508.**

- **Child Molestation** – "A person commits molestation of a child by intentionally or knowingly engaging in or causing a person to engage in sexual contact, except sexual contact with the female breast, with a child who is under fifteen years of age." **A.R.S. § 13-1410.**

- **Kidnapping** – [Restraining someone with the intent to commit a crime against them.] **A.R.S. § 13-1304.**

- **Manslaughter** – [Recklessly or in a heat of passion causing the death of another.] **A.R.S. § 13-1103.**

- **Murder in the first or second degree** – [Murder with or without premeditation. Includes knowing or intentionally engaging in conduct likely to cause death or serious physical injury.] **A.R.S. § 13-1104 and 1105.**

- **Sexual conduct with a minor** – [Sexual intercourse with someone under 18 yrs old.] **A.R.S. § 13-1405.**

- **Sexual assault in the first or second degree** – [Sexual intercourse or oral sex with another person without their consent.] **A.R.S. § 13-1405.**

- **Occupied structure** – means any structure as defined in paragraph 4 in which one or more human beings either is or is likely to be present or so near as to be in equivalent danger at the time the fire or explosion occurs. The term includes any dwelling house, whether occupied, unoccupied or vacant. **A.R.S. § 13-1701(2).**

- **Physical force** – means force used upon or directed toward the body of another person and includes confinement, but does not include deadly physical force. **A.R.S. § 13-105(31). Definitions.**

- **Physical injury** – means the impairment of physical condition. **A.R.S. § 13-105(32). Definitions.**

- **Property** – means anything of value, tangible or intangible. **A.R.S. § 13-105(36). Definitions.**

- **Property** – [as applied to arson] - means anything other than a structure which has value, tangible or intangible, public or private, real or personal, including documents evidencing value or ownership. **A.R.S. § 13-1701(3).**

- **Residence** – means the person's dwelling place, whether permanent or temporary. **A.R.S. § 13-3822(D)(3).**

- **Serious physical injury** – includes physical injury that creates a reasonable risk of death, or which causes serious and permanent disfigurement, serious impairment of health or loss or protracted impairment of the function of any bodily organ or limb. **A.R.S. § 13-105(38). Definitions.**

- **Structure** – means any building, object, vehicle, watercraft, aircraft or place with sides and a floor, used for lodging, business, transportation, recreation or storage. **Arizona Statute 13-1701 (4).**

- **Unlawful** – means contrary to law or, where the context so requires, not permitted by law. **Arizona Statute 13-105 (39). Definitions.**

- **Vehicle** – means a device in, upon or by which any person or property is, may be or could have been transported or drawn upon a highway, waterway or airway, excepting devices moved by human power or used exclusively upon stationary rails or tracks. **Arizona Statute 13-105 (40). Definitions.**

[TEMPLATE Topics We Could Not Find Explained in Statutes or Cases]
(For each of these topics that we could not find addressed in your state's statutes or cases, we suggest you review the same topics in the subchapters of surrounding states. Your state's courts may look to the law of the surrounding states to see how their courts and legislatures have treated that particular self-defense issue.)

[Mutual Combat]
[The provision regarding mutual combat, A.R.S. § 13-462 was repealed in 1977. Case law up to that point referenced the repealed statute.]

[Co-Habitants; Co-Employees – Duty to Retreat]

Pancho's Wisdom

You just might be a Gunnut if . . . you could only have one or the other, you'd rather have a treasure chest full of shiny brass bullets than one full of brilliant gold coins.

Key: ■ commentary ■ original statutes, cases or jury instructions

[Defense of Self and Others] [Non-Deadly Force]
[Defense of Third Persons]

§ ARKANSAS CODE ANNOTATED (A.CA.) § 5-2-606.
Use of physical force in defense of a person.

(a) (1) A person is justified in using physical force upon another person to defend himself or herself or a third person from what the person reasonably believes to be the use or imminent use of unlawful physical force by that other person, and the person may use a degree of force that he or she reasonably believes to be necessary.

(2) However, the person may not use deadly physical force except as provided in § 5-2-607.

[Exceptions to Justifiable Self-Defense]
(b) A person is not justified in using physical force upon another person if:

[Provocation]
(1) With purpose to cause physical injury or death to the other person, the person provokes the use of unlawful physical force by the other person;

[Initial Aggressor]
(2) (A) The person is the initial aggressor.

[Exceptions to the Exceptions][Withdraw and Communicate]
(B) However, the initial aggressor's use of physical force upon another person is justifiable if:

(i) The initial aggressor in good faith withdraws from the encounter and effectively communicates to the other person his or her purpose to withdraw from the encounter; and

(ii) The other person continues or threatens to continue the use of unlawful physical force; or

[Mutual Combat]
(3) The physical force involved is the product of a combat by agreement not authorized by law.

[This is the standard description of the limitations of non-deadly force. You can use as much physical force as is necessary, short of deadly force, to stop the progression of an unlawful act. The exceptions to this rule are the standard exceptions as well, provoking a fight for the purpose of hurting your opponent, being the initial aggressor and agreeing to fight.]

[Deadly Force]

§ A.C. A. § 5-2-607.
Use of deadly physical force in defense of a person.

(a) A person is justified in using deadly physical force upon another person if the person reasonably believes that the other person is:

[Use of Deadly Force to Prevent Serious Felonies]

(1) Committing or about to commit a felony involving force or violence;

(2) Using or about to use unlawful deadly physical force; or

(3) (A) Imminently endangering the person's life or imminently about to victimize the person as described in § 9-15-103 from the continuation of a pattern of domestic abuse.

(B) As used in this section, "domestic abuse" means the same as defined in § 9-15-103. [According to § 9-15-103 "domestic abuse" means any physical harm, bodily injury, assault, or the infliction of fear of imminent physical harm, bodily injury, or assault between family or household members; or any sexual conduct between family or household members, whether minors or adults, that constitutes a crime under the laws of this state. See Domestic Violence Chapter 13 for further information on the subject.]

[Duty to Retreat – Generally – Yes]

(b) A person may not use deadly physical force in self-defense if he or she knows that he or she can avoid the necessity of using deadly physical force with complete safety:
(1) (A) By retreating.

[No Duty to Retreat From Special Places]

(B) However, a person is not required to retreat if the person is:

(i) In the person's dwelling or on the curtilage surrounding the person's dwelling and was not the original aggressor; or

(ii) A law enforcement officer or a person assisting at the direction of a law enforcement officer; or

(2) By surrendering possession of property to a person claiming a lawful right to possession of the property.

(c) As used in this section, "curtilage" means the land adjoining a dwelling that is convenient for family purposes and habitually used for family purposes, but not necessarily enclosed, and includes an outbuilding that is directly and intimately connected with the dwelling and in close proximity to the dwelling.

[You can use deadly force to defend against deadly force or a violent felony, such as being robbed by someone at gunpoint or being threatened with death by a person having a deadly weapon. But you must retreat first, if you can do so in complete safety. So if a person on crutches is threatening you with a knife from a distance of 25 yards and you know you can outrun him, you have to retreat before you cut loose with your Colt. You don't have to retreat from your home, garage or carport ("curtilage") unless you started a fight.

Notice the use of the term "imminent" in connection with "domestic abuse." Even if a woman is the victim of domestic violence (example—"wife beating"), she cannot use deadly force unless the threat is imminent, meaning about to happen. Too often the wife finally snaps, gets her husband's gun while he's in a drunken stupor and puts an abrupt stop to years of abuse with a bullet to the brain. She is ALWAYS arrested and charged with murder or manslaughter and almost always convicted because the threat is not imminent (he's asleep, not up getting ready to beat her again)—see the wife-beating cases reported in Chapter 13. Advocates against spousal abuse are pushing for the repeal of the word "imminent" in the statutes dealing with this issue, but so far the law stands and women who "dust" their abusive husbands are now dusting not-so-fancy furniture in the Big House.]

[Defense of Person(s) in Special Places – Home, Business, Occupied Vehicle]

§ A.C. A. § 5-2-608.
Use of physical force in defense of premises.

(a) A person in lawful possession or control of premises or a vehicle is justified in using nondeadly physical force upon another person when and to the extent that the person reasonably believes the use of nondeadly physical force is necessary to prevent or terminate the commission or attempted commission of a criminal trespass by the other person in or upon the premises or vehicle.

(b) A person may use deadly physical force under the circumstances set forth in subsection (a) of this section if:

(1) Use of deadly physical force is authorized by § 5-2-607 [imminent threat of deadly force against a person on the premises or in a vehicle]; or

(2) The person reasonably believes the use of deadly physical force is necessary to prevent the commission of arson or burglary [attempting to burn or break into a building or vehicle] by a trespasser.

[Notice the distinction in section 608 between defending against a criminal trespass onto property or into a vehicle and defending *persons* in those places from violent crimes. If you are simply defending the premises or vehicle against a trespass, you cannot legally use deadly force. If you are defending persons on the premises or in a vehicle against an imminent threat of deadly force or the dangerous felonies of burglary or arson, you are justified in using deadly force.]

§ A.C. A. § 5-2-620.
Use of force to defend persons and property within home.

(a) The right of an individual to defend himself or herself and the life of a person or property in the individual's home against harm, injury, or loss by a person unlawfully entering or attempting to enter or intrude into the home is reaffirmed as a fundamental right to be preserved and promoted as a public policy in this state. [Like a few other states, Arkansas's Legislature found the right to protect your home so important and fundamental that they actually express it in a statute.]

[Presumption of Reasonableness in Special Places – Home]

(b) There is a legal presumption that any force or means used to accomplish a purpose described in subsection (a) of this section was exercised in a lawful and necessary manner, unless the presumption is overcome by clear and convincing evidence to the contrary.

(c) The public policy stated in subsection (a) of this section shall be strictly complied with by the court and an appropriate instruction of this public policy shall be given to a jury sitting in trial of criminal charges brought in connection with this public policy. [Yea! I want one of these in all of my self-defense cases!! Judges are required to tell juries how important the right of self-defense is.]

[Reckless Injury to Innocent Third Parties]

§ A.C. A. § 5-2-614.
Reckless or negligent force

(a) When a person believes that the use of physical force is necessary for any purpose justifying that use of physical force under this subchapter but the person is reckless or negligent either in forming that belief or in employing an excessive degree of physical force, the justification afforded by this subchapter is unavailable in a prosecution for an offense for which recklessness or negligence suffices to establish a culpable mental state.

(b) When a person is justified under this subchapter in using physical force but he or she recklessly or negligently injures or creates a substantial risk of injury to a third party, the justification afforded by this subchapter is unavailable in a prosecution for the recklessness or negligence toward the third party. [Just because you have a right to self-defense in Arkansas, doesn't mean you can be reckless or careless in exercising that right. **Example:** You can use deadly force to stop the commission of a bank robbery. But if you close your eyes, spray and pray, and hurt innocent people, you could be prosecuted for your carelessness.]

[Civil Liability]

§ A.C. A. § 5-2-621.
Attempting to protect persons during commission of a felony.

No person is civilly liable for an action or omission intended to protect himself or herself or another from a personal injury during the commission of a felony unless the action or omission constitutes a felony. [Legislators in many states are waking up to the ridiculousness of the notion that a criminal injured while committing a felony should be able to sue a person who injures the felon in self-defense. Therefore, more statutes like this are being enacted to protect the innocent from lawsuits by the guilty. Felons and their personal injury attorneys may argue these statutes tend to be punitive in nature. Oh well! Don't do the crime, 'cause if you get injured and sue, you won't win a dime. However, if you are committing a felony, you are not shielded from liability.]

[Defense of Personal Property]

§ **A.C. A. § 5-2-609.**
Use of physical force in defense of property.

A person is justified in using nondeadly physical force upon another person when and to the extent that the person reasonably believes the use of nondeadly physical force is necessary to prevent or terminate the other person's:

(1) Commission or attempted commission of theft or criminal mischief; or

(2) Subsequent flight from the commission or attempted commission of theft or criminal mischief.

[Notice, like in most states, you cannot use deadly force to defend your personal property. It's just not worth the legal risk, unless you want to contribute generously to some attorney's Big-Boy-Toy fund!]

[HELPFUL DEFINITIONS RELATING TO THIS STATE'S SELF-DEFENSE STATUTES]

- **Curtilage** – means the land adjoining a dwelling that is convenient for family purposes and habitually used for family purposes, but not necessarily enclosed, and includes an outbuilding that is directly and intimately connected with the dwelling and in close proximity to the dwelling; **A.C. A. § 5-2-607(c).**

- **Deadly physical force** – means physical force that under the circumstances in which it is used is readily capable of causing death or serious physical injury; **A.C. A § 5-2-601(2).**

- **Dwelling** – means an enclosed space that is used or intended to be used as a human habitation, home, or residence on a temporary or permanent basis; **A.C. A § 5-2-601(3).**

- **Felonies Mentioned Above** – [Arson and burglary are the only felonies specifically mentioned in the statutes above. However, the statute says that deadly force is justifiable against a person "committing or about to commit a felony involving force or violence." **A.C.A. § 5-2-607 (a) (1).** We have included some felonies that would meet this criterion.]

- **Arson** – [Someone who trespasses and recklessly or intentionally sets fire to any property or structure or causes an explosion.] **A.C.A. § 5-38-301.**

- **Aggravated Assault** – [Purposely creating a risk of serious injury or death by displaying a firearm, choking or other means.] **A.C. A. § 5-13-204.**

- **Battery in the 1st or 2nd degree.** [Intentionally causing serious injury to others using a deadly weapon, or to a host of classes of individuals including the elderly over 60, children, unborn children, teachers, doctors, police and correctional officers, medical personnel, firefighters, etc.] **A.C. A. § 5-13-201 and 202.**

- **Burglary** – [Unlawfully entering or remaining in an occupiable residential or commercial structure with the purpose of committing a crime. Arkansas recognizes the difference between a residential and commercial burglary, with residential being a more severe felony, a class B felony rather than a Class C.] **A.C. A. § 5-39-201.**

- **Kidnapping** – [Restraining a person without permission in a way that substantially interferes with their liberty for the purpose of committing a crime.] **A.C. A. § 5-11-102.**

- **Manslaughter or murder** – [Recklessly or intentionally causing death to a person or assisting someone in the process.] **A.C. A. § 5-10-102 - 104.**

- **Robbery** – [Using or threatening the use of force to while in the attempt or process of committing a crime.] **A.C. A. § 5-12-102 & 103.**

- **Minor** – means any person under eighteen (18) years of age; **A.C. A. § 5-2-601 (4).**

- **Occupiable structure** – means a vehicle, building, or other structure:

  (i) Where any person lives or carries on a business or other calling;

  (ii) Where people assemble for a purpose of business, government, education, religion, entertainment, or public transportation; or

  (iii) That is customarily used for overnight accommodation of a person whether or not a person is actually present. A.C. A § 5-2-601 (5) (A).

- **Occupiable structure** – includes each unit of an occupiable structure divided into a separately occupied unit; **A.C. A § 5-2-601 (5)(B).**

- **Physical force** – means any bodily impact, restraint, or confinement; or the threat of any bodily impact, restraint, or confinement; **A.C. A § 5-2-601 (6).**

- **Premises** – means an occupiable structure; or any real property; **A.C. A § 5-2-601(7).**

- **Unlawful physical force** – means physical force that is employed without the consent of the person against whom it is directed and the employment of the physical force constitutes a criminal offense or tort or would constitute a criminal offense or tort except for a defense other than the defense of justification or privilege; **A.C. A. § 5-2-601 (8).**

- **Vehicle** – means any craft or device designed for the transportation of a person or property across land or water or through the air. **A.C. A. § 5-2-601 (9).**

[TEMPLATE Topics We Could Not Find Explained in Statutes or Cases]
(For each of these topics that we could not find addressed in your state's statutes or cases, we suggest you review the same topics in the subchapters of surrounding states. Your state's courts may look to the law of the surrounding states to see how their courts and legislatures have treated that particular self-defense issue.)

[Committing Felony or Unlawful Act]

[Co-Habitants; Co-Employees – Duty to Retreat]

Pancho's Wisdom

You just might be a Gunnut if . . . the aroma of the powder residue in the chamber of your autoloader revs your pleasure meter as high as sausage, eggs and grits with a side of biscuits and gravy.

WARNING: Relying solely upon the language of California's justifiable homicide statute could be legally disastrous! Its meaning has been altered drastically by case law. We believe California's jury instructions provide a much more accurate and understandable description of the law that is applied to defensive incidents than Cali's statutes do. The jury instructions incorporate the law set forth in California's latest self-defense cases.

Our legal database indicates that California's main self-defense statute dealing with the use of deadly force in defense of self and home, §197, was enacted in 1850. Although it has been amended since, crucial phrases in the statute deviate significantly from current case law and the state's most recent self-defense jury instructions. It appears that rather than wait for the California legislature to update self-defense law, the courts have changed the law case by case. The rules of self-defense contained in these cases have been incorporated into jury instructions. As explained in more detail in Chapter 3, jury instructions are statements of law that courts give jurors so jurors can apply the facts of the case to the law. If you were prosecuted in California and claimed self-defense, the jury in your case would not be asked to apply California's bare-bones-self-defense statutes as they appear in California's code books. Instead, they would be given the jury instructions "CALCRIM,"contained in this subchapter or a similar set only available to lawyers through a private publishing company. As far as we can tell, California's criminal jury instructions are better maintained and more frequently updated than any in the country. It is our impression that the trial courts rely upon them heavily and unless there is an extremely good reason seldom deviate from them. The instructions we used appear on the internet at http://www.courtinfo.ca.gov/jury/criminaljuryinstructions. The specific instructions on self-defense are not easy to find. Once found, they are difficult to understand because of all the blanks that need to be filled in. For ease in understanding, we filled in all the blanks and used the pronoun "you" to emphasize personal accountability. The California Judicial Council updates these instructions frequently. If you take the subject of self-defense seriously, we suggest you request information about keeping up with the changes as described in Chapter 19.

Because the focus in California seems to be upon jury instructions rather than updating its statutes, we debated whether to even include the statutes themselves. We omitted many because the jury instructions are easier to understand. However, because we expect Californians to encourage their legislature to update its statutes, we included **§197 Penal** because it is sorely in need of updating. Again, we warn you, despite the broad language of **§197 Penal** you legally:

CANNOT use deadly force to prevent any and *all* felonies,

CANNOT kill any and *all* rioters,

CANNOT kill people committing any and *all* acts of disturbing the peace.

FURTHERMORE, you take a HUGE LEGAL RISK if you harm a trespasser in your home who you know or should know is unarmed, non-threatening and non-violent.

Due to California's heavy reliance upon jury instructions, we had to change the order of our TEMPLATE outline slightly to keep it understandable.

Key: ■ commentary ■ original statutes, cases or jury instructions

---

[Defense of Self and Others] [Non-Deadly Force]
[Defense of Third Person]

[We picked the charge of assault to illustrate the use of the jury instructions relating to non-deadly force. We could just as well have used other crimes involving less-than-lethal force such as exhibiting a dangerous weapon (§417 Penal) or exhibiting an imitation firearm (§417.4). In the jury instructions used in court, you would be referred to as the defendant. We substituted the word "you" for "defendant" to make it easier to understand how all of these instructions apply to you personally. Because the Judicial Council drafted California's jury instructions to be easily understood by non-lawyers, we did not see the need for extensive commentary.]

California Criminal Jury Instructions (CALCRIM) 3470. Right to Self-Defense or Defense of Another (Non-Homicide)

Self-defense is a defense to assault. You are not guilty of assault if you used force against the other person in lawful self-defense or defense of another. You acted in lawful self-defense or defense of another if:

1. You reasonably believed that you or someone else was in imminent danger of suffering bodily injury;

2. You reasonably believed that the immediate use of force was necessary to defend against that danger;

AND

3. You used no more force than was reasonably necessary to defend against that danger.

[You can use a reasonable amount of non-deadly force to respond to an imminent threat of non-deadly force. You cannot use deadly force.]

. . .

When deciding whether your beliefs were reasonable, the jury must consider all the circumstances as they were known to and appeared to you and consider what a reasonable person in a similar situation with similar knowledge would have believed. If your beliefs were reasonable, the danger does not need to have actually existed. . . . [You can be forgiven for mistaken beliefs, if those beliefs were reasonable.]

[No Duty to Retreat – Generally]

CALCRIM 3470. Right to Self-Defense or Defense of Another (Non-Homicide)(Cont.)
You are not required to retreat. You are entitled to stand your ground and defend yourself and, if reasonably necessary, to pursue an assailant until the danger of bodily injury has passed. This is so even if safety could have been achieved by retreating.

[Exceptions to Justifiable Self-Defense] [Mutual Combat] [Initial Aggressor] [Withdraw and Communicate]

[These Exceptions apply to the use of both non-deadly and deadly force.]

CALCRIM 3471. Right to Self-Defense: Mutual Combat or Initial Aggressor
If you are engaged in mutual combat or are the initial aggressor you have a right to self-defense only if:

1. you actually and in good faith try to stop fighting;

AND

2. you indicate, by word or by conduct, to your opponent, in a way that a reasonable person would understand, that you want to stop fighting and that you have stopped fighting,

<Give element 3 in cases of mutual combat>
[AND

3. you give your opponent a chance to stop fighting.

If you meet these requirements, you then have a right to self-defense if your opponent continues to fight.
[This is a very common rule that relates to starting a fight or agreeing to fight. Generally, you cannot claim self-defense if you start or agree to a fight. But if you give up your macho, and make every reasonable attempt to tell your adversary you no longer want to fight, you can legally defend yourself if your adversary continues to fight. At that point, he becomes the aggressor, not you. We find, however, that once it gets this complicated, plan on being arrested and prosecuted.

Notice the following rule allows you to still claim self-defense if you thought you were only agreeing to a fist fight and your opponent suddenly tries to kill you with a deadly weapon.]

. . .

If the jury decides that you started the fight using non-deadly force and the opponent responded with such sudden and deadly force that you could not withdraw from the fight, then you had the right to defend yourself with deadly force and were not required to try to stop fighting. [If a jury believes this is what happened, you can win your case on the theory of self-defense. However, our research shows that anytime you are at fault in starting or agreeing to a fight and your opponent gets hurt or killed, you will be arrested and prosecuted. See Thumbs-Down Chapter 7.]

CALCRIM 3474. Danger No Longer Exists or Attacker Disabled
The right to use force in self-defense or defense of another continues only as long as the danger exists or reasonably appears to exist. When the attacker withdraws or no longer appears capable of inflicting any injury, then the right to use force ends. [This is the flip side of the rule stated immediately above. If your opponent stops fighting and communicates that to you, you must stop as well. Remember our discussion in Chapters 3 and 4, your purpose is not to punish your attacker, only to STOP the progression of force against yourself or another. Once the threat stops, whether it's because your adversary changes his mind or can't hurt you because of severe wounds, you must stop your use of force or else you become the aggressor. This applies to the use of both non-deadly force and deadly force.]

[Provocation]
"[S]elf-defense is not available as a plea to a defendant who has sought a quarrel with the design to force a deadly issue and thus, through his fraud, contrivance, or fault, to create a real or apparent necessity for making a felonious assault." *People v. Hinshaw,* 194 Cal. 1, 26, 227 P. 156 (CA. 1924). [You can't provoke someone with the intent to hurt or kill them when they respond to the provocation. This is a well-established principle in self-defense law throughout the country.]

[Committing Felony or Unlawful Act]
"It is well established that the ordinary self-defense doctrine - applicable when a defendant reasonably believes that his safety is endangered may not be invoked by a defendant who, through his own wrongful conduct (e.g., the initiation of a physical assault or the commission of a felony), has created circumstances under which his adversary's attack or pursuit is legally justified." *In re Christian* S. 30 Cal.Rptr.2d 33 (Cal. 1994) [fn1]. [You cannot claim self-defense after hurting someone forcefully trying to stop you from committing a crime.]

[Deadly Force] [Use of Deadly Force to Prevent Serious Felonies]
[Defense of Others] [Defense of Person(s) in Special Places – Habitation]

[**California Penal Code §197** covers the use of deadly force in the context of self-defense, home-defense and defense of others. It also includes California's fleeing felon statute, suppressing riots and keeping the peace. **YOU MUST NOT RELY UPON THIS STATUTE; THE COURTS HAVE DRASTICALLY CHANGED ITS MEANING.** Refer to the jury instructions following it, beginning with 505. **Justifiable Homicide.** We only cite §197 to show you how important it is for the legislature to amend it to keep citizens from being misled.]

§ **Cal. Penal Code § 197**
Homicide is also justifiable when committed by any person in any of the following cases:

1. When resisting any attempt to murder any person, or to commit a felony, or to do some great bodily injury upon any person; or,

2. When committed in defense of habitation, property, or person, against one who manifestly intends or endeavors, by violence or surprise, to commit a felony, or against one who manifestly intends and endeavors, in a violent, riotous or tumultu-

ous manner, to enter the habitation of another for the purpose of offering violence to any person therein; or,

3. When committed in the lawful defense of such person, or of a wife or husband, parent, child, master, mistress, or servant of such person, when there is reasonable ground to apprehend a design to commit a felony or to do some great bodily injury, and imminent danger of such design being accomplished; but such person, or the person in whose behalf the defense was made, if he was the assailant or engaged in mutual combat, must really and in good faith have endeavored to decline any further struggle before the homicide was committed; or,

4. When necessarily committed in attempting, by lawful ways and means, to apprehend any person for any felony committed, or in lawfully suppressing any riot, or in lawfully keeping and preserving the peace.

[Okay, that was the state self- and home-defense statute. Now notice how drastically the courts have changed it in the following CALCRIM Jury Instructions 505 and 506 (modified for ease in understanding.) These are what you would be judged by if you were arrested for hurting someone in a defensive incident. Of course, if there was a special issue that required changing these slightly, your lawyer would propose the change or amendment to the judge and he would make the final decision as to what law the jury should be instructed to apply in your specific case. But these are the general rules that would be applied.]

CALCRIM 505. Justifiable Homicide: Self-Defense or Defense of Another
You are not guilty of murder or manslaughter if you were justified in killing someone in self-defense or defense of another. You acted in lawful self-defense or defense of another if:

1. You reasonably believed that you or someone else was in imminent danger of being killed or suffering great bodily injury or was in imminent danger of being raped, maimed, robbed or the victim of some other forcible and atrocious crime; [The right to use deadly force to stop "any felony" under §197 has been modified by case law and incorporated into these instructions to only allow deadly force to prevent "forcible and atrocious" crimes such as rape and robbery.]

2. You reasonably believed that the immediate use of deadly force was necessary to defend against that danger; [The use of deadly force was necessary and reasonable. See our discussion of necessity in Chapter 3.]

AND

3. You used no more force than was reasonably necessary to defend against that danger. [NEVER use excessive force or try to execute your adversary to keep him or her from testifying against you. Read Chapters 3 and 4 if you haven't already.]

Belief in future harm is not sufficient, no matter how great or how likely the harm is believed to be. You must have believed there was imminent danger of great bodily injury to yourself or someone else. [If the justification for using deadly force was a forcible and atrocious crime such as rape, we would ask the judge to replace the phrase "imminent danger of great bodily injury" to "imminent danger of being raped."] Your belief must have been reasonable and you must have acted only because of that belief. You are only entitled to use that amount of force that a reasonable person would believe is necessary in the same situation. If you used more force than was reasonable, the killing was not justified. [Again, an admonition not to use excessive force. See our examples in Chapters 3 and 4.]

When deciding whether your beliefs were reasonable, the jury must consider all the circumstances as they were known to and appeared to you and consider what a reasonable person in a similar situation with similar knowledge would have believed. If your beliefs were reasonable, the danger does not need to have actually existed.

Your belief that you were threatened may be reasonable even if you relied on information that was not true. However, you must actually and reasonably have believed that the information was true. [Reasonable reliance upon information is sufficient, even if the information is false.]

[No Duty to Retreat Before Using Justifiable Deadly Force]

You are not required to retreat. You are entitled to stand your ground and defend yourself and, if reasonably necessary, to pursue an assailant until the danger of death, great bodily injury or being the victim of a forcible and atrocious crime has passed. This is so even if safety could have been achieved by retreating.

Great bodily injury means significant or substantial physical injury. It is an injury that is greater than minor or moderate harm. [You don't have to retreat from anywhere you have a legal right to be. But this paragraph also warns that you cannot use deadly force if the harm threatened against you would not cause you serious injury. You can't use a samurai sword to prevent a paper cut.]

[Deadly Force in Defense of Premises (Your Home)]

CALCRIM 506. Justifiable Homicide: Defending Against Harm to Person Within Home or on Property

You are not guilty of murder or manslaughter if you killed to defend yourself or any other person in your home. Such a killing is justified, and therefore not unlawful, if:

1. You reasonably believed that you were defending your home against the person killed, who intended to or tried to commit murder, rape, robbery, or other forcible and atrocious crime [you may obviously defend yourself in your own home against death, serious injury or against serious crimes that could result in serious injury or death] or violently, riotously, or tumultuously tried to enter that home [like the guy in the black ski mask who breaks your window with a crowbar] intending to commit an act of violence against someone inside; [Notice the use of the word "violence" instead of the phrase "threat of serious injury or death." This implies that a lower threshold of potential harm triggers the right to use deadly force in your home as opposed to outside your home when the entry into the home was violent and forceful. But the concept of necessity also applies as explained in paragraphs 3 and 4.]

2. You reasonably believed that the danger was imminent;

3. You reasonably believed that the use of deadly force was necessary to defend against the danger;

AND

4. You used no more force than was reasonably necessary to defend against the danger.

   Belief in future harm is not sufficient, no matter how great or how likely the harm is believed to be. You must have believed there was imminent danger of violence to yourself or someone else. Your belief must have been reasonable and you must have acted only because of that belief. You are only entitled to use that amount of force that a reasonable person would believe is necessary in the same situation. If you used more force than was reasonable, then the killing was not justified.

   When deciding whether your beliefs were reasonable, the jury should consider all the circumstances as they were known to and appeared to you and consider what a reasonable person in a similar situation with similar knowledge would have believed. If your beliefs were reasonable, the danger does not need to have actually existed. [We can't stress enough how important the word "necessary" is in the law of self-defense. You may only use as much force as is necessary to stop the progression of deadly force against you or another and then you must stop your use of such force. If your shots only wound an intruder, but he has stopped his aggression, you must stop yours or you then become the aggressor. See the examples in Chapter 3.

   Pancho's Wisdom – California's jury instructions imply that the threshold of harm when someone violently enters your home is less than "death or serious injury." It would be better if this were made crystal clear. A home defender should not have to waste valuable reaction time trying to conclusively establish if the object in the hand of a person who has just burst into his home is a deadly weapon. By the time he determines for sure that it is, he could be dead. (See Chapter 11 discussing perception and reaction time.) The instruction should say that any threatened violence, "no matter how slight," activates the right to defend persons in the home with deadly force. See the wording of Colorado's home-defense statute. Of course if Californians REALLY wanted to make the home hallowed ground, they would adopt the language of the Florida home-defense statute. See also Chapter 20, The Mother of All Self-Defense Laws. The burden of the legal and physical risks arising out of a home break-in should rest completely upon the home invader, NOT the homeowner.]

[No Duty to Retreat From Home]

CALCRIM 506. (Home Defense Cont.) You are not required to retreat from your home. You are entitled to stand your ground and defend yourself and, if reasonably necessary, to pursue an assailant until the danger of death, bodily injury or the forcible and atrocious crime has passed. This is so even if safety could have been achieved by retreating. [You do not have to retreat from your home before defending yourself with deadly force. However, we could not find for certain whether this rule applies against someone who is not a trespasser, such as a family member or invited guest. We suspect you do not have to retreat, but there is not a presumption of reasonableness against such person as applies against home invaders (see presumptions below). This means that there must be an imminent threat of death or serious injury before you can use deadly force against someone who is not a trespasser. This is a fertile area for arrest and prosecution. See Thumbs-Down Factors, Chapter 7. Consequently we recommend you retreat in such situations, if you can retreat in complete safety.]

. . .

[Presumption of Reasonableness in Your Home]

CALCRIM 3477. Presumption That Resident Was Reasonably Afraid of Death or Great Bodily Injury (Pen. Code, § 198.5)

The law presumes that you reasonably feared imminent death or great bodily injury to yourself, or to a member of your family or household, if:

1. An intruder unlawfully and forcibly entered or was entering your home;
2. You knew or reasonably believed that an intruder unlawfully and forcibly entered or was entering your home;
3. The intruder was not a member of your household or family;

AND

4. You used force intended to or likely to cause death or great bodily injury to the intruder inside the home. *Great bodily injury* means significant or substantial physical injury. It is an injury that is greater than minor or moderate harm.

The State of California has the burden of overcoming this presumption. This means that it must prove that you did not have a reasonable fear of imminent death or injury to yourself, or to a member of your family or household, when you used force against the intruder. If the State of California has not met this burden, a jury must find you reasonably feared death or injury to yourself, or to a member of your family or household. [If an uninvited intruder forces his way into your home, it is presumed you had a reasonable fear of death or serious injury. An unlawful entry is a strict requirement of this rule. The presumption would not apply against an invited guest. If the person had freely come and gone in and out of your home in the past, this could deprive you of the presumption as well, unless it was convincingly established that you had revoked his or her permission to be in your home.]

[Other Issues – Using Deadly Force to Apprehend Fleeing Felons, Preserve the Peace and Prevent Riots]

[We recommend that you do NOT attempt to apprehend fleeing felons or use deadly force to preserve the peace or prevent riots unless there is an imminent threat of serious injury or death to you or a loved one. The personal and legal risks are simply too great. We only mention these issues because paragraph 4 of §197 Penal (the outdated law we cautioned you of above) purports to justify the use of deadly force against persons committing such acts. However, if you read CALCRIM jury instructions 508. Justifiable Homicide: Citizen Arrest and 509. Justifiable Homicide: Non-Peace Officer Preserving the Peace (available at the website we cited in the introduction to this subchapter), you will see that you are NOT justified unless the person you injure or kill posed a threat of serious bodily injury to you or someone else. Because of space constraints, we have not included these two instructions.]

[Reckless Injury to Innocent Third Parties] [Civil Liability]
"[W] e conclude that the doctrine of self-defense is available to insulate one from criminal responsibility where his act, justifiably in self-defense, inadvertently results in the injury of an innocent bystander." *People v. Mathews,* 154 Cal.Rptr. 628, 631 (Cal.App. 1979). "In our view, the rule is simply a recognition that an act resulting in justifiable homicide as defined by Penal Code section 197 is, in legal effect, a privileged act. A privileged act is generally defined as one that would ordinarily be tortious, but which, under the circumstances, does not subject the actor to liability." *Gilmore v. Superior Court,* 230 Cal.App.3d 416, 420 (1991). [As long as you were acting in justifiable self-defense, you won't be held accountable for injury to innocent third parties. However, if your conduct is reckless, you will be held criminally accountable (e.g., manslaughter) and civilly liable. See chapter concerning civil liability, Chapter 15.]

[Defense of Property]

CALCRIM 3475. Right to Eject Trespasser From Real Property
You may request a trespasser to leave your home or property. If the trespasser does not leave within a reasonable time and it would appear to a reasonable person that the trespasser poses a threat to the home or property or you or others on the property, you may use reasonable force to make the trespasser leave.

Reasonable force means the amount of force that a reasonable person in the same situation would believe is necessary to make the trespasser leave.

If the trespasser resists, you may increase the amount of force you use in proportion to the force used by the trespasser and the threat the trespasser poses to you, your guests or the property.

When deciding whether you used reasonable force, the jury will consider all the circumstances as they were known to and appeared to you and consider what a reasonable person in a similar situation with similar knowledge would have believed. If your beliefs were reasonable, the danger does not need to have actually existed.

The State of California has the burden of proving beyond a reasonable doubt that you used more force than was reasonable. If the State of California has not met this burden, the jury must find you not guilty of assault.

[You may use reasonable force to eject trespassers after asking them to leave. Please note you do NOT have the authority to use deadly force. The backwoods sign "Trespassers will be shot; survivors will be prosecuted" is NOT a correct statement of the law in ANY state.]

CALCRIM 3476. Right to Defend Real or Personal Property
You may use reasonable force to protect your real or personal property from imminent harm. You may also use reasonable force to protect the property of a family member/guest/master/servant/ward [a ward is a person who has a guardian] from immediate harm.

Reasonable force means the amount of force that a reasonable person in the same situation would believe is necessary to protect the property from imminent harm.

When deciding whether you used reasonable force, a jury will be instructed to consider all the circumstances as they were known to and appeared to you and consider what a reasonable person in a similar situation with similar knowledge would have believed. If your beliefs were reasonable, the danger does not need to have actually existed.

The State of California has the burden of proving beyond a reasonable doubt that you used more force than was reasonable to protect property from imminent harm. If the State of California has not met this burden, a must find you not guilty of assault.

[You may use non-deadly reasonable force to defend and protect your real and personal property. Rigging a gun to go off to stop burglars is STRICTLY PROHIBITED was the holding of the following landmark case.] "[T]here may be no privilege to use a deadly mechanical device to prevent a burglary of a dwelling house in which no one is present." *People v. Ceballos*, 526 P.2d 241, 246 (Cal. 1974).

[HELPFUL DEFINITIONS RELATING TO THIS STATE'S SELF-DEFENSE STATUTES]

Forcible and Atrocious Crime – A forcible and atrocious crime is any felony that by its nature and the manner of its commission threatens, or is reasonably believed by the defendant to threaten life or great bodily injury so as to instill in him or her a reasonable fear of death or great bodily injury. Murder, mayhem, rape and robbery are forcible and atrocious crimes. (Brackets omitted.) **CALJIC 5.16** (California Jury Instructions Criminal).

Mayhem – Every person who unlawfully and maliciously deprives a human being of a member of his body, or disables, disfigures, or renders it useless, or cuts or disables the tongue, or puts out an eye, or slits the nose, ear, or lip, is guilty of mayhem. **West's Ann.Cal.Penal Code § 203.**

[TEMPLATE Topics We Could Not Find Explained in Statutes or Cases]

(For each of these topics that we could not find addressed in your state's statutes or cases, we suggest you review the same topics in the subchapters of surrounding states. Your state's courts may look to the law of the surrounding states to see how their courts and legislatures have treated that particular self-defense issue.)

[Co-Habitants; Co-Employees – Duty to Retreat]

Key: ■ commentary ■ original statutes, cases or jury instructions

[Defense of Self and Others] [Non-Deadly Force]
[Defense of Third Persons]

§ COLORADO REVISED STATUTES (C.R.S.) § 18-1-704 (1) and (4). Use of physical force in defense of a person.

(1) Except as provided in subsections (2) and (3) of this section, a person is justified in using physical force upon another person in order to defend himself or a third person from what he reasonably believes to be the use or imminent use of unlawful physical force by that other person, and he may use a degree of force which he reasonably believes to be necessary for that purpose. [In other words, a person can use a reasonable amount of non-deadly force to repel a corresponding threat of non-deadly force; but may only use deadly force under the circumstances described under the subheading **[Deadly Force]** below.

. . .

(4) In a case in which the defendant is not entitled to a jury instruction regarding self-defense as an affirmative defense, the court shall allow the defendant to present evidence, when relevant, that he or she was acting in self-defense. If the defendant presents evidence of self-defense, the court shall instruct the jury with a self-defense law instruction. The court shall instruct the jury that it may consider the evidence of self-defense in determining whether the defendant acted recklessly, with extreme indifference, or in a criminally negligent manner. However, the self-defense law instruction shall not be an affirmative defense instruction and the prosecuting attorney shall not have the burden of disproving self-defense. This section shall not apply to strict liability crimes. [This is a very technical rule of law relating to "imperfect self-defense." In Colorado you have to be guiltless to be justified in using force in self-defense. If you act recklessly then you are not guiltless. That means that the prosecutor doesn't have to prove beyond a reasonable doubt that you didn't act in self-defense. There's a different standard of proof under these circumstances which is not something you should be striving to attain. Certainly you don't want to act recklessly and need the court to give this instruction.]

[Deadly Force] [Use of Deadly Force to Prevent Serious Felonies]

§ **C.R.S. § 18-1-704 (2).**
Use of physical force in defense of a person.

. . .

(2) Deadly physical force may be used only if a person reasonably believes a lesser degree of force is inadequate and:

(a) The actor has reasonable ground to believe, and does believe, that he or another person is in imminent danger of being killed or of receiving great bodily injury; or [An immediate threat of deadly force may be repelled by the use of deadly force.]

(b) The other person is using or reasonably appears about to use physical force against an occupant of a dwelling or business establishment while committing or attempting to commit burglary as defined in sections 18-4-202 to 18-4-204; or [A person in a dwelling or business can use deadly force to repel someone committing or attempting to commit a burglary. Even though breaking into a vending machine can be considered a burglary, notice that this section also requires a reasonable belief that physical force his about to be used "against an occupant" of the building, not just the against the vending machine. Bumping off a bumpkin breaking into a bubblegum machine without the threat of physical force to a person is sure to get you convicted and sued.]

(c) The other person is committing or reasonably appears about to commit kidnapping as defined in section 18-3-301 or 18-3-302, robbery as defined in section 18-4-301 or 18-4-302, sexual assault as set forth in section 18-3-402, or in section 18-3-403 as it existed prior to July 1, 2000, or assault as defined in sections 18-3-202 and 18-3-203. [You may use deadly force to prevent the commission of the following serious felonies - kidnapping, robbery, sexual assault or assault with a deadly weapon, IF you reasonably believe a lesser degree of force would be inadequate. For a brief summary of these felonies see [**Helpful Definitions Relating to this State's Self-Defense Statutes**] below.]

[*Pancho's Wisdom* – The phrase "only if a person reasonably believes a lesser degree of force is inadequate" is unique and could cause a defender to hesitate long enough to get himself or herself killed. Why should the defender feel like he has to split hairs if someone is kidnapping his child? In Utah and Florida, you can prevent someone from kidnapping your child by using deadly force. Colorado should stop being mamby pamby about such things. The Colorado Legislature needs to send the message to criminals, " if you don't want to die, don't kidnap people's kids or rob them or sexually assault them - end of story."]

[Exceptions to Justifiable Self-Defense][Initial Aggressor]
[Provocation] [Mutual Combat]

§ **C.R.S. § 18-1-704 (3).**
Use of physical force in defense of a person.

. . .

(3) Notwithstanding the provisions of subsection (1) of this section, a person is not justified in using physical force if:

(a) With intent to cause bodily injury or death to another person, he provokes the use of unlawful physical force by that other person; or [You cannot provoke a person to use physical force against you with the intent to kill or seriously injure that person. To claim self-defense you must be guiltless.]

(b) He is the initial aggressor; except... [You can't start a fight and expect to claim self-defense when the other person uses force to defend himself from your aggression. See heading **[Exceptions to the Exceptions] [Withdraw and Communicate]** below.]

(c) The physical force involved is the product of a combat by agreement not specifically authorized by law. [You're not justified if you tell your opponent to meet you at the O.K. Corral.]

[Exceptions to the Exceptions] [Withdraw and Communicate]

§ **C.R.S. § 18-1-704 (3) (b).**
Use of physical force in defense of a person.

. . .

(3) Notwithstanding the provisions of subsection (1) of this section [§ 18-1-704 above], a person is not justified in using physical force if:

. . .

(b) He is the initial aggressor; except that his use of physical force upon another person under the circumstances is justifiable if he withdraws from the encounter and effectively communicates to the other person his intent to do so, but the latter nevertheless continues or threatens the use of unlawful physical force; or ["Initial aggressor" means "you started it." You are not justified in using deadly force if "you started it" unless you withdraw and make it very clear to that person that you are withdrawing and they continue to try to harm you.]

[No Duty to Retreat – Generally]

"Colorado follows the doctrine of no-retreat, which permits non-aggressors who are otherwise entitled to use physical force in self-defense to do so without first retreating, or seeking safety by means of escape. In Colorado, only initial aggressors must retreat before using force in self-defense." *Cassels v. People*, 92 P. 3d 951, 956 (Colo. 2004) (internal citations omitted). [There is no duty to retreat generally; however, initial aggressors (people who start fights) must retreat.]

[Defense of Person(s) in Special Places – Home, Business, Occupied Vehicle]

§ **C.R.S. § 18-1-704.5.**
Use of deadly physical force against an intruder.

(1) The general assembly hereby recognizes that the citizens of Colorado have a right to expect absolute safety within their own homes. [This introduction gives the

impression that Colorado has a very protective home-defense law. It has even been referred to as Colorado's make-my-day law after the often-quoted Clint Eastwood movie line. A closer look reveals that it is not as protective as you think.]

(2) Notwithstanding the provisions of section 18-1-704 [the general self-defense statute above], any occupant of a dwelling is justified in using any degree of physical force, including deadly physical force, against another person when that other person has made an unlawful entry into the dwelling, AND when the occupant has a reasonable belief that such other person has committed a crime in the dwelling in addition to the uninvited entry, or is committing or intends to commit a crime against a person or property in addition to the uninvited entry, AND when the occupant reasonably believes that such other person might use any physical force, no MATTER HOW SLIGHT, against any occupant [emphasis added]. [Notice the three requirements that must be satisfied before you can use deadly force. First, there must be an unlawful entry when someone enters your home. A reasonable belief that the entry was unlawful is not enough. See general discussion of this requirement in *People v. Janes*, 982 P.2d 300, 302-304 (Colo. 1999). Second, there must be a reasonable belief that a crime is being committed or about to be committed against a person or property and third, the intruder might use physical force, no matter how slight, against any occupant. *Pancho's Wisdom*– The strict requirement that the entry be unlawful seems harsh and places the legal risk on the wrong person. **Example:** A roommate who deserves the Darwin Award puts on makeup to look like the composite drawing of a serial killer who has been strangling his victims. The homeowner enters the home and honestly believes the roommate is the serial killer. As the disguised roommate approaches possessing no apparent weapon, the homeowner drops him with a double tap to the chest. It seems to us unfair to deny the homeowner the theory of home defense because there was no unlawful entry by a roommate who has a right to be in the home. Of course, the homeowner could still claim self-defense on the basis of a threat of serious injury or death at the hands of a serial killer. But a zealous, anti-gun prosecutor could claim that using a firearm against an unarmed person is excessive force. Rather than requiring the entry to be unlawful no matter what the circumstances, this statute should only require a reasonable belief of an unlawful entry.]

(3) Any occupant of a dwelling using physical force, including deadly physical force, in accordance with the provisions of subsection (2) of this section shall be immune from criminal prosecution for the use of such force. [A defendant claiming self-defense is entitled to a pre-trial hearing to determine if his case should be dismissed. The burden is on the defendant to prove by a "preponderance of evidence" that he is entitled to the dismissal. *People v. Guenther*, 740 P.2d 971 (Colo. 1987). A dismissal in the early stages of the prosecution could save an innocent defendant tens of thousands of thousands of dollars.]

. . .

§ C.R.S. § 18-1-705. Use of physical force in defense of premises.

A person in possession or control of any building, realty, or other premises, or a person who is licensed or privileged to be thereon, is justified in using reasonable and appropriate physical force upon another person when and to the extent that it is reasonably necessary to prevent or terminate what he reasonably believes to be the commission or attempted commission of an unlawful trespass by the other person in or upon the building, realty, or premises. However, he may use deadly force only in defense of himself or another as described in section 18-1-704, or when he reasonably believes it necessary to prevent what he reasonably believes to be an attempt by the trespasser to commit first degree arson. [Notice that your workplace or your other real estate isn't held as in high esteem as your home. You can use force to expel a trespasser, but you can only use deadly force as described in section 704 above. This means you may only use deadly force to repel an immediate threat of deadly force or to prevent an arson, a violent felony. In your home, under the right circumstances (see 704.5 above), you may use deadly force to repel a physical attack by someone who doesn't actually have a deadly weapon.]

[No Duty to Retreat From Special Places]

"Colorado follows the doctrine of no-retreat, which permits non-aggressors who are otherwise entitled to use physical force in self-defense to do so without first retreating, or seeking safety by means of escape. . ." *Cassels v. People,* 92 P. 3d 951, 956, 958 (Colo. 2004) (internal citations omitted). [You don't have to retreat in Colorado unless you're the one who started the fight.]

[Civil Liability]

§ **C.R.S. §18-1-704.5 (4).**
Use of deadly physical force against an intruder.

. . .

(4) Any occupant of a dwelling using physical force, including deadly physical force, in accordance with the provisions of subsection (2) of this section shall be immune from any civil liability for injuries or death resulting from the use of such force. [If somebody breaks into your home and you hurt or kill them, neither they nor their heirs can sue you in a civil lawsuit, provided you comply with all of the elements of 704.5 (2), discussed above.]

[Defense of Property]

§ **C.R.S. § 18-1-706.**
Use of physical force in defense of property.

A person is justified in using reasonable and appropriate physical force upon another person when and to the extent that he reasonably believes it necessary to prevent what he reasonably believes to be an attempt by the other person to commit theft, criminal mischief, or criminal tampering involving property, but he may use deadly physical force under these circumstances only in defense of himself or another as described in section 18-1-704. [Cars, fridges and stereos are items of personal property. You can't defend them with deadly force. However, in the event that you are defending an item of personal property and the person threatens serious bodily injury or death, then you can use deadly force if all the elements of self-defense exist as described above.]

[HELPFUL DEFINITIONS RELATING TO THIS STATE'S SELF-DEFENSE STATUTES]

- **Bodily injury** – means physical pain, illness, or any impairment of physical or mental condition. **C.R.S. §18-1-901(3)(c).**

- **Deadly physical force** – means force, the intended, natural, and probable consequence of which is to produce death, and which does, in fact, produce death. **C.R.S. §18-1-901(3)(d).**

- **Deadly weapon** – means any of the following which in the manner it is used or intended to be used is capable of producing death or serious bodily injury:

  (I) A firearm, whether loaded or unloaded; [in most jurisdictions, pointing a gun at someone is considered an assault with a deadly weapon even if the gun is unloaded.]

  (II) A knife;

  (III) A bludgeon; or

  (IV) Any other weapon, device, instrument, material, or substance, whether animate or inanimate. **C.R.S. §18-1-901(3)(e).**

- **Dwelling** – means a building which is used, intended to be used, or usually used by a person for habitation. **C.R.S. §18-1-901(3)(g).**

- **Felonies Mentioned Above** – [As picky as some of the Colorado courts have been in deciding issues of self-defense, we suggest you read and remember the definition of each felony. You can read the actual definitions online by searching the citation given at the end of our summary. These can normally be found by doing a Yahoo or Google Search for Colorado Revised Statutes and then searching the title, chapter and section number. For example, first-degree arson is found in Title 18, Chapter 4, Section 102.]

  - **Arson, first degree** – [Knowingly setting fire to a building or occupied structure of another or damaging it by means of explosives.] **C.R.S. §18-4-102.**

  - **Assault, first and second degree** – [Intentionally or recklessly causing bodily harm to a person with a deadly weapon or without a deadly weapon if serious bodily harm occurs.] **C.R.S. §18-3-202, 203.**

  - **Burglary first and third degree** – [Unlawfully entering or breaking into a building or occupied structure with the intent to commit a crime. Entering or breaking into a vault, safe, cash register, etc.] **C.R.S. §18-4- 202-204.**

- **Kidnapping** – [Seizing or carrying a person from one place to another without consent or "tak[ing], entic[ing], or decoy[ing] away any child" that is not his with the intent to hide that child from the rightful guardian or with intent to commit a crime against that person.] **C.R.S. § 18-3-301,302.**

- **Robbery** – [Knowingly taking anything of value from another by the use of force, threat or intimidation. Aggravated robbery has additional elements, including the use of a deadly weapon.] **C.R.S. §18-4-301,302.**

- **Sexual assault** – [Forcing sex upon someone against their will or having sex with someone who cannot give consent, like a mentally deficient person or child.] **C.R.S. §18-3-402,403.**

- **Motor vehicle** – includes any self-propelled device by which persons or property may be moved, carried, or transported from one place to another by land, water, or air, except devices operated on rails, tracks, or cables fixed to the ground or supported by pylons, towers, or other structures. **C.R.S. § 18-1-901(3)(k).**

- **Serious bodily injury** – means bodily injury which, either at the time of the actual injury or at a later time, involves a substantial risk of death, a substantial risk of serious permanent disfigurement, a substantial risk of protracted loss or impairment of the function of any part or organ of the body, or breaks, fractures, or burns of the second or third degree. **C.R.S. § 18-1-901(3)(q).**

[TEMPLATE Topics We Could Not Find Explained in Statutes or Cases]

(For each of these topics that we could not find addressed in your state's statutes or cases, we suggest you review the same topics in the subchapters of surrounding states. Your state's courts may look to the law of the surrounding states to see how their courts and legislatures have treated that particular self-defense issue.)

[Co-Habitants; Co-Employees – Duty to Retreat]

[Presumption of Reasonableness in Special Places]

[Reckless Injury to Innocent Third Parties]

Connecticut's self and home-defense laws fall in line with most of the states along the North-Eastern Seaboard. They place a complicated heap of conditions on being able to defend yourself from a deadly attack. *Pancho's Wisdom* – During a violent robbery by an armed, vicious predator claiming a right to your Rolex, be sure to pull out Connecticut's list of exceptions to the use of deadly force and carefully check them off with a red pencil, one by one, as proof that you did not take a precious life without serious and sincere intellectual reflection, meticulously weighing the consequences of your potentially dangerous conduct. We'll all be there to sing Yankee Doodle at your funeral.

Key: ■ commentary ■ original statutes, cases or jury instructions

---

[Defense of Self and Others] [Non-Deadly Force]

[Defense of Third Persons]

§ CONNECTICUT GENERAL STATUTE ANNOTATED (C.G.S.A.) § 53A-19. Use of physical force in defense of person.

(a) Except as provided in subsections (b) and (c) of this section, a person is justified in using reasonable physical force upon another person to defend himself or a third person from what he reasonably believes to be the use or imminent use of physical force, and he may use such degree of force which he reasonably believes to be necessary for such purpose; except . . . [You can use reasonable force to defend yourself and others from the imminent threat of non-deadly force, but you may not respond with deadly force.]

[Deadly Force]

[(a) continued . . .] that deadly physical force may not be used unless the actor reasonably believes that such other person is (1) using or about to use deadly physical force, or (2) inflicting or about to inflict great bodily harm. [To be justified in using deadly force there must be an imminent threat of deadly force or serious physical injury. There are no serious felonies in Connecticut that automatically authorize the use of deadly force.]

[Duty to Retreat – Generally – Yes]

[No Duty to Retreat From Special Places – Dwelling, Place of Work]

(b) Notwithstanding the provisions of subsection (a) of this section, a person is not justified in using deadly physical force upon another person if he or she knows that he or she can avoid the necessity of using such force with complete safety (1) by retreating, except that the actor shall not be required to retreat if he or she is in his or her dwelling, as defined in section 53a-100 [a dwelling is where you stay overnight], or place of work and was not the initial aggressor, or if he or she is a peace officer or a special policeman appointed under section 29-18b, a Department of Motor Vehicles inspector appointed under section 14-8 and certified pursuant to section 7-294d, or a private person assisting such peace officer, special policeman or motor vehicle inspector at his or her direction, and acting pursuant to section 53a-22, or (2) by surrendering possession of property to a person asserting a claim of right thereto, or (3) by complying with a demand that he or she abstain from performing an act which he or she is not obliged to perform. [In Connecticut, unless you are in your home or workplace, you must retreat before using deadly force in self-defense, if you can retreat in complete safety. People starting fights (initial aggressors) must also retreat. Certain law enforcement officers listed in the statute need not retreat. Exception (2) "surrendering property to a person claiming a right to it" means you cannot shoot it out with your landlord when he serves you with an eviction notice or the repo man when he repossesses your new Firebird for failing to make payments. The law expects you to work out disagreements such as that in court, not at the OK Corral.

Robbery Warning: After reading the jury instructions for this state, we're concerned that exception (2) might actually be interpreted by Connecticut courts to mean that if a robber tells you to give him all your belongings, he won't hurt you, you've got to do it. The paragraph of concern is 8.2-3 Exceptions to Use of Deadly Physical Force: Duty to Retreat, Surrender Property, Comply with Demand — § 53a-19 (b), paragraph B. Surrender Property which states: "Under this provision, if the assailant's conduct appears motivated by (his/her) claim to property that the defendant possesses and the defendant knows that if (he/she) surrendered the property that the assailant would cease the assault upon the defendant, then the defendant may not use deadly physical force in defense and must surrender the property" (used with permission of the State of Connecticut Judicial Branch, Copyright ©2010, State of Connecticut Judicial Branch). In the instruction, it's not clear whether a robber could have a "claim to property." To us westerners, such an idea is inconceivable. But for us cowboys, having to retreat from a place we have a right to be before using deadly force is pretty hard to swallow as well.

We can imagine an anti-guns prosecutor telling a jury that you should have just given up your whole month's earnings to the creep who robbed you "because we are talking about a human life ladies and gentlemen of the jury!" (Oh, brother. Actually, he had become a vicious predator and assumed the risks of living that life-style.) You live on the Eastern Seaboard and understand the mentality of your neighbors better than we do. Would you feel comfortable being tried by your fellow citizens for shooting a robber who pointed a gun at you and told you he wouldn't hurt you if you gave him all your valuables? As he was distracted by a passing bus, you drew from concealment and performed the "Mozambique" drill you learned competing in IPSC matches, two .40 S&W to the torso, one to the head. Unfortunately, your assailant had an acquaintance video taping the whole incident hoping to score his own reality show to be called, "Connecticut Quick Cash." The audio picks up his offer to let you go if you give him your wallet. As Clint would ask, "Do you feel lucky (being tried under those circumstances by a jury of your peers)?"

We're not 100% sure what it means to abstain from performing an act you are not under an obligation to perform. We could not find cases explaining this, so it must not come up very often. For entertainment, ask your legislator what it means. For whatever it's worth, here's what the jury instruction (simplified - wise cracks by Pancho) says: "Another circumstance under which you are not justified in using deadly physical force in self-defense is when you know that you can avoid the necessity of using such force with complete safety by complying with a demand that you abstain from performing an act which you are not obliged to perform. Under this provision, if your assailant's conduct appears motivated by his insistence that you stop [stop watching while he robs the convenience store] and you were not obliged to [watch while he robs the convenience store] and you knew your assailant would cease [threatening to kill you while tweaking and pointing a gun at you], then you may not use deadly physical force in self-defense and must comply with the demand." http:/ /www.jud.ct.gov/JI/criminal/part2/2.8-3.htm#C (used with permission of the State of Connecticut Judicial Branch, Copyright ©2010, State of Connecticut Judicial Branch). *Pancho's Wisdom* – To the lawyers and judges who drafted this provision of the Model Penal Code adopted by Connecticut, please read our Chapter 11 concerning perception and reaction time.]

[Co-Habitant – Duty to Retreat – Yes]

[Although generally persons do not have a duty to retreat from their homes before defending themselves with deadly force, a co-habitant must retreat before using deadly force against his roommate. *State v. Shaw,* 185 Conn. 372, 382, 441 A.2d 561, 565, 566 (1981), certiorari denied 454 U.S. 1155, 102 S.Ct. 1027, 71 L.Ed.2d 312 (1982).]

[Exceptions to Justifiable Self-Defense][Initial Aggressor]
[Provocation][Mutual Combat] [Exceptions to the Exceptions]
[Withdraw and Communicate]

(c) Notwithstanding the provisions of subsection (a) of this section, a person is not justified in using physical force when (1) with intent to cause physical injury or death to another person, he provokes the use of physical force by such other person, or (2) he is the initial aggressor, except that his use of physical force upon another person under such circumstances is justifiable if he withdraws from the encounter and effectively communicates to such other person his intent to do so, but such other person notwithstanding continues or threatens the use of physical force, or (3) the physical force involved was the product of a combat by agreement not specifically authorized by law. [You cannot win on the theory of self-defense if you provoke a fight as an excuse to hurt or kill, you start a fight or you agree to fight. If you start or provoke a fight, you may be able recover your right to claim self-defense if you stop fighting and tell your adversary that you stopped fighting. If he continues to try to injure you after that, you may be able to fight back to defend yourself and still win on the theory of self-defense. When the facts become this complicated, you will almost always be arrested and prosecuted. Don't start fights if you don't like paying attorneys.]

[Committing Felony or Unlawful Act]

"Even if we were to assume without deciding that this evidence, viewed in the context of all the evidence regarding the killing of the victims, would have permitted a rational jury to find self-defense without resorting to speculation, the defendant was not entitled to an instruction on that theory of defense because he was engaged in robbing the victims when his purported justification for killing them arose." *State v. Lewis*, 717 A. 2d 1140, 1158 (Conn. 1998).

[Raymond Robber goes into a convenience store for some instant cash using a Saturday night special like a debit card. The clerk responds with a Jennings .380 which, as a surprise to us all, misfires. Raymond caps the clerk and then claims self-defense. The judge's response to Raymond's lawyer when he asks the judge to instruct the jury on the theory of self-defense is, "You're joking, right?"]

[Use of Deadly Force to Prevent Serious Felonies]

[Connecticut does not list any specific felonies in its general self-defense statute. Although none are listed, there is a case that suggests that certain common law felonies are incorporated into the definition "serious bodily injury." See *State v. Havican*, 213 Conn. 593 (1990), 569 A.2d 1089, holding that the defendant would be justified in using deadly force to prevent forcible sodomy upon himself. The case suggested that the use of deadly force to stop a rape or sexual assault would be justifiable. What about a kidnapping where the kidnapper runs out of your home claiming your child will not be harmed if you simply pay a ransom? The problem with having to wait for a court to tell citizens specifically what is or is not justifiable is that your case may be the test case. *Pancho's Wisdom* – Connecticut's legislature should add a list of carefully defined forcible felonies to its self-defense statute to take the guesswork out of defending one's self and loved ones. Connecticut has already done this in connection with its home-defense statute below by specifically naming arson as one of the crimes which justifies the use of deadly force. Why not add additional violent felonies to both the self and home defense statutes? See the Mother of All Defense Statutes, Chapter 20.]

[Defense of Persons in Special Places – Home, Business]

§ **C.G.S.A. § 53A-20.**
Use of physical force in defense of premises.

A person in possession or control of premises, or a person who is licensed or privileged to be in or upon such premises, is justified in using reasonable physical force upon another person when and to the extent that he reasonably believes such to be necessary to prevent or terminate the commission or attempted commission of a criminal trespass by such other person in or upon such premises; [You may use reasonable force, but not deadly force to stop a person from trespassing on real estate to or to kick him off the property. We don't suggest you do this because these incidents tend to escalate unexpectedly. Call the police; it's what you pay taxes for.] but he may use deadly physical force under such circumstances only (1) in defense of a person as prescribed in section 53a-19, or (2) when he reasonably believes such to be necessary to prevent an attempt by the trespasser to commit arson or any crime of violence [see definitions below], or (3) to the extent that he reasonably believes such to be necessary to prevent or terminate an unlawful entry by force into his dwelling as defined in section 53a-100 [a dwelling is where you stay overnight], or place of work, and for the sole purpose of such prevention or termination. [This deadly-force section of Connecticut's home-defense statute has three numbered clauses. We explain them by number as follows:

(1) This refers back to Connecticut's self-defense statute (**§53a-19**) which defines the use of deadly force outside of your home as requiring a threat of death or serious injury. You can use deadly force to defend your home or business if an intruder threatens imminent death or serious injury. It doesn't matter if a person threatening you with a firearm is standing in your home, on your porch or on the sidewalk. If the threat is imminent, you can defend yourself with deadly force. If he falls outside of your home with his weapon by his side, you certainly don't have to worry about dragging him back into your home and staining your light-colored acrylic! (Doing that would be tampering with the evidence, a serious crime on its own, which suggests you have a guilty conscience. Don't ever do it.)

(2) Deadly force can be used to stop a trespasser (one who is on your property without your permission) from committing arson or a crime of violence. Arson means intentionally starting a fire or causing an explosion. If someone were trying to throw a Molotov cocktail or toss gasoline into your doorway, you could respond with deadly force to stop the attempt. "Crime of violence" is not defined in the self-defense statutes. It is defined in Connecticut's "Machine Gun" statute (see discussion under definitions below). Keep in mind that the purpose of this statute is to prevent the commission of the crime, NOT to avenge the crime after the fact. In this light, one of the footnotes to Connecticut's jury instructions relating to this statute says that you may use deadly force against an arsonist up until he starts the fire "but not one second after the blaze has begun. . . . Any other interpretation would result in a retaliatory and unlawful use of force." (Emphasis added.) http://www.jud.ct.gov/JI/criminal/ 2.8-4 Defense of Premises — § 53a-20, note 4 (Copyright ©2010).

[Co-Employee – Duty to Retreat]

(3) You can use deadly force without having to retreat to prevent a forcible entry into your home or workplace as long as you are not the "initial aggressor" (the person who started the fight). The right to use deadly force against a forcible unlawful entry does not apply against persons who are on the premises by permission or mistake. If you dust the pushy insurance salesman who simply refuses to leave or your elderly neighbor with Alzheimer's who walks through your unlocked front door and yells, "Honey, I'm home!", you'll end up a proverbial Connecticut Yankee in King Arthur's court. You must retreat from a roommate or intimate partner threatening deadly force if you can do so in complete safety. *State v. Shaw*, 185 Conn. 372, 382, 441 A.2d 561, 565, 566 (1981), certiorari denied 454 U.S. 1155, 102 S.Ct. 1027, 71 L.Ed.2d 312 (1982). We suspect the same rule (the need to retreat if it could be done in complete safety) would apply to a co-worker because he is on the work premises by permission. On the other hand, it seems you would not have to retreat from a co-worker who has been fired and returns to the job site to take revenge. (*Pancho's Wisdom* – We suspect most employers in Connecticut will fire you for violating their "Workplace Violence Policy" if you take a defensive handgun to work. That means if a fired employee goes postal, you will have to fend him off with a staple gun - but at least you don't have to retreat.)]

[Defense of Personal Property]

§ C.G.S.A. § 53A-21.
Use of physical force in defense of property.

A person is justified in using reasonable physical force upon another person when and to the extent that he reasonably believes such to be necessary to prevent an attempt by such other person to commit larceny or criminal mischief involving property, or when and to the extent he reasonably believes such to be necessary to regain property which he reasonably believes to have been acquired by larceny within a reasonable time prior to the use of such force; but he may use deadly physical force under such circumstances only in defense of person as prescribed in section 53a-19 [to stop an imminent threat of death or serious bodily injury].

[HELPFUL DEFINITIONS RELATING TO THIS STATE'S SELF-DEFENSE STATUTES]

- **Building** – in addition to its ordinary meaning, includes any watercraft, aircraft, trailer, sleeping car, railroad car or other structure or vehicle or any building with a valid certificate of occupancy. Where a building consists of separate units, such as, but not limited to separate apartments, offices or rented rooms, any unit not occupied by the actor is, in addition to being a part of such building, a separate building. **C.G.S.A. § 53a-100 (a) (1).**

- **Deadly physical force** – means physical force which can be reasonably expected to cause death or serious physical injury. **C.G.S.A. § 53a-3 (5).**

- **Deadly weapon** – means any weapon, whether loaded or unloaded, from which a shot may be discharged, or a switchblade knife, gravity knife, billy, blackjack, bludgeon, or metal knuckles. The definition of "deadly weapon" in this subdivision shall be deemed not to apply to section 29-38 or 53-206. **C.G.S.A. § 53a-3 (6).**

- **Dangerous instrument** – means any instrument, article or substance which, under the circumstances in which it is used or attempted or threatened to be used, is capable of causing death or serious physical injury, and includes a "vehicle" as that term is defined in this section and includes a dog that has been commanded to attack, except a dog owned by a law enforcement agency of the state or any political subdivision thereof or of the federal government when such dog is in the performance of its duties under the direct supervision, care and control of an assigned law enforcement officer. **C.G.S.A. § 53a-3 (7).**

- **Dwelling** – means a building which is usually occupied by a person lodging therein at night, whether or not a person is actually present. **C.G.S.A. § 53a-100 (a) (2).**

- **Felonies Mentioned Above** –
  - **Arson** – [recklessly or intentionally setting fire or causing an explosion to a building whether you own it or not.] **C.G.S.A. § 53a-113.**

- **Crime of Violence** – ["Crime of Violence" is not defined in the same chapter or even of the Connecticut Statutes that the self-defense laws are in. The only definition for "crime of violence" is found in 53-202 (2) relating to "machine guns." It is not clear whether the courts would apply the definition to a self-defense case. It's this kind of uncertainty that gets a person charged with a crime or sued to "clarify the law." "Crime of violence" in the machine gun statute includes murder, manslaughter, kidnapping, sexual assault and sexual assault with a firearm, assault in the first or second degree, robbery, burglary, larceny and riot in the first degree or an attempt to commit any of these crimes.]

- **Physical injury** – means impairment of physical condition or pain. **C.G.S.A. § 53a-3 (3).**

- **Serious physical injury** – means physical injury which creates a substantial risk of death, or which causes serious disfigurement, serious impairment of health or serious loss or impairment of the function of any bodily organ. **C.G.S.A. § 53a-3 (4).**

[TEMPLATE Topics We Could Not Find Explained in Statutes or Cases]

(For each of these topics that we could not find addressed in your state's statutes or cases, we suggest you review the same topics in the subchapters of surrounding states. Your state's courts may look to the law of the surrounding states to see how their courts and legislatures have treated that particular self-defense issue.)

[Reckless Injury to Innocent Third Parties]

[Presumption of Reasonableness in Special Places]

[Civil Liability]

Pancho's Wisdom

You just might be a Gunnut if . . .

the value of the stuff in yer gun safe exceeds the value of all the stuff in yer garage.

. . . your ring tone on your cell phone plays either a ricochet or the theme from The Good, the Bad and the Ugly.

Key: ■ commentary ■ original statutes, cases or jury instructions

[Defense of Self and Others] [Non-Deadly Force]

§ 11 DELAWARE CODE (DEL.C.) § 464.
Justification – Use of force in self-protection.

(a) The use of force upon or toward another person is justifiable when the defendant believes that such force is immediately necessary for the purpose of protecting the defendant against the use of unlawful force by the other person on the present occasion.

[No Duty to Retreat – Generally (when using non-deadly force)]

(b) Except as otherwise provided in subsections (d) and (e) of this section, a person employing protective force may estimate the necessity thereof under the circumstances as the person believes them to be when the force is used, without retreating, surrendering possession, doing any other act which the person has no legal duty to do or abstaining from any lawful action. [You don't have to retreat when using non-deadly force, but must when using deadly force, see paragraph (e) below.]

[Deadly Force] [Use of Deadly Force to Prevent Serious Felonies]

(c) The use of deadly force is justifiable under this section if the defendant believes that such force is necessary to protect the defendant against death, serious physical injury, kidnapping or sexual intercourse compelled by force or threat. [Deadly force may be used to stop the immediate threat of kidnapping and forcible sexual assault. See definitions below. We commend Delaware for justifying the use of deadly force against forcible sexual intercourse for reasons explain in detail in Chapter 4.]

[Exceptions to Justifiable Self-Defense]

[As indicated below in both statutory law and case law, you can't claim self-defense in Delaware if you start a fight, provoke a fight as an excuse to hurt someone, or agree to fight or duel. These are standard exceptions to self-defense in most states.]

(d) The use of force is not justifiable under this section to resist an arrest which the defendant knows or should know is being made by a peace officer, whether or not the arrest is lawful.

(e) The use of deadly force is not justifiable under this section if:

[Provocation]

(1) The defendant, with the purpose of causing death or serious physical injury, provoked the use of force against the defendant in the same encounter; or

. . .

[Initial Aggressor]

"[S]econd, the general rule is that one who kills another, to be justified or excused on the ground of self-defense, must have been without fault in provoking the difficulty and must not have been the aggressor and must not have provoked, brought on, or encouraged the difficulty or produced the occasion which made it necessary for him to do the killing." *State v. Stevenson,* 188 A. 750, 751 (Del. O. & T. 1936). [Although this rule comes from an old case, it is mentioned again in a recent case, *Smith v. State,* 913 A.2d 1197, 1212 (Del. 2006.)]

[Mutual Combat]

"Where persons engage in a mutual combat it is not material who gives the first blow. And, one who willingly enters into a combat and fights willingly, not for his own protection, but to gratify his passion by inflicting injury upon his opponent, may not invoke in his behalf the doctrine of self-defense." *State v. Bell,* 192 A. 553, 554 (Del. O. & T. 1937).

[Exceptions to the Exceptions] [Withdraw and Communicate]

"Even though you should be satisfied that the prisoner committed the first assault, if you should further believe that he withdrew from the combat and retreated, with the honest intent to escape, and was pursued and unlawfully assaulted, then his assailants became the aggressors, and the prisoner had the right in self-defense to use so much force as was necessary under the circumstances to repel the attack upon him and protect himself." *State v. Miele,* 74 A. 8, 10 (Del. O. & T. 1909).

[Duty to Retreat – Generally – Yes]

§ **11 DEL.C. § 464 (e) (2).**
Justification – Use of force in self-protection.

. . .

(e) The use of deadly force is not justifiable under this section if:

. . .

(2) The defendant knows that the necessity of using deadly force can be avoided with complete safety by retreating, by surrendering possession of a thing to a person asserting a claim of right thereto or by complying with a demand that the defendant abstain from performing an act which the defendant is not legally obligated to perform except that: [There is a duty to retreat before using deadly force, if retreat can be carried out in complete safety. There is no duty to retreat, however, from the home or workplace.]

[No Duty to Retreat From Special Places – Dwelling, Place of Work]

a. The defendant is not obliged to retreat in or from the defendant's dwelling; and

b. The defendant is not obliged to retreat in or from the defendant's place of work, unless the defendant was the initial aggressor; and

c. A public officer justified in using force in the performance of the officer's duties, or a person justified in using force in assisting an officer or a person justified in using force in making an arrest or preventing an escape, need not desist from efforts to perform the duty or make the arrest or prevent the escape because of resistance or threatened resistance by or on behalf of the person against whom the action is directed.

[This self-defense statute is fairly standard in some respects and typically Eastern in others. You can use as much non-deadly force as required to repel non-deadly force and you don't have to retreat before using such force. For example, if someone keeps trying to hit you with their fists, you can use as much force as is necessary to stop them. You cannot use deadly force (a deadly weapon), however. Typically knocking a person down would be an assault, but you are justified in doing so to stop an assault.

You don't have to surrender possession. For example, if someone is trying to steal your lawn mower off of your front lawn, you can stop them. You can't threaten them with a deadly weapon, however.

This statute is "typically Eastern" because of the retreat requirement before using deadly force (many Western States allow a person to "stand their ground" in any place he has a legal right to be - read Utah's statute, for example). In Delaware, you have to retreat before using deadly force if you can do so in complete safety, unless you are in your home or workplace. You have a duty to retreat from those places as well if you were the initial aggressor (you "started it").

Notice also the "claim of right" and "abstain from performing an act" language. The "claim of right" issue could come into play, for example, if your home was being repossessed. You must surrender the property without using deadly force (obviously) and try to resolve the matter in the courts. To explain the "abstain from performing an act" phrase requires some speculation on our part because we have not, in our extensive research, encountered a case that explains this. **Possible Example:** A convenience-store robber says, "Everyone leave right now, we're robbing the store, but if you all leave, no one gets hurt." You have no legal obligation to leave when someone who has no ownership interest in a property tells you to leave. Everyone testifies the robber seemed sincere and they had all exited the store without being harmed when they heard you blazin' away like Bronco Billy with your matching, pearl-handled .45s. When the police arrive they see you spinning and holstering your smoke wagons and the place looks like the private club scene in Kill Bill after Uma tops off the last of the Crazy 88 with her super-samurai sword. You MIGHT need a lawyer. It's this unclear stuff that test cases are made of. *Pancho's Wisdom* – This confusing provision in Delaware's self-defense laws should be repealed and robbery should be added as one of the serious felonies citizens may use deadly force to prevent.]

[Defense of a Third Person]

§ 11 DEL.C. § 465.
Use of force for the protection of other persons.

(a) The use of force upon or toward the person of another is justifiable to protect a third person when:

(1) The defendant would have been justified under § 464 of this title in using such force to protect the defendant against the injury the defendant believes to be threatened to the person whom the defendant seeks to protect; and

(2) Under the circumstances as the defendant believes them to be, the person whom the defendant seeks to protect would have been justified in using such protective force; and

(3) The defendant believes that intervention is necessary for the protection of the other person.

(b) Although the defendant would have been obliged under § 464 of this title to retreat, to surrender the possession of a thing or to comply with a demand before using force in self-protection, there is no obligation to do so before using force for the protection of another person, unless the defendant knows that the defendant can thereby secure the complete safety of the other person.

(c) When the person whom the defendant seeks to protect would have been obliged under § 464 of this title to retreat, to surrender the possession of a thing or to comply with a demand if the person knew that the person could obtain complete safety by so doing, the defendant is obliged to try to cause the person to do so before using force in the person's protection if the actor knows that complete safety can be secured in that way.

(d) Neither the defendant nor the person whom the defendant seeks to protect is obliged to retreat when in the other's dwelling or place of work to any greater extent than in their own.

[The same rules apply to defending a third person as apply to defending yourself. Where you must retreat before using force to defend yourself, you must try to get the third person to retreat if it can be done in complete safety.]

[Defense of Person(s) in Special Places – Dwelling]

§ 11 DEL.C. § 469.
Justification – Person unlawfully in dwelling.

In the prosecution of an occupant of a dwelling charged with killing or injuring an intruder who was unlawfully in said dwelling, it shall be a defense that the occupant was in the occupant's own dwelling [Example: in your own home, hotel room or trailer used as a temporary home—see definition below] at the time of the offense, and:

(1) The encounter between the occupant and intruder was sudden and unexpected, compelling the occupant to act instantly; or [This is a good provision which takes into account how difficult it is to assess the situation when there is little time to react. Just make sure in your haste to throw lead down range, you're not pumping it into a family member who was simply trying to scare you. It has happened.]

(2) The occupant reasonably believed that the intruder would inflict personal injury upon the occupant or others in the dwelling; or [Notice this does not say there was a "threat of serious bodily injury or death." There is a lower threshold for using deadly force when someone is in your home threatening to hurt you or another person in the home. But don't forget, you CANNOT execute a person who has surrendered or been rendered helpless just because they are in your home (see cases in Chapter 7, Thumbs-Down Factors).]

(3) The occupant demanded that the intruder disarm or surrender, and the intruder refused to do so. ["Drop the weapon! Don't come any closer!" If they fail to comply, you are justified in using deadly force, but don't forget to read the Thumbs-Down Factors Chapter anyway.]

[Defense of Property]

§ 11 DEL.C. § 466.
Use of force for the protection of property.

(a) The use of force upon or toward the person of another is justifiable when the defendant believes that such force is immediately necessary:

(1) To prevent the commission of criminal trespass or burglary in a building or upon real property in the defendant's possession or in the possession of another person for whose protection the defendant acts; or

(2) To prevent entry upon real property in the defendant's possession or in the possession of another person for whose protection the defendant acts; or

(3) To prevent theft, criminal mischief or any trespassory taking of tangible, movable property in the defendant's possession or in the possession of another person for whose protection the defendant acts.

(b) The defendant may in the circumstances named in subsection (a) of this section use such force as the defendant believes is necessary to protect the threatened property, provided that the defendant first requests the person against whom force is used to desist from interference with the property, unless the defendant believes that:

(1) Such a request would be useless; or

(2) It would be dangerous to the defendant or another person to make the request; or

(3) Substantial harm would be done to the physical condition of the property which is sought to be protected before the request could effectively be made.

[Deadly Force]

(c) The use of deadly force for the protection of property is justifiable only if the defendant believes that:

(1) The person against whom the force is used is attempting to dispossess the defendant of the defendant's dwelling otherwise than under a claim of right to its possession; [You can use deadly force if someone is attempting to kidnap you from your own home. However, in this day of bank foreclosures, don't be banging bullets into your banker when he tells you you're six payments behind giving him the right to repossess] or

(2) The person against whom the deadly force is used is attempting to commit arson, burglary, robbery or felonious theft or property destruction *and* either:

a. Had employed or threatened deadly force against or in the presence of the defendant; or

b. Under the circumstances existing at the time, the defendant believed the use of force other than deadly force would expose the defendant, or another person in the defendant's presence, to the reasonable likelihood of serious physical injury. [Although this statute mentions the wrongful taking of personal property, such as your car, wallet, skateboard, whatever, notice that it requires a threat of death or serious bodily injury before you can use deadly force. In other words, it's not the taking of your property that triggers the right to use deadly force; it is the threat of serious injury or death to you or another. If there is no threat of death or serious bodily injury DO NOT use or even threaten deadly force! It's not worth it.

Pancho's Wisdom – It amazes us that an imminent threat of arson or burglary wouldn't automatically trigger the right to use deadly force. In many western states, the right to use deadly force under such circumstances would be automatic. This should be changed.]

. . .

[Reckless Injury to Innocent Third Parties]

§ 11 DEL.C. § 470.
Provisions generally applicable to justification

(a) When the defendant believes that the use of force upon or toward the person of another is necessary for any of the purposes for which such relief would establish a justification under §§ 462-468 of this title but the defendant is reckless or negligent in having such belief or in acquiring or failing to acquire any knowledge or belief which is material to the justifiability of the use of force, the justification afforded by those sections is unavailable in a prosecution for an offense for which recklessness or negligence, as the case may be, suffices to establish culpability.

(b) When the defendant is justified under §§ 462-468 of this title in using force upon or toward the person of another but the defendant recklessly or negligently injures or creates a risk of injury to innocent persons, the justification afforded by those sections is unavailable in a prosecution for an offense involving recklessness or negligence towards innocent persons.

[Even though you may be otherwise justified in using non-deadly or deadly force, if you wield such force recklessly, you can be held accountable under criminal statutes that require only proof of recklessness. **Example** – You spray bullets at a robber without noticing the crowd of innocent persons behind him waiting in line to board a bus. If you kill an innocent person under such circumstances, you could be prosecuted and convicted of manslaughter.]

[Civil Liability]

§ 11 DEL.C. § 466 (d).
Use of force for the protection of property.

. . .

(d) Where a person has used force for the protection of property and has not been convicted for any crime or offense connected with that use of force, such person shall not be liable for damages or be otherwise civilly liable to the one against whom such force was used. [You may only be civilly liable if you are convicted of a crime.]

§ 16 DEL.C. § 6830.
Person intervening to protect other persons from certain criminal acts exempt from liability.

Any person who, in good faith, intervenes without compensation to protect other persons against any criminal act involving death, serious physical injury, robbery, burglary, kidnapping or sexual intercourse compelled by force or threat at the scene of said attempted criminal act, shall not be liable for any civil damages resulting from the rendering of such assistance, except acts or omissions amounting to gross negligence or willful or wanton misconduct. [This is a Good-Samaritan law. You can't be sued for saving someone from death, serious injury, robbery, kidnapping or sexual assault unless grossly negligent. However, indiscriminately spraying heavy metal in self-defense with a Beretta 93R (get giddy Googling it) would probably be considered gross negligence.]

[HELPFUL DEFINITIONS RELATING TO THIS STATE'S SELF-DEFENSE STATUTES]

- **Dwelling** – means any building or structure, though movable or temporary, or a portion thereof, which is for the time being the defendant's home or place of lodging. **11 Del.C. § 471(e).**

- **Deadly force** – means force which the defendant uses with the purpose of causing or which the defendant knows creates a substantial risk of causing death or serious physical injury. Purposely firing a firearm in the direction of another person or at a vehicle in which another person is believed to be constitutes deadly force. A threat to cause death or serious bodily harm, by the production of a weapon or otherwise, so long as the defendant's purpose is limited to creating an apprehension that deadly force will be used if necessary, does not constitute deadly force. **11 Del.C. § 471(d).**

- **Felonies Mentioned Above –**
  - **Arson** – [Recklessly or intentionally damaging a building by fire or explosion.] **11 Del.C. § 801.**
  - **Burglary** – [Knowingly enters or remains unlawfully in a building with the intent to commit a crime therein.] **11 Del.C. § 824.**
  - **Felonious theft** – [Stealing property having a value of $1,000 or more, stealing from any individual 62 years of age or older or who is infirm or disabled.] **11 Del.C. § 841.**
  - **Kidnapping** – [Unlawfully restraining a person with the intent to commit a crime against that person.] **11 Del.C. § 783.**
  - **Robbery** – [While committing a theft a person threatens the use of force against another to carry out the theft.] **11 Del.C. § 831.**
  - **Sexual intercourse compelled by force or threat** – [We could not find a statute that uses this exact language so we assume it means what it says. You may use deadly force to prevent a rape or forcible sodomy.]
- **Force** – in addition to its ordinary meaning, includes confinement. **11 Del.C. § 471(a).**
- **Physical force** – means force used upon or directed toward the body of another person. **11 Del.C. § 471(b).**
- **Unlawful force** – means force which is employed without the consent of the person against whom it is directed and the employment of which constitutes an offense or actionable tort or would constitute such offense or tort except for a defense (such as the absence of intent, negligence or mental capacity; duress; youth; or diplomatic status) not amounting to a privilege to use the force. Assent constitutes consent, within the meaning of this section, whether or not it otherwise is legally effective, except assent to the infliction of death or serious bodily harm. **11 Del.C. § 471(c).**

[TEMPLATE Topics We Could Not Find Explained in Statutes or Cases]

(For each of these topics that we could not find addressed in your state's statutes or cases, we suggest you review the same topics in the subchapters of surrounding states. Your state's courts may look to the law of the surrounding states to see how their courts and legislatures have treated that particular self-defense issue.)

[Committing Felony or Unlawful Act]

[Co-Habitants; Co-Employees – Duty to Retreat]

[Presumption of Reasonableness in Special Places]

Pancho's Wisdom

You just might be a Gunnut if . . .

. . . you shot your first deer with a lever-action rifle bought at a hardware store on your twelfth birthday.

. . . the heaviest piece of luggage you own is your Range Bag.

. . . you consider this book required reading.

. . . your instructions to your funeral home director include placing your favorite pistols in your cold, dead hands during your viewing.

DISTRICT OF COLUMBIA

It is unfortunate that the citizens living and traveling in our nation's capital do not have a self-defense statute that defines exactly what their rights are if they become the victims of a violent attack. The rules are contained solely in law cases which are not readily available or easily understood by the general public. In D.C., a person may only use deadly force in self-defense to stop an imminent threat of death or serious bodily injury. Citizens and visitors are afforded no special legal protections in their homes or hotel rooms. In fact, because of the District's reluctance to amend their ordinances to fully comply with the mandates of the landmark U.S. Supreme Court decision *District of Columbia v. Heller,* 128 S. Ct. 2783, 171 L. Ed. 2d 637 (2008), it is still unclear whether residents will be arrested and prosecuted for keeping firearms loaded and within their immediate reach in their own homes. *Heller* struck down D.C.'s gun ban as an unconstitutional infringement on the individual right to keep and bear arms. Of course, travelers are prohibited from taking any firearm into Washington, D.C.

Pancho's Wisdom– For the ultimate in home defense tactics using household items not normally considered weapons, please carefully watch and ponder the strategies employed in the movies *Home Alone* and *Home Alone 2: Lost in New York.* A BB gun to the groin might be a little over the top, however, leaving you at significant risk of arrest and prosecution for possessing an unauthorized weapon. Another clever self-defense idea for D.C. residents—Only venture outside your home when taking strolls with the President of the United States. His Secret Service entourage is equipped to defend the Prez and you (maybe) with the latest model sub-machine guns, like Glock 18s and MP5s.

Key: ■ commentary ■ original statutes, cases or jury instructions

---

[Defense of Self and Others] [Non-Deadly Force] [Deadly Force]

"To justify the use of lethal force, as in this case, there must be evidence that the defendant honestly and reasonably believed that he or a third party was in imminent peril of death or of serious bodily injury, and that the use of lethal force was necessary to save himself or the third party from that harm." *Dorsey v. U.S.*, 935 A2d 288, 291 (D.C. 2007).

[You must (1) actually and (2) reasonably believe that deadly force was (3) necessary to (4) avoid imminent death or serious injury. Notice the word "necessary." Force that is not necessary is considered excessive force and is not justified.

One of the best illustrations of this principle is a D.C. case involving the defense of a woman who was being "stomped and beaten." The judge agreed that this was an imminent threat of serious injury or death. Upon seeing this poor woman's plight, her champion, the defendant in this case, walked up and hit her assailant with an axe that the defendant kept in his tool belt. After the woman-beater was down, however, the defendant continued to chop at his head with the sharp end of the ax. He died from injuries arising from 13 gashes in the back of his head. The court explained he could have ended the assault on the woman with one or two blows with the blunt end of the axe, but continuing to try to chop the woman's assailant to pieces with the sharp edge of the ax after he was down was clearly excessive force. The defendant was convicted of murder despite his original good intentions (and sexy and attractive leather tool belt). *Fersner v. U.S.*, 482 A.2d 387, D.C.,1984.]

(*Pancho's Wisdom* – Apparently District residents have learned to get around the strict weapons' restrictions in D.C. by possessing tools that have legitimate uses, but could be used as a weapon if necessary. If you are a tree trimmer for a power company or a singer with the Village People, you might get away with wearing a tool belt containing an axe.)

[The following paragraph used as an instruction in a jury case further explains the concept of necessity and its relationship to the use of excessive force.]

"Even if the other person is the aggressor and the defendant is justified in using force in self-defense, he may not use any greater force than he actually and reasonably believes to be necessary under the circumstances to prevent the harm he reasonably believes is intended. In deciding whether the defendant used excessive force in defending himself, you may consider all the circumstances under which he acted. A person acting in the heat of passion caused by an assault does not necessarily lose his claim of self-defense by using greater force than would seem necessary to a calm mind. In the heat of passion, a person actually and reasonably may believe something that seems unreasonable to a calm mind." *Higgenbottom v. U.S.*, 923 A.2d 891, 900 (D.C. 2007). [Of course, if you act "in the heat of passion," expect the D.C. heat to place your hot, passionate body under arrest. This is a good ruling, however, because it allows a jury to take into account the adrenaline rush during a violent attack.]

[Defense of Third Persons]

"A defendant may claim defense of a third party where the third party was the innocent victim of an unlawful attack, or, in other words, where the victim of the attack was himself entitled to the defense of self-defense. The defendant must have reasonably believed and actually believed that [the victim] himself had a right of self-defense, and the focus of the inquiry is on the defendant's reasonable perceptions of the situation, not that of the third party. In using deadly force, the defendant must have actually and reasonably believed that [the victim] was in imminent danger of death or bodily harm. The victim's perception of the situation, however, is still relevant to determine what the intervenor's perceptions actually and reasonably were." *Muschette v. U.S.*, 936 A.2d 791, 799 (D.C. 2007). [The risk you take when you intervene to save a third person from injury or death is that the third person may have started the fight and not be entitled to use force until after he or she retreats and communicates her intent to stop fighting to her opponent. Of course, you will be judged on what you perceived, not necessarily upon what the third person knew about the incident. We're just saying, if she started the fight, you're likely to be arrested and prosecuted until it's clear to the prosecutor that you were not aware she started it.]

[Exceptions to Justifiable Self-Defense] [Initial Aggressor] [Provocation]

"A defendant cannot claim self-defense if the defendant was the aggressor, or if s/he provoked the conflict upon himself/herself." *Rorie v. U.S.*, 882 A.2d 763, 772 (D.C.2005). [This is the law in virtually every state.]

[Committing Felony or Unlawful Act]

"One who commits an armed robbery forfeits his right to claim the right of self-defense against either the intended victim of the robbery or any person intervening to prevent the crime." *Taylor v. U.S.*, 380 A.2d 989, 994 (D.C.1977). [Duh!]

[Exceptions to the Exceptions] [Withdraw and Communicate]

"If you find that the defendant was the aggressor, or if he provoked the assault upon himself, he cannot invoke the right of self-defense to justify his use of force. However, if one who provokes a conflict later withdraws from it in good faith, and communicates that withdrawal by words or actions, and he is thereafter pursued, he is justified in using deadly force to save himself from imminent danger of death or serious bodily harm." *Bedney v. U.S.*, 471 A.2d 1022, 1024 (D.C. 1984) [fn2]. [If you start the fight, you have to stop fighting and let the other guy know you have stopped. The safest way to preserve your self-defense claim in a situation like this is to run away while screaming "I give up; don't hurt me!" If after that, your adversary pursues you and tries to hurt you, he becomes the aggressor and you may then legally defend yourself. This type of incident unfortunately always ends up as a he-said-she-said, which, almost without exception, results in arrest and prosecution. If you want to fight, become a boxer and do it in the ring.]

[Duty to Retreat – Generally, No, But . . .]

"The law does not require a person to retreat or consider retreating when s/he actually and reasonably believes that s/he is in danger of death or serious bodily harm and that deadly force is necessary to repel that danger. But the law does say that a person should take reasonable steps, such as stepping back or walking away, to avoid the necessity of taking a human life, so long as those steps are consistent with the person's own safety. In deciding whether the defendant acted reasonable, you should therefore consider whether the defendant could have taken those steps, consistent with his/her own safety." *Broadie v. U.S.*, 925 A.2d 605 (D.C. 2007) [This jury instruction was approved in the case cited. It reflects the law of the D.C. on the issue of retreat. You don't have to retreat BUT the jury can consider whether you had an opportunity to retreat rather than taking a life. Again, we see how important the word "necessary" is. Was it necessary for you to use deadly force or could you have done something less drastic and still have been safe? This rule is so complicated and requires so much analysis in a deadly encounter you might as well program yourself to always retreat rather than use deadly force, if you can do so safely. If you can't do so safely, use only what force is absolutely necessary and then SHUT UP and insist on talking to a lawyer before giving any statements.]

[Defense of Person(s)s in Special Places – Home, Business, Occupied Vehicle] [Duty to Retreat From Special Places]

[As far as we can tell, the same rule applies in the home as outside the home. You don't have a duty to retreat, but . . . see heading above **[Duty to Retreat – Generally, No, But . . .]** *Smith v. U.S.*, 686 A.2d 537, 545 (D.C. 1996)

[Defense of Property]

"It is well settled that a person may use as much force as is reasonably necessary to eject a trespasser from his property, and that if he uses more force than is necessary, he is guilty of assault. This is true regardless of any actual or threatened injury to the property by the trespasser, although this would be a factor in determining the reasonableness of the force used." *Shehyn v. U.S.*, 256 A.2d 404, 406 (D.C.App. 1969) (Footnote omitted). [You can use reasonable force to defend your property, but not deadly force.]

[TEMPLATE Topics We Could Not Find Explained in Statutes or Cases]

(For each of these topics that we could not find addressed in your state's statutes or cases, we suggest you review the same topics in the subchapters of surrounding states. Your state's courts may look to the law of neighboring states to see how their courts and legislatures have treated that particular self-defense issue.)

[Use of Deadly Force to Prevent Serious Felonies]

[Mutual Combat]

[Presumption of Reasonableness in Special Places]

[Co-Habitants; Co-Employees – Duty to Retreat]

[Responsibility to Innocent Third Parties]

[Civil Liability]

[Helpful Definitions Relating to this State's Self-Defense Statutes]

FLORIDA

"Go ahead, make my day."
Inspector Harry Callahan (Clint Eastwood)
in *Sudden Impact*

The national media reported that gun-control advocates and Ivy League law professors had their panties and briefs in a wad over Florida's "Make-My-Day Law." After the law was passed, but before the law went into effect, gun-control fanatics at the Brady Center warned travelers going to Florida of the impending danger:

> The Brady Campaign to Prevent Gun Violence launched a campaign the week of September 19 [2005] to educate Florida tourists and potential Florida tourists that effective October 1 they face a greater risk of bodily harm within the state of Florida.
>
> *Individuals who are unfamiliar with Florida's roads, traffic regulations and customs, or who speak foreign languages, or look different than Florida residents, may face a higher risk of danger*—because they may be more likely to be perceived as threatening by Floridians, and because they are unaware of Florida's new law that says individuals who feel their safety is threatened or their possessions are at risk are legally authorized to use deadly force.
>
> We have placed travel advertisements to warn these tourists and potential tourists in key U.S. gateway cities feeding tourists to Florida, starting with Chicago, Detroit and Boston, and in selected overseas markets beginning with the United Kingdom, that this risk exists. Educational materials about the law were shipped to more than 120 leading U.S. and international journalists as well as trade publication editors in the travel industry and editors at consumer travel magazines. Advertisements in travel sections of U.S. and British newspapers began Sunday, October 2 and the Brady Campaign is pursuing advertising in Germany, Japan, Columbia and Venezuela.
>
> Trained staff are distributing educational materials on this subject to arriving passengers at Miami International Airport and Orlando International Airport, and may be extended to additional airports in the coming weeks. (Emphasis added.)

http://www.shootfirstlaw.org/campaign/.

The law passed anyway, was signed by Governor Bush and went into effect in October of 2005. Well, it's been four years now. If ya'll would please forward a list of all the *people who look different, speak foreign languages and are unfamiliar with Florida's roads, who have been killed as a result of the passage of your state's "horrendously dangerous law,"* we'll make a plaque with their names on it and dedicate this book to their remembrance.

We're not too worried about the additional cost, however. Utah and several other western and southern states have had similar laws for years without blood runnin' in the gutters. And we figure if ONE PERSON who fit the looks-funny-talks-funny description had been killed in Florida, the national press would have been all over it (and we haven't heard a thing). Have ya'll?

Key: ■ commentary ■ original statutes, cases or jury instructions

[Defense of Self and Others] [Non-Deadly Force]

§ FLORIDA STATUTES ANNOTATED (F.S.A.) § 776.012.
Use of force in defense of person.

A person is justified in using force, except deadly force, against another when and to the extent that the person reasonably believes that such conduct is necessary to defend himself or herself or another against the other's imminent use of unlawful force.

[Deadly Force] [No Duty to Retreat – Generally]
[Use of Deadly Force to Prevent Serious Felonies]
[Defense of a Third Person]

However, a person is justified in the use of deadly force and does not have a duty to retreat if:

(1) He or she reasonably believes that such force is necessary to prevent imminent death or great bodily harm to himself or herself or another or to prevent the imminent commission of a forcible felony; or [In Florida, like in every other state in the Union, you may respond with deadly force against the threat of deadly force or serious injury. You may also use deadly force to prevent or stop a forcible felony about to be committed. Florida's forcible felonies are listed and defined in §776.08 immediately below. However, the threat must be imminent and your use of force must be necessary, not excessive. See the explanations of the terms "imminent" and "necessary" in Chapter 3.]

. . .

§ F.S.A. § 776.08.
Forcible felony.

"Forcible felony" means treason; murder; manslaughter; sexual battery; carjacking; home-invasion robbery; robbery; burglary; arson; kidnapping; aggravated assault; aggravated battery; aggravated stalking; aircraft piracy; unlawful throwing, placing, or discharging of a destructive device or bomb; and any other felony which involves the use or threat of physical force or violence against any individual. [See summaries of these listed felonies below.]

[You can use deadly force to defend against felonies involving violence, threats of violence or sexual assault. Notice robbery is specifically included. In Connecticut and other Model Penal Code states, robbers get your Rolex. In Florida, Texas and Utah they are likely to get a robust ration of red-hot lead. *Pancho's Wisdom* – A long-haired anarchist throwing Molotov Cocktails at people might have gotten away with it in Athens (Greece, not Georgia), but in Florida he would have justifiably ended up a Holy Moley! (Groan . . . Geez Pancho).]

[Exceptions to Justifiable Self-Defense]

§ **F.S.A. § 776.041.**
Use of force by aggressor.

The justification described in the preceding sections of this chapter is not available to a person who:

[Committing Felony or Unlawful Act]

(1) Is attempting to commit, committing, or escaping after the commission of, a forcible felony; or

[This exception exists so violent felons can't use Florida's make-my-day law as a shield to implement their dirty work of preying upon the innocent. A bait shop robber can't assert self-defense after blowing away the bait shop owner for attempting to defend his bait shop with a frog gig. Notice, however, the right of self-defense is not eliminated unless the felony is a forcible felony. A person simply committing felony voter fraud doesn't lose his right to defend himself from a militant Breyer County voting judge trying to beat him to death with a shillelagh (heavy Irish walking stick).]

[Initial Aggressor] [Provocation]

(2) Initially provokes the use of force against himself or herself, unless: [You can't start a fight and claim self-defense unless . . .]

[Exceptions to the Exceptions]

(a) Such force is so great that the person reasonably believes that he or she is in imminent danger of death or great bodily harm and that he or she has exhausted every reasonable means to escape such danger other than the use of force which is likely to cause death or great bodily harm to the assailant; or [You get into a fist fight with some handsome city slicker who is flirting with your beautiful, dark-haired southern belle (I married one – they're worth fighting for!) He unexpectedly raises the stakes by sliding a .45 cal. derringer out of his shirt cuff. You might be justified in beaning him with your pool stick if a shooting is imminent. However, if he can't figure out how to shoot a single action and you see an opportunity to safely escape, you must take it. We have found that anytime a person starts a fight, he's likely to be arrested and prosecuted no matter what his excuse. See Chapter 7, Thumbs-Down Factors.]

[Withdraw and Communicate]

(b) In good faith, the person withdraws from physical contact with the assailant and indicates clearly to the assailant that he or she desires to withdraw and terminate the use of force, but the assailant continues or resumes the use of force. [This is a typical exception to the exception applied in most states. If one person surrenders and makes it clear he does, and the other person continues to fight, the other person then becomes the aggressor and the person who started the fight can again claim self-defense. When it gets this complicated, you will almost always be arrested and prosecuted anyway.]

[Defense of Person(s) in Special Places – Dwelling, Residence, Occupied Vehicle]

§ **F.S.A. § 776.013.**
Home protection; use of deadly force; presumption of fear of death or great bodily harm.

[Presumption of Reasonableness in Special Places – Dwelling, Residence, or Occupied Vehicle]

[This is Florida's dynamite home-defense law that caused the lawyers at Harvard's Journal of Legislation to choke on their caviar. They urged Florida to repeal it right after the Governor signed it. What's kind of funny is that despite protests by the nation's "legal elite," not only did Florida not repeal the law, several surrounding states passed the same or similar legislation. Florida's excellent statute is the pattern for our Defense of Special Places comprising the Mother of All Self-Defense Laws, Chapter 20.]

(1) A person is presumed to have held a reasonable fear of imminent peril of death or great bodily harm to himself or herself or another when using defensive force that is intended or likely to cause death or great bodily harm to another if:

(a) The person against whom the defensive force was used was in the process of unlawfully and forcefully entering, or had unlawfully and forcibly entered, a dwelling, residence, or occupied vehicle, or if that person had removed or was attempting to remove another against that person's will from the dwelling, residence, or occupied vehicle; and

(b) The person who uses defensive force knew or had reason to believe that an unlawful and forcible entry or unlawful and forcible act was occurring or had occurred. (Emphasis added.) [Florida expands "special place" protection beyond the home by using the terms "dwelling" and "occupied vehicle." Dwelling includes your porch, hotel room, trailer and even a tent. But please notice all the "and" connectors we have underlined. You have to have all the elements or the presumption doesn't apply. The requirement for the presumption is that the bad guy enters unlawfully and forcibly OR unlawfully and attempts to forcibly remove someone against her will (like a kidnapping) from the home or vehicle. This means the intruder has to be a trespasser, not a roommate, family member or someone who has been invited into the home. An unlawful entry would generally not involve someone who goes in and out freely with your permission when the door is unlocked, like your kids' cousins or friends.

There has been some criticism that Florida's presumption is not a rebuttable presumption ("rebuttable" means the state can show evidence to the contrary), but rather a "conclusive presumption." *Bartlett v. State*, 993 So.2d

157, 163 (Fla.App. 1 Dist.,2008.) Notice the absence of the term "rebuttable" before the word "presumption." Also, the absence of the word "necessary" is particularly offensive to legal eggheads because they contend this gives a homeowner or vehicle owner license to use more force than is necessary, indeed a license to kill. Our advice is not to count on it and to remember someone is going to be the subject of a life-ruining test case—we don't want it to be you. Finally, please don't neglect to read our commentary in Chapter 4 warning you not to shoot an intruder you know for certain to be unarmed, non-threatening and completely harmless. You ARE accountable to God, even if there might be a loophole in the law.

If you are ever unfortunate enough to have to defend your home or vehicle from an intruder or kidnapper, make sure your lawyer spends ample time researching and analyzing how a conclusive presumption and absence of the word "necessary" may help your case. It may mean that if there is physical evidence that any force was used to get into your home (e.g., pry marks on a window or door) and you blow him into the flower bed, the case is over, you win. We remain skeptical, however, until a case that is directly on point reaches the Florida Supreme Court. For example, what if there is evidence you owed the "intruder" money? You invite him over under the guise you intend to pay him what is owed. The intruder shows up. You tell him the door is jammed, to force it open. When he does, you are sitting on the sofa with a double-barreled shotgun, like the scene in *Kill Bill II* where Budd (Michael Madsen) blasts The Bride (Uma Thurman) out of the trailer and into the desert. If there is evidence you set your "intruder" up in this manner (e.g., recorded phone messages and/or a neighbor's video that captures what happened in your home) you will be prosecuted. You'll probably be convicted, because in this example, you invited the "intruder" in, even though he had to force the door to get in. Therefore, technically, his entry was not unlawful. The law's gonna gitcha, Amos, uh huh.]

(2) The presumption set forth in subsection (1) does not apply if:

(a) The person against whom the defensive force is used has the right to be in or is a lawful resident of the dwelling, residence, or vehicle, such as an owner, lessee, or titleholder, and there is not an injunction for protection from domestic violence or a written pretrial supervision order of no contact against that person; or [The presumption doesn't apply if you whack someone who has a property interest in the dwelling or car, like a lien or mortgage owner who may be trying to repossess, foreclose or evict you. The presumption also doesn't apply if you stick a Seminole spear lined with alligator gar teeth through your abusive husband's rib cage and he's still a lawful resident in your home. However, assume your estranged hubby has been ordered by a court to stay away from you and your home during divorce proceedings. In violation of the court order, he attempts to break into your home or kidnap you from your home or car. Under those conditions, the presumption still applies. You would have a much lower risk of being arrested or prosecuted for defending yourself with deadly force than if the court order was not in place.

A pre-make-my-day-law case held that a spouse had no obligation to retreat outside of the home, but should retreat within the home to try to avoid having to use deadly force. *Weiand v. State*,732 So.2d 1044. We're not sure how that all shakes out after the passage of the make-my-day law. Our experience has been that when you use force against someone you know, especially if they live in the same household, you will be arrested and prosecuted. And don't forget, if the law is unclear, you're next in line to pay for a landmark test case, a bankrupting event for those who don't qualify for the public defender.]

(b) The person or persons sought to be removed is a child or grandchild, or is otherwise in the lawful custody or under the lawful guardianship of, the person against whom the defensive force is used; or [Custody disputes must be resolved in court, not Hatfields-versus-McCoys style.]

(c) The person who uses defensive force is engaged in an unlawful activity or is using the dwelling, residence, or occupied vehicle to further an unlawful activity; or [This is pretty broad. You'd best not be cookin', eatin' or smokin' illegal stuff downstairs or the presumption doesn't apply.]

(d) The person against whom the defensive force is used is a law enforcement officer, as defined in §943.10(14), who enters or attempts to enter a dwelling, residence, or vehicle in the performance of his or her official duties and the officer identified himself or herself in accordance with any applicable law or the person using force knew or reasonably should have known that the person entering or attempting to enter was a law enforcement officer. [The SWAT team gets a free pass during a no-knock entry. The presumption doesn't apply if you miraculously live through your attempt to use deadly force against dem BAD BOYS when dey come for you.]

[Finally, even if the presumption doesn't apply, it doesn't mean you can't respond with deadly force to prevent yourself from being killed in your home. For example, unbeknownst to you, your clean-cut-church-going roomy starts eating psychedelic mushrooms. One evening while watching *The Blair Witch Project* together, he jumps out of the sofa, pulls a Ruger P45 out from under his dark trench coat, screams "You're the Devil! You must DIE!" points it at you and pulls the trigger. Fortunately, the gun is on safety. As an IDPA master, you have learned to draw your fully-charged Glock 22 from concealment faster than it takes Mr. Mushroom Head to clumsily work the thumb safety on his weapon. The incident concludes with your psycho roommate lying on the floor outlined by CSI white chalk. Even though the presumption would not apply because he was a co-tenant, you would still probably be justified in using deadly force against his imminent attempt to kill you.]

[No Duty to Retreat – Generally] [No Duty to Retreat From Dwelling, Residence, or Occupied Vehicle]

(3) A person who is not engaged in an unlawful activity and who is attacked in any other place where he or she has a right to be has no duty to retreat and has the right to stand his or her ground and meet force with force, including deadly force if he or she reasonably believes it is necessary to do so to prevent death or great bodily harm to himself or herself or another or to prevent the commission of a forcible

felony. [You do not have to retreat before using force in self-defense as long as you have a right to be where you are when attacked. Trespassers, therefore, must retreat. But notice this paragraph does include the word "necessary" which prohibits the use of excessive force. See our discussion in Chapter 3.]

(4) A person who unlawfully and by force enters or attempts to enter a person's dwelling, residence, or occupied vehicle is presumed to be doing so with the intent to commit an unlawful act involving force or violence. [We were not able to find any cases interpreting this paragraph. It seems to be superfluous (over-kill). An unlawful and forcible entry into a dwelling already triggers the presumption of fear necessary to use deadly force. We don't see how an additional presumption that the intruder was there to commit an unlawful act involving force or violence gets you anywhere if you are already presumed to be acting reasonably by using deadly force. But we suppose it's nice to have an additional presumption, just in case.]

. . .

[No Duty to Retreat from Co-Employees]

"We have further extended the 'castle doctrine' privilege to employees in their place of employment, while lawfully engaged in their occupations. *See Redondo v. State*, 380 So.2d 1107, 1108 (Fla. 3d DCA 1980)(finding employee of convenience store entitled to non-retreat instruction when attacked at his place of business); *State v. Smith*, 376 So.2d 261 (Fla. 3d DCA 1979) (holding manager of store not obligated to retreat when attacked in or immediately adjacent to store). *But see Frazier v. State*, 681 So.2d 824, 825 (Fla. 2d DCA 1996) (agreeing that castle doctrine protects a worker in the workplace but making an exception where the aggressor was a co-worker). To date, this has been the only extension of the 'castle doctrine' protection to a person not attacked in his or her own dwelling or residence." *State v. James*, 867 So.2d 414, 417 (Fla.App. 3 Dist. 2003). [Because all of these cases precede the make-my-day law, we are not sure how a Florida court will deal with the use of force against co-employees. We suspect because you have a right to be at work, there will be no duty to retreat. Co-employees were not mentioned in the statute. We don't think the presumption will apply, just like it doesn't apply against a co-tenant. That means that you should never use deadly force against a co-employee unless you are facing an imminent threat of death or serious injury from that person. Rest assured, however, if you don't retreat even though it's safe to do so, you will probably be arrested and prosecuted, perhaps as THE test case. Pray you never have to experience something like that.]

[Civil Liability]

§ **F.S.A. § 776.032.**
Immunity from criminal prosecution and civil action for justifiable use of force.

(1) A person who uses force as permitted in §776.12, §776.13, or §776.31 is justified in using such force and is immune from criminal prosecution and civil action for the use of such force, unless the person against whom force was used is a law enforcement officer, as defined in §943.10 (14), who was acting in the performance of his or her official duties and the officer identified himself or herself in accordance with any applicable law or the person using force knew or reasonably should have known that the person was a law enforcement officer. As used in this subsection, the term

"criminal prosecution" includes arresting, detaining in custody, and charging or prosecuting the defendant. [This immunity provision requires the court in a criminal prosecution to hold a hearing before trial to determine if the defendant is immune from prosecution. *Peterson v. State*, 983 So.2d 27 (Fla.App. 1 Dist. 2006). Although the defendant has the burden during the hearing of proving by a preponderance of the evidence that he is innocent by reason of self-defense, this has the potential of greatly reducing the cost of his defense. It appears these proceedings can result in a dismissal of charges without a trial.]

(2) A law enforcement agency may use standard procedures for investigating the use of force as described in subsection (1), but the agency may not arrest the person for using force unless it determines that there is probable cause that the force that was used was unlawful.

(3) The court shall award reasonable attorney's fees, court costs, compensation for loss of income, and all expenses incurred by the defendant in defense of any civil action brought by a plaintiff if the court finds that the defendant is immune from prosecution as provided in subsection (1). [If you act within the bounds of the law of self-defense, you cannot be arrested, prosecuted, convicted or have a verdict against you for civil damages. Just make darn sure the person you are defending yourself against is not a police officer in the performance of his or her duties. I had a client once who, in his drunken state, claimed he honestly believed a police officer, in full uniform, making an arrest in the client's front yard, was a mugger. The client ran out the front door with a 12 gauge in his hand, and "racked one in" pointing his shotgun at the officer. Not only did he come within a quarter of a second of being shot dead, but was later convicted of aggravated assault. Alcohol and guns don't mix. See Chapter 7, Thumbs-Down Factors.]

§ F.S.A. § 776.085.
Defense to civil action for damages; party convicted of forcible or attempted forcible felony.

(1) It shall be a defense to any action for damages for personal injury or wrongful death, or for injury to property, that such action arose from injury sustained by a participant during the commission or attempted commission of a forcible felony. The defense authorized by this section shall be established by evidence that the participant has been convicted of such forcible felony or attempted forcible felony, or by proof of the commission of such crime or attempted crime by a preponderance of the evidence.

(2) For the purposes of this section, the term "forcible felony" shall have the same meaning as in §776.08.

(3) Any civil action in which the defense recognized by this section is raised shall be stayed by the court on the motion of the civil defendant during the pendency of any criminal action which forms the basis for the defense, unless the court finds that a conviction in the criminal action would not form a valid defense under this section.

(4) In any civil action where a party prevails based on the defense created by this section:

. . .

(b) The court shall award a reasonable attorney's fee to be paid to the prevailing party in equal amounts by the losing party and the losing party's attorney; however, the losing party's attorney is not personally responsible if he or she has acted in good faith, based on the representations of his or her client. If the losing party is incarcerated for the crime or attempted crime and has insufficient assets to cover payment of the costs of the action and the award of fees pursuant to this paragraph, the party shall, as determined by the court, be required to pay by deduction from any payments the prisoner receives while incarcerated.

. . .

[**Example:** You return unscathed from a quail-hunting trip in Texas with former Vice President Cheney. As you enter the home cradling your 28 gauge over-and-under, you hear your wife screaming in your upstairs bedroom. You load the shotgun as you rush to the rescue finding a stranger trying to force your wife onto the bed. You trip just as you are ready to shoot and your shots hit the panting pervert in the legs. He screams, "Don't kill me" as he stumbles around you toward the stairs. Because of his wounds, he loses his balance and cartwheels down the hardwood stairs to the main floor, suffering a broken neck with resulting paralysis. He is convicted of multiple forcible felonies.

An ambulance-chasing-attorney friend of the would-be rapist urges him to sue you for his injuries. The attorney has delusions of collecting an $8-million-dollar contingency fee because of the enormous damage award potential for a quadriplegic (see the verdict in the Bernard Goetz case reported in Chapter 15.)

Your attorney will be able to get the civil case against you dismissed because of the criminal conviction of your wife's attacker. Because the ambulance chaser brought the lawsuit against you knowing of his client's conviction, his actions were in "bad faith." This means you can collect the cost of your attorney fees equally from the attorney and his client. This statute is a huge disincentive for attorneys to bring lawsuits on behalf of criminals injured during the commission forcible felonies. Good work, Florida Legislature!]

[Defense of Property]

§ **F.S.A. § 776.031**

Use of force in defense of others. [We're not sure why this title says what it does. The statute is primarily about using force to protect PROPERTY – yours or someone else's.]

A person is justified in the use of force, except deadly force, against another when and to the extent that the person reasonably believes that such conduct is necessary to prevent or terminate the other's trespass on, or other tortious or criminal interference with, either real property other than a dwelling or personal property, lawfully in his or her possession or in the possession of another who is a member of his or her immediate family or household or of a person whose property he or she has a legal duty to protect.

However, the person is justified in the use of deadly force only if he or she reasonably believes that such force is necessary to prevent the imminent commission of a forcible felony. A person does not have a duty to retreat if the person is in a place where he or she has a right to be. [This is why people hate reading law. Its like the drafters are playing a trick on you to see how many times you'll go back over it. After 5 readings, this is our best translation: You can use force, but NOT DEADLY FORCE, to stop trespassers on your land or thieves from stealing your property or someone else's you've been given authority to protect. You can only use deadly force to resist a forcible felony, such as robbery, as explained in the statutes above. You don't have a duty to retreat if you're not a trespasser. Our Advice: If initially only property is at stake, call the cops. If you use force to stop a trespass or theft, the criminal may suddenly react by producing a dangerous weapon. If you then brandish or defend yourself with deadly force, the legal mess will cost you more than the property was worth. Read about the *Schanze* case, Chapter 12.]

[HELPFUL DEFINITIONS RELATING TO THIS STATE'S SELF-DEFENSE STATUTES]

- **Assault** – [Unlawful, intentional threat, verbal or non-verbal, coupled with the ability to carry out that threat OR creating a "well-founded" fear that the violence is imminent.] **F.S.A. § 784.011.**

- **Dwelling** – means a building or conveyance of any kind, including any attached porch, whether the building or conveyance is temporary or permanent, mobile or immobile, which has a roof over it, including a tent, and is designed to be occupied by people lodging therein at night. **F.S.A. § 776.013 (5) (a).**

- **F.S.A. § 776.06 Deadly force.**

  (1) The term "deadly force" means force that is likely to cause death or great bodily harm and includes, but is not limited to:

  (a) The firing of a firearm in the direction of the person to be arrested, even though no intent exists to kill or inflict great bodily harm; and

  (b) The firing of a firearm at a vehicle in which the person to be arrested is riding.

  (2) (a) The term "deadly force" does not include the discharge of a firearm by a law enforcement officer or correctional officer during and within the scope of his or her official duties which is loaded with a less-lethal munition. As used in this subsection, the term "less-lethal munition" means a projectile that is designed to stun, temporarily incapacitate, or cause temporary discomfort to a person without penetrating the person's body.

  (b) A law enforcement officer or a correctional officer is not liable in any civil or criminal action arising out of the use of any less-lethal munition in good faith during and within the scope of his or her official duties.

- **Felonies Mentioned Above** –
  - **Aggravated assault** – [An assault with a deadly weapon or with intent to commit a felony but without the intent to kill.] **F.S.A. § 784.021.**
  - **Aggravated battery** – [While committing battery a person intentionally or knowingly causes great bodily harm, uses a deadly weapon, or the victim at the time was pregnant and the offender knew or should have known of the pregnancy.] **F.S.A. § 784.045.**
  - **Aggravated stalking** – [Willfully, maliciously, and repeatedly following, harassing or cyber-stalking another with the intent of creating a reasonable fear in the victim(s)' minds (including children, siblings, spouse, parent or dependents of the victim) of death or bodily injury. Stalking someone under 16 years of age, or stalking in violation of a protective or restrainer order or in violation of probation.] **F.S.A. § 784.048 (3-5) &(7).**
  - **Aircraft piracy** – [Seizing or attempting to take control of any aircraft against the will of people inside by force or violence.] **F.S.A. § 860.16.**
  - **Arson** – [Intentionally using fire or explosion to damage a structure (see broad definition of "structure" below) knowing people may be in the structure or while committing a felony.] **F.S.A. § 860.01.**
  - **Burglary** – [Entering or remaining unlawfully in a dwelling or structure with the intent to commit a crime.] **F.S.A. § 810.02.**
  - **Carjacking** – [Taking or stealing a car by force, violence, assault, or fear.] **F.S.A. § 812.133.**
  - **Home-invasion robbery** – [A robbery committed in and against the occupants of a dwelling.] **F.S.A. § 812.135.**
  - **Kidnapping** – ["Forcibly, secretly, or by threat confining, abducting, or imprisoning" a person against their will with the intent to commit a crime.] **F.S.A. § 787.01.**
  - **Manslaughter** – [Unlawful killing of a human being by way of negligence or with out prior intent (in the heat of passion).] **F.S.A. § 782.07.**
  - **Murder** – [Unlawful killing of a human being which is either premeditated or during the commission of a felony (sometimes referred to as "felony murder.")] **F.S.A. § 782.04.**
  - **Robbery** – [Taking of property with the intent to deprive the owner of it permanently or temporarily, using force, violence, assault, or perpetuating fear.] **F.S.A. § 812.13.**

- **Sexual battery** – Means oral, anal, or vaginal penetration by, or union with, the sexual organ of another or the anal or vaginal penetration of another by any other object; however, sexual battery does not include an act done for a bona fide medical purpose. **F.S.A. § 794.011 (1)(h).**

- **Treason** – [Making war against the state, or giving its enemies aid or comfort. Example – Benedict Arnold.] **F.S.A. § 876.32.**

- **Unlawful throwing/placing/discharge of destructive device or bomb** – [Whether intentional or not, anyone who uses a bomb or destructive device that results in great bodily harm.] **F.S.A. § 790.1615.**

- **Residence** – Means a dwelling in which a person resides either temporarily or permanently or is visiting as an invited guest. **F.S.A. § 776.013 (5) (b).**
- **Vehicle** – Means a conveyance of any kind, whether or not motorized, which is designed to transport people or property. **F.S.A. § 776.013 (5) (c).**
- **Structure** – Means any building of any kind, any enclosed area with a roof over it, any real property and appurtenances thereto, any tent or other portable building, and any vehicle, vessel, watercraft, or aircraft. **F.S.A. § 806.01 (3) Arson.**

[TEMPLATE Topics We Could Not Find Explained in Statutes or Cases]

(For each of these topics that we could not find addressed in your state's statutes or cases, we suggest you review the same topics in the subchapters of surrounding states. Your state's courts may look to the law of neighboring states to see how their courts and legislatures have treated that particular self-defense issue.)

[Mutual Combat]

[Co-Habitant – Duty to Retreat]

[Reckless Injury to Innocent Third Parties]

Pancho's Wisdom

You just might be a Gunnut if . . . you didn't have to be told that sprinkling pepper on the carcass of a deer or antelope will keep flies out of your truck's camper shell.

The Devil went down to Georgia looking for a home to burglarize, "in a violent and tumultuous manner," and came away with his innards exposed to direct sunlight by a good ol' boy named Johnny, packin' a Glock 21SF made in Smyrna!

Key: ■ commentary ■ original statutes, cases or jury instructions

---

[Defense of Self and Others] [Non-Deadly Force]
[Defense of Third Persons]

§ GEORGIA (GA.) CODE ANNOTATED (ANN.) § 16-3-21.

Use of force in defense of self or others, including justifiable homicide; conflicting rules.

(a) A person is justified in threatening or using force against another when and to the extent that he or she reasonably believes that such threat or force is necessary to defend himself or herself or a third person against such other's imminent use of unlawful force; however,

[Deadly Force] [Use of Deadly Force to Prevent Serious Felonies]

except as provided in Code Section 16-3-23 [defense of premises, discussed below], a person is justified in using force which is intended or likely to cause death or great bodily harm only if he or she reasonably believes that such force is necessary to prevent death or great bodily injury to himself or herself or a third person or to prevent the commission of a forcible felony. [You can only use deadly force if it's necessary to prevent death or serious injury. A forcible felony is "any felony which involves the use or threat of physical force or violence against any person."]

[Exceptions to Justifiable Self-Defense]

(b) A person is not justified in using force under the circumstances specified in subsection (a) of this Code section if he:

[Provocation]

(1) Initially provokes the use of force against himself with the intent to use such force as an excuse to inflict bodily harm upon the assailant;
[You cannot do something that makes the other person come after you and later claim self-defense.]

[Committing Felony or Unlawful Act]

(2) Is attempting to commit, committing, or fleeing after the commission or attempted commission of a felony; or

["I was robbin' the convenience store and the clerk pulled a gun on me so I shot him in self-defense." Not hardly!]

[Initial Aggressor] [Mutual Combat]

(3) Was the aggressor or was engaged in a combat by agreement unless . . .

[You can't start a fight or agree to fight and then claim self-defense unless . . .]

[Exceptions to the Exceptions] [Withdraw and Communicate]

. . . he withdraws from the encounter and effectively communicates to such other person his intent to do so and the other, notwithstanding, continues or threatens to continue the use of unlawful force. [You retreat and tell the guy you're fighting that you quit. If he doesn't quit fighting, he then becomes the aggressor. Then you can again claim self-defense if you have to hurt him to stop his aggression.]

(c) Any rule, regulation, or policy of any agency of the state or any ordinance, resolution, rule, regulation, or policy of any county, municipality, or other political subdivision of the state which is in conflict with this Code section shall be null, void, and of no force and effect.

. . .

[This is referred to as a preemption law. It keeps cities, counties, and any other state agencies from making their own rules about your right to defend yourself. Otherwise, these rules would be impossible to keep up with as you travel from one town to another.]

[No Duty to Retreat – Generally]

§ GA. CODE ANN. § 16-3-23.1.

Use of force in defense of habitation, property, self, or others; no duty to retreat.

A person who uses threats or force in accordance with Code Section 16-3-21, relating to the use of force in defense of self or others, Code Section 16-3-21 relating to the use of force in defense of a habitation, or Code Section 16-3-24, relating to the use of force in defense of property other than a habitation, has no duty to retreat and has the right to stand his or her ground and use force as provided in said Code sections, including deadly force.

[This is Georgia's "No Retreat" law. You don't have to retreat before using lawful force to defend yourself.]

[Defense of Person(s) in Special Places – Dwelling, Place of Business, Motor Vehicle]

§ GA. CODE ANN. § 16-3-23.

A person is justified in threatening or using force against another when and to the extent that he or she reasonably believes that such threat or force is necessary to prevent or terminate such other's unlawful entry into or attack upon a habitation [this "means any dwelling, motor vehicle, or place of business"]; however, such person is justified in the use of force which is intended or likely to cause death or great bodily harm only if:

(1) The entry is made or attempted in a violent and tumultuous manner and he or she reasonably believes that the entry is attempted or made for the purpose of assaulting or offering personal violence to any person dwelling or being therein and that such force is necessary to prevent the assault or offer of personal violence;

(2) That force is used against another person who is not a member of the family or household and who unlawfully and forcibly enters or has unlawfully and forcibly entered the residence and the person using such force knew or had reason to believe that an unlawful and forcible entry occurred; or

(3) The person using such force reasonably believes that the entry is made or attempted for the purpose of committing a felony therein and that such force is necessary to prevent the commission of the felony.

[In the case of an extremely violent or unlawful entry by an intruder, notice the threshold to use deadly force is "assault" or "personal violence" as opposed to "death or serious bodily injury." Also, in the home, preventing the commission of a felony as opposed to a forcible felony is sufficient to authorize the use of deadly force. However, if you are certain the felony does not involve force or violence, we strongly recommend against the use of deadly force. **Example:** A carpet bagger with a New York accent is in your home attempting to gather a boatload of personal information to steal your identity under the guise of giving you a better mortgage rate. Your cousin Vinnie calls and warns you of the scam. We advise you to make a quick call to the FBI from another part of your home rather than blowing the scammer away with the double-barreled shotgun you have mounted under your kitchen table. It will not only save you arrest and prosecution, but could save the need for disaster cleanup in your kitchen/dining room. See our caution about using deadly force to stop the progression of non-violent felonies in Chapter 4.]

[No Duty to Retreat From Special Places – Dwelling, Place of Business, Motor Vehicle]

§ GA. CODE ANN. § 6-3-23.1.
A person who uses threats or force . . .

A person who uses threats or force in accordance with... Code Section 16-3-23, relating to the use of force in defense of a habitation..., has no duty to retreat and has the right to stand his or her ground and use force as provided in said Code sections, including deadly force. [Remember that habitation includes dwelling, WORKPLACE and CAR, so you have no duty to retreat from any of those places. We couldn't find any case law on whether or not you have to retreat from co-habitants or co-employees. A plain reading of the statute seems to suggest that you don't need to retreat no matter who your attacker is (as long as you haven't violated any of the exceptions discussed above) – but we can't be 100% sure until the matter is resolved by the Georgia courts. HOWEVER, because such persons are on the premises legally, you may NOT be able to use deadly force against them unless they threaten serious injury or death. In other words, the lower threshold described in §16-3-23 above probably will not apply against co-tenants or co-employees. We find that using force against such persons usually results in arrest and prosecution. See Thumbs-Down Factors, Chapter 7.]

[Civil Liability]

§ GA. CODE ANN. § 16-3-24.2.
Immunity from criminal prosecution where use of threats or force is justified.

A person who uses threats or force in accordance with Code Section 16-3-21, 16-3-23, 16-3-23.1, or 16-3-24 shall be immune from criminal prosecution therefore unless in the use of deadly force, such person utilizes a weapon the carrying or possession of which is unlawful by such person under Part 2 or 3 of Article 4 of Chapter 11 of this title.
[This is an AMAZINGLY wise statute that the Legislatures of ALL states should consider passing to help preserve the right of self-defense. As a result of this code section and a Georgia case, *Fair v. State,* 664 SE2d 227(2008), if the defendant claims self-defense, the court must hold a hearing before trial to determine if charges (murder, manslaughter, aggravated assault or assault) should be dismissed on the grounds of self-defense. This has the potential of greatly reducing the costs of defending the case. This immunity provision does not apply if you are carrying an illegal weapon.]

[Defense of Property]

§ GA. CODE ANN. § 16-3-24.
Use of force in defense of property.

(a) A person is justified in threatening or using force against another when and to the extent that he reasonably believes that such threat or force is necessary to prevent or terminate such other's trespass on or other tortious or criminal interference with real property other than a habitation or personal property:

(1) Lawfully in his possession;

(2) Lawfully in the possession of a member of his immediate family; or

(3) Belonging to a person whose property he has a legal duty to protect.

(b) The use of force which is intended or likely to cause death or great bodily harm to prevent trespass on or other tortious or criminal interference with real property other than a habitation or personal property is not justified unless the person using such force reasonably believes that it is necessary to prevent the commission of a forcible felony. [You can't use deadly force to keep trespassers off of your land or to stop them from stealing something that isn't attached to the land like a lawn mower or chain saw. But you can use deadly force if it's necessary to keep them from committing a forcible felony on your property. "Forcible felony" is defined below. Of course, if they are breaking into your "premises," you can use deadly force under the conditions we discussed in §16-3-24 above.]

[HELPFUL DEFINITIONS RELATING TO THIS STATE'S SELF-DEFENSE STATUTES]

- **Felony** – means a crime punishable by death, by imprisonment for life, or by imprisonment for more than 12 months. **Ga. Code Ann. § 16-1-3 (5).**

- **Forcible felony** – means any felony which involves the use or threat of physical force or violence against any person. **Ga. Code Ann. § 16-1-3 (5).**

- **Habitation** – As used in Code Sections 16-3-23 and 16-3-24, it means any dwelling, motor vehicle, or place of business, and "personal property" means personal property other than a motor vehicle. **Ga. Code Ann. § 16-3-24.1.**

- **Affirmative defense** – means, with respect to any affirmative defense authorized in this title, unless the state's evidence raises the issue invoking the alleged defense, the defendant must present evidence thereon to raise the issue. The enumeration in this title of some affirmative defenses shall not be construed as excluding the existence of others. **Ga. Code Ann. § 16-1-3 (1)** [If there isn't some evidence you acted in self-defense by the end of the prosecution's case (his witnesses get to testify first), your lawyer will have to present evidence of self-defense. Otherwise the court will not allow the jury to consider your theory of self-defense.]

- **Forcible misdemeanor** – means any misdemeanor which involves the use or threat of physical force or violence against any person. **Ga. Code Ann. § 16-1-3 (7).**

- **Person** – means an individual, a public or private corporation, an incorporated association, government, government agency, partnership, or unincorporated association. **Ga. Code Ann. § 16-1-3 (12).**

- **Property** – means anything of value, including but not limited to real estate, tangible and intangible personal property, contract rights, services, choses in action, and other interests in or claims to wealth, admission or transportation tickets, captured or domestic animals, food and drink, and electric or other power. **Ga. Code Ann. § 16-1-3 (13).**

- **Public place** – means any place where the conduct involved may reasonably be expected to be viewed by people other than members of the actor's family or household. **Ga. Code Ann. § 16-1-3 (15).**

- **Reasonable belief** – means that the person concerned, acting as a reasonable man, believes that the described facts exist. **Ga. Code Ann. § 16-1-3 (16).**

[TEMPLATE Topics We Could Not Find Explained in Statutes or Cases]

(For each of these topics that we could not find addressed in your state's statutes or cases, we suggest you review the same topics in the subchapters of surrounding states. Your state's courts may look to the law of neighboring states to see how their courts and legislatures have treated that particular self-defense issue.)

[Co-Habitants; Co-Employees – Duty to Retreat]

[Presumption of Reasonableness in Special Places]

[Reckless Injury to Innocent Third Parties]

Pancho's Wisdom

You just might be a Gunnut if . . .

. . . you hope that Heaven smells a little like morning dew on an alfalfa field in mid Summer or on damp sagebrush mixed with pine in late September.

. . . your morning warm-up stretch involves bending over to pick up your spent pistol brass.

. . . you hunt jack rabbits with your concealed carry pistol rather than a shotgun.

Key: ■ commentary ■ original statutes, cases or jury instructions

[Defense of Self and Others] [Non-Deadly Force]

§ HAWAII REVISED STATUTES (HRS) § 703-304.
Use of force in self-protection.

(1) Subject to the provisions of this section and of section 703-308, the use of force upon or toward another person is justifiable when the actor believes that such force is immediately necessary for the purpose of protecting himself against the use of unlawful force by the other person on the present occasion. [This is standard non-deadly force language, see Chapter 3.]

[Deadly Force] [Use of Deadly Force to Prevent Serious Felonies]

(2) The use of deadly force is justifiable under this section if the actor believes that deadly force is necessary to protect himself against death, serious bodily injury, kidnapping, rape, or forcible sodomy. [Hawaii should be commended for justifying the use of deadly force to prevent forcible sexual assaults. Kidnapping, rape and forcible sodomy are heinous crimes, the prevention of which should justify the use of deadly force.]

[Duty to Retreat – Generally – No, (when using non-deadly force), Yes (when using deadly force)]

(3) Except as otherwise provided in subsections (4) and (5) of this section, a person employing protective force may estimate the necessity thereof under the circumstances as he believes them to be when the force is used without retreating, surrendering possession, doing any other act which he has no legal duty to do, or abstaining from any lawful action. [Be careful not to mistake this provision for a "Dirty-Harry-Make-My-Day" law. This is not one. This no-retreat provision only applies to a person using non-deadly protective force. The stakes change when a human life is at risk. Section (5) below says you have to retreat before using deadly force if you can do so in complete safety. You are not required to retreat from your home or place of work, except under certain circumstances.]

[Exceptions to Justifiable Self-Defense]

(4) The use of force is not justifiable under this section:

(a) To resist an arrest which the actor knows is being made by a law enforcement officer, although the arrest is unlawful; or [You can't resist arrest even if you know it's an unlawful arrest. You have to make it right through the legal system (example—a civil rights lawsuit), not through the use of force.]

(b) To resist force used by the occupier or possessor of property or by another person on his behalf, where the actor knows that the person using the force is doing so under a claim of right to protect the property, [Two people claiming a right to the same piece of real estate should deal with it in court, not with war clubs lined with shark teeth] except that this limitation shall not apply if:

[Exceptions to the Exceptions]

(i) The actor is a public officer acting in the performance of his duties or a person lawfully assisting him therein or a person making or assisting in a lawful arrest; or [If county deputies show up on your beach lot to sell it at a sheriff's sale, you cannot resist their efforts just because you claim a right to stay on your property. Take it up with the judge.]

(ii) The actor believes that such force is necessary to protect himself against death or serious bodily injury. [You tell your neighbor to get off your land. He says it is his land. As you walk away to call your lawyer, you turn around and notice he is coming at you with a samurai sword. Because of Hawaii's strict gun laws, you probably would have no access to your Glock, but you'd be justified in whacking him with your wok if that's all you could get your hands on. But even though you'll ultimately be acquitted (if the jury believes your story over his), we have found that most such disputes result in the arrest and prosecution of both parties. See Chapter 7, Thumbs-Down Factors.]

(5) The use of deadly force is not justifiable under this section if:

[Exceptions to Justifiable Self-Defense] [Provocation]

(a) The actor, with the intent of causing death or serious bodily injury, provoked the use of force against himself in the same encounter; or [You can't hit someone with a coconut hoping he'll come at you with a machete so you can shoot him!]

[Duty to Retreat – Generally – Yes (when using deadly force)]

(b) The actor knows that he can avoid the necessity of using such force with complete safety by retreating or by surrendering possession of a thing to a person asserting a claim of right thereto or by complying with a demand that he abstain from any action which he has no duty to take, except that: [As we mentioned earlier, the stakes are raised when human life is involved. In Hawaii there is a duty to retreat depending on the degree of force one plans on using. This provision requires you to exhaust all possibilities to get away before using any type of *deadly force.* This applies to situations outside your home or place of work (see para (i) below).]

[Exceptions to Justifiable Self-Defense]
[No Duty to Retreat From Dwelling or Place of Work]
[Co-Employees – Duty to Retreat – Yes]

(i) The actor is not obliged to retreat from his dwelling or place of work, unless he was the initial aggressor or is assailed in his place of work by another person whose place of work the actor knows it to be; and [This is Hawaii's "Castle Doctrine." You can defend your home ("castle") and your place of work with deadly force without retreating, unless you start the fight or the force to be used is against one of your co-workers. If one of your co-workers goes postal, you must retreat to the point you can no longer do so in complete safety, and then, and only then, can you legally and justifiably resort to the use of deadly force. Because of Hawaii's strict-to-the-point-of-ridiculousness gun laws, you probably won't have a firearm at your place of employment when you really need one. Hopefully, you can instantly transform yourself into Jackie Chan to defend yourself and co-workers.]

(ii) A public officer justified in using force in the performance of his duties, or a person justified in using force in his assistance or a person justified in using force in making an arrest or preventing an escape, is not obliged to desist from efforts to perform his duty, effect the arrest, or prevent the escape because of resistance or threatened resistance by or on behalf of the person against whom the action is directed.

(6) The justification afforded by this section extends to the use of confinement as protective force only if the actor takes all reasonable measures to terminate the confinement as soon as he knows that he safely can, unless the person confined has been arrested on a charge of crime.

[Defense of a Third Person]

§ HRS § 703-305.
Use of force for the protection of other persons.

(1) Subject to the provisions of this section and of section 703-310 [concerning reckless or negligent behavior—explained below under [**Reckless Injury to Innocent Third Parties**] section], the use of force upon or toward the person of another is justifiable to protect a third person when:

(a) Under the circumstances as the actor believes them to be, the person whom the actor seeks to protect would be justified in using such protective force [You would be justified in defending another if he would be justified to defend himself under Hawaii's self-defense laws]; and

(b) The actor believes that the actor's intervention is necessary for the protection of the other person. ["Necessary" does not mean "Macho." See our discussion of "necessary" in Chapter 3 above.]

(2) Notwithstanding subsection (1):

[Duty to Retreat]

(a) When the actor would be obliged under section 703-304 to retreat, to surrender the possession of a thing, or to comply with a demand before using force in self-protection, the actor is not obliged to do so before using force for the protection of another person, unless the actor knows that the actor can thereby secure the complete safety of such other person; and [Even if you are required to retreat under the rules of self-defense in section 304 above, you are not required to do so when protecting a third person unless you know you can help the third person retreat in complete safety. Of course, the third person does not have to retreat from his home or workplace, except under certain circumstances (see commentary to (c) below).]

(b) When the person whom the actor seeks to protect would be obliged under section 703-304 to retreat, to surrender the possession of a thing or to comply with a demand if the person knew that the person could obtain complete safety by so doing, the actor is obliged to try to cause the person to do so before using force in the person's protection if the actor knows that the actor can obtain the other's complete safety in that way; and [Retreat, retreat, retreat. Who wrote these laws? The French?]

(c) Neither the actor nor the person whom the actor seeks to protect is obliged to retreat when in the other's dwelling or place of work to any greater extent than in the actor's or the person's own. [This is another reinforcement of the castle doctrine when acting on behalf of someone else. The exceptions to this section of the statute are as stated in 703-304. You must retreat if you are the initial aggressor or when "assailed in your place of work by another person whose place of work you know it to be."]

[Defense of Person(s) in Special Places – Dwelling]

§ **HRS § 703-306.**
Use of force for the protection of property.

. . .

(3) The use of deadly force for the protection of property is justifiable only if:

(a) The person against whom the force is used is attempting to dispossess the actor of the actor's dwelling otherwise than under a claim of right to its possession; or [You can use deadly force to keep someone from forcing you out of your home (e.g., a kidnapping) UNLESS it's someone like the landlord with an eviction notice or a banker repossessing your home with a claim of right to the property for some legal reason or another.]

(b) The person against whom the deadly force is used is attempting to commit felonious property damage, burglary, robbery, or felonious theft **AND** either:

(i) Has employed or threatened deadly force against or in the presence of the actor; or

(ii) The use of force other than deadly force to prevent the commission of the crime would expose the actor or another person in the actor's presence to substantial danger of serious bodily injury. [The use of deadly force in protection of property is non-existent unless there is a substantial risk that you or someone else is in threat of death or serious bodily harm by the assailant(s).]

(4) The justification afforded by this section extends to the use of a device for the purpose of protecting property only if:

(a) The device is not designed to cause or known to create a substantial risk of causing death or serious bodily injury; **AND** [this prohibits the use of what used to be known as a "spring gun" which has been the source of multiple prosecutions and lawsuits over the years. Property owners would get tired of being burglarized over and over, so they would set traps consisting of tripwires and devices, like shotguns, that would go off when intruders broke into their garages or homes. The problem is these devices aren't capable of exercising good judgment. They don't distinguish between a burglar and a relative sneaking into the house to surprise the homeowner. An injury or death caused by such a device is not justifiable even if it shoots a burglar.]

(b) The use of the particular device to protect the property from entry or trespass is reasonable under the circumstances, as the defendant believes them to be; **AND**

(c) The device is one **customarily** used for such a purpose or reasonable care is taken to make known to probable intruders the fact that it is used. [We're not aware of any devices customarily used besides burglar alarms or security cameras. However, if it isn't customary, intruders have to be warned. **Example:** "Warning: If you break into our home, our adult son, who unfortunately remains a permanent fixture, will shoot you in the groin with his BB gun like in the movie *Home Alone!* Mahalo."]

(5) The justification afforded by this section extends to the use of confinement as protective force only if the actor takes all reasonable measures to terminate the confinement as soon as the actor knows that the actor can do so with safety to the property, unless the person confined has been arrested on a charge of crime. [If you are using a palm-tree spring net (boing!), you have to cut them down as soon as you can safely do so—like after the blue lights arrive on the scene!]

[Reckless Injury to Innocent Third Parties]

§ HRS § 703-310.
Provisions generally applicable to justification.

(1) When the actor believes that the use of force upon or toward the person of another is necessary for any of the purposes for which such belief would establish a justification under sections 703-303 to 703-309 but the actor is reckless or negligent in having such belief or in acquiring or failing to acquire any knowledge or belief which is material to the justifiability of the actor's use of force, the justification afforded by those sections is unavailable in a prosecution for an offense for which recklessness or negligence, as the case may be, suffices to establish culpability.

(2) When the actor is justified under sections 703-303 to 703-309 in using force upon or toward the person of another but the actor recklessly or negligently injures or creates a risk of injury to innocent persons, the justification afforded by those sections is unavailable in a prosecution for such recklessness or negligence toward innocent persons.

[You cannot be careless or reckless in your use of force. **Example:** You work at the front desk of the luxurious (and fictional) Wahini Molokini. Suddenly a three-hundred-pound former professional linebacker from the Mainland fumin' cause he didn't get full ocean view, leaps over the counter with a Polynesian war club purchased at a souvenir shop. He says he's going to take your da kine Hawaiian head off. You grab the Glock 18 (full auto) out of the lost-and-found box that a U.S. Secret Service agent forgot in the men's restroom. You close your eyes and spray hot 9mms all over the foyer even though you know a busload of tourists just walked through the breezeway. You'd probably be justified in using deadly force against the Howlie (Haole). But if innocents are injured or killed because of your "spray-and-pray" defensive tactics, you could be prosecuted for manslaughter or other crimes that require only proof of criminal negligence or recklessness rather than an intent to kill.]

[Use of Deadly Force to Prevent Serious Felonies]

§ **HRS § 703-308 (1) (b) and (2).**
Use of force to prevent suicide or the commission of a crime.

. . .

(1) (b) The use of deadly force is not in any event justifiable under this section unless:

(i) The actor believes that there is a substantial risk that the person whom the actor seeks to prevent from committing a crime will cause death or serious bodily injury to *another* [e.g., a deranged person whose suicide wish endangers others such as threatening to pull the pin on a hand grenade while on the "Glass Bottom Boat."] unless the commission or the consummation of the crime is prevented and that the use of such force presents no substantial risk of injury to innocent persons; or

(ii) The actor believes that the use of such force is necessary to suppress a riot after the rioters have been ordered to disperse and warned, in any particular manner that the law may require, that deadly force will be used if they do not obey. [We could not find a Hawaiian case discussing the issue of a citizen using deadly force to suppress a riot. Our bet is that this will never happen to you. In any event, we don't recommend you get involved in trying to suppress a violent riot unless it involves the use of deadly force against you or a loved one. Let the police handle it unless your name is Tommy Lee Jones and you're a federal marshal.]

(2) The justification afforded by this section extends to the use of confinement as preventive force only if the actor takes all reasonable measures to terminate the confinement as soon as the actor knows that the actor safely can, unless the person confined has been arrested on a charge of crime.

[Civil Liability]

§ **HRS § 703-301.**
Justification a defense; civil remedies unaffected.

(1) In any prosecution for an offense, justification, as defined in sections 703-302 through 703-309, is a defense.

(2) The fact that conduct is justifiable under this chapter does not abolish or impair any remedy for such conduct which is available in any *civil action*. [Just because you were found not guilty by reason of self-defense in a criminal case, doesn't mean the person you injured in self-defense can't sue you. For more information about this, see Chapter 15 on civil liability.]

[Defense of Property]

§ HRS § 703-306 (1) and (2).
Use of force for the protection of property.

(1) The use of force upon or toward the person of another is justifiable when the actor believes that such force is immediately necessary:

(a) To prevent the commission of criminal trespass or burglary in a building or upon real property in the actor's possession or in the possession of another person for whose protection the actor acts; or

(b) To prevent unlawful entry upon real property in the actor's possession or in the possession of another person for whose protection the actor acts; or

(c) To prevent theft, criminal mischief, or any trespassory taking of tangible, movable property in the actor's possession or in the possession of another person for whose protection the actor acts.

(2) The actor may in the circumstances specified in subsection (1) use such force as the actor believes is necessary to protect the threatened property, provided that the actor first requests the person against whom force is used to desist from the person's interference with the property, unless the actor believes that:

(a) Such a request would be useless; or

(b) It would be dangerous to the actor or another person to make the request; or

(c) Substantial harm would be done to the physical condition of the property which is sought to be protected before the request could effectively be made.

. . .

[Notice there is nothing mentioned about using "deadly force" to defend your property. You can't. If the threat, however, escalates to become an imminent threat of death or serious bodily injury, then you may use deadly force to defend yourself or others on the property.]

[HELPFUL DEFINITIONS RELATING TO THIS STATE'S SELF-DEFENSE STATUTES]

- **Apartment building** – means any structure containing one or more dwelling units which is not a hotel or a single-family residence. **HRS § 708-800.**
- **Believes** – means reasonably believes. **HRS § 703-300.**

- **Bodily injury** – means physical pain, illness, or any impairment of physical condition. **HRS § 707-700.**

- **Building** – includes any structure, and the term also includes any vehicle, railway car, aircraft, or watercraft used for lodging of persons therein; each unit of a building consisting of two or more units separately secured or occupied is a separate building. **HRS § 708-800.**

- **Deadly force** – means force which the actor uses with the intent of causing or which the actor knows to create a substantial risk of causing death or serious bodily harm. Intentionally firing a firearm in the direction of another person or in the direction which another person is believed to be constitutes deadly force. **A threat to cause death or serious bodily injury, by the production of a weapon or otherwise, so long as the actor's intent is limited to creating an apprehension that the actor will use deadly force if necessary, does not constitute deadly force. HRS § 703-300.**

- **Dwelling** – means any building or structure, though movable or temporary, or a portion thereof, which is for the time being a home or place of lodging. **HRS § 703-300.**

- **Enter or remain unlawfully** – A person "enters or remains unlawfully" in or upon premises when the person is not licensed, invited, or otherwise privileged to do so. A person who, regardless of the person's intent, enters or remains in or upon premises which are at the time open to the public does so with license and privilege unless the person defies a lawful order not to enter or remain, personally communicated to the person by the owner of the premises or some other authorized person. A license or privilege to enter or remain in a building which is only partly open to the public is not a license or privilege to enter or remain in that part of the building which is not open to the public. A person who enters or remains upon unimproved and apparently unused land, which is neither fenced nor otherwise enclosed in a manner designed to exclude intruders, does so with license and privilege unless notice against trespass is personally communicated to the person by the owner of the land or some other authorized person, or unless notice is given by posting in a conspicuous manner. **HRS § 708-800.**

- **Felonies Mentioned Above –**

  - **Felonious property damage** – [Knowingly damaging property by the use of dangerous means. Also includes knowingly or intentionally damaging property without consent that exceeds the amount of $1,500.00.] **HRS § 708-820 & 21.**

  - **Felonious theft** – [Taking property from the person of another or the taking of property that exceeds the value of $300.00. Also, theft of agricultural equipment, supplies, or products that exceed $100.00 in value.] **HRS § 708-830.5 & 31.**

  - **Burglary** – [Intentionally entering or remaining unlawfully in a building with the intent to commit a crime against a person or the property rights.] **HRS 708-10 & 11.**

- **Forcible sodomy** – [According to Act 314 of 1986 "... a distinction no longer exists between what was first and second degree rape (see definition below) and sodomy.] **HRS § 707-730, 731, 732.**

- **Kidnapping** – [Intentionally or knowingly restraining a person with the intent to commit some crime against that person or someone else.] **HRS § 707-720.**

- **Rape** – [Sexual intercourse by force or threat. The statutes cited are felony sexual assaults because there is no statute defining rape.] **HRS § 707-730, 731, 732.**

- **Robbery** – [While committing theft a person uses force or threatens the use of force in order to carry out the theft.] **HRS § 708-840.**

- **Death – (Manslaughter or Murder)** – [Unlawful killing of a human whether criminally negligent or intentional.] **HRS § 707-701, 701.5, 702.**

- **Force** – means any bodily impact, restraint, or confinement, or the threat thereof. **HRS § 703-300.**

- **Premises** – includes any building and any real property. **HRS § 708-800.**

- **Property** – means any money, personal property, real property, thing in action, evidence of debt or contract, or article of value of any kind. Commodities of a public utility nature such as gas, electricity, steam, and water constitute property, but the supplying of such a commodity to premises from an outside source by means of wires, pipes, conduits, or other equipment shall be deemed a rendition of a service rather than a sale or delivery of property. **HRS § 708-800.**

- **Property of another** – means property which any person, other than the defendant, has possession of or any other interest in, even though that possession or interest is unlawful; however, a security interest is not an interest in property, even if title is in the secured party pursuant to the security agreement. **HRS§ 708-800.**

- **Restrain** – means to restrict a person's movement in such a manner as to interfere substantially with the person's liberty by means of force, threat, or deception; or if the person is under the age of eighteen or incompetent, without the consent of the relative, person, or institution having lawful custody of the person. **HRS § 707-700.**

- **Serious bodily injury** – means bodily injury which creates a substantial risk of death or which causes serious, permanent disfigurement, or protracted loss or impairment of the function of any bodily member or organ. **HRS § 707-700.**

- **Unlawful force** – means force which is employed without the consent of the person against whom it is directed and the employment of which constitutes an offense or would constitute an offense except for a defense not amounting to a justification to use the force. Assent constitutes consent, within the meaning of this section, whether or not it otherwise is legally effective, except assent to the infliction of death or serious or substantial bodily injury. **HRS § 703-300.**

[TEMPLATE Topics We Could Not Find Explained in Statutes or Cases]
(For each of these topics that we could not find addressed in your state's statutes or cases, we suggest you review the same topics in the subchapters of surrounding states. Your state's courts may look to the law of the surrounding states to see how their courts and legislatures have treated that particular self-defense issue.)

[Mutual Combat]

[Committing Felony or Unlawful Act]

[Withdraw and Communicate]

[Co-Habitants – Duty to Retreat]

[Presumption of Reasonableness in Special Places]

Aloha and Mahalo!

Idaho's self-defense statutes seem a century old and therefore, should be read and applied with the cautions contained in Chapter 3 and 4. Fortunately, the Idaho Supreme Court has taken the initiative to clarify and simplify the law of self-defense by approving jury instructions written by members of the Criminal Jury Instruction Committee who have carefully researched Idaho's self-defense statutes and case law. In October of 2005, the Idaho Supreme Court Issued the following Order:

> NOW, THEREFORE, IT IS HEREBY ORDERED that the Court does hereby accept the recommendation of the Committee, and the revised Idaho Criminal Jury Instructions shall be disseminated for general use by the trial bench and bar in Idaho, to be effective immediately. It is recommended that whenever these revised Idaho Criminal Jury Instructions contain an instruction applicable to a case and the trial judge determines that the jury should be instructed on that subject, the judge should use the instruction contained in the revised Idaho Criminal Jury Instructions, unless the judge finds that a different instruction would more adequately, accurately or clearly state the law.

http://www.isc.idaho.gov/cji_order1005.htm. This means that Idaho trial judges will first look to the approved jury instructions before they look at state statutes or cases to explain to a jury what law should be applied to the facts of any case. For this reason, we included jury instructions along with the state statutes. This made it a little harder for us to apply our TEMPLATE to this state, but we did the best we could under the circumstances.

Key: ■ commentary ■ original statutes, cases or jury instructions

---

[Defense of Self and Others]
[Non-Deadly Force]

§ §19-201. LAWFUL RESISTANCE.

Lawful resistance to the commission of a public offense may be made:

1. By the party about to be injured.

2. By other parties.

§ §19-202. RESISTANCE BY THREATENED PARTY.

Resistance sufficient to prevent the offense may be made by the party about to be injured:

1. To prevent an offense against his person, or his family, or some member thereof.
2. To prevent an illegal attempt by force to take or injure property in his lawful possession.

[Although the language of these two statutes is slightly different from the non-deadly force statutes of most states, it essentially says the same thing. You may use reasonable force, but not deadly force, to defend yourself, others and your property from unlawful interference. Examples would be stopping petty theft of your kids' toys from your front lawn, blocking a punch or pushing someone away who is trying to strike you with his fists. Remember, if you are reacting to simply stop the assault or theft, your actions will be more likely to be justified. On the other hand, if you become angry and your actions go beyond stopping the assault or theft to "teach the creep a lesson," you set yourself up for being charged with an assault or sued for injuries that would not have occurred had you not used excessive force. Although it sounds wimpy, the legally prudent thing to do is to keep a safe distance, draw your cell phone from concealment and call the police.]

[The following jury instruction shows that the same rules of justification apply in the case of a battery (hitting someone in self-defense without using a dangerous weapon) as they do for a homicide (killing of a human). If the person struck in self-defense died, the term "homicide" would be used, if he didn't, the word "battery" would be used.]

Idaho Criminal Jury Instruction (ICJI)1517 Self-Defense

A [homicide] [battery] is justifiable if the defendant was acting in [self-defense] [defense of another].

In order to find that the defendant acted in [self-defense] [defense of another], all of the following conditions must be found to have been in existence at the time of the [killing] [striking]:

1. The defendant must have believed that [the defendant] [another person] was in imminent danger of [death or great bodily harm] [bodily harm]. [See our explanation of the word "imminent" in Chapter 3.]
2. In addition to that belief, the defendant must have believed that the action the defendant took was necessary to save [the defendant] [another person] from the danger presented. [See discussion of the concept of "necessity" in Chapter 3.]
3. The circumstances must have been such that a reasonable person, under similar circumstances, would have believed that [the defendant] [another person] was in imminent danger of [death or great bodily injury] [bodily injury] and believed that the action taken was necessary.

4. The defendant must have acted only in response to that danger and not for some other motivation. [See cases in the Thumbs-Down Chapter 7 describing how motive to kill can defeat a self-defense case. In particular, read the summary of the Idaho case *State v. Turner*, 38 P.3d 1285 (Id. 2001).]

[5. When there is no longer any reasonable appearance of danger, the right of (self-defense) (defense of another) ends.] [See Chapter 3.]

In deciding upon the reasonableness of the defendant's beliefs, you should determine what an ordinary and reasonable person might have concluded from all the facts and circumstances which the evidence shows existed at that time, and not with the benefit of hindsight.

The danger must have been present and imminent, or must have so appeared to a reasonable person under the circumstances. A bare fear of [death or great bodily injury] [bodily injury] is not sufficient to justify a [homicide] [battery]. The defendant must have acted under the influence of fears that only a reasonable person would have had in a similar position.

The burden is on the prosecution to prove beyond a reasonable doubt that the [homicide] [battery] was not justifiable. If there is a reasonable doubt whether the [homicide] [battery] was justifiable, you must find the defendant not guilty.

[Deadly Force] [Use of Deadly Force to Prevent Serious Felonies]

§ §18-4013. DISCHARGE OF DEFENDANT WHEN HOMICIDE JUSTIFIABLE OR EXCUSABLE.

The homicide appearing to be justifiable or excusable, the person indicted must, upon his trial, be fully acquitted and discharged. [If your killing of another is held to be justifiable or excusable (see explanation below), you cannot be convicted of woeful crimes like murder or manslaughter. Please also notice it says "upon his trial." If you go to trial, prepare to mortgage the farm and next year's hay crop to pay your huggable criminal defense lawyer.]

§ §18-4009(1) AND (4). JUSTIFIABLE HOMICIDE BY ANY PERSON.

Homicide is also justifiable when committed by any person in either of the following cases:

1. When resisting any attempt to murder any person, or to commit a felony, or to do some great bodily injury upon any person; or, [Necessarily killing to prevent murder or great bodily harm of an innocent person is a no-brainer. However, since this statute was written, thousands upon thousands of crimes have been added to the law books as felonies. They're everywhere, they're everywhere! (See our discussion in Chapter 4.) For example, suppose grandpa got convicted of domestic violence 30 years ago for ripping the phone out of the wall during a disagreement with grandma. Under federal law, if grandpa is out 30 miles southwest of Blackfoot to teach a grandchild to shoot a .22, he's committing a felony for simply possessing a firearm. Would anyone in his right mind think he could uncork grandpa with his Kalashnikov for teaching little Jimmy to ventilate pop

cans with a rimfire? Doing something kinky like that in Idaho to "prevent the commission of a felony," would not only get you prosecuted for murder, it could get you lynched! Obviously, the reference to "felony" in this statute and in the jury instructions below should be taken to mean violent felonies such as rape and armed robbery.]

. . .

4. When necessarily committed in attempting, by lawful ways and means, to apprehend any person for any felony committed, or in lawfully suppressing any riot, or in lawfully keeping and preserving the peace. [This is Idaho's fleeing-felon statute. For reasons explained in Chapter 4, we recommend you not go after criminals who have committed a felony unless their escape poses an immediate threat to a loved one. Doing so could get you prosecuted, sued or worse, killed. Also, this statute supposedly gives you authority to kill to lawfully suppress a riot or preserve the peace. How far do you think you'd get dubbing yourself the Avenging Angel and thumping rioting skinheads in Coeur d'Alene with a sniper rifle? Or plinking at drunken college kids disturbing the peace?]

§ §18-4012. EXCUSABLE HOMICIDE.

Homicide is excusable in the following cases:

1. When committed by accident and misfortune in doing any lawful act by lawful means, with usual and ordinary caution, and without any unlawful intent.

2. When committed by accident and misfortune, in the heat of passion, upon any sudden and sufficient provocation, or upon a sudden combat when no undue advantage is taken nor any dangerous weapon used, and when the killing is not done in a cruel or unusual manner. [We picture some buff farm boy innocently on the way to the movies with his girlfriend. They walk past a bar and a drunken patron sucker-punches him and threatens to molest his girlfriend. The farm boy, with arm muscles bulging from lifting 100 lb bags of potatoes onto a flatbed all summer, responds by decking his drunken assailant with one mighty blow to the face. The drunken assailant later dies of a brain hemorrhage. A jury guided by an instruction based upon this statute might excuse the accidental and unfortunate death based upon the farm boy's seemingly innocent response to a sudden and unexpected assault. *Pancho's Wisdom* – Then again, they might not. Barney Buff could get himself bunked in an 8 X 10 cubicle for using excessive force. Set aside your macho, push the assailant away, leave the area and call the police if it can be done safely.]

ICJI 1514 Justifiable Homicide Defense

The defendant contends as a defense in this case that the killing was justifiable because the defendant was [description of justification; e.g., an excusable homicide such as attempting to stop the commission of a robbery].

Under the law, homicide is justifiable if . . .

[The following paragraphs in brackets would not all apply to a single case. A judge would pick the paragraph or paragraphs that best apply to any given case.]

[committed while resisting an attempt to murder any person, or to commit a felony, or to do some great bodily injury upon any person.] [See caution above and in Chapter 4 that deadly force should not be used against non-violent, non-threatening felons.]

[committed in defense of habitation, property or person, against one who manifestly intends or endeavors, by violence or surprise, to commit a felony, or against one who manifestly intends and endeavors, in a violent, riotous or tumultuous manner, to enter the habitation of another for the purpose of offering violence to any person therein. However, the bare fear of such acts is not sufficient unless the circumstances are sufficient to create such a fear in a reasonable person and the defendant acted under the influence of such fears alone.] [This paragraph corresponds to Idaho's home-defense statute (see §18-4009(2) below).]

[committed in the lawful defense of the defendant, or of a wife or husband, parent, child, master, mistress or servant of the defendant, when there is reasonable grounds to apprehend a design to commit a felony or to do some great bodily injury and imminent danger of such design being accomplished; but such person, or the person on whose behalf the defense was made, if that person was the assailant or engaged in mortal combat, must really and in good faith have endeavored to decline any further struggle before the homicide was committed. However, the bare fear of such acts is not sufficient unless the circumstances are sufficient to create such a fear in a reasonable person and the defendant acted under the influence of such fears alone.] [This paragraph covers defense of others and exceptions to self-defense. These are all explained in more detail below. Incidentally, "mistress" is simply the feminine form of "master," (probably an employer of household servants) rather than a woman in an adulterous relationship.]

[when necessarily committed in attempting, by lawful ways and means, to apprehend any person for any felony committed, or in lawfully suppressing any riot, or in lawfully keeping and preserving the peace.] [Again, we don't recommend you do any of these things using deadly force.]

The burden is on the prosecution to prove beyond a reasonable doubt that the homicide was not justifiable. If there is a reasonable doubt whether the homicide was justifiable, you must find the defendant not guilty.

ICJI 1518 Self-Defense-Reasonable Force

The kind and degree of force which a person may lawfully use in [self-defense][defense of another] are limited by what a reasonable person in the same situation as such person, seeing what that person sees and knowing what the person knows, then would believe to be necessary. Any use of force beyond that is regarded by the law as excessive. Although a person may believe that the person is acting, and may act, in [self-defense] [defense of another], the person is not justified in using a degree of force clearly in excess of that apparently and reasonably necessary under the existing facts and circumstances. [This statute incorporates the concepts of "necessary" and "excessive force" into Idaho's self-defense laws. A thorough understanding of these concepts is vital to anyone who believes he or she would be willing to use a deadly weapon in defense of self or family. Please read and ponder these topics in Chapters 3 and 4 very carefully.]

[Defense of Third Persons]

§ §19-202A. LEGAL JEOPARDY IN CASES OF SELF-DEFENSE AND DEFENSE OF OTHER THREATENED PARTIES.

No person in this state shall be placed in legal jeopardy of any kind whatsoever for protecting himself or his family by reasonable means necessary, or when coming to the aid of another whom he reasonably believes to be in imminent danger of or the victim of aggravated assault, robbery, rape, murder or other heinous crime. [The use of the phrase "aide of another" suggests that the defense of others might not be limited to just members of your family.]

§ §19-203. RESISTANCE BY OTHER PARTIES.

Any other person, in aid or defense of the person about to be injured, may make resistance sufficient to prevent the offense. [This statute allows the defense of persons not related to you by family or employment.]

§ §18-4009(3). JUSTIFIABLE HOMICIDE BY ANY PERSON.

. . .

3. When committed in the lawful defense of such person, or of a wife or husband, parent, child, master, mistress or servant of such person, when there is reasonable ground to apprehend a design to commit a felony or to do some great bodily injury, and imminent danger of such design being accomplished; but such person, or the person in whose behalf the defense was made, if he was the assailant or engaged in mortal combat, must really and in good faith have endeavored to decline any further struggle before the homicide was committed; or [This is the paragraph in the justifiable homicide statute that deals with the defense of third persons. It also requires people who start fights or agree to fight to withdraw (retreat if necessary) to avoid further risk of injury, if they expect to claim self-defense. This statute is reinforced by the case cited immediately below.]

. . .

[Exceptions to Justifiable Self-Defense][Initial Aggressor] [Provocation]

"A person is not entitled to claim self-defense or justify a homicide when he or she was the aggressor or the one who provoked the altercation in which another person is killed, unless such person in good faith first withdraws from further aggressive action." State v. Turner, 38 P. 3d 1285, 1290 (Idaho Ct. App. 2001).

[Mutual Combat]

ICJI 1521 Self-Defense-Participants in Mutual Combat Instruction No.

The right of self-defense is not available to a person who, by pre-arrangement or agreement, engages in mutual combat, unless and until the person has really and in good faith endeavored to decline further combat, and has fairly and clearly informed the adversary of a desire for peace and that the person has abandoned the contest. If, after the adversary has been so informed and given an opportunity to quit the fight, such adversary continues the combat, such continuance of the fight is a new assault by the adversary, and the person seeking to withdraw from the fight may exercise the right of self-defense. [This instruction says essentially the same thing as the statute above (18-

4009(3)), but is somewhat more explanatory. You can't claim self-defense if you agree to meet the town desperado outside Saloon Diablo at high noon for a live-ammo-fast-draw demonstration, even if he draws first. On the other hand, let's suppose you set your macho aside, text message him that you don't want to go through with the duel (so it's documented on your and his cell phone records) and he comes a gunnin' for you anyway. We suggest you try to retreat if it can be done in safety, while dialing 911. If he catches you after so many documented attempts to avoid the conflict, you should be justified in using deadly force to defend yourself. We have found that anytime it gets this complicated, you will usually be arrested and prosecuted. See Thumbs-Down Chapter 7.) *Pancho's Wisdom* – NEVER go around agreeing to fight anyone, or starting a fight. Even if you intend just a fist fight, if it escalates beyond that, you could get killed, seriously injured, prosecuted and sued. It ain't worth it Cisco.]

[Extra Exception – Fear Alone Not Sufficient]

§ §18-4010. FEAR NOT SUFFICIENT JUSTIFICATION.

A bare fear of the commission of any of the offenses mentioned in subdivisions 2 [home defense] and 3 [defense of a third person] of the preceding section [18-4009], to prevent which homicide may be lawfully committed, is not sufficient to justify it. But the circumstances must be sufficient to excite the fears of a reasonable person, and the party killing must have acted under the influence of such fears alone. [Fear alone is not enough (this statement could very well be interpreted to require an "overt act" before you use force in self-defense — see discussion in Chapter 3). Your fear must be reasonable, not eccentric. Furthermore, your fear must be the only motive, not anger or revenge. **Example** – You walk into the Lost River Inn in Arco. Your big fat neighbor who has been accusing you of stealing his irrigation shares is carving up a rib eye. He's been deer hunting and his 30-06 is perched in his gun rack just outside the door. He notices you walk in and threatens, "As soon as I finish this delectable piece of Black Angus, I'm going to get my rifle and stop your thievin' ways once and for all." You take that as an imminent threat even though you know it will take the lard @$$ fifteen minutes to unwedge his belly from between the table and the back of the booth. So you draw your Peacemaker and do what witnesses claim was a western version of the restaurant scene in the Godfather. Did Dumbo threaten you with death or serious bodily injury? Yes. Did it frighten you? Yes. Was the danger imminent? No, and although he had a gun in the truck, as he was sitting there, he was unarmed. Are you guilty of something ugly like murder? Probably.]

[Exceptions to the Exceptions] [Withdraw and Communicate]

"A person is not entitled to claim self-defense or justify a homicide when he or she was the aggressor or the one who provoked the altercation in which another person is killed, unless such person in good faith first withdraws from further aggressive action." *State v. Turner,* 38 P. 3d 1285, 1290 (Idaho Ct. App. 2001). [This provision appears in most states' self-defense laws. See more detailed discussion in Chapter 4.]

[No Duty to Retreat]

ICJI 1519 Self-Defense – Duty To Retreat

In the exercise of the right of self-defense or defense of another, a person need not retreat. He may stand his ground and defend himself or a third person by the use of all force and means which would appear to be necessary to a reasonable person in a similar situation and with similar knowledge; and a person may pursue the attacker until he or the third person has been secured from danger if that course likewise appears reasonably necessary. This law applies even though the person being attacked or third person being defended might more easily have gained safety by flight or by withdrawing from the scene. [Idaho's make-my-day law is typical for many western and southern states. It is probably somewhat punitive rather than purely defensive. Career criminals are more likely to be killed on the job in a western or southern state with a no-retreat law. We couldn't find an Idaho statute or case that was as clear as this jury instruction.]

[Defense of Person(s)s in Special Places – Habitation]

§ §18-4009(2). JUSTIFIABLE HOMICIDE BY ANY PERSON.

Homicide is also justifiable when committed by any person in either of the following cases:

2. When committed in defense of habitation, property or person, against one who manifestly intends or endeavors, by violence or surprise, to commit a felony, or against one who manifestly intends and endeavors, in a violent, riotous or tumultuous manner, to enter the habitation of another for the purpose of offering violence to any person therein; or, [This is Idaho's home-defense statute. The triggering language that authorizes the use of deadly force is that the assailant attempts to commit a violent felony in one's home or against him or simply tries to enter the home to commit "violence" against a person in the home. The second phrase suggests, like in other western states, that if someone breaks into your home and you fear "violence" from that person, whether he possesses a deadly weapon or not, you may use deadly force.]

[Duty to Retreat From Special Places]

[See jury instruction and explanation under [*No Duty to Retreat*] above.]

[Civil Liability]

§ §6-808. CIVIL IMMUNITY FOR SELF-DEFENSE.

(1) A person who uses force as justified in section 18-4009, Idaho Code, or as otherwise permitted in sections 19-201 through 19-205, Idaho Code, is immune from any civil liability for the use of such force except when the person knew or reasonably should have known that the person against whom the force was used was a law enforcement officer acting in the capacity of his or her official duties. [If you win your criminal case, you can't be sued in a civil case unless your victim was a law enforcement officer acting in his or her official capacity.]

(2) The court shall award reasonable attorney's fees and costs incurred by the defendant in any civil action if the court finds that the defendant is immune from such action pursuant to this section. [If you get sued after you win your criminal case, and you have to hire an attorney to get the civil case dismissed, you can collect fees from the person who sues you.]

(3) As used in this section, "law enforcement officer" means any court personnel, sheriff, constable, peace officer, state police officer, correctional officer, probation or parole official, prosecuting attorney, city attorney, attorney general, or their employees or agents, or any other person charged with the duty of enforcement of the criminal, traffic or penal laws of this state or any other law enforcement personnel or peace officer as defined in chapter 51, title 19, Idaho Code.

[Defense of Personal Property]

ICJI 1522 Defense Of Property – Reasonable Force

When conditions are present which under the law justify a person in using force in defense of [pick the one that applies:] [another] [the person] [the person's family] [property in the person's lawful possession], that person may use such degree and extent of force as would appear to be reasonably necessary to prevent the threatened injury. Reasonableness is to be judged from the viewpoint of a reasonable person placed in the same position and seeing and knowing what the defendant then saw and knew. Any use of force beyond that limit is unjustified.

[We suggest that you NEVER use any type of deadly force whatsoever in defense of your property. The following is the Idaho Supreme Court approving a jury instruction (more explicit than the one we included) that does not tolerate threatening the use of a deadly weapon to protect property or evict a trespasser.]

"In defense of goods or possessions, if a man endeavor to deprive another of them, the other may lay hands on him to protect his goods or possessions. However, this does not authorize the defendant to use a deadly weapon to protect his goods or possessions. . . To merely go upon the lands of another will not justify or excuse a resort to the use of a deadly weapon to drive the intruder off." *State v. Mathewson*, 472 P.2d 638, 641 (Idaho 1970).

[TEMPLATE Topics We Could Not Find Explained in Statutes or Cases]

(For each of these topics that we could not find addressed in your state's statutes or cases, we suggest you review the same topics in the subchapters of surrounding states. Your state's courts may look to the law of neighboring states to see how their courts and legislatures have treated that particular self-defense issue.)

[Committing Felony or Unlawful Act]

[Co-Habitants; Co-Employees – Duty to Retreat]

[Presumption of Reasonableness in Special Places]

[Reckless Injury to Innocent Third Parties]

[Helpful Definitions Relating to this State's Self-Defense Statutes]

Pancho terrorizing civilized folks in Sandy, Utah, with the Sheriff on his heels. (Photo courtesy of the Cold Water Gang, Tremonton, Utah.)

ILLINOIS

Introduction

Illinois' self-defense statutes do not cover many of the issues the statutes in other states address. Therefore, the Illinois courts have had to fill in what the statutes do not define. For example, there is nothing in these statutes that explains whether there is a duty to retreat either in or outside of a person's home. The courts have, however, decided that there is no duty to retreat as long as the defender has a right to be where the defensive incident occurs. The rule evolved through several court cases and has now become part of the pattern jury instructions accepted by the appellate courts of the state.

Key: ■ commentary ■ original statutes, cases or jury instructions

[Defense of Self and Others] [Non-Deadly Force]
[Defense of Third Persons]

§ 720 ILLINOIS COMPILED STATUTES (ILCS) 5/7-1.
Use of force in defense of person.

(a) A person is justified in the use of force against another when and to the extent that he reasonably believes that such conduct is necessary to defend himself or another against such other's imminent use of unlawful force. . .

[Deadly Force] [Use of Deadly Force to Prevent Serious Felonies]

[(a) continued . . .] However, he is justified in the use of force which is intended or likely to cause death or great bodily harm only if he reasonably believes that such force is necessary to prevent imminent death or great bodily harm to himself or another, or the commission of a forcible felony. [You may use deadly force if it is necessary to prevent the imminent use of deadly force against you or a third person or to prevent the commission of a forcible felony. Forcible felonies include treason, murder, criminal sexual assault, robbery, burglary, kidnapping, etc. For a full list and summary of these felonies see **[Helpful Definitions Relating to this State's Self-Defense Statutes]** below.]

[Exceptions to Justifiable Self-Defense] [Mutual Combat]

"This case appears to be a mutual combat situation, where both parties fought willingly upon equal terms. The perfect defense of self-defense is not available in such a situation." *People v. White*, 687 N.E.2d 1179, 1182 (Ill.App. 4 Dist. 1997). [Don't agree to a fight if you expect to claim self-defense later.]

[Initial Aggressor]

"It is well accepted that in order to establish a claim of self-defense, a defendant must prove that unlawful force was used against him, he was not the aggressor, he believed that the danger of harm was imminent, force was necessary to avert the danger, and the amount of force used was necessary." *People v. Williams*, 617 N.E.2d 87, 97 (Ill.App. 1 Dist. 1993). [If you start a fight in which someone is injured or killed, you cannot win a not-guilty verdict on the theory of self-defense.]

[Provocation] [Committing Felony or Unlawful Act]

§ **720 ILCS 5/7-4.**
Use of force by aggressor.

The justification described in the preceding Sections of this Article is not available to a person who:

(a) Is attempting to commit, committing, or escaping after the commission of, a forcible felony; or [You cannot rob a gas station, kill the attendant because he tries to stop the robbery and then claim self-defense when you are prosecuted.]

(b) Initially provokes the use of force against himself, with the intent to use such force as an excuse to inflict bodily harm upon the assailant; [**Example:** You hate your neighbor who loves knives and has a short temper. You kick him in the shin hoping he will pull a knife so you can shoot him. You can't instigate such an attack on yourself for the purpose of injuring or killing someone and then win on the theory of self-defense.] or

(c) Otherwise initially provokes the use of force against himself, unless:

[Exceptions to the Exceptions] [Withdraw and Communicate]

(1) Such force is so great that he reasonably believes that he is in imminent danger of death or great bodily harm, and that he has exhausted every reasonable means to escape such danger other than the use of force which is likely to cause death or great bodily harm to the assailant; or [**Example:** You're at the Chicago Dog stand at the mall and notice the new guy on campus who has been trying to get your girlfriend to go out with him. You shove him and tell him to stay away from her, hoping he'll take a swing at you so you can rearrange his pretty nose. Instead, he pulls out a knife and chases you into an alley. You yell you don't want to fight and retreat until you come to a dead end. You beg him not to hurt you. As he makes his final lunge, intending to slice you from your diaphragm to your belly button, you end his murderous rampage by thrusting a couple of nails sticking out of a broken pallet board into his left temple. You will probably be arrested and prosecuted because you started the fight, but you might be found not guilty by reason of self-defense under this exception.]

(2) In good faith, he withdraws from physical contact with the assailant and indicates clearly to the assailant that he desires to withdraw and terminate the use of

force, but the assailant continues or resumes the use of force. [The exceptions here are pretty standard to the exceptions we have mentioned in Chapter 4. These almost always result in arrest and prosecution, but sometimes, if a jury believes you retreated in good faith and your opponent became the aggressor, you can win the case on the theory of self-defense. But this rarely happens without paying a fortune in attorney fees and spending three years in litigation thinking you might end up rotting in prison.]

[No Duty to Retreat – Generally]

"Although one does not have to retreat from a place where he has a right to be, the nonaggressor may use force likely to cause death or serious bodily harm only if he reasonably believes that the imminently threatened force had placed him in danger of death or great bodily harm." *People v. Manley*, 584 N.E.2d 477, 491 (Ill.App. 1 Dist. 1991). [There is no duty to retreat in Illinois for those who are in a place where they have a right to be AND who are guilt free. If you don't meet this criteria then you must exhaust all efforts to avoid using force, especially deadly force.]

[Defense of Person(s) in Special Places – Dwelling]

§ 720 ILCS 5/7-2.
Use of force in defense of dwelling.

(a) A person is justified in the use of force against another when and to the extent that he reasonably believes that such conduct is necessary to prevent or terminate such other's unlawful entry into or attack upon a dwelling. [The definition of dwelling is fairly broad. It includes places where one lives for a reasonable amount of time, for example, a tent, RV, trailer etc.] However, he is justified in the use of force which is intended or likely to cause death or great bodily harm only if: [The "only if" in this subsection introduces limitations to the use of deadly force in your home or temporary home. There is no authorization to use deadly force if you don't comply with the following:]

(1) The entry is made or attempted in a violent, riotous, or tumultuous manner, and he reasonably believes that such force is necessary to prevent an assault upon, or offer of personal violence to, him or another then in the dwelling, or

(2) He reasonably believes that such force is necessary to prevent the commission of a felony in the dwelling.

[You can use deadly force to keep an unlawful intruder from violently breaking into your home if you reasonably believe it's necessary to keep him from hurting someone. Do you see how the words "prevent an assault upon, or offer of personal violence" create a lower threshold for the use of deadly force than the phrase "prevent serious bodily injury or death?" It doesn't matter that the intruder is unarmed, if it appears he is attempting to cause physical harm to someone in the home. The Illinois criminal jury instructions confirm our interpretation of this lower threshold for the use of deadly force in the home. See Ill. Pattern Jury Instruction–Criminal 24-25.07 (4th ed.). This lower threshold could provide a much-needed tactical advantage for Illinois citizens whose homes are violently invaded. In broad daylight, it is often difficult to identify what's in a person's hands. At night, it's nearly impossible without seeing the object up close and personal. By the time the homeowner is able to identify and object as a firearm, he or she could be shot and killed.

There are several hidden legal traps lurking in this home-defense statute. Notice the entry must be unlawful. If the person is a co-tenant, landlord with the right of entry, a family member (Heaven forbid) or was invited in, the entry is not unlawful. If you are violently attacked by someone whose entry is not unlawful, the threshold reverts back to "an imminent threat of serious injury or death."

Another potential hidden trap exists in paragraph (2) above. The language of that paragraph seems to authorize the use of deadly force to prevent any felony. However, we caution you not to use deadly force against felonies that do not involve a threat of physical harm. Refer to our explanation in Chapter 4 under the heading [**Use of Deadly Force to Prevent Serious Felonies**]. **Example:** You are a big shot in your voting district. A political candidate drops by your home and you invite him in. He offers you $100,000 to endorse him publically. You tell him you would never do such a thing and ask him to leave. He refuses. Assuming the attempted bribe is a felony, can you legally raise his blood lead levels with your Luger? No! He is not committing a violent felony. Furthermore, his entry was lawful. You invited him in.]

[No Duty to Retreat From Special Places]
[Although we could not find any statutes or case law expressly stating you have no duty to retreat from your home, we are under the impression that the no-retreat rule stated above applies in the home as well as out of the home. The only requirement in the Illinois jury instruction saying there is no duty to retreat is that one not be the initial aggressor. Therefore, as long as you are not the initial aggressor or have not provoked the use of force against yourself, you should not have to retreat from your own home. The jury instruction we refer to states:]

24-25.09X NON-INITIAL AGGRESSOR.
No Duty To Retreat.

A person who has not initially provoked the use of force against himself has no duty to attempt to escape the danger before using force against the aggressor.

[Civil Liability]

§ 720 ILCS 5/7-1 (2) (b).
Use of force in defense of person.

. . .

(b) In no case shall any act involving the use of force justified under this Section give rise to any claim or liability brought by or on behalf of any person acting within the definition of "aggressor" set forth in Section 7-4 of this Article, or the estate, spouse, or other family member of such a person, against the person or estate of the person using such justified force, unless the use of force involves willful or wanton misconduct. [This provision is a civil immunity clause. It is repeated word for word at the end of statutes 7-2 and 7-3. If you are justified in using force to defend yourself from an aggressor, neither he nor his heirs, if he dies, should be able to win a civil suit against you.]

[Defense of Property]

§ 720 ILCS 5/7-3.
Use of force in defense of other property.

(a) A person is justified in the use of force against another when and to the extent that he reasonably believes that such conduct is necessary to prevent or terminate such other's trespass on or other tortious or criminal interference with either real property (other than a dwelling) or personal property, lawfully in his possession or in the possession of another who is a member of his immediate family or household or of a person whose property he has a legal duty to protect. However, he is justified in the use of force which is intended or likely to cause death or great bodily harm only if he reasonably believes that such force is necessary to prevent the commission of a forcible felony. [Caution: The inclusion of the concept of deadly force in this provision could be misleading if not understood correctly. The event that triggers the right to use deadly force is NOT the theft or interference with property, it is the commission of a forcible felony by an intruder or thief. Otherwise, deadly force cannot be used. We strongly advise against citizen arrests or citizens chasing lawbreakers except perhaps to carefully follow with a cell phone to keep police informed of the whereabouts of such persons. These types of incidents can too easily explode into a major confrontation with deadly weapons. Your big screen, stereo, iPod, and even your Beamer may not be worth the money you'll spend on attorney fees if you send some thief to the Promised Land courtesy of your Kimber.]

(b) In no case shall any act involving the use of force justified under this Section give rise to any claim or liability brought by or on behalf of any person acting within the definition of "aggressor" set forth in Section 7-4 of this Article, or the estate, spouse, or other family member of such a person, against the person or estate of the person using such justified force, unless the use of force involves willful or wanton misconduct. [After reading this subsection you say, "Good, I can't be sued." Unfortunately this statute has an easy loophole for personal injury attorneys. If you empty your hi-cap Glock into Gone-in-Sixty-Seconds-Gus as he speeds away into heavy traffic, his attorney will simply allege "willful and wanton misconduct." This is even more likely if your stray bullets hit an innocent person.]

[HELPFUL DEFINITIONS RELATING TO THIS STATE'S SELF-DEFENSE STATUTES]

720 ILCS 5/2-6 "Dwelling"

(a) Except as otherwise provided in subsection (b) of this Section, "dwelling" means a building or portion thereof, a tent, a vehicle, or other enclosed space which is used or intended for use as a human habitation, home or residence.

(b) For the purposes of Section 19-3 of this Code, "dwelling" means a house, apartment, mobile home, trailer, or other living quarters in which at the time of the alleged offense the owners or occupants actually reside or in their absence intend within a reasonable period of time to reside.

- **Felonies Mentioned Above (Justifying the Use of Deadly Force) –**

    - **Arson** – [Destroying or damaging real property by fire or explosive without consent.] **720 ILCS 5/20-1. Also see 720 ILCS 5/20-1.2 & 1.3.**

    - **Aggravated arson** – [Destroying or damaging, by fire or explosion, any building, structure house trailer, watercraft, motor vehicle, or railroad car in which the actor knows or has reason to know that it is occupied by a person or if a victim suffers great physical harm. Also, if a fireman, policeman, or correctional officer who is present at the scene acting in the line of duty is injured as a result of the fire or explosion.] **720 ILCS 5/20-1.1.**

    - **Aggravated battery** – [Knowingly or intentionally causing great bodily harm or permanent disability or disfigurement.] **720 ILCS 5/12-4.**

    - **Aggravated criminal sexual assault** – [Committing a sexual assault while threatening with a dangerous weapon, or in the commission of a felony, against a person 60 or older, against a mentally deficient person or child under 9 or 13 years of age depending upon the circumstances , or having caused bodily harm to the victim.] **720 ILCS 5/12-14.**

    - **Aggravated kidnapping** – [Kidnapping for ransom, taking someone under the age of 13 years or mentally retarded person. Also, if the offender inflicts great bodily harm or commits a felony upon his victim; using a weapon or concealing identity in the process of the kidnapping.] **720 ILCS 5/10-2.**

    - **Burglary** – [Unlawfully entering without authority a building, housetrailer, watercraft, aircraft, motor vehicle, railroad car or any part of one with the intent to commit a felony or theft therein.] **720 ILCS 5/19-1.**

    - **Criminal sexual assault** – [Any unlawful sexual penetration by use of force or upon someone or one who is unable to understand the nature of the act. This also seems to include incest.] **720 ILCS 5/12-13.**

    - **First degree murder** – [Unlawful intentional killing of a person. Also, intentionally causing serious bodily harm that is likely to and results in the death of a person.] **720 ILCS 5/9-1.**

    - **Kidnapping** – [Knowingly confining a person against their will. Also would include luring by deceit or enticement person with the intent to confine them against their will.] **720 ILCS 5/10-1.**

    - **Predatory criminal sexual assault of a child** – [A person 17 years or older, by use of force, threatens or by the use of a controlled substance (e.g., drugs), commits an act of sexual penetration upon a victim under the age of 13.] **720 ILCS 5/12-14.1.**

- **Residential burglary** – [Knowingly without authority entering or remaining in a dwelling of another with the intent to commit a felony or theft therein.] **720 ILCS 5/19-3.**
- **Robbery** – [Taking property from a person by force or threat.] **720 ILCS 5/ 18-1.**
- **Second degree murder** – [Unlawful killing of a person. This would include situations involving sudden intense passion or where the offender was seriously provoked and the response results in an accidental or negligent death of another.] **720 ILCS 5/9-2.**
- **Treason** – [Treason against the State. Realistically don't worry about this one. Just don't try to be a "hero" and assassinate someone for political reasons and claim it was to prevent treason. That'd just be plain stupid.] **720 ILCS 5/ 30-1.**

720 ILCS 5/7-8 – Force likely to cause death or great bodily harm.

(a) Force which is likely to cause death or great bodily harm, within the meaning of Sections 7-5 and 7-6 includes:

(1) The firing of a firearm in the direction of the person to be arrested, even though no intent exists to kill or inflict great bodily harm; and

(2) The firing of a firearm at a vehicle in which the person to be arrested is riding.

(b) A peace officer's discharge of a firearm using ammunition designed to disable or control an individual without creating the likelihood of death or great bodily harm shall not be considered force likely to cause death or great bodily harm within the meaning of Sections 7-5 and 7-6.

- **Forcible felony** – means treason, first degree murder, second degree murder, predatory criminal sexual assault of a child, aggravated criminal sexual assault, criminal sexual assault, robbery, burglary, residential burglary, aggravated arson, arson, aggravated kidnapping, kidnapping, aggravated battery resulting in great bodily harm or permanent disability or disfigurement and any other felony which involves the use or threat of physical force or violence against any individual. **720 ILCS 5/2-8.**
- **Reasonable belief** or **reasonably believes** – means that the person concerned, acting as a reasonable man, believes that the described facts exist. **720 ILCS 5/2-19.**

[TEMPLATE Topics We Could Not Find Explained in Statutes or Cases]

(For each of these topics that we could not find addressed in your state's statutes or cases, we suggest you review the same topics in the subchapters of surrounding states. Your state's courts may look to the law of neighboring states to see how their courts and legislatures have treated that particular self-defense issue.)

[Co-Habitants; Co-Employees – Duty to Retreat]

[Presumption of Reasonableness in Special Places]

[Reckless Injury to Innocent Third Parties]

Most of the template topics are contained on one Indiana Statute, § 35-41-3-2. "Use of force to protect person or property." It seems like Indiana legislators have crammed as many self-defense topics as possible into one statute, even covering some rare situations like hijackings. For quick reference, we have broken up IC § 35-41-3-2 to conform to the order of the template topics.

Key: ■ commentary ■ original statutes, cases or jury instructions

[Defense of Self and Others] [Non-Deadly Force]
[Defense of Third Persons]

§ INDIANA CODE (IC) § 35-41-3-2 (a)

(a) A person is justified in using reasonable force against another person to protect the person or a third person from what the person reasonably believes to be the imminent use of unlawful force. However, a person:

[Deadly Force] [Use of Deadly Force to Prevent Serious Felonies]

(1) is justified in using deadly force; and

(2) does not have a duty to retreat; [See retreat section for more information.] if the person reasonably believes that that force is necessary to prevent serious bodily injury to the person or a third person or the commission of a forcible felony. ... [The deadly force you use must have been necessary to prevent serious injury to yourself or another. Forcible felony "means a felony that involves the use or threat of force against a human being, or in which there is imminent danger of bodily injury to a human being." See **[Helpful Definitions Relating to this State's Self-Defense Statutes]** section below.]

. . .

[Exceptions to Justifiable Self-Defense]

§ INDIANA CODE (IC) § 35-41-2 (e)

(e) Notwithstanding subsections (a), (b), and (c), a person is not justified in using force if:

[Committing Felony or Unlawful Act]

(1) the person is committing or is escaping after the commission of a crime; [You're robbing a jewelry store and the owner pulls a gun on you. You can't shoot at him and then claim it was in self-defense.]

[Provocation]

(2) the person provokes unlawful action by another person with intent to cause bodily injury to the other person; or [Don't shove someone, hoping he'll shove you back so you can break his nose. If you do, you won't be able to beat the assault charge on the grounds of self-defense.]

[Initial Aggressor] [Mutual Combat]

(3) the person has entered into combat with another person or is the initial aggressor . . . [Don't go starting fights or agreeing to them and then think you can claim self-defense when things get ugly.]

[Exceptions to the Exceptions] [Withdraw and Communicate]

[(3) continued . . .] unless the person withdraws from the encounter and communicates to the other person the intent to do so and the other person nevertheless continues or threatens to continue unlawful action. [If you start a fight or agree to fight, you might be able to claim self-defense if you stop fighting, retreat and make it very plain to your opponent you don't want to continue to fight. Once you have done that, and your opponent continues, he then becomes the aggressor. You then regain the right to defend yourself. We have found, however, that when it gets this complicated, you will be arrested and prosecuted so the jury can sort out the complicated details.]

[No Duty to Retreat – Generally]

§ IC § 35-41-3-2 (a)

(a) A person is justified in using reasonable force against another person to protect the person or a third person from what the person reasonably believes to be the imminent use of unlawful force. However, a person:

(1) is justified in using deadly force; and

(2) does not have a duty to retreat; if the person reasonably believes that that force is necessary to prevent serious bodily injury to the person or a third person or the commission of a forcible felony. [While some states don't require you to retreat when using non-deadly force, and to retreat before using deadly force, this statute seems to do just the opposite. It expressly allows you to stand your ground when threatened with deadly force or a forcible felony, but it does not cover the issue of retreat when confronted with non-deadly force. The force used must be necessary and reasonable. See discussion in Chapter 3.]

. . .

[Defense of Person(s) in Special Places – Home, Curtilage and Occupied Motor Vehicle] [No Duty to Retreat From Special Places – Home, Curtilage and Occupied Motor Vehicle]

§ IC § 35-41-3-2 (b)

. . .

(b) A person:

(1) is justified in using reasonable force, including deadly force, against another person; and

(2) does not have a duty to retreat; if the person reasonably believes that the force is necessary to prevent or terminate the other person's unlawful entry of or attack on the person's dwelling, curtilage, or occupied motor vehicle. [This home-defense statute is so protective of home owners that we checked the jury instructions to make sure the courts hadn't "watered it down." To our amazement, the jury instructions have incorporated the language of the statute without any major changes. Because of the relatively few requirements and broad language, it is among the strongest home-defense statutes in the country. Notice it does not require a "violent or tumultuous entry" or the "commission of a felony" before deadly force can be used like in many states. Furthermore, it includes the "curtilage" or space immediately around the home or dwelling.

Despite the strength of this self-defense provision, Indiana jurors are still convicting people of murder for defending their homes and occupied vehicles if there are enough thumbs-down factors (See the summaries of the cases, *Hood v. State*, 877 N.E.2d 492 (Ind.App. 2007), (defendant convicted of murder even though he was attacked while in his vehicle), *Birdsong v. State*, 685 N.E.2d 42 (Ind. 1997), (Ind.App. 2007) Chapter 7) (defendant convicted of murder of two persons who forced their way into defendant's apartment with a gun and a can of bug spray. Excessive force seems to have been a big factor in this case.).]

. . .

[Civil Liability]

§ IC § 35-41-3-2 (a) (2)

(a) (2) . . . No person in this state shall be placed in legal jeopardy of any kind whatsoever for protecting the person or a third person by reasonable means necessary. [This appears to be legal immunity against both criminal actions and civil liability provided your actions were completely reasonable and necessary in defense of self or others.]

. . .

[Defense of Property]

§ IC § 35-41-3-2 (c)

. . .

(c) With respect to property other than a dwelling, curtilage, or an occupied motor vehicle, a person is justified in using reasonable force against another person if the person reasonably believes that the force is necessary to immediately prevent or terminate the other person's trespass on or criminal interference with property lawfully in the person's possession, lawfully in possession of a member of the person's immediate family, or belonging to a person whose property the person has authority to protect. [You can use reasonable force, but not deadly force, to keep people from trespassing on your real estate or real estate you are authorized to defend. In *Nantz v. State*, 740 N.E.2d 1276 (Ind.App. 2001) an Indiana jury convicted a drunken (see "Thumbs-Down" Chapter 7 below) property owner of "pointing a firearm" at a trespasser, in spite of the language of this paragraph, and the Indiana Court of Appeals upheld the conviction.]

However, a person:

(1) is justified in using deadly force; and

(2) does not have a duty to retreat; only if that force is justified under subsection (a) [Requiring a threat of deadly force or the commission of a felony before the defender can respond with deadly force when not in his home, curtilage or occupied vehicle].

[Hijacking an Airplane] . . . [Seriously]

§ IC § 35-41-3-2 (d)

. . .

(d) A person is justified in using reasonable force, including deadly force, against another person and does not have a duty to retreat if the person reasonably believes that the force is necessary to prevent or stop the other person from hijacking, attempting to hijack, or otherwise seizing or attempting to seize unlawful control of an aircraft in flight. For purposes of this subsection, an aircraft is considered to be in flight while the aircraft is:

(1) on the ground in Indiana:

(A) after the doors of the aircraft are closed for takeoff; and

(B) until the aircraft takes off;

(2) in the airspace above Indiana; or

(3) on the ground in Indiana:

(A) after the aircraft lands; and

(B) before the doors of the aircraft are opened after landing.

[Oh, my, this subparagraph begs for commentary. We're taking it at face value and assume it applies to both private and commercial aircraft. Of course, one is not allowed to take anything that could be considered a deadly weapon onto a commercial airliner, so the justification to use deadly force seems somewhat hollow unless you are Steven Seagal, Chuck Norris, Jackie Chan or Hulk Hogan!]

. . .

§ IC § 35-41-3-2 (f)

. . .

(f) Notwithstanding subsection (d), a person is not justified in using force if the person:

(1) is committing, or is escaping after the commission of, a crime;

(2) provokes unlawful action by another person, with intent to cause bodily injury to the other person; or

(3) continues to combat another person after the other person withdraws from the encounter and communicates the other person's intent to stop hijacking, attempting to hijack, or otherwise seizing or attempting to seize unlawful control of an aircraft in flight.

[Should you find yourself in a situation where a hijacking is taking place, and you're in a position to take on the hijackers (1) don't be a criminal at the time (we find this a bit bizarre—can't criminals be heroes too? Wouldn't we pat them on the back if, even though breaking parole by getting on the plane, they saved everyone by subduing hijackers?) (2) Don't provoke someone else with the intent to harm them (this is also very strange... don't provoke the hijackers with the intent to hurt them? As in don't walk up to them and pull their whiskers in the hopes they'll lash out so you can hurt them?) and (3) don't keep beating them once they say "okay, please sir, I don't want to hijack anymore."]

[HELPFUL DEFINITIONS RELATING TO THIS STATE'S SELF-DEFENSE STATUTES]

- **Bodily injury** – means any impairment of physical condition, including physical pain. **IC § 35-41-1-4.**

- **Deadly force** – means force that creates a substantial risk of serious bodily injury. **IC § 35-41-1-7.**

- **Dwelling** – means a building, structure, or other enclosed space, permanent or temporary, movable or fixed, that is a person's home or place of lodging. **IC § 35-41-1-10.**

- **Property** – means anything of value. The term includes:
  - a gain or advantage or anything that might reasonably be regarded as such by the beneficiary;
  - real property, personal property, money, labor, and services;
  - intangibles;
  - commercial instruments;
  - written instruments concerning labor, services, or property;
  - written instruments otherwise of value to the owner, such as a public record, deed, will, credit card, or letter of credit;
  - a signature to a written instrument;
  - extension of credit;
  - trade secrets;
  - contract rights, choses-in-action, and other interests in or claims to wealth;
  - electricity, gas, oil, and water;
  - captured or domestic animals, birds, and fish;
  - food and drink; and
  - human remains.

- Property is that "of another person" if the other person has a possessory or proprietary interest in it, even if an accused person also has an interest in that property. **IC § 35-41-1-23.**

- **Felonies Mentioned Above –**
  - **Airplane hijacking** – [Knowingly or intentionally disrupting the operation of an aircraft by threat or violence.] **IC § 35-47-6-1.6.**

- **Forcible felony** – means a felony that involves the use or threat of force against a human being, or in which there is imminent danger of bodily injury to a human being. **IC § 35-41-1-11.**

- **Serious bodily injury** – means bodily injury that creates a substantial risk of death or that causes serious permanent disfigurement, unconsciousness, extreme pain, permanent or protracted loss or impairment of the function of a bodily member or organ, or loss of a fetus. **IC § 35-41-1-25.**

- **Vehicle** – means a device for transportation by land, water, or air. The term includes mobile equipment with provision for transport of an operator. **IC § 35-41-1-28.**

[TEMPLATE Topics We Could Not Find Explained in Statutes or Cases]

(For each of these topics that we could not find addressed in your state's statutes or cases, we suggest you review the same topics in the subchapters of surrounding states. Your state's courts may look to the law of neighboring states to see how their courts and legislatures have treated that particular self-defense issue.)

[Co-Habitants; Co-Employees – Duty to Retreat]

[Presumption of Reasonableness in Special Places]

[Reckless Injury to Innocent Third Parties]

Pancho's Wisdom

You just might be a Gunnut if . . . you have a life membership in a firearms training resort.

Key: ■ commentary ■ original statutes, cases or jury instructions

[Defense of Self and Others] [Non-Deadly Force]
[Defense of Third Persons]

§ 704.3 DEFENSE OF SELF OR ANOTHER

A person is justified in the use of reasonable force when the person reasonably believes that such force is necessary to defend oneself or another from any imminent use of unlawful force.

§ 704.1. REASONABLE FORCE

"Reasonable force" is that force and no more which a reasonable person, in like circumstances, would judge to be necessary to prevent an injury or loss and can include deadly force if it is reasonable to believe that such force is necessary to avoid injury or risk to one's life or safety or the life or safety of another, or it is reasonable to believe that such force is necessary to resist a like force or threat . . . [This is the standard for the state of Iowa, remember this definition whenever you see the words "reasonable force" below.]

[Deadly Force] [Duty to Retreat – Generally – Yes]
[No Duty to Retreat From Special Places – Home or Workplace]
[§ 704.1 continued . . .] Reasonable force, including deadly force, may be used even if an alternative course of action is available if the alternative entails a risk to life or safety, or the life or safety of a third party, or requires one to abandon or retreat from one's dwelling or place of business or employment. [You have a duty to retreat when outside of your home if it can be done without risk to you or the person you may be defending. However, you are not required to retreat from your home or workplace.]

"To justify homicide on the ground that it was committed in self-defense, four elements must be present: (1) the slayer must not be the aggressor in provoking or continuing the difficulty that resulted in the homicide; (2) he must retreat as far as is reasonable and safe before taking his adversary's life, except in his home or place of business; (3) he must actually and honestly believe he is in imminent danger of death or great bodily harm and that the action he takes is necessary for self-preservation-this danger need not be real, but only thought to be real in the slayer's mind, acting as a reasonable prudent person under the circumstances; (4) he must have reasonable grounds for such relief." *State v. Badgett*, 167 N.W.2d 680, 683 (Iowa 1969). [This case confirms the rules stated above and dissects them even further. Notice the requirement that you don't start or continue the fight that resulted in the killing. If you do, a jury will be told that they cannot find you innocent by reason of self-defense.]

[Use of Deadly Force to Prevent Serious Felonies]

§ 704.7 RESISTING FORCIBLE FELONY

A person who knows that a forcible felony is being perpetrated is justified in using, against the perpetrator, reasonable force to prevent the completion of that felony. [See definition of "forcible felony" below. Most states authorize the use of deadly force to stop the progression of a forcible felony. This statute does not expressly go that far. It does not say you can use deadly force to stop a forcible felony. We could not find any cases where informing the jury of this rule made any difference. It leaves us wondering why the Iowa Legislature passed the law in the first place inasmuch as it does not expressly give a defender any additional privilege to use deadly force when confronted by a criminal committing a forcible felony.]

[Exceptions to Justifiable Self-Defense]

§ 704.6 WHEN DEFENSE NOT AVAILABLE

The defense of justification is not available to the following:

[Committing Felony or Unlawful Act]

1. One who is participating in a forcible felony, or riot, or a duel.

[Provocation]

2. One who initially provokes the use of force against oneself, with the intent to use such force as an excuse to inflict injury on the assailant.

[Initial Aggressor]

3. One who initially provokes the use of force against oneself by one's unlawful acts, unless:

[Exceptions to the Exceptions]

a. Such force is grossly disproportionate to the provocation, and is so great that the person reasonably believes that the person is in imminent danger of death or serious injury or [You shove someone for cutting in front of you while waiting in line at the movie theater. He pulls an Uzi submachine gun out of his black trench coat and threatens to shoot you. This subsection says you can respond with deadly force. Whenever you initiate a conflict using physical force, however, you run the risk of arrest and prosecution.]

[Withdraw and Communicate]

b. The person withdraws from physical contact with the other and indicates clearly to the other that the person desires to terminate the conflict but the other continues or resumes the use of force. [This is the standard "exception to the exception;" see discussion in Chapter 4.]

[These exceptions are warnings that if you are at all responsible for starting, continuing or escalating a fight, you run the risk of being found legally responsible for whatever results. If a person dies, you could be found guilty of murder or manslaughter. If he does not die, but is seriously injured, you could be found guilty of an assault that is classified as a felony or attempted murder. If you are going to carry weapons for self-defense, please, leave your machismo in your gun safe.]

§ 704.1. REASONABLE FORCE

"... Reasonable force, including deadly force, may be used even if an alternative course of action is available if the alternative entails a risk to life or safety, or the life or safety of a third party..." [This is a confusing way of saying you have a duty to retreat unless you can't do so in safety. So simply put, you have to retreat if you can retreat safely.]

[Co-habitants – Duty to Retreat – No]

"(T)he fact that the assailant is also an occupant of the home, with an equal right there, does not put upon the one assaulted any duty to retreat." State v. Jacoby, 260 N.W.2d 828, 835 (Iowa 1977). [You don't have to retreat from a co-habitant in your own home. All other restrictions on the use of force would apply, including the requirement that you only use reasonable, necessary force.]

[Civil Liability]

§ 707.6. CIVIL LIABILITY

No person who injures the aggressor through application of reasonable force in defense of the person's person or property may be held civilly liable for such injury.

No person who injures the aggressor through application of reasonable force in defense of a second person may be held civilly liable for such injury.

[You won't be held civilly liable for acting in justifiable self-defense or defense of another person.]

[Defense of Property]

§ 704.4 DEFENSE OF PROPERTY

A person is justified in the use of reasonable force to prevent or terminate criminal interference with the person's possession or other right in property. Nothing in this section authorizes the use of any spring gun or trap which is left unattended and unsupervised and which is placed for the purpose of preventing or terminating criminal interference with the possession of or other right in property. [This code section is similar to other states in that it does not give a property owner the right to use deadly force to protect one's property. It also is careful not to authorize the use of any spring gun or trap, which devices are discouraged and outlawed in most states with some exceptions (see Hawaii's code [Defense of Special Places] for example authorizing devices that are non-lethal and "customarily used.")]

§ 704.5 AIDING ANOTHER IN THE DEFENSE OF PROPERTY

A person is justified in the use of reasonable force to aid another in the lawful defense of the other person's rights in property or in any public property. [This code section gives authority to use reasonable force, but not deadly force, when helping to defend the property of another.]

[HELPFUL DEFINITIONS RELATING TO THIS STATE'S SELF-DEFENSE STATUTES]

- **Deadly force** – means any of the following:
  1. Force used for the purpose of causing serious injury.
  2. Force which the actor knows or reasonably should know will create a strong probability that serious injury will result.
  3. The discharge of a firearm, other than a firearm loaded with less lethal munitions and discharged by a peace officer, corrections officer, or corrections official in the line of duty, in the direction of some person with the knowledge of the person's presence there, even though no intent to inflict serious physical injury can be shown.
  4. The discharge of a firearm, other than a firearm loaded with less lethal munitions and discharged by a peace officer, corrections officer, or corrections official in the line of duty, at a vehicle in which a person is known to be.

As used in this section, "less lethal munitions" means projectiles which are designed to stun, temporarily incapacitate, or cause temporary discomfort to a person without penetrating the person's body. **Iowa Statutes 704.2**

- **Dwelling** – is any building or structure, permanent or temporary, or any land, water or air vehicle, adapted for overnight accommodation of persons, and actually in use by some person or persons as permanent or temporary sleeping quarters, whether such person is present or not. **Iowa Statutes 702.10.**

- **702.11 Forcible felony.**
  1. A "forcible felony" is any felonious child endangerment, assault, murder, sexual abuse, kidnapping, robbery, arson in the first degree, or burglary in the first degree.
  2. Notwithstanding subsection 1, the following offenses are not forcible felonies:
     a. Willful injury in violation of section 708.4, subsection 2.
     b. Sexual abuse in the third degree committed between spouses.
     c. Sexual abuse in violation of section 709.4, subsection 2, paragraph "c", subparagraph (4).
     d. Sexual exploitation by a counselor, therapist, or school employee in violation of section 709.15.
     e. Child endangerment subject to penalty under section 726.6, subsection 6.

- **Forcible Felonies Mentioned Above –**
  - **Arson in the first degree** – [When it can be anticipated that people could be in the building or on the property where the arson is committed or the arson results in the death of a person.] **Iowa Statutes 712.2.**

  - **Assault** – [Intentionally causing pain or injury to another, placing another in fear of immediate injury or pain coupled with the ability to do the act. Also, pointing a gun at someone or threatening with any dangerous weapon.] **Iowa Statues 708.1.**

  - **Burglary in the first degree** – [While in the process of committing burglary (entering or remaining in an occupied structure with the intent to commit a crime therein) a person has on his/her possession an explosive, incendiary device or material, a dangerous weapon; intentionally or recklessly causes injury to another, or attempts to sexually abuse another during the burglary.] **Iowa Statues 713.1.**

  - **Felonious child endangerment** – [Knowingly or willfully putting a child or minor in harms way that is likely deprive that child or minor of physical, mental or emotional health or safety.] **Iowa Statutes 726.6.**

  - **Kidnapping** – [Confining or removing a person from one place to another without authority or consent in order to commit a crime against that person such as, holding that person for ransom, using them as a shield, or interfering with any government function.] **Iowa Statues 710.1.**

  - **Murder** – A person who kills another person with malice aforethought either express or implied commits murder. **Iowa Statutes 707.1.**

  - **Robbery** – [Unlawfully using force or threats of violence to take property from another.] **Iowa Statutes 711.1.**

  - **Sexual abuse** – [Any sex act with a minor or a person suffering from mental defect or incapacity that is done by force against the other person's will.] **Iowa Statutes 709.1.**

- **Occupied structure** – is any building, structure, appurtenances to buildings and structures, land, water or air vehicle, or similar place adapted for overnight accommodation of persons, or occupied by persons for the purpose of carrying on business or other activity therein, or for the storage or safekeeping of anything of value. Such a structure is an "occupied structure" whether or not a person is actually present. However, for purposes of chapter 713, a box, chest, safe, changer, or other object or device which is adapted or used for the deposit or storage of anything of value but which is too small or not designed to allow a person to physically enter or occupy it is not an "occupied structure". **Iowa Statutes 702.12.**

- **Property** – is anything of value, whether publicly or privately owned, including but not limited to computers and computer data, computer software, and computer programs. The term includes both tangible and intangible property, labor, and services. The term includes all that is included in the terms "real property" and "personal property". **Iowa Statutes 702.14.**

- **Serious injury** – means any of the following:
  a. Disabling mental illness.
  b. Bodily injury which does any of the following:
     (1) Creates a substantial risk of death.
     (2) Causes serious permanent disfigurement.
     (3) Causes protracted loss or impairment of the function of any bodily member or organ.
  c. Any injury to a child that requires surgical repair and necessitates the administration of general anesthesia.
     2. "Serious injury" includes but is not limited to skull fractures, rib fractures, and metaphyseal [growth plate] fractures of the long bones of children under the age of four years. **Iowa Statutes 702.18.**

[TEMPLATE Topics We Could Not Find Explained in Statutes or Cases]

(For each of these topics that we could not find addressed in your state's statutes or cases, we suggest you review the same topics in the subchapters of surrounding states. Your state's courts may look to the law of neighboring states to see how their courts and legislatures have treated that particular self-defense issue.)

[Mutual Combat]

[Defense of Person(s) in Special Places (e.g., Home, Business, Occupied Vehicle). We could not find anything other than rules for retreat under this topic. **]**

[Co-Employees – Duty to Retreat]

[Presumption of Reasonableness in Special Places]

[Reckless Injury to Innocent Third Parties]

Pancho's Wisdom

You just might be a Gunnut if . . .

. . . when you were a teething baby, you kicked and screamed because your ma and pa wouldn't let you chew on a live bullet.

. . . during your first geometry test, you answered that the shortest distance between two points is a gun barrel.

. . . you really do work for guns and ammo.

KANSAS

Key: ■ commentary ■ original statutes, cases or jury instructions

[Defense of Self and Others] [Non-Deadly Force]
[Defense of a Third Person]

§ KANSAS STATUTES ANNOTATED (K.S.A.) § 21-3211. Use of force in defense of a person; no duty to retreat.

(a) A person is justified in the use of force against another when and to the extent it appears to such person and such person reasonably believes that such force is necessary to defend such person or a third person against such other's imminent use of unlawful force. [Reasonable belief requires both a belief by the defendant and the existence of facts that would persuade a reasonable person to that belief.

Just before this book went to print, we discovered a Kansas case that held that self-defense does not apply to crimes that involve the threat of force rather than the use of force. Such crimes include brandishing and aggravated assault. The term "threaten" is not found in the Kansas self-defense statute. Therefore, the State's Supreme Court held that a person who threatens deadly force cannot claim self-defense. *State v. Hendrix*, 289 Kan. 859, 218 P.3d 40 (Kan. 2009), followed by *State v. Flint*, 2010 WL 445934 (Kan.App. Jan 29, 2010). Fortunately, we have not found any cases in other states that have followed this reasoning even though several states' self-defense statutes do not expressly address the act of threatening. *Pancho's Wisdom* – This is a harebrained decision. If you have access to legal cases, see Justice Davis' dissent in *Hendrix*. Read UCLA law professor Eugene Volokh's stinging criticism of the *Hendrix* and *Flint* decisions at http://volokh.com/2010/02/12/if-you-brandish-a-gun-in-self-defense-in-kansas-youd-best-shoot-it/. The Kansas Legislature should fix this by substituting the language of Paragraph I (Non-Deadly Force) & II (Deadly Force) of The Mother of All Self-Defense Laws, Chapter XX. We understand there is a push this year to fix this problem. Please stay in touch with your legislators.]

[Deadly Force]

(b) A person is justified in the use of deadly force under circumstances described in subsection (a) if such person reasonably believes deadly force is necessary to prevent imminent death or great bodily harm to such person or a third person.

(c) Nothing in this section shall require a person to retreat if such person is using force to protect such person or a third person.

[Like in most states, you can use deadly force to stop someone posing an immediate threat of death or serious injury to you or another person. You don't have to retreat before using deadly force. Please notice the word "necessary." You must have an honest belief that deadly force is necessary and your belief must be reasonable. Carefully study about the concepts of necessity and reasonableness in Chapter 3.

Kansas does not list any specific serious violent felonies that automatically trigger the right to use deadly force in self-defense. We searched for Kansas cases holding that rape or sexual assault constitutes "great bodily harm" for purposes of justifying the use of deadly force to prevent a rape or sexual assault. We found none. Although other states have held that rape or forcible sexual assault qualify as great bodily harm, without any case law on the subject in Kansas, it's not something a woman (or man for that matter, nowadays) can rely upon.

Pancho's Wisdom – Legislators in Kansas should consider adding sexual assault as justification for the use of deadly force as many states in the West and South have done.]

[Exceptions to Justifiable Self-Defense]

§ K.S.A. § 21-3214.
Use of force by an aggressor.

The justification described in sections 21-3211, 21-32312, and 21-3213, is not available to a person who:

[Committing Felony or Unlawful Act]

(1) Is attempting to commit, committing, or escaping from the commission of a forcible felony; or [This subsection is to prevent felons from committing violent crimes, killing their intended victims if they resist and then claiming self-defense. Forcible felonies include: treason, murder, voluntary manslaughter, rape, robbery, burglary, arson, kidnapping, aggravated battery, aggravated sodomy and any other felony which involves the use or threat of physical force or violence against any person. See definitions section.]

[Provocation]

(2) Initially provokes the use of force against himself or another, with intent to use such force as an excuse to inflict bodily harm upon the assailant; or [**Example:** Your rival for the affections of the beautiful Peggy Sue is a knife aficionado. You know if you irritate him sufficiently, he'll unsheathe his blade, which, you reason, will give you justification to blast him to Beaver City. You yank on his mustache, slap him twice and call him a wussy. As expected, he flicks a shiny, deadly-looking toad stabber and rushes you like a charging rhino. As planned, you whip your Desert Eagle out of your Thunderwear and tap his torso twice with a couple of .50 AEs. You get to spend the rest of your life watching MTV with pretty, pretty, pretty Peggy Sue, Right? Wrong! If all of the facts come to light, the jury will reject your self-defense claim. You provoked the poor, hot-tempered rival as an excuse to lay him to rest.]

[Initial Aggressor]

(3) Otherwise initially provokes the use of force against himself or another [You start a fight.], unless:

[Exceptions to the Exceptions]

(a) He has reasonable ground to believe that he is in imminent danger of death or great bodily harm, and he has exhausted every reasonable means to escape such danger other than the use of force which is likely to cause death or great bodily harm to the assailant; or [If you do start the fight, you must have tried all non-deadly ways to escape the situation; deadly force must be the last possible means of escape.]

[Withdraw and Communicate]

(b) In good faith, he withdraws from physical contact with the assailant and indicates clearly to the assailant that he desires to withdraw and terminate the use of force, but the assailant continues or resumes the use of force. [These two exceptions only apply to subsection three above (when you provoke the use of force against yourself, other than by committing forcible felony on purpose because you want to hurt someone without getting in trouble). (a) and (b) are very similar, except that (a) does not require you to communicate your removal. We think the major difference is that in (a) you have to exhaust every reasonable means of escape, whereas in (b) you must withdraw and communicate your intent to stop fighting.]

[Mutual Combat]

"The doctrine of self-defense cannot be invoked to excuse a killing done in mutual combat willingly entered into. One willingly entering into a mutual combat is not justified or excused in taking life unless he or she has withdrawn in good faith and done all in his or her power to avert the necessity of killing." *State v. Barnes,* 948 P.2d 627, 639 (Kan. 1997) [You can't agree to meet your mortal enemy at high noon outside the saloon downtown to slap leather. If you do, whoever survives is guilty of murder. It won't matter that you both lived in Dodge City.]

[No Duty to Retreat – Generally]

§ K.S.A. § 21-3218.
No duty to retreat; exceptions.

(a) A person who is not engaged in an unlawful activity and who is attacked in a place where such person has a right to be has no duty to retreat and has the right to stand such person's ground and meet force with force. [You don't have to retreat before using force to defend yourself. If you are a trespasser or otherwise committing a crime when attacked, you must retreat.]

(b) This section shall be part of and supplemental to the Kansas criminal code.

[Defense of Person(s) in Special Places – Dwelling, Occupied Vehicle]

§ K.S.A. § 21-3212.
Use of force in defense of dwelling; no duty to retreat.

(a) A person is justified in the use of force against another when and to the extent that it appears to such person and such person reasonably believes that such force is necessary to prevent or terminate such other's unlawful entry into or attack upon such person's dwelling or occupied vehicle. [Person can use non-deadly force to protect what appears to be an unlawful entry or attack on the home or vehicle.]

(b) A person is justified in the use of deadly force to prevent or terminate unlawful entry into or attack upon any dwelling or occupied vehicle if such person reasonably believes deadly force is necessary to prevent imminent death or great bodily harm to such person or another. [Although you are attacked in your home or occupied vehicle, you still have to show an imminent threat of death or great bodily harm before you can respond with deadly force. This is less favorable than in most states in the West and South that presume a person was acting reasonably in using deadly force if an attacker attempts to forcibly break into the defender's special place (usually his home, workplace or car). Many of these states do not require an imminent threat of great bodily harm, but only an imminent threat of an assault or personal violence. *Pancho's Wisdom* – Kansas should consider amending its home-defense laws to explicitly allow the use of deadly force to prevent any threat of an assault, no matter how slight in the event of an unlawful, forcible entry (break-in by a stranger). See, for example, Colorado's home-defense statute.]

[No Duty to Retreat From Dwelling or Occupied Vehicle]

(c) Nothing in this section shall require a person to retreat if such person is using force to protect such person's dwelling or occupied vehicle. [No duty to retreat in the home or your vehicle.]

[Civil Liability]

§ K.S.A. § 21-3219.
Use of force; immunity from prosecution or liability; investigation.

(a) A person who uses force which, subject to the provisions of K.S.A. 21-3214 [can't claim self-defense if you start fight, etc.], and amendments thereto, is justified pursuant to K.S.A. 21-3211, 21-32312, or 21-3213, [defense of self, others, home, occupied car and property] and amendments thereto, is immune from criminal prosecution and civil action for the use of such force, unless the person against whom force was used is a law enforcement officer who was acting in the performance of such officer's official duties and the officer identified the officer's self in accordance with any applicable law or the person using force knew or reasonably should have known that the person was a law enforcement officer. As used in this subsection, "criminal prosecution" includes arrest, detention in custody and charging or prosecution of the defendant. [If you have a valid claim to self-defense, this immunity statute could be very helpful to keep your legal fees from going through the roof. It is a way to cut off the prosecution of your case early on in an evidentiary hearing in which the accused has the burden of proving by a preponderance of the evidence (more likely than not) that he is innocent by virtue of self-defense (or defense of another).]

(b) A law enforcement agency may use standard procedures for investigating the use of force as described in subsection (a), but the agency shall not arrest the person for using force unless it determines that there is probable cause for the arrest. [The standard procedures must be followed in an investigation and there will be no arrest until there is probable cause. Probable cause means more than a possibility, but does not have to be more likely than not.]

(c) A county or district attorney or other prosecutor may commence a criminal prosecution upon a determination of probable cause.

[Defense of Property]

§ K.S.A. § 21-3213.
Use of force in defense of property other than a dwelling.

A person who is lawfully in possession of property other than a dwelling is justified in the threat or use of force against another for the purpose of preventing or terminating an unlawful interference with such property. Only such degree of force or threat thereof as a reasonable man would deem necessary to prevent or terminate the interference may intentionally be used. [You can only use as much force as necessary to stop a thief from stealing your iPod®. Interestingly, it appears the Kansas Legislature left off the last sentence that had been proposed during the passage of this law which prohibited the use of deadly force in defense of real and personal property. The following 1988 case, which has not been overturned to our knowledge, confirmed that it was the intent of the Legislature to permit the use of deadly force when necessary to defend your personal property.

In that case, the defendant saw a person burglarizing his car in his driveway. Afraid the person might find his garage-door opener, he went outside and fired a "warning shot" over the individual's head and another into the ground. The police found a mortally wounded 15 year old with a bullet in his head in the driveway. The kid later died and the homeowner was prosecuted for involuntary manslaughter. The trial court informed the jury of the language of this statute and the jury found the defendant not guilty. The State of Kansas appealed, claiming its legislature exceed its powers by passing a law allowing the use of deadly force in defense of property. The Kansas Supreme Court denied the appeal and said the legislature had the power to do what it did. It stated:

> "The State argues that these statutes are in derogation of the common law which prohibits the use of deadly force in defense of property unless there is a threat of imminent bodily harm prior to the use of such force. At the time of the adoption of the Kansas Criminal Code in 1969, the proposal by the Kansas Judicial Council included the following concluding sentence to the proposed K.S.A. 21-3213:

> "It is not reasonable to intentionally use force intended or likely to cause death or great bodily harm for the sole purpose of defending property other than a dwelling."
>
> That sentence was deleted by the legislature, demonstrating an intent to avoid limitation, thus leaving this section apparently as broad as K.S.A. 21-3212. See the author's comment in Vernon's Kansas Crim.C.Proc. § 21-3213, p. 200 (1971). In adopting that position, the Kansas legislature joined a minority of jurisdictions which permit the use of all reasonably necessary force in the defense of property other than a dwelling." *State v. Clothier*, 753 P.2d 1267, 1269 (Kan. 1988).

Interestingly, in *Clothier*, the prosecutor claimed that Kansas' defense-of-property statute violated the holding in the U.S. Supreme Court case we warned you about in Chapter 4, *Tennesee v. Garner* (which held that a state statute allowing the use of deadly force against a non-threatening, unarmed person violated that person's Fourth Amendment rights against unreasonable seizures (arrest)). The Kansas Supreme Court held that *Garner* did not apply to criminal cases (Warning: Nevada and California have applied the reasoning in Garner to their fleeing felon statutes). The State of Kansas appealed to the Supreme Court of the United States which refused to hear the case.

The Kansas case, *State v. Clothier*, holds a person may use deadly force to protect his property if his use of force is reasonable and necessary. Most states do not allow the use of deadly force to protect property. We do not suggest you defend your property with deadly force. If you do, there will be such a public outcry for your scalp that prosecutors will try to figure out some clever way to prosecute. For example, see our lengthy discussions of the Joe Horn and Tommy Oakes cases in the Texas subchapter. Texas allows the use of deadly force to defend a neighbor's personal property under some circumstances. Nevertheless, both of these men were vigorously (if not viciously) prosecuted for exercising that right. By the time they get done paying their attorneys, they will have spent many times more than the stolen property was worth.

Pancho's Wisdom – You either have a right to defend your property with deadly force or you don't. If the statute says you can, you shouldn't be prosecuted if you do. One way to stop such prosecutions is to pass a law requiring the police department that made the arrest and the prosecutor's office that prosecuted the case to totally reimburse the defendant for all fees, including attorney fees, lost time from work, and any other expenses out of their budgets!]

[HELPFUL DEFINITIONS RELATING TO THIS STATE'S SELF-DEFENSE STATUTES]

- **Dwelling** – means a building or portion thereof, a tent, a vehicle or other enclosed space which is used or intended for use as a human habitation, home or residence. **K.S.A. § 21-3110 (7).**

- **Forcible felony** – includes any treason, murder, voluntary manslaughter, rape, robbery, burglary, arson, kidnapping, aggravated battery, aggravated sodomy and any other felony which involves the use or threat of physical force or violence against any person. **K.S.A. § 21-3110 (8).**

- **Personal property** – means goods, chattels, effects, evidences of rights in action and all written instruments by which any pecuniary obligation, or any right or title to property real or personal, shall be created, acknowledged, assigned, transferred, increased, defeated, discharged, or dismissed. **Iowa Statutes 21-3110 (15).**

- **Property** – means anything of value, tangible or intangible, real or personal. **K.S.A. § 21-3110 (16).**

- **Real property or real estate** – means every estate, interest, and right in lands, tenements and hereditaments [property you can inherit]. **K.S.A. § 21-3110 (20).**

- **Threat** – means a communicated intent to inflict physical or other harm on any person or on property. K.S.A. § 21-3110 (24).

[TEMPLATE Topics We Could Not Find Explained in Statutes or Cases]

(For each of these topics that we could not find addressed in your state's statutes or cases, we suggest you review the same topics in the subchapters of surrounding states. Your state's courts may look to the law of neighboring states to see how their courts and legislatures have treated that particular self-defense issue.)

[Use of Deadly Force to Prevent Serious Felonies]

[Co-Habitants; Co-Employees – Duty to Retreat]

[Presumption of Reasonableness in Special Places]

[Reckless Injury to Innocent Third Parties]

KENTUCKY

In 2006 the Kentucky General Assembly cranked out a major overhaul of its state's self-defense laws. It adopted the same home-defense statute Florida enacted the previous year. Florida's law drew intense criticism from the Harvard Journal on Legislation which claimed Florida homeowners had been given a license to kill that is unprecedented in American jurisprudence. Although we don't agree with the Harvardhood men in tweed that Florida and Kentucky's home-defense statutes are over the top, we agree they may be the most protective in the nation. Congratulations Kentucky for protecting your homeowners rather than worrying about irking the Ivy League.

Kentucky's general self-defense statute actually goes a step further than Florida's by eliminating the requirement of reasonableness. Some legal commentators believe this will reduce the effectiveness of prosecutors who, in the past, have been able to win on theories such as the defender's fears were unreasonable, his assailant's actions were technically lawful or the defender used excessive force. Although you may be able to ultimately win a case because Kentucky eliminated the use of the word "reasonable," we warn that if you harm someone otherwise acting legally, you act unreasonably or use more force than necessary to defend yourself or others, you will most likely be arrested and prosecuted. If a jury believes your actions involved a wanton or reckless disregard for the safety of others, you could be convicted of manslaughter or reckless homicide.

Key: ■ commentary ■ original statutes, cases or jury instructions

---

[Defense of Self and Others]

§ KENTUCKY REVISED STATUES (K.R.S.) § 503.020.
Justification – A defense.

In any prosecution for an offense, justification, as defined in this chapter, is a defense.

§ K.R.S. § 503.050.
Use of physical force in self-protection – Admissibility of evidence of prior acts of domestic violence and abuse.

[Non-Deadly Force]

(1) The use of physical force by a defendant upon another person is justifiable when the defendant believes that such force is necessary to protect himself against the use or imminent use of unlawful physical force by the other person. [One of the unique things about Kentucky's self-defense statute is the omission of the word "reasonable." The Kentucky Crime Commission Commentary reveals this omission

was intentional. This probably makes self-defense incidents harder for prosecutors to prosecute, but our advice is only use whatever force is reasonably necessary to stop the commission of an unlawful act against yourself or others. If you are charged with a crime jurors will likely judge your actions by what they consider to be reasonable whether they are supposed to or not.]

[Deadly Force] [Use of Deadly Force to Prevent Serious Felonies]

(2) The use of deadly physical force by a defendant upon another person is justifiable under subsection (1) only when the defendant believes that such force is necessary to protect himself against death, serious physical injury, kidnapping, sexual intercourse compelled by force or threat, felony involving the use of force, or under those circumstances permitted pursuant to KRS 503.055 [You can use deadly force to stop a threat of serious injury, kidnapping, rape and other felonies using the threat of force, such as a robbery (taking property by force or threat). 503.055 explains how to legally defend your home and occupied vehicle].

(3) Any evidence presented by the defendant to establish the existence of a prior act or acts of domestic violence and abuse as defined in KRS 403.720 by the person against whom the defendant is charged with employing physical force shall be admissible under this section. [See chapter about domestic violence, Chapter 13.]

[No Duty to Retreat – Generally]

(4) A person does not have a duty to retreat prior to the use of deadly physical force. [You don't have to retreat before using justifiable deadly force.]

[Defense of a Third Person]

§ **K.R.S. § 503.070.**
Protection of another.

(1) The use of physical force by a defendant upon another person is justifiable when:

(a) The defendant believes that such force is necessary to protect a third person against the use or imminent use of unlawful physical force by the other person; and [Self-defense is permitted to protect or defend third persons].

(b) Under the circumstances as the defendant believes them to be, the person whom he seeks to protect would himself have been justified under KRS 503.050 [the self-defense statute explained above] and 503.060 [the exceptions-to-self-defense statute explained below] in using such protection. [This is a little confusing. It means that you are justified in defending a third person if the third person would have been justified in defending him or herself under Kentucky's general self-defense statute (above) and not prohibited from defending him or herself under the exceptions below.]

(2) The use of deadly physical force by a defendant upon another person is justifiable when:

(a) The defendant believes that such force is necessary to protect a third person against imminent death, serious physical injury, kidnapping, sexual intercourse compelled by force or threat, or other felony involving the use of force, or under those circumstances permitted pursuant to KRS 503.055; and

(b) Under the circumstances as they actually exist, the person whom he seeks to protect would himself have been justified under KRS 503.050 and 503.060 in using such protection. [You can use deadly force to defend another under the same conditions that justify defending yourself.]

(3) A person does not have a duty to retreat if the person is in a place where he or she has a right to be. [Unless you are trespassing, you can stand your ground and defend another person without retreating.]

[Exceptions to Justifiable Self-Defense]

§ **K.R.S. § 503.060 (2) and (3).**
Improper use of physical force in self-protection.
[These are typical exceptions to being able to claim self-defense. If you share any blame for starting, escalating, or agreeing to a fight, plan on being arrested and prosecuted.]

Notwithstanding the provisions of KRS 503.050, the use of physical force by a defendant upon another person is not justifiable when:

. . .

[Provocation]

(2) The defendant, with the intention of causing death or serious physical injury to the other person, provokes the use of physical force by such other person; or [Simply put, you cannot use self-defense in situations where you started the fight as an excuse to seriously harm or kill.]

[Initial Aggressor]

(3) The defendant was the initial aggressor, except that his use of physical force upon the other person under this circumstance is justifiable when: [Even if you started the fight, self-defense can still be used under certain situations described below in (a) and (b)]

[Exceptions to the Exceptions]

(a) His initial physical force was nondeadly and the force returned by the other is such that he believes himself to be in imminent danger of death or serious physical injury; or [We think this subparagraph could be a little too reassuring. It suggests that you can start a fistfight, but when the other guy pulls a gun, you would be justified in shooting the other guy first. Although you might ultimately be found not guilty, it is our experience that any time the defender is guilty of starting (initiating) or agreeing to a fight (mutual combat) he will be arrested and prosecuted (see Thumbs-Down Factors, Chapter 7).]

[Withdraw and Communicate]

(b) He withdraws from the encounter and effectively communicates to the other person his intent to do so and the latter nevertheless continues or threatens the use of unlawful physical force. [The key to proving this exception would be for you to be seen by multiple witnesses running away from the fight with your hands in the air yelling "I don't want to fight anymore; please don't hurt me! I give up! I give up!"]

[Mutual Combat]

"[W]here one voluntarily enters an actual combat or, as it is called, a mutual affray, with the intention of each participant to kill the other or do him great bodily harm, and that results, neither is entitled to go acquit on the ground of self-defense." [If two stiffs begin to fight with the intent to kill or cause serious harm, they can't claim self-defense.] *Toler v. Commonwealth,* 173 S.W.2d 822, 823 (Ky.App. 1943). [Goodwin entered a restaurant in an angry mood and picked a fight with Toler. Goodwin was drunk and had a gun. The two exchanged insults in the restaurant, and Goodwin invited Toler outside to fight. During the ensuing fight outside, the gun went off, shooting Goodwin in the back, killing him. *Pancho's Wisdom* – Dumb (Toler) and Dumber (Goodwin).]

[Presumption of Reasonableness in Special Places – Dwelling, Residence or Occupied Vehicle]
[No Duty to Retreat From Dwelling, Residence or Occupied Vehicle]

§ **K.R.S. § 503.055.**
Use of defensive force regarding dwelling, residence, or occupied vehicle – Exceptions.

(1) A person is presumed to have held a reasonable fear of imminent peril of death or great bodily harm to himself or herself or another when using defensive force that is intended or likely to cause death or great bodily harm to another if:

(a) The person against whom the defensive force was used was in the process of unlawfully and forcibly entering or had unlawfully and forcibly entered a dwelling, residence, or occupied vehicle, or if that person had removed or was attempting to remove another against that person's will from the dwelling, residence, or occupied vehicle; and

(b) The person who uses defensive force knew or had reason to believe that an unlawful and forcible entry or unlawful and forcible act was occurring or had occurred.

[Normally, to be justified in defending with deadly force, a person has to be threatened with deadly force. However, in your home or car the threshold is lower. Deadly force is presumed if there is an unlawful AND forcible entry. **Example:** A menacing-looking stranger breaks into your home at night by smashing through a window or breaking through a locked door. It's dark and you can't tell if the stranger has a weapon or not. This is a VERY dangerous situation for any homeowner (see discussion in Chapter 11 regarding perception and reaction time). By the time you actually figure out the Sandman's got a weapon, you could be dead. Under those circumstances, we suspect you probably would not even be arrested let alone prosecuted if you bop him with .00 Buck belching from the barrel of your Benelli.

No matter how strong legal commentators argue that the home-defense statutes for Kentucky and Florida and "conclusive presumptions" (suggesting they are not rebuttable), my experience has been that they may indeed be rebuttable under the right set of facts. Let's change the facts a bit. The security camera in the convenience store next door reveals the intruder who breaks in is your annoying VEGAN neighbor who tries to convince EVERYONE in the neighborhood they must give up meat. You own the popular Barbeque around the corner and VEGANS are BAD for business. He bursts into your living room, the lights are on, he has no weapon and he says he crashed into your home to VERBALLY protest the animals killed to provide your restaurant with meat. When he sees your home-defense gun pointed at him, he begs you with his empty hands in the air not to hurt him. You decide this is the perfect opportunity to rid the neighborhood of the annoying rascal so you aerate him like you do your bluegrass. Under those circumstances, in my opinion, the "presumption" that you had a reasonable fear of being seriously injured or killed could very well be rebutted and you could be convicted of murder despite the fact that the intruder unlawfully and forcibly entered your home. If not convicted, you will certainly be arrested and prosecuted as a test case.]

(2) The presumption set forth in subsection (1) of this section does not apply if:

(a) The person against whom the defensive force is used has the right to be in or is a lawful resident of the dwelling, residence, or vehicle, such as an owner, lessee, or titleholder, and there is not an [exceptions to the exception] injunction for protection from domestic violence or a written pretrial supervision order of no contact against that person; [The crux of whether the presumption applies is whether or not the person has a right to be in your home. If you cap someone who has a right to be in your home (example: your spouse right after you pumped up her life insurance by a couple of mil), you will be prosecuted. The exception is when there is an injunction or no contact order telling an abusive husband to stay away from the wife's home until the divorce is final. Under those circumstances, the husband has no right to be in the home. If he breaks into her separate household under such circumstances, it is presumed she acted reasonably by hurling him to Hell in a hand basket courtesy of Hornady. See our chapter discussing the issue of domestic violence, Chapter 13.]

(b) The person sought to be removed is a child or grandchild, or is otherwise in the lawful custody or under the lawful guardianship of the person against whom the defensive force is used; [You're not justified acting out the OK Corral over a dispute over visitation rights of a child or grandchild!]

(c) The person who uses defensive force is engaged in an unlawful activity or is using the dwelling, residence, or occupied vehicle to further an unlawful activity; or [i.e., if you have a meth lab in the home]

(d) The person against whom the defensive force is used is a peace officer, as defined in KRS 466.010, who enters or attempts to enter a dwelling, residence, or vehicle in the performance of his or her official duties, and the officer identified himself or herself in accordance with any applicable law or the person using force knew or reasonably should have known that the person entering or attempting to enter was a peace officer. [Example for (c) and (d): People cookin' up Meth in their basement aren't presumed to be acting reasonably by playing shooting gallery with SWAT officers during a "no knock" entry.]

(3) A person who is not engaged in an unlawful activity and who is attacked in any other place where he or she has a right to be has no duty to retreat and has the right to stand his or her ground and meet force with force, including deadly force, if he or she reasonably believes it is necessary to do so to prevent death or great bodily harm to himself or herself or another or to prevent the commission of a felony involving the use of force. [You do not have a duty to retreat from anywhere you have a right to be in Kentucky before using defensive force, either deadly or non-deadly. Conversely, trespassers must retreat before using such force.]

(4) A person who unlawfully and by force enters or attempts to enter a person's dwelling, residence, or occupied vehicle is presumed to be doing so with the intent to commit an unlawful act involving force or violence. [You can presume a person who forces their way into your home or tries to do so, who has no right to be there, intends to use violence against you or an occupant of the home or car. This, in turn, justifies the use of deadly force. This not only protects persons in their homes and vehicles, it acts as a warning to those who break and enter.]

[Civil Liability]

§ K.R.S. § 503.085.
Justification and criminal and civil immunity for use of permitted force – Exceptions.

(1) A person who uses force as permitted in KRS 503.050 [self-defense], 503.055 [defense of persons in the home and car], 503.070 [defense of third persons], and 503.080 [defense of property] is justified in using such force and is immune from criminal prosecution and civil action for the use of such force, unless the person against whom the force was used is a peace officer, as defined in KRS 446.010, who was acting in the performance of his or her official duties and the officer identified himself or herself in accordance with any applicable law, or the person using force knew or reasonably should have known that the person was a peace officer. As used in this subsection, the term "criminal prosecution" includes arresting, detaining in custody, and charging or prosecuting the defendant. [As of the time we finished writing, there had not been a Kentucky appellate court case explaining exactly how immunity will be administered in criminal cases. In other states, (e.g., Kansas — see immediately previous subchapter) there is a hearing to determine whether the immunity-from-criminal-prosecution statute applies to the defensive incident. If immunity is held to apply in the pre-trial hearing, the case is over. This could save tens of thousands of dollars in attorney fees for a person involved in a defensive incident.]

(2) A law enforcement agency may use standard procedures for investigating the use of force as described in subsection (1) of this section, but the agency may not arrest the person for using force unless it determines that there is probable cause that the force that was used was unlawful. [Law enforcement must play by the rules and cannot make an arrest until there is evidence that show probable cause.]

(3) The court shall award reasonable attorney's fees, court costs, compensation for loss of income, and all expenses incurred by the defendant in defense of any civil action brought by a plaintiff, if the court finds that the defendant is immune from prosecution as provided in subsection (1) of this section. [If a citizen is justified in injuring a criminal, and the criminal sues for damages anyway, the citizen can recover his expenses for having to defend such a lawsuit.]

[Defense of Property]

§ K.R.S. § 503.080.
Protection of property.

Non-Deadly Force

(1) The use of physical force by a defendant upon another person is justifiable when the defendant believes that such force is immediately necessary to prevent:

(a) The commission of criminal trespass, robbery, burglary, or other felony involving the use of force, or under those circumstances permitted pursuant to KRS 503.033, in a dwelling, building or upon real property in his possession or in the possession of another person for whose protection he acts; or

(b) Theft, criminal mischief, or any trespassory taking of tangible, movable property in his possession or in the possession of another person for whose protection he acts.

Deadly Force

(2) The use of deadly physical force by a defendant upon another person is justifiable under subsection (1) only when the defendant believes that the person against whom such force is used is: [The use of deadly force to defend one's property is only justifiable under special circumstances: taking over your home, committing burglary, robbery, or arson. See comment in (3) below]

(a) Attempting to dispossess him of his dwelling otherwise than under a claim of right to its possession; or

(b) Committing or attempting to commit a burglary, robbery, or other felony involving the use of force, or under those circumstances permitted pursuant to KRS 503.055, of such dwelling; or

(c) Committing or attempting to commit arson of a dwelling or other building in his possession.

(3) A person does not have a duty to retreat if the person is in a place where he or she has a right to be. [The mention of deadly force under the heading of this "defense of property statute" should not mislead you into believing you can use deadly force to keep someone from stealing or damaging your personal property, such as your lawn mower, Big Screen, stereo or swing set. Notice the crimes referred to immediately below that justify the use of deadly force are crimes that most states refer to as "forcible felonies" which involve grave risk to persons, not just property. These include kidnapping, burglary, and arson.]

§ K.R.S. § 503.120.
Justification – General provisions.

(1) When the defendant believes that the use of force upon or toward the person of another is necessary for any of the purposes for which such belief would establish a justification under KRS 503.050 to 503.110 but the defendant is wanton or reckless in believing the use of any force, or the degree of force used, to be necessary or in acquiring or failing to acquire any knowledge or belief which is material to the justifiability of his use of force, the justification afforded by those sections is unavailable in a prosecution for an offense for which wantonness or recklessness, as the case may be, suffices to establish culpability. [If you truly believe your use of force is justified, but you are reckless in formulating such a belief, your belief will keep you from being prosecuted for a crime requiring "intent" such as murder, but not crimes only requiring recklessness, like manslaughter. **Example:** You are walking down the street where there are obvious movie camera trucks all over the place. You turn the corner and out of your bank comes a "bank robber." You instinctively draw your gun and shoot to stop the progression of what you believe is a forcible felony – armed robbery. All the while the director is yelling "Cut! Cut!" You immediately find out you shot an actor starring in a bank-robbery role for a movie. If the actor dies and the prosecutor believes you truly didn't intend to do evil, that you were simply grossly unaware of the obvious movie being filmed all around you, he could prosecute you for manslaughter.]

(2) When the defendant is justified under KRS 503.050 to KRS 503.110 in using force upon or toward the person of another, but he wantonly or recklessly injures or creates a risk of injury to innocent persons, the justification afforded by those sections is unavailable in a prosecution for an offense involving wantonness or recklessness toward innocent persons. [**Example:** Someone steals your purse. You pull out the Thompson concealed in your violin case and unload a hundred-round drum at the purse-snatcher in downtown Louisville during the lunch hour.]

[HELPFUL DEFINITIONS RELATING TO THIS STATE'S SELF-DEFENSE STATUTES]

- **Deadly physical force** – means force which is used with the purpose of causing death or serious physical injury or which the defendant knows to create a substantial risk of causing death or serious physical injury. **K.R.S. § 503.010 (1).**

- **Dwelling** – means a building or conveyance of any kind, including any attached porch, whether the building or conveyance is temporary or permanent, mobile or immobile, which has a roof over it, including a tent, and is designed to be occupied by people lodging therein at night. **K.R.S. § 503.010 (2).**

- **Felonies Mentioned Above**
    - **Arson** – [Causing destruction or damage to a building by intentionally starting a fire or explosion.] **K.R.S. § 513.020, 030, 040.**

- **Burglary** – [With intent to commit a crime in a building, knowingly entering or remaining unlawfully.] **K.R.S. § 511.020, 030, 040.**

- **Felony involving the use of force** – [This phrase is used, but not defined. The plain meaning would include any felony involving the use of force upon a victim. This would include what some states refer to as "forcible felonies." For example, see the felonies and definitions for the state of Utah.]

- **Kidnapping** – [Unlawfully restraining a person for the purpose of obtaining ransom, inflicting bodily injury, advancing a felony, or interfering with a governmental political function.] **K.R.S. § 509.040.**

- **Robbery** – [Using or threatening immediate, unlawful physical force to take someone's property.] **K.R.S. § 515.020 & 030.**

- **Sexual Intercourse compelled by force or threat** – [This would include varying degrees of rape, sodomy and sexual abuse.] **Rape: K.R.S. § 510.040,050,060. Sodomy: K.R.S. § 510.080,090,100. Sexual abuse: K.R.S. § 510.110,120,130.**

- **Imminent** – means impending danger, and, in the context of domestic violence and abuse as defined by KRS 403.720, belief that danger is imminent can be inferred from a past pattern of repeated serious abuse. **K.R.S. § 503.010 (3).** [This VERY progressive definition puts Kentucky way out in front of most states in recognizing and responding to the deadly plague of domestic violence that results in the permanent injury, disfigurement and deaths thousands of women a year throughout the country.]

- **Physical force** – means force used upon or directed toward the body of another person and includes confinement. **K.R.S. § 503.010 (4).**

- **Residence** – means a dwelling in which a person resides either temporarily or permanently or is visiting as an invited guest. **K.R.S. § 503.010 (5).**

- **Vehicle** – means a conveyance of any kind, whether or not motorized, which is designed to transport people or property. **K.R.S. § 503.010 (6). 503.010.**

[TEMPLATE Topics We Could Not Find Explained in Statutes or Cases]

(For each of these topics that we could not find addressed in your state's statutes or cases, we suggest you review the same topics in the subchapters of surrounding states. Your state's courts may look to the law of neighboring states to see how their courts and legislatures have treated that particular self-defense issue.)

[Committing Felony or Unlawful Act]

[Co-Habitants; Co-Employees – Duty to Retreat]

[Reckless Injury to Innocent Third Parties]

LOUISIANA

For defensive incidents occurring outside of one's home, business or vehicle, Louisiana's self-defense statutes are unique. Instead of focusing exclusively on the type of threat that a defender is facing, the law turns on whether or not the victim dies, something the defender may have very little control over. To us this seems a little backwards. For example, suppose a woman is approached by a man who tries to pull a cheap, cosmetic bracelet off of her wrist. Unbeknownst to her he has a blood vessel in his brain that is very thin and could burst at the slightest trauma to his head. The woman resists his attempt to grab her bracelet and pushes him away. Unfortunately, he hits his head on a lamppost, the aneurism ruptures and he dies from bleeding into his brain. In most states the woman would not even be charged because she only used as much force as she needed to in order to repel the unlawful attack. In Louisiana, the way the defense-of-homicide statute is written, she would only be justified in killing if she were threatened with serious injury or death. Because the man died and he didn't threaten her with death or serious bodily injury, she could be prosecuted and conceivably convicted of manslaughter or negligent homicide. Although most juries would probably refuse to convict her, the fact that she might be convicted creates an unjust and unmanageable risk in Louisiana's law that should be changed.

Because of the uniqueness of Louisiana's self-defense laws, the **[TEMPLATE]** has been modified. Many of the **[TEMPLATE]** headings appear twice; once in relation to non-homicide cases and then again in relation to homicide.

Key: ■ commentary ■ original statutes, cases or jury instructions

---

[Defense of Self and Others]

§ LOUISIANA STATUTES ANNOTATED – REVISED STATUTES (LSA-R.S.) § 14:19.

Use of force or violence in defense.

[Self-Defense Other than Homicide]

A. The use of force or violence upon the person of another is justifiable when committed for the purpose of preventing a forcible offense against the person or a forcible offense or trespass against property in a person's lawful possession, provided that the force or violence used must be reasonable and apparently necessary to prevent such offense, and that this Section shall not apply where the force or violence results in a homicide. [You will be judged by whether your actions were reasonable and apparently necessary in defending yourself or your property. However, these rules do not apply if your attacker dies. If he or she dies, there must be evidence that you were threatened with serious injury or death. See the **[Deadly Force]** section below.]

[Presumption of Reasonableness in Special Places – Non-Deadly Force]

B. For the purposes of this Section, there shall be a presumption that a person lawfully inside a dwelling, place of business, or motor vehicle held a reasonable belief that the use of force or violence was necessary to prevent unlawful entry thereto, or to compel an unlawful intruder to leave the premises or motor vehicle, if *both* of the following occur:

(1) The person against whom the force or violence was used was in the process of unlawfully and forcibly entering or had unlawfully and forcibly entered the dwelling, place of business, or motor vehicle.

(2) The person who used force or violence knew or had reason to believe that an unlawful and forcible entry was occurring or had occurred.

[Like in most states, Louisiana gives you the benefit of the doubt when keeping intruders from breaking into certain special places. In Louisiana, these special places include your home, business and automobile. There must be someone inside the home, building or vehicle at the time of the break-in or attempted break- in. The entry must be made or attempted by force or violence, such as breaking or trying to break a lock or window or threatening an occupant with violence if the occupant doesn't let the intruder inside. The entry must be unlawful. The presumption that you acted reasonably doesn't apply if the person entering has a right to be there such as your spouse, a live-in relative, or a person who has been given permission to enter.]

[No Duty to Retreat – Non-Deadly Force]

C. A person who is not engaged in unlawful activity and who is in a place where he or she has a right to be shall have no duty to retreat before using force or violence as provided for in this Section and may stand his or her ground and meet force with force. [If you have a right to be where you are when attacked (you're not trespassing), you don't have to retreat before using non-deadly force in self-defense.]

D. No finder of fact shall be permitted to consider the possibility of retreat as a factor in determining whether or not the person who used force or violence in defense of his person or property had a reasonable belief that force or violence was reasonable and apparently necessary to prevent a forcible offense or to prevent the unlawful entry. [Juries and judges are not allowed to consider whether a defendant could have retreated in deciding reasonableness or necessity. Otherwise jurors, when deciding whether a defendant's use of force was necessary, may begin to discuss whether it was really necessary to use force in self-defense when there may have been an opportunity to simply leave and avoid the incident. This paragraph makes such discussions by jurors or consideration by judges improper. This is a great addition to Louisiana law and should be adopted by states that do not have this provision. Hence, we have given Louisiana the distinction of having one of its self-defense provisions included in The Mother of All Self-Defense Statutes, Chapter 20.]

[Up to this point, the discussion has been about the use of non-deadly force.]

[Deadly Force]

LSA - R.S. § 14:20.

§ Justifiable homicide

A. A homicide is justifiable:

(1) When committed in self-defense by one who reasonably believes that he is in imminent danger of losing his life or receiving great bodily harm and that the killing is necessary to save himself from that danger. [This is patterned after virtually every other deadly-force self-defense law in the country. You may only use deadly force if you are facing an imminent threat of serious bodily injury or death.

The more modern self-defense statutes authorize the use of deadly force whereas the older statutes refer to the right to kill in self-defense. Unfortunately, the use of the word "kill" may give the impression that it's justifiable to "finish the job" to keep an assailant-criminal from testifying or suing. Executing an assailant who is injured and harmless to keep him from testifying is NEVER justifiable. No matter the language of the statute, we admonish you to NEVER formulate the intent to kill, but rather only to stop the progression of deadly force against yourself. Your words during such an incident should never suggest an intent to kill. You should say, "Drop the knife or I'll shoot," not "drop the knife *&*#()#, or I'll send your &^*&^&% to Hell!"]

[Use of Deadly Force to Prevent Serious Felonies]

(2) When committed for the purpose of preventing a violent or forcible felony involving danger to life or of great bodily harm by one who reasonably believes that such an offense is *about to be committed* and that such action is necessary for its prevention. The circumstances must be sufficient to excite the fear of a reasonable person that there would be serious danger to his own life or person if he attempted to prevent the felony without the killing. [You are not justified in killing to prevent any old felony. It has to be a felony "involving danger to life or great bodily harm." Furthermore, a reasonable person would have to conclude that if the assailant wasn't killed, it would seriously endanger the defender's life.

Of course, your actions must be reasonable and necessary. With such strict requirements, we're not quite sure how this "forcible felony" paragraph gives Cajuns any additional protection. They can already use deadly force to repel a threat of deadly force under paragraph (1).

Pancho's Wisdom – This paragraph should be amended. Law-abiding citizens defending themselves should have a list of clearly defined crimes which, if committed against them, give them the right to respond with deadly force. As a deterrent, criminals should know what crimes they commit authorize their victims to respond with deadly force. See the right to use deadly force to prevent forcible felonies in the Mother of All Self-Defense Statutes, Chapter 20.]

[Defense of Person(s) in Special Places – Dwelling, Business, Motor Vehicle]

(3) When committed against a person whom one reasonably believes to be likely to use any unlawful force against a person present in a dwelling or a place of business, or when committed against a person whom one reasonably believes is attempting to use any unlawful force against a person present in a motor vehicle as defined in R.S. 32:1(40), while committing or attempting to commit a burglary or robbery of such dwelling, business, or motor vehicle. [This paragraph authorizes you to use deadly force to stop a burglar or robber from harming any person who is lawfully in a home, business or motor vehicle. Simply put, burglary means breaking into one of these special places to commit a felony or theft. Robbery is the taking of someone else's property by force or threat. These two crimes are more specifically defined below and their citations are also given so you can look them up at a local law library if you are that interested.]

(4) (a) When committed by a person lawfully inside a dwelling, a place of business, or a motor vehicle as defined in R.S. 32:1(40), against a person who is attempting to make an unlawful entry into the dwelling, place of business, or motor vehicle, or who has made an unlawful entry into the dwelling, place of business, or motor vehicle, and the person committing the homicide reasonably believes that the use of deadly force is necessary to prevent the entry or to compel the intruder to leave the premises or motor vehicle. [You can use deadly force to keep intruders from breaking or sneaking into your house, business or car without your permission OR once they have entered without your permission, to get them to leave. Unlawful entry would not apply to people who have the right to be in the home because they live there or have a property interest (e.g., a family member, roommate, landlord or tenant) or because you've let them enter in the past without objecting (e.g., your kids' friends who go in and out of your house like it's their house).]

(b) The provisions of this Paragraph shall not apply when the person committing the homicide is engaged, at the time of the homicide, in the acquisition of, the distribution of, or possession of, with intent to distribute a controlled dangerous substance in violation of the provisions of the Uniform Controlled Dangerous Substances Law. [Drug dealers don't have the luxury of using deadly force to stop people from making an illegal entry into their home, business or vehicles.

Although paragraphs (3) and (4) above seem very similar, the Attorney General of the state has interpreted them to be different, as follows:]

The language of the two statutes can be distinguished. The language in LSA-R.S. 14:20 (3) clearly states a person who observes an unlawful entry of a dwelling, a place of business or motor vehicle during the commission of or attempted commission of a burglary or robbery and that person knows or reasonably believes that unlawful force will be used against another person present on such premises or motor vehicle then the homicide is justifiable. On the other hand, LSA-R.S. 14:20(4) allows a person lawfully present inside such a premises or motor vehicle to use deadly force if he reasonably believes it necessary to prevent the unlawful entry or to compel the intruder to leave the premises or motor vehicle. In either case the person present is not required to retreat. Op.Atty.Gen. No. 00-87, June 1, 2000.

[Notice that nothing in paragraphs (3) or (4) authorizes the use of deadly force to keep someone from breaking into a building or stealing a vehicle that is not occupied by someone. These laws exist to protect persons, not buildings or cars.]

[Presumption of Reasonableness in Special Places – Deadly Force]

B. For the purposes of this Section, there shall be a presumption that a person lawfully inside a dwelling, place of business, or motor vehicle held a reasonable belief that the use of deadly force was necessary to prevent unlawful entry thereto, or to compel an unlawful intruder to leave the premises or motor vehicle, if both of the following occur:

(1) The person against whom deadly force was used was in the process of unlawfully and forcibly entering or had unlawfully and forcibly entered the dwelling, place of business, or motor vehicle.

(2) The person who used deadly force knew or had reason to believe that an unlawful and forcible entry was occurring or had occurred.

[The law presumes you had a reasonable belief that you needed to use deadly force if someone who has no permission to enter your home, business or car uses force to try to break in. If someone bashes in your window with a tire iron in the middle of the night, you can presume he's not there to share a cup of gumbo. Don't forget, presumptions can be rebutted. See discussion of rebuttable presumptions in Chapter 4.

Example: Some unarmed dude in a ninja outfit is trying to pry your screen door open when he sees you coming down the hall with your 10 gauge "punt" gun. He immediately runs down the boat landing, screaming, "I'm outta here! I'm unarmed! Don't shoot!!!," and dives into the black bayou with the reckless abandon of a competitor in the TV series *Fear Factor*. Police investigators find him floating face down 62 feet away with 723 BB entrance wounds extending from his bottom up. You've got to anticipate that during your trial jurors are going to discuss whether it was necessary for you to shoot someone who has abandoned his attempt to break in. Entrance holes in the back of any part of an intruder's body could convince a prosecutor that he has a good chance of rebutting the presumption that shooting the intruder was reasonable or necessary. See Thumbs-Down Factors, Chapter 20.]

[No Duty to Retreat – Deadly Force]

C. A person who is not engaged in unlawful activity and who is in a place where he or she has a right to be shall have no duty to retreat before using deadly force as provided for in this Section, and may stand his or her ground and meet force with force.

D. No finder of fact shall be permitted to consider the possibility of retreat as a factor in determining whether or not the person who used deadly force had a reasonable belief that deadly force was reasonable and apparently necessary to prevent a violent or forcible felony involving life or great bodily harm or to prevent the unlawful entry.

[If you have a right to be in the place where you are attacked (you're not trespassing), you don't have to retreat before using deadly force. Some states require you to retreat if it can be done in complete safety, before using deadly force. Louisiana does not. Neither jurors nor a judge, if you waive a jury, are supposed to consider the fact that you didn't retreat when deciding if your actions were reasonable or necessary.]

[Defense of a Third Person]

§ **LSA - R.S. § 14:22.**
Defense of others.

It is justifiable to use force or violence or to kill in the defense of another person when it is reasonably apparent that the person attacked could have justifiably used such means himself, *and* when it is reasonably believed that such intervention is necessary to protect the other person. [David can use the same force to defend Jonathan that Jonathan would have been justified to use to defend himself.]

[Exceptions to Justifiable Self-Defense] [Initial Aggressor]

§ **LSA – R.S. § 14:21.**
Aggressor cannot claim self-defense.

A person who is the aggressor or who brings on a difficulty cannot claim the right of self-defense . . . [Don't be goin' around startin' trouble if you expect to claim self-defense!]

[Exceptions to the Exceptions] [Withdraw and Communicate]
[§14:21 continued . . .] unless he withdraws from the conflict in good faith and in such a manner that his adversary knows or should know that he desires to withdraw and discontinue the conflict. [**Example:** "I changed my mind. I don't want to fight you. I give up, no matter what you say." This sounds good and well, but our re-

search has shown that once the conflict goes this far, if your opponent is injured or killed, you WILL be arrested and prosecuted. Take our advice; don't get sucked into a verbal dispute that could escalate into a fight to the death.]

[Civil Liability]

§ LSA-R.S. 9:2800.19

A. A person who uses reasonable and apparently necessary or deadly force or violence for the purpose of preventing a forcible offense against the person or his property in accordance with R.S. 14:19 or 20 is immune from civil action for the use of reasonable and apparently necessary or deadly force or violence.

B. The court shall award reasonable attorney fees, court costs, compensation for loss of income, and all expenses to the defendant in any civil action if the court finds that the defendant is immune from suit in accordance with Subsection A of this Section.

[This act was passed in 2006 and we could find no cases interpreting how it is to be applied. It simply says that if you are not guilty under the criminal law by reason of self-defense, then you cannot be sued for damages either. It does not address the lower burden of proof in a civil case. In a criminal case, the state must prove beyond a reasonable doubt that you were not justified in defending yourself. In most civil cases, the person bringing the lawsuit need only prove his case by a preponderance of evidence (more likely than not). The Louisiana courts have not decided these issues. Furthermore, you should be somewhat discomforted by a Louisiana case which held that liability insurance does not cover an act of self-defense. *Duplechain v. Turner,* App. 4 Cir.1984, 444 So.2d 1322, writ denied 448 So.2d 114. For further information regarding potential civil liability for an act of self-defense, see Chapter 15.]

[Defense of Property]

[There is a lack of information concerning the amount of force one can use in protection of property. A former Attorney General (AG) has plainly stated that an individual is not warranted in using warning shots from a firearm to deter trespassers and that property owners doing so would be prosecuted for aggravated assault. Op.Atty.Gen., No. 91-69 (March 13, 1991). This AG opinion relates only to trespassers, not burglars, robbers or intruders breaking into occupied buildings or vehicles. Self-defense with respect to such crimes are covered in §§ 14:19&20 above. http://www.ag.state.la.us/Opinions.aspx]

[HELPFUL DEFINITIONS RELATING TO THIS STATE'S SELF-DEFENSE STATUTES]

- **Dangerous weapon** – [Anything, including gas, liquid or other substance or instrumentality, which, in the manner used, is calculated to or likely to produce death or great bodily harm.] **LSA - R.S. § 14:2 (A)(3).**

- **Felonies Mentioned Above – (These are mentioned only in the Home/Dwelling section)**

  - **Burglary** – [Unauthorized entering of a dwelling, vehicle, watercraft, or other structure, movable or immovable, or any cemetery, with the intent to commit a felony or theft therein. There are many specific types of burglary defined in Louisiana.] **LSA - R.S. § 14:60, 62, 62.1,62.2, 62.6.**

  - **Robbery** – [Taking anything belonging to another by use of unlawful force or intimidation.] **LSA - R.S. § 14:64, 64.1,64.3,64.4.**

- **Felony** – is any crime for which an offender may be sentenced to death or imprisonment at hard labor. **LSA - R.S. § 14:2(A)(4).**

- **Motor vehicle** – means every vehicle which is self-propelled, and every vehicle which is propelled by electric power obtained from overhead trolley wires, but not operated upon rails, but excluding a motorized bicycle. "Motor vehicle" shall also include a "low-speed vehicle" which is a four-wheeled, electric-powered vehicle with a maximum speed of not less than twenty miles per hour but not more than twenty-five miles per hour and is equipped with the minimum motor vehicle equipment appropriate for vehicle safety as required in 49 C.F.R. § 571.500. **LSA - R.S. § 32:1(40).**

- **Property** – refers to both public and private property, movable and immovable, and corporeal and incorporeal property. **LSA - R.S. §:2(A)(8).**

[TEMPLATE Topics We Could Not Find Explained in Statutes or Cases]

(For each of these topics that we could not find addressed in your state's statutes or cases, we suggest you review the same topics in the subchapters of surrounding states. Your state's courts may look to the law of neighboring states to see how their courts and legislatures have treated that particular self-defense issue.)

[Committing Felony or Unlawful Act]

[Mutual Combat]

[Co-Habitant; Co-Employees – Duty to Retreat]

[Reckless Injury to Innocent Third Party]

Key: ■ commentary ■ original statutes, cases or jury instructions

[Defense of Self and Others]

§ 17-A M.R.S.A. § 108.
Physical force in defense of a person.

[Non-Deadly Force] [Defense of a Third Person]

1. A person is justified in using a reasonable degree of nondeadly force upon another person in order to defend the person or a 3rd person from what the person reasonably believes to be the imminent use of unlawful, nondeadly force by such other person, and the person may use a degree of such force that the person reasonably believes to be necessary for such purpose. [Reasonable, non-excessive force is justifiable.]

[Exceptions to Justifiable Self-Defense – Non-Deadly Force]

However, such force is not justifiable if:

[Provocation]

A. With a purpose to cause physical harm to another person, the person provoked the use of unlawful, nondeadly force by such other person; or

[Initial Aggressor] [Exception to an Exception]
[Withdraw and Communicate]

B. The person was the initial aggressor, unless after such aggression the person withdraws from the encounter and effectively communicates to such other person the intent to do so, but the other person notwithstanding continues the use or threat of unlawful, nondeadly force; or

[Mutual Combat]

C. The force involved was the product of a combat by agreement not authorized by law.

1-A. A person is not justified in using nondeadly force against another person who that person knows or reasonably should know is a law enforcement officer attempting to effect an arrest or detention, regardless of whether the arrest or detention is legal. A person is justified in using the degree of nondeadly force the person reasonably believes is necessary to defend the person or a 3rd person against a law enforcement officer who, in effecting an arrest or detention, uses nondeadly force not justified under section 107, subsection 1.

[Your reasonable use of non-deadly force is justifiable unless you provoked or started the fight, (unless you withdraw and make it plain you are withdrawing), or you both agree to fight each other (mutual combat), or fight with a cop even if you think the arrest is unlawful.]

[Deadly Force] [Defense of a Third Person]

2. A person is justified in using deadly force upon another person:

   A. When the person reasonably believes it necessary and reasonably believes such other person is:

      (1) About to use unlawful, deadly force against the person or a 3rd person; or [You can use deadly force to repel deadly force. But don't EVER skim over the word "NECESSARY." See our discussion in Chapter 3.]

[Use of Deadly Force to Prevent Serious Felonies]

      (2) Committing or about to commit a kidnapping, robbery or a violation of section 253, subsection 1, paragraph A against the person or a 3rd person; or [These felonies are described below under [**Helpful Definitions**. . .] Section 253 refers to 17-A M.R.S.A. §253 Gross sexual assault.]

[Defense of Person(s) in Special Places – Home]

   B. When the person reasonably believes:

      (1) That such other person has entered or is attempting to enter a dwelling place or has surreptitiously remained within a dwelling place without a license or privilege to do so; AND [an intruder unlawfully enters your home or secretly remains in your home AND (don't forget the Big "AND")]

      (2) That deadly force is necessary to prevent the infliction of bodily injury by such other person upon the person or a 3rd person present in the dwelling place; [and you reasonably believe the intruder is there to inflict bodily injury. Notice that the words "serious" and "death" are omitted. This means you don't have to believe the intruder is there to cause serious bodily injury or death, only that he (or she) is there to cause bodily injury of some degree. This again, is because your home is your castle and you should not have to tolerate someone entering your home unlawfully to hurt you, your family or your guests. Notice in the definitions at the end of this subchapter, the rather narrow definition of "dwelling place" which DOES NOT include the garage or spaces immediately around the home (commonly referred to as the "curtilage") as in other states. Again, don't forget your use of deadly force must have been necessary.]

   C. However, a person is not justified in using deadly force as provided in paragraph A if: [Exceptions repeated here for deadly force.]

      (1) With the intent to cause physical harm to another, the person provokes such other person to use unlawful deadly force against anyone;

(2) The person knows that the person [presumably a third person] against whom the unlawful deadly force is directed intentionally and unlawfully provoked the use of such force; [You are not justified in using deadly force to defend a third person who you know provoked the use of force against himself AS AN EXCUSE to hurt or kill.] or

[Duty to Retreat – Generally – Yes] [No Duty to Retreat from Home]

(3) The person knows that the person or a 3rd person can, with complete safety:

(a) Retreat from the encounter, except that the person or the 3rd person is not required to retreat if the person or the 3rd person is in the person's dwelling place and was not the initial aggressor; [You don't have to retreat from your home unless you or the third person you are defending started the fight. Please notice that "dwelling place" has a narrower meaning than in some states and DOES NOT include the garage or places immediately around the home (commonly referred to as the curtilage).]

(b) Surrender property to a person asserting a colorable claim of right thereto; or [Neither this subparagraph nor paragraph (c) immediately below have been interpreted by a Maine court. **Example:** Your landlord shows up at your apartment with a gun after you have ignored his eviction notices for six months. He threatens, "to aerate your apartment-trash hind end if you don't get your ugly, yella, no-good keester off my property." You blast him with your Bersa and his body falls into a crumpled heap of eviction notices. A tape recorder found upon his body reveals that he told you he would NOT resort to violence if you would simply take your belongings and leave. You might be convicted of murder despite your claim to self-defense. The same scenario might play out if you are behind on your car payments and you rat-tat-tat the repo man.]

(c) Comply with a demand that the person abstain from performing an act that the person is not obliged to perform. [Honestly, we don't know for certain what this means. Connecticut, Delaware, Hawaii, Maine, Nebraska, New Hampshire, New Jersey and Pennsylvania all have a provision like or similar to this. We comment extensively on what this might mean in Connecticut's subchapter.]

"The Pennsylvania Court has wisely stated, 'Life is sacred and if it is merely a question of whether one man should flee or another should die, then certainly the taking of life should be avoided and the person under attack should flee.' Our own rule applicable to retreat when retreat can safely be made requires no less. The law cannot give its sanction to the settling of disputes by the use of deadly weapons." *State v. Millett*, 273 A.2d 504, 510 (Me. 1971). [Maine Supreme Court's rationale for requiring retreat before using deadly force when not in one's home.]

[Co-Habitants – Duty to Retreat – No]

"Given the clear and unambiguous language of section 108, we conclude that the 'dwelling place exception' to the retreat rule is applicable even if the assailant is lawfully present." *State v. Laverty*, 495 A. 2d 831, 833 (Me. 1985). [Even if the person from whom you are protecting yourself has a right to be there, such as a roommate, you do not have to retreat from them unless you were the initial aggressor.]

[Defense of Person(s) in Special Places – Premises, Dwelling]

§ 17-A M.R.S.A. § 104.
Use of force in defense of premises.

1. A person in possession or control of premises or a person who is licensed or privileged to be thereon is justified in using nondeadly force upon another person when and to the extent that the person reasonably believes it necessary to prevent or terminate the commission of a criminal trespass by such other person in or upon such premises. [You can't use deadly force against trespassers.]

2. A person in possession or control of premises or a person who is licensed or privileged to be thereon is justified in using deadly force upon another person when and to the extent that the person reasonably believes it necessary to prevent an attempt by the other person to commit arson. [Arson is one of the property crimes that usually justifies the use of deadly force. This is because of the risk to human life if an assailant uses fire or explosives to damage a building.]

3. A person in possession or control of a dwelling place or a person who is licensed or privileged to be therein is justified in using deadly force upon another person: [You can use deadly force to defend your home . . .]

   A. Under the circumstances enumerated in section 108 [. . . in defense of persons to prevent a deadly attack, kidnapping, robbery, or forcible sexual attack]; or

   B. When the person reasonably believes that deadly force is necessary to prevent or terminate the commission of a criminal trespass by such other person, who the person reasonably believes: [. . . as necessary to stop a trespasser who . . .]

      (1) Has entered or is attempting to enter the dwelling place or has surreptitiously remained within the dwelling place without a license or privilege to do so; and [. . . who is trying to force his way into your home or has sneaked in AND . . .]

      (2) Is committing or is likely to commit some other crime within the dwelling place. [. . . is committing or likely to commit a crime in the home AND comply with paragraph 4 below requiring you to use verbal commands to "leave immediately."]

4. A person may use deadly force under subsection 3, paragraph B only if the person first demands the person against whom such deadly force is to be used to terminate the criminal trespass and the trespasser fails to immediately comply with the demand, unless the person reasonably believes that it would be dangerous to the per-

son or a 3rd person to make the demand. [Notice the threshold for the use of deadly force is lower when someone breaks or sneaks into your home. Rather than requiring you to have a reasonable belief you are facing an imminent threat of deadly force, you only need to have a reasonable belief the intruder is committing a crime or is there to commit a crime. Notice the use of the phrase "other crime." This means that the trespass alone is not enough. He has to be stealing something or threatening someone. A ski mask and latex gloves might provide you with a nice clue. You are required by paragraph 4 to give a verbal command like, "Get Out!!!! Now!!!!" You're not required to do this if it looks like it could be dangerous to give the warning (e.g., he has what looks like a machine gun angled in your direction). Under either of these two scenarios (he fails to leave immediately or the danger of letting your presence be known is obvious) you may let the music begin—play percussion with your POF (clean-running, piston-driven AR-15). However, we caution you again to read Chapter 3 and 4 carefully about the other possible limitations of the use of force.]

5. As used in this section:

   A. Dwelling place has the same meaning provided in section 2, subsection 10; and

   B. Premises includes, but is not limited to, lands, private ways and any buildings or structures thereon. [Please notice that "premises" has a broader definition than dwelling. You may only use deadly force to protect a premises from arson, but you may defend your home with deadly force to prevent a trespass with the intent to commit a crime in addition to the trespass.]

[Defense of Property]

§ 17-A M.R.S.A. § 105.
Use of force in property offenses.

A person is justified in using a reasonable degree of nondeadly force upon another person when and to the extent that the person reasonably believes it necessary to prevent what is or reasonably appears to be an unlawful taking of the person's property, or criminal mischief, or to retake the person's property immediately following its taking; but the person may use deadly force only under such circumstances as are prescribed in sections 104 [defense of premises and dwellings, above], 107 [use of force by law enforcement, not included] and 108 [defense of persons, above].

[As in most states, you may only defend items of personal property (e.g., your big screen, stereo, furniture, bicycle, etc.) with non-deadly force.]

[Reckless Injury to Innocent Third Parties]

§ 17-A M.R.S.A. § 101.
General rules for defenses and affirmative defenses; justification.

. . .

3. Conduct that is justifiable under this chapter constitutes a defense to any crime; except that, if a person is justified in using force against another, but the person recklessly injures or creates a risk of injury to 3rd persons, the justification afforded by this chapter is unavailable in a prosecution for such recklessness. If a defense

provided under this chapter is precluded solely because the requirement that the person's belief be reasonable has not been met, the person may be convicted only of a crime for which recklessness or criminal negligence suffices. [You may be justified to use force, but if you use it recklessly or with criminal negligence, you can be prosecuted for your poor behavior. **Example:** You see bank robbers coming out of a bank holding several tellers hostage and decide to cut loose Banderas-style *(Desperado)* with twin 1911s. If you kill or injure any of the hostages, you could be charged with manslaughter or other crimes that only require proof of recklessness as opposed to an intent to kill (such as murder).]

[Civil Liability]

4. The fact that conduct may be justifiable under this chapter does not abolish or impair any remedy for such conduct which is available in any civil action. [Even if a court finds you innocent of a crime, this doesn't mean you can't be sued. Read Chapter 15, about civil liability.]

[HELPFUL DEFINITIONS RELATING TO THIS STATE'S SELF-DEFENSE STATUTES]

- **Armed with a dangerous weapon** – means in actual possession, regardless of whether the possession is visible or concealed, of:

  (1) A firearm;

  (2) Any device designed as a weapon and capable of producing death or serious bodily injury; or

  (3) Any other device, instrument, material or substance, whether animate or inanimate, which, in the manner it is intended to be used by the actor, is capable of producing or threatening death or serious bodily injury. . . . **Maine Revised Statutes 17-A M.R.S.A. § 2 (9)(B).**

- **Bodily injury** – means physical pain, physical illness or any impairment of physical condition. **Maine Revised Statutes 17-A M.R.S.A. § 2 (5).**

- **Deadly force** – means physical force that a person uses with the intent of causing, or that a person knows to create a substantial risk of causing, death or serious bodily injury. Intentionally or recklessly discharging a firearm in the direction of another person or at a moving vehicle constitutes deadly force. **Maine Revised Statutes 17-A M.R.S.A. § 2 (8).**

- **Dwelling place** – means a structure which is adapted for overnight accommodation of persons, or sections of any structure similarly adapted. A dwelling place does not include garages or other structures, whether adjacent or attached to the dwelling place, which are used solely for the storage of property or structures formerly used as dwelling places which are uninhabitable. It is immaterial whether a person is actually present. **Maine Revised Statutes 17-A M.R.S.A. § 2 (10).**

- **Felonies Mentioned Above –**
  - **Arson** – [Starting, causing or maintaining a fire or explosion on a property with the intent of damaging that property or if done with recklessness that endangers another or property of another.] **Maine Revised Statutes 17-A M.R.S.A. § 802.**
  - **Kidnapping** – [Restraining someone against their will with the intent to use them for ransom, hostage/shield, or commit a crime against them. Kidnapping also includes knowingly restraining a person secretly or restraining someone under circumstances that would expose that person to serious bodily injury.] **Maine Revised Statutes 17-A M.R.S.A. § 301.**
  - **Robbery** – [While committing theft or in the attempt, a person recklessly injures another or threatens force against another to accomplish the theft.] **Maine Revised Statutes 17-A M.R.S.A. § 651.**
  - **Gross sexual assault** – [Compelling someone against their will to have sex.] **Maine Revised Statues 17-A M.R.S.A. §253(1)(A).**
- **Non-deadly force** – means any physical force which is not deadly force. **Maine Revised Statutes 17-A M.R.S.A. § 2 (18).**
- **Serious bodily injury** – means a bodily injury which creates a substantial risk of death or which causes serious, permanent disfigurement or loss or substantial impairment of the function of any bodily member or organ, or extended convalescence necessary for recovery of physical health. **Maine Revised Statutes 17-A M.R.S.A. § 2 (23).**
- **Structure** – means a building or other place designed to provide protection for persons or property against weather or intrusion, but does not include vehicles and other conveyances whose primary purpose is transportation of persons or property unless such vehicle or conveyance, or a section thereof, is also a dwelling place. **Maine Revised Statutes 17-A M.R.S.A. § 2 (24).**
- **Use of a dangerous weapon** – means the use of a firearm or other weapon, device, instrument, material or substance, whether animate or inanimate, which, in the manner it is used or threatened to be used is capable of producing death or serious bodily injury. **Maine Revised Statutes 17-A M.R.S.A. § 2 (9)(A).**

[TEMPLATE Topics We Could Not Find Explained in Statutes or Cases]

(For each of these topics that we could not find addressed in your state's statutes or cases, we suggest you review the same topics in the subchapters of surrounding states. Your state's courts may look to the law of the surrounding states to see how their courts and legislatures have treated that particular self-defense issue.)

[Committing Felony or Unlawful Act]

[Co-Employees – Duty to Retreat]

[Presumption of Reasonableness in Special Places]

Pancho's Wisdom

You just might be a Gunnut if . . .

. . . you refuse to golf unless they let you shoot the balls.

. . . you believe the Big Bang Theory is the solution to violent crime.

MARYLAND

With the exception of a short section on Battered Women's Syndrome, Maryland does not have self-defense statutes. Its courts and lawyers rely heavily upon jury instructions based upon cases handed down by appeals courts over the years. These jury instructions are not readily available to the public, but rather are sold to law firms and law libraries. Because Maryland's self-defense laws were developed in court cases rather than written by Maryland's elected officials, Maryland's citizens have no input into what these laws should say. Furthermore, no one can discover what the rules of self-defense in Maryland are without digging through thousands of pages of dusty law books. We have endeavored to distill Maryland's laws of self-defense from the latest cases we could find involving self-defense.

Pancho's Wisdom – We are as frustrated as you are that the law has to be this difficult. We encourage you to become politically active and have your Legislature codify what presently is Maryland's common (case) law. Self-defense law should be simplified and made available to the public. Also, encourage your elected representatives to make the laws less favorable to carjackers and armed robbers and more favorable to innocent citizens. Although ignorance of the law is no excuse, it's also inexcusable for state officials to hide the rules that govern an inalienable right, the right of self-defense, in thousands of pages of legal mumbo jumbo! Following are rules of self-defense law that we dug out of the cases we could find. This digging reminded us of when our cousin Mike and his friend Thayne got peppered with rock salt shot from a 12 gauge for stealing cherries. They spent hours digging salt crystal out of their stinging BEHINDS! Justifiable or not, the two little hoodlums left Hal's orchard alone and for years believed the word "assault" was spelled "assalt." Anyway, as we dig, we hope you dig because apparently the Maryland Legislature doesn't dig. Maryland lawmakers should read and apply the concluding chapter of this book, The Mother of All Self-Defense Laws, Chapter 20.

Key: ■ commentary ■ original statutes, cases or jury instructions

---

[Defense of Self and Others] [Non-Deadly Force] [Deadly Force]

"Perfect self-defense, we observed, is a complete defense to a charge of criminal homicide and, if credited by the trier of fact, results in an acquittal. It constitutes a justification for the killing." *State v. Smullen*, 844 A.2d 429, 439-40 (Md. 2004). [**Translation:** If you understand and correctly apply the law of self-defense resulting in the death of your attacker, you cannot be convicted of murder, manslaughter or any other crime for that matter. You are innocent.]

"The elements of self-defense are well-settled in Maryland:
"(1) The accused must have had reasonable grounds to believe himself in apparent imminent or immediate danger of death or serious bodily harm from his assailant or potential assailant; [Notice the word "apparent." If the belief is reasonable, even though the appearances are false, a person can still be found not guilty by reason of self-defense. **Example:** You shoot a home invader who aims a gun at you and says, "You're dead, M@#$#% F@$#@%!!!!" It turns out his gun was actually a play gun that was painted to look exactly like a real gun. If anyone in your situation would think the gun was real, you would be justified in using deadly force even though his gun was fake and couldn't hurt you.]

"(2) The accused must have in fact believed himself in this danger; [In the example above, if you knew somehow the gun was a fake, you would not be justified in using deadly force.]

"(3) The accused claiming the right of self-defense must not have been the aggressor or provoked the conflict; and [If you start a fight, you can't claim self-defense. See Exceptions to Justifiable Self-Defense below.]

"(4) The force used must not have been unreasonable and excessive, that is, the force must not have been more force than the exigency demanded." *Christian v. State*, 951 A.2d 832, 843 (Md. 2008). [You cannot use excessive force, or, in the language used in other jurisdictions, more force than is "necessary." **Example:** Your severely disabled neighbor freaks out because you can't take him to an Orioles game like you promised. He attacks you with a tire iron, but you know he is too disabled and weak to hurt you. You have just completed a firearms self-defense course during which your instructor told you a tire iron is a dangerous weapon. You draw your gun and perform a perfectly executed Mozambique drill (two to the body, one to the head) on your hapless and unhappy neighbor. It won't help you that crime scene investigators find his riddled body still clutching the tire iron. Because of his total disability he couldn't hurt you with it, therefore, your use of deadly force was unnecessary. Your self-defense claim will be defeated and you will be convicted of something unpleasant.]

[Use of Deadly Force to Prevent Serious Felonies]

"We have never adopted the view, and are unwilling to do so now, that, other than when acting pursuant to an absolute command of the law, a person may use deadly force against another when the use of that deadly force, at the moment and in the circumstance used, was not necessary to protect against an imminent threat of death or serious bodily injury. Under this view, which is the established Maryland law, the right to use deadly force to resist a robbery, or other attempted or ongoing assault or felony, exists only during the time that the victim of the attack reasonably believes that such force is necessary to repel an imminent danger of death or serious bodily harm-during the time that "the exigency demanded" the use of such force." *Sydnor v. State*, 776 A.2d 669, 675 (Md. 2001). [You cannot just kill a felon because he/she is committing a felony. In order to use deadly force, you have to reasonably believe that you need to use it to repel an imminent threat of death or serious injury. This case, *Snydor*, is described more fully in the Thumbs-Down Chapter 7. Defendant was being robbed and pistol whipped. He took the gun away from the robber and shot him with it as he ran away. But there were several Thumbs-Down Factors that increased the probability of arrest, prosecution and conviction. He had been charged with murder, but was only convicted of manslaughter.]

[Defense of Third Persons]

". . . a third person, who is clearly related to or associated with the person subjected to the excessive and unreasonable force of the counterattack, has a right to go to the defense of that person and to use the same degree and character of force that the person presently being attacked could have used to defend himself." *Tipton v. State*, 232 A.2d 289, 292 (Md.App. 1967). [This is an old case, but as far as we can tell, it's still good law. There are two important things going on here. First, the court is clarifying that you can defend another person to the same degree that person can defend him/herself. Second the court is establishing that you have to have some kind of relationship with the person you are defending. We're not sure how strict the "clearly related to or associated with" language will be interpreted by today's Maryland courts, or why Maryland wouldn't want to encourage people to defend strangers. This creates somewhat of a legal risk if you ever have to defend a total stranger.]

"We instruct you, however, that when a person kills in the defense of another person, such a killing is not made unjustifiable or inexcusable because of the fact that the person he defended provoked a conflict, or was the aggressor, provided that the person acting to defend the other person did not know, and under the circumstances had no reasonable grounds to believe that the person he was defending was at fault for being the aggressor or provoking the conflict. On the other hand, if he knew, or as a reasonable person should have known under the circumstances that the person whom he was acting to defend was the aggressor and had provoked a conflict, then his killing in defense of that person would not be justifiable or excusable." *Tipton v. State*, 232 A.2d 289, 292 (Md.App. 1967). [You can't defend a person whom you know initiated or provoked a conflict. However, if you didn't know, but had a reasonable belief that the person you defended was without fault, you would be justified in defending him. Unfortunately, in our opinion, if there is any question about whether you knew the person you defended was an initial aggressor or provoked the fight, you will always be arrested and prosecuted.]

"Defense of another is a recognized response to a second degree assault charge if: (1) the defendant actually believed that the person defended was in immediate and imminent danger of death or serious bodily harm; (2) the defendant's belief was reasonable; (3) the defendant used no more force than was reasonably necessary to defend the person defended in light of the threatened or actual force; and, (4) the defendant's purpose in using force was to aid the person defended...The intervention must be to aid the victim and not to punish the offender or to avenge the victim...The intervenor's acts "must be judged on his own conduct, based upon his own observation of the circumstances as they reasonably appeared to him." *Choi v. State*, 759 A.2d 1156, 1163 (Md.App. 2000). [While these rules apply specifically to assault cases, they're good guidelines for anyone wanting to use force to help someone else. This case also reminds us that punishment and revenge are not justifiable. Notice that here there is no requirement that you have some kind of relationship to the person you're defending. Although this is basically the same standard as described in the other case in this section, it's recast in different language and can cause confusion. This is why the Maryland Legislature needs to step up and CODIFY THE LAW so that citizens can be clear on what's expected of them.]

[Exceptions to Justifiable Self-Defense] [Initial Aggressor] [Provocation]

" ... (3) The accused claiming the right of self-defense must not have been the aggressor or provoked the conflict." *Marquardt v. State,* 882 A. 2d 900, 926 (Md. App. 2005) [Don't start a fight and expect to claim self-defense.]

[Exceptions to the Exceptions]

"Where one attacks another in a manner not calculated to kill or to do serious bodily harm, and the defender counterattacks, using excessive and unreasonable force in a manner reasonably calculated to cause death or great bodily harm, then the original attacker becomes the defender. If the original assailant is unable to retreat to a place of safety or there is no place of safety available, then he may use whatever force necessary to repel the counterattack of the original defender." *Tipton v. State,* 232 A.2d 289, 292 (Md.App. 1967). [This is known as escalation or a "step-up in force." If you attack someone with non-deadly force, and they respond with deadly force, you can use force in justifiable self-defense as long as you first try to retreat to a place of safety. Whether you ultimately are found not guilty, if you are at all at fault in starting a fight, you will almost always be arrested and prosecuted.]

[Duty to Retreat – Generally – Yes]

"One of the elements of the defense of self-defense is 'the duty of the defendant to retreat or avoid danger if such means were within his power and consistent with his safety.'" *Burch v. State,* 696 A.2d 443, 458 (Md. 1997). [You must retreat before you use force in self-defense if it is safe to do so.]

[Defense of Person(s) in Special Places – Home]

"A man is not bound to retreat from his house. He may stand his ground there and kill any person who attempts to commit a felony therein, or who attempts to enter by force for the purpose of committing a felony, or of inflicting great bodily harm upon an inmate. In such a case the owner or any member of the family, or even a lodger in the house, may meet the intruder at the threshold, and prevent him from entering by any means rendered necessary by the exigency, even to the taking of his life, and the homicide will be justifiable." *Barton v. State,* 420 A.2d 1009, 1012 (Md.App. 1980)(citations omitted). [You can use deadly force to prevent an intruder from entering your house if the intruder is entering to commit a felony or cause serious injury. You don't have to retreat from your own home, Chapter 4.]

"[O]ne need not be the head of the household to avail himself of the 'castle' exception. Rather, we concluded that any member of the household, whether or not he or she has a proprietary or leasehold interest in the property, is within its ambit..." [Any member of the household can invoke the castle doctrine (no duty to retreat, right to use deadly force to protect the dwelling and its inhabitants from people with felonious intent) whether or not they own the dwelling.]

"The phrase 'dwelling place' is used... to denote any building or habitation, or part of it, in which the actor is at the time temporarily or permanently residing and which is in the exclusive possession of the actor, or of a household of which he is a member. Only that part of the building or other habitation which is actually used for residential purposes is a dwelling place. Thus, a man's house is the dwelling place of himself, his family, his servants, and for the time being, the dwelling place of one who is residing, however temporarily, in the house as a guest. It is not the dwelling place of a visitor, social or business, who comes to the house for a particular purpose and not to reside therein." *Barton v. State,* 420 A.2d 1009, 1011 (Md.App. 1980)(Citations and footnotes omitted). [A dwelling is any structure you use for residential purposes, but includes only as much of the building as you use for residing. Everyone who lives there is part of the household, even guests who are temporarily residing there. However, visitors (apparently people who aren't spending the night), are not a part of the household and can't invoke the castle doctrine.]

[No Duty to Retreat From Home]

"[A] man faced with the danger of an attack upon his dwelling need not retreat from his home to escape the danger, but instead may stand his ground and, if necessary to repel the attack, may kill the attacker." *Burch v. State,* 696 A.2d 443, 458 (Md. 1997). [You have no duty to retreat from your own home before using deadly force against an intruder.]

[Civil Liability]

"If an injury was done by a defendant in justifiable self-defense, he can neither be punished criminally nor held responsible for damages in a civil action." *Baltimore Transit Co. v. Faulkner,* 20 A.2d 485, 487 (Md. 1941). [If you legally use deadly force to stop an imminent threat of deadly force, you are not liable for damages for the resulting injury or death. Keep in mind, however, that the injured person's attorney will be claiming you negligently used excessive force against his client. The burden of proof in such a case is "more likely than not" rather than "beyond a reasonable doubt," like it is in a criminal case. See our discussion of civil liability in Chapter 15.]

[Defense of Property]

"A robbery victim is free to use non-lethal force to accomplish the recovery of his property or apprehend the robber." *Sydnor v. State,* 754 A.2d 1064, 1072 (Md.App. 2000). [You can use force, but not deadly force, to protect or recover your personal property.]

[TEMPLATE Topics We Could Not Find Explained in Statutes or Cases]

(For each of these topics that we could not find addressed in your state's statutes or cases, we suggest you review the same topics in the subchapters of surrounding states. Your state's courts may look to the law of the surrounding states to see how their courts and legislatures have treated that particular self-defense issue.)

[Committing Felony or Unlawful Act]

[Mutual Combat]

[Withdraw and Communicate]

[Co-Habitants; Co-Employees – Duty to Retreat]

[Presumption of Reasonableness in Special Places]

[Reckless Injury to Innocent Third Parties]

[Helpful Definitions Relating to this State's Self-Defense Statutes]

Massachusetts is another state in which the statutory law is pathetically deficient in putting innocent citizens on notice as to what is expected of them in situations where they are forced to defend themselves and others. We found one homicide statute dealing with defense of home cited below as **M.G.L.A. 278 § 8A. Killing or injuring a person unlawfully in a dwelling; defense.** Besides this one statute, the rest of Massachusetts' self-defense laws have to be dug out of criminal cases. Most citizens are not trained to do such digging nor do they have ready access to the cases. For a state whose motto is, "By the Sword we Seek Peace, but Peace only under Liberty," we believe its legislature can do better. We encourage Massachusetts legislators (and we hope you folks from Massachusetts join in the effort) to enact and simplify a comprehensive self-defense statute that protects the innocent and imposes serious legal and physical risks upon the guilty. The Mother of All Self-Defense Laws, Chapter 20, would be a good place to start.

Key: ■ commentary ■ original statutes, cases or jury instructions

---

[Defense of Self and Others] [Non-Deadly Force]
[Duty to Retreat – Generally – Yes]

"In a case like this where nondeadly force is used, a defendant is entitled to an instruction on self-defense 'if any view of the evidence would support a reasonable doubt as to whether the prerequisites of self-defense were present,' to wit: (1) the defendant had 'a reasonable concern over his personal safety,' (2) he used all reasonable means to avoid physical combat [phrased later on in the case as a duty to retreat before using force]; and (3) the degree of force used was reasonable in the circumstances, with proportionality being the touchstone for assessing reasonableness." Commonwealth [abbreviated hereafter as *"Com."*] *v. Franchino,* 810 N.E.2d 1251, 1254 (Mass.App.Ct. 2004)(citations omitted). [You may use non-deadly force to repel an attacker using non-deadly force. You must have a reasonable belief your personal safety is in jeopardy, you must retreat if you can safely do so before using force and you may only use as much force as is necessary to stop the non-deadly attack. You may not use deadly force.]

[Deadly Force]

"Deadly force used in self-defense is warranted only in circumstances where one '(1) had reasonable ground to believe and actually did believe that he was in imminent danger of death or serious bodily harm, from which he could save himself only by using deadly force, (2) had availed himself of all proper means to avoid physical combat before resorting to the use of deadly force, and (3) used no more force than was reasonably necessary in all the circumstances of the case.'" *Com. v. Haith,* 894 N.E.2d

1122, 1128 (Mass. 2008). [You may only use deadly force in self-defense in Massachusetts if there is an imminent threat of serious injury or death. You must retreat before using deadly force if at all possible. You can only use as much force as necessary and you must reasonably and honestly believe that you can only save yourself if you use deadly force. There are no felonies mentioned in Massachusetts law that automatically give you the right to use deadly force like in many western and southern states. Massachusetts is one of the few states that expressly require an "overt act" before you resort to the use of deadly force. An "overt act" means some motion that is observable and provides an objective basis from which to measure the reasonableness of the defendant's fear.] "For such a belief to be reasonable, the victim must have committed some overt act against the defendant. If an assault includes the threat of an action that would cause the defendant serious bodily injury, this is sufficient to require such an instruction. Self-defense using deadly force is not justified in the absence of such a threat." *Com. v. Pike,* 701 N.E.2d 951, 955 (Mass. 1998).

[Defense of a Third Person]

"Deadly force against another to protect a third party is justified only when (a) a reasonable person in the actor's position would believe his intervention to be necessary for the protection of the third person, and (b) in the circumstances as that reasonable person would believe them to be, the third person would be justified in using such [deadly] force to protect himself." *Com. v. Haith,* 894 N.E.2d 1122, 1128 (Mass. 2008). [You have to actually believe that Jack needs your help, but you can only use as much force as it reasonably appears Jack needs.]

[Exceptions to Justifiable Self-Defense] [Initial Aggressor]
[Provocation] [Exceptions to the Exceptions]
[Withdraw and Communicate]

"The right of self-defense ordinarily cannot be claimed by a person who provokes or initiates an assault unless that person withdraws in good faith from the conflict and announces his intention to retire." *Com. v. Pring-Wilson,* 863 N.E.2d 936, 947 (Mass. 2007). [If you start the fight, or do something to the other guy in the hopes that he'll attack you so you can kill him, you can't claim self-defense unless you withdraw and make it obvious to your opponent you are quitting the fight. You must sincerely intend to withdraw, not just put on a show of withdrawal so you can revive your claim of self- defense. Usually, if things get this complicated, you can count on being arrested and prosecuted.]

[Mutual Combat]

"When two meet, not intending to quarrel, and angry words suddenly arise, and a conflict springs up in which blows are given on both sides, without much regard to who is the assailant, it is a mutual combat. And if no unfair advantage is taken in the outset, and the occasion is not sought for the purpose of gratifying malice, and one seizes a weapon and strikes a deadly blow, it is regarded as homicide in heat of blood." *Com. v. Clemente,* 893 N.E.2d 19, 42 (Mass. 2008). [This means that the best you can hope for is a second degree murder or manslaughter conviction (homicide in the heat of blood) if you voluntarily agree to fight and end up killing someone. Mutual combat is not justifiable, meaning you cannot be found innocent.]

[Defense of Person(s) in Special Places – Dwelling]
[No Duty to Retreat from Dwelling]

§ MASSACHUSETTS GENERAL LAWS ANNOTATED (M.G.L.A.) 278 § 8A.

Killing or injuring a person unlawfully in a dwelling; defense.

Section 8A. In the prosecution of a person who is an occupant of a dwelling charged with killing or injuring one who was unlawfully in said dwelling, it shall be a defense that the occupant was in his dwelling at the time of the offense and that he acted in the reasonable belief that the person unlawfully in said dwelling was about to inflict great bodily injury or death upon said occupant or upon another person lawfully in said dwelling, and that said occupant used reasonable means to defend himself or such other person lawfully in said dwelling. There shall be no duty on said occupant to retreat from such person unlawfully in said dwelling. [This statute is nothing to brag about. It is simply a codification of common law. At common law a person could use deadly force to repel deadly force and had no duty to retreat from his or her home. Before you can use deadly force in your home you must have a reasonable belief that someone is about to inflict serious injury or death upon you or another person lawfully in your home. There is not a lower threshold for the use of deadly force to defend persons in your home like many of the western and southern states.

We are concerned that the threat of sexual assault or rape may not be considered "great bodily harm" and therefore, not justify the use of deadly force. What if a woman shoots a rapist who survives and testifies he told her that he simply wanted to have sex with her but would take every precaution to prevent sexually transmitted disease? Will some prosecutor in the Bay State argue she was not justified in using deadly force because she had not been threatened with "great bodily injury?" We could not find a Massachusetts case that specifically addresses this issue. Until sexual assault is added to Massachusetts' self and home defense statutes, no woman can ever be 100% sure that a prosecutor will not raise such an argument. This is one of our big complaints about states that do not have well-defined self-defense statutes.]

Important: No-Retreat Rule Does Not Extend to Exterior Stairs and Porches.

"We have since determined that the defense provided by § 8A did not apply to an encounter on the exterior stairs and porch of a dwelling, confirming the inapplicability of the defense here. The language of § 8A and our earlier decisions resolve the issue." *Com. v. Carlino*, 865 N.E.2d 767, 772 (Mass. 2007). [The no-retreat rule of Section 8A does not extend beyond the inside of a person's home or dwelling. Notice the words "in said dwelling." Massachusetts cases have held this language limits the no-retreat rule to inside your home, not to exterior stairs or porches. In Mass. a dwelling is "a place where one is 'temporarily or permanently residing and which is in [one's] exclusive possession.' With reference to an apartment building, the judge stated that 'a tenant's dwelling cannot reasonably be said to extend beyond his own apartment and perhaps any separate areas subject to his exclusive control.'" *Com. v. Albert,* 466 N.E.2d 78, 85 (Mass. 1984).]

[Co-Habitants; Guests – Duty to Retreat – Yes]

[Massachusetts' home-defense statute says you do not have to retreat from your home if you are being threatened by someone unlawfully inside. This exception does not apply to roommates, co-habitants, a spouse and others who have the right to be in your home. *Com. v. Noble,* 707 N.E.2d 819 (Mass. 1999). This is true even if you've invited someone to your home and they suddenly go psycho on you. If that happens, you have a duty to retreat before using deadly force if you can do so in complete safety. *Com. v. Peloquin,* 770 N.E.2d 440, 444 (Mass. 2002).]

[Defense of Property]

"The concept of defense of property has been little explicated in the Commonwealth's case law. It relates to the right to use limited force to defend personal property from theft or destruction and real property from unwelcome invasion... The court held that 'a man may defend or regain his momentarily interrupted possession by the use of reasonable force, short of wounding or the employment of a dangerous weapon.'" *Com. v. Haddock,* 704 N.E.2d 537, 540 (Mass.App.Ct. 1999)(citations omitted).

"The right to defend one's property relates to the right to use reasonable force to defend personal property from theft or destruction and real property from unwelcome invasion." *Com. v. Peterson,* 759 N.E.2d 719, 722 (Mass.App.Ct. 2001).

"If ... a property owner ... tell[s] somebody who doesn't have any other right to be there to get off their property, that person could be called a trespasser.... A person may use reasonable force ... to remove a trespasser from their property after the trespasser has been requested to leave and has refused to do so..." *Com. v. Galvin,* 779 N.E.2d 998, 1001 (Mass.App.Ct.2002).

"As for defense of property (at least in the sense intended here of ejecting trespassers), the relevant inquiry is whether (1) the defendant used only nondeadly force, and (2) the force used was appropriate in kind and suitable in degree, to accomplish the purpose." *Com. v. Haddock,* 704 N.E.2d 537, 540 (Mass.App.Ct. 1999).

"Nevertheless, limits must be set, as to the use of deadly force, against the dangers of uncontrolled vigilantism and anarchistic actions, and particularly against the danger of death or injury of innocent persons at the hands of untrained volunteers using firearms. In our view, for example, there would be no wisdom in approving the unqualified right of a private citizen to use deadly force to prevent the escape of one who has committed a crime against property only." *Com. v. Klein,* 363 N.E.2d 1313, 1317 (Mass. 1977). [These four quotes together mean you can use reasonable force but not deadly force to eject a trespasser, or protect property from damage.]

[TEMPLATE Topics We Could Not Find Explained in Statutes or Cases]

(For each of these topics that we could not find addressed in your state's statutes or cases, we suggest you review the same topics in the subchapters of surrounding states. Your state's courts may look to the law of neighboring states to see how their courts and legislatures have treated that particular self-defense issue.)

[Use of Deadly Force to Prevent Serious Felonies]

[Committing Felony or Unlawful Act]

[Co-Employers – Duty to Retreat]

[Presumption of Reasonableness in Special Places]

[Reckless Injury to Innocent Third Parties]

[Civil Liability]

[Helpful Definitions Relating to this State's Self-Defense Statutes]

Pancho's Wisdom

You just might be a Gunnut if . . . "bowling" to you means shooting five used bowling pins completely off of a flat piece of plywood at 30 feet in under 3 seconds.

MICHIGAN

In 2006, Michigan passed its "Self-Defense Act" (hereafter "SDA") that finally gave its citizens and visitors something concrete they could rely upon in defending themselves. Without a written act, there is no notice, in the constitutional sense, of what is legal self-defense and what is not.

Key: ■ commentary ■ original statutes, cases or jury instructions

[Defense of Self and Others] [Deadly Force]
[No Duty to Retreat – Generally] [Defense of Third Persons]

§ 780.972.
Use of deadly force by individual not engaged in commission of crime; conditions.

Sec. 2.

(1) An individual who has not or is not engaged in the commission of a crime at the time he or she uses deadly force may use deadly force against another individual anywhere he or she has the legal right to be with no duty to retreat if either of the following applies: [When using force in self-defense, you have no duty to retreat as long as you are somewhere you're legally allowed to be, and as long as you're not committing a crime. This applies to both deadly and non-deadly force (see below).]

(a) The individual honestly *and* reasonably believes that the use of deadly force is necessary to prevent the imminent death of or imminent great bodily harm to himself or herself or to another individual. [Before a person can use deadly force, he must believe and his belief must be reasonable (not eccentric) that he is facing an imminent threat of death or serious injury. If a person has an honest belief, but it is not reasonable, it amounts to an "imperfect" self-defense and usually results in a manslaughter conviction. Pay attention to the word "necessary." See our detailed discussion of the concept of necessity in Chapter III.]

[Use of Deadly Force to Prevent Serious Felonies]

(b) The individual honestly and reasonably believes that the use of deadly force is necessary to prevent the imminent sexual assault of himself or herself or of another individual. [Before Michigan's Self-Defense Act, it wasn't clear whether deadly force could be used to prevent a sexual assault.]

[Non-Deadly Force]

(2) An individual who has not or is not engaged in the commission of a crime at the time he or she uses force other than deadly force may use force other than deadly force against another individual anywhere he or she has the legal right to be with no duty to retreat if he or she honestly and reasonably believes that the use of that force is necessary to defend himself or herself or another individual from the imminent unlawful use of force by another individual. [Someone tries pulling you out of line at a Wolverines game. You can use reasonable force to keep from being assaulted, but you cannot shoot or stab the person with a deadly weapon.]

[Exceptions to Justifiable Self Defense]

§ 780.961 (1).
Use of deadly force or force other than deadly force; establishing evidence that individual's actions not justified.

[Committing Felony or Unlawful Act]

Sec. 1.

(1) An individual who uses deadly force or force other than deadly force in compliance with section 2 of the self-defense act and who has not or is not engaged in the commission of a crime at the time he or she uses that deadly force or force other than deadly force commits no crime in using that deadly force or force other than deadly force. [You can't justifiably use either deadly or non-deadly force if you are committing a crime, no matter what happens to you. The reason for this exception is to keep criminals from using force to commit a crime and then claim self-defense.]

. . .

[Initial Aggressor]

"...An initial aggressor (i.e., one who is the first to use deadly force against the other), ... is generally not entitled to use deadly force in self-defense." *People v. Riddle,* 649 N.W.2d 30, 35 (Mich. 2002). [Generally, a person who starts a fight is not justified in using force in self-defense.]

[Provocation]

"If a defendant with malice and hatred in his heart towards another person, seeks to provoke a difficulty, either by acts or words, with the intent to induce such other person to strike the first blow, or to make the demonstration, in order to form a pretext to take his life, then the defendant could not avail himself of the right of self-defense." *People v. Fredericks,* 194 N.W.2d 42, 43 (Mich.App. 1971). [Provocation refers to initiating a conflict as an excuse to hurt or kill when the person who is provoked retaliates. If you provoke a fight, you are not entitled to use force in self-defense.]

[Mutual Combat]

"Second, Michigan law imposes an *affirmative obligation* to retreat upon a nonaggressor only in one narrow set of circumstances: A participant in voluntary mutual combat will not be justified in taking the life of another until he is deemed to have retreated as far as safely possible. One who is involved in a physical altercation in which he is a willing participant—referred to at common law as a "sudden affray" or a "chance medley"—is required to take advantage of any reasonable and safe avenue of retreat before using deadly force against his adversary, should the altercation escalate into a deadly encounter." *People v. Riddle*, 649 N.W.2d 30, 35 (Mich. 2002). [If you willingly enter into a fight, you can't claim justifiable homicide/self-defense no matter what happens or how it escalates. You must do everything you can to retreat before using deadly force.]

[Exceptions to the Exceptions] [Withdraw and Communicate]
"Furthermore, the defense is not available when a defendant is the aggressor unless he withdraws from any further encounter with the victim and communicates such withdrawal to the victim." *People v. Kemp*, 508 N.W.2d 184, 187 (Mich.App.1993). [If you were the initial aggressor, you must quit and make it plain to the other guy you've had enough before you can win on the theory self-defense.]

[Defense of Person(s) in Special Places – Dwelling]

§ 768.21C.
Use of deadly force by individual in own dwelling; "dwelling" defined

Sec. 21c.

[No Duty to Retreat From Dwelling]

(1) In cases in which section 2 of the self-defense act does not apply, the common law of this state applies except that the duty to retreat before using deadly force is not required if an individual is in his or her own dwelling or within the curtilage of that dwelling. [We could not find a case where a Michigan court has interpreted the phrase "cases in which Section 2 of the self-defense act does not apply." However, Section 2 seems to limit the no-retreat rule to circumstances in which you are either facing a deadly threat or a sexual assault AND are not involved in the commission of a crime. At common law, unless you were in your own home, you had a duty to retreat if it could be done in complete safety. Therefore, outside of your home, unless you are facing an imminent threat of deadly force or are being sexually assaulted, it seems you would have a duty to retreat before using defensive force. The same rule would apply if you were defending another person. You would have to try to get that person to retreat unless he or she was facing an imminent threat of death, serious injury or being sexually assaulted.]

(2) As used in this section, "dwelling" means a structure or shelter that is used permanently or temporarily as a place of abode, including an appurtenant structure attached to that structure or shelter.

[Co-Habitants – Duty to Retreat – No]
"Justice Cardozo in *People v. Tomlins* (1914), 213 N.Y. 240, 107 N.E. 496 reasoned: 'It is not now and never has been the law that a man assailed in his own dwelling is bound to retreat. If assailed there, he may stand his ground and resist the attack. He is under no

duty to take to the fields and the highways, a fugitive from his own home. * * * The rule is the same whether the attack proceeds from some other occupant or from an intruder. It was so adjudged in *Jones v. State* (1884), 76 Ala. 8, 14. 'Why,' it was there inquired, 'should one retreat from his own house, when assailed by a partner or cotenant, any more than when assailed by a stranger who is lawfully upon the premises? Whither shall he flee, and how far, and when may he be permitted to return?'" *People v. McGrandy,* 156 N.W.2d 48, 49 (Mich.App. 1967). [This is an old case but has been upheld in *People v. Godsey,* 220 N.W.2d 801 (Mich.App.1974). This case relies heavily on the castle doctrine rule that there is no duty to retreat when attacked in the home from anyone at all.]

[Presumption of Reasonableness in Special Places – Dwelling, Business and Occupied Vehicle]

§ 780.951.
Individual using deadly force or force other than deadly force; presumption; definitions. [See Definitions below under "Helpful Definitions . . . "]

Sec. 1.

(1) Except as provided in subsection (2), it is a rebuttable presumption in a civil or criminal case that an individual who uses deadly force or force other than deadly force under section 2 of the self-defense act has an honest and reasonable belief that imminent death of, sexual assault of, or great bodily harm to himself or herself or another individual will occur if *both* of the following apply:

(a) The individual against whom deadly force or force other than deadly force is used is in the process of breaking and entering a dwelling or business premises or committing home invasion or has broken and entered a dwelling or business premises or committed home invasion and is still present in the dwelling or business premises, or is unlawfully attempting to remove another individual from a dwelling, business premises, or occupied vehicle against his or her will.

(b) The individual using deadly force or force other than deadly force honestly and reasonably believes that the individual is engaging in conduct described in subdivision (a).

[This statute that protects individuals in their homes, businesses and occupied vehicles was obviously patterned after Florida's home-defense-on-steroids law passed a year earlier. We suggest you read our comments regarding Florida's presumption statute in the Florida sub-chapter. If a stranger breaks into your home (e.g., a home invasion), business or occupied vehicle or tries to kidnap you or someone from any of these special places, it will be presumed that you had a reasonable fear of serious injury, death or being sexually assaulted. The following is a recent internet news article about a Michigan man who is reported to have interpreted his rights a little too broadly, was arrested and likely will be prosecuted for something unpleasant:

Michigan Boy Shot While Ringing Doorbells as Prank
Updated: Saturday, 21 Nov 2009, 11:46 PM CST
Published : Saturday, 21 Nov 2009, 2:16 PM CST

Authorities say a 15-year-old boy who was ringing doorbells as a prank in Livingston County was shot by a 69-year-old man at one of the homes.

Green Oak Township police tell WHMI-FM that the boy and three other juveniles were ringing doorbells on Friday night in Green Oak Township when the man confronted the boy and shot him in the lower back.

The boy was taken to University of Michigan Hospital in Ann Arbor, where he was listed in stable condition.

Authorities found the man at his home. He was being held at the Livingston County Jail pending arraignment.

Green Oak Township is about 35 miles northwest of Detroit.

http://www.my65orlando.com/dpp/news/national/
Michigan_Boy_Shot_While_Ringing_Doorbells_as_Prank_23682293.

[Exceptions to Presumption; Co-Habitants; Co-Employees; Domestic Violence Issues]

(2) The presumption set forth in subsection (1) does not apply if any of the following circumstances exist:

(a) The individual against whom deadly force or force other than deadly force is used, including an owner, lessee, or titleholder, has the legal right to be in the dwelling, business premises, or vehicle and there is not an injunction for protection from domestic violence or a written pretrial supervision order, a probation order, or a parole order of no contact against that person. [The presumption does not apply if the person you injure or kill has a right to be in the home, business or occupied vehicle. This could include a spouse, live-in relative, child, co-worker, supervisor or employee. The exception to the exception for a spouse would be if an abusive husband had a protective or restraining order to stay away from his wife, kids, home or apartment while a divorce is pending. Under those circumstances, if he breaks into the wife's separate residence, the presumption that she has a reasonable belief that her life is in danger applies. See Chapter XIII regarding domestic violence.]

[Notice the word "rebuttable" in this statute. This means that even though there is a presumption that you acted reasonably in defending your home, business or occupied vehicle, the district attorney can rebut that presumption if he can prove, for example, that you set up someone to kill him and then claim home defense. **Example:** You scheme to get rid of the rotten SOB (Son of a Brightoner) boyfriend. You leave Romeo a cell phone message, "Hi, hon, sorry we haven't been getting along and that I put that Restraining Order on you and you lost your gun rights. Let me make it up to you. Come over tonight for a good time. Don't forget to take your pistol out of the car. If you get stopped on the way over here, it's a federal felony for anybody with a domestic restraining order against them to get caught with a gun. I'll be waiting. Luv and Kisses." When love-starved boyfriend arrives he notices that the screen door is locked and knocks politely. You say in your sexiest voice, "I'm in the bedroom and can't come to the door, sorry I forget to unlock it. You're a big, strong man; just pull it open and we'll fix the broken door hook after our 'appointment.'" He pulls the screen door lock off the hinges and you appear from the bedroom dressed like G.I. Jane with a .50 Cal. Beowulf screaming, "lock and load MF (Mister Ferguson)!" In the mangled debris after the incident, CSI Detroit finds the broken screen-door hook, a pocketknife and the boyfriend's copy of the restraining order with 3 biggie-sized holes through it. Unfortunately for you, they also check his cell phone messages and find your irresistibly tempting invitation. There is a high probability that the presumption that you were in fear of death or serious bodily harm because your ex "broke and entered" would be rebutted.]

(b) The individual removed or being removed from the dwelling, business premises, or occupied vehicle is a child or grandchild of, or is otherwise in the lawful custody of or under the lawful guardianship of, the individual against whom deadly force or force other than deadly force is used. [The Legislature didn't want disputes over child custody or visitation to escalate into the Duel at Detroit.]

(c) The individual who uses deadly force or force other than deadly force is engaged in the commission of a crime or is using the dwelling, business premises, or occupied vehicle to further the commission of a crime. [**Example:** A prostitute who kills a "John" in her home over payment of her fee for services will not be entitled to the presumption outlined in this code section. The same rule might apply against a person who has an illegal collection of guns in his home.]

(d) The individual against whom deadly force or force other than deadly force is used is a peace officer who has entered or is attempting to enter a dwelling, business premises, or vehicle in the performance of his or her official duties in accordance with applicable law. [The meth-lab owner who survives an exchange of gunfire with the SWAT no-knock-entry team is not entitled to the presumption.]

(e) The individual against whom deadly force or force other than deadly force is used is the spouse or former spouse of the individual using deadly force or force other than deadly force, an individual with whom the individual using deadly force or other than deadly force has or had a dating relationship, an individual with whom the individual using deadly force or other than deadly force has had a child in common, or a resident or former resident of his or her household, and the individual using deadly force or other than deadly force has a prior history of domestic violence as the aggressor. [This is the flip side of the "seductive-estranged-wife" example illustrating paragraph (a) above. In this example, if the person using force has a "history of domestic violence" (whatever that means . . . a conviction of domestic violence? . . . . former charges of domestic violence whether they were dropped or not? . . . the former injured spouse, girlfriend says he was violent, but she never called the police?), injures or kills a person with which he had a domestic or romantic relationship, he is not entitled to the presumption.]

[Other Issues – Retreat, Common Law]

§ 780.973.
Duty to retreat; effect of act on common law.

Sec. 3.

Except as provided in Section 2, this act does not modify the common law of this state in existence on October 1, 2006 regarding the duty to retreat before using deadly force or force other than deadly force. [Sometimes what the law giveth, the law taketh away. Unless your defensive incident is specifically described as a circumstance wherein you don't have a duty to retreat, the common law would apply. Under common law, unless you were attacked in your home, you always had a duty to retreat if you could safely do so before using any force in self-defense. Furthermore, if you are at fault in either starting, provoking or agreeing to fight, you have a duty to retreat. Until the Michigan courts clarify what this section means, we suggest you retreat if attacked outside of your home, business or occupied vehicle if you can do so with complete safety. Let someone else pay to be Michigan's test case.]

§ 780.974.
Right to use deadly force; effect of act on common law.

Sec. 4.

This act does not diminish an individual's right to use deadly force or force other than deadly force in self-defense or defense of another individual as provided by the common law of this state in existence on October 1, 2006. [The Michigan Legislature obviously intended to "beef up" Michigan's self-defense laws by passage of the SDA. This section ensures that nothing in the SDA can be interpreted by the courts to be less protective than Michigan's common-law (case law).]

[Civil Liability]

§ 600.2922B.
Use of deadly force or other than deadly force by individual in self-defense; immunity from civil liability.

Sec. 2922b.

An individual who uses deadly force or force other than deadly force in self-defense or in defense of another individual in compliance with section 2 of the self-defense act is immune from civil liability for damages caused to either of the following by the use of that deadly force or force other than deadly force:

(a) The individual against whom the use of deadly force or force other than deadly force is authorized.

(b) Any individual claiming damages arising out of injury to or the death of the individual described in subdivision (a), based upon his or her relationship to that individual. [See example in next section.]

§ 600.2922C.
Individual sued for using deadly force or force other than deadly force; award of attorney fees and costs; conditions.

Sec. 2922c.

The court shall award the payment of actual attorney fees and costs to an individual who is sued for civil damages for allegedly using deadly force or force other than deadly force against another individual if the court determines that the individual used deadly force or force other than deadly force in compliance with section 2 of the self-defense act and that the individual is immune from civil liability under section 2922b. [A young thug in a downtown Detroit parking lot, who doesn't read and didn't know about the passage of the SDA, assumes it's "business as usual" as you and your girlfriend head to your vehicle with wrapped gifts during the Christmas season. He approaches you with a stiletto and demands, "your gifts, your money and your girlfriend OR your life!" You respond instead by delivering him a Federal Hydra-Shok packaged in .45ACP that accidentally strikes him in his "knife arm" leaving him with a bloody stump below his right elbow. He retains the first injury law firm he sees on TV in rehab and sues for "impaired earning capacity." If your use of force was justified, "Stumpy" not only loses his lawsuit against you, he has to pay your attorney fees for suing you under those circumstances.]

[Defense of Property]

"No man may, in defense of his mere land against trespassers, assault the invaders with a dangerous weapon. The law forbids such a menacing of human life for so trivial a cause... It is an inflexible principle of the criminal law of this state, and we believe of all the states, as it is of the common law, that for the prevention of a bare trespass upon property, not the dwelling house, human life cannot be taken, nor grievous bodily harm inflicted. If in the defense of property, not the dwelling house, life is taken with a deadly weapon, it is murder, though the killing may be actually necessary to prevent the trespass. The character of the weapon fixes the degree of the offense. But if the killing is not with a deadly weapon-if it is with an instrument suited rather for the purpose of alarm, or of chastisement-and there is not an intent to kill, it is manslaughter." *People v. Doud*, 193 N.W. 884, 888 (Mi. 1923). [You cannot use deadly force against someone who is simply trespassing on your real estate (e.g., after a football game members of the crowd walk across your newly planted lawn). You may not use deadly force to defend the destruction or theft of personal property such as a bicycle or unoccupied car.]

[HELPFUL DEFINITIONS RELATING TO THIS STATE'S SELF-DEFENSE STATUTES]

- **Business Premises** – means a building or other structure used for the transaction of business, including an appurtenant structure attached to that building or other structure. **M.C.L.A. 780.951(3)(b).**
- **Dwelling** – means a structure or shelter that is used permanently or temporarily as a place of abode, including an appurtenant structure attached to that structure or shelter. M.C.L.A. 780.951(3)(c).
- **Vehicle** – means a conveyance of any kind, whether or not motorized, that is designed to transport people or property. **M.C.L.A. 780.951(3)(g).**
- **Felonies Mentioned Above –**
  - **Sexual assault** – ["assault with intent to commit criminal sexual conduct."] **Michigan Compiled Laws 600.2157a(c).**

[TEMPLATE Topics We Could Not Find Explained in Statutes or Cases]

(For each of these topics that we could not find addressed in your state's statutes or cases, we suggest you review the same topics in the subchapters of surrounding states. Your state's courts may look to the law of neighboring states to see how their courts and legislatures have treated that particular self-defense issue.)

[Reckless Injury to Innocent Third Parties]

Pancho's Wisdom

You just might be a Gunnut if . . . recoil is as emotionally fulfilling as a warm hug.

Pancho's Wisdom – Minnesota's self-defense laws look more like they originated in a personnel office at a cheese factory rather than emanating from the quills of scribes in a Viking castle!

Key: ■ commentary ■ original statutes, cases or jury instructions

[Defense of Self and Others]

§ MINNESOTA STATUTES ANNOTATED (M.S.A.) § 609.06. Authorized use of force.

Subdivision 1. When authorized. Except as otherwise provided in **subdivision 2** [using force against police officers], reasonable force may be used upon or toward the person of another without the other's consent when the following circumstances exist or the actor reasonably believes them to exist: [You can use reasonable force against another person when the following is happening or you reasonably believe it is happening...]

. . .

[Non-Deadly Force] [Defense of Third Persons]

(3) when used by any person in resisting or aiding another to resist an offense against the person; or [in defense of yourself or another person. . .]

(4) when used by any person in lawful possession of real or personal property, or by another assisting the person in lawful possession, in resisting a trespass upon or other unlawful interference with such property; or [to prevent a trespass on real estate or to prevent theft or destruction of personal property (things, like TV, DVD player, computer, lawn mower, etc.).]

(5) when used by any person to prevent the escape, or to retake following the escape, of a person lawfully held on a charge or conviction of a crime; or [to prevent prisoners from escaping or to catch them after escape.]

[Please notice that NOTHING in these paragraphs authorizes the use of deadly force to protect persons, real or personal property or, catch criminals on the run.]

. . .

[Deadly Force]
[Defense of Person(s) in Special Places – Place of Abode]

§ **M.S.A. § 609.065.**
Justifiable Taking of Life.

The intentional taking of the life of another is not authorized by section 609.06, except when necessary in resisting or preventing an offense which the actor reasonably believes exposes the actor or another to great bodily harm or death, or preventing the commission of a felony in the actor's place of abode. [Outside of your home, the standard for using deadly force is that you must be facing an imminent threat of death or serious bodily injury. There is no mention of serious felonies justifying the use of deadly force outside of your home. *Pancho's Wisdom* – Minnesota's self-defense law falls short of adequate legal protection for those threatened with sexual assault or robbery while venturing outside of their homes. Citizens are raped and robbed outside of the home and should not have to wonder whether such heinous crimes pose a threat of serious bodily harm. (e.g., "I'm not going to hurt you if you give me your wallet/sex." Anyone threatened with sexual assault or robbery should be allowed by law to use deadly force to repel such an attack without having to guess what the new prosecutor on the block will do to him or her.

In the home, deadly force is authorized to prevent the commission of a felony. We interpret this to mean serious felonies, like those crimes considered felonies at common law such as murder, manslaughter, rape, robbery, burglary, kidnapping and arson. By authorizing deadly force to prevent the commission of ANY felony in one's home, the statute may unwittingly cause people to believe that they can use deadly force against even non-violent felonies committed by non-threatening criminals. Such use of force could be legally disastrous for the reasons explained more fully in the subheading "Fleeing Felon and Any-Felony Traps" in Chapter 4 under the template and topic **"[Use of Deadly Force to Prevent Serious Felonies]."**

10 MNPRAC CRIMJIG 7.05 [Jury Instruction – Defense of dwelling/place of abode] No crime is committed when a person takes the life of another person, even intentionally, if the defendant's action was taken in preventing the commission of a felony in the defendant's dwelling/place of abode. In order for a killing to be justified for this reason, three conditions must be met. First, the defendant's action was done to prevent the commission of a felony in the dwelling. Second, the defendant's judgment as to the gravity of the situation was reasonable under the circumstances. Third, the defendant's election to defend (his) (her) dwelling was such as a reasonable person would have made in light of the danger perceived. All three conditions must be met... [Your act of using deadly force against a person must be reasonable and necessary under the circumstances. See our discussion of the terms "reasonable" and "necessary" in Chapter 3.]

[Exceptions to Justifiable Self-Defense] [Initial Aggressor]
"An aggressor in an incident has no right to a claim of self-defense." *Bellcourt v. State*, 390 N.W.2d 269, 272 (Minn. 1986) (Citations omitted) [If you are to blame for starting a fight, you can't claim self-defense if you hurt or kill someone during the fight.]

[Exceptions to Exceptions] [Withdraw and Communicate]

"However, where the defendant is the original aggressor in an incident giving rise to his self-defense claim, an instruction on self-defense will be available to him only if he actually and in good faith withdraws from the conflict and communicates that withdrawal, expressly or impliedly, to his intended victim... If the circumstances are such that it is impossible for defendant to communicate the withdrawal, it is attributable to his own fault and he must abide by the consequences." *Bellcourt v. State,* 390 N.W.2d 269, 272 (Minn. 1986)(Citations omitted). [You have to quit and tell your opponent you've had enough. The "expressly or impliedly" language means either with words or with actions. To be safe, of course, you should not leave your actions up to the interpretation of a jury. You should stop, run away, and scream your head off that you want to quit. If circumstances make it impossible for you to tell your opponent you don't want to fight anymore... too bad for you.]

[Provocation]

"The law does not permit or justify one who intends to commit an assault upon another to design in advance his own defense by instigating a quarrel or a combat with a view thereby to create a situation wherein the infliction of the intended injury will appear to have been done in self-defense." *State v. Love,* 173 N.W.2d 423, 427 (Minn. 1970). [You can't get someone riled up with the intent of making them lash out as an excuse to kill or injure them.]

[Duty to Retreat – Generally – Yes]

"Minnesota has recognized that a person who kills another in self-defense must have attempted to retreat if reasonably possible." *State v. Carothers,* 594 N.W.2d 897, (Minn. 1999).

[No Duty to Retreat From Home] [Co-Habitant]

"There is no duty to retreat from one's own home when acting in self-defense in the home, regardless of whether the aggressor is a co-resident. But the lack of a duty to retreat does not abrogate the obligation to act reasonably when using force in self-defense. Therefore, in all situations in which a party claims self-defense, even absent a duty to retreat, the key inquiry will still be into the reasonableness of the use of force and the level of force under the specific circumstances of each case." *State v. Glowacki,* 630 N.W.2d 392, 402 (Minn. 2001). [You don't have to retreat in the home, even against a co-habitant. But you still have to act reasonably, no matter the situation.]

[Defense of Property]

§ **M.S.A. § 609.06 (4).**
Authorized Use of Force.

Subdivision 1. When authorized. Except as otherwise provided in subdivision 2, reasonable force may be used upon or toward the person of another without the other's consent when the following circumstances exist or the actor reasonably believes them to exist:

. . .

(4) when used by any person in lawful possession of real or personal property, or by another assisting the person in lawful possession, in resisting a trespass upon or other unlawful interference with such property...

. . .

"Taken together, these provisions [This one (609.06) and the deadly force statute above (609.065)] establish that reasonable force may be used when a person reasonably believes that he or she is resisting an offense against a person or a trespass upon lawfully held property. This "reasonable force" includes deadly force only when the offense against a person involves great bodily harm or death or is used to prevent the commission of a felony in one's home." *State v. Pendleton*, 567 N.W.2d 265, 268 (Minn. 1997).

[You can never use deadly force to defend property from a trespasser unless he is threatening you with death or serious injury. At that point you are no longer defending property, you are defending yourself.]

[HELPFUL DEFINITIONS RELATING TO THIS STATE'S SELF-DEFENSE STATUTES]

- **Felony** – means a crime for which a sentence of imprisonment for more than one year may be imposed. **M.S.A. § 609.02(2).**

- **Dangerous weapon** – means any firearm, whether loaded or unloaded, or any device designed as a weapon and capable of producing death or great bodily harm, any combustible or flammable liquid or other device or instrumentality that, in the manner it is used or intended to be used, is calculated or likely to produce death or great bodily harm, or any fire that is used to produce death or great bodily harm. **M.S.A. § 609.02(6).**

- **Bodily harm** – means physical pain or injury, illness, or any impairment of physical condition. **M.S.A. § 609.02(7).**

- **Substantial bodily harm** – means bodily injury which involves a temporary but substantial disfigurement, or which causes a temporary but substantial loss or impairment of the function of any bodily member or organ, or which causes a fracture of any bodily member. **M.S.A. § 609.02(7a).**

- **Great bodily harm** – means bodily injury which creates a high probability of death, or which causes serious permanent disfigurement, or which causes a permanent or protracted loss or impairment of the function of any bodily member or organ or other serious bodily harm. **M.S.A. § 609.02(8).**

[TEMPLATE Topics We Could Not Find Explained in Statutes or Cases]

(For each of these topics that we could not find addressed in your state's statutes or cases, we suggest you review the same topics in the subchapters of surrounding states. Your state's courts may look to the law of neighboring states to see how their courts and legislatures have treated that particular self-defense issue.)

[Use of Deadly Force to Prevent Serious Felonies]

[Committing Felony or Unlawful Act]

[Co-Employees – Duty to Retreat]

[Presumption of Reasonableness in Special Places]

[Reckless Injury to Innocent Third Parties]

[Civil Liability]

Pancho's Wisdom

You just might be a Gunnut if . . . when you get your cholesterol and PSA checked at the lab, you ask 'em to check your blood-lead levels just in case.

MISSISSIPPI

Mississippi attempts to cover the entire field of self-defense and home-defense with one statute. The concepts addressed in the statute do not appear in the same order as most state statutes or in the order that we arranged our TEMPLATE headings. We re-arranged our TEMPLATE headings to fit the statute.

This statute suggests you can use deadly force to prevent any felony, kill rioters or those disturbing the peace. We believe relying on such broad language will get you into big trouble. California and Nevada have similar statutes and their courts have held that these statutes do not mean what they say. We suggest you read our lengthy explanations and warnings related to their statutes. We explain in detail in Chapter 4 why you should not use force that can kill against non-violent felonies or against people committing misdemeanors.

Key: ■ commentary ■ original statutes, cases or jury instructions

---

[Defense of Self and Others]

[Defense of Person(s) in Special Places – Dwelling, Occupied Vehicle, Place of Business or Employment]

§ MISS. CODE ANN. § 97-3-15 (1) (e) and (f).

Homicide; justifiable homicide; use of defensive force; duty to retreat.

(1) The killing of a human being by the act, procurement or omission of another shall be justifiable in the following cases:

[Sub-paragraphs (a) – (d) deal with use of force by police officers and persons acting under their direction, which is beyond the scope of this book.]

. . .

(e) When committed by any person in resisting any attempt unlawfully to kill such person or to commit any felony upon him, or upon or in any dwelling, in any occupied vehicle, in any place of business, in any place of employment or in the immediate premises thereof in which such person shall be; [Mississippi, like every other state, justifies you to use deadly force against someone trying to kill you. The language of the rest of paragraph (e) is misleading when it suggests you can use deadly force to defend against any felony. We explain in detail why the use of the phrase "any felony" is too broad in Chapter 4. We suggest you reserve the use of deadly force to stop the commission of violent felonies, such as burglary, arson, kidnapping, attempted rape or sexual assault.]

[Deadly Force] [Use of Deadly Force to Prevent Serious Felonies] [Defense of a Third Person]

(f) When committed in the lawful defense of one's own person or any other human being, where there shall be reasonable ground to apprehend a design to commit a felony or to do some great personal injury, and there shall be imminent danger of such design being accomplished; [Again, as long as your use of deadly force is for the purpose of stopping an immediate threat of serious injury or violent felony, you are probably justified. If you use a deadly weapon to stop non-violent felonies against obviously unarmed and harmless felons, you might be prosecuted. See Chapter 4. **Example:** On a very hot day, you see two boys in their early teens in swimming trunks force their way through your partially open window to steal popsicles out of your chest freezer. It's absolutely obvious to you that they have no weapons. You Rat Tat Tat their tanned torsos with your Taurus. Even if forcing their way into your home would have been enough to charge them all with felonies, you may find yourself paying a lawyer to defend against charges that non-violent felonies do not justify the use of deadly force.]

. . .

"According to Manuel, this statute (referring to sections (e) and (f))... reflect[s] the law that where an individual is unjustifiably attacked by a larger and unarmed person, and the individual is incapable of coping with that person in a physical confrontation, and the individual reasonably perceives that she will receive serious and great bodily injuries as a result, that individual is justified in killing her attacker with a deadly weapon. Manuel is correct." *Manuel v. State*, 667 So.2d 590, 592 (Miss. 1995). [This Mississippi case is a great case for defense lawyers. It says that just because your big, muscle-bound assailant doesn't have a weapon, doesn't mean you can't use deadly force to defend yourself. The defendant in this case was a woman who used a knife to kill her live-in boyfriend who she claimed had been beating her. But please notice she was prosecuted and convicted and had to get the case overturned on appeal. See Thumbs-Down Chapter and Domestic Violence Chapters for further advice about what facts tend to result in arrest, prosecution and conviction in these types of cases.]

§ MISS. CODE ANN. § 97-3-15.
Homicide . . . (cont.)

(g) When necessarily committed in attempting by lawful ways and means to apprehend any person for any felony committed; [Again, we caution against you relying upon the phrase "any felony." See discussion above. This is Mississippi's fleeing felon statute. We explain in Chapter 4 why we counsel against going after fleeing felons. It not only can get you killed, it can get you sued and imprisoned if you kill a criminal and his family claims you used excessive force. When you have stopped a violent felony by using or threatening to use a deadly weapon, if the assailant runs away, let him go. Get a good description and let the police do their jobs.]

(h) When necessarily committed in lawfully suppressing any riot or in lawfully keeping and preserving the peace. [We could not find any cases interpreting this subparagraph. States like California and Nevada have similar, older statutes that suggest you can kill someone for causing a riot or disturbing the peace. The courts in such states have generally held that despite such wording in the state law, you can only use deadly force against rioters and others if they present an imminent threat of serious injury or death.]

[Presumption of Reasonableness in Special Places – Dwelling, Occupied Vehicle or Place of Business]

§ **MISS. CODE ANN. § 97-3-15.**
Homicide. . . (Cont.)

(3) A person who uses defensive force shall be presumed to have reasonably feared imminent death or great bodily harm, or the commission of a felony upon him or another or upon his dwelling, or against a vehicle which he was occupying, or against his business or place of employment or the immediate premises of such business or place of employment, if the person against whom the defensive force was used, was in the process of unlawfully and forcibly entering, or had unlawfully and forcibly entered, a dwelling, occupied vehicle, business, place of employment or the immediate premises thereof or if that person had unlawfully removed or was attempting to unlawfully remove another against the other person's will from that dwelling, occupied vehicle, business, place of employment or the immediate premises thereof and the person who used defensive force knew or had reason to believe that the forcible entry or unlawful and forcible act was occurring or had occurred . . . [If someone forces his way into your home, place of employment or occupied vehicle, it's presumed you are justified in using deadly force to stop him. A presumption can be rebutted, however. If the evidence shows you invited the person into your home but tampered with the evidence to make it look like he broke in, then the presumption is rebutted and you could be convicted for killing the person you claim broke into your home. The presumption of innocence does NOT protect you legally against people who have a right to be in your home, business or vehicle as explained immediately below.]

[Co-Habitants; Co-Employees – Exception to Presumption]

[(3) continued . . .] This presumption shall not apply if the person against whom defensive force was used has a right to be in or is a lawful resident or owner of the dwelling, vehicle, business, place of employment or the immediate premises thereof or is the lawful resident or owner of the dwelling, vehicle, business, place of employment or the immediate premises thereof or if the person who uses defensive force is engaged in unlawful activity or if the person is a law enforcement officer engaged in the performance of his official duties; [The presumption that you acted reasonably in using deadly force against intruders does not apply against people who have a right to be on the premises. This is obviously because they are NOT intruders. Such persons could include family members, people who have been invited into your home by family members, your landlord, roommates, co-tenants, co-employees, and people with whom you share a ride to work.]

[No Duty to Retreat From Special Places]

"The home is one of the most important institutions of the state, and has ever been regarded as a place where a person has a right to stand his ground and repel, force by force, to the extent necessary for its protection." *Lee v. State*, 100 So.2d 358, 361 (Miss. 1958) (citation omitted). [You have no duty to retreat from your home before defending yourself in it.]

[No Duty to Retreat – Generally] [Committing Felony or Unlawful Act]

§ MISS. CODE ANN. § 97-3-15 (4).

Homicide. . . (cont.)

. . .

(4) A person who is not the initial aggressor and is not engaged in unlawful activity shall have no duty to retreat before using deadly force under subsection (1)(e) or (f) of this section if the person is in a place where the person has a right to be, and no finder of fact shall be permitted to consider the person's failure to retreat as evidence that the person's use of force was unnecessary, excessive or unreasonable. [If you are without fault in starting, escalating or agreeing to fight and if you are not trespassing, you don't have to retreat before using force to defend yourself. This is a very strong no-retreat law. Jurors are not allowed to speculate on whether you could have retreated before using deadly force to defend yourself. **Example:** You are standing in line to attend a pop concert when a man approaches you in a threatening manner with a large knife. He says he's going to cut you to pieces for reasons you don't quite understand. You notice a door behind you through which you might escape. You have no duty to retreat through the doorway before defending yourself. Furthermore, if you were prosecuted, a jury would be instructed that they cannot discuss whether you could have retreated through the nearby doorway into a building. You have no duty to retreat and it's emphasized and reinforced by this statute. That's not to suggest jurors ALWAYS do what's told.]

. . .

[Civil Liability]

§ MISS. CODE ANN. § 97-3-15 (5).

Homicide; justifiable homicide; use of defensive force; duty to retreat.

(5) (a) The presumptions contained in subsection (3) of this section shall apply in civil cases in which self-defense or defense of another is claimed as a defense. [**Example:** You shoot someone who is trying to force his way into your home and you know he hasn't been invited in by anyone in your home. He sues you for injuries. It is presumed, because he unlawfully and forcibly entered or attempted to enter, that you acted reasonably and that you are not liable for his injuries.]

(b) The court shall award reasonable attorney's fees, court costs, compensation for loss of income, and all expenses incurred by the defendant in defense of any civil action brought by a plaintiff if the court finds that the defendant acted in accordance with subsection (1)(e) or (f) of this section. A defendant who has previously been adjudicated "not guilty" of any crime by reason of subsection (1)(e) or (f) of this section shall be immune from any civil action for damages arising from same conduct. [If you are found "not guilty" for shooting the scumbag who broke into your home, if he tries to sue you, his lawsuit should be dismissed. You will then be entitled to sue him to pay for your attorney fees, costs and any other expenses you lost defending the lawsuit he brought against you.]

. . .

[Exceptions to Justifiable Self Defense] [Initial Aggressor]

"Mississippi adheres to the common law rule that an aggressor is precluded from pleading self-defense." *Dean v. State,* 746 So.2d 891, 895 (Miss. App. 1998) (citation omitted). [Juries are told that they cannot find a person innocent on the theory of self-defense if he started the fight that resulted in someone else's injury or death.]

[Provocation]

"This Court has held that [i]f a person provokes a difficulty, arming himself in advance, and intending, if necessary, to use his weapon and overcome his adversary, he becomes the aggressor, and deprives himself of the right of self-defense." *Chandler v. State,* 946 So. 2d 355, 363, (Miss. 2006) (citation omitted). [Provocation generally refers to intentionally goading someone into a fight as an excuse to hurt him and then claim self-defense. If you do this, you forfeit the right to win your case on the theory of self-defense.]

[Committing Unlawful Act]

"Flight is a mode of escaping danger to which a party is not bound to resort, so long as he is in a place where he has a right to be, and is neither engaged in an unlawful act, nor the provoker of, nor the aggressor in, the combat. In such case he may stand his ground and resist force by force, taking care that his resistance be not disproportioned to the attack." *Skinner v. State,* 751 So. 2d 1060, 1074 (Miss. Ct. App. 1999). [If you are committing a crime, you have no right to use force to defend yourself against a law-abiding citizen. If you are committing an unlawful act and someone challenges you, you must retreat.]

[Mutual Combat]

"Taking as true all of the evidence presented that is consistent with the verdict, we find there was sufficient evidence to conclude that Robinson intended to inflict serious physical injury to Parks during the course of mutual combat, and that no self-defense justification existed." *Robinson v. State,* 858 So. 2d 887, 892 (Miss. Ct. App. 2003). [Agreeing to fight cancels out your right to self-defense.]

[Exceptions to the Exceptions] [Withdraw and Communicate]

"It should also be noted that where the accused [the one who started the conflict], acting in good faith, attempts to withdraw from the encounter and abandons his original purpose and intent, then in such case the accused would not be deprived of the right to assert self-defense even though it became necessary thereafter to slay his adversary." *Patrick v. State,* 285 So.2d 165, 169 (Miss. 1973). [Under some circumstances, even if you start a fight, you can recover your right to self-defense. You must withdraw (e.g., retreat), and let your opponent know you have completely abandoned any intent to hurt him. Then, if your opponent continues to try to hurt you, he becomes the aggressor and you regain your right to use force in self-defense. We warn you, however, that if you start a fight, even if you later stop fighting and retreat, if you injure or kill someone, you will be arrested, prosecuted and possibly convicted. See Chapter VII which we have entitled Thumbs-Down Factors.]

[Defense of Property]

"The law regarding defense of habitation is not such that a mere trespasser, having been once warned to vacate the premises, may thereafter be killed by the premises' owner with impunity if he fails to leave the property soon enough to satisfy the desires of the owner." *Lester v. State,* 862 So.2d 582, 585 (Miss.App. 2004).

[You can't just blow someone away for walking through your yard after you've politely asked them to leave.]

[HELPFUL DEFINITIONS RELATING TO THIS STATE'S SELF-DEFENSE STATUTES]

- **Dwelling** – means a building or conveyance of any kind that has a roof over it, whether the building or conveyance is temporary or permanent, mobile or immobile, including a tent, that is designed to be occupied by people lodging therein at night, including any attached porch... **Miss.Code Ann. § 97-3-15 (2)(c)** [This definition of dwelling is exclusive to § 97-3-15 as it is used in subsections (1)(e) and (3).]

[TEMPLATE Topics We Could Not Find Explained in Statutes or Cases]

(For each of these topics that we could not find addressed in your state's statutes or cases, we suggest you review the same topics in the subchapters of surrounding states. Your state's courts may look to the law of neighboring states to see how their courts and legislatures have treated that particular self-defense issue.)

[Non-Deadly Force]

[Co-Habitant; Co-Employees – Duty to Retreat]

[Reckless Injury to Innocent Third Parties]

Pancho's Wisdom

You just might be a Gunnut if . . . you live south of the Mason-Dixon Line (excluding New Orleans); or west of the Mississippi (excluding West Coast States).

Key: ■ commentary ■ original statutes, cases or jury instructions

[Defense of Self and Others]

§ M.R.S. § 563.031 (1) (a) and (c).
Use of force in defense of persons.

[Non-Deadly Force] [Defense of Third Persons]

1. A person may, subject to the provisions of subsection 2 of this section, use physical force upon another person when and to the extent he or she reasonably believes such force to be necessary to defend himself or herself or a third person from what he or she reasonably believes to be the use or imminent use of unlawful force by such other person, unless: [You may use reasonable and necessary force to defend against non-deadly force. You may not use deadly force against non-deadly force.]

[Exceptions to Justifiable Self-Defense] [Initial Aggressor]

(1) The actor was the initial aggressor; except that in such case his or her use of force is nevertheless justifiable provided:

[Exceptions to the Exceptions] [Withdraw and Communicate]

(a) He or she has withdrawn from the encounter and effectively communicated such withdrawal to such other person but the latter persists in continuing the incident by the use or threatened use of unlawful force; or

. . .

(c) The aggressor is justified under some other provision of this chapter or other provision of law;

. . .

[Provocation]

"Miller must establish the following elements to show an entitlement to self defense: "(1) [he] did not provoke the attack..." *State v. Miller,* 91 S.W.3d 630, 635 (Mo.App. 2002). [Provocation usually refers to starting a fight as an excuse to hurt or kill someone when he or she retaliates. Doing so defeats your right to use force in self-defense.]

[Mutual Combat]

"If as Hatfield claims they were engaged in mutual combat with deadly weapons there could be no self-defense." *State v. Hatfield,* 465 S.W.2d 468, 470 (Mo. 1971).

"And it has been held that when two persons engage in mutual combat in such circumstances, the law will regard both as the aggressors." *State v. Williams*, 87 S.W.2d 175, 178 (Mo. 1935). [Agreeing to fight defeats your right to use force to defend yourself.]

[Defense of Third Persons]

§ **M.R.S. § 563.031. (cont.) (2) (3) and 2.**
Use of force in defense of persons.

(2) Under the circumstances as the actor reasonably believes them to be, the person whom he or she seeks to protect would not be justified in using such protective force; [If you believe or should know the third person you are trying to defend would not be justified in using force, then you are not justified in defending him. **Example:** You and your worthless brother-in-law are stealing watermelons from Farmer Brown's field. Old Farmer Brown catches you both red-handed and starts swinging a hoe at your brother-in-law. You know the brother-in-law can easily outrun the old man, but you draw your gun and make a leaker out of Farmer Brown. You are arrested for attempted murder and claim you were defending a third person from the use of deadly force (the hoe) being wielded by Farmer Brown. You will lose because you know or should have known your brother-in-law had no right to use deadly force.]

[Committing Felony or Unlawful Act]

(3) The actor was attempting to commit, committing, or escaping after the commission of a forcible felony. [You rob a convenience store and then shoot the clerk when he uses a weapon to keep you from robbing him or when he tries to chase you down. You will not win on the theory of self-defense.]

[Deadly Force] [Use of Deadly Force to Prevent Serious Felonies]

2. A person may not use deadly force upon another person under the circumstances specified in subsection 1 of this section unless:

   (1) He or she reasonably believes that such deadly force is necessary to protect himself or herself or another against death, serious physical injury, or any forcible felony; [See definition of "forcible felony" below]

[Duty to Retreat – Generally]

[This issue is anything but clear in Missouri law. We found some cases that seemed to suggest there was a duty to retreat before using deadly force, and others that said there was not. We did further research on the issue, but despite our best efforts were unable to come up with a concrete answer. Until the legislature or the courts officially sanction the no-duty-to-retreat rule, it's going to be risky to ever use force in self-defense without first retreating.]

[Defense of Person(s) in Special Places – Dwelling, Residence or Occupied Vehicle]

§ **M.R.S. § 563.031.**
Use of force in defense of persons.

. . .

2. A person may not use deadly force upon another person under the circumstances specified in subsection 1 of this section unless:

. . .

(2) Such force is used against a person who unlawfully enters, remains after unlawfully entering, or attempts to unlawfully enter a dwelling, residence, or vehicle lawfully occupied by such person. [Although the plain words of this paragraph give homeowners the right to use deadly force against intruders unlawfully entering or remaining in their homes, over time Missouri case law and resulting jury instructions have altered the meaning. As recently as 2006 the Missouri Court of Appeals has stated the law as follows:

"In Missouri, defense of premises is a defense of justification. . . . Defense of one's premises is an accelerated form of self-defense. . . . This defense 'authorizes protective acts to be taken *earlier* than they otherwise would be authorized, that is, *at the time when and place where the intruder is seeking to cross the protective barrier of the house.'* . . . However, once the intruder *enters the premises without resistance,* the defender is *no longer entitled to an instruction on defense of premises.* At that point, the principles of self-defense apply." *State v. Goodine,* 196 S.W.3d 607, 613 (Mo.App.S.D. 2006) (citations omitted, emphasis added). [This seems to contradict the language of the statute that says if a person "remains after unlawfully entering [your home]," you can use deadly force. The Missouri courts have added another element that doesn't appear in paragraph (2) above, the reasonable belief that the intruder was entering to kill or inflict serious injury:]

"A defense of premises instruction must be given by the trial court only when there is evidence of attempted unlawful entry and evidence that the lawful occupant reasonably believed: (1) immediate danger of entry existed; (2) *the entry was being attempted in order to kill or inflict serious bodily harm to the occupant;* and (3) deadly force was required to prevent the entry. . . To determine whether a defendant has presented evidence sufficient to inject the issue of defense of premises, it is necessary for him or her to present evidence that under its most favorable construction such evidence supports a finding of defense of premises. 'It is not sufficient solely that the defendant believed in his or her own mind that the other person was attempting to enter the premises to commit a burglary; the belief must also be objectively reasonable.'" *Perkins v. State,* 77 S.W.3d 21 (Mo.App.E.D. 2002)(emphasis added, citations omitted). [*Pancho's Wisdom* – How do the courts of Missouri expect home defenders to know about these COURT ADD-ONS to the state's home defense statute unless they are lawyers and read Appeals Court cases like a newspaper? See how the court in the *Goodine* case changed the plain wording of the definition of "premises" in the definitions section below. Changing the plain meaning of statutes by judicial edict undermines any confidence citizens can have in the wording of their state statutes.]

[No Duty to Retreat from Special Places – Dwelling, Residence or Vehicle]

3. A person does not have a duty to retreat from a dwelling, residence, or vehicle where the person is not unlawfully entering or unlawfully remaining. [You don't have to retreat from your own home, apartment or vehicle. If you are trespassing, you MUST retreat before using any kind of force to defend yourself.]

4. The justification afforded by this section extends to the use of physical restraint as protective force provided that the actor takes all reasonable measures to terminate the restraint as soon as it is reasonable to do so. [If you trap an intruder in your

bathroom after he sneaks into your home, make sure you cut him loose when the cops get there.]

5. The defendant shall have the burden of injecting the issue of justification under this section.

[Reckless Injury to Innocent Third Parties]

"'If ... the perpetrator of the homicide or of the assault had no criminal intent in attempting to injure or kill another person, as where the perpetrator was lawfully defending himself from the harm sought to be inflicted upon him by such other person, the fact that, on that occasion, a third person was unintentionally injured or killed by the perpetrator would not make him liable, unless the perpetrator acted carelessly or without regard to the safety of innocent bystanders.'" *State v. Zumwalt*, 973 S.W.2d 504, 508 (Mo.App. S.D. 1998) (citation omitted). [You have to act reasonably. You cannot spray bullets into a crowd of innocent bystanders just to try and hit the one person who has it out for you.]

[Civil Liability]

§ M.R.S. § 563.074.
Justification as an absolute defense, when.

1. Notwithstanding the provisions of section 563.016, a person who uses force as described in sections 563.031, 563.041, 563.046, 563.051, 563.056, and 563.061 is justified in using such force and such fact shall be an absolute defense to criminal prosecution or civil liability.

2. The court shall award attorney's fees, court costs, and all reasonable expenses incurred by the defendant in defense of any civil action brought by a plaintiff if the court finds that the defendant has an absolute defense as provided in subsection 1 of this section. [This statute says that if you injure or kill someone in justifiable self-defense, you have an "absolute defense" against a civil lawsuit for damages. If you are sued and win, you can collect attorney fees and costs against the person who sued you. But notice the following section seems to say just the opposite. We could not find any cases that discuss either of these two statutes. But because 563.074 is more specific and actually mentions 563.016, it probably will protect a defender from civil liability despite the seemingly opposite language of 563.016. The Missouri Legislature should simply repeal 563.016 and eliminate the uncertainty.]

§ M.R.S. § 563.016.
Civil remedies unaffected.

The fact that conduct is justified under this chapter does not abolish or impair any remedy for such conduct which is available in any civil actions.

[Defense of Property]

§ M.R.S. § 563.041.
Use of physical force in defense of property.

1. A person may, subject to the limitations of subsection 2, use physical force upon another person when and to the extent that he or she reasonably believes it necessary to prevent what he or she reasonably believes to be the commission or attempted commission by such person of stealing, property damage or tampering in any degree. [You can use reasonable force, but not deadly force, to protect your property.]

2. A person may use deadly force under circumstances described in subsection 1 only when such use of deadly force is authorized under other sections of this chapter. [The use of deadly force is NOT justified to recover or protect your personal property such as a stolen car, bicycle or scooter, UNLESS it is justified by any of the code sections above (e.g., imminent threat of death, serious physical injury, or forcible felony, 563.031(1) explained above). In other words, you can't use deadly force unless your defense of personal property ESCALATES to become a DEADLY ENCOUNTER. This is why we discourage the use of ANY force to defend or recover personal property. It can get you killed, prosecuted or sued. And for what, a scooter that you can replace for $1,000?]

3. The justification afforded by this section extends to the use of physical restraint as protective force provided that the actor takes all reasonable measures to terminate the restraint as soon as it is reasonable to do so.

4. The defendant shall have the burden of injecting the issue of justification under this section.

[HELPFUL DEFINITIONS RELATING TO THIS STATE'S SELF-DEFENSE STATUTES]

- **Deadly force** – physical force which the actor uses with the purpose of causing or which he or she knows to create a substantial risk of causing death or serious physical injury; **M.R.S. § 563.011(1).**

- **Dwelling** – any building, inhabitable structure, or conveyance of any kind, whether the building, inhabitable structure, or conveyance is temporary or permanent, mobile or immobile, which has a roof over it, including a tent, and is designed to be occupied by people lodging therein at night; **M.R.S. § 563.011(2).**

- **Forcible felony** – any felony involving the use or threat of physical force or violence against any individual, including but not limited to murder, robbery, burglary, arson, kidnapping, assault, and any forcible sexual offense; **M.R.S. § 563.011(3).**

- **Felonies Mentioned –**
  - **Arson** – [Knowingly damaging a building or inhabitable structure by fire or explosion.] **M.R.S. § 569.040 &050.**
  - **Burglary** – [Knowingly entering or remaining unlawfully in a building or inhabitable structure for the purpose of committing a crime therein.] **M.R.S. § 569.160 & 170.**
  - **Assault (felony)** – [Knowingly causing serious physical injury to another with or without the use of a deadly or dangerous weapon. Also, recklessly causing serious injury to another person.] **M.R.S. § 565.050 & 060.**
  - **Murder** – [Knowingly causing death or killing during the commission or attempt to commit a felony.] **M.R.S. § 565.020 & 021.**
  - **Robbery** – [Taking someone else's property by force.] **M.R.S. § 569.020 & 030.**
  - **Kidnapping** – [Unlawfully removing or confining a person without his or her consent for a substantial period, or for the purpose of ransom, to use that person as a hostage, interfere with governmental or political function, or to commit a felony against that person.] **M.R.S. § 565.110.**
  - **Forcible sexual offense** – [Any sexual offense that is a felony under the law AND involves the use of force, including, but not limited to: 566.030 Forcible rape and attempted forcible rape, 566.060 Forcible sodomy, 566.067 Child molestation 1st degree, 566.068 Child molestation 2nd degree, and 566.070 Deviate sexual assault.] **All of these are found under Missouri Revised Statutes Chapter 566 Sexual Offenses.**
- **Premises** – includes any building, inhabitable structure and any real property; **M.R.S. § 563.011(4).** [Even though the statute plainly includes "any real property," the courts say it DOESN'T mean what it says. *State v. Goodine*, 196 S.W.3d 607, 613, 614 (Mo.App.S.D. 2006). *Pancho's Wisdom* – We consider it EXTREMELY UNFAIR for courts to interpret and apply a statute contrary to its plain meaning. Citizens have access to state statutes, but do not have ready access to case law. Defense attorneys should be screaming "estoppel" and asserting a denial of due process in such cases.]
- **Private person** – any person other than a law enforcement officer; **M.R.S. § 563.011(5).**
- **Remain after unlawfully entering** – to remain in or upon premises after unlawfully entering as defined in this section; **M.R.S. § 563.011(6).**
- **Residence** – a dwelling in which a person resides either temporarily or permanently or is visiting as an invited guest; **M.R.S. § 563.011(7).**
- **Unlawfully enter** – a person unlawfully enters in or upon premises when he or she

enters such premises and is not licensed or privileged to do so. A person who, regardless of his or her purpose, enters in or upon premises that are at the time open to the public does so with license unless he or she defies a lawful order not to enter, personally communicated to him or her by the owner of such premises or by another authorized person. A license to enter in a building that is only partly open to the public is not a license to enter in that part of the building that is not open to the public. **M.R.S. § 563.011(8).**

[TEMPLATE Topics We Could Not Find Explained in Statutes or Cases]

(For each of these topics that we could not find addressed in your state's statutes or cases, we suggest you review the same topics in the subchapters of surrounding states. Your state's courts may look to the law of neighboring states to see how their courts and legislatures have treated that particular self-defense issue.)

[Co-Habitants; Co-Employees –Duty to Retreat]

[Presumption of Reasonableness in Special Places]

Pancho's Wisdom

You just might be a Gunnut if . . . you'd rather pee outdoors than indoors.

The rights of citizens living in and traveling through Montana to defend themselves and their loved ones were boosted considerably in 2009 by Montana House Bill 00228 which has been incorporated into this sub-chapter.

Key: ■ commentary ■ original statutes, cases or jury instructions

---

[Defense of Self and Others] [Non-Deadly Force]

§ MONTANA CODE ANNOTATED (MCA) § 45-3-102.
Use of force in defense of person.

A person is justified in the use of force or threat to use force against another when and to the extent that the person reasonably believes that the conduct is necessary to for self-defense or the defense of another against the other person's imminent use of unlawful force . . . [**Example:** You can push a person away to keep him from striking you with his fist. If he hadn't tried to hit you first, your force would otherwise be an assault.]

[Deadly Force] [Defense of a Third Person]

. . . However, the person is justified in the use of force likely to cause death or serious bodily harm only if the person reasonably believes that the force is necessary to prevent imminent death or serious bodily harm to the person or another or . . . [**Example:** You can use a dangerous weapon to stop an immediate threat from a person with a device that could cause death or serious injury, such as a gun, knife, chain saw, large rock or branding iron.]

[Use of Deadly Force to Prevent Serious Felonies]

. . . to prevent the commission of a forcible felony. [Defined below as any felony that "involves the use or threat of physical force or violence against any individual."]

[Exceptions to Justifiable Self-Defense]

§ MCA § 45-3-105.
Use of force by aggressor.

The justification described in 45-3-102 through 45-3-104 is not available to a person who:

[Committing Felony or Unlawful Act]

(1) is attempting to commit, committing, or escaping after the commission of a forcible felony; or [You can't rob a convenience store and claim self-defense after shoot-

ing the cashier for pulling a gun on you. You can't try to rape a woman and shoot her because she tried to defend herself with a Taser. Duh!]

[Initial Aggressor] [Provocation]

(2) purposely or knowingly provokes the use of force against the person, unless: [Start a fight with someone as an excuse to hurt or kill him.]

[Exceptions to the Exceptions] [Withdraw and Communicate]

(a) such force is so great that the person reasonably believes that the person is in imminent danger of death or serious bodily harm and that the person has exhausted every reasonable means to escape the danger other than the use of force that is likely to cause death or serious bodily harm to the assailant; or [You corner the slicker who stole your girlfriend and begin to bruise his Hollywood good looks . Your intent is not to kill or seriously injure him. Although you have a Freedom Arms mini revolver, it's stuffed deep in your Thunderwear and you have no intent to use it. Infuriated by how the beating might affect his chances of being picked as an extra for a movie being shot under the Big Sky, your rival in romance picks up a tire iron and bears down on you like a charging grizzly. You retreat, begging him not to escalate the fight to a deadly level and telling him you give up. He responds by trying to mash out your headlights and your forearm begins to splinter from the heavy blows. Awkwardly you wrench the mini from the depths of deep concealment without snagging the family jewels and stop the deadly attack. If you can convince a jury this is how it happened, you might be acquitted of murder OR convicted of a lesser crime, manslaughter. But our research shows that when you start a fight, you WILL be arrested, prosecuted and probably convicted of something ugly. See Thumbs-Down Factors, Chapter 7.]

(b) in good faith, the person withdraws from physical contact with the assailant and indicates clearly to the assailant that the person desires to withdraw and terminate the use of force but the assailant continues or resumes the use of force. [This is the standard exception to the exceptions – good faith means you actually wanted to withdraw, you're not faking it just so you can claim self-defense. But in a situation where there are no witnesses and just the two of you, how are you going to prove "good faith?" Again, nothing good can come from starting a fight, even if you didn't intend for it to end up deadly.]

[No Duty to Retreat]

[There is no duty to retreat before using reasonable force, including deadly force, if you have a legal right to be where you were attacked, and you were not the aggressor.] "The given instructions do not specifically preclude persons assaulted in their place of business from benefitting from the defense of justifiable force. Nor do they require retreat of anyone who is not the aggressor...The given instructions properly state the law and the giving of defendant's proposed instruction would be repetitious." *State v. Bingman*, 745 P.2d 342, 348 (Mont. 1987).

[The no-retreat rule found in Montana case law was finally written into a statute in 2009 thanks to the persistence of the champion of Montana's right to keep and bear arms, Gary Marbut, his associates and like-minded lawmakers. (For more information about Gary and accomplishments, see our comments at the end of this sub-chapter.)]

§ MCA § 4-3-110.
No duty to summon help or flee.

Except as provided in 45-3-105, a person who is lawfully in a place or location and who is threatened with bodily injury or loss of life has no duty to retreat from a threat or summon law enforcement assistance prior to using force. The provisions of this section apply to a person offering evidence of justifiable use of force under 45-3-102, 45-3-103, or 45-3-104. [There is no duty to retreat from anywhere you have a right to be unless you start a fight. See [**Exceptions to Justifiable Self-Defense**] above. Trespassers must retreat because they don't have a right to be on the property. You also have no duty to call the police before using justifiable force.

[Defense of Person(s) in Special Places – Occupied Structure]

§ MCA § 45-3-103.
Use of force in defense of occupied structure.

(1) A person is justified in the use of force or threat to use force against another when and to the extent that the person reasonably believes that the use of force is necessary to prevent or terminate the other's unlawful entry into or attack upon an occupied structure. [You can use non-deadly force to prevent or terminate a trespass on your home and other structures which fit into the broad definition of an "occupied structure." See definitions below. If you have a sign on your perimeter that says "Trespassers will be shot, survivors will be prosecuted," you'd best not be relying upon it for legal advice. You can't shoot trespassers unless their actions fall within the parameters of the following paragraph regarding the use of deadly force.]

(2) A person is justified in the use of force pursuant to subsection (1) is justified in the use of force likely to cause death or serious bodily harm only if:

(a) the entry is made or attempted and the person reasonably believes that the force is necessary to prevent an assault upon the person or another then in the occupied structure; or [The intruder enters or attempts to enter without your permission and tries to assault you. Notice the threat does NOT have to be one of serious injury or death, or a threat with a deadly weapon (see the broad definition of "assault" below; it's a misdemeanor). Making someone fear bodily injury is an assault. Montana is one of several states that have lowered the degree of threat necessary to trigger the right of citizens to use deadly force in defense of persons in their home. Because of the word "attempted," you don't have to drag anyone back into the home if your shotgun blasts them out the window and into the patio. In fact, if you do, it's tampering with the evidence, which you must never do. See cases involving tampering with evidence in Chapter 7. Please study and remember our admonition not to injure a non-threatening-unarmed intruder or execute a wounded, completely helpless person to keep him from testifying. See Chapter 4.]

(b) the person reasonably believes that the force is necessary to prevent the commission of a forcible felony in the occupied structure. [A forcible felony would include assault with a deadly weapon, rape, or any other form of sex against one's will. You may only use as much force as is necessary to stop the commission of a violent felony.]

[The term "unlawful" is important. If an assailant had permission to enter and then permission is withdrawn and the homeowner uses force against him, there is a serious doubt that this section applies as a defense to the homeowner. In what is referred to as "Annotator's Notes:" after this section of Montana's code, the following comments appear: "The wording for this section is substantially the same as the Illinois source. Illinois case law indicates that the entry must be unlawful before this section is applicable, thus excluding the possibility of justification under this section where the victim enters lawfully but subsequently engages in unlawful conduct for which the occupant of the dwelling expels the victim. See *People v. Brown,* 19 Ill. App.3d 757, 312 N.E.2d 789 (1974), in which the court held that a defense under this section is untenable where the evidence discloses a lawful entry by the victim, and *People v. Chapman*, 49 Ill. App.3d 553, 364 N.E.2d 577 (1977), in which this section was held inapplicable where the victim was not an unlawful intruder (victim shared apartment with defendant) even if the defendant acted to prevent the commission of a forcible felony by the victim in defendant's home."

Pancho's Wisdom – Don't you love it when hidden traps like this appear in the law? In short, this means your lawyer will not be able to use this defense-of-occupied-structure statute to defend you if you cap your serial-killer roomy with a carbine. You'll have to rely on the imminent-threat-of-death-or-serious-bodily-injury defense. Even then, the legal risks are high. If you are not getting along with someone you live with, move out and get your own place. Make sure you report all threats of violence to the police. Then if he tries to break into your place to hurt you, you can use deadly force if necessary. However, if after you separate, you invite the person over as a ploy to kill or injure him or her, you WILL be caught and prosecuted. If the law don't getcha, rest assured, God and Karma will.]

[Defense of Property]

§ MCA § 45-3-104.
Use of force in defense of other property.

A person is justified in the use of force or threat to use force against another when and to the extent that the person reasonably believes that the conduct is necessary to prevent or terminate the other person's trespass on or other tortious or criminal interference with either real property, (other than an occupied structure), or personal property lawfully in the person's possession or in the possession of another who is a member of the person's immediate family or household or of a person whose property the person has a legal duty to protect. However, the person is justified in the use of force likely to cause death or serious bodily harm only if the person reasonably believes that the force is necessary to prevent the commission of a forcible felony. [You can use reasonable force, but not deadly force to protect your real estate and personal property. If you try to stop the lowlife who is damaging or taking your property and he resorts to deadly force, you may respond with deadly force. But why defend your personal property knowing there is a risk it might turn deadly if the criminal decides to fight back? Doing so could easily cost you more in attorneys' fees than the property is worth. See our discussion on the defense of personal property in Chapter 4.]

[Other Issues – Open Carry, Brandishing, Duty of the Police to Preserve Evidence Supporting Self-Defense, No Destruction of Firearms, Citizen's Arrest, Burden of Proof]

[Although this section extends far beyond the issues we highlight in our TEMPLATE outline, it shows determined citizens can accomplish sweeping positive changes if they persist. Bravo to Gary Marbut his Merry Band of Patriots.]

§ MCA § 45-3-111.
Openly carrying weapon — display — exemption.

(1) Any person who is not otherwise prohibited from doing so by federal or state law may openly carry a weapon and may communicate to another person the fact that the person has a weapon. [You can carry your gun on your hip or in your gun rack in Montana without expecting the SWAT team to repel all around you from black helicopters. This doesn't apply to felons or other persons prohibited by state and federal law from possessing a firearm.]

(2) If a person reasonably believes that the person or another person is threatened with bodily harm, the person may warn or threaten the use of force, including deadly force, against the aggressor, including drawing or presenting a weapon. [If your belief that you are about to be assaulted is reasonable, you can warn the assailant to keep his distance by drawing your gun. Making it legal to access your weapon in response to a threat of physical harm helps solve the problem of perception and reaction time referred to in Chapter 11. Notice this does not appear to give you the right to brandish to protect your personal property.

Pancho's Wisdom – Are we reading this right? Justification to brandish to ward off a simple assault? Spectacular!]

(3) This section does not limit the authority of the board of regents or other postsecondary institutions to regulate the carrying of weapons, as defined in 45-8-361(5)(b), on their campuses. [This means universities can prohibit firearms on campus. *Pancho's Wisdom* – This was probably a concession to legislators with an unnatural fear of guns to get the rest of the bill passed. In Utah, the law expressly prohibits public universities from establishing rules that undercut the rights of students and teachers with concealed weapon permits to defend themselves with a firearm. Utah's statute has been upheld by the Utah Supreme Court. The last time I lectured at a Utah university, the head of the political science department thanked licensed students for bringing their concealed weapons to class and for being prepared to prevent anything similar to Virginia Tech. Of course,

she and her fellow professors were packin' some potent heat as well. How about that? Galileo and Glock in the same lecture hall. Annie Oakley would have been proud.]

§ MCA § 45-3-112.
Investigation of alleged offense involving claim of justifiable use of force.

When an investigation is conducted by a peace officer of an incident that appears to have or is alleged to have involved justifiable use of force, the investigation must be conducted so as to disclose all evidence, including testimony concerning the alleged offense and that might support the apparent or alleged justifiable use of force. [A mandate to law enforcement to not try to sweep evidence of self-defense under the carpet.]

§ MCA § 46-5-313.
Firearm not to be destroyed.

If a firearm possessed by a law enforcement agency was not purchased by the agency for agency use, if it is legal for a private person to own and possess the firearm, and if the legal owner cannot be determined by the agency, the agency may not destroy the firearm and shall sell the firearm to a licensed dealer. The proceeds of the sale must be deposited in the general fund of the governmental entity of which the agency is a part. [No Terminator bubble baths for guns that end up in the hands of the police for one reason or another. You will now know of a certainty that the frying pan you bought at Wal-Mart wasn't once a Smith and Wesson confiscated by police in Montana.]

§ MCA § 70-24-110.
Landlords and tenants — no firearm prohibition allowed.

A landlord or operator of a hotel or motel may not, by contract or otherwise, prevent a tenant or a guest of a tenant from possessing on the premises a firearm that it is legal for the tenant or guest to possess. A landlord or operator of a hotel or motel may prohibit the discharge of a firearm on the premises except in self-defense. [Hotels and motels that post signs prohibiting firearms set their guests up for hotel-room invasions. Why not just post a neon sign out front telling violent criminals your guests are defenseless? Montana no longer allows such nonsense.]

[HELPFUL DEFINITIONS RELATING TO THIS STATE'S SELF-DEFENSE STATUTES]

- **Assault** – (1) A person commits the offense of assault if the person: (a) purposely or knowingly causes bodily injury to another; (b) negligently causes bodily injury to another with a weapon; (c) purposely or knowingly makes physical contact of an insulting or provoking nature with any individual; or (d) purposely or knowingly causes reasonable apprehension of bodily injury in another. (2) A person convicted of assault shall be fined not to exceed $500 or be imprisoned in the county jail for any term not to exceed 6 months, or both. **MCA § 45-5-201.**

- **Bodily injury** – means physical pain, illness, or an impairment of physical condition and includes mental illness or impairment. **MCA § 45-2-101(5).**

- **Felony** – means an offense in which the sentence imposed upon conviction is death or imprisonment in a state prison for a term exceeding 1 year. **MCA § 45-2-101(23).**

  45-3-101. Definitions. (1) **"Force likely to cause death or serious bodily harm"** within the meaning of this chapter includes but is not limited to:

  (a) the firing of a firearm in the direction of a person, even though no purpose exists to kill or inflict serious bodily harm; and

  (b) the firing of a firearm at a vehicle in which a person is riding.

  (2) **"Forcible felony"** means any felony which involves the use or threat of physical force or violence against any individual.

- **Knowingly** – a person acts knowingly with respect to conduct or to a circumstance described by a statute defining an offense when the person is aware of the person's own conduct or that the circumstance exists. A person acts knowingly with respect to the result of conduct described by a statute defining an offense when the person is aware that it is highly probable that the result will be caused by the person's conduct. When knowledge of the existence of a particular fact is an element of an offense, knowledge is established if a person is aware of a high probability of its existence. Equivalent terms, such as "knowing" or "with knowledge", have the same meaning. **MCA § 45-2-101(35).**

- **Negligently** – a person acts negligently with respect to a result or to a circumstance described by a statute defining an offense when the person consciously disregards a risk that the result will occur or that the circumstance exists or when the person disregards a risk of which the person should be aware that the result will occur or that the circumstance exists. The risk must be of a nature and degree that to disregard it involves a gross deviation from the standard of conduct that a reasonable person would observe in the actor's situation. "Gross deviation" means a deviation that is considerably greater than lack of ordinary care. Relevant terms, such as "negligent" and "with negligence", have the same meaning. **MCA § 45-2-101(43).**

- **Occupied structure** – means any building, vehicle, or other place suitable for human occupancy or night lodging of persons or for carrying on business, whether or not a person is actually present, including any outbuilding that is immediately adjacent to or in close proximity to an occupied structure and that is habitually used for personal use or employment. Each unit of a building consisting of two or more units separately secured or occupied is a separate occupied structure. **MCA § 45-2-101(47).**

- **Property** – means a tangible or intangible thing of value. Property includes but is not limited to: [This definition gives nearly 100 examples for property like real estate, money, pets, food and drink, and even microorganisms . . .] **MCA § 45-2-101(61).**

- **Property of another** – means real or personal property in which a person other than the offender has an interest that the offender has no authority to defeat or impair, even though the offender may have an interest in the property. **Montana Statutes 45-2-101(62).**

- **Purposely** – a person acts purposely with respect to a result or to conduct described by a statute defining an offense if it is the person's conscious object to engage in that conduct or to cause that result. When a particular purpose is an element of an offense, the element is established although the purpose is conditional, unless the condition negatives the harm or evil sought to be prevented by the law defining the offense. Equivalent terms, such as "purpose" and "with the purpose", have the same meaning. **MCA § 45-2-101(65).**

- **Serious bodily injury** – means bodily injury that:

  (i) creates a substantial risk of death;

  (ii) causes serious permanent disfigurement or protracted loss or impairment of the function or process of a bodily member or organ; or

  (iii)at the time of injury, can reasonably be expected to result in serious permanent disfigurement or protracted loss or impairment of the function or process of a bodily member or organ.

  (b) The term includes serious mental illness or impairment. **MCA § 45-2-101(66)(a).**

- **Threat** – means a menace, however communicated, to:

  (a) inflict physical harm on the person threatened or any other person or on property;

  (b) subject any person to physical confinement or restraint;

  (c) commit a criminal offense;

  (d) accuse a person of a criminal offense;

  (e) expose a person to hatred, contempt, or ridicule;

  (f) harm the credit or business repute of a person;

  (g) reveal information sought to be concealed by the person threatened;

  (h) take action as an official against anyone or anything, withhold official action, or cause the action or withholding;

  (i) bring about or continue a strike, boycott, or other similar collective action if the person making the threat demands or receives property that is not for the benefit of groups that the person purports to represent; or

  (j) testify or provide information or withhold testimony or information with respect to another's legal claim or defense. **MCA § 45-2-101(76).**

- **Vehicle** – means a device for transportation by land, water, or air or by mobile equipment, with provision for transport of an operator. **MCA § 45-2-101(78).**

[TEMPLATE Topics We Could Not Find Explained in Statutes or Cases]

(For each of these topics that we could not find addressed in your state's statutes or cases, we suggest you review the same topics in the subchapters of surrounding states. Your state's courts may look to the law of neighboring states to see how their courts and legislatures have treated that particular self-defense issue.)

[Mutual Combat]

[Co-Habitants; Co-Employees – Duty to Retreat]

[Presumption of Reasonableness in Special Places]

[Civil Liability]

Gary Marbut has been an inspiration to all of us who struggle to preserve the right to defend ourselves and loved ones in our own states. He is a living testimony of the enormous influence one determined person can have. Although not a lawyer, Gary has been writing and pushing pro-self-defense bills through the Montana legislature for years. He has written several editions of the book *Gun Laws of Montana* which we encourage every person living or traveling in Montana to own. To find out more about Gary, his presidency of the Montana Shooting Sports Association or to order his book, go to www.marbut.com online.

Pancho's Wisdom

You just might be a Gunnut if . . . humidity makes your NRA card stick to your credit card in your sweaty leather wallet.

Key: ■ commentary ■ original statutes, cases or jury instructions

[Defense of Self and Others] [Non-Deadly Force]

§ NEBRASKA REVISED STATUTES (NEB.REV.ST.) § 28-1409.
Use of force in self-protection.

(1) Subject to the provisions of this section and of section 28-1414, the use of force upon or toward another person is justifiable when the actor believes that such force is immediately necessary for the purpose of protecting himself against the use of unlawful force by such other person on the present occasion. [You can use reasonably necessary non-deadly force to defend yourself against unlawful non-deadly force.]

[Exceptions to Justifiable Self-Defense]

(2) The use of such force is not justifiable under this section to resist an arrest which the actor knows is being made by a peace officer, although the arrest is unlawful. [You can't use force to resist arrest even if you believe the arrest is illegal.]

(3) The use of such force is not justifiable under this section to resist force used by the occupier or possessor of property or by another person on his behalf, where the actor knows that the person using the force is doing so under a claim of right to protect the property, except that this limitation shall not apply if: [Disputes over possession of property must be enforced in the courts, not toe to toe with fists, shovels or crowbars on the disputed property line.]

(a) The actor is a public officer acting in the performance of his duties or a person lawfully assisting him therein or a person making or assisting in a lawful arrest; [Police officers are justified in using force to seize property or persons as directed in court orders.]

(b) The actor has been unlawfully dispossessed of the property and is making a reentry or recapture justified by section 28-1411; or [**Example:** Looters throw you out of your own store after a natural disaster and you simply are using force to get back onto your own property. Keep in mind, however, this subparagraph is not referring to deadly force. That comes later; see the discussion below.]

(c) The actor believes that such force is necessary to protect himself against death or serious bodily harm. [Staying with the example in the paragraph above, if the looters are threatening you with baseball bats or tire irons, which could cause death or serious bodily injury, then you would be justified, naturally, to respond with force if necessary to defend yourself, not your property. See Section 4 immediately below for a discussion of deadly force.]

[Deadly Force] [Use of Deadly Force to Prevent Serious Felonies]

(4) The use of deadly force shall not be justifiable under this section unless the actor believes that such force is necessary to protect himself against death, serious bodily harm, kidnapping or sexual intercourse compelled by force or threat, [Like in every other state, you may use deadly force to defend yourself against an imminent threat of death or serious injury. You may also use deadly force to defend against kidnapping, rape or forcible sodomy.] nor is it justifiable if:

[Exceptions to Justifiable Self-Defense] [Provocation]

(a) The actor, with the purpose of causing death or serious bodily harm, provoked the use of force against himself in the same encounter; or [**Example:** There's an old foreigner who is an especially talented salesperson and your main competitor in the used-car business. You want to get rid of the competition. He's very proud of his young, beautiful mail-order bride whom he parades around town. You know he carries a concealed weapon on his ankle, but because of his age, he can't get to it very quickly. You suspect if you insult his wife in front of him, he'll go for his gun, but he's so slow you can beat him to the draw. You meet them on the street and call her a nasty name and then slap her face. He mumbles obscenities that you can't quite make out and then bends over to grab his ankle pistol. You've practiced enough to be able to draw from concealment in under 1 second, so you put four rounds into him before he's able to clear his pant cuff. Self-defense? Not under this statute if the state can prove your provocation was simply an excuse to snuff your able competitor.]

[Duty to Retreat – Generally]

(b) The actor knows that he can avoid the necessity of using such force with complete safety by retreating or by surrendering possession of a thing to a person asserting a claim of right thereto or by complying with a demand that he abstain from any action which he has no duty to take, except that: [You have a duty to retreat before using deadly force if you can retreat "in complete safety." However, you don't have to retreat from your home or workplace. **Retreat:** If you are being robbed on the street by a wobbly drunk with a Swiss Army knife and you hold the Cornhusker record for the 440 yard run, you'd best be sprintin' rather than spinnin' the cylinder on your wheel gun. **Surrender Possession:** A person tells you that you're driving the car someone stole from him, to get out and surrender possession. You can't give him the Mad Max treatment and blow him into Kansas. **Abstain from Action No Duty to Take:** We still haven't figured this out and could find no Nebraska cases to enlighten us. The following example might be something an anti-gun prosecutor might prosecute: You are in a convenience store during a robbery. The robber tells you if you simply leave without looking back, he won't hurt you or the clerk. You exit the glass doors unharmed, but burst through the delivery area with pistolas ablaze like Bronco Billy. An over-zealous prosecutor might argue that by complying with the robber's demand to leave and not interfere with the robbery, you could have avoided the need to use deadly force. Do these nit-picky Nebraska rules leave you somewhat confused? *Pancho's Wisdom* – It's time for Nebraska's legislature to make it easier on law-abiding citizens and more risky for violent criminals instead of the other way around.]

[Defense of Person(s) in Special Places – Dwelling, Place of Work]
[No Duty to Retreat from Home or Workplace] [Co-Employees]

(i) The actor shall not be obliged to retreat from his dwelling or place of work, unless he was the initial aggressor or is assailed in his place of work by another person whose place of work the actor knows it to be; and [You don't have to retreat from your home or place of work before you defend yourself with deadly force unless you started the conflict or the conflict is with a co-worker. If your fellow employee goes "Postal" you must retreat if you can do so with complete safety. You still must retreat before using deadly force if you are on the public sidewalk in front of your home. *State v. Menser,* 382 N.W.2d 18 (Neb. 1986).]

. . .

(5) Except as required by subsections (3) and (4) of this section, a person employing protective force may estimate the necessity thereof under the circumstances as he believes them to be when the force is used, without retreating, surrendering possession, doing any other act which he has no legal duty to do, or abstaining from any lawful action. [This paragraph is confusing at best. It purports to relieve one of the duty to retreat, but it doesn't apply to the use of deadly force. You must still retreat before you use deadly force if you can do so in complete safety unless at home or at work, unless you started the fight at home or at work, or unless the assailant is a co-worker. *Pancho's Wisdom* – About as clear as mud, aye? Hey, just dictate this to your iPod and play it back while being attacked. Your legislators should simplify!]

. . .

[Exceptions to the Exceptions] [Withdraw and Communicate]

"No doubt, a person may actually and bona fide withdraw from a strife of his own seeking, and thereafter, if attacked, if he is without fault, resist the attack, and avail himself of the plea of necessary self-defense." *Hans v. State,* 100 N.W. 419, 422 (Neb. 1904). [Although this case is over 100 years old, our legal research service says it's still good law. It seems to be stating the same law that is applied in most states. Even if you started a fight, if you withdraw and thereafter are attacked, you can defend yourself. We've found, however, if you bear any responsibility for starting or escalating a fight or agreeing to duel and someone is hurt or killed, you will be arrested, prosecuted and probably convicted.]

[Defense of Third Persons]

§ NEB.REV.ST § 28-1410.
Use of force for protection of other persons.

(1) Subject to the provisions of this section and of section 28-1414 [negligent use of defensive force], the use of force upon or toward the person of another is justifiable to protect a third person when:

(a) The actor would be justified under section 28-1409 in using such force to protect himself against the injury he believes to be threatened to the person whom he seeks to protect; [You have to believe you would be justified in using such force if it were you who was being attacked, AND. . .]

(b) Under the circumstances as the actor believes them to be, the person whom he seeks to protect would be justified in using such protective force; and [you have to believe the person you are defending would be justified using the force you are about to use in defending him or herself, AND . . .]

(c) The actor believes that his intervention is necessary for the protection of such other person. [you believe the force you are about to use is necessary to protect the person you are about to protect.]

[This is another complicated section because of all the hurdles. If any one of these requirements is not fulfilled, you would not be justified in defending another person.]

(2) Notwithstanding subsection (1) of this section:

(a) When the actor would be obliged under section 28-1409 to retreat, to surrender the possession of a thing or to comply with a demand before using force in self-protection, he shall not be obliged to do so before using force for the protection of another person, unless he knows that he can thereby secure the complete safety of such other person; [Even if you would have been required to retreat under the general self-defense statute above, you don't have to retreat when defending a third person unless you know you can get him out of the situation in complete safety by retreating. The same rule applies to surrendering possession and complying with a demand, etc.]

(b) When the person whom the actor seeks to protect would be obliged under section 28-1409 to retreat, to surrender the possession of a thing or to comply with a demand if he knew that he could obtain complete safety by so doing, the actor is obliged to try to cause him to do so before using force in his protection if the actor knows that he can obtain complete safety in that way; and [If there is anything you know you can do to end the danger to the third person you intend to defend without using force to protect him, you have to do it.]

(c) Neither the actor nor the person whom he seeks to protect is obliged to retreat when in the other's dwelling or place of work to any greater extent than in his own. [Neither you nor the person you are defending have to retreat from the home of the person you are defending before using deadly force.]

[Civil Liability]

§ NEB.REV.ST § 28-1416.

Justification an affirmative defense; civil remedies unaffected.

(1) In any prosecution based on conduct which is justifiable under sections 28-1406 to 28-1416, justification is an affirmative defense.

(2) The fact that conduct is justifiable under sections 28-1406 to 28-1416 does not abolish or impair any remedy for such conduct which is available in any civil action. [Even though you may be innocent in a criminal trial on the theory of self-defense, it doesn't necessarily shield you from a lawsuit for money damages if you injure or kill someone during a defensive incident.]

[Defense of Property]

§ NEB.REV.ST § 28-1411.

Use of force for protection of property. [This may be the most convoluted and complicated defense of property law in the nation. This section is so filled with exceptions and requirements that you'll never remember it all during an adrenaline rush, so just call the police. But, if you must know . . . here we go . . .]

(1) Subject to the provisions of this section and of section **28-1414** [reckless, negligent use of force], the use of force upon or toward the person of another is justifiable when the actor believes that such force is immediately necessary:

(a) To prevent or terminate an unlawful entry or other trespass upon land or a trespass against or the unlawful carrying away of tangible, movable property; PROVIDED, that such land or movable property is, or is believed by the actor to be, in his possession or in the possession of another person for whose protection he acts; or [Notice, you cannot use deadly force if only property is at risk. Once again, simply call the police. The riding lawn mower that is stolen only costs a fraction of the price of the defense attorney you'll need if you confront the thief, things get ugly and you hurt or kill Mr. Stickyfingers.]

(b) To effect an entry or reentry upon land or to retake tangible movable property; PROVIDED, that the actor believes that he or the person by whose authority he acts or a person from whom he or such other person derives title was unlawfully dispossessed of such land or movable property and is entitled to possession; AND PROVIDED FURTHER, that:

(i) The force is used immediately or on fresh pursuit after such dispossession; or

(ii) The actor believes that the person against whom he uses force has no claim of right to the possession of the property and, in the case of land, the circumstances, as the actor believes them to be, are of such urgency that it would be an exceptional hardship to postpone the entry or reentry until a court order is obtained.

[Again, this statute seems overly complicated. Not only do you have to believe you were unlawfully dispossessed of land or property, you also have to be within the bounds of fresh pursuit, and you have to believe that the other person had no claim to the property and that it would be an "exceptional hardship" to regain the property through the courts. While you could argue that ANYTHING you do through the courts is a hardship, that probably wouldn't fly. But it doesn't stop there. See sections 2 and 3 below for more trip wires.]

(2) For the purposes of subsection (1) of this section:

(a) A person who has parted with the custody of property to another who refuses to restore it to him is no longer in possession, unless such property is movable and was and still is located on land in his possession;

(b) A person who has been dispossessed of land does not regain possession thereof merely by setting foot thereon; and

(c) A person who has a license to use or occupy real property is deemed to be in possession thereof except against the licenser acting under claim of right.

[If you've given your property to someone and they refuse to give it back or you've been evicted or whatever, this is all too complicated to remember for purposes of the use of force . . . so DON'T use force, use a lawyer!]

(3) The use of force is justifiable under this section only if the actor first requests the person against whom such force is used to desist from his interference with the property, unless the actor believes that:

(a) Such request would be useless;

(b) It would be dangerous to himself or another person to make the request; or

(c) Substantial harm will be done to the physical condition of the property which is sought to be protected before the request can effectively be made. [AND you have to request that person knock it off before you can use force, unless it would be useless, dangerous, or the damage would already be done. Now after all of these requirements and exceptions, if you can still remember what you were doing in the first place, you may be able to use force to recover or protect your property. But wait, there is more...]

(4) The use of force to prevent or terminate a trespass is not justifiable under this section if the actor knows that the exclusion of the trespasser will expose him to substantial danger of serious bodily harm.

[Okay, so the Hatfields are trespassing while hunting on your land. You go out with a big iron on your hip to confront them. When the smoke clears, you are the only one left standing. Sounds to us like this paragraph (4) could be used by the DA to deep fry your buns.]

(5) The use of force to prevent an entry or reentry upon land or the recapture of movable property is not justifiable under this section, although the actor believes that such reentry or recapture is unlawful, if:

(a) The reentry or recapture is made by or on behalf of a person who was actually dispossessed of the property; and

(b) It is otherwise justifiable under subdivision (1)(b) of this section.

[If the person was actually dispossessed and trying to get his property back, even if you didn't know it, you can't use force to keep him from getting his property back and call it justifiable. And we haven't even gotten into deadly force; that is next...]

(6) The use of deadly force is not justifiable under this section unless the actor believes that:

(a) The person against whom the force is used is attempting to dispossess him of his dwelling otherwise than under a claim of right to its possession; or [You can use deadly force to keep someone from chasing you or dragging you out of your own home. However, you can't use deadly force against your landlord who is trying to oust you by legal means for being behind on the rent or a mortgage holder who claims you are behind on your house payments.]

[Use of Deadly Force to Prevent Serious Felonies]

(b) The person against whom the force is used is attempting to commit or consummate arson, burglary, robbery or other felonious theft or property destruction [see definitions for these serious felonies] and either:

(i) Has employed or threatened deadly force against or in the presence of the actor; or

(ii) The use of force other than deadly force to prevent the commission or the consummation of the crime would expose the actor or another in his presence to substantial danger of serious bodily harm. [Basically, you must be threatened, not just your property, unless anything less than deadly force would put you at risk of serious bodily harm.]

[*Pancho's Wisdom* – Frankly, it is absurd that Nebraska lawmakers don't think it's bad enough that a person on your property is committing an arson, burglary or robbery. They expect you to take the time to determine if the perpetrator of these otherwise heinous crimes is a deadly threat or whether using force other than deadly force would subject you to serious bodily harm. If a person is an intruder in your home, you could be killed by the time you accurately identify what, if anything, is in his hands. Like in Florida and states that have adopted its home-defense statute, the presumption should be in favor of the law-abiding citizen and against the criminal. If someone breaks into your home, the guessing game for both of you should be over; you live, he dies, period. Nebraska legislators should scrap this wimpy statute and adopt something like Florida's.]

(7) The justification afforded by this section extends to the use of confinement as protective force only if the actor takes all reasonable measures to terminate the confinement as soon as he knows that he can do so with safety to the property, unless the person confined has been arrested on a charge of crime. [If you lock a burglar in your bathroom, you have to let him out as soon as the former-Cornhusker-fullback sheriff arrives to tie him into knots.]

(8) The justification afforded by this section extends to the use of a device for the purpose of protecting property only if:

(a) Such device is not designed to cause or known to create a substantial risk of causing death or serious bodily harm;

(b) Such use of the particular device to protect such property from entry or trespass is reasonable under the circumstances, as the actor believes them to be; and

(c) Such device is one customarily used for such a purpose or reasonable care is taken to make known to probable intruders the fact that it is used.

[This paragraph refers to traps you set to protect your property. It can't be a spring-loaded 10 gauge or any other device that could cause death or serious injury. You have to warn intruders that you are using such a device. **Example:** "Warning: Our son Kevin has a sadistic propensity to torture home burglars. If he is home alone and you attempt to enter these premises, you may be shot in the groin with his pellet gun, suffer third degree burns from grabbing a red-hot door knob, punctured by rusty nails sticking up from creaky stair steps, branded in the forehead with a hot clothes iron or fanged by a frothing tarantula spider!"]

(9) The use of force to pass a person whom the actor believes to be purposely or knowingly and unjustifiably obstructing the actor from going to a place to which he may lawfully go is justifiable if:

(a) The actor believes that the person against whom he uses force has no claim of right to obstruct the actor;

(b) The actor is not being obstructed from entry or movement on land which he knows to be in the possession or custody of the person obstructing him, or in the possession or custody of another person by whose authority the obstructor acts, unless the circumstances, as the actor believes them to be, are of such urgency that it would not be reasonable to postpone the entry or movement on such land until a court order is obtained; and

(c) The force used is not greater than would be justifiable if the person obstructing the actor were using force against him to prevent his passage.

[You can use a straight arm block to do an end run around someone blocking your access to your home and property, but not to trespass onto his property. This does not authorize you to use deadly force or cause more harm than needed to get around the obstructionist than is reasonably necessary.]

[HELPFUL DEFINITIONS RELATING TO THIS STATE'S SELF-DEFENSE STATUTES]

- **Bodily injury** shall mean physical pain, illness, or any impairment of physical condition; **Neb.Rev.St § 28-109 (4).**

- **Building** shall mean a structure which has the capacity to contain, and is designed for the shelter of man, animals, or property, and includes ships, trailers, sleeping cars, aircraft, or other vehicles or places adapted for overnight accommodations of persons or animals, or for carrying on of business therein, whether or not a person or animal is actually present. If a building is divided into units for separate occupancy, any unit not occupied by the defendant is a building of another. **Neb.Rev.St § 28-501.**

- **Deadly force** shall mean force which the actor uses with the purpose of causing or which he knows to create a substantial risk of causing death or serious bodily harm. Purposely firing a firearm in the direction of another person or at a vehicle in which another person is believed to be constitutes deadly force. A threat to cause death or serious bodily harm, by the production of a weapon or otherwise, so long as the actor's purpose is limited to creating an apprehension that he will use deadly force if necessary, shall not constitute deadly force. **Neb.Rev.St § 28-1406(3).**

- **Deadly physical force** shall mean force, the intended, natural, and probable consequence of which is to produce death, or which does, in fact, produce death. **Neb.Rev.St § 28-109 (6).**

- **Deadly weapon** shall mean any firearm, knife, bludgeon, or other device, instrument, material, or substance, whether animate or inanimate, which in the manner it is used or intended to be used is capable of producing death or serious bodily injury. **Neb.Rev.St § 28-109 (7).**

- **Dwelling** shall mean any building or structure, though movable or temporary, or a portion thereof, which is for the time being the actor's home or place of lodging. **Neb.Rev.St § 28-1406(5).**

- **Felonies Mentioned –**
    - **Arson** – [Intentionally setting fire to or damaging by explosives any building or occupied structure.] **Neb.Rev.St § 28-502 & 503.**

    - **Burglary** – A person commits burglary if such person willfully, maliciously, and forcibly breaks and enters any real estate or any improvements erected thereon with intent to commit any felony or with intent to steal property of any value. **Neb.Rev.St § 28-507.**

    - **Felonious property destruction** – [This is not defined under this name in Nebraska statutes. We suspect it refers to destroying property which has enough value to raise the crime from a misdemeanor to a felony. Whatever it means, we recommend you NEVER use deadly force to defend property unless there is a contemporaneous threat of serious injury or death to a person as well as the threat to the property.]

- **Felonious Theft** – [This phrase is not defined in the Nebraska statutes. We suspect it refers to stealing property that has enough value to raise the crime from a misdemeanor to a felony. However, whatever it means, we recommend you NEVER use deadly force to defend property unless there is a contemporaneous threat of serious injury or death to a person as well as the threat to the property.]

- **Kidnapping** – [Abducting another, or after doing so, continuing to retrain him or her with the intent to obtain ransom, use the victim for a shield or hostage, or commit a crime against the victim.] **Neb.Rev.St § 28-313.**

- **Robbery** – [With the intent to steal, the offender takes money or personal property or thing of value by violence, or by creating fear.] **Neb.Rev.St § 28-324.**

- **Sexual intercourse compelled by force** – [This particular phrase is not defined in Nebraska statutes. However, it would certainly include rape and forcible sodomy. The following statutes also fit the general description:]

§ 2 NEB.REV.ST § 28-319.
Sexual assault; first degree; penalty.

(1) Any person who subjects another person to sexual penetration (a) without the consent of the victim, (b) who knew or should have known that the victim was mentally or physically incapable of resisting or appraising the nature of his or her conduct, or (c) when the actor is nineteen years of age or older and the victim is at least twelve but less than sixteen years of age is guilty of sexual assault in the first degree.

§ NEB.REV.ST § 28-320.
Sexual assault; second or third degree; penalty.

(1) Any person who subjects another person to sexual contact (a) without consent of the victim, or (b) who knew or should have known that the victim was physically or mentally incapable of resisting or appraising the nature of his or her conduct is guilty of sexual assault in either the second degree or third degree.

(2) Sexual assault shall be in the second degree and is a Class III felony if the actor shall have caused serious personal injury to the victim.

§ 28-319.01
Sexual assault of a child; first degree; penalty.

(1) A person commits sexual assault of a child in the first degree:

(a) When if he or she subjects another person under twelve years of age to sexual penetration and the actor is at least nineteen years of age or older; or.

(b) When he or she subjects another person who is at least twelve years of age but less than sixteen years of age to sexual penetration and the actor is twenty-five years of age or older.

(2) Sexual assault of a child in the first degree is a Class IB felony with a mandatory minimum sentence of fifteen years in prison for the first offense.

- **Motor vehicle** shall mean every self-propelled land vehicle, not operated upon rails, except self-propelled chairs used by persons who are disabled and electric personal assistive mobility devices as defined in section 60-618.02. **Neb.Rev.St § 28-109 (12).**

- **Recklessly** shall mean acting with respect to a material element of an offense when any person disregards a substantial and unjustifiable risk that the material element exists or will result from his or her conduct. The risk must be of such a nature and degree that, considering the nature and purpose of the actor's conduct and the circumstances known to the actor, its disregard involves a gross deviation from the standard of conduct that a law-abiding person would observe in the actor's situation. **Neb.Rev.St § 28-109 (19).**

- **Serious bodily injury** shall mean bodily injury which involves a substantial risk of death, or which involves substantial risk of serious permanent disfigurement, or protracted loss or impairment of the function of any part or organ of the body. **Neb.Rev.St § 28-109 (20).**

- **Unlawful force** shall mean force, including confinement, which is employed without the consent of the person against whom it is directed and the employment of which constitutes an offense or actionable tort or would constitute such offense or tort except for a defense such as the absence of intent, negligence, or mental capacity; duress; youth; or diplomatic status; not amounting to a privilege to use the force. **Neb.Rev.St § 28-1406(1).**

[TEMPLATE Topics We Could Not Find Explained in Statutes or Cases]

(For each of these topics that we could not find addressed in your state's statutes or cases, we suggest you review the same topics in the subchapters of surrounding states. Your state's courts may look to the law of neighboring states to see how their courts and legislatures have treated that particular self-defense issue.)

[Initial Aggressor]

[Committing Felony or Unlawful Act]

[Mutual Combat]

[Co-Habitants – Duty to Retreat]

[Presumption of Reasonableness in Special Places]

[Reckless Injury to Innocent Third Parties]

Warning: Some of Nevada's self-defense statutes are a century old and give the false impression that you can use deadly force to prevent any and all felonies or to defend your property. You can't! Some residents believe they can use deadly force to chase down fleeing felons. You can't anymore; that law has been repealed. *Pancho's Wisdom* – Exercising your fundamental right to defend your life and the life of your loved ones should not be a gamble, even in Nevada. The Nevada Legislature needs to repeal its old, hard-to-understand self-defense statutes and replace them with statutes that clearly and accurately define what rights Nevadans have in defending themselves. The Mother of All Self-Defense Laws would be a good place for the Legislature to start. See Chapter 20.

Key: ■ commentary ■ original statutes, cases or jury instructions

[Defense of Self and Others] [Non-Deadly Force]

§ NEVADA REVISED STATUTES (N.R.S.) § 193.230.
Lawful resistance to commission of public offense: Who may make.

Lawful resistance to the commission of a public offense may be made:

1. By the party about to be injured.
2. By other parties.

§ N.R.S. § 193.240.
Resistance by party about to be injured.

Resistance sufficient to prevent the offense may be made by the party about to be injured:

1. To prevent an offense against his person, or his family or some member thereof.
2. To prevent an illegal attempt, by force, to take or injure property in his lawful possession.

§ N.R.S. § 193.250.
Resistance by other persons.

Any other person, in aid or defense of a person about to be injured, may make resistance sufficient to prevent the offense.

[These general provisions are vague and not very helpful. We interpret them to mean you can use reasonable force necessary to prevent an unlawful act against you, a family member, your property or another person. Nothing in these statutes specifically authorizes the use of deadly force.]

[Deadly Force]

§ N.R.S. § 200.200.
Killing in self-defense.

If a person kills another in self-defense, it must appear that:

1. The danger was so urgent and pressing that, in order to save his own life, or to prevent his receiving great bodily harm, the killing of the other was absolutely necessary; and [You cannot take someone else's life unless you are about to die or be seriously injured and your use of deadly force is absolutely necessary. Even though this statute refers to killing, remember our counsel in Chapter 3. Your intent should never be to kill anyone, but merely stop the progression of deadly force against yourself or others.]

2. The person killed was the assailant, or that the slayer had really, and in good faith, endeavored to decline any further struggle before the mortal blow was given. [If the person that died from your otherwise justified use of deadly force was the assailant, the theory of self-defense should ultimately save your bacon. If YOU were the aggressor, however, you will probably be arrested and prosecuted. You might not be convicted, however, if you did everything possible to avoid "the mortal blow" including retreating.

   Although the language of this statute is as old and dusty as the old courthouse in Pioche, it seems to convey the same principle that we see in many other states under the exceptions to justification. One who provokes or voluntarily participates in a fight cannot win on the theory of self-defense unless he ceases all hostile conduct, effectively communicates his intent to withdraw and the other person nevertheless continues to try to harm him. Only then is the initial aggressor justified in using deadly force to save himself.]

§ N.R.S. § 200.120.
"Justifiable homicide" defined.

Justifiable homicide is the killing of a human being in necessary self-defense, or in defense of habitation, property or person, against one who manifestly intends, or endeavors, by violence or surprise, to commit a felony, or against any person or persons who manifestly intend and endeavor, in a violent, riotous, tumultuous or surreptitious manner, to enter the habitation of another for the purpose of assaulting or offering personal violence to any person dwelling or being therein.

[This run-on reads like a double-barreled shotgun blast from the past mixing concepts of self-defense, defense of property and home defense together in one sentence. It comes from an era when most felonies against persons, homes and properties were morally wrong and violent. Times have changed and countless non-violent felonies have been added to the law books of most states. Read the excerpt from the Nevada case *State v. Weddell*, 118 Nev. at 211,212 (2002) in Chapter 4 explaining how currently a multitude of non-violent crimes are classified as felonies and do not justify the use of deadly force.

Use of force to prevent a violent or secret entry into one's habitation – We could not find a definition of "habitation" in Nevada's self-defense laws. The context of the word in other Nevada statutes seems to indicate it refers to a structure in which someone lives, such as one's home. This part of the statute purports to authorize the use of deadly force to stop a violent or secretive entry into a habitation by an unlawful intruder who intends to commit an assault or personal violence. This is a lower threshold than the requirement of a threat of death or serious injury. You should know, however, that in 1994 a man was prosecuted and convicted of second degree murder in Nevada for killing an acquaintance with a gun who had entered his camp tent for the fifth time "acting like a madman" to beat him with his fists. *Stroup v. State*, 110 Nev. 525 (1994). Prosecutions and court decisions such as this create substantial doubt that citizens can rely upon the wording of Nevada's self-defense statutes in defending themselves.]

§ N.R.S. § 200.130.
Bare fear insufficient to justify killing; reasonable fear required.

A bare fear of any of the offenses mentioned in NRS 200.120, to prevent which the homicide is alleged to have been committed, shall not be sufficient to justify the killing. It must appear that the circumstances were sufficient to excite the fears of a reasonable person, and that the party killing really acted under the influence of those fears and not in a spirit of revenge.

[You may only use deadly force to stop a violent felony that is in progress or about to happen (imminent); not based upon a fear that it might happen. If the crime has already been committed, you can't use deadly force as revenge.]

§ N.R.S. § 200.150.
Justifiable or excusable homicide.

All other instances which stand upon the same footing of reason and justice as those enumerated shall be considered justifiable or excusable homicide.

[It's only appropriate that the gambling state, Nevada, have a "wild card" provision in its self-defense statute. This statute basically says there may be other reasons which are logical and just under which a person can defend himself other than those specifically referred to in the Nevada self-defense statute. If it's logical and reasonable, the court will recognize it, but you can be certain, even if it's logical and reasonable, if it's unusual, you will probably be arrested and prosecuted. We could find no Nevada cases specifically interpreting this statute to date.]

§ N.R.S. § 200.275.
Justifiable infliction or threat of bodily injury not punishable.

In addition to any other circumstances recognized as justification at common law, the infliction or threat of bodily injury is justifiable, and does not constitute mayhem, battery or assault, if done under circumstances which would justify homicide. (Added to NRS in 1983.) [This statute applies the same rules of self-defense that apply to homicides to incidents in which the attacker is not killed, just injured.]

[Use of Deadly Force to Prevent Serious Felonies]
[Defense of Third Persons]

§ N.R.S. § 200.160.
Additional cases of justifiable homicide.

Homicide is also justifiable when committed:

1. In the lawful defense of the slayer, or his or her husband, wife, parent, child, brother or sister, or of any other person in his presence or company, when there is reasonable ground to apprehend a design on the part of the person slain to commit a felony or to do some great personal injury to the slayer or to any such person, and there is imminent danger of such design being accomplished; or [Yet another statute justifying the use of deadly force to prevent the commission of a felony. Stealing half a million dollars of poker chips from a man's wife at a poker table at a Nevada casino is probably a felony. Does that mean you would be justified in drillin' the measly varmint as he dashes through the maze of slot machines leaving a trail of chips? We suspect if that *happened* in Vegas, you'd be *stayin'* in Vegas for longer than you planned!

   We predict by the language of the *Weddell* case quoted in Chapter 4, the Nevada courts will confine the justification to use deadly force to prevent imminent felonies to those considered "atrocious felonies" at common law. These include murder, manslaughter, rape, mayhem (cutting off a body part), kidnapping and arson. Without a case interpreting this statute in more depth, we cannot give you a more definite statement of the law relating to the use of deadly force to prevent the commission of serious felonies.

   Pancho's Wisdom – We hope Nevada will pass a statute defining exactly which felonies justify the use of deadly force. For example, see Utah's forcible felony definition.]

SUMMARY – JURY INSTRUCTION USED IN RECENT LANDMARK NEVADA SELF-DEFENSE CASE

[The *Runion* case, decided in 2000, is a landmark Nevada self-defense case. If you are involved in a defensive incident in Nevada, the trial judge presiding over your case will carefully review this case before instructing the jury. Although the *Runion* case gave the trial courts some discretion on exactly what to say to jurors, the law applied in this case would be the starting point for any instructions given to a jury in your case.]

"The killing of another person in self-defense is justified and not unlawful when the person who does the killing actually and reasonably believes:

1. That there is imminent danger that the assailant will either kill him or cause him great bodily injury; and

2. That it is absolutely necessary under the circumstances for him to use in self-defense force or means that might cause the death of the other person, for the purpose of avoiding death or great bodily injury to himself.

A bare fear of death or great bodily injury is not sufficient to justify a killing. To justify taking the life of another in self-defense, the circumstances must be sufficient to excite the fears of a reasonable person placed in a similar situation. The person killing must act under the influence of those fears alone and not in revenge.

An honest but unreasonable belief in the necessity for self-defense does not negate malice and does not reduce the offense from murder to manslaughter.

Actual danger is not necessary to justify a killing in self-defense. A person has a right to defend from apparent danger to the same extent as he would from actual danger. The person killing is justified if:

1. He is confronted by the appearance of imminent danger which arouses in his mind an honest belief and fear that he is about to be killed or suffer great bodily injury; and

2. He acts solely upon these appearances and his fear and actual beliefs; and

3. A reasonable person in a similar situation would believe himself to be in like danger.

The killing is justified even if it develops afterward that the person killing was mistaken about the extent of the danger.

If evidence of self-defense is present, the State must prove beyond a reasonable doubt that the defendant did not act in self-defense. If you find that the State has failed to prove beyond a reasonable doubt that the defendant did not act in self-defense, you must find the defendant not guilty." *Runion v. State*, 13 P.3d 52, 58-59 (Nev. 2000).

[Fleeing Felons]

"[I]n repealing NRS 200.160(3), the legislature indicated its disapproval of private persons using deadly force when arresting or attempting the arrest of a person suspected of a felony. In addition, by simultaneously enacting NRS 171.1455 the legislature obviously meant to limit the use of deadly force to police officers and to limit the circumstances under which police officers could employ such force. To conclude otherwise would be unreasonable. The legislature could not have meant to repose what might easily amount to vigilante justice in the hands of private persons while restricting the use of force in making an arrest by those who are charged by law with duties of public safety and protection. By repealing the codification of the fleeing-felon rule and leaving the citizen's arrest statute and the defense of others statute intact, the legislature has abrogated the common law fleeing-felon rule while at the same time affirming that private persons may perform arrests." *State v. Weddell*, 43 P.3d 987, 991 (Nev. 2002). [**Translation:** Yes, you can still make a citizen's arrest. But, as a private citizen, you cannot use deadly force. The old rule which allowed Nevadans to use deadly force in chasing down fleeing felons has been repealed. Because making any arrest could escalate into a deadly confrontation, we strongly advise you not to attempt a citizen's arrest.]

[Exceptions to Justifiable Self-Defense] [Initial Aggressor] [Provocation]

"The right of self-defense is not available to an original aggressor, that is a person who has sought a quarrel with the design to force a deadly issue and thus through his fraud, contrivance or fault, to create a real or apparent necessity for making a felonious assault." *Runion v. State*, 13 P.3d 52, 59 (Nev. 2000). [Don't start or provoke fights if you expect to claim self-defense.]

[Committing Felony or Unlawful Act]

"... If one makes an attack upon another for the purpose of committing a felony and of wreaking his malice upon the person so attacked, and the person thus attacked makes a counter attack and is slain, the plea of self-defense is not available; but, if such attack is not made with a felonious intent, the plea of self-defense is available." *State v. Huber*, 148 P. 562, 564 (Nev. 1915). [Committing a felony can defeat your claim of self-defense. **Example:** You are robbing a liquor store and the clerk pulls a hand gun from beneath the cash register. You substantially elevate his blood-lead levels with your coach gun. You cannot legitimately claim self-defense.]

[Exceptions to the Exceptions] [Withdraw and Communicate]

"It is true that a person must be without fault in bringing on an encounter before he can justify a killing on the ground of self-defense, or else must have endeavored in good faith to decline any further struggle before the mortal blow was given." *State v. Hall*, 13 P.2d 624, 633 (Nev. 1932). [This case is fairly old, and we have seen precious little on the topic since '32. The best advice is not to start a fight.]

[No Duty to Retreat – Generally]

"However, where a person, without voluntarily seeking, provoking, inviting, or willingly engaging in a difficulty of his own free will, is attacked by an assailant, he has the right to stand his ground and need not retreat when faced with the threat of deadly force." *Runion v. State*, 13 P.3d 52, 59 (Nev. 2000). [Needs no explanation.]

[Defense of Person(s) in Special Places – Place of Abode]

§ N.R.S. § 200.160.
Additional cases of justifiable homicide.

Homicide is also justifiable when committed:

2. In the actual resistance of an attempt to commit a felony upon the slayer, in his presence, or upon or in a dwelling, or other place of abode in which he is. [The same cautions should apply to this paragraph as apply to Paragraph 1 above (under this same heading N.R.S.§200.160. Additional cases of justifiable ho-

micide) regarding the right to use deadly force to prevent the commission of a felony. We, of course, recommend you don't do it unless you do it to prevent an imminent threat of serious injury or death. But the rest of the statute seems in line with the majority of states that authorize the use of deadly force to prevent serious felonies in one's own home.]

[Duty to Retreat From Special Places]

[We could not find any cases stating specifically that you don't have to retreat from your home before using deadly force. The general no-retreat rule is stated plainly in *Runion* above under the heading **[No Duty to Retreat - Generally]**. *Runion* involved a shooting at a Vegas intersection. It seems logical that the Nevada courts would apply the same no-retreat rule to citizens defending their own homes.]

§ N.R.S. § 200.190.
Justifiable or excusable homicide not punishable.

The homicide appearing to be justifiable or excusable, the person indicted shall, upon his trial, be fully acquitted and discharged. [If you take the life of another human being and your actions are held to be justifiable or excusable you will not be held criminally responsible.]

[Presumption of Reasonableness in Special Places - Residence, Lodging - for Purposes of Civil Liability Only]

§ N.R.S. § 41.095.
Presumption that person using deadly force against intruder in his residence has reasonable fear of death or bodily injury; residence defined.

1. For the purposes of **NRS 41.085** [Nevada's wrongful death statute] and **41.130** [liability for personal injury] any person who uses, while lawfully in his residence or in transient lodging, force which is intended or likely to cause death or bodily injury is presumed to have had a reasonable fear of imminent death or bodily injury to himself or another person lawfully in the residence or transient lodging if the force is used against a person who is committing burglary or invasion of the home and the person using the force knew or had reason to believe that burglary or invasion of the home was being committed. An action to recover damages for personal injuries to or the wrongful death of the person who committed burglary or invasion of the home may not be maintained against the person who used such force unless the presumption is overcome by clear and convincing evidence to the contrary. [This presumption statute only applies to civil cases for wrongful death or personal injury. If you injure or kill a burglar or home invader in your own home or hotel room, it's presumed you had a reasonable fear of imminent serious injury or of being killed. This presumption must be overcome by clear and convincing evidence for the injured burglar or his heirs to win a lawsuit against you. If there is strong proof you invited someone in for the purpose of killing him, the presump-

tion is overcome and you can be sued by the dead person's heirs. Usually such cases involve a motive such as money owed, a grudge or a domestic dispute. Anytime police investigators find evidence of a motive to kill, they investigate much more thoroughly, as they should.]

2. As used in this section, residence means any house, room, apartment, tenement or other building, vehicle, vehicle trailer, semitrailer, house trailer or boat designed or intended for occupancy as a residence.

[Nevada is a gaming state with millions of visitors a year living in hotel rooms, motor homes, trailers and other temporary forms of a residence. This section permits you to consider these places your castle and defend yourself with deadly force as set forth above without fear of civil liability.

Pancho's Wisdom – This statute only protects you from a lawsuit, not from prosecution by a district attorney. Nevada should add protection from criminal prosecution to this statute, if not completely overhaul Nevada's self-defense laws as we suggested in the introduction to this sub-chapter.]

[Defense of Property]

§ **N.R.S. § 193.240.**
Resistance by party about to be injured

Resistance sufficient to prevent the offense may be made by the party about to be injured:

1. To prevent an offense against his person, or his family or some member thereof.
2. To prevent an illegal attempt, by force, to take or injure property in his lawful possession.

[We found no cases relating to the defense of property. This statute authorizes the use of "resistance." We assume you can use whatever force is reasonable and necessary to protect your property, but not deadly force.]

[HELPFUL DEFINITIONS RELATING TO THIS STATE'S SELF-DEFENSE STATUTES]

- **Felony Mentioned**
    - **Burglary** – A person who, by day or night, enters any house, room, apartment, tenement, shop, warehouse, store, mill, barn, stable, outhouse or other building, tent, vessel, vehicle, vehicle trailer, semitrailer or house trailer, airplane, glider, boat or railroad car, with the intent to commit grand or petit larceny, assault or battery on any person or any felony, or to obtain money or property by false pretenses, is guilty of burglary. **N.R.S. § 205.060(1).**

[TEMPLATE Topics We Could Not Find Explained in Statutes or Cases]

(For each of these topics that we could not find addressed in your state's statutes or cases, we suggest you review the same topics in the subchapters of surrounding states. Your state's courts may look to the law of neighboring states to see how their courts and legislatures have treated that particular self-defense issue.)

[Mutual Combat]

[Co-Habitants; Co-Employees – Duty to Retreat]

[Reckless Injury to Innocent Third Parties]

Pancho's Wisdom

The same people who wouldn't declaw a cat, would disarm a college coed.

Key: ■ commentary ■ original statutes, cases or jury instructions

[Defense of Self and Others] [Non-Deadly Force]

§ NEW HAMPSHIRE REVISED STATUTES (N.H. REV. STAT.) § 627:4. Physical Force in Defense of a Person.

I. A person is justified in using non-deadly force upon another person in order to defend himself or a third person from what he reasonably believes to be the imminent use of unlawful, non-deadly force by such other person, and he may use a degree of such force which he reasonably believes to be necessary for such purpose. [If someone is trying to hit you with his fists, you can use your physical strength to stop him, but you can't shoot or stab him.]
However, such force is not justifiable if: [Here come the exceptions:]

[Exceptions to Justifiable Self Defense] [Provocation]

(a) With a purpose to cause physical harm to another person, he provoked the use of unlawful, non-deadly force by such other person; or [Provocation usually refers to initiating a fight with the intent to do harm to another when he responds to your provocation. If you provoke a fight, you lose the legal right to use force in self-defense. See quote from *State v. Gorham* on page 229.]

[Initial Aggressor] [Exceptions to the Exceptions]
[Withdraw and Communicate]

(b) He was the initial aggressor, unless after such aggression he withdraws from the encounter and effectively communicates to such other person his intent to do so, but the latter notwithstanding continues the use or threat of unlawful, non-deadly force; or [If you start a fight, you lose the right to claim your use of force was in self-defense UNLESS you stop fighting, retreat if necessary and make it plain to your opponent that you no longer want to fight. When the facts get this complicated, you are usually arrested and prosecuted anyway.]

[Mutual Combat]

(c) The force involved was the product of a combat by agreement not authorized by law. [You can't agree to a duel, hurt or kill your opponent and still expect to win the resulting criminal case on the theory of self-defense.]

[Deadly Force] [Defense of Third Persons]

II. A person is justified in using deadly force upon another person when he reasonably believes that such other person:

(a) Is about to use unlawful, deadly force against the actor or a third person; [This is the standard self-defense provision applicable in every state. You can use deadly force to keep yourself or another person from being killed or seriously injured.]

[Use of Deadly Force to Prevent Serious Felonies]

(b) Is likely to use any unlawful force against a person present while committing or attempting to commit a burglary;

[Examples:

(1) Someone you don't know is using a crowbar to pry through your front door.

(2) You have just locked the glass front door at the convenience store where you work and a man throws a rock through the glass and begins to unlock the door. Hopefully, shouting a warning will motivate the burglar to immediately leave so you don't have to use deadly force. "Stop! Leave Now! I'm calling the police!" If he persists, you may have to use deadly force and would be justified in doing so unless other factors exist (see Thumbs-Down Factors, Chapter 7).]

(c) Is committing or about to commit kidnapping or a forcible sex offense; or [Short definitions of kidnapping and forcible sexual offense appear below.]

(d) Is likely to use any unlawful force in the commission of a felony against the actor within such actor's dwelling or its curtilage. [Because the terms force and felony are used in the same sentence, we assume the reference here is to a "forcible felony" which is not defined in New Hampshire's statutes. Courts often look to other states for definitions. Georgia's code contains a good, short definition of forcible felony. "Forcible felony means any felony which involves the use or threat of physical force or violence against any person." Ga. Code Ann.,§16-1-3 (6). As we have pointed out in other states which authorize the use of deadly force to prevent the commission of a felony in one's home, you would not be justified in shooting a salesman sitting peaceably in your living room attempting to commit felony mortgage fraud or sell you a stolen car.]

[Duty to Retreat – Generally – Yes]

III. A person is not justified in using deadly force on another to defend himself or a third person from deadly force by the other if he knows that he and the third person can, with complete safety:

(a) Retreat from the encounter, except that he is not required to retreat if he is within his dwelling or its curtilage and was not the initial aggressor; or [If you are attacked outside of your home and you can retreat in complete safety, you must retreat before using deadly force. The same rule applies if you are defending someone else. You have to try to get them to retreat if they can do so in safety before you can defend them with deadly force. If you are attacked in your own home or its curtilage (area immediately around your home, see definition below), you don't have to retreat before using deadly force as long as you are not the initial aggressor. A New Hampshire case indicates that your home's curtilage includes your driveway. *State v. Pinkham*, 679 A.2d 589 (N.H.1996).]

(b) Surrender property to a person asserting a claim of right thereto; or [If someone like the repo man, your landlord or a mortgage holder are claiming you need to surrender your car, apartment or your home, you must work out any disagreement in court. You cannot duke it out with deadly force.]

(c) Comply with a demand that he abstain from performing an act which he is not obliged to perform; nor is the use of deadly force justifiable when, with the purpose of causing death or serious bodily harm, the actor has provoked the use of force against himself in the same encounter. [We're not exactly sure what the abstain-from-performing-an-act exception means. We found no New Hampshire cases explaining it.

You are not justified in using deadly force if you provoked someone to fight with the intent to kill them as the case summary immediately below explains.]

. . .

"We observe that the charge, and the statute from which it was taken, RSA 627:4 III(c), use the word "provoke." In all the dictionaries we have consulted, and in those cases that have considered the matter... the term "provoke" connotes speech as well as action. In the present case, if the jury concluded after the court's instruction that a defendant's use of words alone to bring about a fight in which he intended at the outset to kill his opponent was sufficient to destroy his legal defense, they were correct." *State v. Gorham*, 412 A.2d 1017, 1019 (N.H. 1980). [Some states' statutes and cases explain that mere words are not enough to make a person an initial aggressor. Other states seem to use the words initial aggressor and provoker interchangeably. This New Hampshire case emphasizes, however, that words alone can be held to constitute provocation. A person who provokes another with the intent to kill is not justified in using deadly force in self-defense. Our research indicates that anytime you are at fault in initiating, provoking, or escalating a conflict to the point that someone is killed or injured, you will be prosecuted.

We, together with our researchers and editors, cannot explain why New Hampshire's non-deadly force statute covers the concepts of initial aggressor, provocation and mutual combat whereas its deadly force section only discusses provocation. To be safe, we suggest that you assume that the same exceptions apply to the use deadly force as they do to the use of non-deadly force. Do not initiate, provoke or agree to fight. If someone gets hurt and you are found to be somewhat at fault, you will be arrested and prosecuted.]

[Defense of Person(s) in Special Places – Premises]

§ N.H. REV. STAT. § 627:7.
Use of Force in Defense of Premises.

A person in possession or control of premises or a person who is licensed or privileged to be thereon is justified in using non-deadly force upon another when and to the extent that he reasonably believes it necessary to prevent or terminate the commission of a criminal trespass by such other in or upon such premises, but he may use deadly force under such circumstances only in defense of a person as prescribed in RSA 627:4 or when he reasonably believes it necessary to prevent an attempt by the trespasser to commit arson. [You can use non-deadly force to prevent interference with your property by a trespasser. You cannot use deadly force to defend your property from trespassers. You can only use deadly force if the other deadly force requirements mentioned in the code sections above are met, or if someone is trying to burn down your house.]

[No Duty to Retreat From Special Places – Dwelling] [Co-Habitants]

"RSA 627:4, III thus codifies the "duty to retreat" doctrine, and makes clear that a person confronted with deadly force is not justified in using deadly force in response if he or she can retreat with complete safety, unless he or she is in his or her dwelling or its curtilage and is not the initial aggressor. The exception to the duty to retreat is premised upon the notion that when a person is in his or her own home or its curtilage, there is no safer place to which to retreat. Given the rationale for this exception, we agree with the defendant that it applies even when the assailant is a cohabitant of the dwelling." *State v. Warren*, 794 A.2d 790, 794 (N.H. 2002). [You don't have to retreat from a co-habitant when attacked with deadly force. This case also stands for the rule, however, that you cannot use deadly force against a cohabitant who is threatening to commit a non-deadly felony. *Id.*]

[Civil Liability]

§ N.H. REV. STAT. § 627:1.
General Rule.

Conduct which is justifiable under this chapter constitutes a defense to any offense. The fact that such conduct is justifiable shall constitute a complete defense to any civil action based on such conduct. [If you're found not guilty under criminal law, you have a complete defense if you're ever sued.]

[Defense of Property]

§ N.H. REV. STAT. § 627:8.
Use of Force in Property Offenses.

A person is justified in using force upon another when and to the extent that he reasonably believes it necessary to prevent what is or reasonably appears to be an unlawful taking of his property, or criminal mischief, or to retake his property immediately following its taking; but he may use deadly force under such circumstances only in defense of a person as prescribed in RSA 627:4. [You can use reasonable force but not deadly force to protect your personal property (TV, CD player, lawn mower, etc.).

We recommend against using any force to defend items of personal property; it's too easy for the situation to escalate into a deadly encounter. You could be killed or have to kill someone. By the time you get done paying a lawyer if you kill or seriously injure a thief, you could have bought whatever was stolen or damaged brand new. Get a good description and call the police.]

[HELPFUL DEFINITIONS RELATING TO THIS STATE'S SELF-DEFENSE STATUTES]

- **Burglary** – [Unlawfully entering a building or occupied structure with the purpose to commit a crime therein.] **N.H. Rev. Stat. § 635:1.**

- **Curtilage** – means those outbuildings which are proximately, directly and intimately connected with a dwelling, together with all the land or grounds surrounding the dwelling such as are necessary, convenient, and habitually used for domestic purposes. **N.H. Rev. Stat. § 627:9(I).**

- **Deadly Force** – means any assault or confinement which the actor commits with the purpose of causing or which he knows to create a substantial risk of causing death or serious bodily injury. Purposely firing a firearm capable of causing serious bodily injury or death in the direction of another person or at a vehicle in which another is believed to be constitutes deadly force. **N.H. Rev. Stat. § 627:9(II).**

- **Dwelling** – means any building, structure, vehicle, boat or other place adapted for overnight accommodation of persons, or sections of any place similarly adapted. It is immaterial whether a person is actually present. **N.H. Rev. Stat. § 627:9(III).**

- **Felonies Mentioned** –

  - **Kidnapping** – [Knowingly confining or abducting another for the purpose of holding them for ransom, hostage or to commit an offense against them.] **N.H. Rev. Stat. § 633:1.**

  - **Forcible sex offense** – [This would include any type of rape or felonious sexual assault.] **See N.H. Rev. Stat. § 632-A:2 and 632-A:3.**

- **Non-deadly Force** – means any assault or confinement which does not constitute deadly force. **N.H. Rev. Stat. § 627:9(IV).**

[TEMPLATE Topics We Could Not Find Explained in Statutes or Cases]

(For each of these topics that we could not find addressed in your state's statutes or cases, we suggest you review the same topics in the subchapters of surrounding states. Your state's courts may look to the law of neighboring states to see how their courts and legislatures have treated that particular self-defense issue.)

[Committing Felony or Unlawful Act]

[Employees – Duty to Retreat]

[Presumption of Reasonableness in Special Places]

[Reckless Injury to Innocent Third Parties]

NEW JERSEY

Like Pennsylvania, New Jersey adopted the self-defense laws drafted as part of the Model Penal Code ("MPC"). Thus, most aspects of New Jersey self-defense law are quite restrictive. They are also so complicated that we can't imagine anyone getting it exactly right when involved in a defensive incident with adrenaline pulsating through his or her veins.

Pancho's Wisdom – Pancho envisions the complicated Model Penal Code to have been written by a committee of law professors and lawyers who not only have never been involved in a heart-stopping defensive incident, but have never participated in handgun competitions that simulate the stress and confusion of a violent attack. They have no concept of the role perception and reaction time play in defending against such incidents (see Chapter 11). Hence, the rules they have written for the Model Penal Code are so complicated with so many exceptions to the exceptions to the exceptions, that no one in real life could ever apply them correctly let alone remember them all when facing a life-threatening defensive emergency. Is it any wonder that very few of the fifty states have adopted the Model Penal Code's self-defense law? Pancho's advice to New Jersey is to chuck these ridiculously complex rules and adopt the Mother of All Self-Defense Laws (Chapter 20). Pancho's "Mother" resolves all issues in favor of the innocent and against the guilty.

Key: ■ commentary ■ original statutes, cases or jury instructions

---

[Defense of Self and Others] [Non-Deadly Force]

§ NEW JERSEY STATUTES ANNOTATED (N.J.S.A.) § 2C:3-4.
Use of force in self-protection.

a. Use of force justifiable for protection of the person. Subject to the provisions of this section and of section 2C:3-9, the use of force upon or toward another person is justifiable when the actor reasonably believes that such force is immediately necessary for the purpose of protecting himself against the use of unlawful force by such other person on the present occasion. [You may use reasonable and necessary non-deadly force to prevent non-deadly force from being used against yourself or another person. **Example:** You grab a purse snatcher and tell him to let go of the woman's purse. If he doesn't, you may use enough force to take it away from him but not so much force to unnecessarily hurt him. You cannot use a deadly weapon. After you get the purse back, you can't punch his lights out to teach him a lesson.]

b. Limitations on justifying necessity for use of force.

(1) The use of force is not justifiable under this section:

. . .

(b) To resist force used by the occupier or possessor of property or by another person on his behalf, where the actor knows that the person using the force is doing so under a claim of right to protect the property, except that this limitation shall not apply if: [Trespassers can't use force against the occupiers of land unless...]

(i) The actor is a public officer acting in the performance of his duties or a person lawfully assisting him therein or a person making or assisting in a lawful arrest; [. . .the trespasser is a cop;]

(ii) The actor has been unlawfully dispossessed of the property and is making a reentry or recaption justified by section 2C:3-6; or [you are actually the owner and are trying to take back your land;]

(iii) The actor reasonably believes that such force is necessary to protect himself against death or serious bodily harm. [The trespasser needs to protect himself from death or serious injury. Remember, this section does not authorize the trespasser to use deadly force against a rightful owner of property.]

[Deadly Force]

(2) The use of deadly force is not justifiable under this section unless the actor reasonably believes that such force is necessary to protect himself against death or serious bodily harm; nor is it justifiable if: [You can only use deadly force to combat imminent deadly force or serious injury. Even in cases where you're facing that kind of force, you can't use deadly force if...]

[Exceptions to Justifiable Self-Defense]

[Initial Aggressor] [Provocation]

(a) The actor, with the purpose of causing death or serious bodily harm, provoked the use of force against himself in the same encounter; or [You started a fight as an excuse to hurt someone when they react to your provocation . . .]

[Duty to Retreat – Generally]

(b) The actor knows that he can avoid the necessity of using such force with complete safety by retreating or by surrendering possession of a thing to a person asserting a claim of right thereto or by complying with a demand that he abstain from any action which he has no duty to take, [(1) If you can safely retreat, you have to retreat instead of using force; (2) if someone's trying to get something from you (i.e. a robber), you must give it up if you can do it safely instead of using force; and (3) if someone is commanding you not to do something, you must do as you're told instead of using force (unless you have a duty to act.)] except that:

(i) The actor is not obliged to retreat from his dwelling, unless he was the initial aggressor; and [You don't have to retreat from your own home unless you started the fight.]

(3) Except as required by paragraphs (1) and (2) of this subsection, a person employing protective force may estimate the necessity of using force when the force is used, without retreating, surrendering possession, doing any other act which he has no legal duty to do or abstaining from any lawful action. [We have no clue what this means. The law lost us somewhere between the exceptions, the exceptions to the exceptions and the exceptions to the exceptions to the exceptions. Can you imagine trying to analyze all this during a violent attack? Sheesh, give the folks of New Jersey a break and adopt the Mother of All Self-Defense Laws, see Chapter 20.]

. . .

[Mutual Combat]

"In addition, although mutual combat under certain circumstances may constitute adequate provocation and reduce murder to manslaughter, the contest must be waged on equal terms. Thus, the offense is not manslaughter where the defendant alone is armed." *State v. Viera*, 787 A.2d 256, 266 (N.J.Super.A.D. 2001). [Although this quote doesn't mention self-defense at all, it basically means that if you agree to fight and kill someone you'll be found guilty of manslaughter. However, if you're armed and your opponent wasn't, you'll be guilty of murder.]

[Exceptions to the Exceptions] [Withdraw and Communicate]

But, if after commencing the assault, the aggressor withdraws in good faith from the conflict and announces in some way to his adversary his intention to retire, he is restored to his right of self-defense. Thus, the aggressor must abandon the fight, withdraw and give notice to his adversary. *State v. Rivers*, 599 A.2d 558, 562 (N.J.Super.A.D. 1991). [If you withdraw and tell the other person you are withdrawing, you may be justified in defending yourself if he continues to pursue you.]

[Defense of a Third Person]

§ N.J.S.A. § 2C:3-5.
Use of force for the protection of other persons.

a. Subject to the provisions of this section 2C:3-9, the use of force upon or toward the person of another is justified to protect a third person when:

(1) The actor would be justified under section 2C:3-4 in using such force to protect himself against the injury he believes to be threatened to the person whom he seeks to protect; and

(2) Under the circumstances as the actor reasonably believes them to be, the person whom he seeks to protect would be justified in using such protective force; and

(3) The actor reasonably believes that his intervention is necessary for the protection of such other person. [This somewhat confusing section sets forth three

standards for defense of another. (1) Whatever force you used to protect the third person has to be force you would have been justified using to protect yourself, (2) The person you're protecting would have been able to use the force you used and (3) you have to actually believe whoever you're helping needs your help.]

b. Notwithstanding subsection a. of this section:

(1) When the actor would be obliged under section 2C:3-4 b. (2)(b) to retreat or take other action he is not obliged to do so before using force for the protection of another person, unless he knows that he can thereby secure the complete safety of such other person, and [Even if you would normally be required to retreat before using defensive force, if you are defending another person, you don't have to retreat unless you know retreating won't jeopardize the safety of the other person.]

(2) When the person whom the actor seeks to protect would be obliged under section 2C:3-4 b. (2)(b) to retreat or take similar action if he knew that he could obtain complete safety by so doing, the actor is obliged to try to cause him to do so before using force in his protection if the actor knows that he can obtain complete safety in that way; and [You've got to try to get the other person to retreat if you believe his retreat can be accomplished in complete safety rather than use force to defend that person.]

(3) Neither the actor nor the person whom he seeks to protect is obliged to retreat when in the other's dwelling to any greater extent than in his own. [Neither you nor the person you are defending is obligated to retreat from his or her home before you use force to defend him or her.

We could not find a case explaining the "not obliged to do so before using force" language. Such confusing and unfortunate language simply increases the risk of using force to defend yourself and loved ones.]

§ N.J.S.A. § 2C:3-4 (c).
Use of force in self-protection.

. . .

c. (1) Notwithstanding the provisions of N.J.S. 2C:3-5, N.J.S. 2C:3-9, or this section, the use of force or deadly force upon or toward an intruder who is unlawfully in a dwelling is justifiable when the actor reasonably believes that the force is immediately necessary for the purpose of protecting himself or other persons in the dwelling against the use of unlawful force by the intruder on the present occasion. [You can use deadly force against an intruder who is unlawfully in your home if you "reasonably believe" you need to use force to keep the intruder from using "unlawful force" against you or anyone else in your home. Sounds simple enough, except that "reasonable belief" is further defined in the subparagraphs below, with additional requirements making what, at first, appears simple to be even more complicated.]

(2) A reasonable belief exists when the actor, to protect himself or a third person, was in his own dwelling at the time of the offense or was privileged to be thereon and the encounter between the actor and intruder was sudden and unexpected, compelling the actor to act instantly and: [The encounter between you and the intruder has to be sudden and unexpected compelling you to act instantly (sheesh) AND . . .]

(a) The actor reasonably believed that the intruder would inflict personal injury upon the actor or others in the dwelling; or [. . .you have to have a second reasonable belief that the intruder is going to hurt someone in your home . . . OR . . .]

(b) The actor demanded that the intruder disarm, surrender or withdraw, and the intruder refused to do so. [. . . you demanded the intruder to throw down his weapon, give up, leave AND the intruder told you to "kiss his @$$."]

[Every time a state adds another condition to its self-defense laws, it's a blank check for a prosecutor to french-fry your butt. The good news about New Jersey's home-defense statute is that if you have the presence of mind to dot all the I's and cross all the T's, it only requires a fear of personal injury or an unlawful act rather than the fear of death or serious injury. This affords residents of New Jersey more protection than in states that still require an imminent fear of death or serious injury for home-defense.]

[No Duty to Retreat From Special Places – Home]

(3) An actor employing protective force may estimate the necessity of using force when the force is used, without retreating, surrendering possession, withdrawing or doing any other act which he has no legal duty to do or abstaining from any lawful action. [We think this means you don't have to retreat from your own home before using defensive force, although only a law graduate from an Ivy League school with an apartment in Jersey would know for sure.]

N.J.S.A. § 2C:3-6.

Use of force in defense of premises or personal property.

§ a. Use of force in defense of premises. Subject to the provisions of this section and of section 2C:3-9, the use of force upon or toward the person of another is justifiable when the actor is in possession or control of premises or is licensed or privileged to be thereon and he reasonably believes such force necessary to prevent or terminate what he reasonably believes to be the commission or attempted commission of a criminal trespass by such other person in or upon such premises. [You can use force to stop a trespass on your land or any of your property, as long as you have the right to be on the property and you think the use of force is necessary to prevent the trespass. But see the limitations below.]

b. Limitations on justifiable use of force in defense of premises.

(1) Request to desist. The use of force is justifiable under this section only if the actor first requests the person against whom such force is used to desist from his interference with the property, unless the actor reasonably believes that:

(a) Such request would be useless;

(b) It would be dangerous to himself or another person to make the request; or

(c) Substantial harm will be done to the physical condition of the property which is sought to be protected before the request can effectively be made.

[You have to ask an interferer to stop interfering unless it would be useless, dangerous, or the property would be substantially harmed in the time it would take make the request.]

(2) Exclusion of trespasser. The use of force is not justifiable under this section if the actor knows that the exclusion of the trespasser will expose him to substantial danger of serious bodily harm. [You can't kick someone off your land if doing so will put him in a situation where he'll get hurt. **Example:** He's being hunted by a gang of bullies and hiding on your land.]

(3) Use of deadly force. The use of deadly force is not justifiable under Subsection a. of this section unless the actor reasonably believes that: [You can use deadly force to defend persons on land or in a building you have a right to be in if . . .]

(a) The person against whom the force is used is attempting to dispossess him of his dwelling otherwise than under a claim of right to its possession; or [You can use deadly force if someone is trying to make you leave your home (except not against a landlord or mortgage holder trying to get his property back if he claims you violated a loan or lease contract). . .]

[Use of Deadly Force to Prevent Serious Felonies]

(b) The person against whom the force is used is attempting to commit or consummate arson, burglary, robbery or other criminal theft or property destruction; except that

(c) Deadly force does not become justifiable under subparagraphs (a) and (b) of this subsection unless the actor reasonably believes that:

(i) The person against whom it is employed has employed or threatened deadly force against or in the presence of the actor; or

(ii) The use of force other than deadly force to terminate or prevent the commission or the consummation of the crime would expose the actor or another in his presence to substantial danger of bodily harm...

[You can use deadly force, but only if the intruder is trying to get you off your land by force, or if the intruder is attempting to commit arson, burglary, or robbery. However, even if one of these things is happening, the intruder still must have threatened or used deadly force, or it must appear that deadly force is the only way for you to stop the intruder without seriously endangering yourself.]

[Presumption of Reasonableness in Special Places – Dwelling]

N.J.S.A. § 2C:3-6.(cont.)

[(ii) continued . . .] An actor within a dwelling shall be presumed to have a reasonable belief in the existence of the danger. The State must rebut this presumption by proof beyond a reasonable doubt. [If you are in your home, the law presumes you had a reasonable belief of being exposed to serious danger.]

[Co-Habitants – Duty to Retreat – Yes]

"New Jersey is among the minority of jurisdictions that impose a duty of retreat on a woman attacked by her cohabitant spouse." *State v. Gratland,* 694 A.2d 564, 569 (N.J. 1997).

"A person need not retreat if the person is attacked in his or her home by someone who is not a cohabitant." *State v. Blanks,* 712 A.2d 698, 701 (N.J.Super.A.D 1998).

[You do not have to retreat from your home before using defensive force against an intruder, but you must retreat if the assailant is a cohabitant. In a domestic situation, the wife must retreat before she can use defensive force against an abusive husband who is still living in the home (provided she can do so in complete safety). See chapter on domestic violence, Chapter 13.]

[Defense of Property]

§ N.J.S.A. § 2C:3-6. (c) and (d).

. . .

c. Use of force in defense of personal property. [Things other than real estate.] Subject to the provisions of subsection d. of this section and of section 2C:3-9, the use of force upon or toward the person of another is justifiable when the actor reasonably believes it necessary to prevent what he reasonably believes to be an attempt by such other person to commit theft, criminal mischief or other criminal interference with personal property in his possession or in the possession of another for whose protection he acts. [You can use force to protect or keep your possessions but...]

d. Limitations on justifiable use of force in defense of personal property.

   (1) Request to desist and exclusion of trespasser. The limitations of subsection b. (1) and (2) of this section apply to subsection c. of this section. [You have to ask an interferer to stop interfering unless it would be useless, dangerous, or the property would be substantially harmed in the time it would take make the request.]

(2) Use of deadly force. The use of deadly force in defense of personal property is not justified unless justified under another provision of this chapter. [Don't get the impression that you can use deadly force to defend items of personal property like your car, TV or stereo. You can't. But in using non-deadly force to defend such items, the situation may escalate to where you would be justified in using deadly force as explained in other provisions above. Then and only then can you use deadly force. For this reason we strongly recommend that you NOT use non-deadly force to defend items of personal property. It's too easy for such situations to escalate to deadly encounters where you could be killed or have to kill. This could subject you to legal expenses which will cost you far more than if you simply let the thief go and buy a new . . .(whatever he stole). Of course, you should call the police and report the theft.]

[Civil Liability]

§ N.J.S.A. § 2C:3-1.
Justification an affirmative defense; civil remedies unaffected.

a. In any prosecution based on conduct which is justifiable under this chapter, justification is an affirmative defense.

b. The fact that conduct is justifiable under this chapter does not abolish or impair any remedy for such conduct which is available in any civil action. [Even if you're justified under the criminal code, you can still be sued under the civil law for hurting or killing someone. That stinks. NJ should enact protection against felons suing law-abiding citizens they try to victimize. See Mother of All Self-Defense Laws, Chapter 20.]

[Reckless Injury to Innocent Third Parties]

§ N.J.S.A. 2C:3-9

a. The justification afforded by sections 2C:3-4 to 2C:3-7 is unavailable when:

(1) The actor's belief in the unlawfulness of the force or conduct against which he employs protective force or his belief in the lawfulness of an arrest which he endeavors to effect by force is erroneous; and

(2) His error is due to ignorance or mistake as to the provisions of the code, any other provisions of the criminal law or the law governing the legality of an arrest or search.
[Ignorance of these complicated laws is no excuse. Uh, so make your legislators simplify them giving the advantage to folks defending their homes and property against criminals. See the Mother of All Self-Defense Laws, Chapter 20.]

b. (Deleted by amendment, P.L.1981, c. 290.)

c. When the actor is justified under sections 2C:3-3 to 2C:3-8 in using force upon or toward the person of another but he **recklessly or negligently injures or creates a risk of injury to innocent persons, the justification afforded by those sections is unavailable in a prosecution for such recklessness or negligence towards innocent persons.** [Closing your eyes to spray (ammo) against an armed robber could get you prosecuted for manslaughter if your actions are deemed to be reckless or criminally negligent and you kill or harm an innocent person.]

[HELPFUL DEFINITIONS RELATING TO THIS STATE'S SELF-DEFENSE STATUTES]

- Bodily harm – means physical pain, or temporary disfigurement, or impairment of physical condition. **N.J.S.A. § 2C:3-11(e).**

- **Deadly force** – means force which the actor uses with the purpose of causing or which he knows to create a substantial risk of causing death or serious bodily harm. Purposely firing a firearm in the direction of another person or at a vehicle, building or structure in which another person is believed to be constitutes deadly force unless the firearm is loaded with less-lethal ammunition and fired by a law enforcement officer in the performance of the officer's official duties. A threat to cause death or serious bodily harm, by the production of a weapon or otherwise, so long as the actor's purpose is limited to creating an apprehension that he will use deadly force if necessary, does not constitute deadly force. **N.J.S.A. § 2C:3-11(b).**

- **Dwelling** – means any building or structure, though movable or temporary, or a portion thereof, which is for the time being the actor's home or place of lodging except that, as used in 2C:3-7, the building or structure need not be the actor's own home or place of lodging. **N.J.S.A. § 2C:3-11(c).**

- **Felonies Mentioned** –

  - **Arson** – [Purposely causing an explosion or unlawful fire on another's or one's own property.] **N.J.S.A. § 2C:17-1.**

  - **Burglary** – [Entering or remaining in a research facility, structure, or a separately secured or occupied portion thereof with the purpose of committing an offense therein.] **N.J.S.A. § 2C:18-2.**

  - **Robbery** – [While in the course of committing theft a person either uses force or inflicts harm on another or puts another in fear of immediate bodily injury by threat.] **N.J.S.A. § 2C:15-1.**

  - **Criminal theft** – [We couldn't find any enlightening definition for this term.]

  - **Other Property Destruction** – [This term seems to suggest any activity that involves damaging property in which a person might be placed under a threat of injury. See crimes under Chapter 17, "Arson, Criminal Mischief, and Other Property Destruction."]

- **Less-lethal ammunition** – means ammunition approved by the Attorney General which is designed to stun, temporarily incapacitate or cause temporary discomfort to a person without penetrating the person's body. The term shall also include ammunition approved by the Attorney General which is designed to gain access to a building or structure and is used for that purpose. **N.J.S.A. § 2C:3-11(f).**

- **Serious bodily harm** – means bodily harm which creates a substantial risk of death or which causes serious, permanent disfigurement or protracted loss or impairment of the function of any bodily member or organ or which results from aggravated sexual assault or sexual assault. **N.J.S.A. § 2C:3-11(d).**

- **Unlawful force** – means force, including confinement, which is employed without the consent of the person against whom it is directed and the employment of which constitutes an offense or actionable tort or would constitute such offense or tort except for a defense (such as the absence of intent, negligence, or mental capacity; duress, youth, or diplomatic status) not amounting to a privilege to use the force. Assent constitutes consent, within the meaning of this section, whether or not it otherwise is legally effective, except as sent to the infliction of death or serious bodily harm. **N.J.S.A. § 2C:3-11(a).**

[TEMPLATE Topics We Could Not Find Explained in Statutes or Cases]

(For each of these topics that we could not find addressed in your state's statutes or cases, we suggest you review the same topics in the subchapters of surrounding states. Your state's courts may look to the law of neighboring states to see how their courts and legislatures have treated that particular self-defense issue.)

[Committing Felony or Unlawful Act]

[Co-Employees – Duty to Retreat]

Pancho's Wisdom

You just might be a Gunnut if . . . you've ever volunteered to be on a firing squad.

WARNING: Relying solely upon the language of New Mexico's justifiable homicide statute, § 30-2-7, could be legally disastrous! It's meaning has been altered drastically by the New Mexico courts. New Mexico judges and lawyers instead look to a uniform set of jury instructions. We found these instructions using our expensive legal data-base search engine. However, we needed some help finding these jury instructions on the internet. With a little help from the kind folks at the new Mexico Compilation Commission, we finally found them at http://www.conwaygreene.com/nmsu/lpext.dll?f=template&fn=main-hit-h.htm&2.0. The Supreme Court of New Mexico authorized a committee of legal scholars to analyze the law of New Mexico. They drafted jury instructions that accurately state New Mexico's law of self-defense. They also wrote "Committee Commentary" that is extremely helpful, as you'll see below.

Key: ■ commentary ■ original statutes, cases or jury instructions

---

[Defense of Self and Others] [Non-Deadly Force]

UJI [Uniform Jury Instruction] 14-5181. SELF-DEFENSE; NONDEADLY FORCE BY DEFENDANT

Evidence has been presented that the defendant [that'd be you] acted in self-defense. The defendant acted in self-defense if:

1. There was an appearance of immediate danger of bodily harm to the defendant as a result of [Johnny Fisthrower swinging his fists at the defendant] and

2. The defendant was in fact put in fear of immediate bodily harm and [struck Johnny Fisthrower] because of that fear; and

3. The defendant used an amount of force that the defendant believed was reasonable and necessary to prevent the bodily harm; and

[4. The force used by defendant ordinarily would not create a substantial risk of death or great bodily harm; and] [The brackets are indicators this paragraph would only be used if Johnny died as a result of you hitting him with your fist (assuming your name isn't Chuck Norris).]

5. The apparent danger would have caused a reasonable person in the same circumstances to act as the defendant did.

   The burden is on the state to prove beyond a reasonable doubt that the defendant did not act in self-defense. If you have a reasonable doubt as to whether the defendant acted in self-defense, you must find the defendant not guilty.

Committee Commentary – It is never reasonable to use deadly force against a nondeadly attack. A person may use a deadly force in self-defense only if defending himself against an attack which creates a substantial risk of death or great bodily harm. . . [This excerpt from the Committee Comments tells you everything you need to know when attacked by someone who does not have a weapon and you reasonably believe your life is not in danger.]

UJI 14-5182. DEFENSE OF ANOTHER; NONDEADLY FORCE BY DEFENDANT

Evidence has been presented that the defendant acted while defending another person. The defendant acted in defense of another if:

1. There was an appearance of immediate danger of bodily harm to [Thelma Thirdperson] as a result of [Johnny Fisthrower swinging his fists at Thelma]; and

2. The defendant believed that [Thelma] was in immediate danger of bodily harm from [Johnny] and [clobbered Johnny] to prevent the bodily harm; and

3. The defendant used an amount of force that the defendant believed was reasonable and necessary to prevent the bodily harm; and

[4. The force used by defendant ordinarily would not create a substantial risk of death or great bodily harm; and] [Again, this paragraph would only be used if Johnny died as a result of you hitting him with your fist. This is why the authors of the jury instructions put Section 4 in brackets.]

5. The apparent danger to [Thelma] would have caused a reasonable person in the same circumstances to act as defendant did.

[Deadly Force]

UJI 14-5171. JUSTIFIABLE HOMICIDE; SELF-DEFENSE

Evidence has been presented that the defendant killed [Ninja McThrowingstar] in self-defense. The killing is in self-defense if:

1. There was an appearance of immediate danger of death or great bodily harm [defined at the end of this subchapter] to the defendant as a result of [Ninja preparing to throw itsy-bitsy star-shaped sharp objects at defendant] and

2. The defendant was in fact put in fear by the apparent danger of immediate death or great bodily harm and killed [Ninja McThrowingstar] because of that fear; and

3. A reasonable person in the same circumstances as the defendant would have acted as the defendant did. [Notice how this jury instruction adds the requirements of fear of death or great bodily harm and acting the same as a reasonable person would have acted under the circumstances. These requirements are not expressly contained in New Mexico's Justifiable Homicide Statute cited (with a warning) below.]

Committee Commentary – Although numerous New Mexico decisions deal with the principles of self-defense, few of the cases discuss the principles in terms of the statutory language. . . . the supreme court has said that these statutes are merely a legislative recognition of the common law. See *Alaniz v. Funk*, 69 N.M. 164, 364 P.2d 1033 (1961). . . that there is no requirement that the jury be instructed in the precise language of the statutes. *State v. Maestas*, 63 N.M. 67, 313 P.2d 337 (1957). [**Translation:** New Mexico's justifiable homicide statute does not mean what it says.]

The elements of this instruction contain some general principles of self-defense which are often given as separate instructions. For example, the principle of apparent necessity. See California Jury Instructions Criminal, 5.51. In addition, the element of "a reasonable man under the same circumstances as the defendant," includes the principle that the defendant's right to use force may end when the danger ceases or the adversary is disabled. See e.g., *State v. Garcia*, 83 N.M. 51, 54, 487 P.2d 1356, 1359 (Ct.App.1971). See also, California Jury Instructions Criminal, 5.52 and 5.53. [We included this commentary to alert you to the fact that judges are hereby given the hint that they can look to California Jury Instructions when the facts of the case justify it. Notice also the reference to the concept of necessity. Please read our comments about necessity in Chapter 3. You would also do well to read and understand California's subchapter inasmuch as New Mexico judges have been given the invitation by these comments to use them when they think it is advisable.]

[No Duty to Retreat – Generally]

UJI 14-5190. SELF-DEFENSE; ASSAILED PERSON NEED NOT RETREAT

A person who is threatened with an attack need not retreat. In the exercise of his right of self-defense, he may stand his ground and defend himself. [There is no duty to retreat from anywhere you have the right to be. However, there is a New Mexico case that says trespassers must retreat to some extent and under most circumstances before they can use force in self-defense, *State v. Southworth*, 52 P.3d 987, 991 (N.M.App. 2002). Although there may be exceptions, we suggest that if you are trespassing, you should retreat if you can safely do so and then count on being arrested and prosecuted. Do NOT give a statement to the police (see Chapter 14 concerning your right to remain silent).]

[Deadly Force (cont.)] [Defense of Third Persons]

UJI 14-5172. JUSTIFIABLE HOMICIDE; DEFENSE OF ANOTHER

Evidence has been presented that the defendant killed [Ninja McThrowingstar] while defending another. The killing was in defense of another if:

1. There was an appearance of immediate danger of death or great bodily harm to [Thelma Thirdperson] as a result of [Ninja preparing to throw itsy-bitsy star-shaped sharp objects at Thelma]; and

2. The defendant believed that [Thelma Thirdperson] was in immediate danger of death or great bodily harm from [Ninja McThrowingstar] and killed [Ninja McThrowingstar] to prevent the death or great bodily harm; and

3. The apparent danger to [Thelma Thirdperson] would have caused a reasonable person in the same circumstances to act as the defendant did.

Committee Commentary – [You will notice in the justifiable homicide statute below that the right to use deadly force to defend another seems to be limited to one's wife and family. The jury instruction above does not limit the defense of others to specific relationships. The Committee Commentary explains: "By eliminating the shopping list of persons who could be defended, it would appear that the legislature clearly intended to broaden the scope of this defense. See generally, Perkins, Criminal Law 1019 (2d ed. 1969)" . . . There is also the question of whether you can defend another if that person technically would not be justified in defending himself (for example, he started the fight - see discussion below). If you didn't know he started the fight but honestly believed he would have been justified in defending himself, it appears you would be justified in defending him according to the following Committee Commentary, "Because the statute uses the term 'reasonable grounds to believe a design exists, etc.,' it appears that New Mexico law does not require the person intervening to know the actual facts, but only to act as a reasonable person under the circumstances. See generally, Perkins, supra, at 1020-21. LaFave & Scott 397 (1972)."]

[Deadly Force (cont.) – New Mexico's Actual Justifiable Homicide Statute]

[WARNING: This statute has been drastically changed by the courts. We included it merely to show you how misleading it is and why it needs to be repealed and re-written to reflect the actual law of self-defense applied by the courts.]

§ NEW MEXICO STATUTES ANNOTATED (N.M.S.A.) § 30-2-7. Justifiable homicide by citizen.

Homicide is justifiable when committed by any person in any of the following cases:

A. When committed in the necessary defense of his life, his family or his property, or in necessarily defending against any unlawful action directed against himself, his wife or family; [To Heck it's justifiable! You have just read pages of jury instructions above that tell you if you believe you can kill to defend your property or to defend yourself or family "from any unlawful" act, you WILL BE FRIED, ROASTED, GRILLED AND POACHED! *Pancho's Wisdom* – These parts of this statute should be repealed and rewritten. Somebody is likely to read these phrases and rely upon them. It's NOT FAIR for state laws to tell you that you can do something and then singe your bacon for doing it!]

[Use of Deadly Force to Prevent Serious Felonies]

B. When committed in the lawful defense of himself or of another and when there is a reasonable ground to believe a design exists to commit a felony or to do some great personal injury against such person or another, and there is imminent danger that the design will be accomplished; or [To the extent this paragraph authorizes the use of deadly force against ANY felony, it is PURE HOGWASH! According to case law and the jury instructions, the felony must involve an imminent threat of death of serious bodily injury.]

C. When necessarily committed in attempting, by lawful ways and means, to apprehend any person for any felony committed in his presence, or in lawfully suppressing any riot, or in necessarily and lawfully keeping and preserving the peace. [The courts don't follow this. You MAY NOT use deadly force to apprehend a felon, suppress a riot or preserve the peace unless your victim was immediately threatening death or serious bodily injury to another.]

[Exceptions to Justifiable Self-Defense] [Initial Aggressor]
[Combat by Agreement]

UJI [Uniform Jury Instructions] 14-5191. SELF-DEFENSE; LIMITATIONS; AGGRESSOR

Self-defense is not available to the defendant if he started the fight or agreed to fight unless: [Starting or agreeing to fight wipes out your right to use force in self-defense.]

[Exceptions to the Exceptions]

1. The defendant was using force which would not ordinarily create a substantial risk of death or great bodily harm; and
2. [Kid Colt] responded with force which would ordinarily create a substantial risk of death or great bodily harm; [If you start a fist fight, believing it's just going to be a fist fight and Kid draws his smoke wagon (Colt Single Action .45), you'd probably be justified in defending yourself with deadly force. See our caution about the use of excessive force in Chapters 3 and 4.]

[OR]

1. The defendant tried to stop the fight;
2. The defendant let [Kid Colt] know he no longer wanted to fight; and
3. [Kid Colt] became the aggressor.

[If the facts are so complicated that you claim that the exceptions to the exceptions apply, it has been our experience that police and prosecutors will file charges intending to let a jury decide who's at fault. If your opponent dies or his injuries are life-threatening, the resulting criminal and civil cases become life-ruining calamities.]

"The law of self-defense, however, does not imply the right to attack, nor will it permit acts done in retaliation or for revenge, and if you believe from the evidence, beyond a reasonable doubt, that the defendant sought, brought on, or voluntarily entered into a difficulty with the deceased for the purpose of engaging him in a conflict with deadly weapons, then the defendant cannot avail himself of the law of self-defense and you should not acquit him on that ground, and it is for you to determine from all the evidence whether the claim of the defendant that he killed deceased in self-defense is made in good faith or is a mere pretense." *State v. Pruett,* 172 P. 1044, 1046 (N.M. 1918). [Although this case is quite old, it still appears to be good law in New Mexico. Provoking a fight as an excuse to hurt or kill someone is not justifiable self-defense. This case also reminds us that use of force in retaliation or revenge is not justifiable self-defense.]

[Defense of Person(s) in Special Places – Habitation – Deadly Force]

UJI 14-5170. JUSTIFIABLE HOMICIDE; DEFENSE OF HABITATION

Evidence has been presented that the defendant killed [Barry Burglar] while attempting to prevent a [burglary] in the defendant's [home]. A killing in defense of [defendant's home] is justified if:

1. The [apartment, for example] was being used as the defendant's dwelling; and

2. It appeared to the defendant that the commission of a burglary was immediately at hand and that it was necessary to kill the intruder to prevent the commission of [the burglary] and [our reading of New Mexico cases, some of which are cited and explained below, suggests to us that to justify the use of deadly force, the crime the intruder is in the act of committing must be a serious felony such as burglary, arson, robbery, rape, kidnapping or murder. Deadly force cannot be used to prevent a mere trespass.]

3. A reasonable person in the same circumstances as the defendant would have acted as the defendant did. [Unfortunately, this is a "blank check" for a prosecutor to prosecute claiming that you acted like a typical cowboy rather than a reasonable person. See the detailed discussion of reasonableness, necessity and excessive force in Chapter 3.]

Committee Commentary – Section 30-2-7A [New Mexico's infamous justifiable homicide statute] provides that a homicide is justifiable when committed in the necessary defense of property. Although this statute has been a part of New Mexico law since 1907, the New Mexico appellate courts have never given the statute a broad interpretation. . . . The New Mexico courts have consistently held, not always referring to the statute, that one cannot defend his property, other than his habitation, from a mere trespass to the extent of killing the aggressor. [**Translation:** New Mexico Courts have held the statute doesn't really mean what it actually says!] *State v. McCracken,* 22 N.M. 588, 166 P. 1174 (1917); *State v. Martinez,* 34 N.M. 112, 278 P. 210 (1929); *State v. Couch,* 52 N.M. 127, 193 P.2d 405 (1946) . . .

The "pure" defense of property, i.e., not including a defense against force and violence, is always limited to reasonable force under the circumstances. See, e.g., *State v. Waggoner,* 49 N.M. 399, 165 P.2d 122 (1946); *Brown v. Martinez,* 68 N.M. 271, 361 P.2d 152 (1961). In *Brown,* the court held that resort to the use of a firearm to prevent a mere trespass or an unlawful act not amounting to a felony was unreasonable as a matter of law. [**Translation:** You can only use reasonable non-deadly force to keep people from trespassing or stealing or destroying personal property such as an unoccupied trailer or wheelbarrow. You may never use deadly force to defend against such crimes which are not dangerous felonies.]

[No Duty to Retreat From Home]

"'When a person is attacked in his own house, he need retreat no further. Here he stands at bay, and may turn on and kill his assailant if this be apparently necessary to save his own life; nor is he bound to escape from his house in order to avoid his assailant.' 'In this sense, and in this sense alone, are we to understand the maxim that 'every man's house is his castle." 'An assailed person, so we may paraphrase the maxim, is not bound to retreat out of his house to avoid violence, even though a retreat may be safely made. But he is not entitled, either in the one case or the other, to kill his assailant unless he honestly and nonnegligently believes that he is in danger of his life from the assault,' or when a felonious assault is being made upon the house, as to commit burglary, arson, or other felony therein or against its inmates." *State v. Couch,* 193 P.2d 405, 409 (N.M. 1946). [This is New Mexico's castle doctrine. You don't have to retreat from your home, even if you can retreat in complete safety. However, even in the home, deadly force can only be used if the person believes his life is in danger or a serious felony is about to be committed against the home or the people lawfully in the home. And don't forget the paragraph in the jury instruction that says you can only use deadly force if a reasonable person under the same circumstances would have. *Pancho's Wisdom* – This places much too much of a burden on the homeowner under what could be extremely stressful circumstances (like a home invasion). By the time you go through the mental checklist of all the nitpicky requirements, a ruthless, dedicated, experienced and violent home invader could kill you. New Mexico needs to adopt a home-defense statute similar to Florida's (see Mother of All Self-Defense Laws, Chapter 20).]

[Reckless Injury to Innocent Third Parties]

[If your use of deadly force is justifiable and you kill an innocent bystander, you are not guilty of a crime. If, however, you are reckless in your use of defensive force (e.g., "spray and pray") you could be found guilty of manslaughter.] See *State v. Sherwood,* 50 P.2d 968 (N.M. 1935).

[Civil Liability]

"We are well aware that all the cases cited above and certain other cases hereinafter cited are criminal cases, whereas the present case is civil. We do not consider this fact to make any difference since our study of the authorities convinces us that rules of law governing the liability of appellee for shooting and wounding appellant while stopping a trespass or the theft of watermelons are the same whether the proceedings be civil or criminal." *Brown v. Martinez,* 361 P.2d 152, 156 (N.M. 1961). [This case provides some authority for the proposition that the rules of self-defense for civil cases are the same as apply to criminal cases in New Mexico. Of course, the burden of proof on the state in a criminal case is higher than the burden for an injured person in a civil case. See Chapter 15 for a detailed discussion of how you could be liable in a civil suit even though you were found not guilty in your criminal case.]

[Defense of Property]

"We have thus gone at length into a review of the law upon this subject, and we deduce from the decided cases and the standard authors that a mere civil trespass upon a man's dwelling house does not justify him in slaying the trespasser; that the owner may resist the trespass, opposing force against force, but the has no right to kill unless it becomes necessary to prevent a felonious destruction of his property or the commission of a felony therein, or to defend himself against a felonious assault against his life or person; that if he kills without reasonable apprehension of immediate danger to his person or property, but in the heat of passion aroused by the trespasser, it will be manslaughter." *State v. Couch*, 193 P.2d 405, 410 (N.M. 1948). [You may not use deadly force to prevent a trespass or to protect personal property.]

[HELPFUL DEFINITIONS RELATING TO THIS STATE'S SELF-DEFENSE STATUTES]

- **Great bodily harm** – means an injury to the person which creates a high probability of death; or which causes serious disfigurement; or which results in permanent or protracted loss or impairment of the function of any member or organ of the body. **N.M.S.A. § 30-1-12 (A).**

- **Deadly weapon** – means any firearm, whether loaded or unloaded; or any weapon which is capable of producing death or great bodily harm, including but not restricted to any types of daggers, brass knuckles, switchblade knives, bowie knives, poniards, butcher knives, dirk knives and all such weapons with which dangerous cuts can be given, or with which dangerous thrusts can be inflicted, including swordcanes, and any kind of sharp pointed canes, also slingshots, slung shots, bludgeons; or any other weapons with which dangerous wounds can be inflicted. **N.M.S.A. § 30-1-12 (A).**

[TEMPLATE Topics We Could Not Find Explained in Statutes or Cases]

(For each of these topics that we could not find addressed in your state's statutes or cases, we suggest you review the same topics in the subchapters of surrounding states. Your state's courts may look to the law of neighboring states to see how their courts and legislatures have treated that particular self-defense issue.)

[Committing Felony or Unlawful Act]

[Co-Habitants; Co-Employees – Duty to Retreat]

[Presumption of Reasonableness in Special Places]

W**arning:** New York laws relating to the possession and carrying of weapons small enough to conceal are very strict and are beyond the scope of this book. Even though you may have the right to defend yourself and others with deadly force, you may not have the right to possess or carry certain deadly weapons to exercise that right. In other words, even though you may not be prosecuted if you justifiably defend yourself with a weapon, if the weapon is illegal to possess, you will be prosecuted for possession of that weapon. See Chapter 23, Additional Resources for help in finding publications that explain New York's strict weapon-possession laws. To keep from cutting New York's main self-defense statute (§ 35.15 Penal) to pieces, we had to alter the order of our **TEMPLATE** sub-headings somewhat.

Key: ■ commentary ■ original statutes, cases or jury instructions

---

[Defense of Self and Others]

[Non-Deadly Force] [Defense of a Third Person]

§ NEW YORK (N.Y.) PENAL LAW § 35.15 PENAL.
Justification; use of physical force in defense of a person.

1. A person may, subject to the provisions of subdivision two (**[Exceptions to Justifiable Self-Defense]** below), use physical force upon another person when and to the extent he or she reasonably believes such to be necessary to defend himself, herself or a third person from what he or she reasonably believes to be the use or imminent use of unlawful physical force by such other person . . . [According to the New York Jury Instructions, to determine whether you reasonably believe physical force is necessary involves a two part test: (1) you must actually believe that an assailant is about to use physical force against you or another, and that your use of physical force is necessary; and (2) a "reasonable person" in your situation would have done the same thing under similar circumstances.]

[Exceptions to Justifiable Self-Defense]

. . . unless: [you can use physical force to defend yourself, unless...]

[Provocation]

(a) The latter's conduct was provoked by the actor with intent to cause physical injury to another person; or [You cannot use physical force to defend yourself if you started the fight as an excuse to hurt another.]

[Initial Aggressor]

(b) The actor was the initial aggressor; . . . [See definition of "initial aggressor" in the definitions section below. You cannot start a fight and then claim self-defense unless . . .]

[Exceptions to the Exceptions] [Withdraw and Communicate]

. . . except that in such case the use of physical force is nevertheless justifiable if the actor has withdrawn from the encounter and effectively communicated such withdrawal to such other person but the latter persists in continuing the incident by the use or threatened imminent use of unlawful physical force; or [This is only an exception to being the initial aggressor. It does not apply to provocation or mutual combat. If you started the fight, but then stop your aggression and tell your opponent you quit, if he continues to fight, then you can defend yourself as if you weren't the aggressor. This situation is fraught with legal risks. Your opponent and his friends are going to say you didn't stop fighting. They'll claim that it was necessary for him to continue his aggression to defend himself from you. Our research reveals that anytime you start a fight, whether you withdraw and communicate your intent to quit or not, you will be arrested and prosecuted. Our advice – don't go around starting fights, capiche?!]

[Mutual Combat]

(c) The physical force involved is the product of a combat by agreement not specifically authorized by law. [You can't agree to fight and then claim self-defense.]

[Deadly Force] [Duty to Retreat – Generally – Yes]

2. A person may not use deadly physical force upon another person under circumstances specified in subdivision one unless: ["Deadly physical force" is defined in the definitions section below.]

(a) The actor reasonably believes that such other person is using or about to use deadly physical force. Even in such case, however, the actor may not use deadly physical force if he or she knows that with complete personal safety, to oneself and others he or she may avoid the necessity of so doing by retreating; except that the actor is under no duty to retreat if he or she is: [You must actually AND reasonably believe it is necessary for you to use deadly force to defend yourself or another, just like the requirement above regarding the use of non-deadly force. If you can retreat in complete safety, you must do so before using deadly force.]

[Defense of Person(s) in Special Places – Dwelling]
[No Duty to Retreat From Dwelling (Home)]

(i) in his or her dwelling and not the initial aggressor; or [You don't have to retreat from your home unless you started the conflict. (See what we consider the best definition of "initial aggressor" we have yet encountered below.)]

(ii) a police officer or peace officer or a person assisting a police officer or a peace officer at the latter's direction, acting pursuant to section 35.30; or [*Pancho's Wisdom:* When was the last time a police officer in New York asked a citizen to shoot someone for him? Because of New York's strict weapons laws, the only people who have guns are the police, the Mafia, muggers, politicians, VIPs and rapists. Everyone else is a sitting duck.]

[Use of Deadly Force to Prevent Serious Felonies]

(b) He or she reasonably believes that such other person is committing or attempting to commit a kidnapping, forcible rape, forcible criminal sexual act or robbery; [You can use deadly force to prevent the imminent commission of one of these serious felonies. We commend New York for doing its citizens a favor and specifically listing which felonies trigger the right to use of deadly force.]

(c) He or she reasonably believes that such other person is committing or attempting to commit a burglary, and the circumstances are such that the use of deadly physical force is authorized by subdivision three of section 35.20. [See paragraph 3 of §35.20 below, authorizing the use of deadly force to prevent a burglary in a building or dwelling.]

[**Caution:** The use of deadly force must be necessary. Notice that paragraph 2 of this statute incorporates the requirements of paragraph 1. Paragraph 1 requires that the use of force be necessary and reasonable. If a criminal committing one of the serious felonies mentioned in paragraph 2 ceases his attempt to commit the crime before you use deadly force, it would be unnecessary for you then to proceed to use deadly force. See our discussion of "necessity" in Chapter 3.]

[Defense of Premises]

§ N.Y. PENAL LAW § 35.20 PENAL.

Justification; use of physical force in defense of premises and in defense of a person in the course of burglary.

1. Any person may use physical force upon another person when he or she reasonably believes such to be necessary to prevent or terminate what he or she reasonably believes to be the commission or attempted commission by such other person of a crime involving damage to premises. [You can use physical force, but not deadly force, to keep someone from unlawfully damaging your premises. Premises is a broader concept than dwelling (a place where you stay overnight) and includes your place of work, a school, trailer and even real estate. See definitions section below.] Such person may use any degree of physical force, other than deadly physical force, which he or she reasonably believes to be necessary for such purpose, and may use deadly physical force if he or she reasonably believes such to be necessary to prevent or terminate the commission or attempted commission of arson. [There are five degrees of arson one of which is not a felony but rather a class A misdemeanor (see New York Consolidated laws § 150.00 Penal through §150.20 Penal). Although it is not stated that one cannot use deadly force to

prevent misdemeanor arson, we highly recommend you shouldn't use deadly force to prevent an act of arson that CLEARLY will NOT put someone else in danger of physical injury. **Example:** If you shoot a teen prankster trying to ignite a bag of doggie dung on your porch, we suspect you will be arrested and prosecuted. Sure, your lawyer will raise the arson defense. Be prepared to pay for his thirty-year anniversary trip to Tahiti without the couple's-retreat discount.]

2. A person in possession or control of any premises, or a person licensed or privileged to be thereon or therein, may use physical force upon another person when he or she reasonably believes such to be necessary to prevent or terminate what he or she reasonably believes to be the commission or attempted commission by such other person of a criminal trespass upon such premises. Such person may use any degree of physical force, other than deadly physical force, which he or she reasonably believes to be necessary for such purpose, and may use deadly physical force in order to prevent or terminate the commission or attempted commission of arson, as prescribed in subdivision one, or in the course of a burglary or attempted burglary, as prescribed in subdivision three. [You can use reasonable force but not deadly force to stop a trespass in your yard or on your Upstate NY farm. You can use deadly force against someone committing or attempting to commit arson (comply with the paragraph above) or burglary (comply with the paragraph below).]

3. A person in possession or control of, or licensed or privileged to be in, a dwelling or an occupied building, who reasonably believes that another person is committing or attempting to commit a burglary of such dwelling or building, may use deadly physical force upon such other person when he or she reasonably believes such to be necessary to prevent or terminate the commission or attempted commission of such burglary. [Deadly force can be used to protect against the commission or attempted commission of burglary. Simplified, burglary is the unlawful entry into a building for the purpose of committing a crime. Carefully study the concept of necessity in Chapter 3. If you use deadly force against someone whom you clearly know is in the building to commit a petty crime (e.g., kids stealing candy, a homeless person stealing a loaf of bread) you will be arrested and prosecuted. Police, prosecutors and ultimately jurors will be asking, "was it necessary to shoot this individual who the defendant knew to be absolutely harmless?"]

"Moreover, a person subjected to a felonious assault in his abode is not expected to engage in a detached analysis of the probabilities, and may destroy 'the person making the felonious attack" *People v. Patterson,* 250 N.Y.S.2d 715, 722 (N.Y.A.D. 1964). [On the other hand, if a person breaks into your home to cause you or a loved one physical harm, New York law permits you to resolve doubts in favor of you and your family's safety. As mentioned in the introduction, however, your possession of the weapon you use for self-defense must be legal. If not, you will be prosecuted for having an illegal weapon, even though you use it in justifiable self-defense.]

§ 35.20 PENAL (CONT.)

4. As used in this section, the following terms have the following meanings:

   (a) The terms "premises," "building" and "dwelling" have the meanings prescribed in section 140.00 [set forth below];

   (b) Persons "licensed or privileged" to be in buildings or upon other premises include, but are not limited to:

      (i) police officers or peace officers acting in the performance of their duties; and

      (ii) security personnel or employees of nuclear powered electric generating facilities located within the state who are employed as part of any security plan approved by the federal operating license agencies acting in the performance of their duties at such generating facilities. For purposes of this subparagraph, the term "nuclear powered electric generating facility" shall mean a facility that generates electricity using nuclear power for sale, directly or indirectly, to the public, including the land upon which the facility is located and the safety and security zones as defined under federal regulations.

      [You are obviously licensed or privileged to be in the building in which you live or work, but so are police officers and security personnel who are hired to protect such places.]

[Cases Interpreting New York's Home-Defense Law]
"In our view the word 'dwelling,' as used in Penal Law § 35.15 (2) (a) (i), refers to a person's residence, and any definition of the term must therefore account for a myriad of living arrangements, from rural farm properties to large apartment buildings. For purposes of section 35.15, the determination of whether a particular location is part of a defendant's dwelling depends on the extent to which defendant (and persons actually sharing living quarters with defendant) exercises exclusive possession and control over the area in question. The term encompasses a house, an apartment or a part of a structure where defendant lives and where others are ordinarily excluded—the antithesis of which is routine access to or use of an area by strangers." *People v. Hernandez*, 98 N.Y.2d 175, (N.Y. 2002.) [What is your "dwelling" and how far does it extend? In this case, the New York Supreme Court held that it depends on how much control you have over the area in question. If you're living in an apartment complex, your dwelling won't include the common stairwell or other area freely used by guests or tenants.]

[Co-Habitants; Guests – Duty to Retreat – No]
"We affirm the castle doctrine in its application to occupants of the same household. This has been our decisional law at least since *Tomlins*, and it has particular importance in cases of domestic violence, most often against women." *People v. Jones*, 821 N.E.2d 955, 958 (N.Y. 2004). [Some states require you to retreat from a co-habitant in your own home. New York does not. For situations involving domestic violence, however, please carefully read Chapter 13.]

"Notwithstanding that defendant maintains that, as a guest and invitee of the family in whose apartment the shooting occurred, he was under no duty to retreat, article 35 of the Penal Law, which sets forth in detail the standards applicable to the defense of justification, does not support his contention. Penal Law § 35.15(2)(a)(i) provides that a person who is not the initial aggressor and is in his own dwelling is not under a duty to retreat in the face of deadly physical force. There is nothing in the statute that extends the words "no duty to retreat" to the dwelling of anyone besides that of the actor." *People v. Van Allen*, 627 N.Y.S.2d 664, 664 (N.Y.A.D. 1995). [When you are a guest in someone else's home, the castle doctrine does not apply to you. You must retreat before using deadly force.]

[Reckless Injury to Innocent Third Parties]

[If you are otherwise justified in using deadly force to defend yourself and accidently kill an innocent bystander, you are not guilty of manslaughter for killing the bystander unless your use of force is proven to be reckless. You will, however, be arrested, prosecuted and sued if you hurt an innocent person. You OWN every bullet that you fire. We suggest before you ever use a firearm for self-defense, you properly train to use it responsibly, safely and accurately. See our recommendations for additional training in Chapter 18.] *People v. Sierra*, 647 N.Y.S.2d 891 (N.Y.A.D. 1996).

[Civil Liability]

"A criminal conviction, whether by plea or after trial, is conclusive proof of its underlying facts in a subsequent civil action and collaterally estops a party from relitigating the issue." *Grayes v. DiStasio*, 560 N.Y.S.2d 636 (N.Y.A.D. 1990). [If you are found guilty of a crime for harming or killing someone or, if you plead guilty, your conviction or guilty plea can be used against you in a lawsuit brought by the injured person or his heirs.]

[Defense of Property]

§ N.Y. PENAL LAW § 35.25 PENAL.

Justification; use of physical force to prevent or terminate larceny or criminal mischief.

A person may use physical force, other than deadly physical force, upon another person when and to the extent that he or she reasonably believes such to be necessary to prevent or terminate what he or she reasonably believes to be the commission or attempted commission by such other person of larceny or of criminal mischief with respect to property other than premises. [You can use force other than deadly force to prevent theft or damage to your personal property that is not real estate, such as a car, DVD player, etc. The problem is a thief or vandal may react by brandishing a weapon. In an instant an encounter not involving the use of deadly force escalates to a deadly confrontation. You could end up killing the thief or vandal or even worse, you could be killed. If there is any claim that you used excessive force in defending your property, the cost of your lawyer in the subsequent criminal and civil cases may well exceed by many times the value of the property you intended to defend. We strongly advise against attempts to defend personal property and recommend you simply call the police.]

[HELPFUL DEFINITIONS RELATING TO THIS STATE'S SELF-DEFENSE STATUTES]

- **Deadly physical force** – means physical force which, under the circumstances in which it is used, is readily capable of causing death or other serious physical injury. **N.Y. Penal Law § 10.00(11).**

- **Initial aggressor** – means the person who first attacks or threatens to attack; that is, the first person who uses or threatens the imminent use of offensive physical force. The actual striking of the first blow or inflicting of the first wound, however, does not necessarily determine who was the initial aggressor. A person who reasonably believes that another is about to use physical force upon her need not wait until she is struck or wounded. She may, in such circumstances, be the first to use [deadly] physical force, so long as she reasonably believed it was about to be used against her or someone else. She is then not considered to be the "initial aggressor," even though she strikes the first blow or inflicts the first wound. Arguing, using abusive language, calling a person names, or the like, unaccompanied by physical threats or acts, does not make a person an initial aggressor and does not justify physical force. A person cannot be considered the initial aggressor simply because she has a reputation for violence or has previously engaged in violent acts. **New York Justification Jury Instructions 35.15 USE OF [DEADLY] PHYSICAL FORCE IN DEFENSE OF A PERSON.** [This is hands down the best definition of initial aggressor we have seen in any state.]

- **Felonies Mentioned**
  - **Arson** – [recklessly or intentionally damaging a building or car by fire or explosives.] **N.Y. Penal Law § 150.05, 150.10, 150.15, 150.20.**

[Listed here is the definition statute specifically related to the offense of arson...]

N.Y. Penal Law § 150.00 Penal. Arson; definitions.

As used in this article, 1. "Building", in addition to its ordinary meaning, includes any structure, vehicle or watercraft used for overnight lodging of persons, or used by persons for carrying on business therein. Where a building consists of two or more units separately secured or occupied, each unit shall not be deemed a separate building.

2. "Motor vehicle", includes every vehicle operated or driven upon a public highway which is propelled by any power other than muscular power, except (a) electrically-driven invalid chairs being operated or driven by an invalid, (b) vehicles which run only upon rails or tracks, and (c) snowmobiles as defined in article forty-seven of the vehicle and traffic law.

  - **Burglary** – [intentionally entering or remaining in a building unlawfully with the intent to commit a crime in the building.] **N.Y. Penal Law § 140.20, 140.25, 140.30.**

[Listed here is the definition statute specifically relating to burglary.]

N.Y. Penal Law § 140.00 Penal. Criminal trespass and burglary; definitions of terms.

The following definitions are applicable to this article:

1. "Premises" includes the term "building", as defined herein, and any real property.

2. "Building," in addition to its ordinary meaning, includes any structure, vehicle or watercraft used for overnight lodging of persons, or used by persons for carrying on business therein, or used as an elementary or secondary school, or an enclosed motor truck, or an enclosed motor truck trailer. Where a building consists of two or more units separately secured or occupied, each unit shall be deemed both a separate building in itself and a part of the main building.

3. "Dwelling" means a building which is usually occupied by a person lodging therein at night.

4. "Night" means the period between thirty minutes after sunset and thirty minutes before sunrise.

5. "Enter or remain unlawfully." A person "enters or remains unlawfully" in or upon premises when he is not licensed or privileged to do so. A person who, regardless of his intent, enters or remains in or upon premises which are at the time open to the public does so with license and privilege unless he defies a lawful order not to enter or remain, personally communicated to him by the owner of such premises or other authorized person. A license or privilege to enter or remain in a building which is only partly open to the public is not a license or privilege to enter or remain in that part of the building which is not open to the public. A person who enters or remains upon unimproved and apparently unused land, which is neither fenced nor otherwise enclosed in a manner designed to exclude intruders, does so with license and privilege unless notice against trespass is personally communicated to him by the owner of such land or other authorized person, or unless such notice is given by posting in a conspicuous manner. A person who enters or remains in or about a school building without written permission from someone authorized to issue such permission or without a legitimate reason which includes a relationship involving custody of or responsibility for a pupil or student enrolled in the school or without legitimate business or a purpose relating to the operation of the school does so without license and privilege.

- **Forcible rape** – [Although this phrase is used extensively throughout New York cases and statutes, there is no offense listed in New York statutes entitled "forcible rape." We suspect it refers to sexual intercourse carried out by force or threat against the victim's will as opposed to statutory rape. Statutory rape is based upon the legal principle that persons under a certain age and incapacitated persons are incapable of legally consenting to sexual relations. **Example:** A father is shocked to find his under-aged daughter willingly making love to her adult boyfriend. The boyfriend is guilty of statutory rape, but not forcible rape. If the angry dad suddenly ends the relationship with a kiss from his Kimber (in .45ACP), the forcible rape justification to use deadly force in **§ 35.15 Penal** above will probably not apply. For examples of both forcible and statutory rape see **N.Y. Penal Law § 130.35 (Rape in the first degree).**]

- **Forcible sexual act** – [There is no specific offense by the title "forcible sexual act." This term is likely to include but not limited to a number of sexual offenses such as sexual abuse, aggravated sexual abuse, and forcible sexual abuse of a child. The term "forcible" is important and describes a crime accomplished against a victim by force or threat.] **N.Y. Penal Law § 130.50 (Criminal sexual act in the first degree). N.Y. Penal Law § 130.55, 130.60, 130.65 (Sexual abuse in the 3rd 2nd and 1st degree). N.Y. Penal Law § 130.65-a, 130.66, 130.67, 130.70 (Aggravated sexual abuse in the 4th, 3rd, 2nd, and 1st degree). N.Y. Penal Law § 130.75, 130.80 (Course of sexual conduct against a child in the 2nd and 1st degree).**

- **Kidnapping** – [Abducting another person.] **N.Y. Penal Law § 135.20, .25.**

- **Robbery** – [Unlawfully taking another's property by force or threat.] **N.Y. Penal Law § 160.05, .10, .15.**

- **Felony** – means an offense for which a sentence to a term of imprisonment in excess of one year may be imposed. **N.Y. Penal Law § 10.00(5).**

- **Physical injury** – means impairment of physical condition or substantial pain. **N.Y. Penal Law § 10.00(9).**

- **Serious physical injury** – means physical injury which creates a substantial risk of death, or which causes death or serious and protracted disfigurement, protracted impairment of health or protracted loss or impairment of the function of any bodily organ. **N.Y. Penal Law § 10.00(10).**

[TEMPLATE Topics We Could Not Find Explained in Statutes or Cases]

(For each of these topics that we could not find addressed in your state's statutes or cases, we suggest you review the same topics in the subchapters of surrounding states. Your state's courts may look to the law of neighboring states to see how their courts and legislatures have treated that particular self-defense issue.)

[Co-Employees – Duty to Retreat]

[Presumption of Reasonableness in Special Places]

[Committing Felony or Unlawful Act]

Pancho's Wisdom

Speak softly, but carry a BIG SIG!

Pancho's Wisdom

You can tell a lot about a man by the calibers he keeps.

Like a few other states on the Eastern Seaboard which have sparse or no self-defense statutes, North Carolina has only a short home-defense statute. Although it has self-defense jury instructions for judges, lawyers and juries to use, they are not readily available to the public except perhaps through a university law library. Unfortunately, this leaves those living in or traveling through the state without adequate notice of what North Carolina's self-defense laws are. The consequences could be disastrous. Fortunately, we've dug most of its self-defense laws out of the state's criminal law cases for you.

Key: ■ commentary ■ original statutes, cases or jury instructions

[Defense of Self and Others] [Non-Deadly Force]

"In the absence of an intent to kill, a person may fight in his own self-defense to protect himself from bodily harm or offensive physical contact, even though he is not put in actual or apparent danger of death or great bodily harm." *State v. Beaver,* 188 S.E.2d 576, 579 (1972). [You can use force but not deadly force to defend yourself against non-deadly force.]

[Deadly Force]

"It is well settled that perfect self-defense excuses a killing when at the time of the killing:

(1) it appeared to defendant and he believed it to be necessary to kill the deceased in order to save himself from death or great bodily harm; and [You have to have an honest and sincere belief that you need to use deadly force to protect yourself from death or serious injury. . .]

(2) defendant's belief was reasonable in that the circumstances as they appeared to him at the time were sufficient to create such a belief in the mind of a person of ordinary firmness; and [Your belief must be reasonable; not that of an overly paranoid person. . .]

(3) defendant was not the aggressor in bringing on the affray, i.e., he did not aggressively and willingly enter into the fight without legal excuse or provocation; and [You didn't start the fight and...]

(4) defendant did not use excessive force, i.e., did not use more force than was necessary or reasonably appeared to him to be necessary under the circumstances to protect himself from death or great bodily harm." *State v. Williams,* 467 S.E.2d 392, 872 (N.C. 1996).

[You cannot use more force than is necessary to stop the threat of death or serious injury.]

[Use of Deadly Force to Prevent Serious Felonies]

"Deadly force may be employed to repel a felonious assault where such force reasonably appears to be necessary to prevent death or great bodily harm." *Hall v. Coplon,* 355 S.E.2d 195, 508 (N.C.App. 1987). [We were not able to find any statutes or cases that authorize the use of deadly force to prevent expressly listed felonies or serious crimes. It appears that no matter what the crime being committed against you, you still have to show an immediate threat of death or serious injury to justify the use of deadly force.]

[Defense of a Third Person]

"In general one may kill in defense of another if one believes it to be necessary to prevent death or great bodily harm to the other and has a reasonable ground for such belief, the reasonableness of this belief or apprehension to be judged by the jury in light of the facts and circumstances as they appeared to the defender at the time of the killing... [T]he right to kill in defense of another cannot exceed such other's right to kill in his own defense as that other's right reasonably appeared to the defendant." *State v. Perry,* 450 S.E.2d 471, 466 (N.C. 1994). [You can kill in defense of another as long as you reasonably believe the use of deadly force is necessary to prevent death or serious injury to that person. You step into the third person's shoes and can use whatever force that that person would have been authorized to use. You cannot use excessive force.]

[Exceptions to Justifiable Self-Defense] [Initial Aggressor] [Provocation]

"The elements of self-defense are:

(3) defendant was not the aggressor in bringing on the affray, i.e., he did not aggressively and willingly enter into the fight without legal excuse or provocation . . ." *State v. Phifer,* 598 S.E2d 172, 128 (N.C. App. 2004). [You can't start a fight and then expect to win on the theory of self-defense.]

[Mutual Combat]

"Where a man provokes a fight by unlawfully assaulting another, and in the progress of the fight kills his adversary, he will be guilty of manslaughter at least, though at the precise time of the homicide it was necessary for the original assailant to kill in order to save his own life. This is ordinarily true where a man unlawfully and willingly enters into a mutual combat with another and kills his adversary. In either case, in order to excuse the killing on the plea of self-defense, it is necessary for the accused to show that he 'quitted the combat before the mortal wound was given, and retreated or fled as far as he could with safety, and then, urged by mere necessity, killed his adversary for the preservation of his own life . . . " *State v. Poland,* 83 S.E. 168 (N.C. 1924). [If you agree to a fight, and find yourself in a situation where you are compelled to use deadly force to save your life, you're going to get hit with at least manslaughter – NO MATTER HOW MUCH YOUR OPPONENT ESCALATED THE FIGHT. The only way to revive your right to claim self-defense is to abandon the fight and telling your opponent you've had enough, which you need to make PERFECTLY CLEAR. Then, if you need to use deadly force to preserve your own life, you might be justified on the theory of self-defense. Whenever you're at fault in starting, agreeing to or escalating a fight, plan on being arrested, prosecuted and probably convicted of something ugly.]

[Exceptions to the Exceptions] [Withdraw and Communicate]
"However, the right of self-defense is only available to a person who is without fault, and if a person voluntarily, that is aggressively and willingly, enters into a fight, he cannot invoke the doctrine of self-defense unless he first abandons the fight, withdraws from it and gives notice to his adversary that he has done so." *State v. Marsh,* 237 S.E.2d 745 (N.C. 1977). [Same rule as in the case above, but a little more succinctly written. Again, self-defense is not available to those involved in mutual combat, unless you make it PERFECTLY CLEAR that you abandoned the fight and communicated the same to your adversary.]

[Duty to Retreat – Generally – Yes/No]
"[t]he general rules of self-defense allow a defendant to use the amount of force 'necessary or apparently necessary to save himself from death or great bodily harm.' State v. Pearson, 288 N.C. 34, 39, 215 S.E.2d 598, 602 (1975). When confronted with an assault that does not threaten the person assaulted with death or great bodily harm, a party claiming self-defense is required to retreat 'if there is any way of escape open to him, although he is permitted to repel force by force and give blow for blow.' Id. at 39, 215 S.E.2d at 602-03. There is no duty to retreat when (1) the person assaulted is confronted with an assault that threatens death or great bodily harm...'" *State v. Pearson,* 215 S.E.2d 598, 602 (N.C. 1975). [You have to retreat against non-deadly force. You don't have to retreat if you're combating deadly force and you are not at fault in any way in starting the conflict. This rule was re-affirmed in 2004 in the North Carolina case *State v. Everett,* 163 N.C.App. 95, 592 S.E.2d 582 (N.C.App., 2004).]

[Defense of Person(s) in Special Places – Home, Place of Residence]

§ NORTH CAROLINA GENERAL STATUTES ANNOTATED (N.C.G.S.A.) § 14-51.1.

Use of deadly physical force against an intruder.

(a) A lawful occupant within a home or other place of residence is justified in using any degree of force that the occupant reasonably believes is necessary, including deadly force, against an intruder to prevent a forcible entry into the home or residence or to terminate the intruder's unlawful entry (i) if the occupant reasonably apprehends that the intruder may kill or inflict serious bodily harm to the occupant or others in the home or residence, or (ii) if the occupant reasonably believes that the intruder intends to commit a felony in the home or residence.

[No Duty to Retreat From Place of Residence]

(b) A lawful occupant within a home or other place of residence does not have a duty to retreat from an intruder in the circumstances described in this section.

. . .

[You don't have to retreat in your home, and may used deadly force as long if you (1) reasonably think the intruder is going to kill or seriously harm yourself or an occupant of your home or (2) reasonably think the intruder is going to commit a felony in your home. We suspect the courts of North Carolina will hold that the reference to felony in this statute means a "violent felony" such as the common law felonies of murder, rape, arson, burglary, kidnapping and armed robbery. Unarmed, non-threatening people often commit non-violent felonies. There is significant legal risk in using deadly force against such people. See discussion of this issue in Chapter 4. **Example:** An unarmed door-to-door salesman trying to sell you ocean front property in Arizona. Although you'd like to smear his lying lard all over your front lawn with your Winchester 1300 Defender, we suspect the North Carolina courts won't let you go that far.]

"There is no duty to retreat when (1) the person assaulted is confronted with an assault that threatens death or great bodily harm or (2) the person assaulted is not confronted with an assault that threatens death or great bodily harm and the assault occurs in the dwelling, place of business, or premises of the person assaulted, provided the person assaulted is free from fault in bringing on the difficulty. *State v. Everett*, 592 S.E. 2d 582, 586 (N.C.App. 2004)(citations omitted). [This makes it pretty clear that you do not have to retreat if you are threatened by an assault of death or serious bodily harm or if the assault occurs in your home.]

[Co-Habitants – Duty to Retreat – No]

"In addition, 'a person is not obliged to retreat when he is assaulted while in his dwelling house or within the curtilage thereof, whether the assailant be an intruder or another lawful occupant of the premises.'" *State v. Everett*, 592 S.E. 2d 582, 586 (N.C.App. 2004)(citations omitted). [You don't have to retreat out of your home before using force in self-defense, even if the person attacking you has a right to be in the home. This is not true for all states.]

[Civil Liability]

"While self-defense and defense of family are seen more often in the context of criminal law, these defenses are nonetheless appropriate in civil actions; if defenses apply, defendant's conduct is considered privileged and defendant is not subject to tort liability for actions taken within the privilege." *Young v. Warren*, 383 S.E.2d 381, 383 (N.C.App. 1989). [This doesn't necessarily say that there is civil immunity for justifiable self-defense. It does imply, however, that a successful defense in a criminal trial will be successful in a civil one.]

[Defense of Property]

"[W]hen a trespasser invades the premises of another, the latter has the right to remove him, and the law requires that he should first request him to leave, and if he does not do so, he should lay his hands gently upon him, and if he resists, he may use sufficient force to remove him, taking care, however, to use no more force than is necessary to accomplish that object." *State v. Withers*, 633 S.E.2d 863, 872 (N.C.App. 2006). [We're not entirely sure what "lay hands gently upon him" means. We interpret this to mean that you may use non-deadly force to remove a trespasser, but not excessive force and certainly not deadly force.]

[HELPFUL DEFINITIONS RELATING TO THIS STATE'S SELF-DEFENSE STATUTES]

- **House and Building** – shall be defined to include mobile and manufactured-type housing and recreational trailers. **N.C.G.S.A. § 14-58.1.**

[TEMPLATE Topics We Could Not Find Explained in Statutes or Cases]

(For each of these topics that we could not find addressed in your state's statutes or cases, we suggest you review the same topics in the subchapters of surrounding states. Your state's courts may look to the law of neighboring states to see how their courts and legislatures have treated that particular self-defense issue.)

[Committing Felony or Unlawful Act]

[Co-Employees – Duty to Retreat]

[Presumption of Reasonableness in Special Places]

[Reckless Injury to Innocent Third Parties]

Pancho's Wisdom

You just might be a Gunnut if . . . rather than play video games you'd rather blast things (not humans) for real.

Key: ■ commentary ■ original statutes, cases or jury instructions

[Defense of Self and Others] [Non-Deadly Force]

§ NORTH DAKOTA CENTURY CODE (N.D.C.C.) § 12.1-05-03.
Self-defense.

A person is justified in using force upon another person to defend himself against danger of imminent unlawful bodily injury, sexual assault, or detention by such other person, [You can use non-deadly force to defend yourself against someone hitting you, trying to sexually assault you or take or detain you against your will.] except that:

1. A person is not justified in using force for the purpose of resisting arrest, execution of process, or other performance of duty by a public servant under color of law, but excessive force may be resisted. [You are not justified in using force to resist arrest or service of a summons on you. The exception is if the officer uses excessive force, you may resist. Notice this does not give you the right to use deadly force to resist. We recommend you never do this because you will be charged with resisting arrest or worse, assault on a police officer. You will be arrested and prosecuted. It will cost you a small fortune even if you ultimately win the case.]

. . .

[See other exceptions below]

[Deadly Force]

[Use of Deadly Force to Prevent Serious Felonies]

§ N.D.C.C. § 12.1-05-07.
Limits on the use of force – Excessive force – Deadly force.

1. An individual is not justified in using more force than is necessary and appropriate under the circumstances. [Please implant the requirement of necessity deep within the grey matter of your gunslingin' brain. This is a blank check for a prosecutor to fry you if he wants to punish you for having the audacity to defend yourself or your loved ones with a gun. See a more complete detailed discussion of the concept of necessity in Chapter 3.]

2. Deadly force is justified in the following instances:

   a. When it is expressly authorized by law or occurs in the lawful conduct of war. [Deadly force can be used if the law says you can use it or if you are at war.]

b. When used in lawful self-defense, or in lawful defense of others, if such force is necessary to protect the actor or anyone else against death, serious bodily injury, or the commission of a felony involving violence.

[Duty to Retreat – Generally – Yes]

The use of deadly force is not justified if it can be avoided, with safety to the actor and others, by retreat or other conduct involving minimal interference with the freedom of the individual menaced... However, the duty to retreat or avoid force does not apply under the following circumstances: [Generally, deadly force is not justified if it can be avoided by retreating or by using some other means to protect oneself.]

(1) A public servant justified in using force in the performance of the public servant's duties or an individual justified in using force in assisting the public servant need not desist from the public servant's or individual's efforts because of resistance or threatened resistance by or on behalf of the other individual against whom the public servant's or individual's action is directed; and [If you somehow get roped into helping a law enforcement officer, you don't need to retreat before you use force against the criminal's resistance.]

. . .

[Defense of a Third Person]

§ N.D.C.C. § 12.1-05-04.
Defense of others.

A person is justified in using force upon another person in order to defend anyone else if:

1. The person defended would be justified in defending himself; [You can defend a third person if he is justified in defending himself. Unfortunately, this means that if he was not justified in defending himself (for example, he provoked the fight), even though you didn't know he wasn't justified, then you also would not be justified in defending him.] and

2. The person coming to the defense has not, by provocation or otherwise, forfeited the right of self-defense. [You can defend another person if he could have defended himself and as long as you personally haven't done anything to provoke the situation.]

5. A person may use force upon another person, about to commit suicide or suffer serious bodily injury, to prevent the death or serious bodily injury of such other person. [Force can be used to prevent suicide.]

[Duty of Third Person to Retreat – Generally – Yes]

§ N.D.C.C. § 12.1-05-07 (2) (b).
Limits on the use of force – Excessive force – Deadly force.

. . .

2(b) ... An individual seeking to protect another individual must, before using deadly force, try to cause the other individual to retreat, or otherwise comply with the requirements of this provision, if safety can be obtained thereby.... [The duty to retreat applies to defense of other people just like it applies to defense of self. You must attempt to convince the other person you are defending to retreat if he could retreat safely to avoid your use of deadly force.]

. . .

[Exceptions to Justifiable Self-Defense]
[Initial Aggressor] [Provocation] [Mutual Combat]

§ **N.D.C.C. § 12.1-05-03.**
Self-defense.

. . .

2. A person is not justified in using force if:

   a. He intentionally provokes unlawful action by another person to cause bodily injury or death to such other person; or [Provoking a fight means starting a fight with someone hoping to use his reaction as justification to hurt or kill him. If you do this, you lose the right to defend yourself.]

[Exceptions to the Exceptions] [Withdraw and Communicate]

   b. He has entered into a mutual combat with another person or is the initial aggressor unless he is resisting force which is clearly excessive in the circumstances. A person's use of defensive force after he withdraws from an encounter and indicates to the other person that he has done so is justified if the latter nevertheless continues or menaces unlawful action. [If the responsive force is excessive — i.e., you flick someone's ear and they come at you with a knife — you can still have a self-defense claim even though you "started it." You can also have a self-defense claim if, after "starting it," you quit, tell your opponent you want to quit, and the guy keeps coming after you. It seems, based on the structure of the statute, that these exceptions to the exceptions only apply to initial aggressor/mutual combat situations — they don't apply if you provoked the conflict as an excuse to use force against someone. However, if things get this complicated in the analysis, you can bet you will be arrested and prosecuted.]

[Defense of Person(s) in Special Places – Dwelling, Workplace, or Occupied Travel Trailer or Motor Home]
[Presumption of Reasonableness in Special Places]

§ **N.D.C.C. § 12.1-05-07.1.**
Use of deadly force – Presumption of fear of death or serious bodily injury.

1. An individual is presumed to have held a reasonable fear of imminent peril of death or serious bodily injury to that individual or another when using deadly force if:

[The presumption applies if...]

   a. The individual against whom the deadly force was used was in the process of unlawfully and forcibly entering, or had unlawfully and forcibly entered and remains within a dwelling, place of work, or occupied motor home or travel trailer as defined in section **39-01-01** [see definitions below], or if the individual had removed or was attempting to remove another against that individual's will from the dwelling, place of work, or occupied motor home or travel trailer as defined in section **39-01-01**; and [It is presumed you are justified in using deadly force if someone who doesn't have a right to be in your home, workplace or travel trailer uses force to enter or attempt to enter by force. Under these circumstances, you do not have a duty to retreat before using deadly force, unless you started the fight or your assailant had a right to be in one of these special places. Examples of someone who has a right to be present in a home, workplace or travel trailer include family members, live-in lovers, co-employees or supervisors, or someone you have given permission to enter, such as a guest.]

b. The individual who uses deadly force knew or had reason to believe that an unlawful and forcible entry or unlawful and forcible act was occurring or had occurred. [This is the second important prerequisite to the presumption that you used deadly force legally. You must know or have reason to believe the person had unlawfully forced his way into your home, workplace or travel trailer. **Examples:** A co-worker you hate (gun owners must not hate) forgets his key one morning and in his frustration to be on time breaks and enters. You can't use deadly force against him just because he forcibly entered because you know he has a right to be in the workplace. Your kid's friend is having a bad influence on your kid, but generally he comes and goes in your house with your child's permission. One day you see him alone in the house and end up strangling him. You didn't know it, but he broke in. You admit to the police you didn't know he had broken in. The presumption does not apply and you will fry.]

2. The presumption in Subsection 1 may be rebutted by proof beyond a reasonable doubt that the individual who used the deadly force did not have a reasonable fear of imminent peril of death or serious bodily injury to that individual or another. [This is the huge difference between North Dakota's presumption law and Florida's after which this statute was patterned. If you read our commentary on Florida's presumption statute, you'll see some suggestion of it being a "conclusive presumption" (i.e., can't be rebutted by police and prosecutors). Florida's statute does not contain a paragraph like this paragraph specifically stating the presumption is rebuttable. Because of this paragraph in North Dakota's statute, it is crystal clear that the prosecutor can put on evidence that you did not believe the intruder posed an imminent threat of death or serious injury to yourself or others in your home. **Example:** You are extremely annoyed by the druggie who lives next door with his parents. He continues to throw used syringes onto your lawn, but you know he has no access to weapons and that he would never hurt anyone. Of course, you've told his parents that he's not welcome in your home or yard. One day you find the front door broken into and he's rummaging through your fridge for munchies. You positively identify the burglar as your annoying, harmless neighbor. You rationalize that he has broken into your home unlawfully by force so you greet him with a shotgun slug to the torso. You admit to police investigators you knew who the intruder was before you pulled the trigger. The presumption that you feared serious imminent harm is rebutted.]

3. The presumption in subsection 1 does not apply if the court finds that any of the following have occurred: [The presumption doesn't apply if...]

   a. The individual against whom the deadly force is used has the right to be in or is a lawful resident of the dwelling, place of work, or occupied motor home or travel trailer as defined in section **39-01-01**, including an owner, lessee, or title-holder, and there is not a temporary or permanent domestic violence protection order or any other order of no contact against that individual; [The "intruder' actually has a right to be there...i.e., cohabitant, guest, co-owner, landlord, mortgage holder, repo man. An exception would be an abusive husband who no longer has a legal right to be in the home because a judge has issued an order keeping him away from you and your home pending a divorce. See our chapter on domestic violence, Chapter 13.]

   b. The individual removed or sought to be removed is a child or grandchild, or is otherwise in the lawful custody or under the lawful guardianship of, the individual against whom the deadly force is used; [You can't settle custody or visitation disputes with deadly violence.]

   c. The individual who uses deadly force is engaged in the commission of a crime or is using the dwelling, place of work, or occupied motor home or travel trailer as defined in section **39-01-01** to further the commission of a crime; or [You are committing crimes in the home, workplace or motor home or you are using these special places to assist you in committing crimes. **Examples:** Using your home or workplace to grow marijuana or cook meth or using a motor home as a brothel on wheels.]

   d. The individual against whom the deadly force is used is a law enforcement officer who enters or attempts to enter a dwelling, place of work, or occupied motor home or travel trailer as defined in section **39-01-01** in the performance of official duties and the officer provided identification, if required, in accordance with any applicable law or warrant from a court, or if the individual using force knew or reasonably should have known that the individual entering or attempting to enter was a law enforcement officer. [**Example:** The SWAT team enters yelling, "Police! Police! Let's see your hands! Get down on the floor!" *Pancho's Wisdom* – The trouble with this provision is that home invaders may enter yelling the same thing. Any state that has this provision should beef-up their penalties against home invaders who would pose as police officers in order to secure an unfair advantage over armed homeowners.]

[No Duty to Retreat From Dwelling, Workplace, Occupied Motor Home or Travel Trailer]

§ N.D.C.C. § 12.1-05-07 Paragraph 2.b.(2).
Limits on the use of force – Excessive force – Deadly force,

. . . However, the duty to retreat or avoid force does not apply under the following circumstances:

. . .

[Co-Habitants; Co-Employees – Duty to Retreat – Yes]

(2) An individual is not required to retreat within or from that individual's dwelling or place of work or from an occupied motor home or travel trailer as defined in section **39-01-01**, unless the individual was the original aggressor or is assailed by another individual who the individual knows also dwells or works there or who is lawfully in the motor home or travel trailer. [You don't have to retreat in your home, an occupied trailer or motor home, or workplace unless you were the initial aggressor or the person attacking you lives with you or works with you and has a right to be in your home or workplace. **Example:** "Fats" Fonzberry, your co-worker at the supermarket butcher shop hears you've been flirting with his flame and comes at you with a meat cleaver. You can easily outrun the not-so-gentle giant. You run to sporting goods, pick up the .338 Win Mag, load it and splatter Fatso like a monster mosquito from Minot. The evidence shows you could have easily outrun him by simply leaving the store. The District Attorney will probably prosecute you claiming you could have safely retreated from your co-worker and therefore, your use of deadly force was not necessary.]

c. When used by an individual in possession or control of a dwelling, place of work, or an occupied motor home or travel trailer as defined in section **39-01-01**, or by an individual who is licensed or privileged to be there, if the force is necessary to prevent commission of arson, burglary, robbery, or a felony involving violence upon or in the dwelling, place of work, or occupied motor home or travel trailer, and the use of force other than deadly force for these purposes would expose any individual to substantial danger of serious bodily injury. [You don't have to retreat from your home, an occupied trailer or motor home (whether you own it or are legally in control of it), or work if you need to use deadly force to repel someone trying to commit arson, burglary, robbery, or a felony involving violence, and not using deadly force would expose you to danger of serious injury. Arson, burglary and robbery are defined at the end of this subchapter.

In the example under paragraph (2) above involving Fats, your attorney might argue that Fats was committing a violent felony (aggravated assault with a meat cleaver). Nevertheless, the way we read the statute, you would still be required to retreat if you could safely do so because Fats is a co-employee.]

[Reckless Injury to Innocent Third Parties]

§ **N.D.C.C. § 12.1-05-01 (2).**
Justification.

. . .

2. If a person is justified or excused in using force against another, but he recklessly or negligently injures or creates a risk of injury to other persons, the justifications afforded by this chapter are unavailable in a prosecution for such recklessness or negligence.

. . .

[If you are reckless or negligent in defending yourself causing injury to an innocent third party, you can still be prosecuted for crimes based upon recklessness and criminal negligence such as manslaughter (N.D.C.C. § 12.1-16-02) or criminal homicide (N.D.C.C. § 12.1-16-03). **Example:** A shotgun wielding robber holds up a convenience store threatening to immediately kill the clerk. You draw your pistol, close your eyes and empty the entire magazine despite the crowds of people waiting to pay. You would probably be justified in using deadly force against the robber. However, if one of your bullets goes astray and hits an innocent bystander, you may be found reckless or criminally negligent.]

[Civil Liability]

§ N.D.C.C. § 12.1-05-07.2. Immunity from civil liability for justifiable use of force.

1. An individual who uses force as permitted under this chapter is immune from civil liability for the use of the force to the individual against whom force was used or to that individual's estate unless that individual is a law enforcement officer who was acting in the performance of official duties and the officer provided identification, if required, in accordance with any applicable law or warrant from a court, or if the individual using force knew or reasonably should have known that the individual was a law enforcement officer. [You have civil immunity if you legally used force in self-defense. This eminently doesn't apply if the person injured was a policeman in performance of official duties who either (a) complied with any legal duty requiring him to provide identification or if (b) you reasonably should have known the "intruder" was a law enforcement officer.]

2. The court shall award reasonable attorney's fees and court costs and disbursements incurred by the defendant in defense of any civil action brought by a plaintiff if the court finds that the defendant is immune from civil liability as provided in subsection 1. [If you are not guilty by reason of self-defense, you are also not liable to the victim of your use of defensive force. If you are sued by a person you injured in self-defense or by his heirs if he is killed, and you win the civil case on the theory of self-defense, you can get your attorney fees and costs back from the person or persons who sued you. See a detailed discussion of the realities of civil liability in Chapter 15.]

[Defense of Property]

§ N.D.C.C. § 12.1-05-06. Use of force in defense of premises and property.

Force is justified if it is used to prevent or terminate an unlawful entry or other trespass in or upon premises, or to prevent an unlawful carrying away or damaging of property, if the person using such force first requests the person against whom such force is to be used to desist from his interference with the premises or property, except that a request is not necessary if it would be useless or dangerous to make the request or substantial damage would be done to the property sought to be protected before the request could effectively be made. [You can use non-deadly force to stop trespassing on your property or stealing personal property as long as you first ask the person to stop. However, you don't have to do this if the request would be useless, put you in danger, or if things were happening so fast that your property would be seriously damaged in the time it would take to issue the request. See a more detailed discussion of the risks of defending personal property in Chapter 4.]

[HELPFUL DEFINITIONS RELATING TO THIS STATE'S SELF-DEFENSE STATUTES]

- **Bodily injury** – means any impairment of physical condition, including physical pain. **N.D.C.C. § 12.1-01-04 (4).**

- **Deadly force** – means force which a person uses with the intent of causing, or which he knows creates a substantial risk of causing, death or serious bodily injury. A threat to cause death or serious bodily injury, by the production of a weapon or otherwise, so long as the actor's intent is limited to creating an apprehension that he will use deadly force if necessary, does not constitute deadly force. **N.D.C.C. § 12.1-05-12(1).**

- **Dwelling** – means any building or structure, though movable or temporary, or a portion thereof, which is for the time being a person's home or place of lodging. **N.D.C.C. § 12.1-05-12(2).**

- **Felonies Mentioned** –

    - **Arson** – [Intentionally starting a fire or causing an explosion with the purpose of destroying a building or inhabited structure or any part of one.] **N.D.C.C. § 12.1-21-01.**

    - **Burglary** – [Willfully entering or remaining surreptitiously in a building or occupied structure or any part of a building closed off to public with the intent to commit a crime therein.] **N.D.C.C. § 12.1-22-02.**

    - **Robbery** – [Inflicting or attempting to inflict bodily injury on another or threatening imminent bodily injury during the attempt or commission of a theft.] **N.D.C.C. § 12.1-22-01.**

- **Force** – means physical action, threat, or menace against another, and includes confinement. **N.D.C.C. § 12.1-05-12(3).**

- **Law enforcement officer or peace officer** – means a public servant authorized by law or by a government agency or branch to enforce the law and to conduct or engage in investigations or prosecutions for violations of law. **N.D.C.C. § 12.1-01-04 (17).**

- **Motor home** – means a motor vehicle which has been reconstructed or manufactured primarily for private use as a temporary or recreational dwelling and having at least four of the following permanently installed systems:

    a. Cooking facilities.

b. Icebox or mechanical refrigerator.

c. Potable water supply including plumbing and a sink with faucet either self-contained or with connections for an external source, or both.

d. Self-contained toilet or a toilet connected to a plumbing system with connection for external water disposal, or both.

e. Heating or air-conditioning system, or both, separate from the vehicle engine or the vehicle engine electrical system.

f. A 110-115 volt alternating current electrical system separate from the vehicle engine electrical system either with its own power supply or with a connection for an external source, or both, or a liquefied petroleum system and supply. **N.D.C.C. § 39-01-01 (27).**

- **Premises** – means all or any part of a building or real property, or any structure, vehicle, or watercraft used for overnight lodging of persons, or used by persons for carrying on business therein. **N.D.C.C. § 12.1-05-12(4).**

- **Property** – includes both real and personal property. **N.D.C.C. § 12.1-01-04 (26).**

- **Public servant** – as used in this title and in any statute outside this title which defines an offense means any officer or employee of government, including law enforcement officers, whether elected or appointed, and any person participating in the performance of a governmental function, but the term does not include witnesses. **N.D.C.C. § 12.1-01-04 (27).**

- **Serious bodily injury** – means bodily injury that creates a substantial risk of death or which causes serious permanent disfigurement, unconsciousness, extreme pain, permanent loss or impairment of the function of any bodily member or organ, a bone fracture, or impediment of air flow or blood flow to the brain or lungs. **N.D.C.C. § 12.1-01-04 (29).**

- **Travel trailer** – means a vehicular unit mounted on wheels, designed to provide temporary living quarters for recreational, camping, or travel use, and of such size or weight as not to require a special highway movement permit when towed by a motorized vehicle. **N.D.C.C. § 39-01-01 (87).**

[TEMPLATE Topics We Could Not Find Explained in Statutes or Cases]

(For each of these topics that we could not find addressed in your state's statutes or cases, we suggest you review the same topics in the subchapters of surrounding states. Your state's courts may look to the law of neighboring states to see how their courts and legislatures have treated that particular self-defense issue.)

[Committing Felony or Unlawful Act]

OHIO

There are several concerns about Ohio's self-defense laws. First, although there is a defense-of-home/occupied-vehicle statute, there is no general self-defense statute. Even though Ohio's criminal cases define Ohio's general law of self-defense, these cases are not easily accessed or understood by non-lawyers. This leaves citizens without any statutory notice of how to conduct themselves in defensive incidents that occur outside of their homes or occupied vehicles.

Ohio is the only state that we are aware of that still requires a defendant to prove the elements of self-defense by a preponderance of evidence (more likely than not). Unfortunately, the United States Supreme Court has held this is permissible. *Martin v. Ohio,* 480 U.S. 228 (1987).

Pancho's Wisdom – We think placing the burden on defendants to prove self-defense discourages citizens from defending themselves and, in turn, encourages attacks against the innocent. The citizens of Ohio should encourage their legislators to change this. Ohio should pass self-defense statutes based upon the Mother of All Self-Defense Laws or parts of it (See Chapter 20).

Key: ■ commentary ■ original statutes, cases or jury instructions

[Defense of Self and Others] [Non-Deadly Force]

"To establish self-defense against nondeadly force, the defendant must establish (1) that the defendant was not at fault in creating the situation giving rise to the altercation and (2) that he had reasonable grounds to believe and an honest belief, even though mistaken, that he was in imminent danger of bodily harm and his only means to protect himself from the danger was by the use of force not likely to cause death or great bodily harm." *State v. D.H.,* 865 N.E.2d 90, 99 (Ohio App. 2006). [It seems so unusual for an attorney to see phrases like "the defendant must establish" or "the defendant must prove" in a discussion of self-defense. Requiring a defendant to prove "an honest belief," pretty much compels him to testify in his own criminal case. We think it's backwards.]

[Deadly Force]

"In order to prove self-defense by means of deadly force, a defendant has to prove that '(1) he was not at fault in creating the situation giving rise to the shootings, (2) he had reasonable grounds to believe and an honest belief that he was in immediate danger of death or great bodily harm and that his only means of escape from such danger was by the use of deadly force, and (3) he had not violated any duty to escape to avoid the danger.'" *State v. Ludt,* 906 N.E.2d 1182, 1188 (Ohio App. 2009)(citation omitted).

[This is THE rule for self-defense cases in Ohio. It's called the *Robbins* Rule, and was formulated in the 1979 case of *State v. Robbins,* 58 Ohio St.2d 74, 388 N.E.2d 755. In developing the rule, the *Robbins* court cites previous cases for each element, some of which go back as far as the 1850's. As you'll notice in the case citation, three requirements are still in effect as of this year: (1) you can't be the initial aggressor, provoker, or instigator of the conflict, (2) you must have a reasonable fear of immediate death or serious injury and honestly believe the only way to avoid it is through use of deadly force and (3) you must retreat before using deadly force if you can do so in complete safety. You do not have a duty to retreat if attacked while in your home or occupied vehicle. For more details about the duty to retreat, see discussion below.]

"Self-defense has both objective and subjective elements. The defendant's fear of immediate death or great bodily harm must be objectively reasonable. In addition, Ohio has adopted a subjective test in determining whether a particular defendant properly acted in self-defense. The defendant's state of mind is crucial to this defense. ... Thus, there must be both reasonable (objective) grounds to believe that harm is imminent, and there must be an honest (subjective) belief that harm is imminent." *State v. Ludt,* 906 N.E.2d 1182, 1188 (Ohio App. 2009). [We're not quite sure how you prove an "honest belief" unless you get on the witness stand, look the jury in the eye and say, "I really believed I was going to die."]

[Defense of a Third Person]
"A person may use appropriate force to defend another person from imminent harm... A defendant invoking the privilege of defense of others is only entitled to use as much force as the person being defended was permitted to use." *State v. Ludt,* 906 N.E.2d 1182, 1188 (Ohio App. 2009).

"Under certain circumstances, a person may use appropriate force to defend another... However, "one who intervenes to help a stranger stands in the shoes of the person whom he is aiding, and if the person aided is the one at fault, then the intervenor is not justified in his use of force ... Moreover, in *State v. Smith...* the Fourth District Court of Appeals held that a person is not entitled to claim defense of another in regard to a physical altercation if the person being defended voluntarily entered the physical altercation." *State v. D.H.,* 865 N.E.2d 90, 99 (Ohio App. 2006).

[If the guy you're thinking of defending started the fight or was otherwise to blame for the conflict, you are not justified in defending him. This puts you at legal risk to rush to another person's defense.]

[Exceptions to Justifiable Self-Defense] [Initial Aggressor]
[Provocation] [Committing Felony or Unlawful Act]
"We have expressly rejected the trial court's view that Turner's involvement in criminal activity at the time of the alleged attack precluded a claim of self-defense. The first prong of a claim of self-defense-that the defendant was not at fault in creating the situation giving rise to the affray-does not preclude the defense if the defendant was engaged in criminal conduct when he was attacked. Rather, it requires a defendant to show that he was not at fault in creating the situation, i.e., that he had not engaged in

such wrongful conduct toward his assailant that the assailant was provoked to attack... As we said in *Turner I*, '[t]hat Turner was engaged in other criminal conduct when he caused the victim's death is immaterial, so long as his criminal conduct did not give rise to the affray and he was not the first aggressor . . .' We have also expressly rejected the view that possession of a firearm rises to a level of wrongdoing such that reasonable persons could not doubt the defendant's criminal liability." *State v. Turner*, 886 N.E.2d 280, 284 (Ohio App. 2008).

[**Translation:** You can't be at fault if you expect to be justified by reason of self-defense. However, this doesn't mean you can't claim self-defense if you were engaged in unlawful activity and didn't start the fight or provoke the attack. **Example:** You are stealing candy bars from a convenience store. Armed robbers come in threatening to kill everyone. You draw a gun and heroically save the day. If you were prosecuted for shooting one of the robbers, the prosecutor could not use the fact you were stealing candy bars to keep you from asserting self-defense. This is because your stealing candy bars had nothing to do with the armed robbery.]

[Exceptions to the Exceptions] [Withdraw and Communicate]

"The plea of self-defense is not available to a person who starts a fight unless, in good faith, he withdraws from the contest and informs the other party or parties of his withdrawal, or, by word or acts reasonably indicates that he has withdrawn and is no longer participating in the fight." *State v. Davis*, 456 N.E.2d 1256, 1260 (Ohio App. 1982). [You must prove you didn't start the fight. If you started it, before you are justified in using force to defend yourself, you must make it clear to the other guy you don't want to fight anymore.]

[Duty to Retreat – Generally – Yes]

"A person may not kill in self-defense if he has available a reasonable means of retreat from the confrontation..." *State v. Miller*, 778 N.E.2d 1103, 1105 (Ohio App. 2002). [You must retreat before using deadly force if it's reasonably safe to do so unless you are in your home or in your car when attacked. See discussion below.]

[Defense of Person(s) in Special Places – Residence, Occupied Vehicle]
[No Duty to Retreat from Home or Occupied Vehicle]

§ **O.R.C. § 2901.09.**
No duty to retreat.

(A) As used in this section, "residence" and "vehicle" have the same meanings as in section 2901.05 of the Revised Code.

(B) For purposes of any section of the Revised Code that sets forth a criminal offense, a person who lawfully is in that person's residence has no duty to retreat before using force in self-defense, defense of another, or defense of that person's residence, and a person who lawfully is an occupant of that person's vehicle or who lawfully is an occupant in a vehicle owned by an immediate family member of the person has no duty to retreat before using force in self-defense or defense of another.

[There is no duty to retreat before using defensive force if you are in your home, car or a car belonging to an immediate family member. Although not mentioned in the statute above, the no-duty-to-retreat rule that applies to one's home and car also applies to one's place of business. See *State v. Peacock,* 40 Ohio St. 333 (Ohio 1883), *Graham v. State, 120 N.E. 232* and *State v. Beach,* 583 N.E.2d 1097 (Ohio App. 8 Dist.1990).]

"In *Walton,* the defendant argued that because the shooting occurred on his front porch, he did not have a duty to retreat. This Court found otherwise and stated, '[a]t the point [defendant] left his apartment and stepped onto the concrete pad, he once again had a duty to retreat. The privilege to use force to repel an intruder does not permit a defendant to leave the sanctuary of his home to go after an anticipated intruder.' *Walton* at 8-9. Furthermore, it is settled law in several other districts that '[f]or purposes of self-defense, a duty to retreat extends to the driveway of one's own home.' *State v. Schumacher* (Nov. 2, 1998), 12th Dist. No. CA97-12-023, citing *Cleveland v. Hill* (1989), 63 Ohio App.3d 194, 199, 578 N.E.2d 509. See, also, *State v. Burns* (Aug. 3, 2000), 8th Dist. No. 69676; *State v. Smith* (June 27, 1995), 10th Dist. No. 94APA12-1702 (applying the Hill driveway analysis in the context of a sidewalk confrontation)." *State v. Lansberry,* not reported in N.E.2d, 2002 WL 1972918 (Ohio App. 9 Dist.2002).

[For purposes of a retreat analysis, your residence does not extend to your front porch. Therefore, you must retreat from your front porch. In other words, if you scare an intruder out of your home with your gun, don't be running out onto the front porch or driveway to shoot at him. Let him go and call the police.]

[Co-Habitants – Duty to Retreat – No]

"There is no duty to retreat from one's own home before resorting to lethal force in self-defense against a cohabitant with an equal right to be in the home." *State v. Ward,* 861 N.E.2d 823, 831 (Ohio App. 2006).

[Some states that recognize the castle doctrine still require you to retreat from a family member, roommate, girl or boyfriend. Ohio does not, but the presumption of reasonableness (explained below) does NOT apply against a co-habitant. So if you dust someone in self-defense who has a right to be in the home, you don't have to prove you couldn't retreat, but you still must prove you were without fault and reasonably believed you were in immediate danger of death or serious bodily injury.]

[Presumption of Reasonableness in Special Places – Residence, Occupied Vehicle]

§ O.R.C. § 2901.05 (B) and (D).

Presumption of innocence; proof of offense; of affirmative defense; as to each; reasonable doubt.

. . .

(B) (1) Subject to division (B)(2) of this section, a person is presumed to have acted in self-defense or defense of another when using defensive force that is intended or likely to cause death or great bodily harm to another if the person against whom the defensive force is used is in the process of unlawfully and without privilege to do so entering, or has unlawfully and without privilege to do so entered, the residence or vehicle occupied by the person using the defensive force.

(2) (a) The presumption set forth in division (B)(1) of this section does not apply if the person against whom the defensive force is used has a right to be in, or is a lawful resident of, the residence or vehicle.

(b) The presumption set forth in division (B)(1) of this section does not apply if the person who uses the defensive force uses it while in a residence or vehicle and the person is unlawfully, and without privilege to be, in that residence or vehicle.

(3) The presumption set forth in division (B)(1) of this section is a rebuttable presumption and may be rebutted by a preponderance of the evidence.

[If you use deadly force against an intruder, you are presumed to have acted in self-defense as long as the intruder is either entering or trying to enter your occupied house or vehicle unlawfully. However, the presumption doesn't apply if the "intruder" has a right to be there, or if you don't have a right to be there.]

. . .

(D) As used in this section:

(2) "Dwelling" means a building or conveyance of any kind that has a roof over it and that is designed to be occupied by people lodging in the building or conveyance at night, regardless of whether the building or conveyance is temporary or permanent or is mobile or immobile. As used in this division, a building or conveyance includes, but is not limited to, an attached porch, and a building or conveyance with a roof over it includes, but is not limited to, a tent. [Note here that dwelling includes, but is not limited to, porch. This means that the presumption extends to your porch. This sub-paragraph seems to conflict with the case we cited above which says you have a duty to retreat when on your porch (as opposed to no duty to retreat if you are in your home when attacked). The way we reconcile the apparent conflict is that you have a presumption that you acted in self-defense on your porch, but that if you're on your porch when attacked, you still must retreat if you can safely do so before using deadly force.]

(3) "Residence" means a dwelling in which a person resides either temporarily or permanently or is visiting as a guest.

(4) "Vehicle" means a conveyance of any kind, whether or not motorized, that is designed to transport people or property.

. . .

[Civil Liability]

[If you do something wrong and someone is injured, you can be held liable for the damages suffered by the injured person (See Chapter 15, Risk of Being Sued for Defending Yourself). Don't feel intellectually inferior if you have to read the statute below (O.R.C. § 2307.60 Civil action for damages for criminal act) sixteen times before you begin to understand it. Our researcher who is in the top 10% of his law class didn't understand this either until we went through it together, word-by-word. Mamas, don't let your babies grow up to write like legislators!

After dissecting the statute below like a frog in biology class, here's what we found out about suing and being sued in Ohio if you use a dangerous weapon to defend yourself:

1. Criminals hurting people are liable to the injured and can be forced to pay damages.

2. If you injure a person in self-defense to keep him from committing a felony or violent misdemeanor, he cannot hold you liable for damages.

3. If you intentionally hurt someone, they can hold you liable. This does not apply to self-defense. Police officers violating a criminal's civil rights (e.g., like the Rodney King case) could still be held liable under federal law.

4. If you wound or kill an innocent person while defending yourself from someone committing a felony or violent misdemeanor, you could be held liable to the innocent person.]

§ O.R.C. § 2307.60.
Civil action for damages for criminal act.

(A)(1) Anyone injured in person or property by a criminal act has, and may recover full damages in, a civil action unless specifically excepted by law, may recover the costs of maintaining the civil action and attorney's fees if authorized by any provision of the Rules of Civil Procedure or another section of the Revised Code or under the common law of this state, and may recover punitive or exemplary damages if authorized by section 2315.21 or another section of the Revised Code.

[If you are injured by a criminal act, you can sue the criminal for your injuries and not only get fair compensation for your damages, but you can get punitive damages to punish the criminal, plus recover your attorney fees. The problem is, how many people that commit violent crimes have enough assets to make it worthwhile to go after? It reminds us of the old saying, "You can't get blood out of a turnip." Most habitual, violent criminals are "turnips." You can win a big money damage award against them, but because they own nothing, the chances of ever collecting on your judgment is slim to none.]

(2) A final judgment of a trial court that has not been reversed on appeal or otherwise set aside, nullified, or vacated, entered after a trial or upon a plea of guilty, but not upon a plea of no contest or the equivalent plea from another jurisdiction, that adjudges an offender guilty of an offense of violence punishable by death or imprisonment in excess of one year, when entered as evidence in any subsequent civil proceeding based on the criminal act, shall preclude the offender from denying in the subsequent civil proceeding any fact essential to sustaining that judgment, unless the offender can demonstrate that extraordinary circumstances prevented the offender from having a full and fair opportunity to litigate the issue in the criminal proceeding or other extraordinary circumstances justify affording the offender an opportunity to relitigate the issue. The offender may introduce evidence of the offender's pending appeal of the

final judgment of the trial court, if applicable, and the court may consider that evidence in determining the liability of the offender.

[If the criminal who injured you gets convicted of a crime for causing your injury, you don't have to re-try a civil case against him. You can use the criminal verdict to prove his liability for your injuries. The only exception would be if the criminal introduces believable evidence that he didn't get a fair criminal trial for some reason. This works both ways. If you get convicted of a felony (e.g., aggravated assault) for what you thought was an act of self-defense, you could be held liable as well.]

(B) (1) As used in division (B) of this section:

(a) "Tort action" means a civil action for damages for injury, death, or loss to person or property other than a civil action for damages for a breach of contract or another agreement between persons. "Tort action" includes, but is not limited to, a product liability claim, as defined in section 2307.71 of the Revised Code, and an asbestos claim, as defined in section 2307.91 of the Revised Code, an action for wrongful death under Chapter 2125. of the Revised Code, and an action based on derivative claims for relief.

(b) "Residence" has the same meaning as in section 2901.05 of the Revised Code.

(2) Recovery on a claim for relief in a tort action [civil lawsuit for damages] is barred [can't sue & win] to any person [a criminal] or the person's legal representative [the criminal's heirs if he dies] if any of the following apply:

(a) The person has been convicted of or has pleaded guilty to a felony, or to a misdemeanor that is an offense of violence, arising out of criminal conduct that was a proximate cause of the injury or loss for which relief is claimed in the tort action. [If you are convicted of or plead guilty to a felony or violent misdemeanor which leads to your injury, you can't sue the person you think is otherwise responsible for your injuries. **Example:** You break into a home and the homeowner severs your spinal cord with a bullet to the neck. You can't sue him for your injury if you are convicted of burglary.]

(b) The person engaged in conduct that, if prosecuted, would constitute a felony, a misdemeanor that is an offense of violence, an attempt to commit a felony, or an attempt to commit a misdemeanor that is an offense of violence and that conduct was a proximate cause of the injury or loss for which relief is claimed in the tort action, regardless of whether the person has been convicted of or pleaded guilty to or has been charged with committing the felony, the misdemeanor, or the attempt to commit the felony or misdemeanor. [This goes a step further than the previous paragraph and says that it doesn't matter that you weren't convicted of a felony or violent misdemeanor. If you were committing an act that would have been a felony or violent misdemeanor and are injured because of it, you can't sue and win damages.]

(c) The person suffered the injury or loss for which relief is claimed in the tort action as a proximate result of the victim of conduct that, if prosecuted, would constitute a felony, a misdemeanor that is an offense of violence, an attempt to commit a felony, or an attempt to commit a misdemeanor that is an offense of violence acting against the person in self-defense, defense of another, or defense of the victim's residence, regardless of whether the person has been convicted of or pleaded guilty to or has been charged with committing the felony, the misdemeanor, or the attempt to commit the felony or misdemeanor. Division (B)(2)(c) of this section does not apply if the person who suffered the injury or loss, at the time of the victim's act of self-defense, defense of another, or defense of residence, was an innocent bystander who had no connection with the underlying conduct that prompted the victim's exercise of self-defense, defense of another, or defense of residence. [**Translation:** If a burglar breaks into your home (a felony) and is injured after you shoot him or at him, he cannot sue you and win damages. However, if you miss and hit an innocent bystander a half a mile away (you used a Barrett .50 BMG), the innocent bystander can still sue you and win.]

(3) Recovery against a victim of conduct that, if prosecuted, would constitute a felony, a misdemeanor that is an offense of violence, an attempt to commit a felony, or an attempt to commit a misdemeanor that is an offense of violence, on a claim for relief in a tort action is barred to any person or the person's legal representative if conduct the person engaged in against that victim was a proximate cause of the injury or loss for which relief is claimed in the tort action and that conduct, if prosecuted, would constitute a felony, a misdemeanor that is an offense of violence, an attempt to commit a felony, or an attempt to commit a misdemeanor that is an offense of violence, regardless of whether the person has been convicted of or pleaded guilty to or has been charged with committing the felony, the misdemeanor, or the attempt to commit the felony or misdemeanor. [This is confusing, but it seems if both the shooter and the shootee are guilty of felonies or violent misdemeanors, neither can recover money damages against the other for injuries.]

(4) Divisions (B)(1) to (3) of this section do not apply to civil claims based upon alleged intentionally tortious conduct, alleged violations of the United States Constitution, or alleged violations of statutes of the United States pertaining to civil rights. For purposes of division (B)(4) of this section, a person's act of self-defense, defense of another, or defense of the person's residence does not constitute intentionally tortious conduct. [If you intentionally injure a criminal, or if a state employee, like a police officer, commits a civil rights violation, then the criminal can still sue and win. But, a legitimate act of self-defense, defense of others or defense of home will not be considered an intentional act.]

§ O.R.C. § 2307.601.
Self-defense.

(A) As used in this section:

(1) "Residence" and "vehicle" have the same meanings as in section 2901.05 of the Revised Code.

(2) "Tort action" has the same meaning as in section 2307.60 of the Revised Code.

(B) For purposes of determining the potential liability of a person in a tort action related to the person's use of force alleged to be in self-defense, defense of another, or defense of the person's residence, if the person lawfully is in that person's residence, the person has no duty to retreat before using force in self-defense, defense of another, or defense of that person's residence, and, if the person lawfully is an occupant of that person's vehicle or lawfully is an occupant in a vehicle owned by an immediate family member of the person, the person has no duty to retreat before using force in self-defense or defense of another. [Just like you can't be found guilty for not retreating out of your home or car, you aren't liable either.]

§ O.R.C. § 2305.40.
Immunity from liability to trespassers.

(A) As used in this section:

(1) "Firearm" has the same meaning as in section **2923.11** of the Revised Code.

(2) "Tort action" means a civil action for damages for injury, death, or loss to person or property other than a civil action for damages for a breach of contract or another agreement between persons.

(3) "Vehicle" has the same meaning as in section **4501.01** of the Revised Code.

(B) (1) The owner, lessee, or renter of real property or a member of the owner's, lessee's, or renter's family who resides on the property is not liable in damages to a trespasser on the property, to a member of the family of the trespasser, or to any other person in a tort action for injury, death, or loss to person or property of the trespasser that allegedly is caused by the owner, lessee, renter, or family member if, at the time the injury, death, or loss to person or property allegedly is caused, all of the following apply:

[You won't be liable for civil damages if you harm a trespasser while defending your home/dwelling, so long as (all of these conditions must be met)...]

(a) The owner, lessee, renter, or family member is inside a building or other structure on the property that is maintained as a permanent or temporary dwelling;

[You're in the house/dwelling...]

(b) The trespasser has made, is making, or is attempting to make an unlawful entry into the building or other structure described in division (B)(1)(a) of this section;

[. . . and someone is coming or is trying to come in unlawfully...]

(c) The owner, lessee, renter, or family member uses reasonably necessary force to repel the trespasser from the building or other structure described in division (B)(1)(a) of this section or to prevent the trespasser from making the unlawful entry into that building or other structure.

[. . . and you use reasonable force.]

(2) For purposes of the immunity created by division (B)(1) of this section, reasonably necessary force to repel a trespasser from a building or other structure that is maintained as a permanent or temporary dwelling or to prevent a trespasser from making an unlawful entry into a building or other structure of that nature may include the taking of or attempting to take the trespasser's life, or causing or attempting to cause physical harm or serious physical harm to the person of the trespasser, if the owner, lessee, or renter of real property or a member of the owners, lessee's, or renters family who resides on the property has a reasonable good faith belief that the owner, lessee, or renter or a member of the owner's, lessee's, or renter's family is in imminent danger of death or serious physical harm to person and that the only means to escape from the imminent danger is to use deadly force or other force that likely will cause physical harm or serious physical harm to the person of the trespasser, even if the owner, lessee, renter, or family member is mistaken as to the existence or imminence of the danger of death or serious physical harm to person.

[Reasonable force can be deadly force as long as there is a reasonable fear of imminent death or serious injury, and there was no other way to escape besides using deadly force. This fear can be based upon a mistaken belief as long as the belief is reasonable. The phrase "only means to escape" makes us a little nervous. It almost implies a duty to retreat despite paragraph (3) immediately below that says you don't have to retreat from your home to qualify for the immunity.]

(3) In order to qualify for the immunity created by division (B)(1), of this section, an owner, lessee, or renter of real property or a member of the owner's, lessee's, or renter's family who resides on the property is not required to retreat from a building or other structure that is maintained as a permanent or temporary dwelling prior to using reasonably necessary force to repel a trespasser from the building or other structure or to prevent a trespasser from making an unlawful entry into the building or other structure.

[There is no duty to retreat in order to qualify for the civil immunity if the building is being used as a dwelling (home).]

(C) The owner, lessee, or renter of real property or a member of the owner's, lessee's, or renter's family who resides on the property is not liable in damages to a trespasser on the property, to a member of the family of the trespasser, or to any other person in a tort action for injury, death, or loss to person or property of the trespasser that allegedly is caused by the owner, lessee, renter, or family member under circumstances not covered by division (B)(1) of this section if, at the time the injury, death, or loss to person or property allegedly is caused, none of the following applies:

[You don't have immunity if...]

(1) The injury, death, or loss to person or property is caused by a physical assault of the owner, lessee, renter, or family member upon the trespasser other than in self-defense or defense of a third person.

[... you injure or kill someone and it's not in self-defense or defense of another ...]

(2) Self-defense or defense of a third person is not involved, and the injury, death, or loss to person or property is caused by a vehicle driven or otherwise set in motion, a firearm shot, or any other item of tangible personal property held, driven, set in motion, projected, or thrown by the owner, lessee, renter, or family member with the intent to cause injury, death, or loss to person or property of the trespasser or with the intent to cause the trespasser to believe that the owner, lessee, renter, or family member would cause injury, death, or loss to person or property of the trespasser.

[. . . if, not in self-defense or defense of another, you drive a car at, shoot at, or do anything else intended to kill or injure a trespasser or put him in fear of death or injury.]

(3) Under circumstances not described in division (C)(1) or (2) of this section, self-defense or defense of a third person is not involved, and the owner, lessee, renter, or family member intends to create a risk of injury, death, or loss to person or property of any trespasser by direct or indirect means, including, but not limited to, the use of spring guns, traps, or other dangerous instrumentalities.

[There is no immunity from liability if you use deadly traps with the intent to create a risk of death or serious injury to a trespasser. Spring guns are generally firearms rigged to fire when someone trips a wire or string. Traps like this don't have the ability to distinguish between a burglar breaking into your house or a bunch of 12 year olds playing Hide-And-Go-Seek. Therefore, the law does not favor their use. You have no civil immunity (your wallet is up for grabs) if you set such traps. In fact, if you injure someone with a deadly trap you will probably be arrested, prosecuted, convicted, sued and be held liable for the injuries.]

. . .

[Defense of Property]

"While a person has a right to protect his property from a trespass, and, after warning or notice to the trespasser, use such force as is reasonably necessary so to do, he cannot unlawfully use fire arms [sic] to expel the intruder where he has no reasonable ground to fear the trespasser will do him great bodily harm... Once again, if a person brandishes a deadly weapon to expel trespassers, then the defense-of-property argument would necessarily need to include proof of his fear of death or great bodily harm, rather than simple fear of any bodily harm." *State v. Ludt*, 906 N.E.2d 1182, 1188 (Ohio App. 2009). [You can use reasonable force to protect your property, but not deadly force. Check out the comprehensive definition of property in the following section.]

[HELPFUL DEFINITIONS RELATING TO THIS STATE'S SELF-DEFENSE STATUTES]

[No Felonies Mentioned]

- **Force** – means any violence, compulsion, or constraint physically exerted by any means upon or against a person or thing. **O.R.C § 2901.01 (A) (1).**

- **Deadly force** – means any force that carries a substantial risk that it will proximately result in the death of any person. **O.R.C § 2901.01 (A) (2).**

- **Physical harm to persons** – means any injury, illness, or other physiological impairment, regardless of its gravity or duration. **O.R.C § 2901.01 (A) (3).**

- **Physical harm to property** – means any tangible or intangible damage to property that, in any degree, results in loss to its value or interferes with its use or enjoyment. "Physical harm to property" does not include wear and tear occasioned by normal use. **O.R.C § 2901.01 (A) (4).**

- **Serious physical harm to persons** – means any of the following:

  (a) Any mental illness or condition of such gravity as would normally require hospitalization or prolonged psychiatric treatment;

  (b) Any physical harm that carries a substantial risk of death;

  (c) Any physical harm that involves some permanent incapacity, whether partial or total, or that involves some temporary, substantial incapacity;

  (d) Any physical harm that involves some permanent disfigurement or that involves some temporary, serious disfigurement;

  (e) Any physical harm that involves acute pain of such duration as to result in substantial suffering or that involves any degree of prolonged or intractable pain. **O.R.C § 2901.01 (A) (5).**

- **Serious physical harm to property** – means any physical harm to property that does either of the following:

  (a) Results in substantial loss to the value of the property or requires a substantial amount of time, effort, or money to repair or replace;

  (b) Temporarily prevents the use or enjoyment of the property or substantially interferes with its use or enjoyment for an extended period of time. O.R.C § 2901.01 (A) (6).

- **Risk** – means a significant possibility, as contrasted with a remote possibility, that a certain result may occur or that certain circumstances may exist. **O.R.C § 2901.01 (A) (7).**

- **Substantial risk** – means a strong possibility, as contrasted with a remote or significant possibility, that a certain result may occur or that certain circumstances may exist. **O.R.C § 2901.01 (A) (8).**

- **Property** – means any property, real or personal, tangible or intangible, and any interest or license in that property. "Property" includes, but is not limited to, cable television service, other telecommunications service, telecommunications devices, information service, computers, data, computer software, financial instruments associated with computers, other documents associated with computers, or copies of the documents, whether in machine or human readable form, trade secrets, trademarks, copyrights, patents, and property protected by a trademark, copyright, or patent. "Financial instruments associated with computers" include, but are not limited to, checks, drafts, warrants, money orders, notes of indebtedness, certificates of deposit, letters of credit, bills of credit or debit cards, financial transaction authorization mechanisms, marketable securities, or any computer system representations of any of them.

  (b) As used in division (A)(10) of this section, "trade secret" has the same meaning as in section 1333.61 of the Revised Code, and "telecommunications service" and "information service" have the same meanings as in section 2913.01 of the Revised Code.

  (c) As used in divisions (A)(10) and (13) of this section, "cable television service," "computer," "computer software," "computer system," "computer network," "data," and "telecommunications device" have the same meanings as in section 2913.01 of the Revised Code. **O.R.C § 2901.01 (A) (10).**

[TEMPLATE Topics We Could Not Find Explained in Statutes or Cases]

(For each of these topics that we could not find addressed in your state's statutes or cases, we suggest you review the same topics in the subchapters of surrounding states. Your state's courts may look to the law of neighboring states to see how their courts and legislatures have treated that particular self-defense issue.)

[Mutual Combat]

[Use of Deadly Force to Prevent Serious Felonies]

[Co-Employees – Duty to Retreat]

[Reckless Injury to Innocent Third Parties]

WARNING: Relying solely upon the language of Oklahoma's justifiable homicide statute, § 21-733, could be legally disastrous! Its meaning has been altered drastically by the Oklahoma courts. Luckily, Oklahoma has a wonderful set of jury instructions available to the public at http://www.okcca.net/online/oujis/oujisrvr.jsp. It is a service provided by a committee appointed by the Oklahoma Court of Appeals. The Committee incorporates the limitations placed upon the law of self-defense by Oklahoma cases. We think this effort by the Oklahoma Appeals Court Committee is a masterful work and we congratulate Committee members on their efforts. As confusing as the statutes and case law are, we are very impressed with how the Committee has boiled each instruction down into a fairly simple statement of the law synthesized from both statutes and cases; a brilliant work in our opinion.

Rather than confuse you with the statutes themselves, some of which have been gutted by case law, for the most part we have simply quoted the jury instructions themselves. In addition to jury instructions there are what is referred to as "Notes on Use" and "Committee Comments" that follow each jury instruction on the website. These were written by the Committee to explain how the jury instructions are used and how the instruction differs from the language of the statute as a result of interpreting case law. These notes and comments are very informative, so we included several in whole and in part. Because of space limitations we left out some of the less relevant jury instructions. For example, instructions concerning excusable homicides are generally used when a killing is an accident or when you use non-deadly force and your assailant unexpectedly dies. Because these instructions do not specifically define your right to use non-deadly versus deadly force, they are more for your attorney's consideration rather than for your self-defense education.

Pancho's Wisdom – The Oklahoma Legislature needs to amend Oklahoma's outdated statutes so that they correctly state the law as interpreted by the courts. Otherwise, citizens may read and rely upon them and conduct themselves contrary to Oklahoma case law which most citizens have no ready access to. It is grossly unfair to misstate the law in a state statute and then hold a citizen accountable for relying upon it. The Committee Notes we included below describe some of the drastic differences between the wording of Oklahoma's self-defense statutes and how the Oklahoma courts have interpreted these statutes.

Key: ■ commentary ■ original statutes, cases or jury instructions

[Defense of Self] [Non-Deadly Force]

OUJI-CR 8-48 – [**Translation:** Oklahoma Uniform Jury Instruction – Criminal 8-48]
DEFENSE OF SELF-DEFENSE –
JUSTIFIABLE USE OF NONDEADLY FORCE

A person is justified in using force in self-defense if that person reasonably believed that use of force was necessary to protect himself from imminent danger of bodily harm. Self-defense is a defense although the danger to personal security may not have been real, if a reasonable person, in the circumstances and from the viewpoint of the defendant, would reasonably have believed that he was in imminent danger of bodily harm. The amount of force used may not exceed the amount of force a reasonable person, in the circumstances and from the viewpoint of the defendant, would have used to prevent the bodily harm. [This is very similar to most states' non-deadly force statutes. Notice how it incorporates the concept of reasonable belief and warns against the use of excessive force. See Chapter 3 for expanded and simplified explanations of these concepts.] **Statutory Authority: 21 O.S. 1991, § 643(3)** [Oklahoma Code Section dealing with the use of non-deadly force].

Committee Comments – Subdivision 3 of section 643 presents the statutory authorization for use of nondeadly force in self-defense. Although the proviso clause of section 643(3) seems to indicate that a person using force to protect himself is limited to the amount of force "sufficient to prevent" bodily harm, and no more, the Court of Criminal Appeals has interpreted section 643(3) to permit a person to use as much force as reasonably appears necessary, even though in reality no force is necessary. [This interpretation by the courts is actually favorable to a defender. Most court interpretations of Oklahoma's self-defense statutes are less favorable to someone defending himself or others, as you will see in the material that follows.] Moreover, section 643(3) permits the use of force in self-defense against any bodily harm that appears imminent, such as a simple assault or a simple battery. Use of nondeadly force is justifiable even though the harm defended against does not reasonably arouse fear of death or great bodily harm. [Following are citations of the cases that interpret Section 643, Oklahoma's non-deadly force self-defense statute. If you are interested in reading Oklahoma's self-defense cases, you can do so in any law-school or court law library. Relying upon the southern hospitality we have experienced, we expect most law librarians or law students studying in these law libraries would be happy to take a moment to point out to you where the books are that contain these cases and how the numbering system works.] *Johnson v. State*, 59 Okl. Cr. 283, 58 P.2d 156 (1936). See *Boston v. Muncie*, 204 Okl. 603, 233 P.2d 300 (1951). Section 643(3) therefore differs from section 733 [Oklahoma's deadly-force or justifiable homicide statute], in two respects: (1) only nondeadly force is permissible under section 643(3) as opposed to deadly force under section 733; and, (2) any bodily harm may be defended against under section 643(3), whereas, under section 733, the harm must potentially be death or great bodily harm.

The amount of nondeadly force permissible under section 643(3) must be reasonably related to the amount of force defended against. Hence, as the amount of force defended against becomes greater, the amount of force which may justifiably be used in response becomes greater. Of course, if the person claiming self-defense uses excessive force, the defense of self-defense does not justify the excessive force. *Easterling v. State*, 267 P.2d 185 (Okl. Cr. 1954). If the force defended against puts a person in reasonable fear of imminent death or great bodily harm, the permissible force in response can be deadly force, and the defense of self-defense changes from self-defense under section 643(3) to self-defense under section 733. Mere threats, however, do not justify the use of force by the defendant, and the defendant could be convicted of assault or battery. Brewer v. State, 84 Okl. Cr. 235, 180 P.2d 848 (1947). [*Pancho's Wisdom* – Oh, that every state could provide such helpful commentary and simple jury instructions on the Internet. Ideally, the website address would be given to EVERY person buying a gun, knife or other object that is customarily used as a weapon (nunchucks, swords, ninja throwing stars, whatever).]

[Defense of Third Persons – Non-Deadly Force (Cont.)]

OUJI-CR 8-4 – DEFENSE OF ANOTHER – JUSTIFIABLE USE OF NONDEADLY FORCE

A person is justified in using force in defense of another if that person reasonably believed that use of force was necessary to protect another from imminent danger of bodily harm. Defense of another is a defense although the danger to the personal security of another may not have been real, if a reasonable person, in the circumstances and from the viewpoint of the defendant, would reasonably have believed that another was in imminent danger of bodily harm. The amount of force used may not exceed the amount of force a reasonable person, in the circumstances and from the viewpoint of the defendant, would have used to prevent the bodily harm. **Statutory Authority: 21 O.S. 1991, § 643(3).**

Committee Comments – . . . the above instruction is practically identical to the instruction on justifiable use of nondeadly force in self-defense. . . one who goes to the aid of another acts at his own peril, for the right to act in defense of that other is coextensive with the other's right to defend himself at that time, under those circumstances. [**Warning:** You only have as much right to defend another as he has to defend himself. If he started a fight, agreed to fight or provoked the fight as an excuse to hurt the person you protect him from, you are not justified in using force to defend him. See the instructions, commentary and explanations below **[Exceptions to Self-Defense]**].

OUJI-CR 8-3 – DEFENSE OF PERSON – JUSTIFIABLE USE OF FORCE TO PREVENT OFFENSE

A person is justified in using reasonable force in aid or defense of another person who is about to be injured during the commission of a crime. **Statutory Authority: 22 O.S. 1991, § 33.**

Notes on Use – This instruction is appropriate where the defendant used reasonable force to prevent a crime in which personal injury was imminent. [Notice there is nothing in this instruction (nor in the statute, §33) that justifies using deadly force. As explained below, you may only use deadly force to prevent the commission of a crime if the crime involves an imminent threat of serious injury or death.]

[Deadly Force]

OUJI-CR 8-46 – DEFENSE OF SELF-DEFENSE – JUSTIFIABLE USE OF DEADLY FORCE

A person is justified in using deadly force in self-defense if that person reasonably believed that use of deadly force was necessary to protect himself from imminent danger of death or great bodily harm. Self-defense is a defense although the danger to life or personal security may not have been real, if a reasonable person, in the circumstances and from the viewpoint of the defendant, would reasonably have believed that he was in imminent danger of death or great bodily harm. **Statutory Authority: 21 O.S. 1991, § 733.** [This jury instruction, as the comments below explain, embodies all that is left of Oklahoma's Justifiable Homicide statute §733 after the Oklahoma courts have whittled away at it for years. The plain language of the statute says you can kill criminals committing felonies, running away after committing felonies, causing riots, and disturbing the peace. We included section 733 below. **READ IT BUT DON'T BELIEVE IT!** We only included it to emphasize how much trouble a citizen would be in if he relied upon the plain meaning of the words in a self-defense incident. After being worn away for years by court decisions, all there is left is that you can only use deadly force if you do so to stop an immediate threat of serious injury or death against yourself or a limited group of persons as explained in the section below. Oklahoma's home-defense statute, patterned after Florida's, is much more protective, however. It is explained under **[Defense of Special Places]** below.]

Committee Comments – . . . [Explaining why §733 doesn't mean what it says.]

Despite the language of subsection 1, "[w]hen resisting any attempt ... to commit any felony upon him," and despite the language of subsection 2, "when there is a reasonable ground to apprehend a design to commit a felony," the Court of Criminal Appeals has held that not every felony permits a person to use deadly force to prevent commission of that felony. In *Mammano v. State,* 333 P.2d 602 (Okl. Cr. 1958), the deceased grabbed the defendant's hands and placed them on his private parts. The defendant killed the deceased and pleaded subsections 1 and 2 in justification. The court held that the acts of the deceased alone did not justify the homicide because the acts of the deceased did not involve imminent danger of death or great bodily harm to the defendant. . . . Only those felonies which involve danger of imminent death or great bodily harm may be defended against by the use of deadly force. . . .

In light of *Mammano,* the Commission has concluded that a homicide is "necessarily committed ... to apprehend any person for any felony" under subsection 3 only when the person attempting to apprehend the felon is put in imminent danger of death or great bodily harm. . . .

Subsection 3 of section 733 also contains the language, "in lawfully suppressing any riot; or in lawfully keeping and preserving the peace." Research has shown . . . that a homicide is "necessarily committed" when preserving the peace only in those situations in which the peacemaker is in imminent danger of death or great bodily harm. . . Similarly, the Commission has concluded that use of deadly force is justifiable when suppressing a riot only in those situations in which [there is an imminent threat of serious injury or death] . . .

Fear alone does not justify a homicide . . . nor may a homicide be justified because of threats or insults by the decedent . . . nor may a defendant kill and be justified when acting simply on subjective honest belief. . . Rather, a homicide is justifiable when a reasonable person would have used deadly force (citations omitted).

[No Duty to Retreat Generally]
[Use of Deadly Force to Prevent Serious Felonies]

OUJI-CR 8-15A – DEFENSE OF PERSON – RIGHT TO STAND YOUR GROUND

A person has no duty to retreat and has the right to stand his ground and meet force with force, including deadly force, if he is not engaged in an unlawful activity and is attacked in any place where he has a right to be, if he reasonably believes it is necessary to do so to prevent death or great bodily harm to himself or another. Or to prevent the commission of a forcible felony). **Statutory Authority: 21 O.S.Supp. 2007, § 1289.25 (D), (F).** [You have no duty to retreat before using defensive force in Oklahoma unless you are a trespasser, start a fight or agree to a fight. Furthermore, paragraph D of the new home-defense statute authorizes the use of deadly force to prevent the commission of a forcible felony whether in or outside of one's home or occupied vehicle. Forcible felony is not defined in the Oklahoma code. A definition that an Oklahoma court might use is found in Georgia's code: "A forcible felony means any felony that involves the use or threat of physical force or violence against any person." Ga. Code Ann., § 16-1-3(b)(6).]

[ACTUAL TEXT OF OKLAHOMA'S DEADLY FORCE STATUTE (for illustrative purposes only)]

[Warning: the following statute has been gutted by Oklahoma cases to the point you can no longer rely upon what it says. See, rather, the jury instructions, comments and explanations in the jury instructions above. We've included this code section simply to show you how misleading these outdated statutes can be.]

21 Okl.St.Ann. § 733 Justifiable homicide by any person [Oklahoma case law has altered the meaning of this statute as follows]

Homicide is also justifiable when committed by any person in either of the following cases:

1. When resisting any attempt to murder such person [yes, you can still use deadly force against someone who is trying to murder you], or to commit any felony upon him [not true, the felony must involve a threat of serious injury or death], or upon or in any dwelling house in which such person is [Not true. Your right to defend your home is as described in the "Defense of Special Places" statute below]; or,

2. When committed in the lawful defense of such person, or of his or her husband, wife, parent, child, master, mistress ["mistress" means woman employer, NOT

paramour], or servant, [These are the only third persons you can defend when using deadly force.] when there is a reasonable ground to apprehend a design to commit a felony [not true, you may only use deadly force to prevent felonies that threaten serious injuries and death], or to do some great personal injury, and imminent danger of such design being accomplished [yes]; or,

3. When necessarily committed in attempting, by lawful ways and means, to apprehend any person for any felony committed [no, only felonies involving serious injury or death]; or in lawfully suppressing any riot [no, only acts threatening imminent death or serious injury]; or in lawfully keeping and preserving the peace [no, only acts threatening imminent death or serious injury].

[Defense of Third Persons – Deadly Force (Cont.)]

OUJI-CR 8-2 – DEFENSE OF ANOTHER – JUSTIFIABLE USE OF DEADLY FORCE

A person is justified in using deadly force in defense of his or her husband, wife, parent, child, master, mistress, and servant [hereinafter "the special person"] if that person reasonably believed that use of deadly force was necessary to protect [the special person] from imminent danger of death or great bodily harm. Defense of another is a defense although the danger to the life or personal security of [the special person] may not have been real, if a reasonable person, in the circumstances and from the viewpoint of the defendant, would reasonably have believed that [the special person] was in imminent danger of death or great bodily harm. **Statutory Authority: 21 O.S. 1991, § 733(2).**

Committee Comments – Since section 733(2) also deals with self-defense, cases that have interpreted the language of the subsection in self-defense cases should be authoritative as to the meaning of the statutory language when defense of another is the defense urged. It must be emphasized that the existence of this defense, defense of another, is dependent upon whether that other would be permitted, under the circumstances, to defend himself. The general rule that an individual who intervenes to abort a difficulty among others stands in the place of the person whom he defends, and must accept all responsibilities and liabilities of the person whom he aids by his intervention, obtains under section 733. Therefore, whether the defendant's conduct is justifiable is dependent upon whether the person defended would be innocent or guilty had he exerted the same degree of force in the same manner in his own defense. . . [in other words, if the person you are defending is guilty of starting a fight, agreeing to fight or provoking a fight in order to hurt his opponent, he can't assert self-defense so neither can you (see exceptions below). It's a huge legal risk to step in to defend one of two or more persons in a fight.]

Use of deadly force in defense of another is limited to instances in which the other person is in imminent danger of death or great bodily harm, even though the statutory language would seem to indicate that deadly force could be used to protect another from "a felony"—any felony. The language "a felony" is limited to those that involve imminent danger of death or great bodily harm to the other person. See *Garrett v. State*, 586 P.2d 754 (Okl. Cr. 1978) (justifiable homicide not warranted where defendant shot deceased and three others to prevent continued statutory rape of her foster daughter;

the daughter was not in imminent danger and defendant had previous knowledge of the relationship); . . .

Numerous cases have held that, when acting in defense of another, the danger need not be actual so long as the defendant reasonably believes the danger to exist and to be imminent. Moreover, these cases also hold that the circumstances are to be considered from the viewpoint of the defendant. E.g., Hendrick v. State, 63 Okl. Cr. 100, 73 P.2d 184 (1937); *Litchfield v. State*, 8 Okl. Cr. 164, 126 P. 707 (1912); *Clemmons v. State*, 8 Okl. Cr. 159. 126 P. 704 (1912).

The statutory language also limits the instances in which use of deadly force in defense of another is justifiable to specific, named persons. The Court of Criminal Appeals has refused to extend the justification beyond the statutory language. *Cowles v. State*, 636 P.2d 342, 345 (Okl. Cr. 1981) (defendant's companion was not within the limited group of persons for whom fatal force in their defense is justifiable); *Haines v. State*, 275 P.2d 347 (Okl. Cr. 1954) (homicide in defense of mistress/paramour not justifiable; mistress in statute means female counterpart of master); *Chapman v. State*, 84 Okl. Cr. 41, 178 P.2d 638 (1947) (alleged common law husband).

[Exceptions to Justifiable Self-Defense] [Initial Aggressor] [Provocation] [Mutual Combat]

[Persons who start, escalate or agree to fight are not entitled to claim self-defense. If you act to defend someone who has started, escalated or agreed to fight, you can't claim defense of another. The exception is if the aggressor withdraws and plainly communicates his or her intent to withdraw. When it gets this complicated, the popo's going to arrest and let the jury sort it out. Don't go around getting into fights expecting to claim self-defense.]

OUJI-CR 8-9 – DEFENSE OF ANOTHER – AGGRESSOR DEFINED

A person is an aggressor when that person by his/her wrongful conduct provokes, brings about, or continues an altercation. The use of words alone cannot make a person an aggressor. [Self explanatory.]

Committee Comments – The above four instructions reflect the case law that one who intervenes on behalf of another intervenes at his own risk. A defendant is entitled to the defense of defense of another only when the person defended is not at fault in the altercation. If the person defended is at fault, even if the defendant is unaware of who is at fault, the defense of defense of another does not exist. Hence, although the defendant is entitled to act on reasonable appearances, he is entitled to the defense of defense of another only as long as he has chosen correctly to act on behalf of the party not at fault in the altercation, or the party who has attempted to terminate the altercation.

OUJI-CR 8-50 – DEFENSE OF SELF-DEFENSE – WHEN DEFENSE NOT AVAILABLE

Self-defense is permitted a person solely because of necessity. Self-defense is not available to a person who or was the aggressor or provoked another with the intent to cause the altercation or voluntarily entered into mutual combat, no matter how great the danger to personal security became during the altercation unless the right of self-defense is reestablished.

OUJI-CR 8-6 – DEFENSE OF ANOTHER – WHEN DEFENSE NOT AVAILABLE

Defense of another is permitted as a defense solely because of necessity. Defense of another is not available to a defendant when the person on whose behalf the defendant intervened was the aggressor or provoked another with the intent to cause the altercation or voluntarily entered into mutual combat, no matter how great the danger to personal security became during the altercation unless the right of defense of another is reestablished. [You're toast if you defend someone who doesn't have the legal right to defend himself.]

[Exceptions to the Exceptions] [Withdraw and Communicate]

OUJI-CR 8-51 – DEFENSE OF SELF-DEFENSE – DEFENSE REESTABLISHED

A person who was the original aggressor or provoked another with intent to cause the altercation or voluntarily entered into mutual combat may regain the right to self-defense if that person withdrew or attempted to withdraw from the altercation and communicated his desire to withdraw to the other participant(s) in the altercation. If, thereafter, the other participant(s) continued the altercation, the other participant(s) became the aggressor(s) and the person who was the original aggressor or provoked another with the intent to cause the altercation or voluntarily entered into mutual combat is entitled to the defense of self-defense. [This the typical exception to the exceptions to self-defense as explained in Chapter 4. You lose the right to use defensive force if you start a fight, start a fight as an excuse to hurt someone when he reacts, or you mutually agree to fight. But you can regain the right if you (1) withdraw (meaning retreat if possible), (2) effectively communicate you are withdrawing and (3) the other guy becomes the aggressor.]

OUJI-CR 8-7 – DEFENSE OF ANOTHER – DEFENSE REESTABLISHED

If the person on whose behalf the defendant intervened was the original aggressor or provoked another with the intent to cause the altercation or voluntarily entered into mutual combat but withdrew or attempted to withdraw from the altercation and communicated his desire to withdraw to the other participant(s) in the altercation, then the defendant would be entitled to the defense of defense of another. [The same rule stated in Jury Instruction 8-51 above applies to the defense of third persons. You have no right to defend one of the special people (spouse, mistress, etc.) if that person initiated, provoked or mutually agreed to fight. But you regain the right if she withdraws, communicates her withdrawal and her opponent becomes the aggressor. In both cases, you will probably be arrested and prosecuted so the jury can sort out the whether all the steps were accomplished to regain the right of self-defense.]

[No Duty to Retreat – Generally]

OUJI-CR 8-52 – DEFENSE OF SELF-DEFENSE – NO DUTY TO RETREAT

A person who was not the aggressor or did not provoke another with intent to cause an altercation or did not voluntarily enter into mutual combat has no duty to retreat, but may stand firm and use the right of self-defense. [If you are completely innocent, you have no duty to retreat before using force in self-defense. However, as explained above, you must retreat if you started a fight, agreed to fight, or provoked a fight. You must also retreat if you were trespassing when attacked. See jury instructions below.]

[Exception – Trespassers Must Retreat]

OUJI-CR 8-54 – DEFENSE OF SELF-DEFENSE – AVAILABILITY TO A TRESPASSER

The defense of self-defense is available to a person who was a trespasser only if the trespasser availed or attempted to avail himself of a reasonable means of retreat from the imminent danger of death or great bodily harm or bodily harm before repelling or attempting to repel an unlawful attack.

OUJI-CR 8-10 -DEFENSE OF ANOTHER – WHEN PERSON AIDED IS A TRESPASSER

Defense of another is available to a defendant when the person on whose behalf the defendant intervened was a trespasser only if the trespasser availed or attempted to avail himself of any reasonably safe means of retreat from the imminent danger of death or great bodily harm or bodily harm before repelling or attempting to repel an unlawful attack. [This instruction shows the risk of defending another person. If you don't know he was trespassing and hadn't retreated before you showed up to save the day, whatever use of force you use to defend the trespasser is not justified. You had better know the facts before you go rushing into a rescue in a blaze of glory. As you can see, defending another person in Oklahoma is fraught with legal risks.]

[Defense of Person(s) in Special Places – Home and Occupied Vehicle]
[Presumption of Reasonableness in Special Places – Home and Occupied Vechicle]

OUJI-CR 8-14 – DEFENSE OF PROPERTY – JUSTIFIABLE USE OF DEADLY FORCE IN DEFENSE OF HABITATION

A person is justified in using deadly force when resisting any attempt by another to commit a felony upon or in any dwelling house in which that person is lawfully present. Defense of habitation is a defense although the danger that a felony would be committed upon or in the dwelling house may not have been real, if a reasonable person, in the circumstances and from the viewpoint of the defendant, would reasonably have believed that there was an imminent danger that such felony would occur. **Statutory Authority: 21 O.S. 1991, § 733(1).** [This jury instruction is based upon § 733 which we told you not to rely upon. To the extent this jury instruction claims to give a person the right to use deadly force to prevent any felony, we are reluctant to believe the courts will give this instruction if, for example, you claim you shot and killed a carpet bagger for sitting at your kitchen table trying to sell you on a fraudulent mortgage agreement. We think you'd be better off reserving your use of deadly force to situations where the felony involves an element of violence such as threatening with a deadly weapon or violently breaking into your home with force. Fortunately, Oklahomans have a second home-defense statute, 21 O.S.Supp. 2008, § 1289.25, summarized below in Oklahoma Jury Instruction OUJI-CR 8-15 – DEFENSE OF PERSON – JUSTIFIABLE USE OF DEADLY FORCE AGAINST INTRUDER. § 1289.25 is patterned after Florida's-home defense statute, arguably the most protective in the country.]

Committee Comments – At common law, the precept that a person's habitation constituted his "castle" gave rise to a privilege to defend his dwelling from felonious attempts, even to the point of exercising deadly force. R. Perkins, *Criminal Law* 1022 (2d ed. 1969). This right of defense on behalf of property which constitutes a dwelling, codified at 21 O.S. 1991, § 733(1), must be distinguished from the far more restricted right of defense of other property, codified at 21 O.S. 1991, § 643(3), which permits only use of nondeadly force.

The Court of Criminal Appeals has consistently interpreted this provision of section 733(1) as extending the right to use deadly force in defense of one's habitation only where the person defending has reason to fear that one who entered unlawfully, a trespasser, intended to perpetrate a felony therein, or to inflict harm upon him or some other person. The position espoused by the court with respect to defense of one's domicile may be summarized as follows:

A person may resist a trespass on real property in his possession, where such trespass does not amount to a felony, and may eject the trespasser therefrom by the use of any reasonable force short of taking or endangering human life; but if he is unable to prevent a trespass, where no felony is attempted, by any means short of taking or endangering human life, he must suffer the trespass and seek redress at the hands of the law rather than commit homicide. [Citations Omitted. An important point in this comment is that you cannot use deadly force to expel a trespasser in your yard or on your land. You can only use non-deadly force. If he doesn't leave, you're going to have to look to the police and the courts to get him to leave or keep him from trespassing. Warning: Some of you may rationalize that you will use non-deadly force to handle the situation, but take a gun with you "just in case." We suggest you avoid the temptation to eject trespassers off of your land. It's too easy for such situations to escalate into a deadly confrontation. You are paying for police protection with your property taxes. Use it.]

Use of the statutory term "dwelling house" would seem to preclude use of deadly force in defense of one's place of business. Although the Court of Criminal Appeals has not considered this issue, claims of appropriate use of deadly force to defend one's business establishment were rejected on other grounds in two cases, in which the court did not isolate this fact as a further ground for the infirmity of the claim. [Citations Omitted. Don't expect to defend your store or business the way Oklahoma allows you to defend your home. If you have a shoplifter, call the police. Of course business owners still have the right under jury instructions OUJI-CR 8-46 and OUJI-CR 8-15A above if they are threatened with imminent deadly force or forcible felony.]

OUJI-CR 8-15 – DEFENSE OF PERSON – JUSTIFIABLE USE OF DEADLY FORCE AGAINST INTRUDER [This jury instruction is based upon Oklahoma's home-defense statute, 21 Okl.St.Ann. § 1289.25, which in turn was copied from Florida's dynamite home-defense statute. We suggest you read our comments and examples in Florida's statute. Just as Florida was passing the law, a student from Harvard Law School wrote a scathing criticism of the statute saying it was too protective. We had to chuckle because within a couple of years several states, including Oklahoma, adopted virtually the same statute. Maybe the Harvard men-in-tweed aren't as influential as they think they are.]

A person is justified in using force that is intended or likely to cause death or great bodily harm to another person who was in the process of unlawfully and forcefully entering or unlawfully and forcibly entered a dwelling, residence or occupied vehicle if the person using the force knew or had reason to believe that an unlawful and forcible entry was occurring or had occurred. [The keys words here are "unlawful" and "forcible." You can use deadly force if someone, who doesn't have permission to be in your home, breaks or tries to break though a door or window. If a person enters with your permission it's not an unlawful entry. The entry does not have to be with a weapon or tool as long as it's forceful. **Example:** A person who does not have permission to be in your home breaks in by slamming his body against a door.

OR

A person is justified in using force that is intended or likely to cause death or great bodily harm if the person against whom the force was used had attempted to remove or was attempting to remove another person against the will of that other person from a dwelling, residence or occupied vehicle [such as an attempted kidnapping] and the person using the force knew or had reason to believe that an unlawful and forcible removal or attempt to remove was occurring or had occurred.

A person is not justified in using force if:

[But you are not allowed to use deadly force if . . .]

The person against whom the force is used has the right to be in or is a lawful resident of the dwelling, residence or occupied vehicle, such as an owner, lessee, or titleholder and there is not a protective order from domestic violence in effect or a written pretrial supervision order of no contact against that person. [You may not use deadly force if the recipient of your use of force has a right to be in the home. Examples would be a co-tenant, roommate, husband or wife, child, landlord or mortgage company employee with a right to inspect after a legal foreclosure. However, if it's an abusive spouse that the courts have issued a written order against, telling the bum to stay out of your home and away from you, you have a right to use deadly force to keep him from forcibly and unlawfully from breaking in.]

OR

The person or persons sought to be removed are children, grandchildren, in the lawful custody or under the lawful guardianship of the person against whom the force is used. [This keeps child-custody disputes from turning into the OK Corral.]

OR

The person who uses force is engaged in or using the dwelling, residence or occupied vehicle to further an unlawful activity. [**Example:** You're cooking meth in your home and the SWAT team breaks in. You can't use deadly force because your use of the home is unlawful.]

[Civil Liability]

21 OKL.ST.ANN. § 1289.25 (CONT.)

F. A person who uses force, as permitted pursuant to the provisions of subsections B [defense of home and occupied vehicle] and D [defense of self and prevention of forcible felonies] of this section, is justified in using such force and is immune from criminal prosecution and civil action for the use of such force. As used in this subsection, the term "criminal prosecution" includes charging or prosecuting the defendant.

G. A law enforcement agency may use standard procedures for investigating the use of force, but the law enforcement agency may not arrest the person for using force unless it determines that there is probable cause that the force that was used was unlawful.

H. The court shall award reasonable attorney fees, court costs, compensation for loss of income, and all expenses incurred by the defendant in defense of any civil action brought by a plaintiff if the court finds that the defendant is immune from prosecution as provided in subsection F of this section.

[If you used force in one of the special places justifiably, then you'll be immune from criminal AND CIVIL trials. Furthermore, a police officer that arrives on the scene cannot arrest you unless he's got a good reason to think that for some reason what you did was unlawful. If any civil suit does get filed against you and it turns out you were justified in your use of force, you will be entitled to recover all court costs, attorney's fees and expenses from the person who sued you or from his heirs if he died.]

[Defense of Property]

OUJI-CR 8-16 – DEFENSE OF PROPERTY – JUSTIFIABLE USE OF NONDEADLY FORCE

A person is justified in using force in preventing or attempting to prevent a trespass or other unlawful interference with real or personal property in his lawful possession. Defense of property is a defense although the danger to the property defended may not have been real, if a reasonable person, in the circumstances and from the viewpoint of the defendant, would reasonably have believed the danger of interference to be imminent. The amount of force used may not exceed that amount of force a reasonable person, in the circumstances and from the viewpoint of the defendant, would have used to prevent the trespass or unlawful interference. **Statutory Authority: 21 O.S. 1991, § 643(3).** [You can use reasonable force to defend property but not deadly force.]

[HELPFUL DEFINITIONS RELATING TO THIS STATE'S SELF-DEFENSE STATUTES]

OUJI-CR 8-12 - DEFENSE OF ANOTHER - DEFINITIONS

- **Altercation** – Heated dispute or controversy. Reference: Black's Law Dictionary 71 (5th ed. 1979). **OUJI-CR 8-56 Defense of Self-Defense - Definitions.**

- **Bodily Harm** – Any touching of a person against **his/her** will with physical force, in an intentional, hostile, and aggressive manner.). Reference: Black's Law Dictionary 222 (Rev. 4th ed. 1968). **OUJI-CR 8-12 – Defense Of Another – Definitions.**

- **Deadly Force** – Force intended or likely to cause death or great bodily injury. References: Gransden v. State, 12 Okl. Cr. 417, 158 P. 157 (1916); R. Perkins, Criminal Law 993 (2d ed. 1969). **OUJI-CR 8-12 – Defense Of Another – Definitions.**

- **Deadly Force** – Force intended or likely to cause death or great bodily injury. Reference: R. Perkins. Criminal Law 993 (2d ed. 1969). **OUJI-CR 8-18 Defense Of Property – Definitions.**

- **Dwelling** – means a building or conveyance of any kind, including any attached porch, whether the building or conveyance is temporary or permanent, mobile or immobile, which has a roof over it, including a tent, and is designed to be occupied by people. **OUJI-CR 8-15 – Defense of Person – Justifiable Use of Deadly Force Against Intruder.**

- **Great Bodily Harm** – Serious and severe bodily injury. Such injury must be of a greater degree than a mere battery. Reference: Roddie v. State, 19 Okl. Cr. 63, 198 P. 342 (1921). **OUJI-CR 8-12 – Defense Of Another – Definitions.**

- **Imminent Danger** – Danger that is pressing, urgent, or immediate. References: Lary v. State, 50 Okl. Cr. 111, 296 P. 512 (1931); Turner v. State, 4 Okl. Cr. 164, 111 P. 988, 998 (1910); R. Perkins, Criminal Law 994 (2d ed. 1969). **OUJI-CR 8-56 Defense of Self-Defense – Definitions.**

- **Master** – Male employer. Reference: Black's Law Dictionary 879 (5th ed. 1979). **OUJI-CR 8-12 – Defense Of Another – Definitions.**

- **Mistress** – Female employer. Reference: Webster's Third New International Dictionary 1446 (1961). **OUJI-CR 8-12 – Defense Of Another – Definitions.**

- **Mutual combat** – A fight between two or more parties into which each party has entered willingly. References: Phelps v. State, 64 Okl. Cr. 240, 78 P.2d 1068 (1938); Weatherholt v. State, 9 Okl. Cr. 161, 131 P. 185 (1913); 27A Words and Phrases 712. **OUJI-CR 8-56 Defense of Self-Defense – Definitions.**

- **Property** – Property includes:

  (a) Real Property – Every estate, interest, and right in lands, including structures or objects permanently attached to the land;

  (b) Personal Property – Money, goods, chattels, effects, evidences of rights in action, and written instruments effecting a monetary obligation or right or title to property. References: 21 O.S. 1991, §§ 102, 103, 104. **OUJI-CR 8-18 DEFENSE OF PROPERTY – DEFINITIONS.**

- **Reasonably Safe Opportunity** – An opportunity to retreat with complete safety. Reference: W. LaFave & A. Scott, Criminal Law § 53, at 396 (1972). **OUJI-CR 8-12 - Defense Of Another – Definitions.**

- **Residence** – means a dwelling in which a person resides either temporarily or permanently or is visiting as an invited guest.] **OUJI-CR 8-15 - Defense of Person - Justifiable Use of Deadly Force Against Intruder.**

- **Servant** – Employee. Reference: Black's Law Dictionary 1227 (5th ed. 1979). **OUJI-CR 8-12 – Defense Of Another – Definitions.**

- **Trespasser** – A person is a trespasser if that person has **([entered without consent]/[is unlawfully] upon the land of another)/(refused to leave the land of another after a lawful request to leave has been made to him/her). OUJI-CR 8-11 – Defense Of Another – Trespasser Defined.**

- **Vehicle** – means a conveyance of any kind, whether or not motorized, which is designed to transport people or property. **OUJI-CR 8-15 – Defense of Person – Justifiable Use of Deadly Force Against Intruder.**

[TEMPLATE Topics We Could Not Find Explained in Statutes or Cases]

(For each of these topics that we could not find addressed in your state's statutes or cases, we suggest you review the same topics in the subchapters of surrounding states. Your state's courts may look to the law of neighboring states to see how their courts and legislatures have treated that particular self-defense issue.)

[Committing Felony or Unlawful Act]

[Co-Habitants; Co-Employees – Duty to Retreat]

[Reckless Injury to Innocent Third Parties]

Pancho's Wisdom

You just might be a Gunnut if . . .

. . . you think of a magazine as something you load; not something you read.

. . . you hope you are part Indian, so that after you die you too can go to the Happy Hunting Grounds. And speaking of death, you'd like to be able to hear after. Huh?

. . . yer ears ring louder than your telephone.

OREGON

Oregon's self-defense laws left us scratching our heads. The wording of its statutes seemed pretty strong at first, until we started reading cases. **Warning:** The Oregon courts have not always interpreted the state's self-defense statutes to mean what they say.

Key: ■ commentary ■ original statutes, cases or jury instructions

[Defense of Self and Others] [Non-Deadly Force]

§ OREGON REVISED STATUTES (O.R.S.) § 161.205.
Use of physical force.

The use of physical force upon another person that would otherwise constitute an offense is justifiable and not criminal under any of the following circumstances:

. . .

(5) A person may use physical force upon another person in self-defense or in defending a third person, in defending property, in making an arrest or in preventing an escape . . . [You can use non-deadly force in self-defense, defense of others, property or to make a citizen's arrest (which we strongly recommend against because of the personal and legal risks, see discussion in Chapter 4).]

§ O.R.S. § 161.209.
Use of physical force in defense of a person.

Except as provided in ORS **161.215** and **161.219**, a person is justified in using physical force upon another person for self-defense or to defend a third person from what the person reasonably believes to be the use or imminent use of unlawful physical force, and the person may use a degree of force which the person reasonably believes to be necessary for the purpose. [You can use force to protect yourself or someone else from the imminent use of unlawful force, as long as it's reasonable.]

[Deadly Force] [Defense of a Third Person]
[Use of Deadly Force to Prevent Serious Felonies]

§ O.R.S. § 161.219.
Limitations on use of deadly physical force in defense of a person.

Notwithstanding the provisions of ORS **161.209**, a person is not justified in using deadly physical force upon another person unless the person reasonably believes that the other person is:

(1) Committing or attempting to commit a felony involving the use or threatened imminent use of physical force against a person; or

(2) Committing or attempting to commit a burglary in a dwelling; or

(3) Using or about to use unlawful deadly physical force against a person.

[The statute says you can only use deadly force if someone is threatening deadly force, committing a violent felony, or a home burglary. This is not exactly how the courts have interpreted it. To justify the use of deadly force the felony has to involve an imminent threat of great bodily injury (see the explanation from the case entitled *State v. Burns* below). Likewise, deadly force may only be used to counter a home burglary if the use of force is absolutely necessary (explained in *State v. Haro* below). It's difficult for citizens to have confidence that they can rely upon the language of their state statutes when the courts keep adding conditions not expressly required by the statutes.

[Additional requirements to be able to use deadly force to stop the commission of a felony involving force or violence as required in *State v. Burns*] "Since the legislature's intention in enacting ORS 161.219 and 161.225(2) was to codify the common law of self-defense and not to articulate a new standard, we conclude that the statutory phrases requiring that there be a 'felony involving the use or threatened imminent use of physical force against a person,' 'unlawful deadly physical force,' or a 'felony by force and violence' are the functional equivalents of the case law's requirement of 'great bodily harm.'" *State v. Burns*, 516 P.2d 748 (Or.App. 1973). [You may only use deadly force to stop felonies that involve an imminent threat of great bodily harm. Where the threat does not pose a risk of great bodily harm, you may not use deadly force to stop a felony in progress despite the broad language of the statute.]

[Additional requirements to be able to use deadly force to stop the commission of a home burglary as required in *State v. Haro*] "ORS 161.219 begins with the phrase, 'Notwithstanding the provisions of ORS 161.209, a person is not justified in using deadly physical force upon another person unless...' That phrase explains that, although ORS 161.209 authorizes the use of physical force in certain circumstances, deadly force is never reasonable, in the absence of any of the additional threatening circumstances described in ORS 161.219. Nothing in the language of ORS 161.219 eliminates the general 'necessity' requirement defined in ORS 161.209. Therefore, even when one or more of the threatening circumstances described in ORS 161.219 is present, the use of deadly force is justified *only* if it does not exceed the 'degree of force which the person reasonably believes to be necessary' in the circumstances. . . The legislature has not created an unlimited right to use deadly force against a burglar." *State v. Haro*, 843 P.2d 966. 968 (Or.App. 1992). [The language of this case is a good reminder of the importance of the concept of necessity when acting in self-defense or defense of another. This case says the necessity requirement of ORS 161.209 (non-deadly force statute above) is incorporated into ORS 161.219 (deadly force statute above). See our detailed discussion of the concept of necessity and excessive force in Chapter 3. Also please review Chapter 7, Thumbs-Down Factors, which contains cases illustrating the concept of excessive force. The bottom line: It doesn't appear to matter whether the statutes allow you to use deadly force against certain felonies (e.g., burglary, arson), the courts are still going to impose the requirement that the force used was reasonable and not excessive.]

[Exceptions to Justifiable Self-Defense]

§ O.R.S. § 161.215.
Limitations on use of physical force in defense of a person.

Notwithstanding ORS **161.209**, a person is not justified in using physical force upon another person if:

[Provocation]

(1) With intent to cause physical injury or death to another person, the person provokes the use of unlawful physical force by that person; or [You can't win on the theory of self-defense if you start a fight as an excuse to hurt someone.]

[Initial Aggressor] [Withdraw and Communicate]

(2) The person is the initial aggressor, except that the use of physical force upon another person under such circumstances is justifiable if the person withdraws from the encounter and effectively communicates to the other person the intent to do so, but the latter nevertheless continues or threatens to continue the use of unlawful physical force; or [You can't start a fight and then win on the theory of self-defense unless you retreat and get the message across that you don't want to fight anymore. Then, if your opponent keeps coming after you and you have to use force to defend yourself, you may have a valid claim self-defense.]

[Mutual Combat]

(3) The physical force involved is the product of a combat by agreement not specifically authorized by law. [The law won't allow you to win on the theory of self-defense if you hurt someone whom you have agreed to fight.]

[No Duty to Retreat Generally] [No Duty to Retreat From Special Places]

". . . we conclude, in short, that the legislature's intent is clear on the face of ORS 161.219: The legislature did *not* intend to require a person to retreat before using deadly force to defend against the imminent use of deadly physical force by another." *State v. Sandoval*, 156 P.3d 60, 64 (Or. 2007). [There is no duty to retreat in Oregon before using deadly force whether you are in your home or occupied vehicle or not.]

[Defense of Person(s) in Special Places – Home, Business, Occupied Vehicle] [Defense of Property]

§ O.R.S. § 161.225.
Use of physical force in defense of premises.

(1) A person in lawful possession or control of premises is justified in using physical force upon another person when and to the extent that the person reasonably believes it necessary to prevent or terminate what the person reasonably believes to be

the commission or attempted commission of a criminal trespass by the other person in or upon the premises. [You can use reasonable force, but not deadly force to keep trespassers off your property.]

(2) A person may use deadly physical force under the circumstances set forth in subsection (1) of this section only:

(a) In defense of a person as provided in ORS 161.219 [regarding the use of deadly force to prevent death or serious bodily injury, felony involving an imminent threat of great bodily harm (see discussion of the *Burns* case above) or burglary (see our caution relating to the *Haro* case above).]; or

(b) When the person reasonably believes it necessary to prevent the commission of arson or a felony by force and violence [meaning felony creating an imminent risk of great bodily harm (see discussion regarding the *Burns* case above).] by the trespasser.

(3) As used in subsection (1) and subsection (2)(a) of this section, "premises" includes any building as defined in ORS 164.205 and any real property. As used in subsection (2)(b) of this section, "premises" includes any building. [We're not exactly sure why the Oregon Legislature would go to the trouble of specifically giving citizens the right to use deadly force to prevent arsons, burglaries and forcible felonies if it still intended to still require proof of the threat of great bodily injury or death. Every state justifies the use of deadly force to prevent great bodily injury. If proof of the threat of great bodily injury is required whether or not a crime is specifically named, why even mention the crime? Oregon needs to adopt The Mother of All Self-Defense Laws, see Chapter 20.]

[HELPFUL DEFINITIONS RELATING TO THIS STATE'S SELF-DEFENSE STATUTES]
Definitions for ORS 164.205 to 164.270. (Offenses against property)

- **Building** – in addition to its ordinary meaning, includes any booth, vehicle, boat, aircraft or other structure adapted for overnight accommodation of persons or for carrying on business therein. Where a building consists of separate units, including, but not limited to, separate apartments, offices or rented rooms, each unit is, in addition to being a part of such building, a separate building. **O.R.S. § 164.205 (1).**

- **Dwelling** – means a building which regularly or intermittently is occupied by a person lodging therein at night, whether or not a person is actually present. **O.R.S. § 164.205 (2).**

- **Premises** – includes any building and any real property, whether privately or publicly owned. **O.R.S. § 164.205 (6).**

- **Felonies Mentioned –**
    - **Arson** – [Intentionally starting a fire or causing an explosion that damages the property of another that exceeds the value of $750 or puts another in danger of serious physical injury.] **O.R.S. § 164.315 and 164.325.**
    - **Burglary** – [Entering or remaining unlawfully in a building with the intent to commit a crime therein.] **O.R.S. § 164.215 and 164.225.**

[TEMPLATE Topics We Could Not Find Explained in Statutes or Cases]

(For each of these topics that we could not find addressed in your state's statutes or cases, we suggest you review the same topics in the subchapters of surrounding states. Your state's courts may look to the law of neighboring states to see how their courts and legislatures have treated that particular self-defense issue.)

[Committing Felony or Unlawful Act]

[Co-Habitants; Co-Employees – Duty to Retreat]

[Presumption of Reasonableness in Special Places]

[Reckless Injury to Innocent Third Parties]

[Civil Liability]

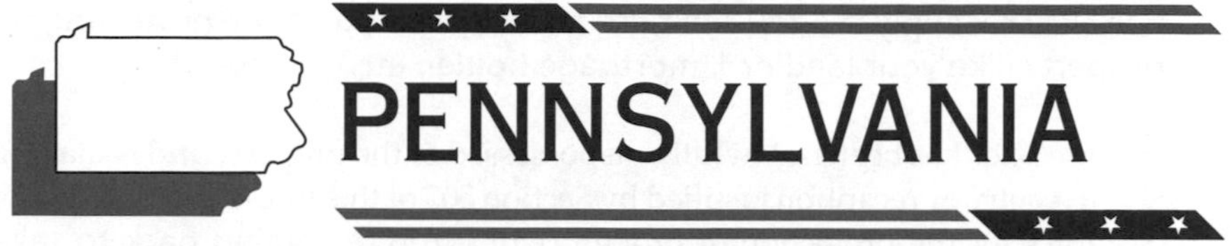

PENNSYLVANIA

As its self-defense law, Pennsylvania has adopted, nearly verbatim, the Model Penal Code ("MPC"). The MPC was published in 1962 with input from law professors and lawyers associated with the American Law Institute.

Pancho's Wisdom – Pancho envisions the complicated Model Penal Code to have been written by a committee of law professors and lawyers who not only have never been involved in a heart-stopping defensive incident, but have never participated in handgun competitions that simulate the stress and confusion of a violent attack. They have no concept of the role perception and reaction time play in defending against such incidents (see Chapter 11). Hence, the rules they have written for the Model Penal Code are so complicated with so many exceptions to the exceptions to the exceptions, that no one in real life could ever apply them correctly let alone remember them all when facing a life-threatening incident. Is it any wonder that very few of the fifty states have adopted the Model Penal Code's self-defense law? Pancho's advice to Pennsylvania is to chuck these ridiculously complex rules and adopt the Mother of All Self-Defense Laws (Chapter 20). It resolves all issues in favor of the innocent and against the guilty.

Key: ■ commentary ■ original statutes, cases or jury instructions

[Defense of Self and Others] [Non-Deadly Force]

§ 18 PENNSYLVANIA CONSOLIDATED STATUTES ANNOTATED (PA.C.S.A.) § 505.

Use of force in self-protection.

(a) Use of force justifiable for protection of the person.

The use of force upon or toward another person is justifiable when the actor believes that such force is immediately necessary for the purpose of protecting himself against the use of unlawful force by such other person on the present occasion. [This is standard non-deadly force language. The MPC uses "immediately necessary" which includes both the imminent and necessary components of the standard we discussed in Chapter 3.]

(b) Limitations on justifying necessity for use of force.

(1) The use of force is not justifiable under this section:

(i) to resist an arrest which the actor knows is being made by a peace officer, although the arrest is unlawful; or

(ii) to resist force used by the occupier or possessor of property or by another person on his behalf, where the actor knows that the person using the force is doing so under a claim of right to protect the property, except that this limitation shall not apply if: [You can't use force against someone protecting his property (like your landlord, mortgage holder, etc.), unless...]

. . .

(B) the actor has been unlawfully dispossessed of the property and is making a reentry or recaption justified by Section 507 of this title (relating to use of force for the protection of property); or [You're coming back to take your property from which you've been unlawfully dispossessed.]

(C) the actor believes that such force is necessary to protect himself against death or serious bodily injury. [. . . or the person defending his property is using deadly force. **Example:** If you start shooting someone simply trespassing on your lawn, he can use force to defend himself. Interestingly, though, he's not expressly authorized to use deadly force in this particular subsection. You'll see later that trespassers must retreat before using deadly force if they can safely do so.]

. . .

[Deadly Force]

[Use of Deadly Force to Prevent Serious Felonies]

§ 18 PA.C.S.A. § 505 (b) (2).
Use of force in self-protection.

. . .

(b) Limitations on justifying necessity for use of force.

(2) The use of deadly force is not justifiable under this section unless the actor believes that such force is necessary to protect himself against death, serious bodily injury, kidnapping or sexual intercourse compelled by force or threat; . . .
[You can use deadly force to defend yourself if you are about to be killed, seriously injured, kidnapped or raped. See [**Exceptions. . .**] and [**Duty to Retreat**] sections below for the exceptions to this rule.]

[Defense of a Third Person]

§ 18 PA.C.S.A. § 506.
Use of force for the protection of other persons.

(a) General rule. – The use of force upon or toward the person of another is justifiable to protect a third person when:

(1) the actor would be justified under section 505 of this title (relating to use of force in self-protection) in using such force to protect himself against the injury he believes to be threatened to the person whom he seeks to protect;

(2) under the circumstances as the actor believes them to be, the person whom he seeks to protect would be justified in using such protective force; and

(3) the actor believes that his intervention is necessary for the protection of such other person.

[This somewhat confusing section sets forth three standards for defense of another. (1) Whatever force you used to protect the third person has to be force you would have been justified using to protect yourself, (2) The person you're protecting would have been able to use the force you used and (3) you have to actually believe whoever you're helping needs your help.]

(b) Exceptions. – Notwithstanding subsection (a) of this section:

(1) When the actor would be obliged under Section 505 of this title to retreat, to surrender the possession of a thing or to comply with a demand before using force in self-protection, he is not obliged to do so before using force for the protection of another person, unless he knows that he can thereby secure the complete safety of such other person. [Even if you would normally be required to retreat before using defensive force, if you are defending another person, you don't have to retreat unless you know retreating won't jeopardize the safety of the other person.]

(2) When the person whom the actor seeks to protect would be obliged under Section 505 of this title to retreat, to surrender the possession of a thing or to comply with a demand if he knew that he could obtain complete safety by so doing, the actor is obliged to try to cause him to do so before using force in his protection if the actor knows that he can obtain complete safety in that way. [You've got to try to get the other person to retreat if you believe his retreat can be accomplished in complete safety rather than use force to defend that person.]

(3) Neither the actor nor the person whom he seeks to protect is obliged to retreat when in the dwelling or place of work of the other to any greater extent than in his own. [Neither you nor the person you are defending is obligated to retreat from his or her home or workplace before you use force to defend him or her.]

[Reckless Injury to Innocent Third Parties]

"[I]f the victim acts outside of the parameters established by the law, then his act is not justified and he may be prosecuted for injury to bystanders or others which he may inflict. Under Section 505 of the Crimes Code, as applied to this case, the defender may use deadly force only if he reasonably believes that such force is necessary to avoid death or serious bodily injury; he did not provoke the use of force against himself in the same incident; and finally, he could not retreat with complete safety. If any of these factors is negated; i.e., the defender did not reasonably believe deadly force was necessary; he provoked the incident, or he could retreat with safety, then his use of deadly force in self-defense was not justifiable and he may be prosecuted for injuries or death he inflicts on the assailants or on bystanders. If his use of deadly force was justifiable, he may not be prosecuted for either. *Com. v. Fowlin*, 710 A.2d 1130, 1134 (Pa. 1998). [If you were justified in using self-defense, you will not be prosecuted for injuries to innocent third parties. In addition to the rule regarding reckless injury, notice how this passage from this case summarizes all of the exceptions you need to be aware of before using deadly force.]

[Initial Aggressor] [Provocation]

§ 18 PA.C.S.A. § 505.

. . .

(2) The use of deadly force is not justifiable... if:

(i) the actor, with the intent of causing death or serious bodily injury, provoked the use of force against himself in the same encounter... [Deadly force is not justified if you start a fight as an excuse to kill or injure someone when he reacts to your provocation.]

[Duty to Retreat – Generally – Yes]

(ii) the actor knows that he can avoid the necessity of using such force with complete safety by retreating or by surrendering possession of a thing to a person asserting a claim of right thereto or by complying with a demand that he abstain from any action which he has no duty to take, except that:

(A) the actor is not obliged to retreat from his dwelling or place of work, unless he was the initial aggressor or is assailed in his place of work by another person whose place of work the actor knows it to be; and

(3) Except as required by paragraphs (1) and (2) of this subsection, a person employing protective force may estimate the necessity thereof under the circumstances as he believes them to be when the force is used, without retreating, surrendering possession, doing any other act which he has no legal duty to do or abstaining from any lawful action.

[This ridiculously confusing section says: (1) you have to retreat before using deadly force if you can retreat in complete safety, (2) if someone is claiming title or a right to property in your possession, you must give it to him rather than resist with deadly force, (3) if someone is commanding you to do something, you have to do it (unless you have a duty not to—e.g., he's trying to force you to commit a crime), rather than use deadly force, (4) if you're the initial aggressor you have to retreat before using deadly force in self-defense even in the home or at work, (5) you have no duty to retreat from an assailant in your home before using deadly force unless you started the fight, and (6) you don't have to retreat at work unless your assailant is a co-worker.

Pancho's Wisdom – Got those rules memorized? Good, you'll feel a sense of accomplishment as you lay dying in a pool of blood because you hesitated .3 seconds too long before using deadly force against a frothing, violent criminal assailant as you mentally tried to apply the long list of rules you've memorized. Could the Pennsylvania legislature make it any more confusing? No wonder over forty-five states have rejected adoption of the Model Penal Code. It seems the professors that drafted it were so focused on preserving the precious lives of common criminals that they lost sight of the fact that innocent citizens could die while trying to remember and apply such complicated rules of self-defense. It's time state legislators stop being politically correct. They need to enact self-defense laws that protect the innocent rather than ensuring the safety of felons. A state's self-defense law should send a message like, "If you commit violent felonies, some law-abiding citizen, who doesn't have to worry about being prosecuted or sued, will blow your worthless, lazy körper into the next county." See Mother of All Self-Defense Laws, Chapter 20.]

(c) Use of confinement as protective force. The justification afforded by this section extends to the use of confinement as protective force only if the actor takes all reasonable measures to terminate the confinement as soon as he knows that he safely can, unless the person confined has been arrested on a charge of crime.

[Defense of Person(s) in Special Places – Dwelling]

§ 18 PA.C.S.A. § 507 (c) (4) and (e).
Use of force for the protection of property.

(c) Limitations on justifiable use of force.

. . .

(4) (i) The use of deadly force is justifiable under this section if:

(A) there has been an entry into the actor's dwelling;

(B) the actor neither believes nor has reason to believe that the entry is lawful; and

(C) the actor neither believes nor has reason to believe that force less than deadly force would be adequate to terminate the entry. [You can use deadly force against an intruder in your home as long as you have no information to believe he's in your home legally and as long as you believe that nothing short of deadly force would stop him/her.]

(ii) If the conditions of justification provided in subparagraph (i) have not been met, the use of deadly force is not justifiable under this section unless the actor believes that: [If you don't meet the above requirements, you can still use deadly force if...]

(A) the person against whom the force is used is attempting to dispossess him of his dwelling otherwise than under a claim of right to its possession; or [The intruder is trying to unlawfully dispossess you of your dwelling. Remember, however, you can't shoot your landlord or mortgage holder if they try to evict you from your home claiming you breached the lease or mortgage agreement. You'll have to fight it out with them in court, not in the OK corral.]

(B) such force is necessary to prevent the commission of a felony in the dwelling. [You are preventing the commission of a felony in your dwelling. We take this to mean violent or serious felonies. See the discussion of cases summarized in Chapter 4 describing the risk of using deadly force against an unarmed, non-threatening felon.]

. . .

(e) Use of device to protect property. – The justification afforded by this section extends to the use of a device for the purpose of protecting property only if:

(1) the device is not designed to cause or known to create a substantial risk of causing death or serious bodily injury;

(2) the use of the particular device to protect the property from entry or trespass is reasonable under the circumstances, as the actor believes them to be; and

(3) the device is one customarily used for such a purpose or reasonable care is taken to make known to probable intruders the fact that it is used. [You can use "booby traps" to protect property, but only if (1) they aren't the kind designed to cause death or serious injury, (2) the use of the device was reasonable under the circumstances and (3) the device is the kind that people usually use or you warn intruders that booby traps are being used. **Example:** Warning! Our child, who has violent, anti-social tendencies, is HOME ALONE with his

sling shot and will not hesitate to shoot you in the groin if the opportunity presents itself.]

[No Duty to Retreat From Dwelling or Place of Work]
[Co-Habitants; Co-Employees]

§ 18 PA.C.S.A. § 505 (b) (1) (ii) (A).

. . .

(A) the actor is not obliged to retreat from his dwelling or place of work, unless he was the initial aggressor or is assailed in his place of work by another person whose place of work the actor knows it to be;. . . [You have no duty to retreat from your home before using deadly force unless you start the fight. You don't have to retreat from your workplace before using deadly force unless the assailant is a co-employee. If your co-employee goes postal, you have to retreat if you can safely do so. You may defend other co-employees, but you must first try to get them to retreat if they can do so in complete safety (see [**Defense of a Third Person**] section above.]

. . .

[Defense of Property]

§ 18 PA.C.S.A. § 507.
Use of force for the protection of property.

(a) **Use of force justifiable for protection of property.** The use of force upon or toward the person of another is justifiable when the actor believes that such force is immediately necessary:

(1) to prevent or terminate an unlawful entry or other trespass upon land or a trespass against or the unlawful carrying away of tangible movable property, if such land or movable property is, or is believed by the actor to be, in his possession or in the possession of another person for whose protection he acts; or [You can use force to prevent a trespass on your property or someone from taking your property as long as you have a right to the property being threatened.]

(2) to effect an entry or reentry upon land or to retake tangible movable property, if: [You can also use force to get your property back as long as...]

(i) the actor believes that he or the person by whose authority he acts or a person from whom he or such other person derives title was unlawfully dispossessed of such land or movable property and is entitled to possession; and [. . .you believe you have a right to the property and...]

(ii) (A) the force is used immediately or on fresh pursuit after such dispossession; or [you're using the force immediately after you've been dispossessed, not a day later and]

(B) the actor believes that the person against whom he uses force has no claim of right to the possession of the property and, in the case of land, the circumstances, as the actor believes them to be, are of such urgency that it would be an exceptional hardship to postpone the entry or reentry until a court order is obtained. [. . . you believe the person has no right to the property. If its land you're trying to get back, you have to believe that it would be a real hardship to have to wait to obtain a court order to get the squatter off.]

. . .

(c) Limitations on justifiable use of force.

(1) The use of force is justifiable under this section only if the actor first requests the person against whom such force is used to desist from his interference with the property, unless the actor believes that: [Even if you meet the above requirements, force isn't justified unless you first ask that the person interfering with your property to stop, unless...]

(i) such request would be useless; [. . . you believe asking the interferer "pretty please" will fall on deaf ears . . .]

(ii) it would be dangerous to himself or another person to make the request; or [. . . you believe it would be dangerous for you to ask the person to stop interfering . . .]

(iii) substantial harm will be done to the physical condition of the property which is sought to be protected before the request can effectively be made. [or, the property will be severely damaged before you can request the interferer to stop.]

(2) The use of force to prevent or terminate a trespass is not justifiable under this section if the actor knows that the exclusion of the trespasser will expose him to substantial danger or serious bodily injury. [You can't send someone off your land if doing so will be the death of him or her. **Example:** It's a blizzard outside and you know the trespasser, a non-threatening homeless person, is in danger of severe hyperthermia if you kick him out of your toasty garage. **Another Example:** An upset and scantily clad (obviously unarmed) woman pounds on your door, begs to come in an pleads for you to call the police. You notice gang-bangers on the street armed with bats, knives and tire irons. The statute seems to say you could be held criminally and civilly liable if you use force to expel these two unfortunate people off of your property and they are killed or injured. Call the authorities instead.]

(3) The use of force to prevent an entry or reentry upon land or the recaption of movable property is not justifiable under this section, although the actor believes that such reentry or caption is unlawful, if:

(i) the reentry or recaption is made by or on behalf of a person who was actually dispossessed of the property; and

(ii) it is otherwise justifiable under subsection (a)(2).

[Notice nothing in this section (507 Protection of Property) authorizes the use of deadly force. We recommend you do not use force to retake property because of the physical and legal risks of the confrontation becoming deadly. If you are ultimately compelled to seriously injure or kill someone who has interfered with your property, the resulting attorney fees could be more than the property is worth. Do yourself and family a favor and let the police apprehend a thief or remove a trespasser.]

. . .

[HELPFUL DEFINITIONS RELATING TO THIS STATE'S SELF-DEFENSE STATUTES]

- **Believes or Belief** – Means "reasonably believes" or "reasonable belief." **18 Pa.C.S.A. § 501.**
- **Deadly force** – Force which, under the circumstances in which it is used, is readily capable of causing death or serious bodily injury. **18 Pa.C.S.A. § 501.**
- **Dwelling** – Any building or structure though movable or temporary, or a portion thereof, which is for the time being the home or place of lodging of the actor. **18 Pa.C.S.A. § 501.**
- **Felonies Mentioned** –
  - **Kidnapping** – [Unlawfully taking or confining a person for the purpose of holding them for reward, hostage, furthering a felony, or causing harm.] **Pennsylvania Statutes 18 Pa.C.S.A. § 2901.**
  - **Sexual intercourse compelled by force** – [Crimes such as rape or forcible sodomy.] **Pennsylvania Statutes 18 Pa.C.S.A. § 3121.**
- **Unlawful force** – Force, including confinement, which is employed without the consent of the person against whom it is directed and the employment of which constitutes an offense or actionable tort or would constitute such offense or tort except for a defense (such as the absence of intent, negligence, or mental capacity; duress; youth; or diplomatic status) not amounting to a privilege to use the force. Assent constitutes consent, within the meaning of this section, whether or not it otherwise is legally effective, except assent to the infliction of death or serious bodily injury. **18 Pa.C.S.A. § 501.**

[TEMPLATE Topics We Could Not Find Explained in Statutes or Cases]

(For each of these topics that we could not find addressed in your state's statutes or cases, we suggest you review the same topics in the subchapters of surrounding states. Your state's courts may look to the law of neighboring states to see how their courts and legislatures have treated that particular self-defense issue.)

[Exceptions to Lawful Self-Defense]

[Committing Felony or Unlawful Act]

[Mutual Combat]

[Exceptions to the Exceptions]

[Withdraw and Communicate]

[Presumption of Reasonableness in Special Places]

[Civil Liability]

Pancho's Wisdom

As for me and my house, we'll continue to cling to our guns and our religion!

RHODE ISLAND

Like many of the Eastern Seaboard States, Rhode Island's self-defense laws leave much to be desired. It only has a presumption statute that relates to the defense of persons occupying certain buildings, including one's home. However, because the presumption statute only applies if an intruder is violating one of several long and complex statutes, remembering all the details could be difficult in a stressful, defensive moment. We encourage the citizens of Rhode Island to lobby for self-defense laws that will be more protective of innocent persons and less protective of criminals. See The Mother of All Self-Defense Laws, Chapter 20.

Key: ■ commentary ■ original statutes, cases or jury instructions

---

[Defense of Self and Others] [Non-Deadly Force]

"The law concerning self-defense in Rhode Island permits persons who believe that they are in imminent peril of bodily harm to use such nondeadly force as is reasonably necessary in the circumstances to protect themselves." *State v. Quarles*, 504 A.2d 473, 475 (R.I.1986)

[Deadly Force]

"Second, the trial justice accurately summarized the circumstances under which defendant was entitled to defend himself with deadly force, explaining that defendant must have a reasonable fear of 'imminent death or serious bodily injury' and must respond reasonably in proportion to that threat, retreating if it is reasonably safe to do so." *State v. Hanes*, 783 A.2d 920, 925 (R.I. 2001) [This court's ruling follows the lead of the other states by requiring two things: (1) a reasonable fear, (2) of imminent death or serious bodily injury.]

[Defense of Third Persons]

"First, the force must be such as the actor could use in defending himself or herself from the harm that he or she believes to be threatened to the third person. In other words, the actor may use the same amount of force that he or she could use to protect himself or herself. Second, the third person must be justified in using such protective force in the circumstances as the actor believes them to be. Thus, if the third person was resisting an arrest by a known police officer, he or she would have no defense and, if the circumstances were known to the actor, the actor would have no defense either. Finally, the actor must believe that his or her intervention is necessary for the protection of the third party." *State v. Beeley*, 653 A.2d 722, 726 (R.I. 1995). [You can use the same force to defend a third person that you could use to defend yourself. You will be judged by what you reasonably believed the situation to be even if you were mistaken.]

[Exceptions to Justifiable Self-Defense] [Initial Aggressor] [Provocation]

"One may not invoke the doctrine of self-defense if he or she has instigated the combative confrontation, as self-defense is grounded on necessity, and one cannot provoke a difficulty, thus creating the necessity, and then justify the resulting homicide or injury as an act of necessity and self-defense." *State v. Linde,* 876 A.2d 1115, 1130 (R.I. 2005). [If you start or provoke a fight, you cannot win the case on the theory of self-defense.]

[Duty to Retreat – Generally – Yes]

"Before resorting to the use of deadly force, the person attacked must attempt retreat if he or she is consciously aware of an open, safe, and available avenue of escape. The only exception in Rhode Island to the obligation to attempt retreat was created by statute. It exempts an individual from the duty to retreat and permits the use of deadly force by an owner, tenant, or occupier of premises against any person engaged in the commission of an unlawful breaking and entering or burglary." *State v. Quarles,* 504 A.2d 473, 475 (R.I. 1986). [You have a duty to retreat before using deadly force if it can be done safely. The exception is if someone is breaking and entering your home as explained below.]

[Defense of Person(s) in Special Places – Dwelling, Business,] [No Duty to Retreat From Dwelling, Business]

§ GENERAL LAWS (G.L.) OF RHODE ISLAND 1956 § 11-8-8.

. . . There shall be no duty on the part of an owner, tenant, or occupier to retreat from any person engaged in the commission of any criminal offense enumerated in §§ **11-8-2 - 11-8-6.** [This is a unique statute among the several states. Most statutes relating to the defense of special places such as the home or business say you do not have to retreat from those places before using defensive force. They do not limit the privilege of not retreating to any specific crimes. Rhode Island limits the doctrine of no-retreat to situations in which the intruder is committing the crimes specifically named in Rhode Island General Laws §§11-8-2 – 11-8-6. Generally these offenses include burglarizing or breaking and entering into a home or business. See detailed summaries of these offenses in the definitions section below.]

[Co-Habitant – Duty to Retreat – Yes]

"Further, 'one need not retreat from [his or her] place of dwelling before using deadly force to repel an assailant.'[....] This exception to the Doctrine of Retreat is not available to repel an attack by a co-tenant or roommate and one must attempt to retreat in the face of a deadly attack by a co-occupant." *Mosby v. Devine,* 851 A.2d 1031, 1043 (R.I. 2004). [If someone you live with attacks you with deadly force, you must retreat before using deadly force if you can retreat with reasonable safety.]

[Presumption of Reasonableness in Special Places]

§ G.L.1956 § 11-8-8 .

In the event that any person shall die or shall sustain a personal injury in any way or for any cause while in the commission of any criminal offense enumerated in §§ **11-8-2 –**

11-8-6, it shall be rebuttably presumed as a matter of law in any civil or criminal proceeding that the owner, tenant, or occupier of the place where the offense was committed acted by reasonable means in self-defense and in the reasonable belief that the person engaged in the criminal offense was about to inflict great bodily harm or death upon that person or any other individual lawfully in the place where the criminal offense was committed . . . [If someone other than a co-tenant breaks and enters your home or your place of business, the law presumes you acted reasonably in defending yourself or others. This applies to criminal cases as well as cases in which the person you injured sues you for his injuries. This presumption can be rebutted. See our discussion in Chapter 4.]

[HELPFUL DEFINITIONS RELATING TO THIS STATE'S SELF-DEFENSE STATUTES]
The following definitions generally define the crimes that an intruder must be in the act of committing before the defending homeowner qualifies for the presumption described in §11-8-8 above. You must retreat from your own home if the intruder is not committing one of these crimes. If the intruder is a co-tenant or he is not committing one of the following offenses, you may only use deadly force to repel an imminent threat of death or serious injury AND you must retreat before using defensive force if it is reasonably safe for you to do so.

Some of the crimes mentioned below are misdemeanors or involve the destruction or theft of property (e.g., stealing chickens!) UNLESS YOU WANT TO BE RHODE ISLAND'S NEXT TEST CASE, we STRONGLY SUGGEST you NOT use deadly force to defend against what you know to be a harmless misdemeanor or prank. Are you going to shoot some kid for breaking into a school library to return a book that is overdue? Kill a poor vagrant for breaking into your chicken coop?

§ 11-8-2. Unlawful breaking and entering of dwelling house [Breaking and entering at any time of the day or night into any dwelling house or apartment, occupied or not, or any outbuilding or garage attached to or adjoining any dwelling house, without the consent of the owner or tenant of the dwelling house, apartment, building, or garage.]

§ 11-8-2.1. Unlawful breaking and entering of dwelling with possession of instruments relating to wrongful setting of fires [Same as above, but pertaining to those who possess the equipment related to the wrongful setting of fires.]

§ 11-8-2.2. Breaking and entering of a dwelling when resident on premises [Breaking and entering into any dwelling house or apartment without the consent of the owner or tenant at a time when the resident or residents of the dwelling house or apartment are on the premises, after having been previously convicted of such an offense.]

§ 11-8-2.3. Breaking and entering of dwelling house of persons 60 years of age or older when resident on premises [Breaking and entering into any dwelling house or apartment, without the consent of the owner or tenant when a resident of the dwelling house or apartment who is sixty (60) years of age or older is there.]

§ 11-8-2.4. Breaking and entering of dwelling house of a person who is severely impaired [Breaking and entering into any dwelling house or apartment, without the consent of the owner or tenant while a person is there who is severely mentally or physically impaired to the extent that the disabled person has considerable difficulty living independently, communicating or providing for himself or herself economically.]

§ 11-8-3. Entry of building or ship with felonious intent [Entering any dwelling house or apartment at any time of day or night or entering a building, ship, or vessel with intent to commit murder, sexual assault, robbery, arson or larceny.]

§ 11-8-4. Breaking and entering business place, public building, or ship with felonious intent [Breaking and entering into any bank, shop, office or warehouse, not adjoining to or occupied as a dwelling house, any meeting house, church, chapel, courthouse, town house, college, academy, schoolhouse, library or other building erected for public use or occupied for any public purpose, or any ship or vessel, with intent to commit murder, sexual assault, robbery or larceny.]

§ 11-8-5. Breaking and entering other buildings with criminal intent—Railroad cars—Tractor trailers [Breaking and entering or entering in the nighttime, with intent to commit larceny or any felony or misdemeanor in it, any barn, stable, carriage house, or other building, for the breaking and entering or entering of which with that intent no punishment is otherwise prescribed by this title, and every person who shall at any time break and enter or enter any railroad car or the trailer portion of a tractor trailer or break any lock or seal on it with intent to commit larceny or other crime.]

§ 11-8-5.1. Unlawful breaking and entering of business place, public building or ship during the daytime [Breaking and entering into any bank, shop, office, or warehouse, not adjoining to or occupied as a dwelling house, any meeting house, church, chapel, courthouse, town house, college, academy, schoolhouse, library, or other building erected for public use or occupied for any purpose, or any ship or vessel during the daytime.]

§ 11-8-6. Entry to steal poultry—Arrest—Fine [Breaking and entering into, or entering in the nighttime without breaking, any building or enclosure in which are kept or confined any kind of poultry, with intent to steal any of the poultry, or entering any building or enclosure in which are kept or confined any kind of poultry, with intent to steal any of the poultry.]

[TEMPLATE Topics We Could Not Find Explained in Statutes or Cases]

(For each of these topics that we could not find addressed in your state's statutes or cases, we suggest you review the same topics in the subchapters of surrounding states. Your state's courts may look to the law of neighboring states to see how their courts and legislatures have treated that particular self-defense issue.)

[Use of Deadly Force to Prevent Serious Felonies]

[Mutual Combat]

[Committing Felony or Unlawful Act]

[Exceptions to the Exceptions]

[Co-Employees – Duty to Retreat]

[Withdraw and Communicate]

[Reckless Injury to Innocent Third Parties]

[Civil Liability]

[Defense of Property]

[History of Violent Behavior]

SOUTH CAROLINA

While South Carolina recently adopted a very protective home-defense statute patterned after Florida's, its general self-defense statute is quite lacking. It still requires a person to retreat before using defensive force and it does not authorize the use of deadly force to stop violent felonies.

Key: ■ commentary ■ original statutes, cases or jury instructions

[Defense of Self and Others] [Non-Deadly Force] [Deadly Force]
"As our precedent recognizes, self-defense requires that a defendant show that (1) he was without fault in bringing on the difficulty; (2) he was in actual imminent danger of losing his life or sustaining serious bodily injury, or he must have actually believed he was in imminent danger of losing his life or sustaining serious bodily injury; (3) a reasonably prudent person of ordinary firmness and courage would have entertained the same belief; and (4) he had no other probable means of avoiding the danger [i.e. retreating, if possible]." *State v. Rye,* 651 S.E.2d 321, 323 (S.C. 2007). [This recent South Carolina case sets forth the four elements of self-defense when not in your home, car or workplace. Notice you must retreat before using defensive force if there is any other probable alternative.]

[Defense of Third Persons]
"Under the theory of defense of others, one is not guilty of taking the life of an assailant who assaults a friend, relative, or bystander if that friend, relative, or bystander would likewise have the right to take the life of the assailant in self-defense." *State v. Starnes,* 531 S.E.2d 907, 913 (S.C. 2007). [You can defend others if they would have been justified in defending themselves as explained in the *Rye* case in the previous paragraph. If the person you end up defending would not be justified in defending herself (e.g., she started the fight), then you would not be justified defending her. This poses a huge legal risk if you are not aware of all of the facts leading up to the conflict between the person you defend and her opponent.]

[Exceptions to Justifiable Self-Defense] [Initial Aggressor]
"'[O]ne who provokes or initiates an assault cannot escape criminal liability by invoking self-defense. . . .' Ferdinand S. Tinio, Comment Note: Withdrawal, After Provocation of Conflict, As Reviving Right Of Self-Defense, 55 A.L.R.3d 1000, 1003 (1974)." Cited with approval in *State v. Bryant,* 520 S.E.2d 319, 322 (S.C. 1999). [If you start a fight or provoke someone as an excuse to hurt him when he reacts, you lose the right to use force in self-defense.]

[Provocation]

"Any act of the accused in violation of law and reasonably calculated to produce the occasion amounts to bringing on the difficulty and bars his right to assert self-defense as a justification or excuse for a homicide. 40 Am. Jur.2d Homicide § 149 (1999)." Cited with approval in *State v. Bryant*, 520 S.E.2d 319, 322 (S.C. 1999).

[Committing Felony or Unlawful Act]

"'[A] robber, who is met with such violent resistance by his victim that he has no opportunity to convince [the] victim that he has abandoned his criminal intentions and only wants to withdraw, may not claim self-defense if he injures or kills his victim.' 55 A.L.R.3d at 1003-04; see also *United States v. Thomas*, 34 F.3d 44 (2d Cir. 1994) (one who commits or attempts a robbery armed with deadly force and kills the intended victim when victim responds with force may not avail himself of the defense of self-defense); *People v. Couch*, 461 N.W.2d 683 (Mich. 1990) (a robber or other wrongdoer engaged in felonious conduct has no privilege of self-defense); *Stiles v. State*, 829 P.2d 984 (Okla.Crim.App. 1994) (one who kills while committing armed robbery is an aggressor and an aggressor is not entitled to a claim of self-defense)." Cited with approval in *State v. Bryant*, 520 S.E.2d 319, 322 (S.C. 1999). [Self-defense is not available for those committing a robbery or felony. If you contribute to the circumstances that eventually lead to you hurting or killing someone, you lose the right to use force in self-defense.]

[Mutual Combat]

"As a general rule, the plea of self-defense is not available to one who kills another in mutual combat. The basic principles governing the doctrine of mutual combat are thus stated in 40 C.J.S. Homicide § 122, p. 996:

"'Where a person voluntarily participates in . . . mutual combat for purposes other than protection, he cannot justify or excuse the killing of his adversary in the course of such conflict on the ground of self-defense, regardless of what extremity or imminent peril he may be reduced to in the progress of the combat, unless, before the homicide is committed, he withdraws and endeavors in good faith to decline further conflict, and either by word or act, makes that fact known to his adversary,. . .'

"We held in *State v. Andrews*, 73 S.C. 257, 53 S.E. 423 that, 'where two persons mutually engaged in combat, and one kills the other, and at the time of the killing it be maliciously done, it is murder; if it be done in sudden heat and passion upon sufficient provocation without premeditation or malice, it would be manslaughter.'" *State v. Graham*, 196 S.E.2d 495, 496 (S.C. 1973). [If you agree to a fight, you lose the right to defend yourself. You might regain the right if you withdraw and communicate that you don't want to fight any longer, but when it gets this complicated, plan on being arrested and prosecuted.]

[Exceptions to the Exceptions] [Withdraw and Communicate]

"'[I]f, after commencing the assault, the aggressor withdraws in good faith from the conflict and announces in some way to his adversary his intention to retire, he is restored to his right of self-defense . . . .' 55 A.L.R.3d at 1003. One's right to self-defense is restored after a withdrawal from the initial difficulty with the victim if that withdrawal is communicated to the victim by word or act. *State v. Graham*, 260 S.C. 449, 196 S.E.2d

495 (1973)." *State v. Bryant,* 520 S.E.2d 319, 322 (S.C.1999). [As mentioned above, self-defense can sometimes be available if you withdraw (e.g., retreat), and effectively communicate to the other person that you no longer want to fight. Under those circumstances, if your opponent continues to come after you, you may be justified in defending yourself. Our advice is, however, never start or escalate a fight. Always try to de-escalate any conflict so that you do not have to use force in defending yourself if at all possible.]

[Duty to Retreat – Generally – Yes]

"A jury also could have found Jackson had no other probable means of preventing serious bodily injury or death once the fight began. Unless the incident occurred in the accused's home or business or on the curtilage thereof, the accused generally has a duty to retreat." *State v. Jackson,* 681 S.E.2d 17, 21 (S.C. App. 2009) [South Carolina case law says you have a general duty to retreat before using defensive force unless you are in your home, business or occupied vehicle. In June of 2006 a new statute went into effect that says you don't have to retreat before using defensive force as long as you have a right to be in the place where you are attacked. That statute was not mentioned in the *Jackson* case mentioned above. The incident in that case occurred in October of 2003 before the new law was passed and the South Carolina courts have refused to apply the new law to defensive incidents preceding the passage of the new law. For example, see the discussion in the Dickey case mentioned below. Until the South Carolina courts answer the question of whether the no-duty-to-retreat rule has been expanded, we suggest you retreat before using defensive force if you can safely do so if attacked outside of your home, business or vehicle. See detailed discussion below in section entitled **[No Duty to Retreat From Dwelling, Business, Occupied Vehicle.]**

[Defense of Person(s) in Special Places – Home, Businesses and Vehicles]

§ S.C. CODE ANN. § 16-11-420.
Intent and findings of General Assembly.

(A) It is the intent of the General Assembly to codify the common law Castle Doctrine which recognizes that a person's home is his castle and to extend the doctrine to include an occupied vehicle and the person's place of business.

(B) The General Assembly finds that it is proper for law-abiding citizens to protect themselves, their families, and others from intruders and attackers without fear of prosecution or civil action for acting in defense of themselves and others.

(C) The General Assembly finds that Section **20**, Article **I** of the South Carolina Constitution guarantees the right of the people to bear arms, and this right shall not be infringed.

(D) The General Assembly finds that persons residing in or visiting this State have a right to expect to remain unmolested and safe within their homes, businesses, and vehicles.

(E) The General Assembly finds that no person or victim of crime should be required to surrender his personal safety to a criminal, nor should a person or victim be required to needlessly retreat in the face of intrusion or attack.

[*Pancho's Wisdom* – We don't want to confuse you, but the phrase "codify the common law Castle Doctrine" has the potential of weakening the application of South Carolina's statute by the state's courts. South Carolina recently patterned its castle doctrine after Florida's, perhaps the most protective in the nation. Florida's law expanded the castle doctrine far beyond the common law rule. The common law rule said you didn't have to retreat from your home (castle in those days), but had to retreat before using deadly force if you were attacked while anywhere besides your home. Florida's castle law extends the no-retreat rule to occupied vehicles and every other place a person has a right to be. See our comments on Florida's home-defense statute in Florida's subchapter. Mentioning the common law in South Carolina's statute could give the South Carolina Courts an excuse to apply less protective common law rules rather than more expansive Florida rules. We suggest the South Carolina Legislature remove every reference to the common law in this statute during the next legislative session.]

[Presumption of Reasonableness in Special Places – Dwelling, Residence or Occupied Vehicle]

§ S.C. CODE ANN. § 16-11-440.

Presumption of reasonable fear of imminent peril when using deadly force against another unlawfully entering residence, occupied vehicle or place of business.

(A) A person is presumed to have a reasonable fear of imminent peril of death or great bodily injury to himself or another person when using deadly force that is intended or likely to cause death or great bodily injury to another person if the person:

(1) against whom the deadly force is used is in the process of unlawfully and forcefully entering, or has unlawfully and forcibly entered a dwelling, residence, or occupied vehicle, or if he removes or is attempting to remove another person against his will from the dwelling, residence, or occupied vehicle; and

(2) who uses deadly force knows or has reason to believe that an unlawful and forcible entry or unlawful and forcible act is occurring or has occurred.
[If a stranger breaks into your home and you splatter him all over the wall, it is presumed you acted lawfully. The "splatteree's" entrance must be unlawful (without your permission) as well as his entry by force (e.g., breaking and entering). Presumptions can, however, be rebutted. Please read our caution in Chapter 4 to never use deadly force against someone whom you know for a fact is unarmed and non-threatening. If your pesky, harmless, bipolar neighbor gets disoriented and breaks into your home from time to time thinking his key is defective and you juice him, it is possible for the presumption to be rebutted and for you to be convicted of murder.]

(B) The presumption provided in subsection (A) does not apply if the person:

(1) against whom the deadly force is used has the right to be in or is a lawful resident of the dwelling, residence, or occupied vehicle including, but not limited to, an owner, lessee, or titleholder; or [The presumption doesn't apply if the person against whom the force is used has a right to be in the residence or vehicle. There is no presumption that you acted reasonably if you dust your room-

mate, spouse (after you bought that humongous life insurance policy), live-in mother-in-law, landlord who showed up to collect the rent, etc., etc.]

(2) sought to be removed is a child or grandchild, or is otherwise in the lawful custody or under the lawful guardianship, of the person against whom the deadly force is used; or [The law will not let you settle custody disputes with deadly force. You have no presumption in your favor if you ventilate your ex when she picks up the kids, even if she is in violation of the visitation order.]

(3) who uses deadly force is engaged in an unlawful activity or is using the dwelling, residence, or occupied vehicle to further an unlawful activity; or [You can't be committing crimes in the home if you want the presumption to apply. A prostitute who tries to kill a john who refuses to pay for services rendered will not be entitled to a favorable presumption.]

(4) against whom the deadly force is used is a law enforcement officer who enters or attempts to enter a dwelling, residence, or occupied vehicle in the performance of his official duties, and he identifies himself in accordance with applicable law or the person using force knows or reasonably should have known that the person entering or attempting to enter is a law enforcement officer. [If you're cookin' meth or growing weed, don't expect the law to presume you acted reasonably if you try to pop a cap on the popo during a no-knock entry.]

[No Duty to Retreat From Dwelling, Businesses, Occupied Vehicle]
[Use of Deadly Force to Prevent Serious Felonies]

(C) A person who is not engaged in an unlawful activity and who is attacked in another place where he has a right to be, including, but not limited to, his place of business, has no duty to retreat and has the right to stand his ground and meet force with force, including deadly force, if he reasonably believes it is necessary to prevent death or great bodily injury to himself or another person or to prevent the commission of a violent crime as defined in Section **16-1-60**. [This is where it gets complicated. We believe the intent of subparagraph (C) was to do away with the duty to retreat if you have a right to be in the place where you are attacked. (e.g., grocery store parking lot). Unfortunately, § 16-11-420 (A) above states, "It is the intent of the General Assembly to codify the common law Castle Doctrine . . ." The problem is common law *required* a person to *retreat* when attacked outside of his home. Therefore, despite what we think is the intent of subparagraph (C), *you still might be required to retreat* before using defensive force when not in your home, occupied vehicle or business.

There are no South Carolina cases that have clarified this since the legislation was signed into law on June 9, 2006. The South Carolina Court of Appeals refused to apply the law retroactively in the case *State v. Dickey,* 669 S.E.2d 917, 924 (S.C.App. 2008). In that case the appeals court held that the defendant, who was on a public sidewalk when attacked, had a duty to retreat before using deadly force unless it would have made it more dangerous for him to retreat. But the shooting occurred before the new law went into effect. South Carolina attorneys should start asserting this subparagraph as authority for a jury instruction that says you don't have to retreat if you have a right to be in the place you are attacked.

It will be interesting to see how the South Carolina Courts will interpret the two seemingly conflicting concepts—the duty to retreat under common law and the language of this paragraph that eliminates the duty to retreat when in a place you have a right to be. Until the South Carolina Supreme Court definitively answers the no-retreat question, we suggest you retreat before using defensive force if you can safely do so if you are not in your home, vehicle or business when attacked.

If the South Carolina courts don't misread this sub-section, it also says you can use deadly force without retreating to prevent the commission of a violent crime as defined in the definitions at the end of this subchapter. That's a huge advantage to law abiding citizens if the courts will validate it. Until the S.C. courts validate it, however, we suggest you not attempt to stop a violent crime outside of your home or occupied vehicle which does not involve an imminent threat of death or serious injury.]

(D) A person who unlawfully and by force enters or attempts to enter a person's dwelling, residence, or occupied vehicle is presumed to be doing so with the intent to commit an unlawful act involving force or a violent crime as defined in Section **16-1-60.** [It's presumed if someone uses force to enter your home or vehicle without your permission, that he intends to commit the type of crime that triggers (pun intended) your right to defend with deadly force. Don't ever forget, however, that presumptions can be rebutted.]

(E) A person who by force enters or attempts to enter a dwelling, residence, or occupied vehicle in violation of an order of protection, restraining order, or condition of bond is presumed to be doing so with the intent to commit an unlawful act regardless of whether the person is a resident of the dwelling, residence, or occupied vehicle including, but not limited to, an owner, lessee, or titleholder. [This is the exception to subparagraph (B)(1) above. The most common scenario this paragraph applies to is when a wife accuses a husband of domestic violence. In such cases the court issues an order telling the husband to stay out of the house and away from the wife. If the husband violates the court order, it's presumed he is doing so with the intent to commit a crime. If he tries to force his way into the home, the law presumes the wife had the justification to use deadly force even though, at one time, he had a right to be in the home. See a more detailed discussion in the chapter on domestic violence, Chapter 13.]

[Civil Liability]

§ S.C. CODE ANN. § 16-11-450.

Immunity from criminal prosecution and civil actions; law enforcement officer exception; costs.

(A) A person who uses deadly force as permitted by the provisions of this article or another applicable provision of law is justified in using deadly force and is immune from criminal prosecution and civil action for the use of deadly force, unless the person against whom deadly force was used is a law enforcement officer acting in the performance of his official duties and he identifies himself in accordance with applicable law or the person using deadly force knows or reasonably should have known that the person is a law enforcement officer. [If you comply with South Carolina's law of self-defense, you are immune from criminal prosecution or civil lawsuits for damages. These protections do not apply if you injure or kill a police officer who properly identifies himself.]

(B) A law enforcement agency may use standard procedures for investigating the use of deadly force as described in subsection (A), but the agency may not arrest the person for using deadly force unless probable cause exists that the deadly force used was unlawful. [You can only be arrested if there is probable cause that the deadly force you used was unlawful, but you will always be investigated if death or serious injury results from your defensive act.]

(C) The court shall award reasonable attorneys' fees, court costs, compensation for loss of income, and all expenses incurred by the defendant in defense of a civil action brought by a plaintiff if the court finds that the defendant is immune from prosecution as provided in subsection (A). [If you are found "not guilty" for shooting the scumbag who broke into your home, if he tries to sue you, his lawsuit will be dismissed. You will then be entitled to sue him to pay for your attorney fees, costs and any other expenses you lost defending the lawsuit he brought against you.]

[Defense of Property]

"A person in possession of property, either as owner, or as the agent or servant of the owner, may justify a charge of assault and battery by proving that, in defense of the property, and to protect it from threatened and impending injury or destruction at the hands of the person assaulted, he used such force as was necessary, and no more than was necessary, to prevent the injury or loss." *State v. Martin,* 147 S.E. 606, 615 (S.C. 1929).

[There is a surprising lack of case law on this area in South Carolina. Although this case is 80 years old, as far as we can tell it is still good law. Please notice that it does not say you can use deadly force to defend your property.]

[HELPFUL DEFINITIONS RELATING TO THIS STATE'S SELF-DEFENSE STATUTES]

- **Dwelling** – means a building or conveyance of any kind, including an attached porch, whether the building or conveyance is temporary or permanent, mobile or immobile, which has a roof over it, including a tent, and is designed to be occupied by people lodging there at night. **S.C. Code Ann. § 16-11-430 (1).**

- **Great bodily injury** – means bodily injury which creates a substantial risk of death or which causes serious, permanent disfigurement, or protracted loss or impairment of the function of a bodily member or organ. **S.C. Code Ann. § 16-11-430 (2).**

- **Residence** – means a dwelling in which a person resides either temporarily or permanently or is visiting as an invited guest. **S.C. Code Ann. § 16-11-430 (3).**

- **Vehicle** – means a conveyance of any kind, whether or not motorized, which is designed to transport people or property. **S.C. Code Ann. § 16-11-430 (4).**

- **Violent Crime** – For purposes of definition under South Carolina law, a violent crime includes the offenses of: murder (Section 16-3-10); criminal sexual conduct in the first and second degree (Sections 16-3-652 and 16-3-653); criminal sexual conduct with minors, first and second degree (Section 16-3-655); assault with intent to commit criminal sexual conduct, first and second degree (Section 16-3-656); assault and battery with intent to kill (Section 16-3-620); kidnapping (Section 16-3-910); voluntary manslaughter (Section 16-3-50); armed robbery (Section 16-11-330(A)); attempted armed robbery (Section 16-11-330(B)); carjacking (Section 16-3-1075); drug trafficking as defined in Section 44-53-370(e) or trafficking cocaine base as defined in Section 44-53-375(C); manufacturing or trafficking methamphetamine as defined in Section 44-53-375; arson in the first degree (Section 16-11-110(A)); arson in the second degree (Section 16-11-110(B)); burglary in the first degree (Section 16-11-311); burglary in the second degree (Section 16-11-312(B)); engaging a child for a sexual performance (Section 16-3-810); homicide by child abuse (Section 16-3-85(A)(1)); aiding and abetting homicide by child abuse (Section 16-3-85(A)(2)); inflicting great bodily injury upon a child (Section 16-3-95(A)); allowing great bodily injury to be inflicted upon a child (Section 16-3-95(B)); criminal domestic violence of a high and aggravated nature (Section 16-25-65); abuse or neglect of a vulnerable adult resulting in death (Section 43-35-85(F)); abuse or neglect of a vulnerable adult resulting in great bodily injury (Section 43-35-85(E)); accessory before the fact to commit any of the above offenses (Section 16-1-40); attempt to commit any of the above offenses (Section 16-1-80); and taking of a hostage by an inmate (Section 24-13-450). Only those offenses specifically enumerated in this section are considered violent offenses.

[TEMPLATE Topics We Could Not Find Explained in Statutes or Cases]

(For each of these topics that we could not find addressed in your state's statutes or cases, we suggest you review the same topics in the subchapters of surrounding states. Your state's courts may look to the law of neighboring states to see how their courts and legislatures have treated that particular self-defense issue.)

[Co-Habitants; Co-Employees – Duty of Retreat]

[Reckless Injury to Innocent Third Parties]

SOUTH DAKOTA

Warning: If you rely upon the plain meaning of certain parts of South Dakota's self-defense statutes you could get into serious trouble. South Dakota's courts have said that some sections of the states statutes do not mean what they say.

Key: ■ commentary ■ original statutes, cases or jury instructions

[Defense of Self and Others] [Deadly Force]
[Use of Deadly Force to Prevent Serious Felonies]

§ SOUTH DAKOTA CODIFIED LAWS (SDCL) § 22-16-34.

Homicide is justifiable if committed by any person while resisting any attempt to murder such person, or to commit any felony upon him or her, or upon or in any dwelling house in which such person is. [The first part of this law is standard in every state. You can use deadly force to resist someone trying to murder you. The second part of the statute is troubling because it seems to authorize you to kill anyone committing "any felony" against you or in your home. South Dakota's cases say that is NOT true.]

[The following quotes are from the landmark South Dakota case *State v. Pellegrino.* It seriously limits the scope of SDCL § 22-16-34, South Dakota's deadly force statute.]

"He [The defendant] seems to argue that if one commits any felony in or upon a home, death may be imposed without qualification, even without apparent necessity. If this is what the statute truly intends, then he may be entitled to acquittal as a matter of law as he asserts. This statute, however, obviously codifies the common law and therefore must be read in comprehension of it and our other statutes controlling the use of deadly force... If we interpret 'any felony' in SDCL 22-16-34 literally, one might justifiably be shot while forging a check in someone's home. '[I]n view of the large number of felonies today and the inclusion of many that do not involve a danger of serious bodily harm, a literal reading of the section is undesirable.'" *State v. Pellegrino*, 577 N.W.2d 590, 596 (S.D. 1998) (citing *People v. Ceballos*, 526 P.2d 241, 244-45 (1974)). [This case says that only felonies involving serious danger of bodily harm justify the use of deadly force in self-defense. You may not use it for felonies that do not involve serious bodily harm, such as forging checks. In addition, deadly force to be necessary and not excessive. See our lengthy discussion on the concept of necessity in Chapter 3.]

[Defense of a Third Person]

§ SDCL § 22-16-35.

Homicide is justifiable if committed by any person in the lawful defense of such person, or of his or her husband, wife, parent, child, master, mistress, or servant if there is reasonable ground to apprehend a design to commit a felony, or to do some great personal injury, and imminent danger of such design being accomplished. [You can use deadly force to defend against an imminent threat of great personal injury. The language that grants the right to use deadly force to prevent "a felony," goes too far, however. As the *Pellegrino* case above explains, despite this wording, you only have the right to use deadly force to prevent felonies involving great bodily harm.

This statute limits the right to defend others to only those classes of persons named, i.e., husbands, wives, parents, etc. To date we have not found a case that expands the right to defend others beyond the specific classes of persons described. For example, if you use deadly force to defend your brother, you run the legal risk of becoming South Dakota's first test case on this issue. Incidentally, in other states with similar restrictions on defending third persons, the term "mistress" does not mean a woman with whom you are having an adulterous relationship. It means the opposite of "master," referring to an employer of some sort, the exact nature of which we cannot tell you because the terms are not defined in the South Dakota statutes or cases.]

§ SDCL § 22-16-33.

Homicide is justifiable if necessarily committed in attempting by lawful ways and means to apprehend any person for any felony committed, or in lawfully suppressing any riot, or in lawfully keeping and preserving the peace. [Despite the extremely broad language of this statute, you cannot use deadly force against fleeing felons, rioters or those disturbing the peace unless they pose an immediate threat of serious bodily injury or death to you or someone in the class of persons described above (husband, wife, child, parent, etc.). Furthermore, as we explain in Chapter 4, we highly recommend you do not chase fleeing felons unless it is absolutely necessary to protect a loved one.]

[Exceptions to Justifiable Self-Defense] [Initial Aggressor]
[Provocation]

"Generally, the aggressor, or the one who produces the circumstances which make it necessary to take another's life, is not entitled to assert self-defense." [There is no right of self-defense for a person who starts a fight.] *State v. Woods,* 374 N.W.2d 92, 97 (S.D. 1985).

[No Duty to Retreat – Generally]

§ SDCL § 22-18-4.

. . . A person does not have a duty to retreat if the person is in a place where he or she has a right to be. [There is no duty to retreat before using defensive force if you have a right to in the place where you are attacked. Trespassers, however, must retreat if they can safely do so before using defensive force.]

[Defense of Person(s) in Special Places – Home, Dwelling]
"The feudal concept of home as castle was borne of an age when inhabitants were compelled to turn their dwellings into fortified strongholds. The idea endures into modern times. But in our legal tradition, except at its uncivilized beginnings, people were not entitled to kill an assailant unless they honestly and reasonably believed their lives were in danger from assault, 'or when a felonious assault is being made upon the house, as to commit a burglary, arson, or other felony therein or against the inmates.' *Id*. (quoting Lord Hale in Pleas to the Crown (1 Hale, P.C. 484)); R. Perkins, *Criminal Law* 1022, n. 1 (2d ed. 1969). Over the years, confusion arose from a too broad interpretation of the castle doctrine: under the common law this precept was merely a 'limitation on the duty to retreat.' Home is a shelter and a refuge, not 'a free-fire zone.'

Pellegrino [defendant] contends that McKee [victim] committed a burglary, and, as a result, deadly force was justified. We find nothing in the record to intimate that McKee had violence in mind when he arrived at the home. Whether he entered uninvited was even open to question. Leetch testified that Pellegrino opened the door to let them in. Salvatore's testimony on this point was contradictory. Even under the defense version, McKee did not enter in a violent or tumultuous manner; he and Leetch simply opened the screen door and stepped inside. In no version did Pellegrino shoot McKee to prevent him from entering, so this was not an instance where a homeowner was attempting to repel a felonious outside intruder. One has no right to later kill a person simply for having made an illegal entry, as that would not be an act in self-protection, but an execution." *State v. Pellegrino*, 577 N.W.2d 590, 595 (S.D.1998) (citations omitted). [The *Pellegrino* case limits the right to use deadly force in your home to situations where you are at least threatened with great bodily harm (serious bodily injury) or death.]

[No Duty to Retreat From Special Places – Home]
"Persons in their own homes assaulted or placed in apparent imminent danger of great personal injury, have the right to stand their ground and meet force with force, even to the extent of taking life if such persons actually believe, and the circumstances and surrounding conditions are such that a reasonably cautious and prudent person would believe, danger of death or great personal injury to be imminent at the hands of the assailant." *State v. Pellegrino*, 577 N.W.2d 590, 596 (S.D. 1998). [You do not have to retreat from your own home before using deadly force. Notice, however, that even in the home, a person has to believe that there is an imminent danger of great personal injury. A homeowner cannot use deadly force on an intruder if there is no danger of serious bodily injury.]

[Defense of Property]

§ SDCL § 22-18-4.

Any person is justified in the use of force or violence against another person when the person reasonably believes that such conduct is necessary to prevent or terminate the other person's trespass on or other criminal interference with real property or personal property lawfully in his or her possession or in the possession of another who is a member of his or her immediate family or household or of a person whose property he or she has a legal right to protect. However, the person is justified in the use of deadly force only as provided in §§ **22-16-34** and **22-16-35** . . . [Force is justified to prevent a trespass or criminal interference with your property or a family member's property. Deadly force is not authorized for the protection of property.]

"Persons in their own homes assaulted or placed in apparent imminent danger of great personal injury, have the right to stand their ground and meet force with force even to the extent of taking life if such persons actually believe, and the circumstances and surrounding conditions are such that a reasonably cautious and prudent person would believe, danger of death or great personal injury to be imminent at the hands of the assailant." *State v. Pellegrino*, 577 N.W.2d 590, 596 (S.D. 1998). [A person assaulted at home does not have to retreat and can use deadly force if he reasonably believes he is in danger of death or serious bodily harm.]

[TEMPLATE Topics We Could Not Find Explained in Statutes or Cases]

(For each of these topics that we could not find addressed in your state's statutes or cases, we suggest you review the same topics in the subchapters of surrounding states. Your state's courts may look to the law of neighboring states to see how their courts and legislatures have treated that particular self-defense issue.)

[Non-Deadly Force]

[Committing Felony or Unlawful Act]

[Mutual Combat]

[Exceptions to the Exceptions]

[Withdraw and Communicate]

[Co-Habitants; Co-Employees – Duty to Retreat]

[Presumption of Reasonableness in Special Places]

[Reckless Injury to Innocent Third Parties]

[Civil Liability]

[Helpful Definitions Relating to this State's Self-Defense Statutes]

TENNESSEE

Key: ■ commentary ■ original statutes, cases or jury instructions

[Defense of Self and Others] [Non-Deadly Force]
[No Duty to Retreat – Generally]

§ TENNESSEE CODE ANNOTATED (T.C.A.) § 39-11-611 (b). Self-defense.

. . .

(b) (1) Notwithstanding the provisions of Section **39-17-1322**, a person who is not engaged in unlawful activity and is in a place where such person has a right to be has no duty to retreat before threatening or using force against another person when and to the degree the person reasonably believes the force is immediately necessary to protect against the other's use or attempted use of unlawful force.

[Deadly Force] [No Duty to Retreat – Generally]

(2) Notwithstanding the provisions of Section **39-17-1322**, a person who is not engaged in unlawful activity and is in a place where such person has a right to be has no duty to retreat before threatening or using force intended or likely to cause death or serious bodily injury if:

(A) The person has a reasonable belief that there is an imminent danger of death or serious bodily injury;

(B) The danger creating the belief of imminent death or serious bodily injury is real, or honestly believed to be real at the time; and

(C) The belief of danger is founded upon reasonable grounds.

[To be justified in using deadly force in self-defense without retreating a person must (1) not be doing anything illegally, (2) have a reasonable belief he is threatened with an imminent threat of death or serious bodily injury, (3) have an honest belief the danger is real and (4) the belief must be based upon facts and logic. **Example:** You don't trust Greeks (I can use this racial example because I'm Greek). You are walking down the sidewalk with your wife near several Greek restaurants and a few of the men look at your wife admiringly and speak in their native tongue (which is totally Greek to you!), laughing and raising their eyebrows as you all go by. Based upon this conduct you draw your gun and open fire. You explain to the police that you were convinced these men, based upon their suspicious conduct, intended to kill you and have their way with your beautiful wife. Justifiable self-defense? Hardly, strike three! Your belief there is an imminent danger is not reasonable, the danger is not real, you may have, in your twisted mind, honestly believed the danger was real, but your belief is not founded upon reasonable grounds. One question you should always ask yourself (quickly, hopefully, if the threat is imminent) is: Are there several facts I can describe that would lead a clear-thinking person to believe that his or her life is in immediate danger. **Example:** The maniac has a knife. He is shouting angrily at me and coming toward me making slashing motions. He is within twenty feet. I've told him to stop and he keeps coming. I retreat and he follows saying he is going to kill me. These are all facts, when considered together, that lead me to logically conclude the threat is imminent and that it is absolutely necessary to employ deadly force to survive the next few seconds.

The reference to 39-17-1322 is to the Tennessee Weapon Code which creates a defense to a weapon violation if the person is possessing or using a weapon to defend himself or another from a crime: "**39-17-1322. Defenses.** – A person shall not be charged with or convicted of a violation under this part [illegal weapons] if the person possessed, displayed or employed a handgun in justifiable self-defense or in justifiable defense of another during the commission of a crime in which that person or the other person defended was a victim."]

[Defense of a Third Person]

§ T.C.A. § 39-11-612.
Defense of third person.

A person is justified in threatening or using force against another to protect a third person, if:

(1) Under the circumstances as the person reasonably believes them to be, the person would be justified under § 39-11-611 [the use of both deadly and non-deadly force in self-defense explained above] in threatening or using force to protect against the use or attempted use of unlawful force reasonably believed to be threatening the third person sought to be protected; and

(2) The person reasonably believes that the intervention is immediately necessary to protect the third person.

[You can defend another person under the same circumstances you can defend yourself if you reasonably believe your actions are necessary.]

[Defense of Person(s) in Special Places – Home, Business, Occupied Vehicle]
[Presumption of Reasonableness in Special Places]

§ T.C.A. § 39-11-612 (c) and (d).

. . .

(c) Any person using force intended or likely to cause death or serious bodily injury within a residence, business, dwelling or vehicle is presumed to have held a reasonable belief of imminent death or serious bodily injury to self, family, a member of the household or a person visiting as an invited guest, when that force is used against another person, who unlawfully and forcibly enters or has unlawfully and forcibly entered the residence, business, dwelling or vehicle, and the person using defensive force knew or had reason to believe that an unlawful and forcible entry occurred. [This is somewhat similar to Florida's presumption statute. It creates a presumption that the person defending the special place has a reasonable fear of impending death or serious injury from an intruder who illegally forces his way in.]

(d) The presumption established in subsection (c) shall not apply, if:

[Co-Habitants; Co-Employees – Exception to Presumption]

(1) The person against whom the force is used has the right to be in or is a lawful resident of the dwelling, business, residence, or vehicle, such as an owner, lessee, or titleholder; provided, that the person is not prohibited from entering the dwelling, business, residence, or occupied vehicle by an order of protection, injunction for protection from domestic abuse, or a court order of no contact against that person; [The presumption does not apply if the intruder has a right to be in the special place, such as a roommate or co-employee. When the presumption does not apply, it means that you may not use deadly force unless faced with an imminent threat of deadly force as explained in §611 above. The presumption still applies, however, if a domestic partner has been denied the right to be in the home. If a court has ordered an abusive husband to stay out of the home and away from his estranged wife, she is presumed to have a reasonable fear of death or serious injury if he violates the protective order and forces his way into her home.]

(2) The person against whom the force is used is attempting to remove a person or persons who is a child or grandchild of, or is otherwise in the lawful custody or under the lawful guardianship of, the person against whom the defensive force is used; [Custody disputes must be resolved in court, not Hatfields-versus-McCoys style.]

(3) Notwithstanding Section **39-17-1322,** the person using force is engaged in an unlawful activity or is using the dwelling, business, residence, or occupied vehicle to further an unlawful activity; or [Special place cannot be used for an unlawful purpose, such as a meth lab in the garage.]

(4) The person against whom force is used is a law enforcement officer, as defined in Section **39-11-106,** who enters or attempts to enter a dwelling, business, residence, or vehicle in the performance of the officer's official duties, and the officer identified the officer in accordance with any applicable law, or the person using force knew or reasonably should have known that the person entering or attempting to enter was a law enforcement officer. [The presumption does not apply if the intruder is a law enforcement officer acting in his or her official capacity.]

[No Duty to Retreat From Special Places]

"However, a person is under no duty to retreat in his own home, even if he can safely do so, but may stand his ground and use reasonable force to prevent or stop an invasion of his home or habitation. One's own home or dwelling includes the curtilage [see definitions below] thereof. While a person assaulted in his own home is not bound to retreat, his right to invoke the doctrine of defense of home and habitation depends upon his being without fault in bringing on the difficulty." *State v. Bottenfield*, 692 S.W.2d 447, 452 (Tenn.Cr.App. 1985). [There is no duty to retreat from your own home.]

[Exceptions to Justifiable Self-Defense]

§ T.C.A. § 39-11-611 (e).

. . .

(e) The threat or use of force against another is not justified:

[Mutual Combat]

(1) If the person using force consented to the exact force used or attempted by the other individual;

[Provocation]

(2) If the person using force provoked the other individual's use or attempted use of unlawful force, unless:

[The use of force is not justified if you have agreed to fight or if you initiated the fight.]

[Exceptions to the Exceptions] [Withdraw and Communicate]

(A) The person using force abandons the encounter or clearly communicates to the other the intent to do so; and

(B) The other person nevertheless continues or attempts to use unlawful force against the person; or
[You may still claim self-defense even though you started the fight if you CLEARLY communicate your intent to quit fighting, you actually do quit and your opponent keeps fighting even though you have stopped.]

(3) To resist a halt at a roadblock, arrest, search, or stop and frisk that the person using force knows is being made by a law enforcement officer, unless:

(A) The law enforcement officer uses or attempts to use greater force than necessary to make the arrest, search, stop and frisk, or halt; and

(B) The person using force reasonably believes that the force is immediately necessary to protect against the law enforcement officer's use or attempted use of greater force than necessary.
[You may not resist any lawful detention unless the law officer over steps his authority and uses excessive force AND you reasonably believe that immediate force is necessary to protect yourself from the excessive force. However, resisting arrest or detention is a no-win situation and could get you shot with a gun or Taser.]

[Reckless Injury to Innocent Third Parties]

§ T.C.A. § 39-11-604.
Reckless injury of innocent third person.

Even though a person is justified under this part in threatening or using force or deadly force against another, the justification afforded by this part is unavailable in a prosecution for harm to an innocent third person who is recklessly injured or recklessly killed by the use of such force. [Although you may be justifiably using force against a "bad guy," if you are reckless in the use of that force, you could be convicted of manslaughter. **Example:** You try to stop a robbery on a busy public sidewalk and empty the entire hi-cap magazine in your Glock 17, injuring or killing an innocent bystander.]

[Civil Liability]

§ T.C.A. § 39-11-605.
Civil remedies unaffected.

The fact that conduct is justified under this part does not abolish or impair any remedy for the conduct that is or may be available in a civil suit. [The burden of proof in civil cases is lower than in criminal cases (see Chapter 15 on civil liability). You could be found not guilty but civilly liable for money damages. The following two statutes make money damage awards less likely, however.]

§ T.C.A. § 39-11-622.
Justification for use of force – Exceptions – Immunity from civil liability.

(a) (1) A person who uses force as permitted in §§ **39-11-611** [self-defense] – **39-11-614** [defense of property] or § **29-34-201**, [protection from lawsuits by criminals] is justified in using such force and is immune from civil liability for the use of such force, unless:

(A) The person against whom force was used is a law enforcement officer, as defined in § **39-11-106** who:

(i) Was acting in the performance of the officer's official duties; and

(ii) Identified the officer in accordance with any applicable law; or

(iii) The person using force knew or reasonably should have known that the person was a law enforcement officer; or

(B) The force used by the person resulted in property damage to or the death or injury of an innocent bystander or other person against whom the force used was not justified.

[When using force, you will be protected from civil liability unless you use force against a law enforcement officer who is performing his duties, and identified himself as an officer or you should have reasonably known he was an officer. Also, if your use of force results in the injury or death of a bystander or property damage, you are not immune from liability.]

(b) The court shall award reasonable attorney's fees, court costs, compensation for loss of income, and all expenses incurred by a person in defense of any civil action brought against the person based upon the person's use of force, if the court finds that the defendant was justified in using such force pursuant to §§ **39-11-611 – 39-11-614** or § **29-34-201**.

§ T. C. A. § 29-34-201.
Felonies; commission or attempt; injuries to perpetrator.

[If criminals get injured while committing the ugly felonies listed in this statute on they can't sue and win. It doesn't bar innocent bystanders from suing you, however. If you cause bullets to fly, make sure you have scanned the area for those who are present but not involved in committing a crime against you or your property.]

(a) Any person who is injured while committing a felony or attempting to commit a felony on the real property of another is barred from recovery of actual or punitive damages resulting from injuries, either accidentally or intentionally inflicted by the owner, lawful occupier or tenant of such property, which the person receives while committing or attempting to commit a felony.

(b) (1) A person who accidentally or intentionally causes property damage to or inflicts injury or death upon the perpetrator of a criminal offense is absolutely immune from civil liability for or the payment of monetary damages from such person's actions if at the time such damage, injury or death occurred:

(A) The person was preventing or attempting to prevent the perpetrator from committing the offense or was apprehending the perpetrator of the offense; and

(B) The perpetrator was committing one (1) or more of the offenses specified in subdivision (c)(1)-(9) or was attempting to commit one (1) or more of the offenses specified in subdivision (c)(10).

(2) The immunity conferred by this subsection shall only apply to property damage caused to or injury or death inflicted upon a perpetrator of an enumerated offense and only under the conditions set out in this subsection. Such immunity shall not be construed to extend to property damage caused to or injury or death inflicted upon a bystander or other person who is not the perpetrator of an enumerated offense.

(c) The offenses for which such immunity applies are:
(1) Any criminal homicide;
(2) Aggravated rape;
(3) Kidnapping;
(4) Aggravated kidnapping;
(5) Especially aggravated kidnapping;
(6) Especially aggravated burglary;
(7) Aggravated robbery;
(8) Especially aggravated robbery;
(9) Carjacking; and
(10) Attempt to commit first or second degree murder.

[Defense of Property]

§ T. C. A. § 39-11-614.
Property; Protection.

(a) A person in lawful possession of real or personal property is justified in threatening or using force against another, when and to the degree it is reasonably believed the force is immediately necessary to prevent or terminate the other's trespass on the land or unlawful interference with the property. [Force can be used to protect against a trespass, but not excessive or deadly force.]

(b) A person who has been unlawfully dispossessed of real or personal property is justified in threatening or using force against the other, when and to the degree it is reasonably believed the force is immediately necessary to reenter the land or recover the property, if the person threatens or uses the force immediately or in fresh pursuit after the dispossession:

(1) The person reasonably believes the other had no claim of right when the other dispossessed the person; and

(2) The other accomplished the dispossession by threatening or using force against the person.

(c) Unless a person is justified in using deadly force as otherwise provided by law, a person is not justified in using deadly force to prevent or terminate the other's trespass on real estate or unlawful interference with personal property.

[Force may be used to repossess land or personal property, but it must be in the moment of dispossession or in "fresh" pursuit. Deadly force may not be used unless justified by the statutes above.]

§ T. C. A. § 39-11-615.
Protection of third person's property.

A person is justified in threatening or using force against another to protect real or personal property of a third person, if, under the circumstances as the person reasonably believes them to be, the person would be justified under § **39-11-614** in threatening or using force to protect the person's own real or personal property. [You can use force to defend the property of others under the same conditions as you could to defend your own property.]

§ T. C. A. § 39-11-616.
Use of device to protect property.

(a) The justification afforded by §§ **39-11-614** and **39-11-615** extends to the use of a device for the purpose of protecting property, only if:

(1) The device is not designed to cause or known to create a substantial risk of causing death or serious bodily harm;

(2) The use of the particular device to protect the property from entry or trespass is reasonable under the circumstances as the person believes them to be; and

(3) The device is one customarily used for such a purpose, or reasonable care is taken to make known to probable intruders the fact that it is used.

(b) Nothing in this section shall affect the law regarding the use of animals to protect property or persons.

[Devices can be used to protect property if they do not create a substantial risk of death or serious bodily harm. **Example:** A shotgun with a trip wire to defend your garage is not legal because it could cause death or serious injury. A large canine with a biological honing device for the crown jewels of a male burglar is allowed.]

[HELPFUL DEFINITIONS RELATING TO THIS STATE'S SELF-DEFENSE STATUTES]

- **Curtilage** – means the area surrounding a dwelling that is necessary, convenient and habitually used for family purposes and for those activities associated with the sanctity of a person's home. **T.C.A. § 39-11-611 (2).**

- **Dwelling** – means a building or conveyance of any kind, including any attached porch, whether the building or conveyance is temporary or permanent, mobile or immobile, that has a roof over it, including a tent, and is designed for or capable of use by people. **T.C.A. § 39-11-611 (3).**

- **Residence** – means a dwelling in which a person resides, either temporarily or permanently, or is visiting as an invited guest, or any dwelling, building or other appurtenance within the curtilage of the residence. **T.C.A. § 39-11-611 (4).**

- **Vehicle** – means any motororized vehicle that is self-propelled and designed for use on public highways to transport people or property. **T.C.A. § 39-11-611 (5).**

- **Deadly force** – means force that is intended or known by the defendant to cause or, in the manner of its use or intended use, is capable of causing death or serious bodily injury; and **T.C.A. § 39-11-602 (2).**

[TEMPLATE Topics We Could Not Find Explained in Statutes or Cases]

(For each of these topics that we could not find addressed in your state's statutes or cases, we suggest you review the same topics in the subchapters of surrounding states. Your state's courts may look to the law of neighboring states to see how their courts and legislatures have treated that particular self-defense issue.)

[Use of Deadly Force to Prevent Serious Felonies]

[Initial Aggressor]

[Committing Felony or Unlawful Act]

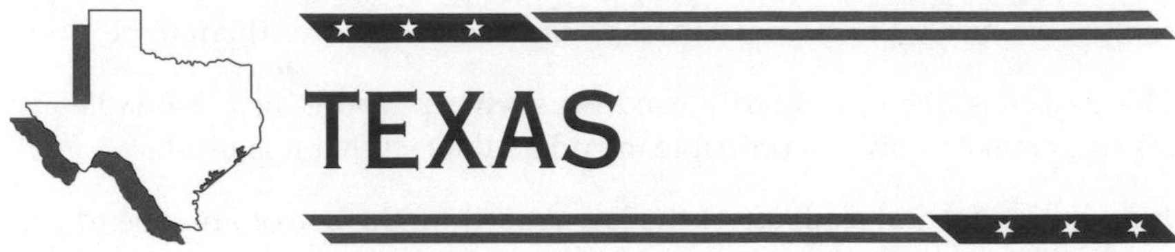

WARNING to CRIMINALS: Don't MESS with TEXAS! The self-defense laws of Texas are very protective. From news reports, a few criminals have caught on too slowly and have reaped the proverbial whirlwind. Texas law allows for the use of deadly force to defend property under limited circumstances not allowed in most states, but there is a price to pay.

Note to Reader: Texas was one of those states that we could not pigeon hole into our TEMPLATE very easily. Rather than cut and scramble the statutes to fit our TEMPLATE, we have for the most part, left the statutes intact and have inserted our TEMPLATE headings to alert you to the topics being dicsussed.

Key: ■ commentary ■ original statutes, cases or jury instructions

[Defense of Self and Others]

[Notice that most of the provisions in the following section (§9.31) relating to non-deadly force in defense persons are identical to those in §9.32 Deadly Force in Defense of Persons. To avoid needless repetition, we confined our comments to §9.32 Deadly Force, and omitted them in §9.31 (non-deadly force).]

[Non-Deadly Force]

§ TEXAS PENAL CODE ANNOTATED § 9.31.
Self-Defense.

(a) Except as provided in Subsection (b), a person is justified in using force against another when and to the degree the actor reasonably believes the force is immediately necessary to protect the actor against the other's use or attempted use of unlawful force.

[Defense of Person(s) in Special Places]
[Presumption of Reasonableness in Special Places – Occupied Habitation, Vehicle, Place of Business]

The actor's belief that the force was immediately necessary as described by this subsection is presumed to be reasonable if the actor:

(1) knew or had reason to believe that the person against whom the force was used:

(A) unlawfully and with force entered, or was attempting to enter unlawfully and with force, the actor's occupied habitation, vehicle, or place of business or employment;

(B) unlawfully and with force removed, or was attempting to remove unlawfully and with force, the actor from the actor's habitation, vehicle, or place of business or employment; or

(C) was committing or attempting to commit aggravated kidnapping, murder, sexual assault, aggravated sexual assault, robbery, or aggravated robbery;

(2) did not provoke the person against whom the force was used; and

(3) was not otherwise engaged in criminal activity, other than a Class C misdemeanor that is a violation of a law or ordinance regulating traffic at the time the force was used.

[Exceptions to Justifiable Self-Defense]

(b) The use of force against another is not justified:

(1) in response to verbal provocation alone;

(2) to resist an arrest or search that the actor knows is being made by a peace officer, or by a person acting in a peace officer's presence and at his direction, even though the arrest or search is unlawful, unless the resistance is justified under Subsection (c);

[Mutual Combat]

(3) if the actor consented to the exact force used or attempted by the other;

[Provocation]

(4) if the actor provoked the other's use or attempted use of unlawful force, unless:

[Exceptions to the Exceptions] [Withdraw and Communicate]

(A) the actor abandons the encounter, or clearly communicates to the other his intent to do so reasonably believing he cannot safely abandon the encounter; and

(B) the other nevertheless continues or attempts to use unlawful force against the actor; or

(5) if the actor sought an explanation from or discussion with the other person concerning the actor's differences with the other person while the actor was:

(A) carrying a weapon in violation of Section 46.02; or

(B) possessing or transporting a weapon in violation of Section 46.05.

(c) The use of force to resist an arrest or search is justified:

(1) if, before the actor offers any resistance, the peace officer (or person acting at his direction) uses or attempts to use greater force than necessary to make the arrest or search; and

(2) when and to the degree the actor reasonably believes the force is immediately necessary to protect himself against the peace officer's (or other person's) use or attempted use of greater force than necessary.

(d) The use of deadly force is not justified under this subchapter except as provided in Sections 9.32, 9.33, and 9.34.

[No Duty to Retreat – Generally]

(e) A person who has a right to be present at the location where the force is used, who has not provoked the person against whom the force is used, and who is not engaged in criminal activity at the time the force is used is not required to retreat before using force as described by this section.

(f) For purposes of Subsection (a), in determining whether an actor described by Subsection (e) reasonably believed that the use of force was necessary, a finder of fact may not consider whether the actor failed to retreat.

[Deadly Force]

§ TEX. PENAL CODE ANN. § 9.32.
Deadly Force in Defense of Person.

(a) A person is justified in using deadly force against another:

(1) if the actor would be justified in using force against the other under Section 9.31 [the non-deadly force section above]; and

(2) when and to the degree the actor reasonably believes the deadly force is immediately necessary:

(A) to protect the actor against the other's use or attempted use of unlawful deadly force; or

[Use of Deadly Force to Prevent Serious Felonies]

(B) to prevent the other's imminent commission of aggravated kidnapping, murder, sexual assault, aggravated sexual assault, robbery, or aggravated robbery. [These crimes are described below. You can use deadly force to stop someone from committing these crimes whether or not you know for sure they are using a deadly weapon to carry out the crime. Such provisions in a statute can give a defender a head start to access his or her weapon and get ahead, rather than be behind, the perception and reaction curve. This could make the difference between life and death. See Chapter 11 on perception and reaction time.]

[Defense of Person(s) in Special Places – Occupied Home, Vehicle, Place of Business] [Presumption of Reasonableness in Special Places]

(b) The actor's belief under Subsection (a)(2) that the deadly force was immediately necessary as described by that subdivision is presumed to be reasonable if the actor:

(1) knew or had reason to believe that the person against whom the deadly force was used:

(A) unlawfully and with force entered, or was attempting to enter unlawfully and with force, the actor's occupied habitation, vehicle, or place of business or employment; [Unlawful means entering without your permission; trespassing. But trespassing alone is NOT enough. The entry has to be forceful. In other words, if someone forces their way into your home, vehicle or workplace without your permission, it is presumed you had a reasonable belief that deadly force was necessary to stop them. Notice, however, that your belief that the person was in the place unlawfully and forced his way in must be reasonable as well.]

(B) unlawfully and with force removed, or was attempting to remove unlawfully and with force, the actor from the actor's habitation, vehicle, or place of business or employment; or [Something akin to kidnapping you or another out of one of these protected places.]

(C) was committing or attempting to commit an offense described by Subsection (a)(2)(B); [If you injure or kill someone to prevent the commission of aggravated kidnapping, murder, sexual assault, aggravated sexual assault, robbery, or aggravated robbery, the law presumes you acted reasonably. The definitions and references to these crimes are found below under the heading **[Helpful Definitions . . .]**.]

[Exceptions to Justifiable Self-Defense Presumption of Reasonableness]

(2) did not provoke the person against whom the force was used; and [You cannot provoke a person to fight as an excuse to hurt or kill him and still claim self-defense.]

(3) was not otherwise engaged in criminal activity, other than a Class C misdemeanor that is a violation of a law or ordinance regulating traffic at the time the force was used. [You can't assert self-defense if you were committing any unlawful act when the necessity for self-defense arose. The only time this doesn't apply is if you were committing a class C misdemeanor, or a minor traffic violation.]

[No Duty to Retreat in General and From Special Places]

(c) A person who has a right to be present at the location where the deadly force is used, who has not provoked the person against whom the deadly force is used, and who is not engaged in criminal activity at the time the deadly force is used is not required to retreat before using deadly force as described by this section.

(d) For purposes of Subsection (a)(2), in determining whether an actor described by Subsection (c) reasonably believed that the use of deadly force was necessary, a finder of fact may not consider whether the actor failed to retreat. [Any good criminal defense attorney would be thankful to have this reassurance that his client will not be condemned for failing to retreat, even if he had an opportunity to do so. The way we read this subparagraph, judges should tell juries that it would be HIGHLY INAPPROPRIATE to even discuss the possibility of retreat in their deliberations in the jury room behind closed doors.]

[Defense of Third Persons]

§ TEX. PENAL CODE ANN. § 9.33.
Defense of Third Person.

A person is justified in using force or deadly force against another to protect a third person if:

(1) under the circumstances as the actor reasonably believes them to be, the actor would be justified under Section 9.31 or 9.32 in using force or deadly force to protect himself against the unlawful force or unlawful deadly force he reasonably believes to be threatening the third person he seeks to protect; and

(2) the actor reasonably believes that his intervention is immediately necessary to protect the third person.

[A person may use the same force to defend another as he is justified in using to defend himself. The actor must reasonably believe that it is immediately necessary to use force or deadly force in order to protect a third person from injury or death. The same presumptions apply here as in 9.31 and 9.32. It is presumed that such a belief is reasonable if you're using force against someone breaking into your house, business, or occupied vehicle while it's occupied, or against someone trying to remove you by force from any such place, or against someone who was committing or attempting to commit aggravated kidnapping, murder, sexual assault, aggravated sexual assault, robbery, or aggravated robbery. Furthermore, under the circumstances as you believe them to be, the person you're trying to protect must not have provoked the conflict and must not be engaged in unlawful conduct when the necessity for self-defense arises. The statute suggests that if you mistakenly believe that the person you're defending was not a provoker or engaged in unlawful activity, that's okay as long as your belief was reasonable.]

[Reckless Injury to Innocent Third Parties]

§ TEX. PENAL CODE ANN. § 9.05.
Reckless Injury of Innocent Third Person.

Even though an actor is justified under this chapter in threatening or using force or deadly force against another, if in doing so he also recklessly injures or kills an innocent third person, the justification afforded by this chapter is unavailable in a prosecution for the reckless injury or killing of the innocent third person. [Firing wildly at a fleeing carjacker on a crowded street could get you charged with the reckless injury or death of an innocent person.]

[Civil Liability]

§ TEX. PENAL CODE ANN. § 9.06.
Civil Remedies Unaffected.

The fact that conduct is justified under this chapter does not abolish or impair any remedy for the conduct that is available in a civil suit. [Just because you were found not guilty by reason of self-defense, doesn't mean you will win a civil lawsuit if the person you injured sues you. See our discussion of civil liability in Chapter 15.]

[Defense of Property – Non-Deadly Force]

§ TEX. PENAL CODE ANN. § 9.41.
Protection of One's Own Property

(a) A person in lawful possession of land or tangible, movable property is justified in using force against another when and to the degree the actor reasonably believes the force is immediately necessary to prevent or terminate the other's trespass on the land or unlawful interference with the property. [You can use non-deadly force to prevent a trespass or interference with real estate or personal property.]

(b) A person unlawfully dispossessed of land or tangible, movable property by another is justified in using force against the other when and to the degree the actor reasonably believes the force is immediately necessary to reenter the land or recover the property if the actor uses the force immediately or in fresh pursuit after the dispossession and: [You can use non-deadly force to re-enter real estate that you were forced off of and to recover personal property that was stolen.]

(1) the actor reasonably believes the other had no claim of right when he dispossessed the actor; or [You weren't forced off the property by a landlord evicting, or a mortgage company foreclosing, or a finance company repossessing your car claiming late payments. If it was something like this, you have to work it out in court, not the boxing ring.]

(1) the other accomplished the dispossession by using force, threat, or fraud against the actor. [Non-deadly force can be used to get your property back from bullies and cheats.]

[Defense of Land or Personal Property with Deadly Force]

§ TEX. PENAL CODE ANN. § 9.42.
Deadly Force to Protect Property.

A person is justified in using deadly force against another to protect land or tangible, movable property:

(1) if he would be justified in using force against the other under Section **9.41** [Under the non-deadly force statute above]; and

(2) when and to the degree he reasonably believes the deadly force is immediately necessary: [Don't forget, police, prosecutors and jurors are going to be ask-

ing themselves, more so than with the defense of persons, was it really NECESSARY to take a life in this situation?]

(A) to prevent the other's imminent commission of arson, burglary, robbery, aggravated robbery, theft during the nighttime, or criminal mischief during the nighttime; or

(B) to prevent the other who is fleeing immediately after committing burglary, robbery, aggravated robbery, or theft during the nighttime from escaping with the property; and

(3) he reasonably believes that:

(A) the land or property cannot be protected or recovered by any other means; or

(B) the use of force other than deadly force to protect or recover the land or property would expose the actor or another to a substantial risk of death or serious bodily injury.

[It is not unusual to see a state statute authorizing the use of deadly force to prevent the commission of arson, burglary, or robbery. These are dangerous and violent felonies which can endanger human life. It IS unusual for a state to authorize the use of deadly force to prevent the commission of misdemeanors like criminal mischief or theft. We just HAD to research this unbelievable provision to see if the courts would somehow try to find a way not to apply it. We found the following language in a case which confirmed that this indeed is Texas law and which defined criminal mischief, but also emphasized the need of satisfying ALL of the elements of the defense:]

"The language of section 9.42 requires that all three of its statutory circumstances exist in order for a person to be justified in employing deadly force against another to protect property. . . The relevant portion of section 9.41 of the Penal Code provides under subsection (a) that: "[a] person in lawful possession of land . . . is justified in using force against another when and to the degree the actor reasonably believes the force is immediately necessary to prevent or terminate the other's trespass on the land or unlawful interference with the property." "Criminal mischief," as referred to in subsection (2) of section 9.42, is defined in section 28.03 as follows: "[a] person commits an offense if, without the effective consent of the owner: (1) he intentionally or knowingly damages or destroys the tangible property of the owner." *Leach v. State*, 983 S.W.2d 45, 47 (Tex.App.-Tyler 1998).

[Although Texas law authorizes the use of deadly force to prevent such misdemeanors or to recover property after the fact, we STRONGLY urge you NOT to use deadly force under such circumstances. If you kill someone to recover a $300 propane grill there will be a public outcry for your prosecution. Even if you are not indicted, you will have spent so much on attorney fees you could have bought the darn thing 100 times. The Joe Horn and Tommy Oakes cases, summarized and compared in the next section, make our point.]

[Defense of Property of a Third Person – Non-Deadly and Deadly Force]

§ TEX. PENAL CODE ANN. § 9.43.
Protection of Third Person's Property.

A person is justified in using force or deadly force against another to protect land or tangible, movable property of a third person if, under the circumstances as he reasonably believes them to be, the actor would be justified under Section **9.41** or **9.42** in using force or deadly force to protect his own land or property and: [All the conditions for the use of non-deadly and deadly force described in the two preceding statutes must exist AND . . .]

(1) the actor reasonably believes the unlawful interference constitutes attempted or consummated theft of or criminal mischief to the tangible, movable property; or

(2) the actor reasonably believes that:

(A) the third person has requested his protection of the land or property; [This provision may have had some influence upon the grand jury which refused to indict Joe Horn.]

(B) he has a legal duty to protect the third person's land or property; or [An example would be a person working for a security company that has a contractual obligation to defend someone's property who has paid for the service.]

(C) the third person whose land or property he uses force or deadly force to protect is the actor's spouse, parent, or child, resides with the actor, or is under the actor's care. [The property you are seeking to protect belongs to your wife/husband, mom or dad, kid, a person who lives with you or you are caring for, like an elderly neighbor.]

[Because of the headache and heartache described in the two cases below, we strongly recommend that you do not use deadly force to defend your property (or anyone else's for that matter), but rather get a good description and then leave it to the men and women of law enforcement. **Example:** You look out the window and see thugs stuffing your neighbor's big screen into their rusty van. You call the police. Law enforcement doesn't arrive until an hour later because a bridge is out due to flooding. They never recover the big screen. Your neighbor submits the claim to his insurance company and a woman with an annoying accent informs him he was 2 days late on his premiums, he had no coverage. Dig $2,500 out of your buried stash, hand it to your neighbor and go buy yourself a huge Porterhouse Steak as a reward for wisely saving yourself at least $20 Grand by not shooting the Big-Screen Burglars.]

The Joe Horn and Tommy Oakes Cases
Two men in Texas, less than a year apart, were prosecuted for killing to defend their neighbors' property. One was not indicted by a grand jury while the other was indicted for negligent homicide. What was the difference?

The first man, Joe Horn, a 61 year-old white resident of Pasadena, TX, called 911 when he realized two burglars were stealing property from his neighbor's home. After the police did not arrive for almost five minutes, Horn told the 911 operator he was going to stop the men. He left his house and confronted the two would-be burglars with a shotgun. When one of the two ran at Horn and then angled away from him, Horn shot him in the back, killing him. Horn fired at the other burglar as he ran down the street, hitting him in the back and killing him as well. The men Horn killed were from Columbia and in the U.S illegally and both had criminal records. A grand jury decided not to indict Joe Horn on any charge. *Man Kills Suspects While On Phone With 911 – CBS News,* Nov. 17, 2007, http://www.cbsnews.com/stories/2007/11/17/national/main3517564.shtml?source=mostpop_story; John Floyd, *Joe Horn Free of Criminal Liability,* July 1, 2008, http://www.johntfloyd.com/comments/july08/01a.htm.

The second man, Tommy Oakes, a 64 year-old white resident of Kingsland, TX, saw three men he believed to be burglars stealing property from his neighbor's home. Oakes left his house to confront the men with a handgun. When the men tried to drive away, Oakes followed the car down the street, shooting at the vehicle several times. Oakes hit one man in back of the neck, which led to his death after several months in a hospital. The man Oakes killed was a young white man from a nearby area. In contrast to Horn, one grand jury indicted Oakes on a lesser charge and a second indicted him for negligent homicide. Press Release, James Wheat, Attorney at Law for Tommy Oakes, Llano District Attorney Asks for Another Swing at the Bat, Seeks Second Indictment for Kingsland Homeowner (March 4, 2009) (on file with author).

In November of 2009, more than a year after the incident, Mr. Oaks pled "No Contest" to the charge of Misdemeanor Deadly Conduct. He will serve a year of probation, pay a $2,000 fine, lose his concealed weapon permit and forfeit the handgun used in the incident. You may read more about the case and plea bargain in *The Llano News,* "Oaks Agrees to Plea Deal in Shooting Incident," by Jodi Lehman, http://www.llanonewss.com/news/article/23171.

Both men had several thumbs-down factors against them: both shot and killed unarmed suspects, both approached the suspects and escalated the conflict, both shot the suspects in back of the body, both used a deadly weapon to protect personal property-a neighbor's property, and neither retreated, although Texas law does not require it.

So what caused the different grand jury outcome in the two cases? Why did one grand jury return no indictment for Horn, while a different grand jury found it proper to indict Oakes for negligent homicide?

Grand jury proceedings are much different than regular court room proceedings. The goal of the jury is not to find the defendant innocent or guilty, but to determine if there is enough evidence against him to justify going to trial. The defendants still have an opportunity to defend themselves, but not at this point. Very few people are allowed to be present: the prosecutor, the jurors, and the witnesses when testifying. There is no judge, no defense attorney, and no defendant present for any of the proceedings. *See* TEX. CODE CRIM. PROC. ANN. arts. 20.011(a), 20.19 (Vernon 2009).

We may likely never know exactly what happened during the grand jury proceedings. Texas grand jury proceedings are held in secret, and no information regarding the evidence or the thoughts and reasoning of the jurors can be disclosed. After the proceedings are finished, no one, not even the jurors themselves, can talk about what happened during the proceedings. *See id*. at 20.02. However, there are many inferences that can be made from the facts. While some have argued that race or circumstances made the difference in the two cases, there is no concrete evidence to that effect.

There were some sympathy factors in the Joe Horn case that did not exist in Tommy Oakes' case. The men Joe Horn killed were adults that were in the country illegally, and each had a history of breaking the law. On the other hand, the man Tommy Oakes killed was a nearby resident. He was the son of a local woman and the boyfriend of a local girl. The grand jurors may have believed that because he was young and may have simply made a mistake, it would not be right to allow Oakes to walk away without an indictment.

Texas self-defense laws may protect law-abiding citizens better than any other state in the nation. In Texas, there are some circumstances in which the law will justify a person using deadly force to protect his neighbor's property from thieves who are trying to steal it. One such set of circumstances occurs when the defender acts immediately to recover stolen property and reasonably believes five things: (1) that the force is immediately necessary, (2) that the suspect has no right to it, (3) that deadly force is immediately necessary to prevent the suspect from escaping with the property, (4) that the use of any force other than deadly force would expose the defender to a risk of death or serious injury, and (5) that the suspect is committing theft. *See* TEX. PENAL CODE ANN. §§ 9.41-9.43.

By applying this law to the Horn case and the Oakes cases, we see that both men were arguably justified in their actions under Texas law.

Joe Horn acted immediately after the two suspects had stolen his neighbor's property; he confronted them outside the home they had just allegedly burglarized. Horn likely believed that force was necessary to recover the stolen property and that the two men walking away with his neighbor's property had no right to it. When one of the men ran at him, and the other ran in the opposite direction, Horn claimed he had to use deadly force to stop them or he would have exposed himself to serious danger. From his conversation with the 911 operator, it was clear he believed that the men were committing theft of his neighbor's property.

Similarly, Tommy Oakes approached the suspects at his neighbor's home before they had even left the driveway. After the suspects ignored his questions about what they were doing and tried to drive away, it seems evident that force was necessary to recover the stolen property. Oakes did not recognize the car, and had no reason to believe that those driving it had any claim to the property they had taken. Oakes would have been unable to prevent the suspects' escape without using his gun. He was outnumbered and on foot. Trying to use less than deadly force on the suspects whom he said he saw stooping over reaching for weapons could have put him at risk of serious injury or death. From his statements through his attorney, he clearly believed that the suspects were committing theft of his neighbor's property.

Because of Texas' statute authorizing the use of deadly force to defend a neighbor's property under some circumstances, the prosecution would have faced quite a challenge proving its case beyond a reasonable doubt against Tommy Oakes. But as most trial lawyers will tell you, you never know the outcome until the jury passes a note to the bailiff that they have reached a verdict. It is a time of extremely high anxiety for everyone involved. "Tommy gave up a very significant right of going to trial, but he just wants to get this matter behind him and go back to being retired," his attorney stated. *Id.*]

§ TEX. PENAL CODE ANN. § 9.44.
Use of Device to Protect Property.

The justification afforded by Sections **9.41** and **9.43** applies to the use of a device to protect land or tangible, movable property if:

(1) the device is not designed to cause, or known by the actor to create a substantial risk of causing, death or serious bodily injury; and

(2) use of the device is reasonable under all the circumstances as the actor reasonably believes them to be when he installs the device.

[You can use booby traps as long as whatever you've rigged up does not pose a risk of serious bodily injury or death.]

[Other Issues – Threatening Deadly Force, Confinement]

§ TEX. PENAL CODE ANN. § 9.04.
Threats as Justifiable Force.

The threat of force is justified when the use of force is justified by this chapter. For purposes of this section, a threat to cause death or serious bodily injury by the production of a weapon or otherwise, as long as the actor's purpose is limited to creating an apprehension that he will use deadly force if necessary, does not constitute the use of deadly force. [The THREAT of deadly force is not the same as the USE of deadly force. This raises the question: Can a person threaten deadly force to defend him or herself from simple assault by unarmed assailants or to protect his or her property? Because we couldn't find a Texas case that directly answers this question, we feel compelled to tell you probably shouldn't do it unless you believe it's absolutely necessary. Obviously, if you can get the assailant(s) to leave without shooting, the potential charges will be lower than if you shoot at them (see table illustrating plausible responses to threats in Chapter 10). In any event, this statute gives your lawyer additional legal ammo if you are charged with a crime for drawing your gun to persuade unarmed but threatening hoodlums to leave you alone.]

§ TEX. PENAL CODE ANN. § 9.03.
Confinement as Justifiable Force.

Confinement is justified when force is justified by this chapter if the actor takes reasonable measures to terminate the confinement as soon as he knows he safely can unless the person confined has been arrested for an offense. [You can lock a burglar in a closet, but be sure to let him out when the Texas Rangers ride in to save the day.]

[HELPFUL DEFINITIONS RELATING TO THIS STATE'S SELF-DEFENSE STATUTES]

- **Bodily injury** – means physical pain, illness, or any impairment of physical condition. **Tex. Penal Code Ann. § 1.07 (a)(8).**
- **Building** – means any enclosed structure intended for use or occupation as a habitation or for some purpose of trade, manufacture, ornament, or use. **Tex. Penal Code Ann. § 30.01 (2).**
- **Deadly force** – means force that is intended or known by the actor to cause, or in the manner of its use or intended use is capable of causing, death or serious bodily injury. **Tex. Penal Code Ann. § 9.01 (3).**
- **Death** – includes, for an individual who is an unborn child, the failure to be born alive. **Tex. Penal Code Ann. § 1.07 (a)(49).**
- **Felonies Mentioned** –
  - **Aggravated kidnapping** – [Intentionally or knowingly abducting a person with the intent to hold her for ransom, use her as a shield or hostage, facilitate the commission of a felony or flight from one, inflict bodily injury, etc. **Tex. Penal Code Ann. § 20.04.**
  - **Aggravated robbery** – [While in the commission of a robbery (theft by threat or force (see **Texas Statues § 29.02**) a person causes serious bodily injury to another, uses a dangerous weapon, or causes bodily injury, threatens, or places another who is 65 yrs or older or disabled in fear of imminent bodily injury or death.] **Tex. Penal Code Ann. § 29.03.**
  - **Aggravated sexual assault** – [Same as sexual assault briefly defined below, but carried out through the use of a deadly weapon, death threats, threats of kidnapping or against a very young or very old victim.] **Tex. Penal Code Ann. § 22.021.**
  - **Arson** – [Intentionally starting a fire or causing an explosion with intent to destroy or damage a building, habitation or vehicle.] **Tex. Penal Code Ann. § 28.02.**

   - **Burglary** – [Entering or remaining in a habitation or building (including portions of a building not open to the public) without the consent of the owner with the intent to commit a felony, theft or assault therein.] **Tex. Penal Code Ann. § 30.02.**

   - **Criminal mischief during the nighttime** – [Criminal mischief means intentionally or knowingly damaging or destroy tangible property of an owner without his/her consent. **Tex. Penal Code Ann. § 28.03.** Nighttime means 30 minutes after sunset until 30 minutes before sunrise. (*Laws v. State*, 10 S.W. 220 (Tex.Ct.App. 1888)].

   - **Murder** – [Intentionally or knowingly causing the death of an individual.] **Tex. Penal Code Ann. § 19.02.**

   - **Robbery** – [While committing a theft, a person intentionally, knowingly or recklessly causes bodily injury to another or places another in fear of imminent bodily injury or death.] **Tex. Penal Code Ann. § 29.02.**

   - **Sexual assault** – [Any non-consensual sexual penetration of any kind to another person or child. Consent explained at length in the actual statute.] **Tex. Penal Code Ann. § 22.011.**

   - **Theft during the nighttime** – [An unlawful taking of movable or non-movable property at night. Nighttime means 30 minutes after sunset until 30 minutes before sunrise. **Tex. Penal Code Ann. § 31.03.** (*Laws v. State*, 10 S.W. 220 (Tex.Ct.App. 1888).]

- **Felony** – means an offense so designated by law or punishable by death or confinement in a penitentiary. **Tex. Penal Code Ann. § 1.07 (a)(23).**

- **Habitation** – means a structure or vehicle that is adapted for the overnight accommodation of persons, and includes:

  (A) each separately secured or occupied portion of the structure or vehicle; and

  (B) each structure appurtenant to or connected with the structure or vehicle.
  Tex. Penal Code Ann. § 30.01 (1). [e.g., This would include a motor home and a porch attached to the motor home.]

- **Peace officer** – means a person elected, employed, or appointed as a peace officer under Article 2.12, Code of Criminal Procedure, Section 51.212 or 51.214, Education Code, or other law. T**ex. Penal Code Ann. § 1.07 (a)(36).**

- **Possession** – means actual care, custody, control, or management. **Tex. Penal Code Ann. § 1.07 (a)(39).**

- **Reasonable belief** – means a belief that would be held by an ordinary and prudent man in the same circumstances as the actor. **Tex. Penal Code Ann. § 1.07 (a)(42).**

- **Serious bodily injury** – means bodily injury that creates a substantial risk of death or that causes death, serious permanent disfigurement, or protracted loss or impairment of the function of any bodily member or organ. **Tex. Penal Code Ann. § 1.07 (a)(46).**

- **Vehicle** – includes any device in, on, or by which any person or property is or may be propelled, moved, or drawn in the normal course of commerce or transportation, except such devices as are classified as "habitation." **Tex. Penal Code Ann. § 30.01 (3).**

[TEMPLATE Topics We Could Not Find Explained in Statutes or Cases]

(For each of these topics that we could not find addressed in your state's statutes or cases, we suggest you review the same topics in the subchapters of surrounding states. Your state's courts may look to the law of the surrounding states to see how their courts and legislatures have treated that particular self-defense issue.)

[Committing Felony or Unlawful Act]

[Initial Aggressor]

[Co-Habitants; Co-Employees – Duty to Retreat]

Pancho's Wisdom

You just might be a Gunnut if . . . when a golfer mentions a hole-in-one with a nine iron, you picture yourself making a hole in one armed carjacker with your 9mm Glock.

UTAH

. . . And it shall be said among the wicked: Let us not go up to battle against Zion, for the inhabitants of Zion are terrible; wherefore we cannot stand.
– Doctrine & Covenants 45: 67 & 70.

For the most part, Utah's lawmakers have refused to disarm or tie the hands of the innocent so that they cannot defend themselves. Utah is the only state that has unequivocally established the right of public school teachers with concealed firearm permits to carry concealed weapons in class, from kindergarten through college, to protect themselves and their students. Self-reliance and trusting law-abiding citizens are two values that pervade Utah's self-defense laws making them among the most protective in the country.

Key: ■ commentary ■ original statutes, cases or jury instructions

---

[Defense of Self and Others]

§ UTAH CODE ANNOTATED § 76-2-402.
Force in defense of person – Forcible felony defined.

[Non-Deadly Force]

(1) (a) A person is justified in threatening or using force against another when and to the extent that the person reasonably believes that force or a threat of force is necessary to defend the person or a third person against another person's imminent use of unlawful force. [This first sentence applies to the use of non-deadly force. You can use as much non-deadly force as reasonably necessary to stop the progression of unlawful force against you or another person.]

[Deadly Force]

(1) (b) A person is justified in using force intended or likely to cause death or serious bodily injury only if the person reasonably believes that force is necessary to prevent death or serious bodily injury to the person or a third person as a result of another person's imminent use of unlawful force, or to prevent the commission of a forcible felony. [You can't use deadly force unless you reasonably believe there is an immediate threat of being seriously injured or killed. You may also used deadly force to prevent (but not avenge) the commission of a forcible felony. Forcible felonies are defined below. This applies as well to defense of third persons.]

[Exceptions to Justifiable Self-Defense]

(2) (a) A person is not justified in using force under the circumstances specified in Subsection (1) if the person: [you cannot claim self-defense if you . . .]

[Provocation]

(i) initially provokes the use of force against the person with the intent to use force as an excuse to inflict bodily harm upon the assailant; [provoke someone so you have an excuse to hurt them . . .]

[Committing Felony or Unlawful Act]

(ii) is attempting to commit, committing, or fleeing after the commission or attempted commission of a felony; or [you're committing a felony, like an armed robbery, duh!]

[Initial Agressor] [Combat by Agreement]

(iii) was the aggressor [you started it] or was engaged in a combat by agreement ["meet me behind the Wal-Mart at high noon!"], unless

[Exceptions to the Exceptions]

the person withdraws from the encounter and effectively communicates to the other person his intent to do so ["Hey, I didn't mean it, I'm sorry, I'm now retreating, pleeeeeeze let me go in peace."] and, notwithstanding, the other person continues or threatens to continue the use of unlawful force.

(b) for purposes of Subsection (2)(a)(iii) the following do not, by themselves, constitute "combat by agreement":

(i) voluntarily entering into or remaining in an ongoing relationship; [Marrying or living with that violent bum (your parents warned you he was a creep!) doesn't make it combat by agreement. However, our research tends to show that when you put the worthless dopebag out of his misery while he's sleeping or in a drunken stupor, you will almost ALWAYS be arrested and prosecuted and probably convicted of something, manslaughter, if not murder.] or

(ii) entering or remaining in a place where one has a legal right to be. [It's not combat by agreement just because you didn't retreat from a place you have a right to be like your place, the grocery store, mall, on a public street.]

[No Duty to Retreat]

(3) A person does not have a duty to retreat from the force or threatened force described in Subsection (1) in a place where that person has lawfully entered or remained, except as provided in Subsection (2)(a)(iii). [You don't have to retreat unless you provoked the fight, are committing a felony or dueling by agreement.]

[Use of Deadly Force to Prevent Serious Felonies]

(4) (a) For purposes of this section, a forcible felony includes aggravated assault, mayhem, aggravated murder, murder, manslaughter, kidnapping, and aggravated

kidnapping, rape, forcible sodomy, rape of a child, object rape, object rape of a child, sexual abuse of a child, aggravated sexual abuse of a child, and aggravated sexual assault as defined in Title 76, Chapter 5, Offenses Against the Person, and arson, robbery, and burglary as defined in Title 76, Chapter 6, Offenses Against Property.

(b) Any other felony offense which involves the use of force or violence against a person so as to create a substantial danger of death or serious bodily injury also constitutes a forcible felony.

(c) Burglary of a vehicle, defined in Section **76-6-204,** does not constitute a forcible felony except when the vehicle is occupied at the time unlawful entry is made or attempted.

[If your assailant(s) is (are) doing any of these things (except burglary of a non-occupied vehicle), you can defend yourself or others with deadly force. See definitions below. Keep in mind that although you can use deadly force to STOP the progression of a sexual assault on a child, you may NOT legally use deadly force to AVENGE the sexual abuse of a child.]

(5) In determining imminence or reasonableness under Subsection (1), the trier of fact may consider, but is not limited to, any of the following factors:

(a) the nature of the danger; [did assailant have an AK-47 or a chalk eraser?]

(b) the immediacy of the danger; [man pointing gun at you (immediate danger) or knife at 100 yards (not so immediate)?]

(c) the probability that the unlawful force would result in death or serious bodily injury [98 pound Elvis impersonator threatening to slap you with the palm of his hand for helping to fund California's Proposition 8 (improbable serious injury) versus a 350 pound muscle-bound professional wrestler swearing an oath to crush you with the barber chair he just ripped out of the floor for brushing against his tattoo with a permanent marker (probable injury or death).];

(d) the other's prior violent acts or violent propensities [although this clause seems to suggest you would have to know about your assailant's violent traits, at least one clever Utah attorney has used it to introduce the assailant's criminal record into evidence to show that the assailant criminal was likely the aggressor where there were no independent eye witnesses. The court allowed this even though the defendant could not have known of the victims' violent tendencies because he didn't know them from Adam. However, the court also instructed the jury that this evidence could only be used in helping them to decide "who started it," NOT whether defendant believed he was facing an imminent threat.]; and

(e) any patterns of abuse or violence in the parties' relationship [the abusive relationship—again, this almost always results in at least arrest and prosecution UNLESS the abused gets OUT of the relationship, OUT of the same household AND he attacks her in HER OWN NEW HOME! She should report to the police EVERY act of abuse or threat of abuse in the past and get a court order telling him to say the HECK away from her and off the premises of her new home. Only then do the favorable presumptions take affect as she defends her "habitation" (see discussion below).]

[Threatening Deadly Force]

§ U.C.A. § 76-10-506.
Threatening with or using dangerous weapon in fight or quarrel.

(1) As used in this section, "threatening manner" does not include:

(a) the possession of a dangerous weapon, whether visible or concealed, without additional behavior which is threatening; or

(b) informing another of the actor's possession of a deadly weapon in order to prevent what the actor reasonably perceives as a possible use of unlawful force by the other and the actor is not engaged in any activity described in Subsection 76-2-402 (2)(a).

(2) Except as otherwise provided in Section 76-2-402 and for those persons described in Section 76-10-503, a person who, in the presence of two or more persons, draws or exhibits a dangerous weapon in an angry and threatening manner or unlawfully uses a dangerous weapon in a fight or quarrel is guilty of a class A misdemeanor.

(3) This section does not apply to a person who, reasonably believing the action to be necessary in compliance with Section 76-2-402, with purpose to prevent another's use of unlawful force:

(a) threatens the use of a dangerous weapon; or

(b) draws or exhibits a dangerous weapon.

[§ UCA 76-10-506 was amended during the 2010 session of the Utah Legislature and became effective on May 11. The changes simply clarify existing law. Carrying a firearm on your hip is not a threat; it's simply cowboy. Informing someone you have a gun is not a crime unless you start a fight or agree to fight as described in Utah's self-defense statute. A concealed firearms permit holder who accidently displays his gat when reaching for the Doritos on the top shelf at Smith's is not committing a crime.

This law allows a citizen, under some circumstances, to draw his gun and threaten deadly force if necessary to prevent a simple assault. It does NOT, however, allow you to shoot at or shoot an unarmed person. The concepts of reasonable and necessary apply to this law because of the reference to Utah's self-defense statute, §U.C.A. 76-10-402 above. If you threaten someone with a deadly weapon for foolish reasons, you will be prosecuted. Examples would be when a person cuts in front of you at a Jazz Game entrance or some kid trespasses on your lawn to retrieve his soccer ball. Although, in our opinion, Utah law has always permitted a reasonable and necessary threat of deadly force to prevent a simple assault, police and prosecutors have almost NEVER believed it. Those who have drawn firearms on unarmed assailants have either been charged with brandishing or, if the weapon was pointed at the assailant's body, with aggravated assault, a felony. We suspect it will take a long time for police and prosecutors to swallow this concept. It will be several years before this law is interpreted by the Utah Supreme Court. Don't become the first test case unless you want to contribute heavily to the Utah Criminal Defense Attorney Hawaii Vacation Fund.]

[Defense of Special Places – Habitation]

§ U.C.A. § 76-2-405. FORCE IN DEFENSE OF HABITATION.

["Habitation" is not defined in this chapter but it is defined in Chapter 6 of the Utah's Criminal Code which states, "for purposes of this Chapter (meaning Chapter 6 not Chapter 2) 'Habitable structure' means any building, vehicle, trailer, railway car, aircraft, or watercraft used for lodging or assembling persons or conducting business whether a person is actually present or not." It's unclear whether a definition expressly intended for one chapter of the Utah Code is binding in another chapter. A similar Georgia statute also defines habitation as including vehicles and workplaces. Ga Code 16-3-24.1. It's these kinds of unanswered questions that burn the money of the people whose cases have to be appealed. However, we certainly conclude that "habitation" means your home or temporary home.]

(1) A person is justified in using force against another when and to the extent that he reasonably believes that the force is necessary to prevent or terminate the other's unlawful entry into or attack upon his habitation; however, he is justified in the use of force which is intended or likely to cause death or serious bodily injury only if:

(a) the entry is made or attempted in a violent and tumultuous manner, surreptitiously, or by stealth [e.g., breaking or sneaking into your house], and he reasonably believes that the entry is attempted or made for the purpose of assaulting or offering personal violence [notice that this only requires a reasonable fear of an "assault" or "personal violence" rather than "force likely to cause serious bodily injury or death."] to any person, dwelling, or being in the habitation *and* he reasonably believes that the force is necessary to prevent the assault or offer of personal violence; or [Under the general self-defense statute, before deadly force can be used, you must be facing an imminent threat of serious bodily injury, death or a forcible felony (see self-defense statute, 76-2-402, above). In your home, you are only required to have a reasonable fear of being assaulted (a threat accompanied by an immediate show of force, such as when someone raises a fist at you or approaches you with no weapon, but threatens to hurt you). Fortunately, the law doesn't require you to make the fine distinction whether your attacker's intent is to harm you severely or slightly; any reasonable fear of harm justifies the use of deadly force on your part in your home. We would argue vigorously that any intruder in your home who refuses to show his empty hands immediately upon command or keeps coming at you despite your command to, "Stop right there!" creates an immediate fear of assault or personal violence in the mind of any reasonable person.]

(b) he reasonably believes that the entry is made or attempted for the purpose of committing a felony in the habitation *and* that the force is necessary to prevent the commission of the felony.

[Notice, section (b) purports to not require a forcible felony like in the general self-defense statute, but rather any felony is enough. This is what it says, but beware of the "Caution" in Chapter 4 under the heading "Use of Deadly Force to Prevent Serious Felonies." In that section we cautioned you about the Supreme Court case *Tennessee v. Garner* which held that a state statute permitting the use of deadly force to apprehend unarmed, non-dangerous suspects was unconstitutional. Since then at least a couple of states have held that their "fleeing felon" statutes do not give a person the right to use deadly force against an unarmed, non-dangerous felon committing a non-violent felony. This portion of Utah's "defense of habitation" statute is somewhat different than the statutes in the states just referred to. However, if a person is in your home committing a non-violent felony, and it's absolutely clear to you this person is not there to hurt anyone, you should not use deadly force. For example, you catch a burglar about to walk out your front door with your new LCD big screen. He's wearing a swimming suit so you know he is unarmed. He weighs 120 pounds soaking wet and when he sees your Winchester 1300 defender with heat shield and pistol grip, he drops the TV, gets on his knees and begs you not to kill him, holding his hands high in the air showing you he has no weapon. You recognize him as the fifteen-year old kid who lives two houses down from you. Are you going to test the ballistics of your new 12 gauge rifled slugs or are you going to hold him for the police? If he panics and bolts, are you going to shoot him in the back as he runs out the door without the LCD? If you do, you will spend 50 times more than your LCD is worth paying attorneys to defend you in the criminal and civil cases brought against you. You would probably be convicted of murder under those facts.]

[This section does not require a violent or secretive entry or the use of a dangerous weapon by an assailant. Deadly force is justified if (1) you reasonably believe the entry is for the purpose of committing a felony involving force or violence, and (2) the force you use is necessary to prevent the commission of the crime.]

[Presumption of Reasonableness in Special Places]

(2) The person using force or deadly force in defense of habitation is presumed for the purpose of both civil and criminal cases to have acted reasonably and had a reasonable fear of imminent peril of death or serious bodily injury if the entry or attempted entry is unlawful and is made or attempted by use of force, or in a violent and tumultuous manner, or surreptitiously or by stealth, or for the purpose of committing a felony.

[If a guy who resembles Jack Nicholson thrusts a shining ax through your front door with an "I'm-home" look on his face, cackling like the Joker, you'd probably be justified in pumping enough .357's into his diabolical presence to knock him off the porch and onto your front sidewalk. Would you have to drag his bloody corpse back onto your interior white carpet to prove justification? NO! Notice the statute says, "entry made or *attempted.*" You don't need to haul an appropriately-dealt-with felon into your home after you ventilate his bad-boy bod during an attempt.

You think CSI wouldn't see the "skid marks" on your textured white Saxony anyway? That would be tampering with the evidence, a felony in and of itself. It would suggest you had a guilty conscience. Don't EVER tamper with the evidence!

Now let's suppose "Jack" makes it into your living room before your fourth shot severs his spine above the arms and he's lying helplessly, paralyzed from the neck down screaming how he's going to, "sue yer @#*@##," that he's going to tell the cops you shot him on the public sidewalk, and only then did he attack you with the ax to try to defend himself —"You started it!" Dead men tell no tales—Right? Well, yes, but WRONG ANSWER! Notice the statute says "force *necessary* to prevent the assault or felony." He's down and helpless. At this point you have prevented the commission of any assault or felony and any ADDITIONAL force would be considered EXCESSIVE FORCE. Let CSI do their job and they will prove he is lying about what happened. (If there is conflicting evidence like this—he says, you say—you won't be able to talk your way out of an arrest. If you try to, you may very well talk your way into prison. Shut up and let your lawyer handle it from that point on. Tell the police that you'd like to talk to them, but you'd like to speak to a lawyer first. If they persist, politely tell them it's improper for them to try to question you now that you have asserted your right to counsel. Please read Chapter 14, carefully, Statements Made after a Defensive Incident.

If you execute someone to prevent them from testifying, you will have committed murder, obstructing justice and probably fifteen other heinous crimes that will insure your residence at the Big House adjacent to Widow Maker Mountain (uh, which is closer to Brokeback Mountain than most of us want to think). The law does NOT give you justification to kill or execute (even though an ocular cavity "failure drill" shot is almost 99.9999% likely to kill). The law only gives you authority to STOP THE PROGRESSION of deadly force. Once the deadly threat is no longer present, you must halt your use of deadly force. Comprehende?

Finally, while reading EVERY self-defense law in the country, we discovered that the two states, Nevada and Georgia, have a nearly identical phrase to Utah's home defense statute that reads, ". . . *assaulting or offering personal violence to any person, dwelling, or being* in the habitation . . . ." Nevada and Georgia's laws leave out the comma between "person" and "dwelling" which changes the meaning considerably. The statutes of those two states only allow you to use deadly force in defense of a person dwelling or being in the habitation (presumably living in or visiting). The Utah statute purports to justify the use of force in defense not only persons, but the dwelling and "beings" as well. "Being" is not defined in the Justification section of the code. Its dictionary definition includes "something that actually exists." Does this mean you can use deadly force to prevent an assault on your cactus plant, your dog? If you do, you will be inviting a district attorney to prosecute you for murder in order to "clarify the law." But we'd rather have the comma than not; it gives your attorney an additional possible defense, "he was defending his purebred Collie puppies!" We'll refer to it as our "warm, fuzzy defense."]

[Defense of Persons on Real Property]

§ U.C.A. § 76-2-407. DEADLY FORCE IN DEFENSE OF PERSONS ON REAL PROPERTY.

[This statute relating to the defense of persons on real property has wording similar to the home-defense statute and was undoubtedly passed to expand the legal protection of the home-defense statute to the borders of your real estate. CAUTION: IT HAS NEVER BEEN INTERPRETED by an appeals court to our knowledge and there is nothing exactly like this in any other state. YOURS could be the first American-Dream-ruining test case if you pop a person like a prairie dog at 400 yards for jumping your perimeter fence with a Howa on his Honda. Contrary to what some uninformed souls may believe, this statute DOES NOT give justification to shoot persons simply trespassing. Acting on the threat "Trespassers will be shot; survivors will be prosecuted!" is a sure-fired pass to Purgatory (if you live near St. George)!]

(1) A person is justified in using force intended or likely to cause death or serious bodily injury against another in his defense of persons on real property other than his habitation if:

(a) he is in lawful possession of the real property;

(b) he reasonably believes that the force is necessary to prevent or terminate the other person's trespass onto the real property; [We wonder if the hapless defendant in the Fillmore case (Chapter 2) who allegedly told his X-girlfriend that he could "kill trespassers" was mislead by this subsection? He denied saying this, but if he believed it, he certainly was not aware of the other conditions in (c) and (d) that had to be met. By following the two young men down the road, away from the cabin community, there could not have possibly been a reasonable belief that the use of deadly force was necessary to prevent an assault or offer of personal violence on anybody's real property; the two kids were on a public road at the time of the shooting!]

(c) the trespass is made or attempted by use of force or in a violent and tumultuous manner; *and* [but notice there is an "*and*" here which means all four elements , (a) – (d), must apply before a person can use deadly force in defense of persons on real estate.]

(d) (i) the person reasonably believes that the trespass is attempted or made for the purpose of committing violence against any person on the real property and he reasonably believes that the force is necessary to prevent personal violence; or

[Paragraph (1) is probably the most expansive provision of this code section. It allows you to use deadly force against a trespasser who poses an imminent threat of "personal violence" to someone on the real estate. This is clearly a lower threshold than the requirement in the self-defense statute (402) and paragraph (1)(d)(ii) below, both of which require an imminent threat of death or serious bodily injury or of a forcible felony. So your daughter's boyfriend drives his monster truck through your wrought-iron gate and text messages the threat that he is coming to spank her butt black and blue for dating another guy. Does this mean you can drill his hulking haunches with your new Barrett .50 BMG as his big wheels cross the creek over the bridge between the white-fenced corral and the thoroughbred stables? I guess we'll have to wait to find out. In the meantime, mortgage the farm and the horses before you give me a call to defend your case. I'll remain concerned about the potential impact on the jury of the crime scene photos and whether the use of a Barrett was necessary. I KNOW, he didn't suffer!

(ii) the person reasonably believes that the trespass is made or attempted for the purpose of committing a forcible felony as defined in Section **76-2-402** that poses imminent peril of death or serious bodily injury to a person on the real property and that the force is necessary to prevent the commission of that forcible felony.

(2) The person using deadly force in defense of persons on real property under Subsection (1) is presumed for the purpose of both civil and criminal cases to have acted reasonably and had a reasonable fear of imminent peril of death or serious bodily injury if the trespass or attempted trespass is unlawful and is made or attempted by use of force, or in a violent and tumultuous manner, or for the purpose of committing a forcible felony.

§ U.C.A. § 76-2-406. FORCE IN DEFENSE OF PROPERTY.

[You can't use deadly force to protect your property like you can to protect persons ON your property. Although arson and burglary could technically be called property crimes, the justification for the use of deadly force against these forcible felonies is the risk of harm to humans, not property.]

(1) A person is justified in using force, other than deadly force, against another when and to the extent that the person reasonably believes that force is necessary to prevent or terminate another person's criminal interference with real property or personal property:

(a) lawfully in the person's possession

(b) lawfully in the possession of a member of the person's immediate family; or

(c) belonging to a person whose property the person has a legal duty to protect.

(2) In determining reasonableness under Subsection (1), the trier of fact shall, in addition to any other factors, consider the following factors:

(a) the apparent or perceived extent of the damage to the property;

(b) property damage previously caused by the other person;

(c) threats of personal injury or damage to property that have been made previously by the other person; and

(d) any patterns of abuse or violence between the person and the other person.

[You cannot use deadly force to protect property. I have had clients arrested for threatening deadly force to prevent a simple assault or to protect property. In all of these cases the desired result was achieved. The "bad guy(s)" left without further trouble. And most of the clients have "squeaked by" with a dismissal, not-guilty verdict or misdemeanor. Nevertheless, attorneys fees are NOT pretty (well, to me they stinketh not). This statute should be amended to make it clear that a person can defend his property by threatening deadly force as follows:

- [A person is justified in *threatening or* using force, other than the use of deadly force.]

[Civil Liability]

§ U.C.A. § 78B-3-110. DEFENSE TO CIVIL ACTION FOR DAMAGES RESULTING FROM COMMISSION OF CRIME.

(1) A person may not recover from the victim of a crime for personal injury or property damage if the person:

(a) entered the property of the victim with criminal intent and the injury or damage occurred while the person was on the victim's property; or

(b) committed a crime against the victim, during which the damage or injury occurred.

(2) The provisions of Subsection (1) do not apply if the person can prove by clear and convincing evidence that:

(a) his actions did not constitute a felony; and

(b) his culpability was less than the person from whom recovery is sought.

(3) Subsections (1) and (2) apply to any next-of-kin, heirs, or personal representatives of the person if the person is disabled or killed.

(4) Subsections (1), (2), and (3) do not apply if the person committing or attempting to commit the crime has clearly retreated from the criminal activity.

(5) "Clearly retreated" means that the person committing the criminal act has fully, clearly, and immediately ceased all hostile, threatening, violent, or criminal behavior or activity.

[This statute protects you from civil damages if you injure someone committing a felony against you or on your property. Beware, however, that the "clearly retreated" provision in this statute strongly suggests that all entrance holes be in the front of the felon and all exit holes be in the back instead of vice versa. A computer search into our legal database did not find any cases in Utah where this statute had come into play.]

[Other Issues – Citizens Arrest]

§ U.C.A. § 76-2-403. FORCE IN ARREST.

Any person is justified in using any force, except deadly force, which he reasonably believes to be necessary to effect an arrest or to defend himself or another from bodily harm while making an arrest. [The "except deadly force" clause creates a vicious legal trap for anyone using a firearm when attempting to arrest someone committing a crime. If the person you are attempting to arrest pulls a weapon or refuses to stop when coming at you and you use deadly force, the police and prosecutor could point to this clause as a reason to chill your heiny in the hoosegow. For this reason, we suggest you call the police and avoid trying to make an arrest yourself. If your assailant pulls a weapon, yes, you have the Defense-of-Persons statute above to point to. BUT the prosecutor can also point to this statute. When there is a conflict of statutes that can be applied, the case is ripe for arrest and prosecution. It will cost you a bundle. We strongly recommend AGAINST going after a fleeing felon. Be a keenly observant witness and then let the police do their job.]

[HELPFUL DEFINITIONS RELATING TO THIS STATE'S SELF-DEFENSE STATUTES]

- **Bodily injury** – [means physical pain, illness, or any impairment of physical condition.] **U.C.A. § 76-1-601(3).**

- **Serious bodily injury** – [means bodily injury that creates or causes serious permanent disfigurement, protracted loss or impairment of the function of any bodily member or organ, or creates a substantial risk of death.] **U.C.A. § 76-1-601(11).**

- **Substantial bodily injury** – [means bodily injury, not amounting to serious bodily injury, that creates or causes protracted physical pain, temporary disfigurement, or temporary loss or impairment of the function of any bodily member or organ.] **U.C.A. § 76-1-601(12).**

- **Felonies Mentioned –**
  - **Aggravated assault** – [Intentionally causing serious bodily injury or using a dangerous weapon likely to cause death or serious bodily injury.] **U.C.A. § 76-5-103.**
  - **Aggravated kidnapping** – [Kidnapping while using a deadly weapon, holding someone for ransom.] **U.C.A. § 76-5-302.**
  - **Aggravated murder** – [Killing another person under a host of aggravating circumstances defined in U.C.A. 76-5-202 including sexual assault of a child, killing for money, killing while kidnapping, poisoning, torturing, etc.] **U.C.A. § 76-5-202.**

- **Arson** – [Damaging, by fire or explosive, property of another or doing so with the intention of defrauding an insurer.] **U.C.A. § 76-6-102.**
- **Burglary** – [Entering or remaining unlawfully in a building or any portion of a building with the intent to commit a crime.] **U.C.A. § 76-6-202-204.5.**
- **Kidnapping** – [Everyone knows what this is.] **U.C.A. § 76-6-203.**
- **Manslaughter** – [Recklessly but not intentionally killing another.] **U.C.A. § 76-5-205.**
- **Mayhem** – [Cutting off or disabling a member of the body or slitting someone's nose, ear or lip.] **U.C.A. § 76-5-105.**
- **Murder** – [intentional killing of another person.] **U.C.A. § 76-5-203.**
- **Rape** – [when an actor has sexual intercourse without consent from the other person. This applies even if the actor is married to the victim. Caution: for reasons described in the Domestic Abuse section above, if you claim you shot your husband because he raped you, you will still be arrested and vigorously prosecuted.]
- **Other Sex Crimes Related to Rape (non-consensual violent crimes)** – [The titles of the following sex crimes describe in sufficient detail the nature of the sicko crimes. The term "aggravated" usually means a weapon was used to commit the crime, the victim was seriously injured or was kidnapped:]
  - Forcible sodomy, U.C.A. § 76-5-403.
  - Object rape, U.C.A. § 76-5-402.2.
  - Object rape of a child, U.C.A. § 76-5-402.3.
  - Sexual abuse of a child, U.C.A. § 76-5-404.1.
  - Aggravated sexual abuse of a child, U.C.A. § 76-5-404.1.
  - Aggravated sexual assault, U.C.A. § 76-5-405.
  - Rape of a child, U.C.A. § 76-5-402.1.
- **Robbery** – [Taking or attempting to take personal property of another in his possession or immediate possession, against his will, by force or fear.] **U.C.A. § 76-6-301, 302.**

Pancho's Wisdom

You just might be a Gunnut if . . . the types of bullets exceed the types of coins between the cushions of your living-room couch.

VERMONT

Pancho's Wisdom

GUN CONTROL and RAPE are not about guns or sex, they're about CONTROL; but we've GOT GUNS and we refuse to be CONTROLLED or RAPED!

Anyone who is not prohibited by federal law can legally carry a firearm openly or concealed in Vermont as long as it's not for the purpose of committing an unlawful act. As a result, it seems everyone knows to leave everyone else alone. Consequently the violent crime rate in Vermont is low compared to most U.S. states. Perhaps this is why its self-defense statutes and cases are not as highly developed as in other states. Vermont's self-defense statute is short and leaves many unanswered questions, as does its case law.

Key: ■ commentary ■ original statutes, cases or jury instructions

---

[Defense of Self and Others]
[Deadly Force] [Defense of a Third Person]
[Use of Deadly Force to Prevent Serious Felonies]

§ **13 V.S.A. § 2305.**
Justifiable homicide.

If a person kills or wounds another under any of the circumstances enumerated below, he shall be guiltless:

(1) In the just and necessary defense of his own life or the life of his or her husband, wife, parent, child, brother, sister, master, mistress, servant, guardian or ward; or

(2 In the suppression of a person attempting to commit murder, sexual assault, aggravated sexual assault, burglary or robbery, with force or violence . . .

[The phrase "just and necessary" makes this statute slightly different in wording than other self-defense statutes. However, as shown in the quote out of the Vermont case cited immediately below, its application is fairly standard. You must actually believe you need to use deadly force to save yourself and that belief must be reasonable. This statute limits the defense of a third person to those closely related to you and your master, mistress and servant. Neither Vermont's statutes nor its cases define these terms, but they are probably archaic descriptions of domestic employers (master and mistress) of employees or servants. We checked out Vermont's self-defense jury instructions and they limit defense of third persons to those named in the statute as well. It's hard to believe, but if you save the innocent 16 year old girl who works at the convenience store during an armed robbery, you might be risking criminal prosecution and civil damages because strangers are not named in this group of third persons! Time for a legislative update perhaps?

Paragraph 2 of this statute lists certain felonies that justify the use of deadly force. Specifically listing forcible sexual assault eliminates the need for a woman to ask herself the question whether rape constitutes an imminent threat of serious bodily injury.]

. . .

"... for self-defense to be "just and necessary," a defendant's belief that he faces imminent peril, and his belief in the need to employ deadly force to repel that peril, must be reasonable. A defendant must have an honest belief of imminent peril, but that honest belief by itself is insufficient to invoke the defense. The belief must be grounded in reason." *State v. Shaw*, 721 A.2d 486, 489 (Vt.1998). [Before you use deadly force you must honestly and reasonably believe serious injury or death is about to happen.]

§ 13 V.S.A. § 1024. Aggravated assault.

a) A person is guilty of aggravated assault if the person:

(5) is armed with a deadly weapon and threatens to use the deadly weapon on another person. ["Even though you can't see it, I have a gun, so get off my property" equals felony assault unless uttered in necessary defense of life or to prevent one of the serious felonies described in the next paragraph.]

. . .

(d) Subdivision (a)(5) of this section shall not apply if the person threatened to use the deadly weapon:

(1) In the just and necessary defense of his or her own life or the life of his or her husband, wife, civil union partner, parent, child, brother, sister, guardian, or ward; [The use of the word "life" suggests the threat has to be one of death or those crimes listed below. Notice how the category of third persons described differ slightly from the justifiable homicide statute above. This statute leaves out the terms "master, mistress and servant" but adds "civil union partner." We are not sure why the legislature doesn't expressly permit the defense of strangers like most other states do.]

(2) In the suppression of a person attempting to commit murder, sexual assault, aggravated sexual assault, burglary, or robbery; or [This permits you to legally use the threat of deadly force to stop the progression of these serious felonies.]

(3) In the case of a civil or military officer lawfully called out to suppress a riot or rebellion, prevent or suppress an invasion, or assist in serving legal process, in suppressing opposition against him or her in the just and necessary discharge of his or her duty. [Police and soldiers can lawfully threaten deadly force to stop riots and rebellions.]

(e) Subsection (d) of this section shall not be construed to limit or infringe upon defenses granted at common law. [If your attorney can think of other defenses available at common law, then more power to you. This doesn't help you avoid arrest and prosecution, however, because police and prosecutors generally brainstorm to nail you rather than bail you.]

§ 13 V.S.A. § 4011. Aiming gun at another.

Any person who shall intentionally point or aim any gun, pistol or other firearm at or towards another, except in self-defense or in the lawful discharge of official duty, shall be punished by fine not exceeding $50.00. Any person who shall discharge any such firearm so intentionally aimed or pointed shall be punished by imprisonment for not more than one year or fined not more than $100.00, or both. [So it's a felony to tell someone you have a gun, but if you actually point or shoot at them, it's only a misdemeanor? Given the fact that the police and prosecutors get to pick the statute they want to prosecute you under, we suggest you don't even tell people you have a gun to prevent a property crime or a simple assault (a "simple" assault is an assault without the use of a dangerous weapon.)]

[Exceptions to Justifiable Self-Defense] [Initial Aggressor]
[Exception to the Exception]

"[A]n aggressor, – that is, the person who starts the fight - is generally not entitled to raise the defense of self-defense. There is an exception to this rule. That exception applies when the aggressor starts the fight using only non-deadly force, and is then met with unjustified deadly force. In this situation, the aggressor may reasonably defend himself against the unjustified deadly force. This is so because the person using unjustified deadly force is using excessive force and is therefore acting unlawfully. However, deadly force is not unjustified or unlawful if it is reasonably necessary to protect a person from death or serious bodily injury." *State v. Trombley,* 174 Vt. 459 (2002) [The person who starts a fight cannot claim self-defense. An exception is where you start what you think is going to be exclusively a fist fight and the other guy pulls out a gun or knife. If you quickly bean him with a cue ball, you might escape conviction under this exception to the exception, but our research shows that you will probably be arrested and prosecuted.]

"The law of self-defense does not imply the right of attack in the first instance, nor does it permit an action to be done in retaliation or for revenge." *State v. Verrinder,* 637 A.2d 1382, 1396 (Vt. 1993) (jury instruction).

[Provocation]

"One cannot support claim of self-defense by self-generated necessity to kill; right of homicidal self-defense is granted only to those free from fault in the difficulty." *State v. McGee,* 665 A.2d 729, 733 (Vt. 1995). [You can't legally provoke someone into a fight for the purpose of killing them.]

[Committing Felony or Unlawful Act]

"If defendant was acting while in the course of an attempted felony, he was not entitled to the benefit of self-defense because his own conduct brought about the difficulty..." *State v. McGee*, 665 A.2d 729, 733 (Vt. 1995). [People committing felonies do not have the right of self-defense against the victims of their felonies. Their only choice is to surrender.]

[Duty to Retreat – Generally – If possible]
[Duty to Retreat from Home – Uncertain]

[Because the duty to retreat was not addressed in the self-defense statutes, we searched further. We found two cases, one quite old (1917), and one more recent (1997). In the more recent case, although the defendant admitted he didn't retreat, the court gave the instruction, "if defendant honestly and reasonably believed 'it was immediately necessary to use deadly force to protect himself from an imminent threat of death or bodily injury, the law does not require him to retreat.'" *State v. Hatcher,* 706 A.2d 429, 435 (1997). That issue wasn't appealed and therefore it would be difficult for us to conclude this represents the rule of law on the issue of retreat in Vermont. In the older case there was a claim that defendant was assaulted in his home by a trespasser whom he wounded. In analyzing the legal issues the court stated:

"The right of self-defense is founded in the first law of nature, and as applied to human affairs it presupposes that the party interposing the defense has been assaulted. 'The law abhors the use of force, either for attack or defense, and never permits its use unnecessarily,' and if the party assaulted has other means of avoiding the assault that are available, and that appear to him at the time as sufficient, and are in fact available, then he cannot use force in his self-defense." *State v. Albano,* 102 A. 333, 334 (Vt. 1917) (citations omitted).

[Defense of Property]

[We found nothing but an old case holding that you can't assault a trespasser to force him to leave your property unless you ask him to leave first. If he refuses, you can then use whatever non-deadly force is necessary to get him to leave. Of course, if the trespasser tries to assault you first, you can defend yourself with whatever non-deadly force to prevent the assault. We paraphrased because the language of the case was somewhat awkward.] *State v. Bean,* 180 A. 882 (Vt. 1935).

[Other Issues – Intoxication]

"The court instructed the jury to disregard defendant's intoxication. This was proper. Although individual attributes, such as age, size, strength, stamina, courage and assertiveness, are relevant to whether defendant's beliefs are reasonable, voluntarily induced states of mind such as those caused by drug and alcohol ingestion are not." *State v. Wheelock*, 609 A.2d 972 (Vt.1992). [Drunkenness is no excuse. The law does not recognize the "reasonably prudent" drunk. Any form of alcohol, whether stirred OR shaken, doesn't mix well with gun powder. As we told you in Chapter 7, alcohol can seriously affect your judgment and cause you to act stupidly.]

[HELPFUL DEFINITIONS RELATING TO THIS STATE'S SELF-DEFENSE STATUTES]

- **Felonies Mentioned –**
  - **Aggravated sexual assault** – [While in the process of committing a sexual assault, the offender causes serious bodily injury to another, is assisted by another in restraining or assaulting the victim, kidnaps the victim or uses a deadly weapon.] **Vermont Statutes 13 V.S.A. § 3253.**
  - **Burglary** – [Breaking or sneaking into a building or structure with the intent to commit a crime.] **Vermont Statutes 13 V.S.A. § 1201.**
  - **Murder** – [Intentional unlawful killing of a person.] **Vermont Statutes 13 V.S.A. § 2301 and 2311.**
  - **Robbery** – [Assaulting someone with or without a dangerous weapon to take property by force.] **Vermont Statutes 13 V.S.A. § 608 (Assault and robbery).**
  - **Sexual assault** – [Using force or threats to commit a sexual act upon someone.] **Vermont Statutes 13 V.S.A. § 3252.**

[TEMPLATE Topics We Could Not Find Explained in Statutes or Cases]

(For each of these topics that we could not find addressed in your state's statutes or cases, we suggest you review the same topics in the subchapters of surrounding states. Your state's courts may look to the law of neighboring states to see how their courts and legislatures have treated that particular self-defense issue.)

[Non-Deadly Force]

[Mutual Combat]

[Exceptions to the Exceptions]

[Withdraw and Communicate]

[Defense of Person(s) in Special Places – (e.g., Home, Business, Occupied Vehicle)]

[Duty to Retreat From Home]

[Co-Habitants; Co-Employees – Duty to Retreat]

[Presumption of Reasonableness in Special Places]

[Reckless Injury to Innocent Third Parties]

[Civil Liability]

VIRGINIA

Virginia's self-defense law is contained solely in case law rather than in statutes like most other states. All the following references to Virginia self-defense law refer to holdings of Virginia cases. As you will see, Virginia is sorely in need of a self-defense statute to give citizens adequate and precise notice of when and under what circumstances they may legally use force in defense of themselves and their loved ones.

Key: ■ commentary ■ original statutes, cases or jury instructions

---

[Defense of Self and Others] [Deadly Force]

"A defendant must reasonably fear death or serious bodily harm to himself at the hands of his victim. It is not essential that the danger should in fact exist. If it reasonably appears to a defendant that the danger exists, he has the right to defend himself against it to the same extent, and upon the same rules, as would obtain in case the danger is real. A defendant may always act upon reasonable appearance of danger, and whether the danger is reasonably apparent is always to be determined from the viewpoint of the defendant at the time he acted." *Couture v. Commonwealth*, 656 S.E.2d 425, 428 (Va.App. 2008). [You cannot use deadly force unless faced with an imminent threat of death or serious injury. Virginia unequivocally requires an *overt act* for imminence to exist. See discussion of *overt act* under the topic heading IMMINENCE in Chapter 3. Notice that even if the threat of death was not real (example, someone points an unloaded gun at you and says they are going to kill you with it), if your belief is reasonable (because of what he said, you thought it was loaded and had no reason to believe otherwise), absent any negative factors (see discussion below), you would be justified in blasting his Yankee sass into the Chesapeake Bay.]

[Use of Deadly Force to Prevent Serious Felonies]

"Homicide in defense of person or property, under certain circumstances of necessity; which is justifiable by the permission of the law. [This first incomplete sentence is a sub-title out of a treatise (like an encyclopedia) on criminal law, *Davis's Criminal Law*, referenced in the Virginia case cited below.] This takes place when a man, in defense of his person, habitation or property, kills another, who manifestly intends and endeavors, by violence or surprise, to commit a forcible or atrocious felony upon either. [We do not read this to mean you can kill to protect property, but rather persons on property for heinous property crimes such as arson and burglary.] In the cases to which this ground of justification applies, no felony has been committed, but only attempted; and the homicide is justifiable in order to prevent it.

All felonies may not be so prevented. A distinction is made between such felonies as are attended with force, or any extraordinary degree of atrocity, which in their nature betoken such urgent necessity as will not allow of any delay, and others of a different kind and unaccompanied by violence on the part of the felon. Those only which come within the former description may be prevented by homicide; as murder, rape, robbery, arson, burglary and the like. In the attempt to commit either of these, the party whose person or property is attacked is not obliged to retreat, but may pursue his adversary until he has secured himself from all danger, and if he kill him in so doing, it is called justifiable self-defense. And the same justification extends to homicide committed in the mutual and reciprocal defense of such as stand in the relations of husband and wife, parent and child, master and servant; for the act of the assistant shall have the same construction in such cases as the act of the party assisted should have had, if it had been done by himself, in consequence of the relation between them." *Dodson v. Commonwealth*, 167 S.E. 260, 261 (Va. 1933) (Citing with approval *Davis's Criminal Law*). [This old case seems to indicate you can use deadly force to prevent the commission of the heinous common-law felonies, murder, rape, robbery, arson and burglary. However, the following quote from a much more recent case creates some doubt about this. It says there still has to be an imminent threat of death or serious injury. We hate such confusion as much as you do. Unless you want to be the "test case," we suggest you not use deadly force in Old Dominion unless facing an imminent threat of deadly force.]

". . . the test is not whether Gordon used reasonable force against a person who manifestly intended and endeavored by violence to commit a felony on him, but whether he reasonably feared death or serious bodily harm to himself at the hands of such person" *Gordon v. Commonwealth*, 184 S.E.2d 814, 815 (Va. 1971).

[Defense of a Third Person]

"Generally... this privilege is not limited to family members and extends to anyone, even a stranger who is entitled to claim self-defense..." *Foster v. Commonwealth*, 412 S.E.2d 198, 201 (Va.App. 1991). [You don't have to be related to a third person to defend them from an unlawful and imminent threat of injury.]

"We hold that the law pertaining to defense of others is that one may avail himself or herself of the defense only where he or she reasonably believes, based on the attendant circumstances, that the person defended is without fault in provoking the fray." *Foster v. Commonwealth*, 412 S.E.2d 198, 202 (Va.App. 1991). [But you cannot defend someone whom you know provoked a fight.]

"In order to justifiably defend another, the defendant must reasonably believe that the person being defended was free from fault; whether the defended person was, in fact, free from fault is legally irrelevant..." *Foster v. Commonwealth*, 412 S.E.2d 198, 202 (Va.App. 1991). [A reasonable belief that the third person you are defending is free from fault is sufficient justification for you to claim self-defense.]

[Exceptions to Justifiable Self-Defense] [Initial Aggressor]; [Provocation]

"Like self-defense, the circumstances in which the protection of others may be raised as a defense are carefully circumscribed so as to preclude such a claim in situations where one has instigated the fray in order to provide an excuse for assaulting or murdering his enemy." *Foster v. Commonwealth*, 412 S.E.2d 198, 201 (Va.App. 1991). [Like in most states, you can't provoke a fight with the intent to kill your adversary and expect to claim self-defense.]

"If an accused is even slightly at fault in creating the difficulty leading to the necessity to kill, the killing is not justifiable homicide. Any form of conduct by the accused from which the fact finder may reasonably infer that the accused contributed to the affray constitutes fault." *Smith v. Commonwealth,* 435 S.E.2d 414, 416 (Va.App. 1993) (citations omitted). [If you are at fault in causing a chain of events that leads to someone getting killed, you will not be allowed to win your case on the theory of self-defense.]

[Mutual Combat]

"When two persons enter willingly into a combat, not for self protection but to gratify their passion by inflicting injury upon each other, the doctrine of self-defense cannot be invoked on behalf of either." *Jones v. Commonwealth,* 82 S.E.2d 482, 485 (Va. 1954)(citations omitted).

"The Supreme Court has held that when a homicide is committed in the course of a sudden quarrel or broil, or mutual combat, ... and without any previous grudge, the offence may be murder or manslaughter, according to the circumstances of the case. Thus, it is perfectly true that where homicide occurs in the course of a sudden quarrel, mutual combat, ... and the killing is from passion growing solely out of the provocation, the offense is manslaughter and not murder." *Rhodes v. Commonwealth,* 583 S.E.2d 773, 778 (Va.App. 2003)(Citations omitted). [In Virginia, if you engage in mutual combat you lose the privilege to claim self-defense whether you used non-deadly or deadly force. If the person you are fighting dies, you could be convicted of murder or manslaughter depending on how the jury perceives the situation. Killing in a heat of passion after being provoked generally leads to a conviction of manslaughter rather than murder, but it still gets you a dismal view of the world from behind bars.].

[Exception to the Exceptions] [Withdraw and Communicate]

"Excusable homicide in self-defense occurs where the accused, although in some fault in the first instance in provoking or bringing on the difficulty, when attacked retreats as far as possible, announces his desire for peace, and kills his adversary from a reasonably apparent necessity to preserve his own life or [to] save himself from great bodily harm." *Smith v. Commonwealth,* 435 S.E.2d 414, 416 (Va.App. 1993) (citations omitted). [Although you are not entitled to claim self-defense if you start a fight, if you withdraw from the conflict, make it plain to your opponent that you no longer want to fight, and then he tries to filet your fanny, you can defend yourself with deadly force. Our experience has been that if you share any blame for starting a fight, the Popo-Five-O and DAs will do their thing and let the jury sort it out.]

[No Duty to Retreat]

"In the case of justifiable homicide, '[in which] the accused is free from fault in bringing on the fray, the accused need not retreat, but is permitted to stand his [or her] ground and repel the attack by force, including deadly force, if it is necessary.'" *Gilbert v. Commonwealth,* 506 S.E.2d 543, 546 (1998) (quoting Foote v. Commonwealth, 396 S.E.2d 851, 855 (1990)). [There is no duty to retreat unless you are at fault in the chain events that lead to the assault or killing. The use of the word "necessary," however, makes us believe that if you could have retreated safely without killing someone, you will probably be required to do so.]

[Defense of Person(s) in Special Places – Home "Castle Doctrine"]
[No Duty to Retreat from Home]

"One in his own curtilage [the space immediately surrounding one's home], who is free from fault in bringing on the combat, when attacked by another, has the same right of conduct, without any retreat (i.e., to stand at bay and resist assault), even to the taking of life, that one has when within his own home . . .. But in no case, even within one's own home or curtilage, is a person wholly justified in taking the life of another who has entered the home or curtilage peaceably, on an implied license [if you voluntarily let him in], merely to punish or subdue him, or to compel him to leave the premises, where there is no apparent intent on the part of the latter to commit any felony. . . . The general rule is that, while a man may use all reasonable and necessary force to defend his real and personal estate, of which he is in the actual possession, against another who comes to dispossess him without right, he cannot innocently carry this defense to the extent of killing the aggressor [you can't simply kill a trespasser because he won't leave; you have to resort to the courts. **Translation:** You and Me can't strangle Dupree for overstaying his welcome (even though we'd like to)]. If no other way is open to him, he must yield, and get himself righted by resort to the law. A seeming exception to this rule is the **Defense of the Castle.** In the early times our forefathers were compelled to protect themselves in their habitations by converting them into holds of defense; and so the dwelling house was called the castle. To this condition of things the law has conformed, resulting in the familiar doctrine that, while a man keeps the doors of his house closed, no other may break and enter it, except in particular circumstances to make an arrest or the like—cases not within the line of our present exposition. From this doctrine is derived another, namely: That the persons within the house may exercise all needful force to keep aggressors out, even to the taking of life. As observed by Campbell, J., in Michigan [notice how courts in one state look to other states for a rule of law]: 'A man is not obliged to retreat if assaulted in his dwelling, but may use such means as are absolutely necessary to repel the assailant from his house or prevent his forcible entry, even to the taking of life.'" *Fortune v. Com.,* 112 S.E. 861, 867 (Va. 1922). [This is an old case, but is one of the clearest statements of the doctrine of home defense that we could find in Virginia. It says you can use deadly force to keep an intruder from breaking and entering into your home.]

[Defense of Property]

". . . the owner of land has no right to assault a mere trespasser with a deadly weapon... a deadly weapon may not be brandished solely in defense of personal property." *Commonwealth v. Alexander,* 531 S.E.2d 567, 569 (2000). [You can't threaten deadly force, let alone use deadly force, to defend your personal property or real estate.]

[TEMPLATE Topics We Could Not Find Explained in Statutes or Cases]

(For each of these topics that we could not find addressed in your state's statutes or cases, we suggest you review the same topics in the subchapters of surrounding states. Your state's courts may look to the law of neighboring states to see how their courts and legislatures have treated that particular self-defense issue.)

[Non-Deadly Force]

[Committing Felony or Unlawful Act]

[Co-Habitants; Co-Employees – Duty to Retreat]

[Presumption of Reasonableness in Special Places]

[Reckless Injury to Innocent Third Parties]

[Civil Liability]

[Helpful Definitions Relating to this State's Self-Defense Statutes]

Pancho's Nomination for the Darwin Award

"... guns don't belong in the classroom ...In an academic environment, we believe you should be free from fear.. . . we think it's a common-sense policy for the protection of students, staff and faculty . . . this will help parents, students, faculty and visitors feel safe on our campus." Warm-Fuzzy Statement by Virginia Tech spokesman, Larry Hincker upon hearing that the Virginia Legislature would allow Virginia Tech to maintain a "gun free campus" a year before the Virginia Tech shooting.

Pancho's Wisdom

Gun FREE zones COST innocent lives.

WASHINGTON

Key: ■ commentary ■ original statutes, cases or jury instructions

[Defense of Self and Others] [Non-Deadly Force]

[Washington State gives cops, bus drivers, train operators, mental hospital employees, those making citizens' arrests and others the right to manhandle people in ways described below. These situations do not involve the use of deadly force. We rearranged our TEMPLATE slightly to avoid having to carve up Washington's statutes.]

§ REVISED CODE OF WASHINGTON (RCW) § 9A.16.020
Use of Force – When lawful.

The use, attempt, or offer to use force upon or toward the person of another is not unlawful in the following cases:

(1) Whenever necessarily used by a public officer in the performance of a legal duty, or a person assisting the officer and acting under the officer's direction; [e.g., police officers.]

(2) Whenever necessarily used by a person arresting one who has committed a felony and delivering him or her to a public officer competent to receive him or her into custody; [e.g., citizens' arrest of felons. We STRONGLY recommend against doing this unless someone's life is in danger. See our commentary in Chapter 4.]

(3) Whenever used by a party about to be injured, or by another lawfully aiding him or her, in preventing or attempting to prevent an offense against his or her person, or a malicious trespass, or other malicious interference with real or personal property lawfully in his or her possession, in case the force is not more than is necessary; [The use of non-deadly force to prevent an assault or trespass. If you use more force than necessary, it is considered excessive force. This could subject you to the conviction of a crime or civil damages.]

(4) Whenever reasonably used by a person to detain someone who enters or remains unlawfully in a building or on real property lawfully in the possession of such person, so long as such detention is reasonable in duration and manner to investigate the reason for the detained person's presence on the premises, and so long as the premises in question did not reasonably appear to be intended to be open to members of the public; [Use of non-deadly force to deal with trespassers in a building not open to the public.]

(5) Whenever used by a carrier of passengers or the carrier's authorized agent or servant, or other person assisting them at their request in expelling from a carriage, railway car, vessel, or other vehicle, a passenger who refuses to obey a lawful and reasonable regulation prescribed for the conduct of passengers, if such vehicle has first been stopped and the force used is not more than is necessary to expel the offender with reasonable regard to the offender's personal safety; [Using non-deadly force to throw troublemakers off of the bus or train.]

(6) Whenever used by any person to prevent a mentally ill, mentally incompetent, or mentally disabled person from committing an act dangerous to any person, or in enforcing necessary restraint for the protection or restoration to health of the person, during such period only as is necessary to obtain legal authority for the restraint or custody of the person. [Non-deadly force to deal with the mentally incompetent if necessary.]

[Deadly Force] [Defense of a Third Person]

§ REVISED CODE OF WASHINGTON (RCW) 9A.16.050

Homicide—By other person—When justifiable.

Homicide is also justifiable when committed either:

(1) In the lawful defense of the slayer, or his or her husband, wife, parent, child, brother, or sister, or of any other person in his presence or company, when there is reasonable ground to apprehend a design on the part of the person slain to commit a felony or to do some great personal injury to the slayer or to any such person, and there is imminent danger of such design being accomplished; or [The language of this statute is archaic (old), but it says basically the same thing that other state's deadly force statutes say. You can use deadly force to defend yourself and others from an imminent threat of serious bodily injury or death. Although it looks like you can use deadly force to prevent felonies, this has been limited to violent felonies described in the *Nyland* case immediately following paragraph (2) below.]

[Defense of Person(s) in Special Places – Home or Temporary Home]

(2) In the actual resistance of an attempt to commit a felony upon the slayer, in his presence, or upon or in a dwelling, or other place of abode, in which he is. [You can use deadly force to prevent someone from committing one of the violent felonies described in the *Nyland* case below, either against you, in your presence or in your home or temporary home.]

"The class of crimes in prevention of which a man may, if necessary, exercise his natural right to repel force by force to the taking of the life of the aggressor, are felonies which are committed by violence and surprise; such as murder, robbery, burglary, arson, breaking a house in the day time with intent to rob, sodomy, and rape..." *State v. Nyland*, 287 P.2d 345 (1955) (citing *State v. Moore*, 31 Conn. 479, quoted with approval in *State v. Marfaudille*, 92 P. 939 (1907)).

[Use of Deadly Force to Prevent Serious Felonies]

§ RCW 9A.16.110 (1)

No person in the state shall be placed in legal jeopardy of any kind whatsoever for protecting by any reasonable means necessary, himself or herself, his or her family, or his or her real or personal property, or for coming to the aid of another who is in imminent danger of or the victim of assault, robbery, kidnapping, arson, burglary, rape, murder, or any other violent crime as defined in RCW 9.94A.030. [You may use deadly force to protect yourself and others from violent felonies like the ones listed in this statute, which are defined below.]

[Exceptions to Justifiable Self-Defense] [Initial Aggressor] [Provocation]

"No person may, by any intentional act reasonably likely to provoke a belligerent response, create a necessity for acting in self-defense and thereupon use, offer or attempt to use force upon or toward another person. Therefore, if you find beyond a reasonable doubt that the defendant was the aggressor, and that defendant's acts and conduct provoked or commenced the fight, then self-defense is not available as a defense." *State v Riley,* 976 P.2d 624 (1999). [If you start a fight for the purpose of hurting someone, you can't claim self-defense after you hurt him or her.]

"If there is credible evidence that the defendant made the first move by drawing a weapon, the evidence supports the giving of an aggressor instruction." *State v. Thompson,* 733 P.2d 584 (1987). "An aggressor instruction is appropriate if there is conflicting evidence as to whether the defendant's conduct precipitated a fight." *State v. Davis,* 835 P.2d 1039 (1992). "We hold that words alone do not constitute sufficient provocation." *State v. Riley,* 976 P.2d 624 (1999). [The rules of law in these three cases refine the law related to starting or provoking a fight. If there is some evidence that you started the fight or provoked it for the purpose of hurting someone, the judge will instruct the jury on that theory. If the jury finds you started or provoked the fight, you would not be entitled to a not-guilty verdict on the theory of self-defense. Furthermore, you can't use force or deadly force against someone who simply calls you names.]

[Exceptions to the Exceptions] [Withdraw and Communicate]

"However, in general, the right of self-defense cannot be successfully invoked by an aggressor or one who provokes an altercation, unless he or she in good faith first withdraws from the combat at a time and in a manner to let the other person know that he or she is withdrawing or intends to withdraw from further aggressive action." *State v. Craig,* 514 P.2d 151 (1973). [You can't claim self-defense if you start a fight unless you first withdraw from the fight and tell the other person you intend to withdraw. This is a fairly consistent rule throughout the entire country.]

[No Duty to Retreat – Generally]

"It is lawful for a person who is in a place where that person has a right to be and who has reasonable grounds for believing that he is being attacked to stand his ground and defend against such attack by use of lawful force. The law does not impose a duty to retreat." *State v. Prado,* 181 P.3d 901 (2008). (jury instructions). [You don't have to retreat from anywhere you have a legal right to be before using reasonable force, including deadly force. There is no language that would suggest that the same rule of no retreat does not apply to defense of one's home as well.]

[Civil Liability]

RCW 9A.16.110

§ **Defending against violent crime—Reimbursement.**

[This is a one-of-a-kind statute that saves a person found not guilty by reason self-defense from bankruptcy after paying attorney fees. If the judge smells a fish in the defendant's conduct, he doesn't have to allow the reimbursement. The judge can also award reimbursement for the days, if not weeks, sitting in court as well as other costs. If the court doesn't reimburse, the legislature can. Every state should have this provision. The cost of defending a criminal case can be financially ruinous. This financial burden sometimes forces innocent citizens to plead guilty to keep their house, car or furniture from being foreclosed upon or to keep themselves from having to take out bankruptcy. Making the state pay attorney fees of the innocent places the burden back upon the state and probably dissuades prosecutors, at least in some small degree, from prosecuting those who appear to have acted in self-defense. This keeps district attorneys from shirking their duty to properly screen cases rather than placing the burden on juries.]

(1) No person in the state shall be placed in legal jeopardy of any kind whatsoever for protecting by any reasonable means necessary, himself or herself, his or her family, or his or her real or personal property, or for coming to the aid of another who is in imminent danger of or the victim of assault, robbery, kidnapping, arson, burglary, rape, murder, or any other violent crime as defined in **RCW 9.94A.030.**

(2) When a person charged with a crime listed in subsection (1) of this section is found not guilty by reason of self-defense, the state of Washington shall reimburse the defendant for all reasonable costs, including loss of time, legal fees incurred, and other expenses involved in his or her defense. This reimbursement is not an independent cause of action. To award these reasonable costs the trier of fact must find that the defendant's claim of self-defense was sustained by a preponderance of the evidence. If the trier of fact makes a determination of self-defense, the judge shall determine the amount of the award.

(3) Notwithstanding a finding that a defendant's actions were justified by self-defense, if the trier of fact also determines that the defendant was engaged in criminal conduct substantially related to the events giving rise to the charges filed against the defendant the judge may deny or reduce the amount of the award. In determining the amount of the award, the judge shall also consider the seriousness of the initial criminal conduct.

Nothing in this section precludes the legislature from using the sundry claims process to grant an award where none was granted under this section or to grant a higher award than one granted under this section.

(4) Whenever the issue of self-defense under this section is decided by a judge, the judge shall consider the same questions as must be answered in the special verdict under subsection (4) [(5)] of this section.

(5) Whenever the issue of self-defense under this section has been submitted to a jury, and the jury has found the defendant not guilty, the court shall instruct the jury to return a special verdict in substantially the following form:

Answer
Yes or No

1. Was the finding of not guilty based upon self-defense? _____
2. If your answer to question 1 is no, do not answer the remaining question.
3. If your answer to question 1 is yes, was the defendant:
   a. Protecting himself or herself? _____
   b. Protecting his or her family? _____
   c. Protecting his or her property? _____
   d. Coming to the aid of another who was in imminent danger of a heinous crime? _____
   e. Coming to the aid of another who was the victim of a heinous crime? _____
   f. Engaged in criminal conduct substantially related to the events giving rise to the crime with which the defendant is charged? _____

[Defense of Personal Property]

§ RCW 9A.16.020

The use, attempt, or offer to use force upon or toward the person of another is not unlawful in the following cases: [You can use reasonable force to defend your property, but not deadly force.]

. . .

(3) Whenever used by a party about to be injured, or by another lawfully aiding him or her, in preventing or attempting to prevent an offense against his or her person, or a malicious trespass, or other malicious interference with real or personal property lawfully in his or her possession, in case the force is not more than is necessary;

(4) Whenever reasonably used by a person to detain someone who enters or remains unlawfully in a building or on real property lawfully in the possession of such person, so long as such detention is reasonable in duration and manner to investigate the reason for the detained person's presence on the premises, and so long as the premises in question did not reasonably appear to be intended to be open to members of the public;

. . .

"One of the defenses to a charge of assault is that the act was committed in the defense of property of the actor, or of one whom he is under a legal duty to protect. It is the generally accepted rule that a person owning, or lawfully in possession of, property may use such force as is reasonably necessary under the circumstances in order to protect that property, and for the exertion of such force he is not liable either criminally or civilly" *State v. Bland,* 116 P.3d 428 (2005) fn3. (citing *Peasley v. Puget Sound Tug & Barge Co.,* 125 P.2d 681 (1942)). [You can even assault someone to prevent damage to or the taking of property. But you cannot use more force than is necessary, and certainly not deadly force.]

[HELPFUL DEFINITIONS RELATING TO THIS STATE'S SELF-DEFENSE STATUTES]

- **Necessary** – means that no reasonably effective alternative to the use of force appeared to exist and that the amount of force used was reasonable to effect the lawful purpose intended. **Revised Code of Washington, RCW 9A.16.010 (1).**

- **Deadly force** – means the intentional application of force through the use of firearms or any other means reasonably likely to cause death or serious physical injury. **Revised Code of Washington RCW 9A.16.010 (2).**

- **Felonies Mentioned –**

    - **Assault** – [Intentionally or recklessly causing or threatening bodily harm or injury to another.] **RCW 9A.36.011 (first degree), RCW 9A.36.021 (second degree) RCW 9A.36.031 (third degree).**

    - **Robbery** – [The taking of property from another or against his will by the use of threat or force, violence or fear of injury.] **RCW 9A.56.190, RCW 9A.56.200 (first degree) RCW 9A.56.210 (second degree).**

    - **Kidnapping** – [The intentional abduction of another. Under the Washington criminal code "abduct means to restrain a person by either secreting or holding him in a place where he is not likely to be found, or using or threatening to use deadly force." RCW 9A.40.010] **RCW 9A.40.020 (first degree), RCW 9A.40.030.**

    - **Arson** – [Knowingly or maliciously causing a fire or explosion in a building "or any structure or erection appurtenant to or joining any building, or any wharf, dock, machine, engine, automobile, or other motor vehicle, watercraft, aircraft, bridge, or trestle, or hay, grain, crop, or timber, whether cut or standing or any range land, or pasture land, or any fence, or any lumber, shingle, or other timber products, or any property."] **RCW 9A.48.020 (first degree), RCW 9A.48.030 (second degree).**

    - **Burglary** – [Intentionally entering or remaining unlawfully in a building or residence with the intent to commit a crime therein.] **RCW 9A.52.020 (first degree burglary), RCW 9A.52.025 (residential burglary) , RCW 9A.52.030 (second degree burglary).**

    - **Rape** – [This would include all felonies regarding any form of the offense of rape. These are all cited below. The generic definition of rape could be defined as: When a person engages in nonconsensual sexual intercourse with another outside of marriage and where the victim in word or conduct communicated the nonconsensual nature of the act.] **RCW 9A.44.040, 050, 060, 073, 076, 079.**

- **Murder** – [The unlawful killing of another.] **RCW 9A.32.010, 030, 050, 055, 060, 070.**

[TEMPLATE Topics We Could Not Find Explained in Statutes or Cases]
(For each of these topics that we could not find addressed in your state's statutes or cases, we suggest you review the same topics in the subchapters of surrounding states. Your state's courts may look to the law of the surrounding states to see how their courts and legislatures have treated that particular self-defense issue.)

[Combat by Agreement]

[Committing Felony or Unlawful Act]

[Co-Habitants; Co-Employees – Duty to Retreat]

[Presumption of Reasonableness in Special Places]

[Duty to Retreat in Special Places]

Pancho's Wisdom

You just might be a Gunnut if . . . you have a semi-circular scar just over the eye-brow of your dominant eye.

. . . you have a long straight dent across the hood of your truck that ends with a rifle caliber hole.

. . . when making that dent, you discovered that yer scope and yer gun barrel ain't lookin' at the same thing at close distances.

West Virginia has no self-defense statutes. It's all case law. The cases do not cover all the topics we outlined in our TEMPLATE. We were actually surprised how protective West Virginia's case law has developed compared to some of the disappointments we noticed in Virginia.

Key: ■ commentary ■ original statutes, cases or jury instructions

---

[Defense of Self and Others] [Non-Deadly Force] [Deadly Force]
"The amount of force that can be used in self-defense is that normally one can return deadly force only if he reasonably believes that the assailant is about to inflict death or serious bodily harm; otherwise, where he is threatened only with non-deadly force, he may use only non-deadly force in return." *State v. Jason H.*, 599 S.E.2d 862, 865 (W.Va. 2004.) [This is a very typical statement of the law. You may only use non-deadly force to repel an attack of non-deadly force, and deadly force versus deadly force.]

[Defense of a Third Person]
"Under the laws of this state, if the Defendant was not the aggressor, and had reasonable grounds to believe and actually did believe that he or others were in imminent danger of death or serious bodily harm from which he could save himself or others only by using deadly force against his assailant or assailants, then he had the right to employ deadly force in order to defend himself or others. By deadly force is meant force which is likely to cause death or serious bodily harm". *State v. Dinger,* 624 S.E.2d 572, 576 (W.Va. 2005) fn4.

"In *State v. Best* 113 S.E. 919, 925 (1922), this Court alluded to the alter ego rule when it was said that 'the right of a person to defend another does not ordinarily exceed such person's right to defend himself.'" *State v. Cook,* 515 S.E.2d 127, 135 (W.Va. 1999).
[You can use the same degree of force to defend a third person that the third person could legally have used to defend him or herself.]

[Exceptions to Justifiable Self-Defense] [Initial Aggressor] [Provocation]
"In order for the Defendant to have been justified in the use of deadly force in self-defense or in defense of others, he must not have provoked the assault on him or have been the aggressor. Mere words, without more, do not constitute provocation or aggression." *State v. Dinger,* 624 S.E.2d 572, 576 (W.Va. 2005). [This is the general rule that if you start a fight or provoke a fight as an excuse to hurt or kill someone, you can't claim self-defense. But mere words, without more, will not defeat your right

to claim self-defense. We believe, however, if your words are very inflammatory, you might be arrested, prosecuted or convicted. See Thumbs-Down Factors, Chapter 7.]

[Committing Felony or Unlawful Act]

"We hold that self-defense and provocation instructions are not available in response to a charge of felony-murder where the predicate felony is the delivery of a controlled substance." *State v. Wade,* 200 W. Va. 637, 645 (1997). [Victim, who is trying to buy drugs, almost runs into car of drug-dealer friend of defendant. Defendant shoots victim when the drug deal goes bad. Court held defendant can't claim self-defense under those circumstances.]

[Exceptions to the Exceptions] [Withdraw and Communicate]

"If a person voluntarily, that is aggressively and willingly, enters into a fight, he cannot invoke the doctrine of self-defense unless he first abandons the fight, withdraws from it, and gives notice that he has done so." *State v. Brooks,* 591 S.E.2d 120, 125 (W.Va. 2003). [This is the classic exception to the exception. See discussion in Chapter 4.]

[No Duty to Retreat – Generally]

"This Court long ago recognized that it is only the faultless, who are exempt from the necessity of retreating while acting in self-defense. Those in fault must retreat, if able to do so; if from the fierceness of the attack or for other reasons they are unable to retreat, they will be excused by the law for not doing so." *State v. Dinger,* 624 S.E.2d 572, 576 (W.Va. 2005). [If you are without fault, you don't have to retreat. If you are at fault and try to retreat, but can't for some reason, you are excused from retreating. However, we find when it gets this complicated, you will be arrested, prosecuted and there is a good chance you will be convicted of a felony if your actions resulted in someone dying.]

[Defense of Person(s) in Special Places – Home]

"We believe that there are sound policy reasons for permitting the homeowner to repel with deadly force a violent intrusion into his home where he has reasonable grounds to believe the intruder will commit a felony or personal injury on the occupant and that deadly force is the only means available to prevent it. First, there is still basic vitality to the ancient English rule that a man's home is his castle, and he has the right to expect some privacy and security within its confines. This rule arises from a societal recognition that the home shelters and is a physical refuge for the basic unit of society the family. In the criminal law there is a marked recognition of this fact, as shown by the difference in the right to arrest a criminal without a warrant as between his home and a public place.

Second, we believe that from the standpoint of the intruder the violent and unlawful entry into a dwelling with intent to injure the occupants or commit a felony carries a common sense conclusion that he may be met with deadly force, and that his culpability matches the risk of danger. We also recognize that there is often a certain vulnerability to the occupant of a dwelling who is forced to confront the unlawful intruder in the privacy of his home, without any expectation of a public response or help.

Finally, while it can be acknowledged that one element of a mature criminal justice system is to narrow the areas where individuals may resort to self-help in the infliction of punishment or the taking of life, no court has seen fit to abolish the concept of self-defense." *State v. W.J.B.*, 276 S.E.2d 550, 612 (W.Va. 1981). [In this decision, the West Virginia appeals court held that an unlawful entry and threat of a violent assault in one's home are enough to activate the right to use deadly force in self-defense. It did not require a showing of a threat of serious injury or death. This lower threshold for the use of deadly force in the home is in line with the law in many southern and western states.]

[No Duty to Retreat From Your Home]

"We have recognized that a person in his own home who is subject to an unlawful intrusion and placed in immediate danger of serious bodily harm or death has no duty to retreat but may remain in place and employ deadly force to defend himself." *State v. W.J.B.*, 166 W. Va. 602, 606 (1981). [There is no duty to retreat from your own home. The West Virginia Supreme Court of Appeals recently held in *State v. Harden*, 679 S.E.2d 628 (W.Va.,2009) that you don't even have a duty to retreat from a co-occupant of the home if facing a threat of serious injury or death (in that case an abusive husband). Whenever it gets that messy, however, the defender is going to be arrested and vigorously prosecuted.]

[Civil Liability]

§ WEST VIRGINIA CODE § 55-7-22.
Civil relief for persons resisting certain criminal activities.

[This statute protects from civil lawsuits only. It does not have anything to do with criminal charges.]

(a) A lawful occupant within a home or other place of residence is justified in using reasonable and proportionate force, including deadly force, against an intruder or attacker to prevent a forcible entry into the home or residence or to terminate the intruder's or attacker's unlawful entry if the occupant reasonably apprehends that the intruder or attacker may kill or inflict serious bodily harm upon the occupant or others in the home or residence or if the occupant reasonably believes that the intruder or attacker intends to commit a felony in the home or residence and the occupant reasonably believes deadly force is necessary. [You cannot be sued for using deadly force against a forcible or illegal entry into your home if you have a reasonable belief the intruder will kill or cause serious injury OR he intends to commit a felony and you believe deadly force is necessary. This statute has not been interpreted by any court.]

(b) A lawful occupant within a home or other place of residence does not have a duty to retreat from an intruder or attacker in the circumstances described in subsection (a) of this section. [Under civil law, there is no duty to retreat from an intruder in your home under the circumstances described in (a) above.]

(c) A person not engaged in unlawful activity who is attacked in any place he or she has a legal right to be outside of his or her home or residence may use reasonable and proportionate force against an intruder or attacker: *Provided,* That such person may use deadly force against an intruder or attacker in a place that is not his or her residence without a duty to retreat if the person reasonably believes that he or she or another is in imminent danger of death or serious bodily harm from which he or she or another can only be saved by the use of deadly force against the intruder or attacker. [Under civil law, you can only use deadly force against an attacker outside of your home (where you have a right to be) without retreating if you reasonably believe that you or another person is in danger of death or serious bodily injury, and you can only avoid being injured by usings deadly force.]

(d) The justified use of reasonable and proportionate force under this section shall constitute a full and complete defense to any civil action brought by an intruder or attacker against a person using such force. [If you are justified under this section, you have a complete defense in civil action. This does NOT mean you can't be sued; it just means you have a defense in case you are sued in civil court.]

(e) The full and complete civil defense created by the provisions of this section is not available to a person who:

(1) Is attempting to commit, committing or escaping from the commission of a felony; [You are not exempt from civil liability if you try to commit, commit or try to escape after committing a felony;]

(2) Initially provokes the use of force against himself, herself or another with the intent to use such force as an excuse to inflict bodily harm upon the assailant; or [You are not exempt from civil liability if your provoke someone as an excuse to hurt or kill him or her;]

(3) Otherwise initially provokes the use of force against himself, herself or another, unless he or she withdraws from physical contact with the assailant and indicates clearly to the assailant that he or she desires to withdraw and terminate the use of force, but the assailant continues or resumes the use of force. [Exception to the Exception: You MIGHT still be exempt even if you provoked IF you withdraw, communicate your intent to stop fighting and the other person continues to fight. If it gets this complicated, count on being sued.]

(f) The provisions of this section do not apply to the creation of a hazardous or dangerous condition on or in any real or personal property designed to prevent criminal conduct or cause injury to a person engaging in criminal conduct. [This does not apply if you create a dangerous condition to prevent criminal activity. This is talking about setting up a dangerous contraption to catch, injure or kill criminals trespassing on your property. Such devices are generally frowned upon. The most infamous of such traps consists of a spring gun that shoots trespassers as they trespass into a building. Any of the traps set by the precocious little imp in the movie *Home Alone* would subject you to possible civil liability if you set such traps in West Virginia.]

(g) Nothing in this section shall authorize or justify a person to resist or obstruct a law-enforcement officer acting in the course of his or her duty.

[Defense of Property]

"Of course, reasonable interference to prevent destruction of property is always justified. But completed destruction of or damage to property is not, alone, sufficient to justify an assault." *State v. Allen* 49 S.E.2d 847, 53 (W.Va. 1948).

"A proprietor may order a trespasser off his premises and, if he refuses to go, he may use such reasonable force as may be necessary to expel him. But if he exceeds the bounds of reasonable force he is guilty of an assault.

The right to eject an intruder is not limited to one's dwelling house, but applies to any property of which he has lawful possession." *State v. Flanagan,* 86 S.E. 890, 890 (W.Va. 1915).

[You may use non-deadly force to defend your property, but not deadly force.]

[HELPFUL DEFINITIONS RELATING TO THIS STATE'S SELF-DEFENSE STATUTES]

[None, there are no statutes!]

[TEMPLATE Topics We Could Not Find Explained in Statutes or Cases]

(For each of these topics that we could not find addressed in your state's statutes or cases, we suggest you review the same topics in the subchapters of surrounding states. Your state's courts may look to the law of neighboring states to see how their courts and legislatures have treated that particular self-defense issue.)

[Use of Deadly Force to Prevent Serious Felonies]

[Combat by Agreement]

[Co-Habitants; Co-Employees – Duty to Retreat]

[Presumption of Reasonableness in Special Places]

[Civil Liability]

[Reckless Injury to Innocent Third Parties]

WISCONSIN

Key: ■ commentary ■ original statutes, cases or jury instructions

[DEFENSE OF SELF AND OTHERS] [NON-DEADLY FORCE]

§ WISCONSIN STATUE (WIS. STAT.) § 939.48.
Self-defense and defense of others.

(1) A person is privileged to threaten or intentionally use force against another for the purpose of preventing or terminating what the person reasonably believes to be an unlawful interference with his or her person by such other person. The actor may intentionally use only such force or threat thereof as the actor reasonably believes is necessary to prevent or terminate the interference. . . [Non-deadly force may be used to oppose non-deadly force.]

[Deadly Force]

§ WIS. STAT. § 939.48 continued . . .

The actor may not intentionally use force which is intended or likely to cause death or great bodily harm unless the actor reasonably believes that such force is necessary to prevent imminent death or great bodily harm to himself or herself. [Deadly force may be used to oppose deadly force. The use of force must be reasonable, imminent and necessary. Read Chapter 3 carefully.]

. . .

"Although intentionally pointing a firearm at another constitutes a violation of s. **941.20**, under sub. (1) a person is privileged to point a gun at another person in self-defense if the person reasonably believes that the threat of force is necessary to prevent or terminate what he or she reasonably believes to be an unlawful interference." *State v. Watkins*, 647 N.W.2d 244, 256 (Wis. 2002). [This case is somewhat of an amazing find. As you can see from the pattern of self-defense in Wisconsin and in most other states, it is clear that a person can threaten non-deadly force to defend against non-deadly force (e.g., physical strength vs. physical strength) or deadly force against deadly force (e.g., deadly weapon vs. deadly weapon). But as we have mentioned throughout the book, most police and prosecutors will arrest and prosecute if a defender threatens deadly force in response to non-deadly force, calling it excessive force (e.g., you walk out onto your porch and rack a shell into your 12 gauge to keep several unarmed, but combative toughs from coming into your yard). *Watkins* held that under some circumstances it might be reasonable to point a gun at a person or persons to keep them from assaulting you with their fists. Some examples might be a woman who is obviously smaller and weaker than a 250 lb male menacing "muss o' massle" or store owners defending their businesses from mobs of angry looters (e.g., Vietnamese shopkeepers on their roofs with AK-47s during the Rodney King riots). Don't misunderstand what we are saying here. You will probably be arrested and prosecuted for threatening or assault with a deadly weapon for pointing a gun at an unarmed assailant. However, cases such as this can greatly help your attorney prepare jury instructions that can give you an advantage at trial. If you go to trial, be sure to tightly hang onto your wallet during the wild ride into the American Criminal Justice System!]

[Defense of a Third Person]

§ **WIS. STAT. § 939.48 (4).**
Self-defense and defense of others.

. . .

(4) A person is privileged to defend a 3rd person from real or apparent unlawful interference by another under the same conditions and by the same means as those under and by which the person is privileged to defend himself or herself from real or apparent unlawful interference, provided that the person reasonably believes that the facts are such that the 3rd person would be privileged to act in self-defense and that the person's intervention is necessary for the protection of the 3rd person.

. . .

[A recent Wisconsin case explains what courts tell juries about both self-defense and defense of third persons, citing Wisconsin Jury Instructions 805 (self-defense) and 830 (defense of others):] ". . . compare Wis JI-Criminal 805 (self-defense) and Wis JI-Criminal 830 (defense of others), both involving use of force intended or likely to cause death or bodily harm. Under Instruction 805, the defendant must show: (1) the defendant believed that there was an actual or imminent unlawful interference with the defendant's person; (2) the defendant believed that the amount of force the defendant used or threatened to use was necessary to prevent or terminate the interference; and (3) the defendant's beliefs were reasonable. Under INSTRUCTION 830, the defendant must show: (1) the defendant believed that there was an actual or imminent unlawful interference with the person of another; (2) the defendant believed that the amount of force used or threatened by the defendant was necessary for the protection of the third person; (3) the defendant believed that the third person was entitled to use or to threaten to use force in self-defense; and (4) the defendant's beliefs were reasonable." *State v. Davila*, 766 N.W.2d 242, (Wis. App., 2009).

[You are justified in defending another under the same circumstances you would be justified in defending yourself. The threat must be imminent and your actions reasonable and necessary.]

[Exceptions to Justifiable Self-Defense] [Provocation]
[Initial Aggressor] [Mutual Combat]
[Committing Felony or Unlawful Act]

§ **WIS. STAT. § 939.48 (2).**
Self-defense and defense of others.

(2) Provocation affects the privilege of self-defense as follows:

(a) A person who engages in unlawful conduct of a type likely to provoke others to attack him or her and thereby does provoke an attack is not entitled to claim the privilege of self-defense against such attack, except when the attack which ensues is of a type causing the person engaging in the unlawful conduct to reasonably believe that he or she is in imminent danger of death or great bodily harm. In such a case, the person engaging in the unlawful conduct is privileged to act in self-defense, but the person is not privileged to resort to the use of force intended or likely to cause death to the person's assailant unless the person reasonably believes he or she has exhausted every other reasonable means to escape from or otherwise avoid death or great bodily harm at the hands of his or her assailant. [If you create the need to defend yourself, you can't claim self-defense unless the attack is one that threatens death or serious bodily injury. If that happens, you can defend yourself but not with deadly force unless you've retreated and done everything you could to not have to use deadly force.]

[Exceptions to the Exceptions] [Withdraw and Communicate]

(b) The privilege lost by provocation may be regained if the actor in good faith withdraws from the fight and gives adequate notice thereof to his or her assailant. [You can regain your right to use self-defense even if you started it if you quit the fight and tell your opponent you're quitting. Whether the notice was "adequate" may become a sticky issue. If for some reason you find yourself in this situation, you better shout out your desire to quit as loud as possible. If it gets this tangled, you will usually be arrested and prosecuted so the jury can sort it out.]

(c) A person who provokes an attack, whether by lawful or unlawful conduct, with intent to use such an attack as an excuse to cause death or great bodily harm to his or her assailant is not entitled to claim the privilege of self-defense.

[You can't win on the theory of self-defense if you provoked a fight as an excuse to kill or seriously injure another person.]

[Duty to Retreat – Generally – Yes]

"While Wisconsin has no statutory duty to retreat, whether the opportunity to retreat was available may be a consideration regarding whether the defendant reasonably believed the force used was necessary to prevent or terminate the interference."

"There is no duty to retreat. However, in determining whether the defendant reasonably believed the amount of force used was necessary to prevent or terminate the interference, you may consider whether the defendant had the opportunity to retreat with safety, whether such retreat was feasible, and whether the defendant knew of the opportunity to retreat." *State v. Wenger*, 593 N.W.2d 467, 471 (Wis.App. 1999). [Even though the rule says there is no duty to retreat, the explanation leaves the impression that if you could have retreated, you should have.]

[*Pancho's Wisdom* – We hate it when courts "double talk." What good is it to tell people they have no duty to retreat but the jury can consider the opportunity to retreat while deciding if the force used was necessary? Double Talk! Wisconsin citizens should pressure their legislature to pass a self-defense law that eliminates the duty to retreat from anywhere a person has a legal right to be. Furthermore, the law should state that the prosecutor is prohibited from even suggesting a citizen has a duty to retreat, and that if he does, he should PERSONALLY have to pay the attorney fees to have the case retried! One bankrupted prosecutor would keep the rest of them from pulling such monkey business. See Chapter 20, Mother of All Self-Defense Statutes.]

[Defense of Person(s) in Home] [No Duty to Retreat from Your Home]
"Some states impose a duty to take reasonable measures to retreat as a limitation on the privilege of self-defense. The duty has often been modified by the rule that those assaulted in their own homes may stand their ground without losing the privilege of self-defense. Justice Cardozo's poignant explanation for the rule is set out in *Gainer:* 'It is not now and never has been the law that a man assailed in his own dwelling is bound to retreat. If assailed there, he may stand his ground and resist the attack. He is under no duty to take to the fields and the highways, a fugitive from his own home.... Whither shall he flee, and how far, and when may he be permitted to return?'" *State v. Herriges,* 455 N.W.2d 635, 637 (Ct.App.1990). [You don't have a duty to retreat from your own home unless you provoked the fight. See discussion below.]

"The castle rule recognizes the importance of home as sanctuary but it is not without limits. The doctrine is for defensive and not offensive purposes." *State v. Herriges,* 455 N.W.2d 635, 637 (Wis. App.1990).

"We ...adopt the rule that if there has been provocation by the one assaulted, even if that provocation occurs in the home, successful assertion of self-defense requires a reasonable belief that one cannot retreat before force likely to cause death or great bodily harm may be used." *State v. Herriges,* 455 N.W.2d 635, 639 (Wis. App.1990). [If you started it, even if you're in the home, you've got to retreat unless retreating would cause you death or serious bodily injury. The bottom line is you are going to be arrested and prosecuted if you provoked a fight.]

[Reckless Injury to Innocent Third Parties]

§ **WIS. STAT. § 939.48.**
Self-defense and defense of others

. . .

(3) The privilege of self-defense extends not only to the intentional infliction of harm upon a real or apparent wrongdoer, but also to the unintended infliction of harm upon a 3rd person, except that if the unintended infliction of harm amounts to the crime of first-degree or 2nd-degree reckless homicide, homicide by negligent handling of dangerous weapon, explosives or fire, first-degree or 2nd-degree reckless injury or injury by negligent handling of dangerous weapon, explosives or fire, the actor is liable for whichever one of those crimes is committed.

. . .

[If you accidently injure an innocent person while using justifiable force to defend yourself, you are not guilty of a crime. **Example:** By the time you realize you're being attacked by a knife-wielding crazy person, you barely have time to draw your concealed weapon and fire. The bullet goes through the assailant and hits an innocent person you did not notice in the stress of the moment. You probably would not be charged with a crime. Of course, this would not make you feel any better about hurting someone who didn't deserve to be injured nor will it necessarily keep you from being sued. But if you are reckless or criminally negligent, you could be charged with certain crimes that do not require proof on intent. These crimes are named in paragraph 3 above. **Example:** Same facts as above, but you close your eyes and empty a full 15 round magazine at your assailant, 13 shots of which miss and hit others after your assailant was already on the ground. Getting tactical training at facilities like those described in Chapter 18 (e.g., Front Sight Firearms Training Institute) could help reduce the number of mistakes you make during a sudden violent attack.]

[Civil Liability]

"Examining both criminal and civil law because the tort rules on self-defense are virtually identical to those of the criminal law... the right of self-defense is only available to a person who is without fault, and if a person voluntarily, that is aggressively and willingly, enters into a fight, he cannot invoke the doctrine of self-defense unless he first abandons the fight, withdraws from it and gives notice to his adversary that he has done so." *Root v. Saul,* 718 N.W.2d 197, 203 (Wis.App. 2006). [The rules of self-defense with all of their exceptions are the same for civil lawsuits as they are for criminal cases. If your actions are justifiable, the assailant you injured while defending yourself cannot win money damages against you. On the other hand, if you start a fight and injure someone you will not be able to defend yourself from a money-damage-award on the theory of self-defense.]

[Defense of Property]

§ WIS. STAT. § 939.49.
Defense of property and protection against retail theft.

(1) A person is privileged to threaten or intentionally use force against another for the purpose of preventing or terminating what the person reasonably believes to be an unlawful interference with the person's property. Only such degree of force or threat thereof may intentionally be used as the actor reasonably believes is necessary to prevent or terminate the interference. It is not reasonable to intentionally use force intended or likely to cause death or great bodily harm for the sole purpose of defense of one's property. [You can use force but not deadly force to defend property.]

(2) A person is privileged to defend a 3rd person's property from real or apparent unlawful interference by another under the same conditions and by the same means as those under and by which the person is privileged to defend his or her own property from real or apparent unlawful interference, provided that the person reasonably believes that the facts are such as would give the 3rd person the privilege to defend his or her own property, that his or her intervention is necessary for the protection of the 3rd person's property, and that the 3rd person whose property the person is protecting is a member of his or her immediate family or household or a person whose property the person has a legal duty to protect, or is a merchant and the actor is the merchant's employee or agent. An official or adult employee or agent

of a library is privileged to defend the property of the library in the manner specified in this subsection. [You can defend another person's property if you (1) reasonably think he could have legally defended it (2) reasonably think it was necessary to use force to protect it and (3) the property belongs to an immediate family member, member of the household, or you have a legal duty to protect the property, or you work for the guy/woman who owns the property (i.e., you're a cashier in his/her store). The statute expressly allows you to defend library property if you happen to work at one. Nothing in this section justifies the use of deadly force.]

(3) In this section "unlawful" means either tortious or expressly prohibited by criminal law or both.

[HELPFUL DEFINITIONS RELATING TO THIS STATE'S SELF-DEFENSE STATUTES]

- **Unlawful** – means either tortuous [causing damage that one can sue for] or expressly prohibited by criminal law or both. **Wis. Stat. § 939.48(6) and § 939.49(3).**

[TEMPLATE Topics We Could Not Find Explained in Statutes or Cases]

(For each of these topics that we could not find addressed in your state's statutes or cases, we suggest you review the same topics in the subchapters of surrounding states. Your state's courts may look to the law of the surrounding states to see how their courts and legislatures have treated that particular self-defense issue.)

[Use of Deadly Force to Prevent Serious Felonies]

[Presumption of Reasonableness in Special Places]

[Co-Habitants; Co-Employees – Duty to Retreat]

Pancho's Wisdom

You just might be a Gunnut if . . . a vampire ever bit you, he'd die of lead poisoning after Twilight, but before the New Moon.

WYOMING

Although Wyoming's self-defense statute is pretty wimpy for a western state, we give its legislature a thumbs-up for adopting in 2008 an extremely protective home-defense statute patterned after Florida's controversial home-defense law.

Key: ■ commentary ■ original statutes, cases or jury instructions

§ WYOMING STATUTES (W.S.) § 6-1-102 (b).

Common-law crimes abolished; common-law defenses retained.

. . .

(b) Common-law defenses are retained unless otherwise provided by this act.

[Wyoming's self-defense statute only covers defense of people in special places. It does not address self-defense outside of these special places. Because there is no statute covering self-defense outside of special places like the home, this statute says common-law rules apply. At common law a person was required to retreat before using deadly force when not in his home. Therefore, unlike many, if not most Western and Southern states, Wyoming juries may consider whether the defender could have retreated during a incident where he used deadly force. See further discussion below under **[Deadly Force] – [Duty to Retreat.]]**

[Defense of Self and Others] [Non-Deadly Force]

"It is lawful for a person who is being assaulted to defend himself from attack if he has reasonable grounds for believing and does believe that bodily injury is about to be inflicted upon him. In doing so she may use all force which would appear to a reasonable person, in the same or similar circumstances, to be necessary to prevent the injury which appears to be imminent." Jury instruction from *Farmer v. State,* 124 P.3d 699 (Wyo. 2005). "... it is not necessary that the danger was real . . . so long as the defendant had reasonable cause to believe and did believe [the threat was real]." Wyoming Pattern Instruction 8.11 entitled Actual Danger Not Necessary To Claim Of Self-Defense, taken from *Holloman v. State,* 51 P.3d 214, 219 (2002). [Although this jury instruction is a little wordy, it is the same rule regarding non-deadly force in just about any other state. You can use reasonable force to defend yourself from unlawful force. If the threat isn't real, but looks real, you can still defend yourself with reasonable force.]

[Deadly Force]

(Jury Instruction) Instruction No. 18

"If the defendant had reasonable grounds to believe and actually did believe that he or another was in imminent danger of death or serious bodily harm from which the defendant could save himself or another only by using deadly force against the other person, the defendant had the right to use deadly force in self-defense of himself or defense of another. 'Deadly force' means force which is likely to cause death or serious bodily harm."

"The circumstances under which the defendant acted must have been such as to produce in the mind of a reasonably prudent person, similarly situated, the reasonable belief that the other person was about to kill the defendant or another or do serious bodily harm to the defendant or another. The danger must have been apparent, present and imminent or must have appeared to be so under the circumstances."

"If the defendant believed that he or another was in imminent danger of death or serious bodily harm, and that deadly force was necessary to repel such danger, and if a reasonable person in a similar situation seeing and knowing the same facts would be justified in believing that he was in similar danger, the defendant would be justified in using deadly force in self-defense of himself or defense of another. The defendant would be justified even though the appearance of danger later proved to be false and there was actually neither purpose on the part of the other person to kill the defendant or another or do the defendant or another serious bodily harm, nor imminent danger that it would be done, nor actual necessity that deadly force be used in self-defense of himself or defense of another. If the person so confronted acts in self-defense or defense of another upon such appearance of danger from honest belief, the right of self-defense of himself or defense of another is the same whether the danger is real or merely apparent." *Farmer v. State,* 124 P.3d 699 (Wyo. 2005)fn3. (jury instruction). [This is essentially what a judge would tell a jury if you were charged with murder and were claiming self-defense. In short, it says that if your belief is reasonable, you may repel an imminent threat of deadly force with deadly force. You may not use excessive force, only as much force as is necessary to repel the deadly attack. This jury instruction was adapted from case law, not any provision in a Wyoming statute.]

[Defense of a Third Person]

"One asserting the justification of defense of another steps into the position of the person defended. Defense of another takes its form and content from defense of self. The defender is not justified in using force unless he or she reasonably believes the person defended is in immediate danger of unlawful bodily harm, and that the force is reasonable and necessary to prevent that threat." *Leeper v. State,* 589 P.2d 379, 383 (Wyo. 1979). [The language of this case shows how closely related defense of another is to defense of self. The defense of another has to be reasonable and necessary.]

[Exceptions to Justifiable Self-Defense] [Initial Aggressor] [Provocation] [Exceptions to the Exceptions] [Withdraw and Communicate]

"Generally, the right to use self-defense is not available to one who is the aggressor or provokes the conflict. However, if one who provokes a conflict thereafter withdraws from it in good faith and informs his adversary by words or actions that he wants to end the conflict, and he is thereafter attacked, he then has the same right of self-defense as any other person. This right of self-defense extends not only against the actual assailant, but also to those acting in concert with the assailant." *Farmer v. State,* 124 P.3d 699

(Wyo. 2005) fn3. (Jury instruction) [This is the typical rule that one who initiates or provokes a fight cannot claim self-defense unless he withdraws and effectively communicates his intent to withdraw.]

"One who has reasonable grounds to believe that another will attack him, and that the anticipated attack will be of such a character as to endanger his life or limb, or to cause him serious bodily harm, has a right to arm himself for the purpose of resisting such attack. If the defendant armed himself in reasonable anticipation of such an attack, that fact alone does not make the defendant the aggressor or deprive the defendant of the right of self-defense." *Farmer v. State,* 124 P.3d 699 (Wyo. 2005) fn3. (Jury instruction) [Arming yourself does not necessarily make you the aggressor. Good Night! Everyone carries a gun in Wyoming. Who'd believe this would even be an issue in a case?]

[Mutual Combat]

"Our case law also provides that two individuals who mutually agree to fight are both considered aggressors, making a self-defense theory unavailable to either of them." *Coburn v. State,* 20 P.3d 518 (Wyo. 2001). [Remember the movie *Shane,* Alan Ladd starred as Shane, the good-guy gunslinger with a white hat, and Jack Palance played the bad-guy gunslinger, Wilson, who not only had a black hat, but a weird black glove on his right hand. Under current Wyoming law, it would NOT BE LEGAL for Shane, to agree to a quick-draw duel against Wilson at the creepy old saloon silhouetted against the Tetons. With Shane quick and Wilson dead, Cowboy State officials would nowadays prosecute Shane for murder even though Wilson went for his pearl handles first after Shane called him "a low-down Yankee liar!" In the shootout following the quick-draw contest, Shane also guns down Wilson's boss and another hired gun lurking in the shadows on the second floor of the bar, who tries to shoot Shane in the back. Some modern prosecutors would probably charge Shane with the murder of these two men as well. After all, the gunfight with those two resulted from the mutual combat between Shane and Wilson. Our experience has been that police and district attorneys prosecute such legally complicated scenarios and let the jury sort it all out. If you don't want to mortgage the ranch to pay criminal-defense fees in a murder trial, don't be duped into participating in anything that remotely resembles mutual combat while carrying a gun. (Video clip found searching "Alan Ladd Shane Clips" on YouTube.)]

[Duty to Retreat – Generally – Yes]

"We have stated that the law in Wyoming requires that, prior to resorting to deadly force, a defendant has a duty to pursue reasonable alternatives under the circumstances, and that among those reasonable alternatives may be the duty to retreat." *Baier v. State,* 891 P.2d 754 (Wyo. 1995). [Wyoming juries can consider retreat as a reasonable alternative to using deadly force. Unless you are in your own home, if you can do so without a significant risk of being injured, always retreat before using deadly force.]

[*Pancho's Wisdom* – It seems to us unusual that the "Cowboy State" requires retreat from places where people have a right to be before defensive force can be used. We think this encourages rather than discourages criminal behavior and should be changed to conform to the "No Retreat" provisions of the self-defense laws of other western states.]

[Defense of Person(s) in Special Places – Residence]
[No Duty to Retreat From Residence]

"You are instructed that, if the defendant at her place of residence had reasonable ground to believe and actually did believe that she was in imminent danger of death or serious bodily harm and that the use of deadly force was necessary to repel such danger, she was not required to retreat or to consider whether she could safely retreat. The defendant was entitled to stand her ground and use such force as was reasonably necessary under the circumstances to save her life or protect herself from serious bodily harm." Jury Instruction used in *Miller v. State*, 67 P.3d 1191, 1196 (Wyo. 2004). [You don't have to retreat from your own home in Wyoming before defending yourself or others with deadly force.]

[Presumption of Reasonableness in Special Places – Home/Habitation]

§ **W.S. § 6-2-602.**
Use of force in self-defense.

[This is Wyoming's home-defense statute. It is patterned after Florida's excellent home defense statute. We suggest you read the commentary in Florida's subchapter. It presumes your use of deadly force is reasonable when someone unlawfully forces his way into your home or tries to kidnap someone from your home. Notice that this presumption doesn't apply if you harm a person who has a right to be in the home or who has an arguable interest in the property.]

(a) A person is presumed to have held a reasonable fear of imminent peril of death or serious bodily injury to himself or another when using defensive force that is intended or likely to cause death or serious bodily injury to another if:

(i) The intruder against whom the defensive force was used was in the process of unlawfully and forcefully entering, or had unlawfully and forcibly entered, another's home or habitation or, if that intruder had removed or was attempting to remove another against his will from his home or habitation; and

(ii) The person who uses defensive force knew or had reason to believe that an unlawful and forcible entry or unlawful and forcible act was occurring.

(b) The presumption set forth in subsection (a) of this section does not apply if:
[You won't be presumed to have acted reasonably if you shoot anyone in the following classes of persons in your home:]

(i) The person against whom the defensive force is used has a right to be in or is a lawful resident of the occupied structure, such as an owner, lessee or titleholder, and there is not an injunction for protection from domestic violence or a written pretrial supervision order of no contact against that person; [Someone who has an interest in the property besides you. It could be a co-owner, like your wife. The classic case is the husband who buys additional life insurance on his wife and then claims he shot her by accident thinking she was an intruder. The "injunction from domestic violence" refers to a husband who has been abusing his wife and the court kicks him out of the home and tells him to stay away from her until the divorce issues are settled. Even though he may have a property interest in the home, if he breaks in and she shoots him, she still has the presumption that she acted reasonably. This is because he violated the court order to stay away from her. Landlords and mortgage companies cannot use deadly force to settle a civil dispute over payment of rent or the foreclosure of a mortgage and vice versa. Evicted tenants and foreclosed homeowners can't either.]

(ii) The person sought to be removed is a child or grandchild, or is otherwise in the lawful custody or under the lawful guardianship of, the person against whom the defensive force is used; or [Parents and grandparents can't expect to be presumed to have acted reasonably if they try to resolve custody or guardianship matters with force.]

(iii) The person against whom the defensive force is used is a peace officer who enters or attempts to enter another's home or habitation in the performance of his official duties. [If the SWAT team enters your home yelling "police, get down, let us see your hands," you can't shoot at them and expect any favorable presumptions under the law. Unfortunately, home invaders are now shouting the same thing when they enter a home and this makes it more likely that homeowners will shoot anyone who enters their home by force. This creates a dangerous situation for police. Under this statute it seems even if you thought the SWAT team were home invaders, you will probably not be entitled to any presumption of reasonableness if you unload your 870 at them (not to mention that you may not survive another 3 seconds if you do).]

(c) A person who unlawfully and by force enters or attempts to enter another's home or habitation is presumed to be doing so with the intent to commit an unlawful act involving force or violence.

[Civil Liability]

§ W.S. § 6-1-204.
Immunity from civil action for justifiable use of force.

Except as provided by W.S. **6-1-103**(a), a person who uses force as reasonably necessary in defense of his person, property or abode or to prevent injury to another is immune from civil action for the use of the force. [If you are justified in using force in self-defense under the criminal law, you can't be sued for damages under the civil law. But W.S. **6-1-103**(a) allows you to sue a criminal who either injures you or damages your property. This statute protects the good guys from being sued for damages if they hurt someone in self-defense, but makes criminals accountable if they injure someone while committing a crime.]

[Defense of Property]

"You are instructed that a person using force in defense of property may use such degree and extent of force as would appear to a reasonable person, placed in the same position, and seeing and knowing what the resisting person then sees and knows, to be reasonably necessary to prevent imminent injury threatened to the property. Any use of force beyond that limit is regarded by the law as excessive and unjustified, and a person using such excessive force is legally responsible for the consequences thereof." *Horn v. State*, 554 P.2d 1141, 1143 (Wyo. 1976) (jury instruction). [Like in most states, you can't use deadly force to protect your personal property. Personal property means things like your car, DVD player or iPod. If you use excessive force, the criminal and civil laws will punish you. **Example:** You wrest your wallet back from a pickpocket. Then, in anger, you punch him in the nose so hard that bone fragments pierce his brain causing permanent injury. You will be sued for negligent use of excessive force and could have an enormous civil judgment awarded against you.]

[HELPFUL DEFINITIONS RELATING TO THIS STATE'S SELF-DEFENSE STATUTES]

- **Bodily injury** – means physical pain, illness or any impairment of physical condition. **W.S. § 6-1-104 (a)(i).**

- **Deadly weapon** – means but is not limited to a firearm, explosive or incendiary material, motorized vehicle, an animal or other device, instrument, material or substance, which in the manner it is used or is intended to be used is reasonably capable of producing death or serious bodily injury. **W.S. § 6-1-104 (a)(iv).**

- **Occupied structure** – means a structure or vehicle whether or not a person is actually present:

  (A) Where any person lives or carries on business or other calling;

  (B) Where people assemble for purposes of business, government, education, religion, entertainment or public transportation;

  (C) Which is used for overnight accommodation of persons; or

  (D) In which a person may reasonably be expected to be present. **W.S. § 6-1-104 (a)(v).**

- **Property** – means anything of value whether tangible or intangible, real or personal, public or private. **W.S. § 6-1-104 (a)(viii).**

- **Serious bodily injury** – means bodily injury which creates a substantial risk of death or which causes miscarriage, severe disfigurement or protracted loss or impairment of the function of any bodily member or organ. **W.S. § 6-1-104 (a)(x).**

- **Vehicle** – means any device by which persons or property may be moved, carried or transported over land, water or air. **W.S. § 6-1-104 (a)(xi).**

- **Violent felony** – means murder, manslaughter, kidnapping, sexual assault in the first or second degree, robbery, aggravated assault, aircraft hijacking, arson in the first or second degree or aggravated burglary or a violation of W.S. 6-2-314(a)(i) or 6-2-315(a)(ii). **W.S. § 6-1-104 (a)(xii).**

[TEMPLATE Topics We Could Not Find Explained in Statutes or Cases]

(For each of these topics that we could not find addressed in your state's statutes or cases, we suggest you review the same topics in the subchapters of surrounding states. Your state's courts may look to the law of the surrounding states to see how their courts and legislatures have treated that particular self-defense issue.)

[Use of Deadly Force to Prevent Serious Felonies] – [Wyoming does not authorize the use of deadly force to prevent the commission of certain felonies. If you are outside your home, you must be facing an imminent threat of serious bodily injury or death before you are justified in using deadly force.]

[Use of Deadly Force to Prevent Serious Felonies]

[Committing Felony or Unlawful Act]

[Co-Habitants; Co-Employees – Duty to Retreat]

[Reckless Injury to Innocent Third Parties]

Pancho's Wisdom

You just might be a Gunnut if . . . The Armed Citizen is the first article you read when you get your monthly NRA magazine.

Pancho's Wisdom

If you become euphoric while pumping lead down range, you're probably committing a federal felony!

6

STATE DEADLY FORCE COMPARISON CHART

(Caution: Quick-reference guide only – see each state's subchapter for details)

STATES	Duty to Retreat Before Using Deadly Force Outside of Special Places	Crimes Justifying Use of Deadly Force Outside of Special Places	Duty to Retreat When Occupying Special Places - - - - Special Places Mentioned in Statute such as Home, Workplace, Occupied Vehicle, etc.	Presumption of Reasonableness in Special Places - - - - Unlawful Acts Justifying Use of Deadly Force in Special Places	Immunity from Civil Liability	Notable Provisions of this State's Self-Defense Law
Alabama	No	Burglary, kidnapping, 1st and 2nd degree assault, robbery, forcible rape, forcible sodomy	No - - - - Dwelling, premises	Yes - - - - Arson	Yes, but possible exceptions (see Alabama sub-chapter)	
Alaska	Yes, unless in defense of family member or child	Kidnapping, sexual assault, sexual abuse of minor, robbery	No - - - - Premises owned or leased by defender, his perm or temp residence, or workplace	Yes - - - - Arson, carjacking, theft of occupied car	Yes	
Arizona	No, not when threatened with forcible felonies named in next column.	Forcible felonies/Arson of occupied structure, 1st & 2nd degree burglary, kidnapping, murder, manslaughter, sexual assault, sexual conduct with a minor, child molestation, armed robbery, aggravated assault	No - - - - Need not retreat from threat of death, serious physical injury or forceful removal from residential structure or occupied vehicle	Yes	Yes	
Arkansas	Yes	Felony involving force or violence	No - - - - Dwelling or curtilage	Yes - - - - Arson, burglary	Yes	

STATES	Duty to Retreat Before Using Deadly Force Outside of Special Places	Crimes Justifying Use of Deadly Force Outside of Special Places	Duty to Retreat When Occupying Special Places - - - - - - Special Places Mentioned in Statute such as Home, Workplace, Occupied Vehicle, etc.	Presumption of Reasonableness in Special Places - - - - - - Unlawful Acts Justifying Use of Deadly Force in Special Places	Immunity from Civil Liability	Notable Provisions of this State's Self-Defense Law
California	No	"Atrocious felony" i.e., murder, mayhem, rape, and robbery	No	Yes - - - - - - "Atrocious felony" i.e., murder, mayhem, rape, and robbery	Yes, case law	WARNING: §197, California's deadly force statute, has been changed drastically by case law and jury instructions WARNING: Defense of third person limited to specific persons. See state's sub-chapter.
Colorado	No	Kidnapping, robbery, sexual assault, assault with a deadly weapon, assault with intent to cause serious injury	No - - - - - - Dwelling or building	No - - - - - - Burglary	Yes, under home-defense statute	Occupant of dwelling or building may use deadly force if he reasonably believes unlawful intruder might use <u>any</u> physical force, no matter how slight, against any occupant
Connecticut	Yes	No specific crimes mentioned	No - - - - - - Dwelling (where you stay at night) or place of business – see exceptions in state's sub-chapter	Presumption not mentioned - - - - - - Arson or crime of violence against person in dwelling or place of work	No	May use deadly force to the extent reasonably necessary to prevent or terminate an unlawful entry by force into dwelling . . . or place of work, and for the sole purpose of such prevention or termination
District of Columbia	Best to retreat; law is confusing	Not mentioned	Best to retreat; law is confusing	No	No	Case law only and the state and federal cases sometimes conflict

STATES	Duty to Retreat Before Using Deadly Force Outside of Special Places	Crimes Justifying Use of Deadly Force Outside of Special Places	Duty to Retreat When Occupying Special Places - - - - - - - Special Places Mentioned in Statute such as Home, Workplace, Occupied Vehicle, etc.	Presumption of Reasonableness in Special Places - - - - - - - Unlawful Acts Justifying Use of Deadly Force in Special Places	Immunity from Civil Liability	Notable Provisions of this State's Self-Defense Law
Delaware	Yes	Kidnapping or sexual intercourse compelled by force or threat	No - - - - - - - Dwelling or place of work	No - - - - - - - Arson, burglary, robbery or felonious theft or property destruction (combined with threat of serious injury or death)	Yes, under home-defense statute	A threat to cause death or serious bodily harm, by the production of a weapon or otherwise, so long as the defendant's purpose is limited to creating an apprehension that deadly force will be used if necessary, does not constitute [use of] deadly force
Florida	No (received consider-able publicity as Florida's "Make My Day" law)	Forcible Felony = treason; murder; manslaughter; sexual battery; carjacking; home-invasion robbery; robbery; burglary; arson; kidnapping; aggravated assault; aggravated battery; aggravated stalking; aircraft piracy; unlawful throwing, placing, or discharging of a destructive device or bomb; and any other felony which involves the use or threat of physical force or violence against any individual	No - - - - - - - Dwelling, residence, occupied vehicle	Yes - - - - - - - When unlawful entry plus forcible entry OR unlawful and forcible attempt to remove persons from dwelling, residence or occupied vehicle	Yes	Unusually strong home defense statute
Georgia	No	Forcible Felonies	No	No - - - - - - - Felony (forcible felony if on real property that is not your dwelling)	Yes	

STATES	Duty to Retreat Before Using Deadly Force Outside of Special Places	Crimes Justifying Use of Deadly Force Outside of Special Places	Duty to Retreat When Occupying Special Places / Special Places Mentioned in Statute such as Home, Workplace, Occupied Vehicle, etc.	Presumption of Reasonableness in Special Places / Unlawful Acts Justifying Use of Deadly Force in Special Places	Immunity from Civil Liability	Notable Provisions of this State's Self-Defense Law
Hawaii	Yes	Kidnapping, rape, forcible sodomy	No / Home and Workplace	No / Felonious property damage, burglary, robbery, or felonious theft AND either intruder is using deadly force or defending with anything less than deadly force would result in death or serious bodily injury	No, civil remedies still apply	
Idaho	No, ICJI (Idaho Criminal Jury Instruction) #1519	Aggravated assault, robbery, rape, murder or other heinous crime (violent felony)	No, ICJI (Idaho Criminal Jury Instruction) #1519	No	Yes	WARNING: Defense of third person limited to specific persons. See state's sub-chapter.
Illinois	No (Ill. Jury Instruc-tions)	Forcible felony	No (Ill. Jury Instructions)	No / Unlawful and Forcible entry plus act of violence against a person in dwelling	Yes	
Indiana	No	Forcible felony or during hijacking of airplane	No / Dwelling, curtilage, occupied vehicle	No / To terminate unlawful entry into or attack on dwelling, curtilage or occupied vehicle	Yes	
Iowa	Yes	Forcible felony	No / Home, place of business or employment	Not mentioned / Not mentioned	Yes	Before any force is used a person is required avoid the confrontation by seeking an alternative course of action (with the exception of retreating from your home or workplace)
Kansas	No	Not mentioned	No / Dwelling or occupied vehicle	No / To terminate unlawful entry into or attack on dwelling, curtilage or occupied vehicle; to prevent forceful removal from dwelling	Yes	Immunity from Criminal Prosecution. Self-defense is not a defense to brandishing or threatening with a deadly weapon (recent case law)

STATES	Duty to Retreat Before Using Deadly Force Outside of Special Places	Crimes Justifying Use of Deadly Force Outside of Special Places	Duty to Retreat When Occupying Special Places - - - - - - Special Places Mentioned in Statute such as Home, Workplace, Occupied Vehicle, etc.	Presumption of Reasonableness in Special Places - - - - - - Unlawful Acts Justifying Use of Deadly Force in Special Places	Immunity from Civil Liability	Notable Provisions of this State's Self-Defense Law
Kentucky	No	Kidnapping, sexual intercourse compelled by force or threat, felony involving the use of force	No - - - - - - Dwelling, residence, occupied vehicle	Yes - - - - - - When unlawful entry plus forcible entry OR unlawful entry plus forcible attempt to remove persons from dwelling, residence or occupied vehicle	Yes	Kentucky has adopted Florida's extremely protective home and vehicle defense statute
Louisiana	No	Violent or forcible felony involving danger to life or great bodily harm	No - - - - - - Dwelling, business, occupied vehicle	Yes - - - - - - Any unlawful force against a person present in a dwelling or a place of business, or occupied vehicle, burglary, robbery, or other felony involving the use of force	Yes/For self-defense and home-defense (may not apply to defense of a third person)	Unusual statute; see introduction to states subchapter
Maine	Yes	Kidnapping, robbery, gross sexual assault	No - - - - - - Dwelling place	No - - - - - - Unlawful entry of dwelling with intent to commit a crime, arson, kidnapping, robbery or forcible sexual attack	No	
Maryland	Yes	Felonies involving imminent threat of death or serious bodily harm	No - - - - - - Home	No - - - - - - To prevent unlawful entry for purpose of committing a violent felony	Yes	No Self-Defense Statutes – only case law and jury instructions
Massachusetts	No	Not mentioned	No - - - - - - Dwelling	No	No	Imminence requires "overt act"

STATES	Duty to Retreat Before Using Deadly Force Outside of Special Places	Crimes Justifying Use of Deadly Force Outside of Special Places	Duty to Retreat When Occupying Special Places / Special Places Mentioned in Statute such as Home, Workplace, Occupied Vehicle, etc.	Presumption of Reasonableness in Special Places / Unlawful Acts Justifying Use of Deadly Force in Special Places	Immunity from Civil Liability	Notable Provisions of this State's Self-Defense Law
Michigan	No	Sexual Assault	No / Dwelling, business premises, occupied vehicle	Yes / Sexual Assault, breaking and entering or invasion of home, business or occupied vehicle, OR unlawfully attempting to remove individual from a dwelling, business premises, or occupied vehicle against his or her will	Yes	
Minnesota	Yes (case law)	Not mentioned/ There remains a question whether sexual assault qualifies as "great bodily harm" justifying use of deadly force	No / Home (case law)	Violent felony in place of abode	No	
Mississippi	No	Felony, suppressing a riot, keeping the peace (see caution in Chapter 4)	No / Home	Yes / Committing a violent felony against the person, his dwelling, occupied vehicle	Yes	Reimbursement for attorney fees for having to defend against a civil lawsuit if the court finds you were justified in using force to defend yourself
Missouri	Best to retreat; law is confusing	Forcible felonies: Murder robbery, burglary, arson, kidnapping, assault, and any forcible sexual offense	No / Dwelling, Residence or Occupied Vehicle	No / Unlawful attempt or entry into dwelling, residence or occupied vehicle	Probably. See discussion of conflicting statutes in this state's subchapter	Very technical rule for defending residence; we strongly suggest not using deadly force unless there is an imminent threat of deadly force even in your home
Montana	No	Forcible felony	No	No / Forcible felony or violent assault in the home	No	Statute let's you tell people you have a gun or exhibit a weapon without the SWAT team or Black Helicopters immediately swarming you

STATES	Duty to Retreat Before Using Deadly Force Outside of Special Places	Crimes Justifying Use of Deadly Force Outside of Special Places	Duty to Retreat When Occupying Special Places Special Places Mentioned in Statute such as Home, Workplace, Occupied Vehicle, etc.	Presumption of Reasonableness in Special Places Unlawful Acts Justifying Use of Deadly Force in Special Places	Immunity from Civil Liability	Notable Provisions of this State's Self-Defense Law
Nebraska	Yes	Kidnapping, forced sexual intercourse	No Dwelling or place of work	No Attempt to dispossess you of your dwelling, arson, burglary, robbery or other felonious theft or property destruction AND either intruder is using deadly force or defending with anything less than deadly force would result in death or serious bodily injury	No	
Nevada	No (case law)	Violent felony	No (case law)	No, not for criminal cases; yes, for civil lawsuits, burglary, home invasion Deadly force may be used in dwelling or place of abode against violent felonies	Yes, for home defense unless overcome by clear and convincing evidence	It must appear that the killing was "absolutely necessary" and killer "endeavored to decline any further struggle before mortal blow given"
New Hampshire	Yes	Burglary, kidnapping, forcible sex offense	No Home or curtilage	No Arson, forcible felonies	Yes	
New Jersey	Yes	Not mentioned	No	Yes Arson, burglary, robbery	No	
New Mexico	No		No Dwelling	No Burglary, arson, robbery, rape, kidnapping	No	Statute says you can kill in defense of property, but NM courts have limited that to defense of home
New York	Yes	Kidnapping, forcible rape, forcible sexual act, robbery	No Dwelling	No May use deadly force to defend "premises" from arson burglary, attempted burglary	Yes	
North Carolina	No when facing deadly threat, yes for non-deadly threat	Felonies involving threat of death or serious bodily injury	No Dwelling, premises, place of business	No Violent felonies	Yes	

STATES	Duty to Retreat Before Using Deadly Force Outside of Special Places	Crimes Justifying Use of Deadly Force Outside of Special Places	Duty to Retreat When Occupying Special Places - - - - - - Special Places Mentioned in Statute such as Home, Workplace, Occupied Vehicle, etc.	Presumption of Reasonableness in Special Places - - - - - - Unlawful Acts Justifying Use of Deadly Force in Special Places	Immunity from Civil Liability	Notable Provisions of this State's Self-Defense Law
North Dakota	Yes	Violent felonies	No, Unless assailant had right to be in special place - - - - - - Home, place of work, occupied motor home or travel trailer	Yes - - - - - - Arson, burglary, robbery, or a felony involving violence [kidnapping]	Yes	
Ohio	Yes	Not mentioned	No - - - - - - Home, car, place of business	No	Yes, if using force in defense of self in structure used as a permanent or temporary dwelling or preventing commis-sion of violent felony or violent misde-meanor	Only state which places burden on defendant to prove self-defense by preponderance of the evidence
Oklahoma	No	Forcible felony	No - - - - - - Dwelling, residence, occupied vehicle	Yes - - - - - - When unlawful entry plus forcible entry OR unlawful entry plus forcible attempt to remove persons from dwelling, residence or occupied vehicle	Yes	WARNING: Defense of third person limited to specific persons. See state's sub-chapter.
Oregon	No	Felony involving the use or threatened imminent use of physical force against a person	No - - - - - - Premises	No - - - - - - Arson, burglary or [forcible felony]	No	

STATES	Duty to Retreat Before Using Deadly Force Outside of Special Places	Crimes Justifying Use of Deadly Force Outside of Special Places	Duty to Retreat When Occupying Special Places --- Special Places Mentioned in Statute such as Home, Workplace, Occupied Vehicle, etc.	Presumption of Reasonableness in Special Places --- Unlawful Acts Justifying Use of Deadly Force in Special Places	Immunity from Civil Liability	Notable Provisions of this State's Self-Defense Law
Pennsylvania	Yes	Kidnapping or sexual intercourse compelled by force or threat	No --- Dwelling place or work	No --- You cannot believe or have reason to believe that force less than deadly force would be adequate to terminate the entry OR you must believe intruder is about to commit a felony or attempt to dispossess you of your dwelling	No	
Rhode Island	Yes	Not mentioned	Yes, unless you're an owner, tenant or guest threatened with burglary or breaking and entering – see details in state subchapter	Yes, but presumptions only apply to burglary or breaking and entering types of offenses – see details in state subchapter	Same presump-tions apply in civil cases and in criminal cases	
South Carolina	Yes, until the S. Carolina courts clarify the new castle doctrine	Not mentioned	No --- Dwelling, Residence, occupied vehicle, place of business	Yes --- When unlawful entry plus forcible entry OR unlawful and forcible attempt to remove persons from dwelling, residence or occupied vehicle	Yes, at least with respect to defense of persons at their residences, places of business or in occupied vehicles	
South Dakota	No	Murder, serious violent felonies	No --- Home	No --- Violent felony	No	WARNING: Defense of third person limited to specific persons. See state's sub-chapter.
Tennessee	No	Not specifically mentioned	No --- Residence, business, dwelling or vehicle	Yes --- Unlawful and forcible entry	Yes, with specific exceptions	

STATES	Duty to Retreat Before Using Deadly Force Outside of Special Places	Crimes Justifying Use of Deadly Force Outside of Special Places	Duty to Retreat When Occupying Special Places Special Places Mentioned in Statute such as Home, Workplace, Occupied Vehicle, etc.	Presumption of Reasonableness in Special Places Unlawful Acts Justifying Use of Deadly Force in Special Places	Immunity from Civil Liability	Notable Provisions of this State's Self-Defense Law
Texas	No	Aggravated kidnapping, murder, sexual assault, aggravated sexual assault, robbery, or aggravated robbery	No Occupied habitation, vehicle, or place of business or employment	Yes (A) to prevent the other's imminent commission of arson, burglary, robbery, aggravated robbery, theft during the nighttime, or criminal mischief during the nighttime; or (B) to prevent the other who is fleeing immediately after committing burglary, robbery, aggravated robbery, or theft during the nighttime from escaping with the property[we strongly recommend AGAINST chasing fleeing felons!]	No	Texas is famous for it's statutes allowing use of deadly force to defend property under some circumstances; given the indictments or attempted indictments in two recent high profile cases involving deadly force in defense of property we HIGHLY recommend against use of deadly force to defend property
Utah	No	Aggravated assault, mayhem, aggravated murder, murder, manslaughter, kidnapping, aggravated kidnapping, rape, forcible sodomy, rape of a child, object rape, object rape of a child, sexual abuse of a child, aggravated sexual abuse of a child, aggravated sexual assault, arson, robbery, and burglary including burglary of an occupied vehicle	No Habitation, dwelling	Yes Assault or personal violence or a felony in the habitation	Yes, if person injured is committing a felony against a defender. Does not apply if felon has "clearly retreated."	

STATES	Duty to Retreat Before Using Deadly Force Outside of Special Places	Crimes Justifying Use of Deadly Force Outside of Special Places	Duty to Retreat When Occupying Special Places - - - - - - Special Places Mentioned in Statute such as Home, Workplace, Occupied Vehicle, etc.	Presumption of Reasonableness in Special Places - - - - - - Unlawful Acts Justifying Use of Deadly Force in Special Places	Immunity from Civil Liability	Notable Provisions of this State's Self-Defense Law
Vermont	Uncertain, probably should retreat if it can be accomplished safely.	Murder, sexual assault, aggravated sexual assault, burglary or robbery, with force or violence	Uncertain, probably should retreat if it can be accomplished safely.	No	No	WARNING: Defense of third person limited to specific persons. See state's sub-chapter.
Virginia – case law only – no statutes	No	Not mentioned other than imminent threat of death or serious injury	No			Imminence requires showing of an "overt act" on the part of the assailant before deadly force can be used
Washington	No (case law)	Assault, robbery, kidnapping, arson, burglary, rape, murder, or any other violent crime as defined in RCW **9.94A.030**, see state sub-chapter	No	No - - - - - - Burglary, arson, breaking and entering with intent to rob, commit sodomy or rape	No	Reimbursement of legal fees for criminal case after a verdict of "not guilty" by virtue of self-defense!
West Virginia	No	Not mentioned	No	No - - - - - - Unlawful entry with intent to commit injury or violent felony	No	
Wisconsin	Confusing at best, probably should retreat	Not Mentioned	No - - - - - - Home	No	No	
Wyoming	Yes, if retreat is a reasonable alternative	Not Mentioned	No - - - - - - Home, habitation	Yes - - - - - - Unlawful and forcible entry or attempted forceful removal from home or habitation	Yes	

States in Red Require Retreat Before
Using Deadly Force Outside of Special Places.
WASHINGTON
OREGON
CALIFORNIA
NEVADA
IDAHO
MONTANA
WYOMING
UTAH
ARIZONA
COLORADO
NEW MEXICO
NORTH DAKOTA
SOUTH DAKOTA
NEBRASKA
KANSAS
OKLAHOMA
TEXAS
MINNESOTA
IOWA
MISSOURI
ARKANSAS
LOUISIANA
WISCONSIN
ILLINOIS
MISS.
MICHIGAN
INDIANA
KENTUCKY
TENNESSEE
ALABAMA
GEORGIA
FLORIDA
OHIO
WEST VIRG.
VIRGINIA
NORTH CAROLINA
SOUTH CAROLINA
PENNSYLVANIA
NEW YORK
MAINE
NEW HAMPSHIRE
VERMONT
MASSACHUSETTS
RHODE ISLAND
CONNECTICUT
NEW JERSEY
DELAWARE
MARYLAND
ALASKA
HAWAII
Duty to Retreat
No Duty to Retreat Outside of Special Places
Duty Varies or Unclear
(See Deadly Force Chart and States Subchapter)

7

THUMBS-DOWN FACTORS

What to Avoid to Reduce Chances of Arrest, Prosecution and Conviction

"You've got to learn from the mistakes of others because you'll never live long enough to make them all yourself." – Author Unknown

After reviewing what seems like countless self-defensive cases, we noticed certain recurring fact patterns that increase the chances of arrest, prosecution and conviction. We refer to them as "thumbs-down" factors, meaning you should try to avoid them if at all possible. We are *not* claiming that these are the *only* factors that could lead to arrest, prosecution or conviction; these are just the ones we saw over and over during our research.

In the first part of this chapter, we list and explain the factors. In the second half, we summarize some of the cases we found that helped us compile this list. Carefully compare these cases to the incidents in the following chapter that did not result in arrest or conviction. Remember, these are real cases involving real people, many of whom thought they had a legal right to do what they did.

Common Fact Patterns Resulting in Arrest, Prosecution and Conviction:

1. **Armed defendant; Unarmed assailant(s)** – This is one of the most common reasons for arrest in our experience. The defendant feels threatened by one or more unarmed, but dangerous-looking and acting assailants, so he draws his gun and tells them to stop. Either the assailants or witnesses call the police from a cell phone reporting a "man with a gun." You may have heard firearms instructors claiming that you are justified in threatening or using deadly force if you are at a disadvantage in strength or numbers (often referred to as a "disparity of strength" or a "disparity of numbers"). It has been our experience that, regardless of the disparity, the person with the gun is usually arrested and prosecuted because his attacker or attackers did not have weapons. Here in Utah, pointing a weapon at any part of the body usually results in a felony charge (aggravated assault), whereas simply showing the weapon results in a serious misdemeanor charge referred to in most states as "brandishing." In our experience, if you threaten deadly force or use deadly force against an unarmed person, you will

be at least arrested, probably prosecuted and could be convicted. There are two possible exceptions. The first is in defense of persons in the home in those states that allow deadly force against intruders threatening assault or personal violence. The second is in states that permit the use of deadly force against a forcible sexual assault.

[Another variation of the armed defender/unarmed assailant is where an unarmed defender takes a weapon away from the armed assailant and kills him with his own gun or knife. Focusing on the fact that the assailant is no longer armed when the defender uses deadly force, these cases do not usually turn out well for the defender as you will notice in the cases described in this chapter.]

2. **Initiating, provoking or escalating a fight** – You may recognize these often overlooked factors as **[Exceptions to Justifiable Self-Defense]** addressed in the individual states' subchapters. Remember, we warned you that you lose the right to defend yourself if you initiate, provoke or agree to fight, even in your own home. You risk losing the right of self-defense if you allow yourself to actively participate in any of the following types of disputes:

   a. Road rage,

   b. Domestic violence,

   c. Love triangles and jealousy,

   d. Gang fights and defending one's machismo ("he disrespected me"),

   e. Neighbor boundary disputes, or

   f. Fighting over money or debts owed.

   If you are responsible for starting or escalating a fight that eventually leads to the use of or threatened use of deadly force, you will almost always be arrested and prosecuted. The majority of brandishing cases we have defended have arisen from situations where the client's temper got the best of him.

3. **Shooting anyone in the back of any part of the body** – What have we learned by watching television and the movies? Cowards shoot people in the back, right? Logically, if you were really being attacked, the entrance wounds would be in the front of the body and exit wounds in the back. If the forensic evidence shows it was just the opposite, it adds fuel to the prosecutor's argument that the person was retreating when shot and deadly force was not *necessary*.

4. **Mixing drugs or alcohol with weapons, drug deals gone bad** – Judgment and a clear mind are critical in applying the complicated rules of

self-defense during an angst-filled instant. In many states, simply possessing a firearm while under the influence of drugs or alcohol is a crime. Making life-altering decisions when under the influence of drugs or alcohol is as crazy as racing up Pike's Peak blindfolded. Notice how many cases illustrated below involved drinking. Finally, no matter how clever your lawyer is, it's hard for jurors to side with anyone messing with drugs and guns.

5. **Unnecessary use of excessive force –**

   a. **During an incident – Example:** The mouthy neighbor kid takes a swing at you with a flimsy piece of wall molding and you respond with a 12 gauge slug.

   b. **After the threat ceases – Example:** "Further, the manner in which Davis shot his brother—26 times, including 16 times in the head and neck, after having reloaded his gun with an extra ammunition clip — belies his claim of self-defense." *U.S. Ex Rel. Davis v. Gramley*, p. 9 (N.D.Ill. 3-26-2008).

6. **Engaging in unlawful activity, including possessing illegal weapons** – If you are committing a serious felony, you obviously lose the right to defend yourself against those trying to stop you from committing the crime. Also, if you possess a weapon illegally, you will be arrested for that crime, even if the act of self-defense was justified. It could cause detectives to take a lot closer look at your claim of self-defense.

7. **Failing to call 911 and let the police handle it if time permits** – You'll notice that the phrase "call the police" is not in any of the self-defense statutes. Yet prosecutors continuously argue that defendants should have called the police rather than using defensive force. Although we believe it's objectionable for district attorneys to impose conditions on self-defense not contained in state statutes, they often get away with it. It definitely can be a negative factor in your case if you have time to call the police but don't.

8. **Use of "spring guns" or traps** – These devices cannot distinguish between the innocent and the guilty. This is why most states outlaw such contraptions, especially those that could kill or maim. Paper Boy: "Sorry Mr. Brown, didn't mean to throw your paper into your garage! ... I'll get it ... Blam!!!!"

9. **Motive to kill –**

   a. "Of course I'll pay you that gambling debt I owe you. Just come on over and pull hard on the screen door; it gets stuck (you locked it to feign a break in). I'll be waiting in the kitchen," as you chuckle silently to yourself, "Heh, heh."

b. "Accidentally" shooting your wife claiming you thought she was a burglar soon after you insured her for $1M (and then bragged about it to your adulterous girlfriend).

10. **Hate speech, then hate crime** – Spewing verbal or written hatred against any race, religion, national origin or sexual orientation could become a link in a prosecutor's chain of evidence proving pre-meditation if you later injure a member of the group you despise. In the civil suit against New York Subway Vigilante Bernhard Goetz (Chapter 15), the plaintiff's attorney claimed Goetz acted out of racial bias. This obviously did not sit well with a racially mixed jury that handed down a multi-million dollar civil verdict against him.

11. **Not retreating, even though your state says you don't have to retreat** – This should *not* be a reason for a jury to convict in states that have eliminated the duty to retreat. But it's hard to get this out of a juror's mind if he or she believes you could have avoided killing someone by simply backing off or walking away.

12. **Fleeing after incident, tampering with evidence or witnesses, lying to the police** – When you run and hide after you have killed someone, bury the body in a shallow grave, dump it in the Briar Patch, wipe away finger prints or ask a witness to lie for you, *doesn't this suggest you have a guilty conscience?* Tampering with evidence or witnesses is a felony in most jurisdictions. In one recent case, picking up spent brass after a shooting was held to be tampering with evidence. Asking a witness to forget what he or she saw or heard you say would be tampering with a witness. We suggest you read your state's witness tampering and obstruction of justice statutes very carefully so that you do not make these kinds of mistakes after a defensive incident.

13. **Use of deadly weapon to protect personal property** – We strongly recommend not threatening with or using a deadly weapon to protect items of personal property such as an unoccupied vehicle, stereo, or a television. You'll be sellin' all your Big-Boy Toys to pay attorney fees. See the discussion of the Joe Horn and Tommy Oakes cases in the Texas subchapter.

14. **Big/ugly criminal record** – If lifting a bound volume of your criminal history could cause a lower abdominal hernia, it could cut against you in a case of "who started it?"

15. **A child or teen is killed or seriously injured** – Absent unusual circumstances, persons defending their homes and families against intruders usually get a free pass from police and prosecutors. An exception to this general rule exists when the victim/intruder is a child or teen who

has broken into the home to steal rather than physically harm someone. Often there is such a public outcry against the homeowner for lighting up a teenage-mutant-ninja burglar that prosecutors feel compelled to prosecute.

The "Case-Study" Method

Law professors insist that their students understand and remember the law better by reading how it is applied in cases rather than simply trying to memorize the words of statutes. This is known as the case-study method. Most lawyers agree it's easier to remember a dramatic story than to memorize some abstract rule of law. Why do you suppose the good Lord gave us Bible stories and not just the Ten Commandments? We think you'll remember the thumbs-down factors better if you read how they have affected the outcome of actual court cases. The more thumbs-down factors during a claimed defensive event, the more likely the defender will be arrested, prosecuted and convicted. Prepare your mind for a fascinating journey into the annals of armed conflict in America.

Thumbs-Down Factors in the Harmon Case

The defendant in the *Harmon* case described in Chapter 2 believed his actions were justifiable against two younger, stronger men he claimed intended to overpower him and take his gun away. But his perception was only part of the story. The case involved several thumbs-down factors which undoubtedly lead to arrest, prosecution and ultimately contributed to his conviction. To discover some of these factors, it was necessary to spend a day and a half reading 1500 pages of transcript available at the Millard County, Utah Courthouse. 1. Harmon was armed with a .45 pistol; his claimed assailants did not have weapons. 2. He shot at and hit Thomas while Thomas was running away. Undisputedly, he had an exit hole in the front of his arm and jacket. Was he trying to kill the witness who ultimately testified against him? 3. Harmon had been drinking. 4. Harmon gave several seemingly inconsistent versions of what he claimed happened including the 911 call and multiple statements to investigators. Giving any statement, let alone multiple statements before re-visiting the scene with your attorney is a bad idea. 5. The DA argued Harmon had time to call the police before using deadly force. From the time he kicked the two intruders off his property until he confronted them with a gun on a dirt road outside of the cabin community, they had traveled a half mile on foot. 6. Although he denied saying it, there was testimony that he had told his former girlfriend that the law allowed him to "kill" trespassers. Chasing down and killing someone after they commit a misdemeanor is excessive force. 7. The jury may have understood him to be the initial aggressor. Although he claimed the victims tried to enter his cabin, there was certainly no evidence that they were aggressive toward him until after he drove down the road, parked in front of them and showed them a gun. Even then, it may have appeared to jurors that the two were simply headed toward town thinking he had no reason to be serious about using a gun against them. 8. It wasn't clear, but there was some suggestion that his former girlfriend, who testified against him, had spent time with the man Harmon shot first. Love triangle? Jealousy? Who knows, but harmful innuendo such as this can contribute to an unfavorable verdict, especially when combined with several other thumbs-down factors. Like we said, the more thumbs-down factors, the greater likelihood of a conviction.

Additional Cases Containing Thumbs-down Factors

The following cases from several different states contain multiple thumbs-down factors. Every case involved both a trial and an appeal. Unless you are represented by a public defender, having your case tried and appealed could cost a fortune. As you are reading these case summaries, ask yourself if you think pride, anger, or revenge had anything to do with what happened. If you had been a juror in any of these cases, would your decision have been any different? As you read the facts, what thumbs-down factors can you indentify?

Over-the-Top Delaware Home Defense – *Warrington v. State,* 840 A.2d 590 (Del. 2003).

Facts and Verdict: The defendants are brothers (Wes and Drew). Wes owed an acquaintance, Pecco, approximately $800 for *drugs* that Wes had consumed instead of selling. The defendants claimed Pecco unlawfully entered their home and assaulted Wes with a knife. Drew smacked Pecco from behind, causing him to let go of the knife. Wes stabbed Pecco multiple times with the knife and Drew struck him repeatedly with a fireplace poker. Pecco had 13 stab wounds, including one in the left lung, and one through his pathetic, drug-dealing heart. He also suffered eight blunt-force blows to the head, a skull fracture, and blood on the brain. Pecco had deep slices through his hands, characteristic of defensive wounds. During the struggle, a 911 call was made from the Warrington residence. DNA from blood marks found on the telephone indicated Pecco made the call. Drew said that it was he who dialed the number, only to have Pecco knock the phone from his hands. Unbeknownst to the brothers, the 911 call continued to be taped. The tape revealed that Pecco was pleading with the brothers to stop attacking him. He asked, "Why are you guys trying to kill me?" to which one of the brothers responded, "Good reasons." As he died, Pecco said, "Wes, show me some love. Give me a hug before I die. Give me a hug." The recording demonstrated that Drew responded by kicking him in the face and telling him to shut up. Their lawyer claimed they had the right to defend their home with deadly force against a knife-wielding intruder. The jury found Wes and Drew guilty of first-degree murder.

Thumbs-Down Factors

i. **Use of excessive force after threat ceased:** The main issue in this case was whether Delaware's home-defense statute gave homeowners the right to *execute* an armed intruder who initially attacked one of them, but who, after they carved him up like a jigsaw puzzle with a couple of pieces missing, no longer had a weapon and was no longer a threat. The Court said, "No!" and instructed the jury, "if the defendant overcame Jesse Pecco so that the defendant no longer believed he was in danger of physical injury or personal injury, and therefore, the defendant knew the use of deadly force was *no longer necessary,* then the continued use of deadly force was not justified." The most important thumbs-down factor, therefore, is the use of deadly force after the attacker had been totally disabled, and they killed him (. . . the only part that wasn't bloody was the soles of the big man's feet) as he begged for a little compassion.

ii. **Drugs, illegal activity –** A drug deal gone bad presents a horrible obstacle for a defense attorney to overcome.

iii. **Failing to call 911 to let the police handle it if time permits** – There was time for a 911 call, but it was Pecco, not the defendants who made it. Certainly, if Pecco had time for a 911 call, the defendants did as well.

iv. **Motive to kill** – Wes owed Pecco $800.

v. **Lying to police** – They fibbed about who called 911. How do we know they didn't invite Pecco into the house with the intent to kill him? These guys were so dishonest about so many things, how can we believe with confidence the knife was even Pecco's? Nowadays, if you do something wrong, technology can nail you. It could be a surveillance camera in a nearby store, a Rodney-King-home-style video, a video cam on a cell phone, a voice message on a cell phone, or a recorded 911 call like in this case. If these types of technology don't record the criminal act, the Crime Scene Investigation (CSI) technology can recreate it. If you fudge on the truth, the jury will think you have a guilty conscience. If you decide to speak to the police (which we advise against - see Chapter 14), don't lie or even exaggerate! If you do, science and technology gonna-gitchu!

Less-than-Perfect Home Defense in Idaho – *State v. Turner,* 38 P.3d 1285 (Id. 2001).

Facts and Verdict: George Turner (Defendant) and Danny Pratt (victim) were in Turner's apartment arguing over money that Pratt allegedly owed Turner. Two other men were present (witness A and witness B). Witness A began an argument with Pratt that turned into a physical scuffle. Turner broke up the fight by hitting Pratt on the shoulder with a hammer a couple times. Pratt sat down on the couch and continued arguing with Turner, calling him a "f***ing liar." Turner, a paraplegic, wheeled to his bedroom, assembled and loaded a .22 caliber pistol and returned to the living room. He pointed the loaded weapon directly at Pratt and said to him "Now who you calling a f***ing liar?" Pratt responded with "you better get me before I get you," and started to stand up. Turner fired one shot at Pratt, hitting him in the head, killing him. Turner later testified, "I panicked, I thought he was going to get me." Witness A was on the ground still recovering from the fight, and wasn't paying attention. Witness B had put his head down when Turner appeared with the weapon, so neither witness actually saw whether Pratt tried to attack Turner as claimed. None of the men present called the police to report the incident. Pratt's body was found over *a month later* near a local creek. Subsequent investigation led the police to those involved in the shooting. George Turner was convicted of first-degree murder and sentenced to life in prison.

Thumbs-Down Factors:

i. **Armed defendant; Unarmed assailant** – Turner had a weapon and Pratt did not. Turner's defense was that because of his disability, he had reason to believe that Pratt would easily overpower him and use his own weapon against him. He claimed the shooting was in self-defense. However, because there was no evidence that Pratt attacked Turner, and since Turner was the one who introduced a gun into an already volatile situation, the judge refused to instruct the jury on self-defense.

ii. **Defendant was the initial aggressor** – This was perhaps Turners biggest mistake in the incident. He was the one who introduced deadly force into the situation. Being called a "f***ing liar" is not a good reason to point a loaded gun at someone. In fact, it's a good reason NOT to inject a deadly weapon into an already volatile situation. Turner should have kicked Pratt out of his apartment, or called the police to solve the dispute. Instead, he took the time to wheel into his bedroom, assemble and load his weapon, and then point a gun at Pratt. The jury saw this as a premeditated act resulting in a first-degree murder conviction.

iii. **Unnecessary use of excessive force** – It was indeed unnecessary and excessive for Turner to get and point a gun at Pratt in response to being called a "f***ing liar."

iv. **Failing to call 911 to let the police handle it if time permits** – The shooting was definitely avoidable. Turner had plenty of time to call the police and let them handle the situation. The only threat was the pistol that Turner foolishly introduced into the disagreement, like sparking a match around an uncapped powder keg!

v. **Killing someone you have a motive to kill** – The whole argument started from a dispute about Pratt owing Turner money. Both the judge and the jury believed that this plus the insult were the reason Turner pulled the trigger.

vi. **Fleeing after the incident, tampering with the evidence or witnesses** – If a person is confident he has acted in self-defense, why would he try to hide the assailant's body? Confined to a wheelchair, Turner probably didn't accomplish this himself. This implies he conspired with one or both of the witnesses (although the case does not say).

Having your handgun taken away by an angry assailant could be a legitimate concern. Even police officers have been disarmed and killed with their own duty weapons. It is an issue that shouldn't be lightly dismissed. We don't agree with the judge not giving a self-defense instruction. But even if he had, juries seem to reject this defense. Being overpowered and losing his weapon was the same concern the defendant had in the *Harmon* case in Chapter 2. Remember, *Harmon* claimed the two strangers ignored his warnings to stop their approach. The trial judge in Harmon gave a self-defense instruction, but the jury didn't buy it. From what we've seen, the I-was-afraid-he-would-kill-me-with-my-own-gun defense rarely works after shooting an unarmed person.

"I thought he was reaching for a weapon" in Vermont – *State v. Wheelock*, 609 A.2d 972 (Ver. 1992).

Facts and Verdict: Wheelock (defendant) and Brillon (victim) had been consuming alcohol, cocaine, valium and marijuana all night at Brillon's girlfriend's house. Throughout the evening Wheelock and Brillon had multiple confrontations. As early morning approached, Wheelock entered the living room with a shotgun. He fired one round at Brillon at close range and the chest shot killed him. Wheelock testified that he believed Brillon had a knife and that the shooting was in self-defense. However, the police found no knife near the crime scene. When Wheelock was apprehended, he possessed a bottle of partially consumed Scotch. Wheelock was convicted of second-degree murder.

Thumbs-Down Factors:

i. **Armed Defendant; Unarmed assailant** – Though Wheelock claimed Brillon had a knife, evidence suggests otherwise. (Notice that this thumbs-down factor has been present in every case so far).

ii. **Involvement of the defendant in either initiating or provoking a fight that escalates from a verbal dispute to a potentially deadly encounter** – Wheelock and Brillon had been arguing and confronting each other all night. Wheelock's anger from the multiple arguments may have been the catalyst that caused him to pull the trigger.

iii. **Mixing drugs or alcohol with weapons** – Both men were stoned out of their minds. Wheelock claimed that he honestly believed Brillon posed a threat to his life. He was either lying or his perception was severely compromised by the chemicals marinating his brain. Most people understand the danger of driving while intoxicated. To the slogan, "don't drink and drive" we add, "don't drink, smoke, pop, snort, sniff or inject anything you know you shouldn't and then pack heat."

iv. **Engaging in unlawful activity** – Wheelock's violation of the law by using illegal substances may have been a factor in affecting the jury's analysis of his character.

Where Does Self-Defense End and Aggression Begin in Maryland? – *Sydnor v. State*, 776 A.2d 669 (Md. 2001).

Facts and Verdict: Sydnor (defendant) was out with some friends when Jackson (victim) approached and asked if he could buy some "weed." When Sydnor responded in the negative, Jackson pulled a gun and demanded Sydnor's gold chain. After hitting Sydnor on the head with the gun and threatening to kill him, Jackson took $30 in cash from him and was about to take the gold chain when Sydnor, assisted by his friends, grabbed the gun and, after a struggle, was able to take it from Jackson. As Jackson then attempted to flee, Sydnor chased Jackson, fired five shots at him, hitting him four times - once in the front of his thigh, once in the forearm, and twice in his back (not necessarily in that order). Jackson collapsed and died in the street 40 to 50 yards from where the robbery occurred. Five bullet casings were found in the street near where Jackson collapsed (indicating that the shots were fired near where the body was found). One witness said she heard people running followed by five or six gunshots. Another witness said she saw Jackson "[try] to run and he [Sydnor] shot him in his back and then he ran in the opposite direction." Several police officers, who were in the vicinity, responded to the shots and saw Sydnor running away. They gave chase and eventually apprehended him, still in possession of the gun. At the police station,

Sydnor gave a formal, taped statement. He claimed he panicked as soon as he took the gun from Jackson. Sydnor added that he did not know whether Jackson had another gun, but that "I was already aggravated over the fact that he said he was going to kill me." In a later part of his statement, he said that Jackson acted like he was getting ready to "go back in his jacket," and "[s]o I panicked even more and just got to shooting." Sydnor was convicted of voluntary manslaughter and use of a handgun in the commission of a felony.

Thumbs-Down Factors:

i. **Armed defendant; Unarmed assailant** – The issue here is timing. Both individuals were armed, but at different times in the conflict. When the shots were fired, only Sydnor was armed. Though he claimed that he thought Jackson was going to pull another gun, no other gun was found nor did anyone report having seen another gun.

ii. **Shooting anyone in the back of any part of the body** – A witness testified that she saw Sydnor shoot Jackson in the back and ballistics confirmed it. If the initial aggressor is retreating, no matter how upset you are from their attack, once the threat of imminent danger is gone, you need to keep your cool and stop polluting Mother Earth with toxic lead pellets.

iii. **Not retreating** – Unless you are in your own home, in Maryland there is a duty to retreat before using deadly force. Not only did Sydnor not retreat, he and his friends chased Jackson 40 to 50 feet before Sydnor shot him in the back. Some might think that the verdict would be different in a state where there is no duty to retreat. But there are so many thumbs-down factors in this case, we are fairly positive the defendant would have been arrested and prosecuted even in a no-retreat state.

iv. **Fleeing after the incident** – It's understandable that Sydnor was scared, but view this from the perspective of an investigating officer. You hear gunshots, rush to the scene, observe a bloody corpse in the street and witness a man with a gun running away. What conclusion would you make?

v. **Using a deadly weapon to protect items of personal property** – Although this was a robbery, the use of deadly force by the victim ended when the defendant took the gun away from him. After that, the victim was killed to avenge the taking of a gold chain.

vi. **Excessive use of force after the threat ceased** – Because the immediate threat was over, there was no need to shoot Jackson in self-defense, nor was there any reason to shoot him multiple times, including twice in the back.

vii. **Spilling guts to police before talking to his attorney** – Snydor told police he was already aggravated that Jackson said he was going to kill him. That suggests he acted out of revenge rather than out of fear of being injured. Your statements to the police can give the prosecutor evidence to prove his case that he cannot get anywhere else. Authors re-write sentences several times (including this one) before publishing. We don't always say exactly what we mean the first time. Neither can you after a horrendous self-defense incident. Let your attorney explain what happened after you've both visited the scene together. See our detailed advice in this regard in Chapter 14 below.

Deadly Force Against a Not-So-Imminent Threat in Iowa – *State v. Elam*, 328 N.W.2d 314 (Iowa. 1980);

Facts and Verdict: Defendant Elam had been bowling one evening with two women. After bowling, the three purchased marijuana and went to the home of one of the women. Shortly thereafter, Stevens (the victim), who had been keeping company with one of the women, arrived at the house and proceeded to interrogate her as to where she had been that evening. This conversation culminated with Stevens striking her in the face. When she threatened to call the police, Stevens left. On his way out, he violently broke the glass in the storm door causing a splinter of glass to lodge in Elam's eye. Later, when Elam left the woman's house, he saw Stevens standing near a window. At this time, Stevens accused Elam of being involved with the woman, which Elam denied. As Elam walked away, Stevens informed him that he knew where he lived.

Elam then returned to the apartment complex where he resided. He went to his grandfather's apartment in the same apartment complex and unsuccessfully attempted to borrow a shotgun. He then asked his aunt for a pistol which she claimed not to have. Later in the evening, Elam heard Stevens asking an acquaintance where he was. Elam testified he believed that Stevens was after him. Elam then approached Stevens with an ax and asked him why he was chasing him. Stevens replied, "That [the ax] ain't going to do you no good." Elam then retreated to his aunt's apartment. Stevens approached the door of that apartment and invited Elam to come out. Elam did not come out at Steven's request and ultimately Stevens left the area as the clock continued to tick, tick, hint, hint.

A "friend," Jones, finally convinced Elam's grandfather to lend Elam the shotgun. Elam and Jones then proceeded outside the apartment complex armed with the shotgun. Outside the building, they encountered Stevens. Stevens ran toward Elam who tried to fire the shotgun, but it did not go off. Stevens then turned, raising his hands, and Jones yelled at Elam to lookout. At this point, Elam successfully fired the shotgun killing Stevens. Elam testified that he believed Stevens had a weapon, but one was never found. Following the shooting, Jones returned to Elam's grandfather's apartment where he washed the shotgun and concealed it under a mattress. Elam returned to his apartment and changed clothes. Elam and Jones then left the apartment complex. Later Elam traveled to St. Louis where he remained a couple months. He finally and gave himself up to the police. Elam was convicted of first-degree murder.

Thumbs-Down Factors:

i. **Armed defendant; Unarmed assailant** – Even though Stevens was the initial aggressor, Elam was the one who introduced deadly force into the situation. Although some would argue Stevens got what he deserved, the fact that he was unarmed turned out to be a significant thumbs-down factor for Elam's case.

ii. **Mixing drugs or alcohol with weapons** – Elam had been in possession of marijuana that night. The case doesn't say whether or not he was under the influence of drugs at the time of the shooting, but his mere involvement with drug related activity could have been viewed negatively by the jury.

iii. **Failing to call 911 to let the police handle it if time permits** – Being threatened and hunted by a determined adversary is understandably terrifying. But the whole incident between Elam and Stevens took place over the course of hours. The jury saw this as time for deliberation, premeditation, and formation of malice on the part of Elam, and therefore, saw grounds for a first-degree murder conviction. Elam should have called the police and had them apprehend Stevens for assaulting the girl. Elam was the one who kept showing up with weapons.

iv. **Not retreating** – Again, Elam had plenty of time to get away from imminent danger. When the shooting occurred, Elam was the one who actually went outside with the shotgun looking for Stevens.

v. **Unnecessary use of excessive force** – The victim was found dead with no weapon. He had been killed by a shotgun blast. Some might consider that excessive force.

vi. **Fleeing after the incident, tampering with the evidence or witnesses** – Elam skipped town and didn't turn himself in for over two months. His friend Jones washed the shotgun and then hid it.

No Way for a Hood to Handle the Truth in Indiana – *Hood v. State,* 877 N.E.2d 492 (Ind.App. 2007).

Facts and Verdict: Hood (not the best name for a defendant) and Earls had just finished buying beer from a liquor store, when a driver careened into the parking lot, narrowly missing the two men. Hood and the driver, whose last name was Truth (honest), exchanged profanities. Earls urged Hood to leave. Truth approached Hood on foot. Hood reached into his own car, retrieved a handgun and shot Truth twice. When Truth did not fall, Hood shot him four more times. The driver died of massive blood loss. Hood got into his minivan and drove away. He did not stop when police tried to pull him over. He jumped out of the minivan while it was still moving and was chased down by police. Investigators later found from the way the shots entered the victim's body that he was twisting and trying to get away. The defendant was charged with murder. The jury found Hood guilty of voluntary manslaughter.

Thumbs-Down Factors

i. **Armed defendant; Unarmed assailant(s)** – Although the defendant claimed the victim was reaching for a gun, the victim was unarmed. (How many cases have you read so far where this defense was shot down? Can you imagine detectives and prosecutors saying, "Yeah, Right!)

ii. **Initiating, provoking or escalating a fight** – The victim may have been ready to get physical with the defendant, but he never indicated he intended to take this to a deadly level. The defendant claims that the victim said, "I've got something for your @#$," but that, in the jury's view, did not excuse the killing. It did, however, reduce the verdict from murder to manslaughter.

iii. **Shooting any part of the body from behind** – Investigators testified the victim was twisting, trying to avoid the bullets.

iv. **Mixing drugs or alcohol with weapons** – Coming out of a liquor store while drunk reduces the chances your conduct will be judged favorably.

v. **Unnecessary use of excessive force during the incident** – Multiple shots fired at an unarmed man is hard to justify.

vi. **Fleeing after incident** – This could help you get a non-speaking role in an episode of *The World's Wildest Police Chases*, but it's not good for your case.

Home Defense and Teenage Victims – *Quaggin v. State*, 752 So.2d 19, (Fla. App. 2000) (a guilty verdict overturned on appeal and then an acquittal); *Texas v. Gonzalez* (an acquittal).

These two cases show the legal risk of shooting a teen intruder who is not committing a violent felony.

Quaggin involved a 76 year old man living in a home surrounded by trailers and old parade floats (made by Quaggin) containing piles of horded papers and personal belongings. Two boys, one 14 and the other 10, trespassed onto the lot, entered several of the trailers without permission and began gathering items without permission. They eventually wandered into the old man's home. When they finally encountered Quaggin, there was a pile of clutter between him and them. They claimed they entered his home to ask permission to gather lumber to build a fort in the woods. Mr. Quaggin perceived them as burglars and tragically shot the 14-year-old dead. He was convicted of manslaughter and sentenced to 15 years in prison. He won a new trial because of faulty jury instructions that had been given. He was found not guilty in the second trial, but his daughter told the media he later died broke because of the dreadful legal expense. Six years later Florida beefed up its home-defense law to give homeowners a presumption of innocence when using deadly force to defend against an unlawful and forcible entry (see Florida's subchapter and The Mother of All Self-Defense Laws, Chapter 20).

Gonzales – Just when we thought it was safe in Texas to defend one's home from any intruder, the state brought murder charges against Jose Gonzales, age 63. On an evening in July of 2007, he killed one of three teenagers who broke into his home to "rummage for snacks and soda." Although Mr. Gonzales was found not guilty, he had to endure the emotional nightmare and astronomical cost (assuming he wasn't represented by a public defender) of a murder trial. "Man cleared in killing of intruder sneaking snack." *Deseret News* at deseretnews.com, 28 September 2008.

Although *Quaggin* preceded Florida's dynamite new home-defense statute, Florida and Texas have had comparatively strong home defense laws for years. No matter how strong your state's self-defense statutes appear, a community uproar fueled by a sensationalized media "investigation" can put pressure on an elected District Attorney to prosecute. Every agency that arrests or prosecutes should be required to pay the attorney fees, out of its own budget, of any defendant who is found not guilty on the theory of self-defense or defense of others. The State of Washington has a similar provision as part of its self-defense statute. See Chapters 5 and 20.

Excessive Force Trumps Home Defense in Indiana – *Birdsong v. State,* 685 N.E.2d 42 (Ind. 1997).

Facts and Verdict: McDowell, a resident of an apartment complex, saw Miller and a woman named Colquit, arguing in the hallway. Colquit appeared falling-down drunk. Miller threw a bottle at Colquit and told her to leave.

Colquit managed to get back into the apartment building and she began knocking on defendant Birdsong's door. He let her in, but a few minutes later, McDowell heard Colquit screaming. He looked out of his door and saw Birdsong dragging Colquit down the stairs by her legs. They were punching at each other, and Birdsong socked Colquit in the mouth.

Minutes later, McDowell heard Colquit kicking on Birdsong's door. He noticed Colquit was carrying a can of wasp spray and Miller was with her carrying a gun by its barrel. The door of defendant's apartment opened and Colquit and Miller went inside.

Colquit was inside the defendant's apartment, but McDowell saw Miller raise his right hand, the hand with the gun in it. Miller then slipped on a carpet by the door and dropped the gun. McDowell saw Birdsong strike Miller three or four times in his head with an axe. As Birdsong was striking Miller with the axe, McDowell, who was still standing in his own doorway, called to Birdsong, 'What the hell are you doing?' In response, Birdsong shot at McDowell, hitting the doorframe near McDowell's head. McDowell heard five more shots as he ran out of the building.

When the police arrived at the scene, Birdsong led them to the bodies of Miller and Colquit which had both been chopped by an axe and shot. He admitted to the killings claiming home defense. *Birdsong v. State*, 685 N.E.2d 44-45 (Ind. 1997). Defendant was convicted of the murders of Miller and Colquit and attempted murder of McDowell, the witness.

Thumbs-Down Factors:

i. **Unnecessary use of excessive force** – We categorized Indiana's home-defense statute as very protective. It allows a person to use deadly force if he "reasonably believes that the force is necessary to prevent or terminate the other person's unlawful entry of or attack on the person's dwelling, curtilage…" [Curtilage is the area immediately around the home.] There is no duty to retreat from one's home before using deadly force. With such a protective home-defense statute, some might predict the defendant would have been acquitted. After all, the pistol possessed by Miller and wasp spray Colquit was brandishing could have caused serious injury.

   The fact that Birdsong was convicted emphasizes the importance of the terms "reasonable" and "necessary." The appeals court conceded that Birdsong had presented strong evidence of home-defense. He was in a place he had a right to be, he was in fear of serious bodily injury, the victims were the initial aggressors. Birdsong was preventing an unlawful entry into his home. However, despite compliance with these technicalities, the court affirmed the convictions on the grounds that Birdsong had used "unreasonable force" (the crime scene photos must have been hideous). Specifically the court pointed out Colquit was armed only with a can of wasp spray, Miller was holding his gun by the barrel, and then dropped it. The court also stated, "… Miller and Colquit were chopped and shot several times, even after they were incapacitated." Id. at 46.

Pancho's Wisdom

When did the game "Paper, Rock, Scissors" become "Wasp Spray, Axe, Gun?"

ii. **Armed defendant; Unarmed assailant/witness** – McDowell was simply a witness and was unarmed. Birdsong took a pot shot at McDowell who was standing in his own doorway across the hall and posed no threat. The court said, "With respect to the attempted murder conviction, there also existed evidence that defendant employed unreasonable force and, thus, did not validly act in self-defense. For example, McDowell was unarmed and standing across the hallway in his own doorway when defendant shot at him." Id. at 46.

Road rage

Criminal defense attorneys must wonder if road rage is the root of all brandishing cases. Gun owners rationalize that because their antagonist's vehicle could be considered a dangerous weapon, they have a right to threaten with a weapon. The following description is out of an actual case I handled.

Two vehicles were stopped for a red light at 9000 South 450 West. One of the vehicles was a pick-up truck and the other was a passenger car. The passenger car, driven by [my client (MC)], was stopped in the #2 lane. The pick-up truck, driven by [other guy (OG)], was stopped in the #3 lane. At approximately 500 West and 9000 South, the #3 lane merges into the #2 lane. The truck in lane #3 accelerated in an attempt to merge in front of the vehicle in the #2 lane. As the two vehicles were side by side, MC and OG both flipped each other off. . . OG said that MC started waiving a gun around inside his car. OG described the gun as a black semi-auto Glock Handgun. MC did not threaten OG with the gun, but waved the gun around inside the window so he could easily see it.

Our client was charged with threatening with a dangerous weapon in a fight or quarrel, also known as brandishing. Because of certain technicalities in Utah's law, I got the case dismissed. Fortunately, the defendant had not pointed the gun at OG or he could have been charged with felony assault. Unfortunately, the dismissal didn't keep the defendant from incurring attorney fees. Carrying a gun should be the reason to *de-escalate* a situation like this, not escalate it.

I could relate dozens of similar stories. Similar circumstances; different client. The vehicles of MC and OG almost collided where two lanes merged into one. Tempers flared and angry words were exchanged (like a severe cosmic disturbance caused by the collision of two parallel universes. Sometimes I feel like I'm entering . . . ominous music. . . The Twilight Zone!). MC followed OG home. OG emerged with a knife and his live-in girlfriend (two witnesses to one – ugh). They called the police claiming MC pointed a gun at them during the standoff in front of OG's yard. MC said he never showed the gun. Problem was, OG and his girlfriend were able to describe MC's gun fairly accurately ("It was a black gun!" I would have given anything had MC's pistol been purple.) MC was initially accused of assault with a deadly weapon, a felony. Fortunately, MC's charges were later dismissed, but not before increasing my tax liability. Please read and internalize Chapter 9.

Pancho's Wisdom

Pancho sleeps with two colts under his pillow; one gives him a STIFF NECK!

8

JUSTIFIABLE ACTS OF SELF-DEFENSE

By the time you get to this part of the book you might be asking yourselves, "What's the use of even having a gun for self-defense?" Yes, defending with deadly force is a serious legal and personal risk and should be reserved as your last option. But defensive incidents do occur without arrest and prosecution. How are such incidents different from those in the previous chapter? Is there such a thing as a "Thumbs-Up Factor?"

It's easy for us to report defensive incidents gone bad because they end up as cases reported in law books. The facts come from sworn testimony and are summarized by judges who write fairly well. In contrast, incidents that do not result in conviction are extremely difficult to report for several reasons. First, they are not always reported to the authorities. The good guys may not call the police for fear of legal repercussions. The bad guys don't dial 911 because they possess illegal weapons, drugs or their criminal records are as thick as a Webster's Dictionary. Even if these incidents are reported to the police, they generally are not featured in any media source. If they are, the facts can be distorted in an attempt to sensationalize and sell the story. The self-defense aspect of the incident is often not even mentioned. This phenomenon is well documented in John Lott's book, *The Bias Against Guns*. For example, compare the media coverage of the Virginia Tech shooting or Columbine, to the incident in Colorado where a concealed firearm permit holder, Jeanne Assam, is credited with saving hundreds of parishioners in a large Christian congregation. "Who? What?" you say. It did appear in the national media, but not to the extent of the two school shootings mentioned above. The primary reason was there were not as many lives lost. We know the facts of Ms. Assam's incident only because it was related in detail in the minutes of the Colorado Senate. Finally, even if self-defense incidents are reported in a media source, such as a newspaper or magazine (e.g., *The Armed Citizen* feature in the NRA magazines), there is rarely any follow-up to determine if the defender eventually was arrested or prosecuted. When police investigate but don't arrest, the investigative papers are usually kept confidential. The defender is typically advised by his attorney not to discuss the facts with anyone, particularly the news media. In sum, it's downright tough to find out what really happened. With this disclaimer, we proceed.

Summary of Thumbs-Up Factors

Those defending themselves and others against random mass shootings are not generally prosecuted. Two recent examples are the Colorado church shooting mentioned above and the shooting at Trolley Square Mall in Salt Lake City, Utah. In both, the attacker had a weapon and was using deadly force against innocents. The defenders were credited with saving innocent lives and neither defender was ever arrested. Both of these incidents are described in more detail below.

Another fairly common scenario nowadays is where a business owner defends his business against an attack or robbery. Convenience stores, pawn shops and jewelry stores are often the targets. It's not uncommon for the assailant to enter the store firing a round to terrorize the employees into submission. Under those circumstances, responding with deadly force is generally deemed justifiable as long is it is necessary to stop a robbery carried out with a deadly weapon. Unfortunately, many businesses not only prohibit their employees from possessing self-defense weapons, but will actually fire employees for offering any resistance or assistance during violent encounters. For example, see *Feliciano v. 7-eleven*, 210 W. Va. 740 (2001), where an employee was fired for wrestling a handgun away from a female armed robber and *Bruley v. Village Green Management Company*, 592 F.Supp.2d 1381 M.D. Fla. (2008). in which an employee of an apartment complex was fired for, among other things, responding with his shotgun to the aid of a tenant who had been shot. Finally, absent any of the thumbs-down factors mentioned in the preceding chapter, persons defending their homes or temporary homes often avoid arrest and prosecution, especially in states with highly protective home-defense laws.

The Jeanne Assam Incident

In December of 2007, Jeanne Assam, a church volunteer carrying a concealed weapon at the invitation of her pastor, is credited with saving hundreds of worshipers during an attempted mass killing at her church. She was honored by the Colorado Legislature in Joint Resolution 08.019. Here are the facts reported in the legislative record without all the whereases:

> On December 9, 2007, Matthew Murray drove to the Youth With A Mission campus in Arvada, Colorado. At approximately 12:30 A.M., the gunman, Matthew Murray, shot four students, killing two of them. Following the shooting in Arvada and later that day, the gunman drove to New Life Church in Colorado Springs, Colorado. At approximately 1 P.M. on December 9, 2007, the gunman entered the parking lot of New Life Church, as a church service was concluding. The gunman carried as many as one thousand rounds of ammunition for his assault rifle, with the apparent intent to cause a great loss of life and injury. The gunman began to open fire on the

> members of the congregation as they exited the church, injuring two and killing two members of the same family. Jeanne Assam, a volunteer security guard, was inside the church when she became aware of the shooting taking place and rushed toward the scene. Upon witnessing the gunman entering the church and firing his weapon, Jeanne Assam, putting herself in harm's way and risking her own life, drew her weapon, believing God was with her, and stepped into the gunman's line of fire. Jeanne Assam shot Mr. Murray and thereby stopped him from harming any more of the hundreds of people in the church.

Colorado Senate Joint Resolution 08.019. Her own words to a news outlet have been posted on a website honoring her courage:

> I want to extend my sympathy to the families of the victims and the gunman, and I mean that very sincerely. What happened yesterday at church: I heard shots fired, and there was chaos and there were a lot of people in the church, and people were running away from where the shots were fired. The shots were so loud, I thought he was inside. He wasn't even inside yet when I heard the rounds. It seems like the halls cleared out, I saw him coming through the doors. I took cover, and I waited for him to get closer, then I came out of cover, and I identified myself, and engaged him, and took him down. I give the credit to God, and I mean that, I say that very humbly. God was with me… this has got to be God, because of the firepower that he had versus what I had, was God. I did not run away, and did not think for a minute to run away, I just knew that I was given the assignment to end this before it got too much worse. I just prayed for the Holy Spirit to guide me, I just said Holy Spirit be with me. My hands weren't even shaking. Honestly, I was very focused, and it was chaotic, it was so loud, I will never forget the gunshots, it was so loud. I was just focused; I just knew I was not going to wait for him to do any further damage. I just knew what I had to do.

Barry Bourbonnais, a Vietnam combat veteran witnessed the commotion. He did not have a gun, but was courageously attempting to distract the shooter when Ms. Assam came into the picture.

> I saw him [the shooter] in the hallway...I saw the rifle go up… My only option was to distract the gunman... To my left, she came through the doors... It was the bravest thing I'd ever seen, including my 14 months in Vietnam… She was heroic... she was like an angel, I mean, it was unbelievable, and she was fully exposed, I hear him firing, and she's returning fire, and she's yelling, surrender, surren-

> der and she just starts calmly, like she's walking to her car in the parking lot, firing round after round... After we met at his slumped-over body, I said, "You were so calm." She said, "I was praying to the Holy Spirit the whole time."
>
> http://jeanneassamfanclub.blogspot.com/

We have followed this event closely since it occurred and have found nothing to indicate that the police ever considered arresting Ms. Assam or that the district attorney screened the incident with any serious intent of prosecuting.

Thumbs-Up – Calling upon Deity for Divine Assistance – This is not the first account of the innocent calling upon Deity for help and protection during a violent attack. See the historical account of Medal of Honor winner Sergeant Alvin York by Dave Kopel in *America's 1st Freedom,* February 2006. Under heavy machine gun fire during WWI, York, with one rifle and one pistol almost single-handedly captured 128 German enlisted men and 4 officers, killed 25 and knocked 35 German machine-gun nests out of commission. When an officer later asked York how he did it he responded, "[S]ir, it is not man power. A higher power than man power guided and watched me and told me what to do." Id. p. 41. Other well-known accounts include General Washington praying at Valley Forge and a multitude of incidents described in Holy Writ, particularly the Old Testament and Book of Mormon. Pardon the leap of faith, but there is some historical precedent to the effect that calling upon God during a terrifying, imminent attack could help you to do the right thing at the right time.

Trolley Square Shooting – The following detailed description of the incident comes from a Salt Lake Tribune article investigated and reported by veteran reporters Kristen Moulton and Russ Rizzo:

> Staring down on a gunman's carnage at Trolley Square, Ogden police officer Kenneth Hammond had a choice: retreat to safety with his pregnant wife or confront a killer. He chose to act. Off-duty but armed with a .45-caliber handgun, he exchanged fire with 18-year-old Sulejman Talovic, who had killed five people and wounded four in less than six minutes at the Salt Lake City mall…Hammond and his wife, Sarina Hammond, had finished a pre-Valentine's Day dinner at Rodizio Grill on the mall's upper floor. Married just a few months, Hammond was waiting on a bench outside the restaurant for his wife…He heard popping noises that he thought were from construction, but when he looked over the balcony, he saw bodies on the floor below and a man with a shotgun leaving a store. He told Sarina, an Ogden Police dispatcher, to return to Rodizio, "lock down" the restaurant and call 911. Sarina said Tuesday that she bor-

> rowed a waiter's cell phone to tell Salt Lake police that her husband was an off-duty officer, not a second gunman. She described what he was wearing, hoping to protect her husband from officers' fire. Hammond drew his .45-caliber handgun, but did not dare put it back in his holster to pull out his badge. To let mall customers and clerks know he was not a second gunman, Hammond said, "I was yelling and screaming as loudly as I possibly could . . . Officer Hammond, off-duty OPD!" and "Get down! Get down!" "It was tense for a few seconds," he said. Then he and the gunman traded shots, Hammond on the second floor and the shooter down below. Hammond said he moved to another part of the balcony and lost sight of the gunman. He lay flat, but soon realized the gunman could come up the escalator behind him. No words were exchanged. In fact, Hammond said he couldn't even describe the shooter. "I was so focused on that gun." When he looked down again, he saw a Salt Lake City officer below and shouted out that he was an off-duty officer. "I didn't know him. He didn't know me." Hammond went down the escalator and together the two officers pursued the gunman. They fired at him and Hammond said there was silence for five to 10 seconds, before he heard rapid gunfire—apparently from the SWAT team—and looked up to see glass falling and the gunman down. In about nine minutes, the massacre was over. . . Salt Lake City police Chief Chris Burbank called it "amazing." . . . "There is no question his quick actions saved the lives of numerous other people."

"Trolley Square: The Hero Cop – Six-Year Veteran Having A Romantic Dinner With Wife Stalled Shooter Until SWAT Arrived." *The Salt Lake Tribune,* 02/14/2007. Notice the extent of efforts made by both Hammond and his wife to inform responding police officers that he was a defender and not the mass shooter.

Like with the New Life Church and Trolley Square incidents, there have been other random mass shootings where citizens intervened to either stop the shooters or help apprehend them. These include school shootings in Pearl, Mississippi and Edinboro, Pennsylvania. We have found no information to indicate that the armed citizens who intervened were arrested, prosecuted or sued.

Home Defense

There are numerous newspaper accounts throughout the country every week where law-abiding citizens defend persons inside their homes and are actually praised by the police for having done so. These accounts of home defense are often re-printed in the National Rifle Association magazine, *America's 1st Freedom.* A section of the magazine entitled "The Armed Citizen" summarizes news stories from all over the U.S. in which armed individuals have defended themselves, their homes, businesses and others. Law enforcement officials often announce there will be no arrest or prosecution. However, this is hard to confirm. Nevertheless, our experience and research indicates that those defending persons in their homes are generally not arrested or prosecuted absent unusual circumstances, like those described in the previous chapter.

Pancho's Wisdom

You just might be a Gunnut if . . . when your teens come home late after you've gone to bed, they roll twice across the kitchen floor, just in case they wake you up!

9
CONFLICT AVOIDANCE

Winning a case on the theory of self-defense will put another feather in your defense attorney's cap, but it's not really something you want to experience during your lifetime. I encourage my concealed-carry students to forgo the adventure altogether by (1) being aware of their surroundings, (2) avoiding dangerous places and situations, (3) dressing as if concealing weapons and (4) avoiding confrontations and de-escalating conflicts.

Awareness of surroundings – Those who would harm you have predatory instincts. What are the traits of the animals that end up as lunch on Africa's Great Serengeti Plain? They are the inattentive, the weak, and the helpless. Likewise, human predators attack those they perceive to be easy targets. One indication of a pushover is a person who appears clueless of what is going on around him or her. Self-defense instructors often refer to this state of obliviousness as condition white. Predators salivate at the prospect of pouncing upon the inattentive before they can even begin to conceptualize defensive moves or plan a means of escape. One way to avoid and discourage such attacks is to be aware of your surroundings. If you look alert, predators may pass you up in hopes of finding someone else they can more easily dominate using the element of surprise.

Avoiding dangerous places and dangerous situations – If we told you about a pretty young woman, without a gun, who was mugged and raped while walking down a dark, deserted alley in a high-crime area at 3am, the more callous might say something like, "she was asking for it! Tragic! Why would anyone in their right mind do anything so stupid?" Unless you are a paid decoy for the local vice squad or are horribly self-destructive, why would you intentionally subject yourself to such danger? Unless you absolutely must, avoid high crime areas, traveling alone at night, and dark, unguarded parking lots.

If you don't have a weapon, at least look like you might be carrying one – A young attorney who worked for me in downtown Salt Lake rode the mass transit train (TRAX) back and forth from his home in the suburbs. He often worked until after dark. His exit was near a poorly lit city park. One evening, as he crossed through the park thinking about work, he didn't notice two young men running towards him. One of them stopped abruptly in front of him with his arm outstretched. The lawyer asked the stranger what he had in his hand, to which the mugger responded, "What the [expletive] do you think it is? It's a gun!" They demanded his wallet and he it handed over. They hesitated for a moment with the gun still pointed at his face. He wondered if they were going to kill him.

Luckily they just ran off with his wallet. A brave Sandy City police officer single-handedly arrested them at the next train stop after the young attorney quickly dialed 911 (Wow, great response time!). Talking freely about their misadventure, the captured criminals revealed truths that gun owners should know about the predatory mind. Other potential victims had been allowed to pass by without attack, "because they seemed like the types who might be carrying concealed weapons." Isn't that an interesting comment? Evidently, some of the first people off the train didn't fit the victim profile they were looking for. They picked on someone who was pre-occupied with his thoughts and wasn't dressed like a person who might be carrying a gun.

Be keenly aware of your surroundings. If you don't have a weapon, look as if you might. Wear a fanny pack, a concealment vest or loose clothing. A cell phone mounted on your belt where some people keep a gun holster could prove to be a visual repellant. Usually, when concealed weapon permit holders change positions like getting off of a bus or train, they check or adjust the position of their weapons. Getting into the habit of adjusting your cell phone or pager on your belt could give the impression you might be armed. Of course, the best solution is to be armed if legally possible, educated in the law of self-defense and well-trained with your defensive weapon.

Avoid Confrontations and De-Escalate Disagreements – *Blessed are the Peacemakers for they shall be called the children of God. Matthew 5:9.* I have a few Colt Peacemakers in my possession, but that's not what this passage is referring to. If you seek peace rather than conflict, you will be blessed legally as well as spiritually. And how about this one? *A soft answer turneth away wrath: but grievous words stir up anger.* Proverbs 15:1.

Isn't the purpose of carrying a firearm for self-defense to make it home each night without being injured? If so, why would you let your macho initiate or aggravate a situation that could turn deadly? At age 59, I have rarely found that, with a little humility, I couldn't apologize my way out of a conflict. OK, so I'm a silver-tongued lawyer. Believe me *anyone* can do it.

Pardon the narration of a couple of personal experiences. Remember we discussed earlier the tendency of road rage to turn kindly gentlemen into frothing, rabid monsters? One afternoon while backing out of a convenience store parking lot, I didn't see the strapping construction worker in my blind spot. Luckily my backup aid was working and I avoided a collision. Stomping my brakes, I immediately turned and begged the individual's pardon, "I'm sorry, I didn't notice you." Rather than accept the apology, the stout fellow, still irritated, blared, "You're sorry alright!" (as in "you're a sorry-excuse for a driver.") I was packing a full-sized Glock that would have easily made up for our difference in size. But knowing from the sad experience of a number of clients that brandishing a firearm wasn't the right way to handle the situation, I retorted, "Honest, I'm sorry and I really do apologize." I knew it was my fault and the hulking stranger perceived my sincerity. He immediately pardoned my poor driving and we both parted company having mutual respect.

But what if you know you weren't at fault? I changed lanes to the right on the interstate preparing to exit. When I heard a high-pitched eeeeeeeee, I thought I was having car problems. A bullet bike appeared from my right rear at a speed almost twice that of the flow of traffic. The rider's face was redder than a GOP-dominated county on a political map. He raised a fist accusing me of changing lanes without looking. I had looked, but at his speed he appeared out of nowhere. As an experienced trial lawyer, I was certainly capable of precisely verbalizing why I believed the near mishap was his fault. My "carsenal" had an ample selection of thug thumpers from which I could have chosen to back up my argument. Again, memory of cases past helped me avoid the temptation of allowing my righteous indignation to override my good sense. I threw up my hands in surrender and mouthed an animated apology through a closed window. Sensing my desire to diffuse the potential conflict with finality and no argument, the cyclist nodded approval and sped away visibly satisfied that I had accepted full responsibility for the near collision.

At the risk of this sounding like a Sunday-Go-To-Meetin' (OK, so we're Tim Tebow fans), a relevant reminder that ought to be engraved on the back strap of every defensive pistol: *"Pride goeth before destruction, and an haughty spirit before a fall.* Proverbs 16:8. Be alert, armed, confident, humble and apologetic. Always try to de-escalate any quarrel before grabbing for the gat.

Pancho's Wisdom

You just might be a Gunnut if . . . your wife never washes a load of clothes without finding at least one bullet in the washer or dryer.

10

STEP UP IN FORCE

Any force used in self-defense must be reasonable and necessary. You can never be absolutely certain how a judge or jury may decide these issues. Therefore, it is best, if time permits, to step up or ratchet up your responses to your opponents' threats only as needed. This way, if you are wrong in your assumption that your actions are justified, you minimize the ultimate crime of which you could be convicted. Peace officers are trained to do it this way. If you do things their way, it increases the chance they will judge your behavior to have been appropriate.

The visual below illustrates what we mean. Your potential responses range from avoidance maneuvers to the use of deadly force. Notice how the potential charges become more severe as responses become potentially more deadly. Also, give heed to where the felony line is positioned.

DETAILED PLAUSIBLE RESPONSES TO INCREASING POTENTIAL THREATS

Assailant's Conduct	Level of Your Threats or Force	Your Response	Potential Charges if your Actions are Found NOT to be Justified
Lurking in areas where predators (murderers, robbers, rapists) feel comfortable.	1	Avoid such areas if possible.	None.
Predator considers you a potential victim.	2	Not acting like a victim; awareness of your surroundings; looking like the type of individual who might be armed.	None.
Approaching from a distance.	3	Your awareness of your surroundings, your training and "that voice inside of you" tells you "something's not right here." You make an avoidance maneuver (e.g., cross the street, head for the nearest home or business).	None.

Assailant's Conduct	Level of Your Threats or Force	Your Response	Potential Charges if your Actions are Found NOT to be Justified
Reacts to your avoidance maneuver by continuing to approach.	4	More drastic avoidance; yell, "Stop, don't come any closer!" Head quickly to a place of safety; dial 911.	None.
Continues to approach trying to distract or confuse you with assurances or questions.	5	Yell, "No! I said Stop!" Position hand on or near firearm without exhibiting it. If his hands are not visible you should be yelling "show me your hands" being ready to draw in case he displays a weapon. A .38 "hammerless" (to avoid hanging up on pocket lining material) pointed at assailants from inside jacket pocket is a favorite of police officers encountering potential threats at this level.	None.
Continues to approach.	6	Shout, "I have a gun!" Retreat "to the wall" if possible, even though in many states you are not required to do so. Tactically retreating puts more distance between you and your assailant. It makes your actions seem more reasonable to police, prosecutors and juries.	Possible misdemeanor. But either not a crime or not usually prosecuted in most jurisdictions, particularly in Western or Southern states.
POSSIBLE		**FELONY**	**LINE**
Begins to rush you, refuses to show his hands, approaches so close you realize he could overpower you before you get your gun out. See discussion of 21 foot rule, Chapter 11.	7	Draw gun to low ready (45 degree angle, not pointed directly at assailant), yelling "Stop or I'll shoot!"	If police believe your actions were not justified, you could be charged with brandishing, a serious misdemeanor in most states, or aggravated assault, also known as assault with a deadly weapon, a felony.
Threateningly enters 21 foot safety zone.	8	Point gun at assailant with finger on the trigger. **Alternatives:** Retreat, use a taser, pepper spray or other non-lethal alternative.	Aggravated Assault or Assault with a Deadly Weapon, a felony, unless justified. **Alternatives:** Less likely to be charged with a crime in most states than if you point a gun.
Assailant reveals deadly weapon.	9	If you have retreated to the wall and an assault with a deadly weapon is imminent, in most states you would be justified to use deadly force.	Ugly Potential charges if not justified include Manslaughter, Attempted Murder, or Murder.
If assailant dispenses with in-between steps and displays a deadly weapon threatening deadly force.	10	You may draw and fire if deadly threat is imminent. See explanation of "imminent" in Chapter 3.	Potential charges if not justified include Manslaughter, Attempted Murder, or Murder.

Crime statistics show that when a criminal predator suspects his intended victim has a gun, he will abandon his attack 98% of the time without a shot being fired.

> If national surveys are correct, 98 percent of the time that people use guns defensively, they merely have to brandish a weapon to break off an attack. Such stories are not hard to find: pizza deliverymen defend themselves against robbers, carjackings are thwarted, robberies at automatic teller machines are prevented, and numerous armed robberies on the streets and in stores are foiled, though these do not receive the national coverage of other gun crimes.

Lott, John R., Jr. *More Guns, Less Crime* (1998): 3.

By the time you get to Level 5 above, most predators will strongly suspect you are armed and let you be. In most states, you will not have committed what could be charged as a crime until you raise your response to Level 6. Once, however, you have raised your response to Level 6, exhibiting a weapon, you run the risk of being charged with brandishing, threatening with a weapon or worse, assault with a deadly weapon, a felony. The Felony Line exists somewhere between levels 6 and 8 in most states. If your attacker gets the hint at level 4 and leaves, you will have accomplished your purpose without even having committed a potential crime.

The following examples illustrate how you might be able to convince an attacker to leave without committing a crime. Both of these individuals reacted brilliantly under extreme stress.

Example #1: Curt exited a restaurant in downtown Salt Lake City late at night with his wife holding on to his arm. As he walked toward his car on the city sidewalk, three individuals approached from the opposite direction. As they passed Curt, one of them reached over and elbowed him in the arm. Curt quickly motioned his wife behind him and faced the aggressors. Unbeknownst to them, he had his hands positioned on his Colt .38 Special legally concealed in the pocket of his trench coat. The three apparently unarmed trouble makers taunted him with their hands to, "Come on!" The defender stood his ground stating something like, "I don't want trouble, but if you start it, I'll finish it!" The mouthy trio looked him in the eye and then looked at his concealed hands. They repeated this several times while he stood his ground. Finally, they put their hands in the air, turned around and left without further provocation. Had Curt committed a crime? No, but his actions were threatening enough to convince three would-be muggers to leave. Had he shown his weapon, he would have risked being charged with brandishing, or worse. This was a brilliant maneuver under intense pressure that convinced multiple threatening individuals to stop their aggression. Too often when the gun owner draws his gun under these conditions, the antagonists draw their cell phones and dial 911. The SWAT team then arrives to shove the gun owner's nose (and pretty gun) into the pavement.

Example 2: Danny was driving home from work when he struck a dog that darted in front of his car. His 1911 .45 was legally hidden under a typical concealment vest. As he stood in front of his vehicle staring in shock at the poor, lifeless pooch, he noticed two men approaching, one of whom had a baseball bat. "He killed our dog! Let's get him!" Danny, realizing the imminent threat of a potentially deadly weapon, positioned his hand by his vest without actually showing his pistol. He shouted in a commanding voice, "It's just a dog! Get out of here!" Both men noticed his hand positioned by his concealment vest. Getting the message, they immediately ceased their aggression, turned around and disappeared into the neighborhood as suddenly as they had appeared. Once again, a concealed weapon permit holder had successfully conveyed the warning that further aggression could be disastrous and yet, in doing so, had not committed a crime. Because the assailants had a potential weapon, Danny was probably justified brandishing his pistol. Had he done so, however, and someone had called the police, he may have been arrested and prosecuted.

Both men used their weapons prudently without actually brandishing. Why raise your response Level to 5, 6 or 7 if you don't have to?

Pancho's Wisdom

You just might be a Gunnut if . . . shirts you've donated to the Goodwill have large, shredded, burnt holes blown through the bottom right front flap (as you've attempted to take perception and reaction time from concealment to a level where no man has ever gone before).

11

PERCEPTION AND REACTION TIME AND THE NON-FIREARM DEADLY THREAT

One of the major beefs we have with the self-defense laws of most states is that they do not take into account the problem of perception and reaction time. Judges and state legislators seem to have all grown up believing the fantasy perpetuated by Hollywood westerns that the good guys can always outdraw bad guys. Police training academies spend a considerable amount of time and effort busting this myth.

Do you remember learning about perception and reaction time in drivers' education? *Perception time* refers to the time it takes your eyes to see and your brain to register that you are encountering a threat to your personal safety. *Reaction time* is a measurement of how long it takes your body to respond to the "OH CWAP!!!!" message from your brain.

Example: A car runs a stop sign and moves directly in front of your vehicle. The time it takes you to see the threat and realize that you must take action is the perception time. Although individuals differ, three quarters of a second (.75 seconds) is often used as the average time it takes a person to perceive a threat. Reaction time is the time it takes to move your foot to the brake. Reaction time also differs from person to person, but .75 seconds is the accepted average. Experts say 1.5 seconds is a typical perception and reaction time for a reasonably skilled driver to react to an emergency in an automobile.

Is the perception and reaction time involved in applying a car brake comparable to the perception and reaction time needed to draw a gun from a concealed holster? We don't think it is. How many times have you applied the brakes in a vehicle during an emergency? Hundreds, perhaps thousands? Now compare that astronomical number to the relatively few number of times you have practiced drawing your pistol or revolver from concealment. For most hombres there is no comparison. It's our assertion that perceiving what could be a deadly threat and drawing from a concealed holster will ordinarily take much longer than the over-learned application of brakes during an emergency. Furthermore, how many times have you heard or read about people who survived a mass shooting say, "I thought it was a stunt or a joke," "I didn't think the gun was real," "It sounded like balloons popping, or a nail gun?" It appears it takes additional time for ordinary people to actually believe they are witnessing a deadly attack.

A. Action Beats Reaction – Police trainers teach their officers, "action always beats reaction." This phenomenon is often demonstrated as follows: Police trainers give two trainees dart guns, assigning one of them to be a cop and the other the bad guy. The cop trains his dart gun on the bad guy with his finger on the trigger. The bad guy raises his hands with the dart gun still in his hands and his finger on the trigger. The cop tells the bad guy to drop his gun. The bad guy says, "OK, don't shoot!" The trainer has secretly instructed the bad guy to shoot the cop rather than drop the dart gun. As the bad guy looks as if he's setting the dart gun down, he suddenly points and shoots. The cop is surprised when the bad guy is able to shoot him with the dart gun before the cop can pull the trigger of a gun already aimed at the bad guy. This is a result of the additional time it takes to perceive and react. Some trainers refer to the phenomenon as "being behind the perception and reaction curve." Defenders who don't account for this time lag when reacting to a deadly threat could acquire unhealthy blood-lead levels at 1500 fps. On the other hand, if courts don't allow defense attorneys and their experts to educate jurors about this factuality, innocents who understood and applied the concept during an attack will be unjustly convicted. We intend to continue to push the courts to allow expert testimony about this issue and give jurors instructions to take perception and reaction time into account in deciding what is reasonable and necessary.

B. The Non-Firearm Deadly Threat and the Tueller Drill – What if your opponent has an edged weapon or a blunt object? No problem, right? We've all heard the admonition, "Never bring a knife to a gun fight." Studies reveal how grave of a danger at close quarters a person with a knife or blunt object can be. A former Salt Lake County deputy by the name of Dennis Tueller has become nationally, if not internationally renowned for a study he undertook a number of years ago to find out why officers with guns were being severely injured or killed by assailants with edged weapons and bludgeons. Tueller's research and testing revealed that a person of average physical capability can begin at a dead stop and cover 21 feet in 1.5 seconds. He also found that it takes a typical officer at least 1.5 seconds to draw his pistol from an open holster and place two hits into the torso of a man-sized target. Tueller expressed his concern that two center torso hits do not always stop an attacker. His article was published in the March 1983 issue of SWAT Magazine.

The last thing you want when you're defending your life and your health is a tie. The law of self-defense should not require us to sustain a lethal blow just to prove that we are the good guys. Therefore, many concealed weapon instructors in Utah now consider the danger zone to be as far as 30 feet. That's just slightly more than 10 paces. This is especially relevant to the defender if he has no escape route. Unfortunately, we have not found any jury instructions or statutes that specifically address this concern. We continue the crusade to assert that there is no way the jury can understand or appreciate the perception-and-reaction problem unless the defendant is allowed to present expert-witness testimony. We used the defendant's concealed weapon instructor as an expert witness in the Schanze brandishing case, an abbreviated transcript of which appears in the following chapter. Understanding perception and reaction time is not only important to help you survive a violent attack, it's vital information for those judging your actions after the fact.

Pancho's Wisdom

IF judges had S-T-R-E-T-C-H-E-D the Right of Self-Defense as far as they've S-T-R-E-T-C-H-E-D the Interstate Commerce Clause, they would have made it a CRIME for citizens NOT to shoot rapists, robbers, kidnappers and carjackers ON SIGHT!

Pancho's Wisdom

You just might be a Gunnut if . . . your total PERCEPTION AND REACTION time is .15 seconds rather than 1.5 seconds.

12

THE "SUPERDELL" SCHANZE BRANDISHING CASE

Brandishing Incidents Common

Several national polls have measured the number of defensive uses of a firearm by American citizens to be between 760,000 to 3.6 million annually (Lott, John R., Jr., *More Guns, Less Crime* (1998) at 11). Ninety-eight percent of the time, the adversary leaves without a shot being fired (Lott, *More Guns, Less Crime, supra*, at 3). If these estimates are true, you are much more likely to be involved in a brandishing incident than in a shooting. You will eventually cause someone to lose his or her temper because of a mistake you made while driving. What happened in this case could happen to you. As you study the following case, ask yourself:

- If this happened to me, how might my responses calm rather than aggravate another who appears to be out of control?
- Assuming I have to "make ready" to prepare to defend myself or a loved one, am I prepared for the aftermath of the incident?
- Do I know what to say or not to say?
- If police interpret my actions as threatening deadly force to defend my property, what are the chances that I will be arrested or prosecuted?
- If the issue is the defense of property, is it worth it to assert my rights?

Who is "SUPERDELL?"

Consumers in the Salt Lake City area had the pleasure (or displeasure) of watching and hearing commercials on television and radio by a master of marketing who calls himself "SUPERDELL." In the matter of a few short years, Dell Buck Schanze became one of the most successful salesmen of desktop computers in the Intermountain West. His commercials were considered to be both tacky and brilliant because consumers remembered them. He was an ardent supporter of the right to keep and bear arms and championed the cause whenever he could work the topic into one of his radio or TV ads. Unfortunately, at the height of his notoriety, he was arrested for brandishing. It is a serious misdemeanor for which a person can lose his permit to carry a concealed weapon. Because of Mr. Schanze's notoriety, his case was elevated to high profile in the media in the Salt Lake City and Northern Utah area. He retained our firm to defend his case.

Charges and Elements of the Crime

Mr. Schanze was charged with violation of Utah's brandishing law which, at the time, required proof beyond a reasonable doubt that he had *drawn or exhibited a dangerous weapon in an angry and threatening manner or unlawfully used it in a fight or quarrel.* The story is told in two strikingly different accounts in the opening statements of the Deputy District Attorney (DDA) and defense counsel (Yours Truly). Opening statements generally consist of an easy-to-follow, story-book version of an incident. For simplicity, we've included only the opening statements. Witness testimony and closing arguments can be found by going to our website at www.firearmslaw.com.

Interesting Tactic for Defense Attorneys – Many criminal defense attorneys would try to exclude anyone remotely related to law enforcement from the jury. Answers to a jury questionnaire submitted to potential jurors before trial hinted that current and former police offers could be our most favorable jurors. They all strongly agreed that they would be willing to use a firearm to defend themselves or family members if necessary. Most of the other potential jurors did not answer the same question unequivocally. We kept all current and former police officers on the jury.

Orientation – Diagram and Photos

The accompanying diagram and photos in the following pages will help you understand the narrative and opening statements.

Narrative: On his way to take his daughter paragliding, Mr. Schanze (Defendant) drove his black Jaguar quite fast through a neighborhood adjacent to a paragliding recreation area. Three residents, upset about Schanze's speed, Clint S. and Scott T. in one vehicle, and Rob T. (not related to Scott) in another, drove to the paragliding park to express their displeasure. By the time they arrived, Mr. Schanze and his 8 year-old daughter had gotten out of the car. Clint and Scott confronted Schanze at **Position A** looking for an apology.

Unhappy about Schanze's response, Clint headed back towards the black Jaguar, at some point picking up a rock. He admitted threatening to break out the tail lights of the Jaguar. Mr. Schanze followed Clint and stopped at **Position B** with the black garbage cans between himself and Clint. As a result of Clint picking up the rock, Mr. Schanze took his pistol out of concealment as a precaution. Clint and Scott testified that Clint dropped the rock straight down after seeing Mr. Schanze's pistol. The rock was discovered by police and photographed at **Position C**. Clint testified he was at **Position D**, directly behind the

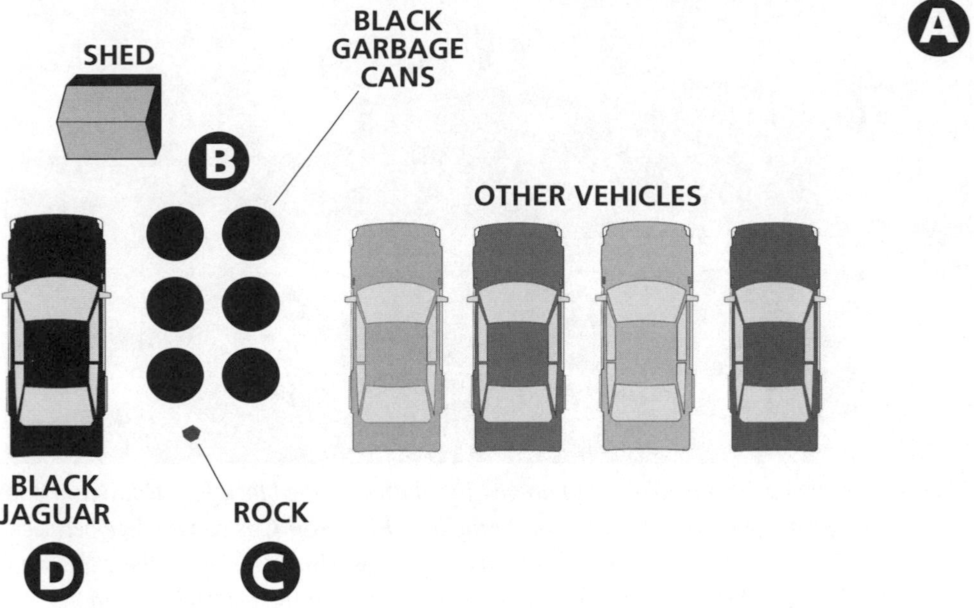

A Where Schanze was first confronted by Clint and Scott near where witness Jenny was sitting.

B Where Schanze ended up after he followed Clint toward the Jaguar and where he was seen holding a pistol.

C Where police found the rock which Clint said he dropped "straight down." We believe Clint was here when he faced Schanze with the rock.

D Clint said he was standing behind the Jaguar with the rock.

---

car, when he dropped the rock. No explanation was ever given why the rock was found at **Position C**. It was undisputed that Mr. Schanze's gun did not come out of his pocket until after Clint picked up the rock.

Witness Jenny C. was somewhere near **Position A** when she saw a gun in Mr. Schanze's hand. Schanze's daughter was nearby when Clint and Scott first confronted Schanze at **Position A**, but the testimony was unclear as to where she went from that instant. A friend of the family, a young boy named Cameron, was thought to be somewhere near the small storage shed that looks like an outhouse when Schanze followed Clint to the car.

Shows how the garbage cans were arranged in relation to the black Jag. ***Position B*** *is shown just over the hood of the car and to the left.* ***Position C*** *is somewhere between the tall, bald officer and the officer with the cap.* ***Position A*** *is near the chair and umbrella shown in the background. The neighborhood is in the far background.*

Shows officers standing at ***Position C****. The rock is visible between the feet of the officer with the cap and with his back to the photographer.*

Another view of the rock.

Prosecutor's Opening Statement

Key: ■ commentary ■ actual transcript

Mr. Bown: [The Deputy District Attorney, an aggressive advocate who uses a "folksy" style that is very effective.] Good morning. The reason why we're here today is because the defendant over there threatened somebody with a gun not in self-defense and then lied about it. [A skilled prosecutor will kick you in the teeth right out of the chute like a Brahma bull on steroids.] On May 21, 2005 up at the hang-gliding park at the South of the valley, three individuals, Rob T., Scott T. and Clint S. saw somebody going through their neighborhood at excessive speed in a black Jaguar. Concerned about it, they followed that car. There's only one way to go up Steep Mountain Drive to the park... Now Rob T. went separately.

He showed up first, confronts the defendant and asked him why he drove through the neighborhood so fast. In the meantime, he's yelling through his car door, ...still seated... He says, "What are you doing, why are you doing this?" At that point, the defendant—he's with his daughter, she has a harness on, probably to go paragliding—walk away from Rob. Now, at that point Scott and Clint come up. They drove up in Clint's car; they are neighbors; they live right next to each other. They show up and ask Rob - because he had parked right next to this black Jaguar—"where is the driver of that vehicle?" ... He points in the direction. They go up and ask the defendant, "Can we talk to you?" And they start to have the discussion again about the excessive speed ... he was going through the neighborhood. There is yelling, arguing. If you wonder where his daughter is, she's walked away at this point. They say their piece and then Mr. Schanze goes, "If you have $1000 each, I'll teach you how to drive." [I'm sure the jury did not like this answer coming from what they perceived to be a rich computer super-salesman. We were stuck with this statement and the DDA made good use of it early in his Opening Statement.] ...

Clint says, "Fine we'll just call it even and I'll break out your tail lights." And he walks away from him. Now at some point a rock is picked up—the witnesses will not be clear on where the rock is picked up. But they're walking away from him. As they get closer to the defendant's vehicle, there is another argument where Clint and the defendant argue about the excessive speed again.

Editing Disclaimer: There was no court-reporter-generated written transcript, only an audio DVD. Our transcribers reported that the audio was difficult to understand. They often had to guess about what was said. When I proofread the typed transcript, many words and phrases were obviously erroneous. There were hundreds of superfluous words, and the testimony contained poor grammar, stuttering, and questions and answers that were corrected in the middle of a sentence. To aid in understanding, these errors were omitted. Marking all the changes would have been annoying. First names of witnesses were used to keep it simple. Our intent was to clarify without changing the substance of what was said. Argument and testimony not related to the brandishing charge were omitted. The transcript is a public record for anyone who wants to buy and listen to the whole thing.

Clint's looking for an apology. Doesn't get it again. He walks to the back of the vehicle, with his back turned or [at] least not looking at Mr. Schanze. He picks up the rock—that's what they'll say—after which there is a paraglider who comes in. Now they never found this paraglider. Scott watches this paraglider come down, and as the paraglider is walking between Scott and Clint he says, "He has a gun!" After which they turn around and they see the gun.

We also have an eyewitness who wasn't involved in the altercation. Her name is Jenny C. She doesn't know anybody, the defense, or the victims in this case. She'll tell you that he pointed the gun at a 90° angle like this. [Positioning with one hand, elbow cocked and gun pointed forward, like in a quick draw.] Clint who sees it a little bit later says the gun is up here, like a "don't you dare" look. [Gun laying against chest with barrel pointed up toward left shoulder, but high enough over the garbage can Mr. Shanze was standing behind that Clint could see it.] Clint and Scott never threatened the defendant. They never threatened bodily injury to him. They never even touched him. That's why he's charged with threatening with a dangerous weapon in a fight or quarrel. Because he pulled a weapon after them when there was no self-defense. [The state's theory was that the gun was exhibited to threaten in *defense of property,* not in defense of any person.]

[. . . argument re false statement omitted.]

And for those reasons...I'll be asking you to convict the defendant of threatening with a dangerous weapon in a fight or quarrel... Now just a caution—this may be disappointing to you—but this won't be like CSI, it won't be like Law and Order. [There won't be music] that rises to [a crescendo to] let you know when an important point is being made. You will not have the ominous music right before the verdict comes in, and you won't solve this in one act. So I ask you to listen to the evidence and at the end, I'll ask you to convict the defendant. Thank you.

Judge: Thank you Mr. Bown. Mr. Vilos.

Defense Opening Statement

Mr. Vilos: Thank you, Your Honor.

Your Honor, Counsel, good morning ladies and gentlemen of the jury. [These are the most exciting words a trial lawyer speaks during his career. Most trial attorneys believe that the opening statement is the most important part of the case. It's a time when jurors begin to form mental images about the story. Humans tend to believe most what we hear first. After such a powerful opening by the DDA, it was crucial to get our point across right here, right now or lose the case! Time to stand and deliver or all is lost!]

...

This is *not* [italics shows voice emphasis] a case of threatening with a weapon. *This is a case of a man taking reasonable precautions to protect himself, two children, and his property from three angry strangers acting like vigilantes, taking the law into their own hands.* [My one-sentence summary of the case to counter the DDA's. Notice I characterized the "victims" as vigilantes and rode that theme like a buckaroo through the whole case.] One of whom had a rock, big and sharp enough to cause serious bodily injury or death; and he was within the distance that he could do that in a heartbeat. [When I said "that" I acted out throwing a rock like a baseball.]

Now, before I get into the story on the Steep Mountain, let me talk to you about what preceded this. Years ago, when Mr. Schanze got his concealed weapons permit, he came to know, like many or most of Utah's 68,000 concealed weapon permit holders, that a rock in the hand is more lethal than a gun in the pocket at any distance under 30 feet. [As I ran this case by everyone who would listen before the trial, they kept saying, "Rock vs. gun, come on, gun wins every time." It was vital I put that misconception to rest right up front.] Some of you [speaking directly to the law enforcement guys on the jury] may recognize the principle referred to in law enforcement circles as the Tueller drill. Sometimes it's referred to as the 21-foot rule. The principle is that a man with a sharp object or an edged weapon can traverse 21 feet and kill an officer before the officer can take his gun out of his open holster. [Three current or former law enforcement officers were now seated on our jury.] Now the concealed weapon permit industry has extended that distance for obvious reasons. Because when you're carrying a concealed defensive firearm, that firearm is not readily accessible; it's concealed. So the procedure taught to students is that you take the defensive firearm from a *position of difficult access* and you take it out of concealment to a *place of ready access*. Just in case the unspeakable happens. *The purpose of taking your firearm out of concealment is not to threaten with a weapon.* The purpose is to *make sure that you have ready access so you can react*... it's like taking your foot off the accelerator if you see someone moving through a stop sign and think they might go through—you take a *reasonable precaution.* [Giving the non-law-enforcement jurors something they could identify with—perception and reaction time related to everyday driving.]

Now let me go to that fateful day, May 21st, 2005. Mr. Schanze [is] a very busy man. It's difficult for people to find time to spend with their children. He made arrangements to take his daughter, who is eight years old . . . paragliding. For her first flight, she would fly with an instructor. He was late that day and he had promised her and it was getting late. [It was important to humanize the defendant whom the DDA had portrayed as a reckless, uncaring speed demon.] This happened at about 6:30 in the evening. And so he's in a hurry. He rushes home, picks her up and they're driving to the park and he does speed. And he has, prior to this argument in this case pled guilty to 50 miles an hour in a 25 mile an hour speed zone.

Now, the evidence will show that when Mr. Schanze went through this neighborhood, his was the only black Jaguar that had passed through. Nobody else said anything about any other black Jaguar. The evidence will show that when Mr. Rob T., the first confronter, goes to the hang gliding park, he is very angry. And he drives up and he sees Mr. Schanze's car parked there. It's the only black Jaguar among all the cars in the park. And the license plate is very visible to Mr. T. At that point we have a positive ID on the car. He parks right behind the car, rolls down his window, and starts yelling profanities at Mr. Schanze in the presence of his daughter. Now Mr. Schanze's object that day was not to confront him. His object was to have a daddy-daughter date and to avoid any conflict, and so he walks away with his daughter. Just before that, however, the 11 year old boy whose family had been visiting Mr. Schanze had greeted Mr. Schanze and was standing in the area where you'll see there is a little hang glider storage shed, there is a sign here, some garbage cans and Mr. Schanze's car is here—this is not to scale [I make a rough drawing of the bird's eye view of the incident, similar to the drawing above.]. 11-year-old Cameron is right here [somewhere between the storage shed and the Jag] greets Mr. Schanze and is in this area, he's playing in this area. Now, the evidence will show Mr. Schanze walking away. He's walking over here **[Position A]** ... Miss Jenny C. is watching the paragliders ... She says she sees two very angry men coming up to Mr. Schanze and his daughter, and again they're using profanities. And yes Mr. Schanze did finally say something. He didn't threaten; he didn't make any physical threats; he didn't make any verbal threats. He's trying to get to the hangliding lesson and ... Clint doesn't like what he says so at that point Jenny says Clint picks up a rock and threatens to kick [kicking with my foot to show jury] out the tail lights of the car.

So there is no dispute as to whether a rock was picked up. There is one thing that you will absolutely know at the end of this trial. It is that *at no time did the gun come out of the pocket until Clint picked up the rock.* As soon as the rock was dropped and Mr. Schanze was *confident that there was no longer a danger, the gun went back in the pocket.*

Mr. Schanze then went and took his daughter on a hang-gliding flight and tried to avoid the conflict. [We re-wrote this opening statement at least a dozen times; every word was calculated to elicit a favorable response.] The evidence will show—one of the elements of this crime is you've got to be angry and threatening—it wasn't Mr. Schanze who was angry and threatening it was Clint. He was aggressive, he was *angry,* he was *unpredictable,* and he was violent. Violence is violence. And Mr. Schanze didn't know what Clint was liable to do because he didn't know him. And he was within this distance [referring to a drawing showing how close **Position C** is to **Position B**.]. We'll see from the evidence it was Clint who picked the fight, it was Clint who went "Postal," it was Clint who first picked up a deadly weapon.

...Clint started walking towards this area here [from **Position A** toward **Position B**]. We don't know where the little girl went specifically, but we know that she was there [at **Position A** for an instant]. And I think Jenny ... women ... watch where the children are, shall say that the daughter was here [**Position A**] and 11 year-old Cameron was over here [near storage shed]. And as Clint was walking towards the storage shed, he was also walking towards 11-year-old Cameron. So Mr. Schanze follows him. When you're involved in an incident like this, fight or flight, and you've got adrenaline flowing, you fall back on your training. [Police officers hear this in training all the time – I know, I've trained with them.] And his training taught him to get behind cover, and he went behind cover behind the garbage cans [**Position B**]. Clint will say that he left this area [**Position A**] and at some point he saw Mr. Schanze following him. Keep in mind he said, "I'm going to <u>kick</u> out your tail lights." He didn't say, "I'm going to bust them out" like the prosecutor said. You'll see that his original statement was, "I'm going to *kick* out your tail lights." So then he looks back and sees Mr. Schanze coming behind him and he picks up a rock. Well if the *shoe is for the tail lights, what's the rock for?*

And he's within a car length [from Mr. Schanze], probably less. You'll see where the rock was. He said he dropped the rock. You'll see that he was facing Mr. Schanze with the rock positioned like this within probably 15 to 20 feet, let alone 30 feet. And within a heartbeat that rock can become a missile. The law doesn't require a man, a father, to take that kind of risk and not take reasonable precautions.

The evidence will show that of the three confronters, three men against one, *two out of the three didn't even see the gun*. And not only that, the evidence will show that the third man may not have even seen a gun if the paraglider hadn't seen it. Now the paraglider didn't come forth and say, "Gee, someone's threatening me with a gun." The evidence is going to be that *it was happenstance that Clint even saw the gun*. And that's because the gun was not held up to threaten. It was held for easy access just in case the unspeakable happened as a result of the actions of a very irrational person, in a very short period of time. So the evidence will show that there was no attempt to threaten and the evidence will show that Mr. Schanze simply took reasonable precautions to protect himself, the two children and his property. And if your actions are reasonable, they are justifiable and if they are justifiable, ladies and gentlemen, *there is no crime*. I look forward to reviewing the evidence with you in this case today. Thank you very much. [That last phrase was NOT an Elvis impersonation. Honest.]

[After a day and a half of testimony from Clint, Scott, Rob, Jenny, a number of police officers, our expert and Mrs. Schanze, the jury was instructed by the judge and the attorneys gave their closing arguments. We intend to post at least an abbreviated transcript of the trial and closing arguments on our website shortly after this book is published. I made a tactical decision to not have Mr. Schanze testify and explained why in our closing argument.]

The Verdict on the Issue of Brandishing

[After the arguments everyone packs up, leaves the courthouse and the attorneys give the judge's clerk their cell phone number. It's nice to have such grueling work like a trial behind you. Most people don't realize the time it takes to prepare and conduct one of these cases. It's exhausting. So anyway, everyone goes out for a snack, lunch, dinner, whatever and breathes a sigh of relief. But when that cell phone jingles and the clerk's expressionless voice confirms, "We have a verdict," the ol' ticker throttles into a fusillade of arrhythmias reminiscent of the drum solo in *Wipeout*!]

May 11, 2006; 2:12:54 pm.

Judge: This is the continuation of the jury trial in the matter of State vs. Dell Buck Schanze. . . .I have been advised by the bailiff that the jury has reached a verdict and that's why we have reassembled everyone here. . .

Bailiff: All rise... [The jury enters. Both attorneys and the defendant forget they're not breathing. The courthouse EMTs are standing behind my fat a## with the paddles ready just in case this old dog slumps.] Please be seated.

Judge: Let the record reflect that we have been joined by the jury in this matter the defendant is present, Mr. Schanze. He is represented by counsel, Mr. Vilos. Counsel for the state, Mr. Bown is present, as are all 6 of our jurors. We dismissed out 2 alternate jurors, I have met with them, thanked them for their service. We invited the 6 remaining jurors to deliberate. . . .And have you reached a verdict in this case?

Jury Foreperson: Yes, we have Your Honor.

Judge: Would you hand that to the bailiff?

Judge: Let's see, I would invite the defendant, Mr. Schanze, Mr. Vilos if you would like to stand and I am going to invite the clerk to read the verdict . . .

Clerk: The State of Utah v. Dell Buck Schanze. We the jury in the above case find the defendant, Dell Buck Schanze, ***NOT GUILTY*** Of Threatening With Or Using A Dangerous Weapon In A Fight Or Quarrel as charged in Count One of the information. [Whew! We considered this a major victory for gun owners in the State of Utah. A jury had agreed under these circumstances that accessing a concealed weapon when confronted by an armed, threatening person was a reasonable precaution and not brandishing. Every gun owner in the state owes Dell Schanze a "thank you" for hanging tough on this issue. This verict sends a message to police and prosecutors that jurors may consider it reasonable for citizens to access their concealed weapons as a precaution.]

13

DOMESTIC VIOLENCE AND BATTERED WOMAN'S SYNDROME

A. The Social Problem

To tell you the truth, we've been losing sleep trying to decide how to present the topic of domestic violence in a way that makes a difference. By "make a difference" we mean making family life in our country safer from acts of violence against wives, girlfriends and children. We're not sexist and recognize that it may occasionally be the wife that is abusive. But most often it involves abusive husbands who treat their wives and children as property or, worse yet, cattle. In most cases, substance abuse, particularly alcoholism, increases the potential lethality. We hear about murder-suicides frequently in the news. If wives and girlfriends are not killed, they are often tortured and mutilated. Jealous boyfriends become obsessed with the thought, "If I can't 'have' her, no one will." In their twisted tyranny they have shot, slashed or burned girlfriends to ensure that no other man would ever want the ghastly-disfigured object of their obsession. The problem is so horrible that the legal community must do more.

As the unfortunate *Sands* case below shows, some women take the abuse until they explode with uncharacteristic deadly fury. Wives can become so convinced of their worthlessness that they can't imagine living without their strong, dominating, but cruel husbands. The abusive cycle occurs over and over without the spiritually broken wife being able to muster enough courage and strength to get out of the destructive relationship. To add to her reluctance, he tells her that if she leaves he'll kill her, the kids, her family and maybe even himself. After several beatings, the wife begins to develop a sixth sense about when threats shift to acts of physical violence. The injuries become increasingly more painful and severe. Finally, she cannot imagine herself surviving if she waits until his next attack. So she ventilates his virileness while he's burping Budweiser or cogitating cocaine, hovering horizontal, in a state of ahhhhh after his latest sexual assault that has left her bleeding, bruised, broken, and hopeless.

When they snap, these gals shoot, stab, run over, or burn their husbands with gasoline. Some have hired hit men. Almost all of these women are convicted of murder or manslaughter. If they are acquitted, it's usually by reason of insanity that involves incarceration in a mental institution.

B. The Legal Problem

Before we look at possible solutions, let us give you a more in depth look at the shocking facts from actual cases. It's hard to imagine this kind of brutality in a supposedly civilized society. *Commonwealth v. Sands*, 553 S.E.2d 733 (Va. 2001) is an appalling case of years of physical beatings and prison-like domination. Following are the facts recited by the appeals court. We substituted the woman's first name instead of using her legal designation, appellant.

> [T]he evidence showed that Victoria [the wife] and Sands [the husband] were married in 1983. Two years after they were married, Sands began beating Victoria. The beatings became progressively worse over time and, at the end, they occurred on a daily basis. Sands was not gainfully employed for the last eight to ten years of their marriage, during which time he used and sold cocaine, marijuana and moonshine. [Not your typical small business owner scratching out a living from home. So you ask, "Why didn't she just leave the dirt-bag drug dealer?" The next couple of paragraphs provide some insight.]
>
> Victoria wanted to take her four-year-old son, leave Sands and get a divorce. Sands told her she could not leave and threatened repeatedly to kill her and her parents if she did. She said she believed Sands would have found and killed her if she had gone to a shelter. Sands also refused Victoria's requests that he leave the marital residence.
>
> Whenever she broached the subject of divorce, he beat her. . .
>
> On August 12, 1998, Victoria spoke to her parents and asked for their help in trying to get Sands arrested for his illegal activities, in the hope that his arrest and conviction would free her from his repeated abuse and threats. However, on August 17, before Victoria's parents were able to take any significant action, they were seriously injured in an automobile accident. Victoria knew she couldn't do anything further on that front because, if she took any direct action to report Sands' activities to the police herself, she believed Sands would find out and kill her.
>
> On August 17, 1998, Sands accompanied Victoria to the hospital in North Carolina to visit her injured parents. Sands returned home that day while Victoria remained with her parents. When Victoria and Sands spoke several times that week, Sands expressed his an-

ger at the fact that Victoria wanted to stay to care for her hospitalized parents rather than to come home to him. When Victoria returned home on the evening of Saturday, August 22, 1998, intending to stay only overnight before returning to help her parents in North Carolina, Sands was angry because she had been gone and did not call to say she was coming home. Sands said he had been up all week since returning home the previous Monday. Sands went into a rage, beat Victoria, and threatened to kill her, saying, "you will die, I promise you, you will die." Victoria did not flee the marital home because she was afraid Sands would come after her and kill her as he had threatened. Between Saturday night and Sunday morning, Sands hit Victoria "[h]undreds and hundreds of times," and threatened her with a gun he always carried, which he repeatedly put up her nose.

At approximately 11:00 a.m. on Sunday, August 23, Victoria tried to hide Sands' gun, and the couple got into another argument on the back porch of their home. Despite the fact that Victoria held the firearm during this time, Sands pushed her into a sink and threw her down five or six concrete steps. Victoria found herself lying on the ground with Sands sitting on top of her holding the firearm. After Sands pinned Victoria to the ground, he again told her he would kill her, and he fired two shots into the ground near her. [Can you believe this happens in modern-day America?]

. . .

Shortly thereafter, Victoria's aunt, Sallie Hodges, came to the house to get the couple's son so she could care for him while Victoria returned to North Carolina to look after her parents. Victoria appeared "sad" and the side of her face looked bruised. Sands was pacing and calling Victoria derogatory names. Sands told Hodges he would not allow Victoria to leave. He then said to Hodges, "I'll kill you and your whole family... I've knocked off a few [people] and I can knock off a few more too." Victoria refused to allow Hodges to take the couple's son, and Hodges left.

When Victoria's brother arrived to take Victoria to visit their parents, Sands would not allow Victoria to leave and told her brother that he would take Victoria to North Carolina himself.

Sands remained home all day, where he used cocaine and drank alcohol. Periodically, he lay down to watch television in the bedroom for five or ten minutes, but he always got up to beat Victoria again and threaten her with the gun. He continued this pattern throughout the day. As the day progressed, Sands continued to tell Victoria he was going to kill her, and Victoria said she believed he was going to do it.

At about 10:00 p.m., Victoria was able to use the telephone. She called Hodges to come get the couple's four-year-old son and take him to her house. While Victoria was on the phone with Hodges, Donald Wright, the couple's neighbor, came to the couple's house and agreed to take the child to Hodges' house. Victoria said she wanted her son away from the house because she "sensed" Sands was going to kill her. After Victoria called Hodges, she then called her sister-in-law, Angela Shelton, and asked Shelton to come to her house. Before Shelton arrived, Sands beat Victoria again. During this beating, which Victoria described as the "longest," Sands hit Victoria's head with the butt of his gun and again put the barrel of the gun up her nose. He then returned to his position in the bedroom in front of the television.

When Shelton arrived, Victoria was crying and upset. Shelton and Victoria went into the bathroom where Shelton helped Victoria undress so they could look at Victoria's bruised and beaten body. After seeing the extent of her injuries, Victoria started shaking and said, "the devil, look at what the devil's done to me. I've got to get this devil out of my house. He's evil." Victoria then "ran out of the bathroom and the door of the living room, . . . came back to the kitchen, . . . opened the cabinet door, . . . got the gun, . . . went to the bedroom and . . . shot [Sands]" five times while he was lying in bed, awake, watching television. After Victoria shot Sands, she walked out of the bedroom, laid the gun down, and called the police.

An officer who saw Victoria at the scene after the shooting testified that her bruises were readily apparent and that her nose was "twisted to the side." He thought her ribs and nose were broken.

After the shooting, Victoria was examined by an emergency room physician, who found that she had "multiple bruises and contusions throughout her body, most of which were extensive in the upper arms and in the flanks." The deceased had bruising on the first and second knuckles of his right hand and on the first knuckle of his left hand.

Victoria's mother, aunt, and sister-in-law testified that they had seen bruises on Victoria numerous times in the months preceding the shooting, and Victoria's aunt and sister-in-law testified that they observed bruises on her the day of the shooting. Internal citations omitted. *Sands v. Com.*, 536 S.E.2d 461, 463-466, Va.App.,2000. [Don't forget, there are usually two different stories in cases like this. The story just recited was in a light most favorable to Victoria because of a legal requirement. Because defendant's testimony attacked the "victim's" character, the state probably put on rebuttal evidence through members of his family that he was the perfect husband, sang in the church choir every Sunday, never laid a hand on the woman and that white powder CSI found all over the house was either her cocaine (her bruises were from getting high and running into doors!), or a sugar substitute he used on the cereal he ate three times a day because she refused to cook for His Royal Highness!]

Victoria was convicted of first-degree murder. [What!?] Her conviction was upheld by the Supreme Court of Virginia saying she was not entitled to a self-defense jury instruction because His Excellency was reclined in front of the flat screen, high on cocaine instead of committing an imminent, "overt act" like attacking her with a weapon. Without a jury instruction telling them they could find her not guilty by reason of self-defense, the jury had no choice but to convict Victoria. This shocking case illustrates how the traditional definition of imminence falls short of giving abused women a shot at convincing juries they had no choice but to resort to the use of deadly force. Virginia's self-defense law gave this woman two choices, assuming she truly believed her husband's death threats: (1) Try to leave and take the chance of him killing her and her family, (2) Kill him and spend the next several decades in prison while someone else raised her little boy. She chose the latter.

What is Battered Woman Syndrome?

Black's law dictionary describes battered woman syndrome as "a constellation of medical and psychological conditions of a woman who has suffered physical, sexual, or emotional abuse at the hands of a spouse or lover." (Black's Law Dictionary 8th ed. 2004). A Maryland court recently penned a learned discourse on the subject of battered woman's syndrome as follows:

> "Dr. Lenore Walker, an academic and clinical psychologist, is usually credited with first describing the battered spouse syndrome, which she called the "battered woman syndrome." *See* Lenore E. Walker, THE BATTERED WOMAN (1979); also THE BATTERED WOMAN SYNDROME (1984) and *Battered Woman Syndrome and Self-Defense,* 6 Notre Dame J.L. Ethics & Pub. Pol'y 321 (1992). Dr. Walker identified a "battered woman" as one who is repeatedly subjected to any forceful physical or psychological behavior by a man in order to coerce her to do something he wants her to do without any concern for her rights. She described three phases to the battering cycle, which, she said, may vary in both time and intensity. Phase I she referred to as the "tension-building" phase, in which minor incidents of physical, sexual, or emotional abuse occur. The woman is not severely abused, but the batterer begins to express hostility toward her. *See* Hope Toffel, *Crazy Women, Unharmed Men, and Evil*

Children: Confronting the Myths About Battered People Who Kill Their Abusers, And The Argument For Extending Battering Syndrome Self-Defenses To All Victims Of Domestic Violence, 70 S. Cal. L.Rev. 337, 349 (1996), citing Walker, THE BATTERED WOMAN SYNDROME, *supra,* at 95. Phase II consists of an acute battering incident, in which the batterer "typically unleashes a barrage of verbal and physical aggression that can leave the woman severely shaken and injured." Toffel, supra, 70 S. Cal. L.Rev. at 349, citing Walker, THE BATTERED WOMAN SYNDROME, *supra,* at 96. Phase III is a contrition stage, in which the batterer apologizes, seeks forgiveness, and promises to change. The apparent transformation of the abuser back into a loving partner, according to Walker, "provides the positive reinforcement for remaining in the relationship." *Id.*

The essence of the syndrome is that this cycle repeats, and, indeed, Walker asserts that the syndrome does not exist unless it has repeated at least once. Worse, perhaps, than the mere repetition, is the fact that, over time, the cycle becomes more intense, more frequent, more violent, and often more lethal." *State v. Smullen,* 844 A.2d 429 at 440 and 441 (Md. 2004).

Reasonableness and Imminence Can Be Different for Battered Women

The following quote from an open-minded Oklahoma court explains how the concept of reasonableness and imminence can be different for the battered woman:

> "For the battered woman, if there is no escape or sense of safety, then the next attack, which could be fatal or cause serious bodily harm, is imminent. Based on the traditionally accepted definition of imminent and its functional derivative, a battered woman, to whom the threat of serious bodily harm or death is always imminent, would be precluded from asserting the defense of self-defense.
>
> Under our "hybrid" reasonableness standard, the meaning of *imminent* must necessarily envelope the battered woman's perceptions based on all the facts and circumstances of his or her relationship with the victim. In *Women's Self-defense Cases: Theory and Practice* (1981), Elizabeth Bochnak writes:
>
> > The battered woman learns to recognize the small signs that precede periods of escalated violence. She learns to distinguish subtle changes in tone of voice, facial expression, and levels of danger. She is in a position to know, perhaps with greater certainly than someone attacked by a stranger, that the batterer's threat is real and will be acted upon.

> Thus, according to the author, an abused woman may kill her mate during the period of threat that precedes a violent incident, right before the violence escalates to the more dangerous levels of an acute battering episode. Or, she may take action against him during a lull in an assaultive incident, or after it has culminated, in an effort to prevent a recurrence of the violence. And so, the issue is not whether the danger was in *fact* imminent, but whether, given the circumstances as she perceived them, the defendant's *belief was reasonable that the danger was imminent.*" (Emphasis in original.) *Bechtel v. State*, 840 P.2d 1 (Okl.Cr. 1992).

Although the Oklahoma court refers to the standard as a "hybrid" standard, it is not so awfully different from a concept we see in the homicide instructions of some of the states. For example, California's jury instruction, **505. Justifiable Homicide: Self-Defense or Defense of Another,** provides in part:

> When deciding whether defendant's beliefs were reasonable, you [the jury] must consider **all the circumstances as they were known to and appeared to the defendant** and consider what a **reasonable person in a similar situation with similar knowledge** would have believed. (Emphasis added.)

It's still a reasonable person standard in a sense. But it's a reasonable person having experienced the same treatment under the same circumstances for the same amount of time as the defendant. Did she act reasonably by killing her husband believing she would die if she waited for an "overt act" such as him picking up a gun and aiming at her head? It would be hard to imagine jurors understanding how years of abuse can alter a person's perceptions of reasonableness or imminence unless courts allow expert testimony from learned professionals who have studied the effects of years of serious physical abuse. Unfortunately, not all courts in all states allow expert testimony.

We don't want to give the impression that abused wives never win their cases. They do, but very seldom. In stark contrast to the *Sands* case above, a court in Virginia's sister state, West Virginia, overturned a conviction of first degree murder of a woman who shot her husband during a night of terror chillingly comparable to the facts in *Sands.* Following is an excerpt from *State v. Harden*, 679 S.E.2d 628 (W.Va.,2009):

> On September 5, 2004, the defendant was arrested upon her admission to having shot and killed her husband, Danuel Harden. At trial, the defendant asserted a claim of self-defense, arguing that her actions precipitously followed a "night of domestic terror" that ended only when the defendant shot and killed the decedent... the decedent, while drinking heavily (with a blood alcohol count ultimately

reaching 0.22% at the time of his death) subjected the defendant to a several-hour-long period of physical and emotional violence. This violence included the decedent brutally beating the defendant with the butt and barrel of a shotgun, brutally beating the defendant with his fists, and sexually assaulting the defendant. An emergency room physician at Cabell Huntington Hospital, who examined the defendant on the morning of the shooting, testified that the defendant "had contusions of both orbital areas, the right upper arm, a puncture wound with a foreign body of the right forearm, contusions of her chest, left facial cheek, the left upper lip" and that "X-rays done at the time demonstrated a nasal fracture."

In addition to the physical violence summarized above, the evidence adduced at trial also showed that the decedent repeatedly threatened to kill the defendant and the defendant's nine-year-old son B.H., ten-year-old daughter A.H., and ten-year-old B.K. (a friend of A.H.'s who had been invited for a "sleep over"). This evidence included testimony from two of the children. B.H. testified to seeing and hearing the decedent say to the defendant "I am going to go get the gun and shoot you" and that the decedent did, in fact, go to a back room in the defendant's home and get a shotgun, and returned to the room with the gun where the decedent subsequently struck the defendant with the butt of the gun in the shoulders and arms while she was seated in a recliner. In addition to B.H.'s testimony, B.K. also testified that she was frightened by what she could hear from her bedroom and had difficulty falling asleep, and that after finally falling asleep, she was awakened by more sounds of fighting, at one point over-hearing the defendant say to the decedent that "she didn't want to get killed with her two kids."

It is conceded by the State that the defendant suffered a "night of domestic terror." During its opening statement the State described the evening's violence as a "knock-down-drag-out" fight. By the time of the State's closing argument, the State conceded to the jury that "Yes, she had a night of terror." In its brief to this Court, the State concedes that the decedent's death followed an "evening of physical and sexual abuse."

Notwithstanding the fact that it does not dispute that the defendant endured a night of extreme violence at the hands of the decedent, the State nonetheless argues that the defendant's claim of self-defense is "untenable." In its closing argument, the State argued to the jury that "the law ... on self-defense says that in order to use deadly force in self-defense you must find that the apprehension existed at the time the defendant attacked, or in this case shot, the [decedent]." In addition, the State maintained that the defendant did not have a reasonable basis to apprehend any danger from the decedent at the time she used deadly force against the decedent because there had been a "cooling off" period, and the evidence showed that the decedent was lying down on a couch possibly "asleep" or, alternately, possibly "passed out drunk" when the defendant shot him. The State further argued to the jury that the defendant's use of deadly force was not reasonable because the defendant could have retreated from any danger posed by the decedent, evidenced by the fact that the decedent "is on that couch with a BAC of .22 [blood alcohol content – two to three times higher than legally drunk in many states] and she has got control of that shotgun, she ... could have called the law, and she could have walked out of that trailer. Period. But she didn't."

State v. Harden, 679 S.E.2d 628, 631-633. After her conviction of murder, in an appeal to the Supreme Court of West Virginia, Mrs. Harden insisted she had killed her husband in self-defense. The court agreed:

"Our law entitled the defendant under the circumstances of this case to her subjective belief that she was in imminent danger of death or serious bodily injury and to abate that threat, without retreating, with the use of deadly force. Under the circumstances shown by the evidence in this case, the defendant's use of deadly force to protect herself, without retreating, is *subjectively* reasonable... Additionally, the overwhelming evidence demonstrates that *any reasonable person similarly situated* would have believed that death or serious bodily injury were imminent." (Emphasis added.)

State v. Harden, 679 S.E.2d 628, 647 (W.Va. 2009). The court in *Harden* set forth a subjective and objective test for reasonableness and imminence and held that the defendant had met both tests.

"First, a defendant's belief that death or serious bodily injury was imminent must be shown to have been subjectively reasonable, which is to say that a defendant actually believed, based upon all the circumstances perceived by him or her at the time deadly force was used, that such force was necessary to prevent death or serious bodily injury. Second, that the defendant's belief must be objectively reasonable when considering all of the circumstances surrounding the defendant's use of deadly force, which is to say that another person, similarly situated, could have reasonably formed the same belief."

State v. Harden, 679 S.E.2d 628, 634 (W.Va. 2009).

E. Recent Improvements

Fortunately, more states' self-defense laws are beginning to broaden their statutory definitions of imminence to take into account the case of repeated abuse and a history of violence. For example, Kentucky law has a spousal abuse clause that says, "imminent can be inferred from a past pattern of repeated serious abuse."

Before states like West Virginia and Kentucky addressed this issue and expanded the definition of "imminent," it was quite impossible for a woman to win a case of self-defense unless the jury was so shocked by the abuse that they disregarded the law (sometimes referred to as "juror nullification"). Now at least there is a possibility of a not-guilty verdict, although far too few states have expanded their self-defense laws to address spousal abuse. Maryland and Ohio have adopted a helpful definition of Battered Woman Syndrome (BWS) in their codes. Unfortunately, in Ohio, the defendant to prove self-defense by a preponderance of evidence (more likely than not), which somewhat lessens the advantage of allowing evidence of BWS to be admitted. Despite improvements in the law, you'll notice that in virtually every case we've reported, the defendant wife was tried, convicted and had to appeal.

F. Our Advice

If an abused woman is threatened with serious injury or death, she must (1) call the local police, report the threat and describe in detail her husband/boyfriend's history of abuse, (2) immediately file for a Protective Order requiring him to stay away and not possess weapons, (3) establish a *separate* household.

Warning About Protective Orders – Unfortunately, far too many women believe that a court order will protect them from physical harm. IT WON'T! The dirty, mean, cantankerous, abusive, possessive, dominating, tyrannical SOB is either willing to do life without parole for murder, wants to die in a blaze of glory in a gun battle with police, or plans on putting a bullet through his own head after he puts her backside on ice. Do you think he cares that violating the protective order could result in a felony conviction?

Why in the world would we suggest she get a protective order if it won't protect her physically? It's to protect her LEGALLY if she later has to pockmark his posterior with platinum pellets. The holding of an older Pennsylvania case supports the wisdom of an abused spouse getting a separate residence if she thinks she may have to use deadly force to survive her husband's attempt to kill her:

> In the instant case, however, the mere fact that deceased and defendant were husband and wife does not compel the application of the ordinary rules of self-defense on the theory that each had an equal right to be on the premises. *Here the defendant and deceased had been separated and defendant had maintained her separate residence.*

> Because of the estrangement and separation of the husband and wife, it does not appear that both had an equal right to be there. *Clearly, the husband, under the circumstances, could be regarded as an intruder in his wife's home,* and the jury should have been instructed that if they found the husband was an intruder and that the defendant had reason to believe and did believe that what she did was necessary for the safety of her own life or to protect her from great bodily harm, she was not obliged to retreat or attempt to escape; and that the killing under such circumstances constituted justifiable homicide, entitling her to acquittal. (Emphasis Added.)

Com. v. Fraser, 369 Pa. 273, 278 (1952). Tragically, notice the wife was still prosecuted, convicted and had to appeal. We assume she either had a rich daddy or one dynamite pubic defender. Of course, this case happened in the old days when a woman could get a lawyer like Perry Mason without selling her entire one-half ownership interest in Gigantous Corporation.

In the event you are unlucky enough to discover this book after a defensive incident, tell your lawyer about the following jury instruction. He might be able to use it depending upon the facts and the law in your state. This rule of law should be applicable to your case unless you can beat your husband 9 out of 10 times in an arm-wrestling match.

> The Court instructs the jury that if the deceased, Wendell Norris, was a much larger and stronger man than the defendant, Nancy Manuel, so much so that the Defendant was wholly and absolutely incapable of coping with him in a physical combat, and was liable to receive serious and great bodily injuries at the hands of the deceased in the event that they became engaged in combat, then the Defendant was justified in using a deadly weapon to protect himself [sic] from an unjustifiable and deadly attack of the deceased even though the deceased was wholly unarmed, and the Defendant was in no danger from the deceased except such as might be inflicted by the deceased with his hands or feet. *Manuel v. State,* 667 So.2d 590, 591 (Miss. 1995).

The court held this instruction was a correct statement of the law and should have been given in a case involving a boyfriend who allegedly attacked his much smaller girlfriend. Even though he was unarmed, she said he threatened to kill her. She stabbed and killed him with a knife, claiming self-defense. The foregoing instruction was refused by the trial court, but the Mississippi Supreme Court held it should have been given and sent the case back to the trial court for another trial.

Women. Anytime a man threatens, "if I can't have you, no one will," it's time to stop fooling yourself, quit feeling sorry for the jerk and establish a separate household no matter what it takes. It might be harder to do if you have fallen into the cycle of Battered Women's Syndrome. If you have, we hope and pray the real-life tragedies described in this chapter will help you recognize the personal risk you are taking by remaining in a relationship that is destined to crash and burn. It's time to get a gun, firearms training and face reality. You should study the law of self-defense so you can apply it in a split second. You must not buy into the fantasy that the police can respond in time to save you. If you do, you may end up looking down upon them from another realm as they outline your lifeless form with white chalk. Every state, county, city and town has dozens of public servants and volunteers who stand ready to help you break out of the dead-end cycle of Battered Women's Syndrome. Find them and let them help you. But don't expect them to shoulder the personal responsibility you have to prepare to defend yourself.

Pancho's Wisdom

If judges are SERIOUS about protecting victims of violent domestic abuse, they'll issue them protective orders made of Kevlar®, Tasers, and gift certificates to firearms training institutes!

Pancho's Wisdom

When women BEAR ARMS, domestic abusers and sexual predators will keep HANDS OFF!

14

STATEMENTS MADE AFTER A DEFENSIVE INCIDENT

We have been involved in and have read countless cases where the defendant would have never been prosecuted had he not discussed his case with others before he talked to his lawyer. Remember, the Fifth Amendment of the U.S. Constitution says you do not have to say anything that could incriminate you in a court case later.

A. Beware of the Good Cop, Bad Cop routine.

You just survived the most traumatic moment of your life (aside from giving your daughter's hand in marriage to "Easy Rider"). Your heart will be aching to talk to someone—anyone. Police officers are trained to capitalize on such feelings of remorse. At least one of them will tell you how sorry he is you had to go through this, how you were really a victim and "good people like you have a right to defend yourselves." His voice will sound so soothing, comforting and consoling. "You'll be okay, I have a partner that just went through this. I know how you feel. The scumsucker you just riddled has a police record as long as the Bay Bridge; he's lucky you didn't make him suffer. Let's go down to the office for a video-taped statement and then we'll let you go home to your family (as he crosses the fingers on his left hand behind him!)" Your response should be: "I'm sorry officer, I don't feel very well. I need to call my lawyer; I'm sure you'll understand."

He does understand because in his department's training last week, he roll played a simulated "officer-involved-shooting" with police investigators and district attorneys. They all reminded him to SAY NOTHING until he talks to a lawyer! In fact, some police departments have regulations that will not allow their officers to talk to anyone except a lawyer for at least 24 hours after a shooting. He won't admit it, but he wouldn't talk if he were you. But he'll do what he's trained to do and say, "I'm sorry too. If you won't talk, I'll just have to arrest you now. Lock your fingers behind your neck, please." He will place the cuffs on you and begin to lead you away. Then he'll stop and say, "Look, I know you're the good guy. The dirt bag is lying over there. Just give me a statement so I can finish my report and go home and get some sleep and I'll let you go too." If you give him the statement, he may leave the cuffs on and say, "You're under arrest for First (Second—whatever) degree Murder." You respond, "Wait! I thought you said I could go if I gave you a statement?" His reply, "That's before I knew what you had to say. Your admissions tonight just gave me probable cause to arrest you for murder."

If you don't give him the statement and he arrests you anyway, at least you haven't given away the house, the barn and all the furniture. So he arrests you. Unless the physical evidence at the scene and witnesses are enough to establish murder, you'll be out on bail in the morning. Your lawyer will feed information about your case to the prosecutor as needed to convince the DA he has no case. Your defense attorney will have a winnable case because you didn't spill your guts when you shouldn't have.

B. Miranda Doesn't Apply to Pre-Arrest Statements

Some have the misconception that anything they say before they are "Mirandized" (You have the right to remain silent, the right to an attorney, anything you say can blah, blah blah), cannot be used against them in court. This is not true. The first police officers on the scene don't know what happened. They will start asking everyone questions, including you. At this point, you are not under arrest. *Miranda* only applies *after* you have been arrested. Of course, what constitutes an arrest and when it happened is a hotly debated issue in the courts.

If you start running your mouth before you are arrested, the statements you make that incriminate you will be admissible in court. **Example:** *Police Officer:* Look, we know Victor lying over there has a criminal record as long as the barrel on your Casull. Just give me a short statement so we can both go home and get some sleep." *Naive You:* "The SOB owed me money. We got into an argument and he told me he was going to bash my head in with his fists. I believed him, so I shot him in self-defense." *Police Officer:* "Why did you shoot him 5 times?" *Naive You:* "That's all the bullets my gun holds." *Police Officer:* You're under arrest! You have the right to remain silent (Oh, wonderful, nice of him to tell you that now! Great timing!)...

Your lawyer's response when he first reads the police report, sees the crime scene photos and your revolver that looks like it needs a turret: "Oh, Crap!" Then, as he turns to the subject of your retainer, you notice his countenance changes. His facial expression reminds you of the Little Man hitting the Big Jackpot at the Cheap Casino on the outskirts of Pahrump, Nevada as he leans forward and asks, "How much equity do you have in your home?" Look, you have a Fifth Amendment right not to say anything that will incriminate you. What good is the right if you don't exercise it?

C. Statements to Others

Did you know that *any* statement you make to *anyone* (not just the police) right after a self-defense incident could be admissible in court against you? Admissions of guilt to anyone after the event are probably admissible as exceptions to the hearsay rule. This includes the 911 call, casual conversations with ambulance crew members, doctors, nurses and witnesses on the scene. And take it from us, not everything that is written in medical records is accurate! Doctors and nurses are more concerned about treating your injury than correctly writing down every fact you tell them about an incident. And certainly none of these people are going to give you a Miranda warning. You are getting your warning from us right now, so don't forget it!

Although most states recognize some form of a physician/patient privilege for the purposes of improving communications related to treatment, there is no guarantee that what you tell health care providers will come within the protection of that privilege. This is especially true if what you say has nothing to do with improving your medical care. If you need someone's shoulder to cry on after a defensive incident, call your criminal defense lawyer! It may cost you, but it could save you a fortune if you talk to him rather than someone else who is later called as a witness to nail the coffin shut on your case.

Pancho's Wisdom

You just might be a Gunnut if . . . before Christmas you give your family your calibers rather than your clothing sizes.

Pancho's Wisdom

You just might be a Gunnut if . . .

. . . your vehicle's GPS is programmed to only take you through those states that recognize your state's concealed weapon permit.

15

RISK OF BEING SUED FOR DEFENDING YOURSELF

Criminal law involves punishing a wrongdoer for committing a crime. On the other hand, the primary purpose of civil law is to make a wrongdoer adequately compensate the victim of his wrongful act. If the actions of a person who defends himself or another are not justified, he can be punished both under the criminal law and made to compensate the victim under civil law. The *Harmon* case keynoted in Chapter 2 involved both criminal punishment (conviction of first-degree felony murder with a life sentence) and civil damages. The mother of the young man killed and his friend who was shot obtained a combined civil judgment of $1.5 million dollars. All of the defendant's assets, including his cabin, were sold to satisfy the judgment. As a consequence, Mr. Harmon now sits penniless in prison doing life without parole.

You can win the criminal trial but lose the civil lawsuit. This is what happened to Bernhard Goetz, the infamous subway vigilante. Four young men approached Goetz on the New York subway. One of them brandished a screwdriver and asked for five dollars. Goetz, who was illegally concealing a revolver, drew it and shot at all four, hitting two of them in the back. Goetz found Darryl Cabey, lying wounded on a subway bench and shot him again. The wounds left Cabey permanently paralyzed and brain damaged. New York prosecutors charged Goetz with attempted murder. The jury acquitted Goetz of attempted murder charge, convicting him only of possessing an illegal weapon. Cabey later sued Goetz for civil damages. During the civil trial, Cabey's personal injury lawyer argued that Goetz shot Cabey after he was so badly injured that he no longer posed a threat. The jury returned a verdict against Goetz for $43 million dollars.

Injuries caused intentionally are not covered by liability insurance nor will bankruptcy discharge the damage award. Under such circumstances, if the victim's attorney can find assets owned by the shooter, he can attach and sell them. Large civil damage verdicts can relegate the defendant to a lifetime of poverty.

Civil damages for personal injury can include past medical expenses, future projected medical expenses, past lost wages, future lost earning capacity, loss of enjoyment of life, pain and suffering and the cost of attendant care for severely disabled persons. Unless the defendant has valuable assets, the plaintiff's attorney usually hopes to find insurance coverage of some sort to cover the incident. This can be tricky because insurance contracts will not pay for injuries that result from an intentional act. For this reason, wise plaintiffs' attorneys will allege negligent self-defense in hopes of keeping insurance money available to their clients. For example, if an initial aggressor was using non-deadly force and the defender responds with deadly force, "negligent use of excessive force" can be alleged to keep the insurance company in the case. If the injury really was intentional, the insurance company will bring a declaratory judgment action. Its lawyers will request a court order relieving the company of the responsibility to defend the lawsuit or pay money damages. If the insurance company wins, it's off the hook. Then the injured person and his attorney are back to trying to collect the judgment from the person who caused the injury.

Homeowners' insurance covers a homeowner for negligence even if he's off of his property at the time of an incident. If you carry a firearm for self-defense, you would do well to have a large homeowner's liability policy. If you have a large underlying policy, say as much as three hundred thousand dollars, it is then possible, for a surprisingly small sum per month, usually less than $100, to get an additional $1,000,000 of coverage. Higher amounts can be purchased. The higher the insurance limits, the lower the premium is per thousand dollars of coverage. All who keep a gun for self-defense should have a nice long chat with their homeowners' insurance agent about getting additional coverage.

As seen in Chapter 5, many states are now enacting laws to protect citizens who act in justifiable self-defense from civil lawsuits. As explained in Chapter 4, this protection comes in the form of statutes providing immunity from lawsuits and presumptions of innocence. Finally, a few states, like Utah, severely limit the ability of those injured while committing felonies from bringing lawsuits against the intended victims of their crimes. Every state's law is different in this respect and plaintiffs' attorneys often cleverly find ways around the intended statutory protections. The word to the wise is to have adequate homeowners or business insurance just in case your act of self-defense causes serious injury and the injured person's attorney finds a way around your state's immunity statute. The following cases illustrate how using excessive force, acting out of revenge or trying to shoot fleeing felons can expose you to the risk of civil liability.

A. Act of Revenge Against Mouthy Teenager Reaps Lawsuit.

Estep, an attractive schoolteacher, was taking a spin in the country and encountered a slow-moving tractor driven by Williams, a teenager. When Estep pulled along side to pass, Williams, stirred by her resplendence, howled like a lovesick coyote. Not impressed, Estep backed up and furiously chastised him. Hurt and offended, the teenager asked Estep if she wanted her neck broken. He then drove away on his tractor. Apparently fed up with mouthy teenagers, she pulled a .410 shotgun out of her trunk and chased the impertinent youngster. Overtaking Williams, she forced him to the ground at gunpoint. Confronted with the unfriendly end of a scattergun, Williams dropped to his knees pleading forgiveness. Screaming you "no good S.O.B.," she motioned him to crawl away on his knees. Aiming near his legs, she fired and reloaded twice claiming, with 20 years of shooting experience, that she only intended to scare him.

After the shooting, Williams' doctors were not able to remove all of the pellets from the boy's legs and they testified he would be permanently affected by his body's reactions to the lead. Estep's defense was that Williams had provoked her. She had earlier been convicted of an unspecified crime related to the incident (probably something like assault with a deadly weapon with injuries, a serious felony) and had come before the federal district court asking permission to settle the case for $10,000. The court refused to approve the settlement stating a jury would probably find the shooting unjustified and award damages for far more than what she was offering to pay. Although the case does not mention it, because her actions were clearly out of anger rather than negligence, the $10,000 offered almost assuredly was coming out of her pocket as would any verdict in the case. Her homeowner's insurance company probably told her to "pound sand" (take a hike) citing the intentional-acts exclusion in her policy.

It's not funny when a teenage boy threatens to break a woman's neck. But such a comment does not justify what happened here. Estep was not in imminent danger from Williams. Her actions quickly transformed her from victim to aggressor. She should have simply driven away and reported the teen's threat to the police. *Estep v. Williams,* 431 F.Supp. 75 (E.D. Tenn. 1976).

B. Bubba Shoots Jukebox Ninja During Combat by Agreement, Verdict Exceeds Homeowner's Insurance Limits.

Harris and pistol-packing Pineset got into an argument over one of them using the other's 25 cent juke box credits. Harris invited Pineset to step outside and Pineset accommodated. (Are you kidding me?!!!! Dude, you have a gun! You're agreeing to fight someone mano a mano so you can have your gun jarred loose and he can shoot you with your own pistola? We're talking about a dispute over 25, 50 maybe 75 cents! Wow!) While tussling in the parking lot, Pineset drew his pistol (oh, brilliant). Although disputed, some evidence suggests that Harris tried to grab the gun, but it fired, striking him in the stomach. Surgeons had to remove part of his large bowel. Harris' attorney probably claimed negligent self-defense rather than assault to keep Pineset's homeowners' insurance in the case. The trial court found Pineset negligent and awarded Harris

$203,728 in damages including $38,728 in medical expenses. Unfortunately, Pineset only had $100,000 of homeowner's insurance coverage. Pineset appealed claiming he was justified in defending himself with a pistol because Harris threatened to use karate on him. The appeals court disagreed that Pineset was justified in defending with deadly force. However, it explained that Harris was negligent for urging Pineset to go outside to fight, so it assessed 10% fault to him and reduced the verdict by that percentage. Pineset still ended up owing over $83,000 out of his personal assets to satisfy the verdict. There were two major problems in this case for Pistolero Pineset. First, he agreed to fight (remember combat by agreement takes away your right to claim self-defense) and second, he used a weapon against someone who had no weapon (oh, okay, his hands were "registered," good try, no cigar!) He couldn't have been too worried Harris' hands were deadly weapons. He voluntarily stepped outside to lock horns with Harris. *Harris v. Pineset*, 499 So. 2d 499 at 503 (La. App. 2d Cir. 1986).

C. Gas Station Attendant Shoots Fleeing Robber, Robber Runs into Innocent Motorist, Gas Station gets Sued (Cause and Effect – Welcome to Earth, Third Rock from the Sun!)

Binder, a night manager at a Cleveland, Ohio gas station, lugged a .45 revolver in his overalls while on duty (bet that was uncomfortable). Three men in an Oldsmobile pulled up, wielded a shotgun and demanded cash. Fearing for his life, Binder handed over $400. The robbers told Binder not to move as they slowly drove away. Before the thugs pulled onto the street, Binder drew his handgun and blasted through the back window of the car. The slug penetrated the front seat and plunged deep into the driver's back, perforating his spleen, stomach and heart. Mortally wounded, the driver's legs stiffened, propelling the gas pedal to the floor. The Oldsmobile screeched into the street accelerating rapidly. A block and a half from the station, it crashed head on into a Cadillac driven by Strother, an innocent motorist, causing serious injuries. (Stuff happens! Yes, this is a real case.) As usual, the criminals had no money or insurance so Strother sued Binder and his employer under the theory of negligent self-defense.

Strother's attorney argued that Binder didn't need to shoot to protect himself; the criminals were almost out of the driveway when Binder began shooting, as evidenced by a shot through the back. His actions, he alleged, created an unnecessary and unreasonable risk of harm to others. Despite his eloquent presentation, the trial court concluded Binder was not liable to Strother. The appeals court agreed with the trial court, pointing out that the getaway car was still in the gas station parking lot when Binder fired. It held Binder could not have foreseen the Oldsmobile would have lunged out of the parking lot to strike an oncoming car. Although there are exceptions, negligence law holds that a person is not liable if he cannot foresee that his actions will cause injury.

We agree that it would be difficult to foresee that the bullet would hit the driver in the back, cause him to stiffen up, slam on the gas, speed down the street and take out another vehicle. Nevertheless, it is foreseeable that when you are shooting at somebody pulling away in a car, he might panic, stomp on it to get away, and cause an accident. This is the very reason many police departments forbid their officers to engage in dangerous, high-speed chases. Certainly Binder could have foreseen some injury, although not the manner or extent of the injury. His bullet could have missed and struck an innocent bystander (see the following case). Under negligence law, if a person's actions are unreasonable and he can foresee some injury, he is liable even though he cannot foresee exactly how the injury will occur or the seriousness of the injury. This was a close case. Another court in another state might have found Binder and his employer liable. *Strother v. Hutchinson,* 423 N.E.2d 467 (Ohio 1981).

D. Shots Fired Wildly into the Dark Kill Innocent Bystander Resulting in Wrongful Death Lawsuit.

Another tragic case involving an alleged negligent self-defense occurred in Nashville, Tennessee. Late one night in 1956, sixty-eight year old Norman Goodrich was walking home from work through a dark, heavily populated residential area. Meanwhile, a woman named Morgan heard a window rattling and thought it could be a prowler. She grabbed her pistol and went outside to sit on her front porch swing. She spotted a man peeping through a basement window at a woman undressing. Infuriated, Morgan pointed the handgun and cut loose with several shots. As bullets whizzed by, the intruder fled into the street and disappeared into the dark. Morgan heard someone call out "I've been shot." A bullet struck Mr. Goodrich in the chest, ultimately killing him.

Mrs. Goodrich, wife of the deceased, sued Ms. Morgan for negligence, but the trial court dismissed the case. The appeals court, however, sent the case back for a new trial, criticizing Morgan for shooting into the dark without knowing where her bullets would strike. The rule of law that the court applied to the case was that "a person using a firearm or other weapon in the exercise of ... self-defense is not liable for any injury unintentionally inflicted upon a bystander unless [she] is guilty of some negligence or folly in the use of the weapon." The Restatement of Torts, a highly-respected legal treatise, explains the rule of law with the following example:

> A points a pistol at B, threatening to shoot him. B attempts to shoot A, but his bullet goes astray and strikes C, an innocent bystander. B is not liable to C unless, taking into account the exigency [emergency] which A's act placed B, B fired his self-defensive shot in a manner unnecessarily dangerous to C (emphasis added).

Restatement Second, Torts § 75 (Illustration 1). Unfortunately for Morgan, there was no evidence to show that the intruder was armed or about to commit a sexual assault. He ran away after the first shot. The shots into the street were not intended to defend as much as they were intended to frighten or punish a criminal. *Goodrich v. Morgan*, 291 S.W.2d 610 (Tenn.App. 1956). As a practical matter, any time you injure an innocent bystander, plan on getting sued.

E. Bartender held Liable for Shooting Patron in Foot.

The facts giving rise to this case occurred in 1948 in Wisconsin. Oshogay, a reservation Indian, had started a fight in the defendant's tavern a couple of weeks earlier. When he revisited the bar, Shultz, the bar owner, refused to serve him alcohol. He asked Oshogay to leave, but Oshogay refused (ostensibly a misdemeanor trespass). Finally, Shultz pulled a pistol and shot near Oshogay's feet. The bullet struck Oshogay in the foot. A jury awarded damages in the sum of $1,223.70, a sizeable verdict in 1950. The appeals court upheld the verdict, explaining that the bar owner had not asked anyone to help remove the belligerent patron, nor had he summoned the police. Oshogay had not threatened anyone with deadly force. The bartender was not justified in responding with deadly force. *Oshogay v. Schultz*, 43 N.W.2d 485 (Wis. 1950).

Pancho's Wisdom

You just might be a Gunnut if . . . when you're in Vegas "pullin'" the slots, you get homesick for your Dillon 650 reloading press.

16

TASER: A LESS-LETHAL ALTERNATIVE

Taser International manufactures a civilian version of a stunning device known as the Taser that many, if not most, police agencies are now using. The official name of the civilian version of this device is the TASER® C2™ electronic control device (hereinafter C2). Its advantage over a normal stun gun is that it contains a cartridge that propels two darts up to a distance of 15 feet carrying a charge of 50,000 volts. Ouch! This way, you never have to get within arms length of your attacker to deliver the juice.

As the cases in the previous chapters illustrate, a perplexing situation is one in which threatening individuals are not brandishing weapons, but the defender believes they might be armed or could overpower him and use his gun against him. Under these circumstances, if the defender draws, exhibits, points or shoots a firearm, he or she could be charged with a serious crime. In several states, if you threaten someone with a toy, fake or unloaded gun, you can be charged as if it were a loaded gun. One solution to this dilemma might be to carry a C2 Taser; it doesn't look like a gun. It looks more like a TV channel changer or electric razor. This reduces the chance of being charged with felony assault with a deadly weapon. The court in *Hennigan v. Taser,* 2001 WL 185122 (S.D.N.Y. Feb. 26, 2001) referred to the Taser as "[a] stun gun, a non-lethal self-defense device." This, however, does not mean that other states might not consider Taser a deadly weapon. Discussions with prosecutors here in Utah lead us to believe that in our state, use of a Taser carries far less legal risk than pointing or shooting a gun at someone.

Its shape and lightweight construction make the C2 comfortable to carry and easy to conceal. A direct hit with both Taser darts generally causes the attacker to drop immediately, not always the case with a handgun, even with well-placed torso shots. We are not saying the Taser is better than a handgun. We are saying it has unique features that, from a legal standpoint, might better allow you to deal with an attacker who has not displayed a weapon but refuses to obey your verbal commands to stop. If the only weapon you have is a gun and the assailant continues to advance despite your warnings, if you shoot him, your world could collapse around you. In contrast, if you score a direct hit with the C2, the bad guy falls to the ground, you drop the Taser and it continues the voltage for 30 seconds while you run away. Afterwards, you submit a copy of the police report to Taser International and the company will replace the device at no charge.

We are not suggesting that the device is harmless. Injuries and death have occurred. If serious injury results, you could still be charged with a felony or sued. A fall could cause injury and a dart in the face could damage an eyeball. People with medical conditions or on stimulant drugs like methamphetamines have died when tased. Paying a little extra for the laser-pointer accessory will help you avoid hitting your assailant in the face. Even if your assailant hurts himself in the fall and you are charged with a crime, the level of the charge will generally be less than if you shoot someone with a gun.

As effective as the Taser is, it is unfortunate that many states such as Hawaii, New York and others either prohibit the use of Tasers by private citizens or severely limit its use.

Pancho's Wisdom

You just might be a Gunnut if . . .

. . . you learned to use a screw driver by taking your dad's guns apart.

. . . you learned to read by reading a gun safety manual.

. . . you learned to shoot before you learned to read.

17

SELF-DEFENSE FROM ANIMALS

Pancho's Wisdom

The Second Amendment does NOT say, "The right of the BEARS (and other creatures with dripping fangs) to gnaw off your ARMS shall not be infringed."

We are often asked whether persons attacked by dangerous animals have a right of self-defense. The most common statutes that generate prosecution for killing animals include the federal Endangered Species Act, various state animal cruelty laws and state wildlife "poaching" statutes. It would be beyond the scope of this book to try to analyze every state animal cruelty statute and wildlife code, but we have compiled the Endangered Species Act, the Federal Code relating to defense from grizzly bears and a few state cases that have addressed the right of self-defense vis-à-vis the states' animal cruelty laws. Be forewarned. These cases are investigated with the same care using the same techniques employed in cases involving the homicide of humans.

Key: ■ commentary ■ original statutes, cases or jury instructions

A. The Endangered Species Act
16 U.S.C. § 1540. Penalties and enforcement

. . .

(a) Civil penalties

(1) Any person who knowingly violates . . .any provision of this chapter . . . may be assessed a civil penalty by the Secretary of not more than $25,000 for each violation . . .

(b) Criminal violations

(1) Any person who knowingly violates any provision of this chapter . . . shall, upon conviction, be fined not more than $50,000 or imprisoned for not more than one year, or both. Any person who knowingly violates any provision of any other regulation issued under

this chapter shall, upon conviction, be fined not more than $25,000 or imprisoned for not more than six months, or both . . . [Although killing an animal listed as endangered is a misdemeanor under the federal code, the states can make the same crime a felony (e.g., see **Utah Code Annotated 23-20-4. Wanton destruction of protected wildlife...**). Therefore, it's extremely important that you understand what your rights and responsibilities are when defending yourself from endangered animals.]

. . .

(3) Notwithstanding any other provision of this chapter, it shall be a defense to prosecution under this subsection if the defendant committed the offense based on a good faith belief that he was acting to protect himself or herself, a member of his or her family, or any other individual, from bodily harm from any endangered or threatened species. [The right of self-defense is specifically preserved in the federal Endangered Species Act. Notice the threshold to defend yourself from an endangered animal is "bodily harm" rather than "serious bodily harm or death." We didn't find any cases that change this threshold by judicial edict (which would be plain wrong and unfair). Most states' departments of wildlife resources have listings of the endangered animals in their state.]

B. Self-Defense Against Grizzly Bears
50 C.F.R. § 17.40 Special rules – mammals.

. . .

(b) Grizzly bear (Ursus arctos) [*Pancho's Wisdom* – This is Latin for "You are my little Arctic Circle treat!"] – (1) Prohibitions. The following prohibitions apply to the grizzly bear:

(i) Taking.

(A) Except as provided in paragraphs (b)(1)(i)(B) through (F) of this section, no person shall take [euphemism for "kill"] any grizzly bear in the 48 conterminous states of the United States.

(B) Grizzly bears may be taken in self-defense or in defense of others, but such taking shall be reported, within 5 days of occurrence, to the Assistant Regional Director, Division of Law Enforcement, U.S. Fish and Wildlife Service, P.O. Box 25486, Denver Federal Center, Denver, Colorado 80225 (303/236-7540 or FTS 776-7540), if occurring in Montana or Wyoming, or to the Assistant Regional Director, Division of Law Enforcement, U.S. Fish and Wildlife Service, Lloyd 500 Building, Suite 1490, 500 Northeast Multnomah Street, Portland, Oregon 97232 (503/ 231-

6125 or FTS 429-6125), if occurring in Idaho or Washington, and to appropriate State and Indian Reservation Tribal authorities. Grizzly bears or their parts taken in self-defense or in defense of others shall not be possessed, delivered, carried, transported, shipped, exported, received, or sold, except by Federal, State, or Tribal authorities. [This regulation adds the requirement that any act of self-defense against a grizzly be reported within 5 days. It is interesting that if you shoot a person, you have a Fifth Amendment right against self-incrimination, but not if you shoot a grizzly. Although violation of this regulation is a misdemeanor, the civil and criminal penalties can be as high as $50,000. Check out the following case to see how this law has been applied and prosecuted. It ain't funny if you blow apart Fuzzy Wuzzy and it wazzn't self-defense.]

C. Inconsistent Testimony Defeats Case of Self-Defense in Shooting of Grizzly Bear.

[The following quotes are out of the federal appeals court case, *United States of America v. Clavette*, 135 F.3d 1308 (9th Cir. 1998). We included a considerable portion of the case to show the reader how much effort goes into the investigation and how the courts tend to analyze the evidence to render their opinions.]

> On September 20, 1995, U.S. Fish and Wildlife Service Special Agent Tim Eicher began investigating the killing of a grizzly bear at a campsite southwest of Big Sky, Montana. At the campsite, Eicher discovered two pine trees with a pole suspended by rope between them. This was a "meat pole," used for stringing up and skinning large game animals. Underneath it, Eicher found traces of moose blood and hair, indicating that a moose had recently been dressed there. Eicher found the dead grizzly bear approximately 170 yards away, lying in a large pool of blood. The bear had been shot at least four times. Looking for bullets or spent shell casings, Eicher searched a conical area extending about 25 yards beyond the bear toward the campsite; he found one .7 mm casing by the meat pole [This suggests that the first bullet may have been fired from where the defendant was cleaning the moose. The fact that the bear was found dead 170 yards away from the meat pole is very damaging to the defendant's case unless he has a logical explanation for it.] and two bullets, one buried about two inches in the dirt at the base of a tree near the bear, and one on the surface of the ground next to the pool of the bear's blood.

Eicher located two bow hunters who had stopped at the campsite on September 17, 1995, to visit with an Oregon man skinning a freshly killed moose. The man seemed to be in a hurry and did not say anything about confronting or killing a grizzly. He did ask the bow hunters what would happen to someone who shot a grizzly bear. The bow hunters told him he had better be prepared to prove it was in self-defense. [You see that anything you tell anyone about a potential crime can come back to haunt you. Please don't get the impression we're trying to explain how to get away with poaching animals. We're not. It's a despicable crime and we condemn it. We're simply showing how statements made to other persons besides the police can be damaging, especially if you are innocent and they either misunderstood what you said or have some incentive to get you into trouble.]

Through these bow hunters and Montana hunting license records, Eicher identified the defendant, Paul Clavette, as the man at the campsite on September 17, 1995. Agents of the U.S. Fish and Wildlife Service in Portland, Oregon, obtained and executed a search warrant in defendant's home on November 2, 1995. During the course of that search, and after full Miranda warnings, Clavette admitted to killing the grizzly, claiming that it was in self-defense. [Without his and his wife's statements to investigators, this might have been a tough case to prove. This suspect should have immediately contacted a lawyer. I recently had a case where, after the detective discovered my client had an attorney, he called me and asked if he could take my client's statement. I told him, "No." Without an admission he couldn't "connect the dots" and was forced to drop the case against the client. The Fifth Amendment of the U.S. Constitution guarantees that citizens have no obligation to testify against themselves, which makes us wonder whether the requirement that a person contact the federal government within five days after shooting a bear in self-defense can pass constitutional muster. This constitutional defense was not raised by Clavette or his attorney. We could not find a case that had decided that issue.]

After a bench trial, the [judge] found Clavette guilty of illegally killing a grizzly bear. Clavette was sentenced to three years' probation. Additionally, Clavette was ordered to pay a fine of $2,000 and restitution of $6,250 to the United States Fish & Wildlife Service... To find Clavette guilty of knowingly taking (or killing) an endangered species, the Government must prove, beyond a reasonable doubt, that: (1) Clavette knowingly killed a bear; (2) the bear was a grizzly;

(3) Clavette had no permit from the United States Fish & Wildlife Service to kill a grizzly bear; and (4) Clavette did not act in self-defense or in the defense of others. [These are the elements of the crime. Notice the government has the burden of proving beyond a reasonable doubt that it was not self-defense.] Pursuant to the regulations, a grizzly bear may be taken in self-defense or defense of others [16 U.S.C. § 1540], but any such taking must be reported within five days to the U.S. Fish and Wildlife Service. [50 C.F.R. § 17.40 (b)(i)(B).]

There is no dispute that Clavette knowingly killed a grizzly bear without first obtaining a permit from the Fish & Wildlife Service. The only issue at trial was whether he acted in self-defense or in defense of his wife. Because Clavette presented evidence that he acted in self-defense, the Government had to disprove self-defense beyond a reasonable doubt.

Clavette and his wife changed their story multiple times. Clavette initially described his trip to Montana to Agent Earl Kisler as follows:

Clavette said that as he was skinning a moose he had killed, he sensed something was wrong. He looked up and saw a seven- or eight-foot bear standing on its hind legs about 25 yards away from him, across a creek that ran past the campsite. He made noises to try to drive the bear away and fired a warning shot with his .7 mm rifle. Then, Clavette said, the bear began to circle the campsite, and Clavette was sure it was going to come forward. He told Kisler that he was terrified. Clavette's wife had retreated into the pickup truck. Clavette stated that when the bear was 40 to 75 yards away from the campsite, he shot it. The first shot hit the bear on the left side and appeared to paralyze its hindquarters, but it kept struggling, trying to get up, and so he emptied his rifle into it, reloaded, and fired more rounds into the bear.

[This may have been the truth given the autopsy findings. But then he and his wife gave different versions of what happened and it killed their credibility.] Clavette later stated that there were two bears, although his wife still said that there had been one bear. Then, at trial, Clavette's wife testified that not only were there two bears, but that the second one charged her husband at a dead run. When asked why she had not mentioned two bears before, she explained that only one bear was shot. Clavette himself testified at trial that he had in fact told Agent Kisler about the second bear during their first discussion; Clavette surmised that it must have slipped their minds. He also testified that the second bear charged straight at him and that he crippled it with his first shot at 33 yards. [Then why weren't there any holes in the front of the bear?] Clavette said he saw the bear spin 180 degrees and dig with its front paws, trying to move away from him. The bear looked as if it was paralyzed in its hindquarters but actually ran another hundred yards away from him, without bleeding, so as to die in the spot where the bear was found by the agents.

Although he could not identify the order in which the shots occurred, Keith Aune, a wildlife laboratory supervisor for the Montana Department of Fish, Wildlife and Parks, testified that the shots Clavette described were inconsistent with his own observations and measurements gathered during the necropsy. *No entry wounds appeared on the head, chest or front legs, as would be expected if the bear had been approaching at high speed; all the entry wounds were in the rear portion* (emphasis added). [It's just as hard to convince people of your self-defense claim after shooting an animal in the back, as it is if you shoot a human in the back.] The stories were also inconsistent with the physical evidence found by Agent Eicher at the site.

Given the physical evidence and the inconsistencies in the Clavettes' stories, a reasonable person could have found beyond a reasonable doubt that Clavette had not killed the bear in self-defense.

[Therefore, the court of appeals refused to overturn Clavette's conviction for killing the bear. One wonders if this defendant may have killed the bear to keep it from taking his harvested moose. As you'll see in the next case, killing a grizzly to defend property is not justified.]

Key: ■ End of original statutes and cases relating to Endangered Species Act.

D. Defense of Property Not Justifiable Reason to Kill Grizzly

While federal law permits the use of deadly force to defend *persons* against an animal attack, defense of one's *domestic animals* has been held not to be a defense. In *Christy v. Hodel*, 857 F.2d 1324 (9th Cir. 1988) the Ninth Circuit Court of Appeals refused to expand the self-defense provision of the Endangered Species Act to include defense of livestock, namely sheep. Grizzly bears had killed 20 of Mr. Christy's sheep. They were attacking his flock on a nightly basis. A U.S. Fish and Wildlife employee had failed to trap the responsible bears. One night a bear, not deterred by the presence of Mr. Christy or the Wildlife Officer, headed directly for the frightened sheep. Christy shot the bear at a distance of 60-100 yards. He was fined $3,000 by the feds. He brought suit claiming that he was being deprived of his property, his sheep, without due process if he was unable to defend them against marauding grizzlies. Both the federal district court and federal court of appeals disagreed with him.

E. California Court Holds Self-Defense Applies to State's Animal Cruelty Law Even Though Not Specifically Mentioned in the Statute.

The California Court of Appeals held that California's self-defense instructions could be adapted to incorporate threats from animals, *People v. Lee*, 131 Cal. App. 4th 1413 (2005). In that case, a retired deputy sheriff walking her dog was approached by two dogs she perceived as vicious. She thought they were preparing to attack her or her old, defenseless dog. She pulled her pistol out of her purse and after pausing several times and shouting at the dogs to leave, she fired one shot into the ground. The ricochet hit a parked car [Oh, wonderful - nothing like unintentionally inviting the SWAT team to the party]. Several police officers [what did we tell you?] arrested her at gunpoint for, among other things, felony negligent discharge of a firearm and attempted animal cruelty. She pled self-defense. The state produced witnesses who testified that the dogs were not threatening. After a deadlocked jury in her first trial, the judge in her second trial refused to allow her to claim self-defense, and the jury found her guilty. She appealed. The appellate court reversed saying the jury in the second case should have been allowed to consider the theory of self-defense. [Two trials and an appeal to win the right to argue self-defense. It's good that her case established this right in California, but can you imagine what she paid in attorney fees?]

F. Further Close Encounters of a Dog Kind

We were consulted on two dog-attack cases here in Utah. One was dismissed and the other was never filed by the police. For us, these cases emphasized two important points for people attacked by animals to remember. First, if you are going to talk to the police (which we strongly discourage), tell the truth. Secondly, the Thumbs-Down Factors mentioned in Chapter 7 apply to animal-attack cases as well.

1. **.45 ACP Educates Pit Bull** – The case that was never filed shows how telling the truth can shift the dynamics of the investigation and decision whether or not to prosecute in your favor. On the other hand, stretching the truth can have just the opposite affect. One Saturday, I was taking my daily exercise walk when a call came to my cell phone. It was a gentleman whom I had never met, but who had heard of my work defending gun owners in criminal matters. He said he was having his Beamer serviced in downtown Salt Lake City when, during the wait, he took a walk around a city block near the dealership. As he approached a yard with a beware-of-dog sign, a large pit bull started

going berserk and looked like it would jump over or plow through the fence. Trying always to live in trouble-avoidance mode, the gentleman crossed the street hoping the big dog would calm down. Despite crossing completely across the wide roadway and having walked almost 100 meters from the yard, the dog jumped the fence and stretched out at top speed. With very little time to think, he drew his compact 1911 .45 from concealment and pointed hoping the dog would somehow get the hint and stop its attack. When it was apparent he would either have to shoot or be bitten, he scanned behind the dog to make sure no people, homes, or vehicles were in line with his gun sights. He led the dog slightly and fired. As the gun recoiled, the dog's head bobbed down and his fanny teeter-tottered up. The bullet clipped a tuft of hair from the dog's rear near its tail. The frothing bulldog yipped, spun 180 degrees and retreated home. The dog owner and the defender went for their cell phones intent on beating the other to a 911 operator.

After reporting the incident, the man immediately called me. I advised him to not talk to the police. He said he felt he was completely in the right and intended to explain what happened. The officer verified that the bullet had struck the pavement exactly where the man said he shot at the dog. The woman who owned the dog, however, told the police that the man had shot at her dog near her home. She wanted to press charges for animal cruelty and firing a gun in the city limits.

We were told when the officer saw that the physical evidence supported our potential client's version and belied the dog owner's, he refused to arrest or ticket the defender. The best we can tell, the policeman was completely turned off by the woman's lack of candor and told the defender his actions were completely justified. Needless to say, we were amazed to see such an attitude from an urban police officer. Like most firms that defend gun cases, we had become so accustomed to the man with the gun being demonized from the get-go as the next dog-case story confirms.

2. **Naughty Rotty Gets Beamed Up by Scotty** – The following dog incident happened in a suburb of Salt Lake City. Our client owned a Shih Tzu and his back-yard neighbor had a young Rottweiler. The yards were separated by a fence made of vertical redwood slats. About a week or so before the incident, the Rottweiler had broken through the fence and killed the Shih Tzu. The incident was reported, but the authorities in the small city suburb were slow to do anything about it. Our client bought a new Shih Tzu puppy.

   The dog-shooting incident occurred during an outdoor barbeque hosted in our client's backyard. He invited friends with small children. As the children were playing with the new Shih Tzu puppy, the Rottweiler again started battering the fence which had since been repaired. It looked to our client that the dog would again break through and cause havoc during the backyard get-together. The client immediately went to his truck and grabbed his .45 while the other grownups yelled to the Rottweiler's owner to call off his dog. The Rotty's owner never responded, apparently not at home. A twelve-year-old girl picked up an infant that was close by and also the puppy and started to run for a trampoline so they would be out-of-reach of the big dog. As the Rottweiler burst through the planks, the client fired one shot which pierced its skull and neck. It quickly retreated to its own yard where it either died or had to be euthanized. Unfortunately, the client was so upset at having to shoot the dog; he tried to calm himself with an alcoholic beverage (the Thumbs-Down Factor in this case). When the police arrived, they smelled alcohol on his breath. They cited him for animal cruelty, discharging a firearm in the city limits, and possessing a firearm while under the influence of alcohol. Although we had become accustomed to urban police and prosecutors demonizing gun owners, we were truly surprised this man had been charged under the circumstances. After all, when the Rottweiler burst through the fence, an infant and pre-teen female had been in imminent danger of being bitten.

As I interviewed witnesses, I picked one who had seen the whole event and was able to describe it in vivid detail. I asked her to dress appropriately for the pre-trial conference that the prosecutor had asked the arresting officer to attend. I invited the prosecutor and police officer to interview the witness in my presence and ask her anything they wanted. After hearing the frightening details of the dog attack, the prosecutor stood up and said, "I'm dismissing all charges!" The arresting officer agreed. The client had taken a fairly sizable hit for attorney's fees [Hey, I don't come cheap!], but was relieved to be walking away with his concealed weapon permit and right to keep and bear arms intact. Had the children and other people not been present during the attack, the result could have been different. Unless your state has a very protective statute allowing you to shoot stray dogs chasing your animals on your property, you run the risk of prosecution and arrest if you shoot a dog in the city limits. And don't forget, many of the states have made animal cruelty a felony. This is not to say we have bought into the claim that shooting an animal is cruel. If that were the case, shooting any animal during a hunt would be cruel.

Before you convince yourself that all is well because state and federal jurisdictions seem to be allowing those charged with killing animals to plead self-defense, check out the following news story we pulled off of the internet as the ink was drying on this chapter:

> **Rapid River man shot his neighbor's dog.**
>
> Wednesday, February 25, 2009 at 7:32 p.m.
>
> RAPID RIVER — The Rapid River man charged with animal cruelty for shooting his neighbor's dog was found guilty of the charge on Wednesday afternoon in Escanaba. Fifty-year-old Kenneth Seiler had claimed he shot and killed the dog in self-defense because he had been bitten by the dog before. The dog's owners denied that their pet had ever bitten anyone. The jury deliberated for two hours and found Seiler guilty. He could face up to four years in prison. Sentencing will be scheduled within the next six weeks.

http://www.uppermichiganssource.com/news/news_story.aspx?id=265433.

A later article about the incident reported:

> **Kenneth Seiler was sentenced to time in jail and probation.**
>
> Tuesday, April 14, 2009 at 5:33 p.m.
>
> ESCANABA — A Rapid River man will spend the next few months behind bars for shooting and killing his neighbor's dog back in August. Tuesday, 50-year-old Kenneth Seiler was sentenced to 6 months in the Delta County Jail and 18 months probation. In February, a jury found Seiler guilty of killing and torturing an animal, which is a felony. Seiler claimed it was self-defense, but the dog owners, who spoke in court today, felt it was an unjust act. "When Mr. Seiler senselessly and in cold blood shot and killed our loving dog, Pups, he took more from us than the adored member of our family; he took away our children's trust in others. It is impossible to explain to a then 12 year old, let alone a 5 year old, why someone would destroy their beloved pet," said dog owner, Jeannie Pearson. "What I see is a cruel and vindictive man who killed his neighbor's dog in cold blood," commented the Honorable Judge Stephen Davis with the Delta County Circuit Court. Seiler will be credited for 11 days already spent in jail. His attorney says he will appeal his case.

http://www.uppermichiganssource.com/news/news_story.aspx?id=286836.

18

ADDITIONAL RESOURCES

A. **Other Gun-Law Books** – There are so many state and federal laws related to firearms that it would be impossible for one attorney to keep up with them all. Fortunately, attorneys and authors throughout the country have taken it upon themselves to become experts in the laws of the various states, federal laws and laws related to travel. One of the easiest ways to find publications related to gun law is to visit Alan Korwin's website www.gunlaws.com which lists for sale a multitude of books related to federal and state gun laws. Alan and others have published the gun laws of several of the states. Scott Kappas, an attorney in Kentucky, has published several editions of *The Traveler's Guide* that gives a one-page description of the laws relating to possession of a firearm as one travels through each state. This book is also available for purchase at gunlaws.com. We suggest you carry it when you travel with firearms.

B. **Applying Your Legal Knowledge to a Defensive Incident** – Knowing the law will keep you from being burned by your state's criminal and civil law. It can also prevent you from hesitating, wondering if you have justification when, in fact, you do. For maximum effectiveness in defending yourself and loved ones, however, you need to develop good gun-handling skills. Although there are several shooting academies available throughout the country, we are most familiar with the excellent tactical and shooting instruction available at Front Sight, Nevada. See www.frontsight.com. Part of the training one typically gets with such instruction is what we in the industry refer to as shoot-no-shoot scenarios. Students are trained to make responsible choices whether to use deadly force while experiencing frightening encounters. You owe it to yourselves to experience such training. It will help you correctly apply the legal rules you have studied in this book. If you shoot too early, too late or at the wrong person during training, you won't die, be arrested or get sued. You want to make your legal and tactical mistakes during training so you don't make the same mistakes if and when it really counts.

Pancho's Wisdom

Pancho describes action shooting to non-shooters as being like golf with an adrenaline rush.

C. **Activities That Will Help You Develop Shooting Skills To Survive A Defensive Incident** – Shooting pop cans or targets when completely relaxed is one thing. Hitting the broad side of a barn during a heart-stopping, adrenaline-filled, life-threatening emergency is another. You may ask, "How can I find anything to simulate that?" Our reply, "Have you ever tried competitive action shooting?" Although the experience is not exactly the same as being involved in a defensive incident and the targets don't shoot back, at least you experience an adrenaline high while trying to hit something with a handgun, rifle or shotgun. We would hope that as you become more competent shooting under stress, you will be able to expend less mental energy worrying about whether you can hit your threat, and devote more thought to whether you have legal justification to use force in the first place.

International Defensive Pistol Association (IDPA), in our opinion, provides competitive scenarios most like you might encounter in real life. The competitions generally require you to draw a handgun from a concealed holster while being timed on a shot timer. Every phase of the competition has a story line. You might pretend you are in a bank with a child (a large doll) in a stroller when four armed suspects burst in shooting. You have to grab the child with one hand while shooting with the other as you move to cover. You are expected to "slice the pie" when you shoot from impenetrable cover like a brick wall. This means you must shoot multiple bad guys in the order they appear to you as you carefully adjust your stance to view them one at a time. You are taught not to expose your body to additional assailants until you have neutralized the one you are able to see.

If there is no cover, you learn to knock the assailants down in tactical sequence. To help you remember what this means, experienced shooters tell you it's the school-lunch theory. Each assailant gets one helping (of lead), before anyone gets seconds. This way you learn not to waste time and ammunition shooting one of several assailants while the others empty their guns on you. One dramatic, but humorous scenario involves a shooter sitting on a toilet in a stall when three assailants holding knives kick down the stall door. Competitors quickly figure out the best place to put their concealed weapons (we're talkin' GUNS here folks! Don't get distracted!), so that they can respond in the quickest and most accurate way possible. **Hint:** You don't leave it in your holster flopping half way into the next stall. Anyway, you get the picture—it's A BLAST!!! For more information see idpa.com.

If you don't have an IDPA club near you, you can either organize one or see if you can find an IPSC (International Practical Shooting Federation) group that shoots nearby. IPSC is similar to IDPA, but with more emphasis on shooting speed and athletic ability and less emphasis on tactics and concealed carry. To enhance speed, many competitors do not use equipment that could be easily concealed (often referred to as "space guns and holsters" resembling something you'd see in a Star Wars movie). Nevertheless, the more IPSC matches you compete in, the faster and more accurately you will learn to shoot under stress. **Caution:** Justifiable self-defense is not emphasized. For the sake of practicing more often, some shooters compete in both IPSC and IDPA. See ipsc.org.

The rules of Cowboy Action Shooting are governed by the Single Action Shooting Society. You can win the competition with speed and accuracy, but it seems most of the folks are there to have a *great time,* sporting a most amazing collection of Old-West-style pistols, lever-action rifles and stagecoach shotguns. Members are required to assume an alias with clothing to match, hence "Pancho Vilos." Although most of us will never experience a stage-coach holdup in real life, learnin' to shoot while yer a shakin' could come in mighty handy some day, ol' Pard. For a club near you, check out www.sassnet.com.

Pancho's Wisdom

You just might be a Gunnut if . . . you have adopted a Cowboy Action Shooting alias.

Pancho's Wisdom

You just might be a Gunnut if . . . your kids' friends know they don't have to talk your kids into sneaking into your guns because you've told them you will take them shooting any time they want with their parents' permission.

19

ABOUT FUTURE EDITIONS

Writing a book about the laws of 51 different jurisdictions including Washington D.C. is necessarily a work in progress. The legislatures of the various states convene at different times. Laws can change overnight. Judges' case interpretations can change what appears to be the plain meaning of a state's self-defense statute. It is important to stay updated on the law of your state. Ignorance of the law is no excuse. We will continue to update this book in subsequent editions as we become aware of changes in the law. You will find something new and exciting in each subsequent edition. If you would like to receive notification of new editions of this book, please send us an email and we will notify you when the new edition is available. Go to www.firearmslaw.com and scroll down to the "signup for updates" tab.

Our goal is to be the MOST RELIABLE source of information about the law of self-defense in the country. We can only achieve this with the help of our readers. Please contact us at the email address in the previous paragraph with information about changes you've heard about involving your state's self-defense laws, questions about anything you find unclear, if you believe we've made an error or suggestions for topics in future editions.

We look forward to discussing any self-defense issues with attorneys from other states who are as enthusiastic about the inalienable right of self-defense as we are. We, of course, reserve the exclusive right to control the content of our book. We have thoroughly enjoyed our association with and have found success in working with attorneys from others states on cases within our areas of expertise. Ultimately, our intent is to maintain the most comprehensive and accurate compilation self-defense laws ever written.

UNCLE PANCHO WANTS YOU

To Be Part of His Revolution to Establish The Mother of All Self-Defense Laws In Every State

20

CONCLUSION: THE MOTHER OF ALL SELF-DEFENSE LAWS

You might compare this Chapter to an all-star team where the most talented players from the best teams are chosen to create a "Dream Team." Likewise, we have chosen the most favorable provisions from the most protective self-defense statutes in the country. We call it the Mother of All Self-Defense Laws. If your state's self-defense statute doesn't measure up in comparison (none of them do), you can either slump on your sofa like a sports-channel-anesthetized three-toed sloth or be like Gary Marbut, the Man from La Mancha, er we mean Montana. Gary, a non-lawyer, a self-appointed political steamroller has been *the* driving force in improving Montana's gun laws for years. Behind most of the positive gun laws we see in our nation today were teams of men and women like Gary, most of them non-lawyers, working hard to make their state's laws more protective of the innocent. Some examples are Alan Korwin in Arizona; Clark Aposhian, Woody Powell, John Spangler, Curt Oda, and Charles Hardy in Utah; Former Representative Dr. Suzanna Gratia Hupp from Texas and John Cahill (yes, a Democrat and proud of it) and Dr. Ignatius Piazza in Nevada. We encourage you to join these men and women and thousands of other true patriots who, together with the NRA and other Second Amendment advocacy groups, have made their states' self-defense and gun laws more protective of innocent citizens and more dangerous for violent criminals.

One of the first questions your legislators will ask about changing your state's self-defense law is "has any other state done this?" This book is the first of its kind (with the exception of hard-to-understand legal encyclopedias) to compile all of the nation's self-defense laws under one cover. It's a perfect tool to use to assure legislators that the changes you are proposing have been passed elsewhere without plunging states into anarchy and chaos with blood running in the streets.

So without further ado, may we introduce to you, the act you've anticipated through all the ages, or pages, The Mother of All Self-Defense Laws!

Key: ■ commentary ■ original statutes, cases or jury instructions

DEFENSE OF SELF AND OTHERS

I. Non-Deadly Force

A person is justified in threatening or using force against another when and to the extent that he or she reasonably believes that force is necessary to defend himself or a third person against such other's imminent use of unlawful force. [Utah Code Annotated § 76-2-402. Virtually every state authorizes the use of non-deadly force to respond to an imminent threat of unlawful, non-deadly force. However, two recent Kansas Supreme Court decisions say that those committing threat crimes, such as brandishing or assault with a deadly weapon, are not entitled to claim self-defense because the term "threat" does not appear in the Kansas statute. See discussion under this TEMPLATE subheading (Non-Deadly Force) in Chapter 4. The term "threatening" is included here to avoid the absurdity of the Kansas court rulings.

The use of the term "threatening" here, but not in the following section regarding the use of deadly force, shows legislative intent to legally allow a defender to threaten deadly force against an unarmed attacker if necessary to prevent an imminent violent, physical assault. This concept of justifying a threat with a deadly weapon against an unarmed assailant is strengthened in the "defensive-display" section below (Section V).

This section justifies the defense of all third persons, not just family or work associates (e.g., California, Idaho). Also, it allows for the defense of third persons whom the defender reasonably believes are entitled to defend themselves, even if they are not (e.g., initial aggressors). Defenders of third persons should not be punished for a technicality of which they are unaware, provided they are acting upon a reasonable belief.]

II. The Use of Deadly Force to Prevent Death or Serious Bodily Injury to Self or Third Persons and to Prevent Forcible Felonies

A person is justified in using force intended or likely to cause death or serious bodily injury only if he or she reasonably believes that force is necessary to prevent death or serious bodily injury to himself or a third person as a result of the other's imminent use of unlawful force, or to prevent the commission of a forcible felony as defined in the definitions below. [Adapted from Utah Code Annotated § 76-2-402. Like in most states, the use of deadly force is limited to circumstances involving an imminent threat of death or serious bodily injury. However, unlike many states, this statute allows citizens to use deadly force to prevent the commission of forcible felonies. Forcible felonies are listed in the definitions section below. Deadly force may be used to defend any third person whom the defender reasonably believes is imminently threatened with deadly force.] In determining imminence or reasonableness under Subsection I and II, the trier of fact [meaning a jury or a judge if you waive a jury] may consider, but is not limited to, any of the following factors [See Utah Code Annotated § 76-2-402.]:

A. the nature of the danger;

B. the immediacy of the danger;

C. the probability that the unlawful force would result in death or serious bodily injury;

D. the other's previous violent acts or violent propensities. If the defendant was not aware of the other's prior violent acts or violent propensities, then this evidence is only admissible to aid the trier of fact to determine whether the defendant or the alleged victim was the initial aggressor. [This definition of imminence gives the trier of fact broader discretion to consider guilt or innocence than in many states (e.g., Massachusetts, Virginia).]; and

[Other Issues – e.g., Domestic Violence]

E. any patterns of abuse or violence in the parties' relationship; [This relates to an abusive relationship. The following subparagraphs taken from Ohio's code recognizes the special needs of domestic violence victims. See Chapter 13.]

   1. The [state's legislature] hereby declares that it recognizes both of the following, in relation to the "battered woman syndrome:"

      a. That the syndrome currently is a matter of commonly accepted scientific knowledge;

      b. That the subject matter and details of the syndrome are not within the general understanding or experience of a person who is a member of the general populace and are not within the field of common knowledge.

   2. If a person is charged with an offense involving the use of force against another and the person, as a defense to the offense charged, raises the affirmative defense of self-defense, the person may introduce expert testimony of the "battered woman syndrome" and expert testimony that the person suffered from that syndrome as evi-

dence to establish the requisite belief of an imminent danger of death or great bodily harm that is necessary, as an element of the affirmative defense, to justify the person's use of the force in question. The introduction of any expert testimony under this division shall be in accordance with [the state's] Rules of Evidence.

F. The trier of fact must consider that a person acting during an emergency is not required to exercise the judgment of one who has time for calm deliberation. Furthermore, a person defending himself or another is not required to hesitate before using defensive force to the extent that it would create an unreasonable risk of injury to himself or the third person he is defending. Having time to perceive and react to danger is an important principle for the trier of fact to consider. The defendant may introduce expert testimony concerning the perception and reaction time needed to access a defensive weapon. Expert testimony may be introduced to assist the trier of fact to view the imminence of the danger and reasonableness of defendant's actions from the standpoint of someone with similar education and training in the discipline of self-defense as the defendant. [This paragraph combines the "emergency doctrine" found in many civil jury instructions with an admonition that jurors consider the realities of perception and reaction time as it relates to accessing a defensive weapon. It also gives a jury an opportunity to view the incident from the standpoint of someone who had received self-defense training similar to that of the defendant.]

III. Exceptions to Justifiable Self-defense - Initial aggressor, Provocation, Committing Felony or Unlawful Act, and Combat by Agreement; Exceptions to the Exceptions

A person is not justified in using force under the circumstances specified in paragraphs I or II above if he or she:

A. initially provokes the use of force against himself/herself with the intent to use force as an excuse to inflict bodily harm upon the assailant;

B. is attempting to commit, committing, or fleeing after the commission or attempted commission of a felony; or

C. was the aggressor or was engaged in a combat by agreement, unless he or she withdraws from the encounter and effectively communicates to the other person his/her intent to do so and notwithstanding, the other person continues or threatens to continue the use of unlawful force.

D. For purposes of Subsection C. the following do not, by themselves, constitute "combat by agreement":

a. voluntarily entering into or remaining in an ongoing relationship, or [relating to Domestic Violence, Chapter 13.]

b. entering or remaining in a place where one has a legal right to be.

[Adapted from Utah Code Annotated § 76-2-402. Paragraph B is particularly important. It prevents felons from committing crimes, hurting or killing their victims and then claiming self-defense when the victims use force to stop the crimes. Notice that the exception to the exception in Paragraph C does not apply to paragraphs A and B.]

IV. No Duty to Retreat

A person does not have a duty to retreat from the force or threatened force described in Subsections I or II in a place where that person has lawfully entered or remained, except as provided in Subsection III.C. [Adapted from Utah Code Annotated § 76-2-402.] No finder of fact shall be permitted to consider the possibility of retreat as a factor in determining whether or not the person who used deadly force had a reasonable belief that deadly force was reasonable and apparently necessary to prevent a violent or forcible felony involving life or great bodily harm or to prevent the unlawful entry. [Louisiana Statutes Annotated – Revised Statutes (LSA-R.S.) § 14:20. Justifiable homicide. There is a concern that jurors may find the use of force unnecessary if a defender fails to retreat. But when a state statute eliminates the duty to retreat, defenders should be able to rely upon that statute without worrying that jurors might require retreat anyway. This provision, given as a strong admonition in a jury instruction, should remind jurors that they cannot punish a defendant for not retreating under any circumstances.]

V. Defensive Display – Defense of Persons in or upon Premises

A. An individual who is not prohibited from possessing a firearm by federal or state law may:

i. openly carry a firearm; and

ii. communicate to another person the fact that the individual has a firearm.

B. If an individual who is carrying a firearm reasonably believes that the individual or another person is threatened with bodily harm, the individual may lawfully warn or threaten the use of force, including deadly force against the aggressor, including drawing or exhibiting the firearm.

C. If a peace officer is conducting an investigation of an incident that appears to have or is alleged to have involved the justifiable use of force under subsection B, the officer shall conduct the investigation so as to disclose all evidence, including testimony, concerning the alleged offense that might support the apparent or alleged justifiable use of force.

D. Except as otherwise provided in Subsections A and B and for those persons prohibited from possessing a dangerous weapon by state or local law, an individual who draws or exhibits a dangerous weapon, not in self-defense of the individual or another person, in an angry and threatening manner or unlawfully uses the weapon in a fight or quarrel is guilty of a class A misdemeanor. [This is a combination of an amendment proposed in 2010 to Utah's Brandishing statute U.C.A. 76-10-506 adding the concept of defensive display similar to Montana's bill HB0228 that was passed in 2009. For a similar defensive display statute read Arizona Revised Statutes §13-407. Justification; use of physical force in defense of premises.]

VI. Presumption of Reasonableness in Dwelling, Residence, Business or Occupied Vehicle]

[This is patterned after Florida's presumption statute, F.S.A. § 776.013 Home Protection; Use Of Deadly Force; Presumption Of Fear Of Death Or Great Bodily Harm. For similar defense-of-special-place statutes see also the subchapters of Alabama, Kentucky, Oklahoma, Michigan, South Carolina and Wyoming. These states passed similar statutes in spite of a scathing criticism of Florida's statute that appeared in the *Harvard Journal of Legislation.* One of the primary concerns of the *Harvard Journal* article was that the statute created a "conclusive presumption" of reasonableness (innocence) if a homeowner uses deadly force in home defense. One of the reasons for this conclusion is the absence of the term "necessary" in the main body of the statute (Paragraph A. below). The *Journal* laments that children, innocently wandering into a Florida home, could be shot and killed without the homeowner being subjected to criminal or civil accountability, 43 *Harv. J. on Legis.* 199 (2006).

Pancho's Wisdom: If Willie Nelson were asked to sing a logical response to the Harvard argument, he would probably pen the words, "Mamas don't let you babies grow up to "wander" into other people's homes in Bama or Florida." There are countless places that exist in our modern world that could prove fatal for children. Parents and teens in New York understand that if the kids play hide-n-seek in an active subway tunnel, they could be crushed. San Diego families don't let their kids play laser tag on Interstate 5 at 3am. Moms and dads all over this land teach their kids not to trespass into power sub-stations surrounded by high chain-link fences topped with barbed wire, surrounded by signs warning "Danger: High Voltage." Concerned career-criminal parents nurturing, burgeoning burglars-in-embryo need only remind their offspring to add *someone-else's home* to the list of places where they know that uninvited intrusion could lead to sudden death. What's so hard about that?

Reality Check: Self-defense statutes are only as protective as the courts interpret them to be. As strongly worded as Florida's statute is, we posed questions in Florida's subchapter that leave room for interpretation. Any concerns we expressed about Florida's statute would also apply to the states listed above that have patterned their statutes after Florida's. Nevertheless, the presumption of reasonableness and the absence of the word "necessary" as pointed out in the Harvard study, makes Florida's defense-of-persons-in-special-places law perhaps the most protective in the entire country. Careful, some of the states that patterned their defense-of-special-places statutes after Florida's, reinserted the word *necessary,* thus increasing the legal risk to the defender. For maximum protection of homeowners, we recommend the word *necessary* be kept out of the statute.]

A. A person is presumed to have held a reasonable fear of imminent peril of death or great bodily harm to himself or herself or another when using defensive force that is intended or likely to cause death or great bodily harm to another if:

   1. The person against whom the defensive force was used was in the process of unlawfully and forcefully entering, or had unlawfully and forcibly entered, a dwelling, residence, or occupied vehicle, or if that person had removed or was attempting to remove another against that person's will from the dwelling, residence, business [we added "business" as did Michigan's statute] or occupied vehicle; and

   2. The person who uses defensive force knew or had reason to believe that an unlawful and forcible entry or unlawful and forcible act was occurring or had occurred. (Emphasis added.)

B. The presumption set forth in subsection (1) does not apply if:

   1. **Co-Habitants, Co-Employees and Co-Occupants** – The person against whom the defensive force is used has the right to be in or is a lawful resident of the dwelling, residence, business or vehicle, such as an owner, lessee, or titleholder, and there is not an injunction for protection from domestic violence or a written pretrial supervision order of no contact against that person; or [This does not eliminate the use of deadly force against a co-tenant or co-worker, who threatens deadly force, it simply eliminates

the presumption. In other words, the threshold for the use of deadly force requires an imminent threat of death or serious injury rather than simply an unlawful or violent entry. The presumption would not be lost in the case of a fired former employee unlawfully on the premises going postal.]

2. The person or persons sought to be removed is a child or grandchild, or is otherwise in the lawful custody or under the lawful guardianship of, the person against whom the defensive force is used; or [This keeps people who Rambo their relatives over a custody dispute from claiming the protection of the presumption.]

3. The person who uses defensive force is engaged in an unlawful activity or is using the dwelling, residence, or occupied vehicle to further an unlawful activity; or [This prevents lawbreakers from claiming a presumption of innocence while using their special places to harbor nefarious activities.]

4. The person against whom the defensive force is used is a law enforcement officer, as defined in [this state's statutes], who enters or attempts to enter a dwelling, residence, business or vehicle in the performance of his or her official duties and the officer identified himself or herself in accordance with any applicable law or the person using force knew or reasonably should have known that the person entering or attempting to enter was a law enforcement officer.

C. **No Duty to Retreat From Home, Business, or Occupied Vehicle** – A person who is not engaged in an unlawful activity and who is attacked in any other place where he or she has a right to be has no duty to retreat and has the right to stand his or her ground and meet force with force, including deadly force if he or she reasonably believes it is necessary to do so to prevent death or great bodily harm to himself or herself or another or to prevent the commission of a forcible felony. [No-Retreat provisions similar to this are now in effect in most jurisdictions.]

D. A person who unlawfully and by force enters or attempts to enter a person's dwelling, residence, business or occupied vehicle is presumed to be doing so with the intent to commit an unlawful act involving force or violence. [This is simply recognition of the reality that someone who breaks into a home using unlawful force is probably not there to play Monopoly.]

E. Protection of Activities in Private Vehicles

[This subsection is patterned after a recent Utah law that prohibits employers and other commercial entities from establishing policies preventing Utah employees or customers from keeping firearms in their own vehicles while parked on the property of an employer or other commercial entity. It recognizes an employee's own vehicle as a special place where the employee has a right to defend himself, particularly in the trip to and from work where an employer has no duty to provide security for the employee. See UCA § 34-45-101-107. For brevity's sake we left out the reference to the right to keep religious materials in vehicles, but in a religious state like Utah, it was easier to pass the bill relating to firearms because the bill also prohibited discrimination against an employee's religion. Legislative strategy is a fascinating topic for another book another time.]

1. No person, including employers, may establish, maintain, or enforce any policy or rule that has the effect of:
   a. prohibiting any individual from transporting or storing a firearm in a motor vehicle on any property designated for motor vehicle parking, if:
      (1) the individual is legally permitted to transport, possess, purchase, receive, transfer, or store the firearm;
      (2) the firearm is locked securely in the motor vehicle or in a locked container attached to the motor vehicle while the motor vehicle is not occupied; and
      (3) the firearm is not in plain view from the outside of the motor vehicle.
2. A person who owns or controls a parking area that is subject to this chapter and that complies with the requirements of paragraph 1 is not liable in any civil action for any occurrence resulting from, connected with, or incidental to the use of a firearm, by any person, unless the use of the firearm involves a criminal act by the person who owns or controls the parking area. [Employers who comply with this law are protected from lawsuits (unless, of course, they use a firearm to injure their own employee). If they don't comply, they could get their butts sued as provided in the following paragraph.]
3. An individual who is injured, physically or otherwise, as a result of any policy or rule prohibited by paragraph 1, may bring a civil action in a court of competent jurisdiction against any person that

violates the provisions of paragraph 1. Any individual who asserts a claim under this subsection is entitled to request:

a. declaratory relief;

b. temporary or permanent injunctive relief to prevent the threatened or continued violation;

c. recovery for actual damages sustained; and

d. punitive damages, if:

  (1) serious bodily injury or death occurs as a result of the violation of subparagraph 1; or

  (2) the person who violates subparagraph 1 has previously been notified by the attorney general that a policy or rule violates subparagraph 1.

e. The prevailing party in an action brought under paragraph 3 may recover its court costs and reasonable attorney fees incurred.

f. Nothing in this chapter shall be construed or held to affect any rights or claims made in relation to [this state's] Workers' Compensation Act.

[Paragraph 3 warns owners of parking lots, including employers, that if they create no weapon policies in violation of paragraph 1, they risk being sued civilly, including for punitive damages. This provides a financial disincentive for violating this provision.]

VII. Defense of Persons on Real Property

[This statute is based upon Utah U.C.A. § 76-2-407. Deadly Force In Defense Of Persons On Real Property. It expands the protections given to persons in the home to the borders of a person's real property. Thus, it prevents arguments about where the curtilage begins and ends. It does not give justification to use deadly force against persons simply trespassing. At a minimum, to justify the use of deadly force there must be a forcible act of trespass or a violent entry and a reasonable belief that the intruder intends to commit an assault against someone on the real property.]

A. A person is justified in using force intended or likely to cause death or serious bodily injury against another in his defense of persons on real property other than his habitation if:

1. he is in lawful possession of the real property;

2. he reasonably believes that the force is necessary to prevent or terminate the other person's trespass onto the real property;

3. the trespass is made or attempted by use of force or in a violent and tumultuous manner; and

   a. the person reasonably believes that the trespass is attempted or made for the purpose of committing violence against any person on the real property and he reasonably believes that the force is necessary to prevent personal violence; or

[Paragraph A is probably the most expansive provision of this code section. It allows an owner of real estate to use deadly force against a trespasser who poses an imminent threat of "personal violence" to someone on the real estate. This is clearly a lower threshold than the requirement of an imminent threat of death or serious bodily. Real estate owners should not have to submit to being physically assaulted on their own properties. The terms *necessary* and *reasonable* guard against the misuse of this protective statute or the use of excessive force.

   b. the person reasonably believes that the trespass is made or attempted for the purpose of committing a forcible felony as defined in Section below that poses imminent peril of death or serious bodily injury to a person on the real property and that the force is necessary to prevent the commission of that forcible felony. [Property owners are allowed to defend themselves against heinous felonies under this provision.]

B. The person using deadly force in defense of persons on real property under Subsection A. is presumed for the purpose of both civil and criminal cases to have acted reasonably and had a reasonable fear of imminent peril of death or serious bodily injury if the trespass or attempted trespass is unlawful and is made or attempted by use of force, or in a violent and tumultuous manner, or for the purpose of committing a forcible felony. [Property owners should not have to worry about being criminally prosecuted or sued civilly for using deadly force against unlawful, violent intruders.]

VIII. Reckless Injury to Innocent Third Parties

[Alabama's Code, § 13A-3-21 modified. You own any bullet that leaves your barrel. If it happens to strike an innocent person, you can count on a lawsuit—period. If you negligently start a gunfight and innocents are struck by someone else's bullet, you will end up the defendant in a civil suit, even if you are not prosecuted.]

A. Defense. – Except as otherwise expressly provided, justification or excuse under this article is a defense.

B. Danger to innocent persons. – If a person is justified or excused in using force against a person, but he recklessly or negligently injures or creates a substantial injury to another person, the justifications afforded by this article are unavailable in a prosecution for such recklessness or negligence.

C. Civil remedies for innocent persons unimpaired. – Except as specifically provided herein, any justification or excuse within the meaning of this article does not abolish or impair any right of action that arises out of negligent or reckless conduct causing bodily injury to innocent persons. An "innocent person" does not include any person committing, aiding or abetting in the commission of, or assistance in fleeing after any violent felony or misdemeanor at the time of that person's injury. [This is different than Alabama's subparagraph to ensure it only relates to the injury of innocent persons and does not give those committing crimes the right to bring civil suits. The following paragraph provides additional protection against civil lawsuits.]

IX. Civil Liability

[Based upon Utah statute, U.C.A. § 78B-3-110. Defense To Civil Action For Damages Resulting From Commission Of Crime. Persons injured committing felonies can't win personal injury damages against the intended victims of their crimes. If the criminal dies from injuries sustained during the criminal act, wrongful death lawsuits brought by their heirs will be doomed as well. A defender who shoots a home invader or carjacker should not need to worry about being sued under this statute unless (1) his culpability in bringing about the incident was greater than or equal to the felon injured or killed, or (2) the felon was "clearly retreating." Smoking some bloke in the back of the head at 1,400 yards in 45-90 with your Quigley rig as his wagon crests the hill might be construed to have been an act of "clearly retreating."]

A. A person may not recover from the victim of a crime for personal injury or property damage if the person:

   1. entered the property of the victim with criminal intent and the injury or damage occurred while the person was on the victim's property; or

   2. committed a crime against the victim, during which the damage or injury occurred.

B. The provisions of Subsection A do not apply if the person can prove by clear and convincing evidence that:

   1. his actions did not constitute a felony; and

   2. his culpability was less than the person from whom recovery is sought.

C. Subsections A and B apply to any next-of-kin, heirs, or personal representatives of the person if the person is disabled or killed.

D. Subsections A, B, and C do not apply if the person committing or attempting to commit the crime has clearly retreated from the criminal activity.

E. "Clearly retreated" means that the person committing the criminal act has fully, clearly, and immediately ceased all hostile, threatening, violent, or criminal behavior or activity.

F. A person who uses force [consistent with this state's self and home defense statutes] is immune from criminal prosecution and civil action for the use of such force, unless the person against whom force was used is a law enforcement officer who was acting in the performance of such officer's official duties and the officer identified the officer's self in accordance with any applicable law or the person using force knew or reasonably should have known that the person was a law enforcement officer. As used in this subsection, "criminal prosecution" includes arrest, detention in custody and charging or prosecution of the defendant. [Section (6) is adapted from K.S.A. (Kansas) § 21-3219. Use of Force; Immunity From Prosecution Or Liability; Investigation. This statute claims to prohibit arresting a person just because a weapon was used and someone was hurt if it appears the force was used in self-defense. The following two paragraphs describe the strength of the evidence that must exist against the defender before an arrest can be made. If you have a valid claim to self-defense, this immunity statute could be very helpful to keep your legal fees from going through the roof. The accused has the burden of proving by a preponderance of evidence (more likely than not) that he is innocent by virtue of self-defense (or defense of another). Any prosecution ends once this burden is met. If the defendant does not meet his burden and the prosecution goes forward, the burden then shifts to the state to prove beyond a reasonable doubt that the defendant did not act in self-defense.]

   1. A law enforcement agency may use standard procedures for investigating the use of force as described in subsection F, but the agency shall not arrest the person for using force unless it determines that

there is probable cause for the arrest. [The standard procedures must be followed in an investigation and there will be no arrest until there is probable cause. Probable cause means more than a possibility, but does not have to be more likely than not.]

2. A county or district attorney or other prosecutor may commence a criminal prosecution upon a determination of probable cause.

X. Defense of Personal Property – Non-Deadly Force

[Patterned after Tex. Penal Code Ann. § 9.41.]

[Texas has the most protective defense-of-property statutes. Under some (not all) circumstances, a person is legally permitted to use deadly force not only to defend his own property, but to defend his neighbor's property as well. Nevertheless, we continue to advise **not** to use deadly force to defend property. Review the Joe Horn and Tommy Oaks case summaries in Texas' subchapter. If you kill or injure someone in defense of a flat screen or gas grill, ugh! By the time you get done paying an attorney to defend you, even if you beat the charges, you could have bought fifty (50!) brand new flat screen TVs for yourself, your kids and your neighbors! The good news is if you've used deadly force to defend against what you thought was a violent felony and the person ends up not being armed, it's always good for your attorney to have a strong defense-of-property statute like Texas' to fall back on. Texas has several statutes.

Pancho's Wisdom – Let's just say that Texas hasn't bought into the American trend of providing career criminals with an ideally safe place to work.]

A. **Protection of One's Own Property** – (a) A person in lawful possession of land or tangible, movable property is justified in using force against another when and to the degree the actor reasonably believes the force is immediately necessary to prevent or terminate the other's trespass on the land or unlawful interference with the property.

1. A person unlawfully dispossessed of land or tangible, movable property by another is justified in using force against the other when and to the degree the actor reasonably believes the force is immediately necessary to reenter the land or recover the property if the actor uses the force immediately or in fresh pursuit after the dispossession and:

   a. the actor reasonably believes the other had no claim of right when he dispossessed the actor; or

   b. the other accomplished the dispossession by using force, threat, or fraud against the actor. [Most states authorize the reasonable and necessary use of non-deadly force to defend real and personal property. This statute is not out of the ordinary.]

XI. Defense of Land or Personal Property with Deadly Force

[Patterned after Tex. Penal Code Ann. § 9.42.]

A. A person is justified in using deadly force against another to protect land or tangible, movable property:

1. if he would be justified in using force against the other under [your state's deadly force statute]; and

2. when and to the degree he reasonably believes the deadly force is immediately necessary:

   a. to prevent the other's imminent commission of arson, burglary, robbery, aggravated robbery, theft during the nighttime, or criminal mischief during the nighttime; or

   b. to prevent the other who is fleeing immediately after committing burglary, robbery, aggravated robbery, or theft during the nighttime from escaping with the property; and

3. he reasonably believes that:

   a. the land or property cannot be protected or recovered by any other means; or

   b. the use of force other than deadly force to protect or recover the land or property would expose the actor or another to a substantial risk of death or serious bodily injury.

[The following case confirms that deadly force can be used to prevent a criminal mischief, if the other conditions of the statute are met. One of the other conditions is an imminent threat of death or serious injury under the state's deadly force statute. So this statute is not that unusual. It gives property owners an added degree of legal protection in the event they believe deadly force is necessary to defend property, which can be dangerous (which is why we recommend against it).]

"The language of section 9.42 requires that all three of its statutory circumstances exist in order for a person to be justified in employing deadly force against another to protect property. . . The relevant portion of section 9.41 of the Penal Code provides under subsection (a) that: "[a] person in lawful possession of land . . . is justified in using force against another when and to the degree the actor reasonably believes the force is immediately necessary to prevent or terminate the other's trespass on the land or unlawful interference with the property." "Criminal mischief," as referred to in subsection (2) of section 9.42, is defined in section 28.03 as follows: "[a] person commits an offense if, without the effective consent of the owner: (1) he intentionally or knowingly damages or destroys the tangible property of the owner." *Leach v. State,* 983 S.W.2d 45, 47 (Tex.App.-Tyler 1998).

XII. Defense of Property of a Third Person – Non-Deadly and Deadly Force [Patterned after Tex. Penal Code Ann. § 9.42.]

A. A person is justified in using force or deadly force against another to protect land or tangible, movable property of a third person if, under the circumstances as he reasonably believes them to be, the actor would be justified under Section **XI** or **XII** in using force or deadly force to protect his own land or property and: [All the conditions for the use of non-deadly or deadly force described in the two preceding statutes must exist and, in addition...]

1. the actor reasonably believes the unlawful interference constitutes attempted or consummated theft of or criminal mischief to the tangible, movable property; or
2. the actor reasonably believes that:
    a. the third person has requested his protection of the land or property; [This provision may have had some influence upon the grand jury which refused to indict Joe Horn.]
    b. he has a legal duty to protect the third person's land or property; or
    c. the third person whose land or property he uses force or deadly force to protect is the actor's spouse, parent, or child, resides with the actor, or is under the actor's care.

XIII. Reimbursement for criminal defense costs

[In the state of Washington, part of the state budget is earmarked to reimburse the attorney fees of those found innocent on grounds of defense of self, home or others (RCW 9A.16.110 Defending against violent crime—Reimbursement). We recommend carrying it a step further. The reimbursement should come out of the budget of those who insist on arresting and prosecuting. Having to pay the fees and costs of an acquitted defendant makes it less likely an agency will cave in to pressure from the families of criminals killed while committing violent crimes.]

A. No person in the state shall be placed in legal jeopardy of any kind whatsoever for protecting by any reasonable means necessary, himself or herself, his or her family, or his or her real or personal property, or for coming to the aid of another who is in imminent danger of or the victim of assault, robbery, kidnapping, arson, burglary, rape, murder, or any other forcible felony as defined.

B. When a person is found not guilty by reason of self-defense, [the arresting and prosecuting agencies] shall reimburse [out of their yearly budgets] the defendant for all reasonable costs, including loss of time, legal fees incurred, and other expenses involved in his or her defense. This reimbursement is not an independent cause of action. To award these reasonable costs the trier of fact must find that the defendant's claim of self-defense was sustained by a preponderance of the evidence. If the trier of fact makes a determination of self-defense, the judge shall determine the amount of the award. [The reference to "preponderance of the evidence" means that a jury could find a defendant not guilty and still not award fees. This would result if jurors believed the prosecution did not prove it's case beyond a reasonable doubt, but that the innocence of the defendant appeared more probable than not. Thus, reimbursement is based upon an entirely different burden of proof than the issue of guilt or innocence.]

C. Notwithstanding a finding that a defendant's actions were justified by self-defense, if the trier of fact also determines that the defendant was engaged in criminal conduct substantially related to the events giving rise to the charges filed against the defendant the judge may deny or reduce the amount of the award. In determining the amount of the award, the judge shall also consider the seriousness of the initial criminal conduct.

   Nothing in this section precludes the legislature from using the sundry claims process to grant an award where none was granted under this section or to grant a higher award than one granted under this section.

D. Whenever the issue of self-defense under this section is decided by a judge, the judge shall consider the same questions as must be answered in the special verdict under subsection E. of this section.

E. Whenever the issue of self-defense under this section has been submitted to a jury, and the jury has found the defendant not guilty, the court shall instruct the jury to return a special verdict in substantially the following form:

Answer Yes or No

1. Was the finding of not guilty based upon self-defense? _______
2. If your answer to question 1 is no, do not answer the remaining questions.
3. If your answer to question 1 is yes, was the defendant:
   a. Protecting himself or herself? _______
   b. Protecting his or her family? _______
   c. Protecting his or her property? _______
   d. Coming to the aid of another who was in imminent danger of a heinous crime? _______
   e. Coming to the aid of another who was the victim of a heinous crime? _______
   f. Engaged in criminal conduct substantially related to the events giving rise to the crime with which the defendant is charged? _______ [A "yes" in this box would either reduce or eliminate reimbursement for costs and fees altogether.]

[Helpful Definitions Relating to this State's Self-Defense Statutes]

- **Deadly force** – means force which the defendant uses with the purpose of causing or which the defendant knows creates a substantial risk of causing death or serious physical injury. Purposely firing a firearm in the direction of another person or at a vehicle in which another person is believed to be constitutes deadly force. A threat to cause death or serious bodily harm, by the production of a weapon or otherwise, so long as the defendant's purpose is limited to creating an apprehension that deadly force will be used if necessary, does not constitute deadly force. **11 Delaware Code § 471(d).**
- **Dwelling** – means a building or conveyance of any kind, including any attached porch, whether the building or conveyance is temporary or permanent, mobile or immobile, which has a roof over it, including a tent, and is designed to be occupied by people lodging therein at night. **F.S.A. § 776.013 (5) (a).**
- **Forcible Felonies** – For purposes of Section II above, a forcible felony includes aggravated assault, mayhem, aggravated murder, murder, manslaughter, kidnapping, and aggravated kidnapping, rape, forcible sodomy, rape of a child, object rape, object rape of a child, sexual abuse of a child, aggravated sexual abuse of a child, and aggravated sexual assault as de-

fined in [fill in appropriate state code sections], and arson, robbery, and burglary as defined in [fill in appropriate state code sections]. Any other felony offense which involves the use of force or violence against a person so as to create a substantial danger of death or serious bodily injury also constitutes a forcible felony. Burglary of a vehicle, defined in [fill in appropriate state code sections], does not constitute a forcible felony except when the vehicle is occupied at the time unlawful entry is made or attempted. [This definition of "Forcible Felony" comes from the Utah self-defense statute, 76-10-402. Each state legislature may decide what serious felonies it wishes to add to this list.]

- **Imminent** – means impending danger, and, in the context of domestic violence and abuse as defined by [your state's domestic abuse statute], belief that danger is imminent can be inferred from a past pattern of repeated serious abuse. **Kentucky Statutes 503.010 (3).** [This very progressive definition puts Kentucky above most states in recognizing and responding to the deadly plague of domestic violence that results in the permanent injury, disfigurement and deaths of thousands of women a year throughout the country.]

- **Initial aggressor** – means the person who first attacks or threatens to attack; that is, the first person who uses or threatens the imminent use of offensive physical force. The actual striking of the first blow or inflicting of the first wound, however, does not necessarily determine who was the initial aggressor. A person who reasonably believes that another is about to use physical force upon her need not wait until she is struck or wounded. She may, in such circumstances, be the first to use [deadly] physical force, so long as she reasonably believed it was about to be used against her or someone else. She is then not considered to be the "initial aggressor," even though she strikes the first blow or inflicts the first wound. Arguing, using abusive language, calling a person names, or the like, unaccompanied by physical threats or acts, does not make a person an initial aggressor and does not justify physical force. A person cannot be considered the initial aggressor simply because she has a reputation for violence or has previously engaged in violent acts. **New York Justification Jury Instructions 35.15 USE OF [DEADLY] PHYSICAL FORCE IN DEFENSE OF A PERSON.** [This is hands down the best definition of initial aggressor we have seen in any state.]

Pancho's Wisdom – There you are my compatriots, a veritable smorgasbord of the best of the best. If your legislators refuse to eat the whole elephant, with the help of lobbyists from the National Rifle Association and similar groups, you can feed it to them one bite at a time. Another option would be to adopt the entire self-defense laws of a protective neighboring state such as Florida, Utah or Texas. Sometimes it's easier for a state legislature to accept a neighboring state's statutes that have not lead to that state's total societal collapse.

This has been a monumental effort on our part taking the best part of two years. We've now done everything we could to give you a vision of what is possible. We would like citizens all over the country to have the right to defend themselves, their families and their loved ones like we do here in Utah. You may have noticed that Utah's statutes seem to be over-represented in this chapter. It's either because we are biased or Utah has some of the most protective self-defense statutes in the country. You decide. Your involvement is indispensible if you want the law in your state to be more protective for the innocent and less protective for violent criminals. Your legislators need to know you want change. Please be polite, not threatening (you don't want to feed their perception of gun owners as raving maniacs on a power trip). But it's time to get off the couch, turn off the sports network and get to work. Vaya Con Dios, God be with you, my Compatriots. Pancho V.

Pancho's Wisdom

You just might be a Gunnut if . . . you understand that the best way to protect your children from accidental shootings is to educate them and satisfy their curiosity.

21
ABOUT THE AUTHORS

James D. "Mitch" Vilos is a prominent Utah trial lawyer. He has the notable distinction of being a member of the Million Dollar Advocates Forum for having obtained numerous six and seven figure recoveries for his injured clients involving tractor-trailer accidents, car and motorcycle accidents, birth injuries, medical malpractice, products liability, and on-the-job injuries. His focus has been on brain, spinal cord, burns and other serious injuries, including those caused by firearms. He has been nominated by his peers (attorneys, judges) as one of Utah's Top Lawyers for 2008 & 2009 as reported in Utah Business Magazine.

Mitch's success as a personal injury lawyer has allowed him to delve into a unique area of the law in which he has an interest and passion - firearms law. In May of 2006 Mitch won a not guilty jury verdict to the charge of brandishing in a case highly publicized in the Salt Lake City area; the case of computer store magnate Dell "SUPERDELL" Schanze. Another notable victory for Mr. Vilos was his participation in the defense of premier candle company, Salt City Candle Company. It was sued for $150 Million dollars by a related company. Mr. Vilos was retained by Salt City's team of attorneys as lead trial counsel and was instrumental in getting the majority of the claims against his client completely dismissed.

James D. "Mitch" Vilos is a graduate of J. Reuben Clark Law School at Brigham Young University. He has practiced law since 1978. He has authored and co-authored articles relating to personal injury litigation and insurance law in legal publications such as the Utah State Bar Journal and Utah Trial Lawyers Journal. He is the author of *Utah Gun Law: Good, Bad and Ugly, Utah Gun Law II: Pancho's Wisdom, Utah Gun Law, 3rd ed.* and the *Utah Spotlighting and Night Hunting Manual.*

Mr. Vilos has participated in educating the public, including on radio and television, about legal topics such as negligence law, medical malpractice, insurance law, representing people with traumatic brain injuries, constitutional law, self-defense and firearms law.

Mitch is a Utah State authorized concealed weapon instructor, a graduate of the Ogden Metro Swat Basic Training Course (affectionately known as "Hell

Week") and Davis County Sheriff's Citizen's Academy. Mitch has a Federal Firearms License (FFL), is a member of the National Rifle Association and Single Action Shooting Society (Badge No. 10,586, Alias "Pancho Vilos"). He recently received the honor of being the first alumnus to be invited to participate in Utah State University's Distinguished Alumni Speaker Series.

Evan Vilos is a graduate of Brigham Young University, Hawaii Campus with a B.A. in political science and minors in girls, surfing, 80's-Rock guitar and beach parties (but hey, how wild could it have been at BYU?)

Pancho's Wisdom

You just might be a Gunnut if . . . If, with tears streaming down your cheeks, you've ever hugged your kids and told 'em you love 'em while sitting around a campfire discussing the truths of eternity in a place where the Milky Way isn't obscured by city lights. Maybe being a Gunnut (or a Redneck) isn't so bad after all.

NOTES

NOTES

NOTES

NOTES

NOTES

NOTES